ACTIVE
MANAG

MW01097350

Library of Congress Cataloging-in-Publication Data

Grinold, Richard C.
    Active portfolio management : a quantitative approach for providing
    superior returns and controlling risk
    / by Richard C. Grinold and Ronald N. Kahn.—2nd ed.
        p.   cm.
    Includes bibliographical references and index.
    ISBN 0-07-024882-6
    1. Portfolio management—Mathematical models.   I. Kahn, Ronald N.
II. Title.
HG4529.5.G75   1999
332.6′015′1—dc21   99-21967
                                                                 CIP

McGraw-Hill

A Division of The McGraw·Hill Companies

1 2 3 4 5 6 7 8 9 0   DOC/DOC   9 0 9 8 7 6 5 4 3 2 1 0 9

ISBN 978-1-26-591971-9

The sponsoring editor for this book was Stephen Isaacs, the editing supervisor was Paul R. Sobel, and the production supervisor was Elizabeth J. Strange. It was set in Palatino by ATLIS Graphics and Design.

McGraw-Hill books are available at special quantity discounts to use as premiums and sales promotions, or for use in corporate training programs. For more information, please write to the Director of Special Sales, McGraw-Hill, 11 West 19th Street, New York, NY 10011. Or contact your local bookstore.

*To Leilani
and to Bonnie*

CONTENTS

PREFACE

Why a second edition? Why take time from busy lives? Why devote the energy to improving an existing text rather than writing an entirely new one? Why toy with success?

The short answer is: our readers. We have been extremely gratified by *Active Portfolio Management*'s reception in the investment community. The book seems to be on the shelf of every practicing or aspiring quantitatively oriented investment manager, and the shelves of many fundamental portfolio managers as well.

But while our readers have clearly valued the book, they have also challenged us to improve it. Cover more topics of relevance to today. Add empirical evidence where appropriate. Clarify some discussions.

The long answer is that we have tried to improve *Active Portfolio Management* along exactly these dimensions.

First, we have added significant amounts of new material in the second edition. New chapters cover *Advanced Forecasting* (Chap. 11), *The Information Horizon* (Chap. 13), *Long/Short Investing* (Chap. 15), *Asset Allocation* (Chap. 18), *The Historical Record for Active Management* (Chap. 20), and *Open Questions* (Chap. 21).

Some previously existing chapters also cover new material. This includes a more detailed discussion of risk (Chap. 3), dispersion (Chap. 14), market impact (Chap. 16), and academic proposals for performance analysis (Chap. 17).

Second, we receive exhortations to add more empirical evidence, where appropriate. At the most general level: how do we know this entire methodology works? Chapter 20, on *The Historical Record for Active Management*, provides some answers. We have also added empirical evidence about the accuracy of risk models, in Chap. 3.

At the more detailed level, readers have wanted more information on typical numbers for information ratios and active risk. Chapter 5 now includes empirical distributions of these statistics. Chapter 15 provides similar empirical results for long/short portfolios. Chapter 3 includes empirical distributions of asset level risk statistics.

Third, we have tried to clarify certain discussions. We received
feedback on how clearly we had conveyed certain ideas through
at least two channels. First, we presented a talk summarizing the
book at several investment management conferences.[1] "Seven
Quantitative Insights into Active Management" presented the key
ideas as:

1. Active Management is Forecasting: consensus views lead
   to the benchmark.
2. The Information Ratio (*IR*) is the Key to Value-Added.
3. The Fundamental Law of Active Management:
   $IR = IC \cdot \sqrt{Breadth}$.
4. Alphas must control for volatility, skill, and expectations:
   Alpha = Volatility · IC · Score.
5. Why Datamining is Easy, and guidelines to avoid it.
6. Implementation should subtract as little value as
   possible.
7. Distinguishing skill from luck is difficult.

This talk provided many opportunities to gauge understanding
and confusion over these basic ideas.

We also presented a training course version of the book, called
"How to Research Active Strategies." Over 500 investment professionals from New York to London to Hong Kong and Tokyo have
participated. This course, which involved not only lectures, but
problem sets and extensive discussions, helped to identify some
remaining confusions with the material. For example, how does the
forecasting methodology in the book, which involves information
about returns over time, apply to the standard case of information
about many assets at one time? We have devoted Chap. 11, *Advanced
Forecasting*, to that important discussion.

Finally, we have fixed some typographical errors, and added
more problems and exercises to each chapter. We even added a
new type of problem—applications exercises. These use commercially available analytics to demonstrate many of the ideas in the

---

[1] The BARRA Newsletter presented a serialized version of this talk during 1997 and
1998.

book. These should help make some of the more technical results accessible to less mathematical readers.

Beyond these many reader-inspired improvements, we may also bring a different perspective to the second edition of *Active Portfolio Management*. Both authors now earn their livelihoods as active managers.

To readers of the first edition of *Active Portfolio Management*, we hope this second edition answers your challenges. To new readers, we hope you continue to find the book important, useful, challenging, and comprehensive.

Richard C. Grinold
Ronald N. Kahn

ACKNOWLEDGMENTS

Many thanks to Andrew Rudd for his encouragement of this project while the authors were employed at BARRA, and to Blake Grossman for his continued enthusiasm and support of this effort at Barclays Global Investors.

Any close reader will realize that we have relied heavily on the path breaking work of Barr Rosenberg. Barr was the pioneer in applying economics, econometrics and operations research to solve practical investment problems. To a lesser, but not less crucial extent, we are indebted to the original and practical work of Bill Sharpe and Fischer Black. Their ideas are the foundation of much of our analysis.

Many people helped shape the final form of this book. Internally at BARRA and Barclays Global Investors, we benefited from conversations with and feedback from Andrew Rudd, Blake Grossman, Peter Algert, Stan Beckers, Oliver Buckley, Vinod Chandrashekaran, Naozer Dadachanji, Arjun DiVecha, Mark Engerman, Mark Ferrari, John Freeman, Ken Hui, Ken Kroner, Uzi Levin, Richard Meese, Peter Muller, George Patterson, Scott Scheffler, Dan Stefek, Nicolo Torre, Marco Vangelisti, Barton Waring, and Chris Woods. Some chapters appeared in preliminary form at BARRA seminars and as journal articles, and we benefited from broader feedback from the quantitative investment community.

At the more detailed level, several members of the research groups at BARRA and Barclays Global Investors helped generate the examples in the book, especially Chip Castille, Mikhail Dvorkin, Cliff Gong, Josh Rosenberg, Mike Shing, Jennifer Soller, and Ko Ushigusa.

BARRA and Barclays Global Investors have also been supportive throughout.

Finally, we must thank Leslie Henrichsen, Amber Mayes, Carolyn Norton, and Mary Wang for their administrative help over many years.

ACTIVE PORTFOLIO MANAGEMENT

CHAPTER 1

Introduction

The art of investing is evolving into the science of investing. This evolution has been happening slowly and will continue for some time. The direction is clear; the pace varies. As new generations of increasingly scientific investment managers come to the task, they will rely more on analysis, process, and structure than on intuition, advice, and whim. This does not mean that heroic personal investment insights are a thing of the past. It means that managers will increasingly capture and apply those insights in a systematic fashion.

We hope this book will go part of the way toward providing the analytical underpinnings for the new class of active investment managers. We are addressing a fresh topic. Quantitative active management—applying rigorous analysis and a rigorous process to try to beat the market—is a cousin of the modern study of financial economics. Financial economics is conducted with much vigor at leading universities, safe from any need to deliver investment returns. Indeed, from the perspective of the financial economist, active portfolio management appears to be a mundane consideration, if not an entirely dubious proposition. Modern financial economics, with its theories of market efficiency, inspired the move over the past decade away from active management (trying to beat the market) to passive management (trying to match the market).

This academic view of active management is not monolithic, since the academic cult of market efficiency has split. One group now enthusiastically investigates possible market inefficiencies.

1

Still, a hard core remains dedicated to the notion of efficient markets, although they have become more and more subtle in their defense of the market.[1]

Thus we can look to the academy for structure and insight, but not for solutions. We will take a pragmatic approach and develop a systematic approach to active management, assuming that this is a worthwhile goal. Worthwhile, but not easy. We remain aware of the great power of markets to keep participants in line. The first necessary ingredient for success in active management is a recognition of the challenge. On this issue, financial economists and quantitative researchers fall into three categories: those who think successful active management is impossible, those who think it is easy, and those who think it is difficult. The first group, however brilliant, is not up to the task. You cannot reach your destination if you don't believe it exists. The second group, those who don't know what they don't know, is actually dangerous. The third group has some perspective and humility. We aspire to belong to that third group, so we will work from that perspective. We will assume that the burden of proof rests on us to demonstrate why a particular strategy will succeed.

We will also try to remember that this is an economic investigation. We are dealing with spotty data. We should expect our models to point us in the correct direction, but not with laserlike accuracy. This reminds us of a paper called "Estimation for Dirty Data and Flawed Models."[2] We must accept this nonstationary world in which we can never repeat an experiment. We must accept that investing with real money is harder than paper investing, since we actually affect the transaction prices.

PERSPECTIVE

We have written this book on two levels. We have aimed the material in the chapters at the MBA who has had a course in investments

---

[1] A leading academic refined this technique to the sublime recently when he told an extremely successful investor that his success stemmed not from defects in the market but from the practitioner's sheer brilliance. That brilliance would have been as well rewarded if he had chosen some other endeavor, such as designing microchips, recombining DNA, or writing epic poems. Who could argue with such a premise?

[2] Krasker, Kuh, and Welch (1983).

or the practitioner with a year of experience. The technical appendices at the end of each chapter use mathematics to cover that chapter's insights in more detail. These are for the more technically inclined, and could even serve as a gateway to the subject for the mathematician, physicist, or engineer retraining for a career in investments. Beyond its use in teaching the subject to those beginning their careers, we hope the comprehensiveness of the book also makes it a valuable reference for veteran investment professionals.

We have written this book from the perspective of the active manager of institutional assets: defined-benefit plans, defined-contribution plans, endowments, foundations, or mutual funds. Plan sponsors, consultants, broker-dealers, traders, and providers of data and analytics should also find much of interest in the book. Our examples mainly focus on equities, but the analysis applies as well to bonds, currencies, and other asset classes.

Our goal is to provide a structured approach—a process—for active investment management. The process includes researching ideas (quantitative or not), forecasting exceptional returns, constructing and implementing portfolios, and observing and refining their performance. Beyond describing this process in considerable depth, we also hope to provide a set of strategic concepts and rules of thumb which broadly guide this process. These concepts and rules contain the intuition behind the process.

As for background, the book borrows from several academic areas. First among these is modern financial economics, which provides the portfolio analysis model. Sharpe and Alexander's book *Investments* is an excellent introduction to the modern theory of investments. *Modern Portfolio Theory*, by Rudd and Clasing, describes the concepts of modern financial economics. The appendix of Richard Roll's 1977 paper "A Critique of the Asset Pricing Theory's Tests" provides an excellent introduction to portfolio analysis. We also borrow ideas from statistics, regression, and optimization.

We like to believe that there are no books covering the same territory as this.

STRATEGIC OVERVIEW

Quantitative active management is the poor relation of modern portfolio theory. It has the power and structure of modern portfolio theory without the legitimacy. Modern portfolio theory brought economics, quantitative methods, and the scientific perspective to the study of investments. Economics, with its powerful emphasis on equilibrium and efficiency, has little to say about successful active management. It is almost a premise of the theory that successful active management is not possible. Yet we will borrow some of the quantitative tools that economists brought to the investigation of investments for our attack on the difficult problem of active management.

We will add something, too: separating the risk forecasting problem from the return forecasting problem. Here professionals are far ahead of academics. Professional services now provide standard and unbiased[3] estimates of investment risk. BARRA pioneered these services and has continued to set the standard in terms of innovation and quality in the United States and worldwide. We will review the fundamentals of risk forecasting, and rely heavily on the availability of portfolio risk forecasts.

The modern portfolio theory taught in most MBA programs looks at total risk and total return. The institutional investor in the United States and to an increasing extent worldwide cares about active risk and active return. For that reason, we will concentrate on the more general problem of managing relative to a benchmark. This focus on active management arises for several reasons:

- Clients can clump the large number of investment advisers into recognizable categories. With the advisers thus pigeonholed, the client (or consultant) can restrict searches and peer comparisons to pigeons in the same hole.
- The benchmark acts as a set of instructions from the fund sponsor, as principal, to the investment manager, as agent. The benchmark defines the manager's investment neighborhood. Moves away from the benchmark carry substantial investment and business risk.
- Benchmarks allow the trustee or sponsor to manage the aggregate portfolio without complete knowledge of the

[3]Risk forecasts from BARRA or other third-party vendors are unbiased in that the process used to derive them is independent from that used to forecast returns.

holdings of each manager. The sponsor can manage a mix of benchmarks, keeping the "big picture."

In fact, analyzing investments relative to a benchmark is more general than the standard total risk and return framework. By setting the benchmark to cash, we can recover the traditional framework.

In line with this relative risk and return perspective, we will move from the economic and textbook notion of *the market* to the more operational notion of *a benchmark*. Much of the apparatus of portfolio analysis is still relevant. In particular, we retain the ability to determine the expected returns that make the benchmark portfolio (or any other portfolio) efficient. This extremely valuable insight links the notion of a mean/variance efficient portfolio to a list of expected returns on the assets.

Throughout the book, we will relate *portfolios* to *return forecasts* or *asset characteristics*. The technical appendixes will show explicitly how every asset characteristic corresponds to a particular portfolio. This perspective provides a novel way to bring heterogeneous characteristics to a common ground (portfolios) and use portfolio theory to study them.

Our relative perspective will focus us on the residual component of return: the return that is uncorrelated with the benchmark return. The information ratio is the ratio of the expected annual residual return to the annual volatility of the residual return. The information ratio defines the opportunities available to the active manager. The larger the information ratio, the greater the possibility for active management.

Choosing investment opportunities depends on preferences. In active management, the preferences point toward high residual return and low residual risk. We capture this in a mean/variance style through residual return minus a (quadratic) penalty on residual risk (a linear penalty on residual variance). We interpret this as "risk-adjusted expected return" or "value-added." We can describe the preferences in terms of indifference curves. We are indifferent between combinations of expected residual return and residual risk which achieve the same value-added. Each indifference curve will include a "certainty equivalent" residual return with zero residual risk.

When our preferences confront our opportunities, we make investment choices. In active management, the highest value-added achievable is proportional to the square of the information ratio.

The information ratio measures the active management opportunities, and the square of the information ratio indicates our ability to add value. Larger information ratios are better than smaller. Where do you find large information ratios? What are the sources of investment opportunity? According to the fundamental law of active management, there are two. The first is our ability to forecast each asset's residual return. We measure this forecasting ability by the information coefficient, the correlation between the forecasts and the eventual returns. The information coefficient is a measure of our level of skill.

The second element leading to a larger information ratio is breadth, the number of times per year that we can use our skill. If our skill level is the same, then it is arguably better to be able to forecast the returns on 1000 stocks than on 100 stocks. The fundamental law tells us that our information ratio grows in proportion to our skill and in proportion to the square root of the breadth: $IR = IC \cdot \sqrt{breadth}$. This concept is valuable for the insight it provides, as well as the explicit help it can give in designing a research strategy.

One outgrowth of the fundamental law is our lack of enthusiasm for benchmark timing strategies. Betting on the market's direction once every quarter does not provide much breadth, even if we have skill.

Return, risk, benchmarks, preferences, and information ratios are the foundations of active portfolio management. But the practice of active management requires something more: expected return forecasts different from the consensus.

What models of expected returns have proven successful in active management? The science of asset valuation proceeded rapidly in the 1970s, with those new ideas implemented in the 1980s. Unfortunately, these insights are mainly the outgrowth of option theory and are useful for the valuation of dependent assets such as options and futures. They are not very helpful in the valuation of underlying assets such as equities. However, the structure of the options-based theory does point in a direction and suggest a form.

The traditional methods of asset valuation and return forecasting are more ad hoc. Foremost among these is the dividend discount model, which brings the ideas of net present value to bear on the valuation problem. The dividend discount model has one unambiguous benefit. If used effectively, it will force a structure on the investment process. There is, of course, no guarantee of success. The outputs of the dividend discount model will be only as good as the inputs.

There are other structured approaches to valuation and return forecasting. One is to identify the characteristics of assets that have performed well, in order to find the assets that will perform well in the future. Another approach is to use comparative valuation to identify assets with different market prices, but with similar exposures to factors priced by the market. These imply arbitrage opportunities. Yet another approach is to attempt to forecast returns to the factors priced by the market.

Active management is forecasting. Without forecasts, managers would invest passively and choose the benchmark. In the context of this book, forecasting takes raw signals of asset returns and turns them into refined forecasts. This information processing is a critical step in the active management process. The basic insight is the rule of thumb Alpha = volatility · IC · score, which allows us to relate a standardized (zero mean and unit standard deviation) score to a forecast of residual return (an alpha). The volatility in question is the residual volatility, and the IC is the information coefficient—the correlation between the scores and the returns. Information processing takes the raw signal as input, converts it to a score, then multiplies it by volatility to generate an alpha.

This forecasting rule of thumb will at least tame the refined forecasts so that they are reasonable inputs into a portfolio selection procedure. If the forecasts contain no information, IC = 0, the rule of thumb will convert the informationless scores to residual return forecasts of zero, and the manager will invest in the benchmark. The rule of thumb converts "garbage in" to zeros.

Information analysis evaluates the ability of any signal to forecast returns. It determines the appropriate information coefficient to use in forecasting, quantifying the information content of the signal.

There is many a slip between cup and lip. Even those armed with the best forecasts of return can let the prize escape through

inconsistent and sloppy portfolio construction and excessive trading costs. Effective portfolio construction ensures that the portfolio
effectively represents the forecasts, with no unintended risks. Effective trading achieves that portfolio at minimum cost. After all, the
investor obtains returns net of trading costs.

The entire active management process—from information to
forecasts to implementation—requires constant and consistent
monitoring, as well as feedback on performance. We provide a
guide to performance analysis techniques and the insights into the
process that they can provide.

This book does not guarantee success in investment management. Investment products are driven by concepts and ideas. If
those concepts are flawed, no amount of efficient implementation
and analysis can help. If it is garbage in, then it's garbage out; we
can only help to process the garbage more effectively. However,
we can provide at least the hope that successful and worthy ideas
will not be squandered in application. If you are willing to settle
for that, read on.

REFERENCES

Krasker, William S., Edwin Kuh, and William S. Welsch. "Estimation for Dirty
    Data and Flawed Models." In *Handbook of Econometrics* vol. 1, edited by
    Z. Griliches and M.D. Intriligator (North-Holland, New York, 1983), pp.
    651–698.
Roll, Richard. "A Critique of the Asset Pricing Theory's Tests." *Journal of Financial
    Economics*, March 1977, pp. 129–176.
Rudd, Andrew, and Henry K. Clasing, Jr. *Modern Portfolio Theory*, 2d ed. (Orinda,
    Calif.: Andrew Rudd, 1988).
Sharpe, William F., and Gordon J. Alexander, *Investments* (Englewood Cliffs, N.J.:
    Prentice-Hall, 1990).

PART ONE

Foundations

Consensus Expected Returns: The Capital Asset Pricing Model

INTRODUCTION

Risk and expected return are the key players in the game of active management. We will introduce these players in this chapter and the next, which begin the "Foundations" section of the book.

This chapter contains our initial attempts to come to grips with expected returns. We will start with an exposition of the capital asset pricing model, or CAPM, as it is commonly called.

The chapter is an exposition of the CAPM, not a defense. We could hardly start a book on active management with a defense of a theory that makes active management look like a dubious enterprise. There is a double purpose for this exploration of CAPM. First, we should establish the humility principle from the start. It will not be easy to be a successful active manager. Second, it turns out that much of the analysis originally developed in support of the CAPM can be turned to the task of quantitative active management. Our use of the CAPM throughout this book will be independent of any current debate over the CAPM's validity. For discussions of these points, see Black (1993) and Grinold (1993).

One of the valuable by-products of the CAPM is a procedure for determining consensus expected returns. These consensus expected returns are valuable because they give us a standard of comparison. We know that our active management decisions will be driven by the difference between our expected returns and the consensus.

The major points of this chapter are:

- The return of any stock can be separated into a systematic (market) component and a residual component. No theory is required to do this.
- The CAPM says that the residual component of return has an expected value of zero.
- The CAPM is easy to understand and relatively easy to implement.
- There is a powerful logic of market efficiency behind the CAPM.
- The CAPM thrusts the burden of proof onto the active manager. It suggests that passive management is a lower-risk alternative to active management.
- The CAPM provides a valuable source of consensus expectations. The active manager can succeed to the extent that his or her forecasts are superior to the CAPM consensus forecasts.
- The CAPM is about expected returns, not risk.

The remainder of this chapter outlines the arguments that lead to the conclusions listed above. The chapter contains a technical appendix deriving the CAPM and introducing some formal notions used in technical appendixes of later chapters.

The goal of this book is to help the investor produce forecasts of expected return that differ from the consensus. This chapter identifies the CAPM as a source of consensus expected returns.

The CAPM is not the only possible forecast of expected returns, but it is arguably the best. As a later section of this chapter demonstrates, the CAPM has withstood many rigorous and practical tests since its proposal. One alternative is to use historical average returns, i.e., the average return to the stock over some previous period. This is not a good idea, for two main reasons. First, the historical returns contain a large amount of sample error.[1] Second,

---

[1]Given returns generated by an unvarying random process with known annual standard deviation σ, the standard error of the estimated annual return will be $\sigma/\sqrt{Y}$, where Y measures the number of years of data. This result is the same whether we observe daily, monthly, quarterly, or annual returns. Since typical volatilities are ~35 percent, standard errors are ~16 percent after 5 years of observations!

the universe of stocks changes over time: New stocks become available, and old stocks expire or merge. The stocks themselves change over time: Earnings change, capital structure may change, and the volatility of the stock may change. Historical averages are a poor alternative to consensus forecasts.[2]

A second alternative for providing expected returns is the arbitrage pricing theory (APT). We will consider the APT in Chap. 7. We find that it is an interesting tool for the active manager, but not as a source of *consensus* expected returns.

The CAPM has a particularly important role to play when selecting portfolios according to mean/variance preferences. If we use CAPM forecasts of expected returns and build optimal mean/variance portfolios, those portfolios will consist simply of positions in the market and the risk-free asset (with proportions depending on risk tolerance). In other words, optimal mean/variance portfolios will differ from the market portfolio and cash if and only if the forecast excess returns differ from the CAPM consensus excess returns.

This is in fact what we mean by "consensus." The market portfolio is the consensus portfolio, and the CAPM leads to the expected returns which make the market mean/variance optimal.

SEPARATION OF RETURN

The CAPM relies on two constructs, first the idea of a market portfolio M, and second the notion of beta, β, which links any stock or portfolio to the market. In theory, the market portfolio includes all assets: U.K. stocks, Japanese bonds, Malaysian plantations, etc. In practice, the market portfolio is generally taken as some broad value-weighted index of traded domestic equities, such as the NYSE Composite in the United States, the FTA in the United Kingdom, or the TOPIX in Japan.

Let's consider *any* portfolio P with excess returns r_P and the market portfolio M with excess returns r_M. Recall that excess returns

---

[2]For an alternative view, see Grauer and Hakansson (1982).

are total returns less the total return on a risk-free asset over the same time period. We define[3] the beta of portfolio P as

$$\beta_P = \frac{\text{Cov}(r_P, r_M)}{\text{Var}(r_M)} \tag{2.1}$$

Beta is proportional to the covariance between the portfolio's return and the market's return. It is a forecast of the future. Notice that the market portfolio has a beta of 1 and risk-free assets have a beta of 0.

Although beta is a forward-looking concept, the notion of beta—and indeed the name—comes from the simple linear regression of portfolio excess returns $r_P(t)$ in periods $t = 1, 2, \ldots, T$ on market excess returns $r_M(t)$ in those same periods. The regression is

$$r_P(t) = \alpha_P + \beta_P r_M(t) + \epsilon_P(t) \tag{2.2}$$

We call the estimates of β_P and α_P obtained from the regression the *realized* or *historical* beta and alpha in order to distinguish them from their forward-looking counterparts. The estimate shows how the portfolios have interacted in the past. Historical beta is a reasonable forecast of the betas that will be realized in the future, although it is possible to do better.[4]

As an example, Table 2.1 shows 60-month historical betas and forward-looking betas predicted by BARRA, relative to the S&P 500, for the constituents of the Major Market Index[5] through December 1992:

Beta is a way of separating risk and return into two parts. If we know a portfolio's beta, we can break the excess return

---

[3]For a discussion of variance, covariance, and other statistical and mathematical concepts, please refer to Appendix C at the end of the book.

[4]See Rosenberg (1985) for the empirical evidence. There is a tendency for betas to regress toward the mean. A stock with a high historical beta in one period will most likely have a lower (but still higher than 1.0) beta in the subsequent period. Similarly, a stock with a low beta in one period will most likely have a higher (but less than 1.0) beta in the following period. In addition, forecasts of betas based on the fundamental attributes of the company, rather than its returns over the past, say, 60 months, turn out to be much better forecasts of future betas.

[5]The Major Market Index consists effectively of 100 shares of each of 20 major U.S. stocks. As such, it is not capitalization-weighted, but rather share-price-weighted.

T A B L E 2.1

Betas for Major Market Index Constituents

Stock	Historical Beta	BARRA Predicted Beta
American Express	1.21	1.14
AT & T	0.96	0.69
Chevron	0.46	0.66
Coca Cola	0.96	1.03
Disney	1.23	1.13
Dow	1.13	1.05
Dupont	1.09	0.90
Eastman Kodak	0.60	0.93
Exxon	0.46	0.69
General Electric	1.30	1.08
General Motors	0.90	1.15
IBM	0.64	1.30
International Paper	1.18	1.07
Johnson & Johnson	1.13	1.09
McDonalds	1.06	1.03
Merck	1.06	1.11
MMM	0.74	0.97
Philip Morris	0.94	1.00
Procter & Gamble	1.00	1.01
Sears	1.05	1.05

on that portfolio into a market component and a residual component:

$$r_P = \beta_P r_M + \theta_P \tag{2.3}$$

In addition, the *residual return* θ_P will be uncorrelated with the market return r_M, and so the variance of portfolio P is

$$\sigma_P^2 = \beta_P^2 \sigma_M^2 + \omega_P^2 \tag{2.4}$$

where ω_P^2 is the residual variance of portfolio P, i.e., the variance of θ_P.

Beta allows us to separate the excess returns of any portfolio into two uncorrelated components, a market return and a residual return.

So far, no CAPM. *Absolutely no theory or assumptions are needed to get to this point.* We can always separate a portfolio's return into a component that is perfectly correlated with the market and a component that is uncorrelated with the market. It isn't even necessary to have the market portfolio M play any special role. The CAPM focuses on the market and says something special about the returns that are residual to the market.

THE CAPM

The CAPM states that the expected residual return on all stocks and any portfolio is equal to zero, i.e., that $E\{\theta_P\} = 0$. This means that the expected excess return on the portfolio, $E\{r_P\} = \mu_P$, is determined entirely by the expected excess return on the market, $E\{r_M\} = \mu_M$, and the portfolio's beta, β_P. The relationship is simple:

$$E\{r_P\} = \beta_P E\{r_M\} = \beta_P \mu_M \qquad (2.5)$$

Under the CAPM, the expected residual return on any stock or portfolio is zero. Expected excess returns are proportional to the stock's (or portfolio's) beta.

Implicit here is the CAPM assumption that all investors have the same expectations, and differ only in their tolerance for risk.

Notice that the CAPM result *must* hold for the market portfolio. If we sum (on a value-weighted basis) the returns of all the stocks, we get the market return, and so the value-weighted sum of the residual returns has to be exactly zero. However, the CAPM goes much further and says that the expected residual return of each stock is zero.

THE CAPM IS SENSIBLE

The logic behind the CAPM's assertion is fairly simple. The idea is that investors are compensated for taking necessary risks, but not for taking unnecessary risks. The risk in the market portfolio is necessary: Market risk is inescapable. The market is the "hot potato" of risk that must be borne by investors in aggregate. Residual risk, on the other hand, is self-imposed. All investors can avoid residual risk.

We can see the role of residual risk by considering the story of three investors, A, B, and C. Investor A bears residual risk because he is overweighting some stocks and underweighting others, relative to the market. Investor A can think of the other participants in the market as being an investor B with an equal amount invested who has residual positions exactly opposite to A's and a very large investor C who holds the market portfolio. Investor B is "the other side" for investor A. If the expected residual returns for A are positive, then the expected residual returns for B must be negative! Any theory that assigns positive expected returns to one investor's residual returns smacks of a "greater fool" theory; i.e., there is a group of individuals who hold portfolios with negative expected residual returns.

An immediate consequence of this line of reasoning is that investors who don't think they have superior information should hold the market portfolio. If you are a "greater fool" *and* you know it, then you can protect yourself by not playing! This type of reasoning, and lower costs, has led to the growth in passive investment.

> **Under the CAPM, an individual whose portfolio differs from the market is playing a zero-sum game. The player has additional risk and no additional expected return. This logic leads to passive investing; i.e., buy and hold the market portfolio.**

Since this book is about active management, we will not follow this line of reasoning. The logic conflicts with a basic human trait: Very few people want to admit that they are the "greater fools."[6]

THE CAPM AND EFFICIENT MARKETS THEORY

The CAPM isn't the same as efficient markets theory, although the two are consistent. Efficient markets theory comes in three strengths: weak, semistrong, and strong. The weak form states that investors cannot outperform the market using only historical price

---

[6]As part of a class exercise at the Harvard Business School, students were polled about their salary expectations and the average salary people in the class would receive. About 80 percent of the students thought they would do better than average! This pattern of response has obtained in each year the questions have been asked.

and volume data. The semistrong form states that investors cannot outperform the market using only publicly available information: historical prices plus fundamental data, analysts' published recommendations, etc. The strong form of the efficient markets hypothesis states that investors can never outperform the market: Market prices contain all relevant information.

The CAPM makes similar statements, although perhaps from a slightly different perspective. For any investor whose portfolio doesn't match the market, there must (effectively) be another investor with exactly the opposite deviations from the market. So, as long as there are no "greater fools," we shouldn't expect either of those investors to outperform the market. Efficient markets theory argues that there are no "greater fools" because market prices reflect all useful information.

EXPECTED RETURNS AND PORTFOLIOS

We have just described the CAPM's assumption that expected residual returns are zero, and its implication that passive investing is optimal. As the technical appendix will treat in detail, in the context of mean/variance analysis, we can more generally exactly connect expected returns and portfolios. If we input expected returns from the CAPM into an optimizer—which optimally trades off portfolio expected return against portfolio variance—the result is the market portfolio.[7] Going in the other direction, if we start with the market portfolio and assume that it is optimal, we can back out the expected returns consistent with that: exactly the CAPM expected returns. In fact, given any portfolio defined as optimal, the expected returns to all other portfolios will be proportional to their betas with respect to that optimal portfolio.

For this reason, we call the CAPM expected returns the consensus expected returns. They are exactly the returns we back out by assuming that the market—the consensus portfolio—is optimal.

Throughout this book, we will find the one-to-one relationship between expected returns and portfolios quite useful. An active

---

[7]Depending on an individual investor's trade-off between return and risk, the resulting portfolio is actually a combination of the market and cash, or of the market and the minimum variance portfolio under the constraint of full investment.

manager, by definition, does not hold the market or consensus portfolio. Hence, this manager's expected returns will not match the consensus expected returns.

EX POST AND EX ANTE

The CAPM is about expectations. If we plot the CAPM-derived expected return on any collection of stocks or portfolios against the betas of those stocks and portfolios, we find that they lie on a straight line with an intercept equal to the risk-free rate of interest i_F and a slope equal to the expected excess return on the market μ_M. That line, illustrated in Fig. 2.1, is called the *security market line*.

The picture is drawn for a risk-free interest rate of 5 percent and an expected excess return on the market of 7 percent. The four points on the line include the market portfolio M and three portfolios P_1, P_2, and P_3 with betas of 0.8, 1.15, and 1.3, respectively.

If we look at the ex post or after the fact returns (these are called realizations), we see a scatter diagram of actual excess return against portfolio beta. Figure 2.2 shows a rather small scatter of three portfolios along with the market portfolio and the risk-free asset. We can always draw a line connecting the risk-free return and the realized market return. This ex post line might be dubbed an "insecurity" market line. The ex post line gives the component of return that the CAPM would have forecast *if* we had known

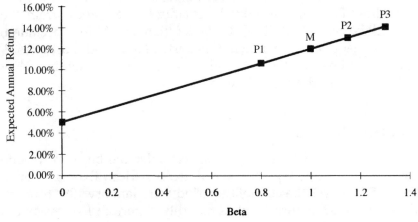

Figure 2.1 The security market line.

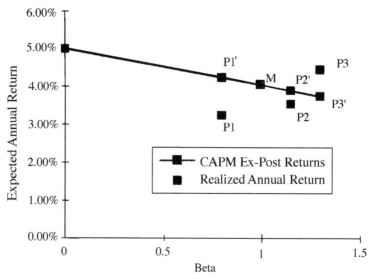

Figure 2.2 An ex-post market line.

how the market portfolio was going to perform. In particular, the line will slope downward in periods in which the market return is less than the risk-free return.

Notice that we have put P_1', P_2', and P_3' along the line. The actual returns for the portfolios were P_1, P_2, and P_3. The differences $P_1 - P_1'$, $P_2 - P_2'$, and $P_3 - P_3'$ are the residual returns on the three portfolios. The value-weighted deviations of all stocks from the line will be zero. Portfolio P_3 did better than its CAPM expectation, so its manager added value in this particular period. Portfolios P_1 and P_2, on the other hand, lie below the ex post market line. They did worse than their CAPM expectation.

AN EXAMPLE

As an example of CAPM analysis, consider the behavior of one constituent of the Major Market Index, American Express, versus the S&P 500 over the 60-month period from January 1988 through December 1992. Figure 2.3 plots monthly American Express excess returns against the monthly excess returns to the S&P 500.

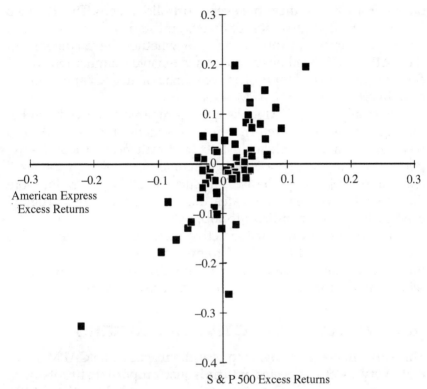

Figure 2.3 Realized excess returns.

Using regression analysis [Eq. (2.2)], we can determine the portfolio historical beta to be 1.21 with a standard error of 0.24. The CAPM predicts a residual return of zero. In fact, over this historical period, the realized residual return was -78 basis points per month with a standard error of 96 basis points: not significant at the 95 percent confidence level. The standard deviation of the monthly residual return was 7.05 percent. For this example, the regression coefficient R^2 was 0.31.

HOW WELL DOES THE CAPM WORK?

The ability to decompose return and risk into market and residual components depends on our ability to forecast betas. The CAPM goes one step further and says that the expected residual return on every stock (and therefore every portfolio) is zero. That last step is controversial. A great deal of theory and statistical sophistication have been thrown at this question of whether the predictions of the CAPM are indeed observed.[8] An extensive examination would carry us far from our topic of active management. "Chapter Notes" contains references on CAPM tests.

Basically, the CAPM looks good compared to naïve hypotheses, e.g., the expected returns on all stocks are the same. It does well, although less well, against abstract statistical tests of the hypothesis in Eq. (2.5), where the alternatives are "reject hypothesis" and "cannot reject hypothesis." The survival of the CAPM for more than twenty-five years indicates that it is a robust and rugged concept that is very difficult to topple.

The true question for the active manager is: How can I use the concepts behind the CAPM to my advantage? As we show in the next section, a true believer in the CAPM would have to be schizophrenic (or very cynical) to be an active manager.

RELEVANCE FOR ACTIVE MANAGERS

The active manager's goal is to beat the market. The CAPM states that every asset's expected return is just proportional to its beta, with expected residual returns equal to zero. Thus, the CAPM appears to be gloomy news for the active manager. A CAPM disciple would give successful active management only a 50-50 chance. A CAPM disciple would not be an active manager or, more significantly, would not hire an active manager.

The CAPM can help the active manager. The CAPM is a theory, and like any theory in the social sciences, it is based on assumptions that are not quite accurate. In particular, market players have differential information and thus different expectations. Superior information offers managers superior opportunities. We need not despair. There is an opportunity to succeed, and the CAPM provides some help.

---

[8]Most recently, Fama and French (1992) have generated significant publicity by claiming to refute the CAPM. But for an alternative interpretation of their results, and a discussion of the remaining uses of CAPM machinery, see Black (1993) and Grinold (1993).

The CAPM in particular and the theory of efficient markets in general help active managers by focusing their attention on how they expect to add value. The burden of proof has shifted to the active manager. A manager must be able to defend why her or his insights should produce superior returns in a somewhat efficient market. While bearing the burden of proof may not be pleasant, it does force the manager to dig deeper and think more clearly in developing and marketing active strategy ideas. The active manager is thus on the defensive, and should be less likely to confuse luck with skill and more likely to eliminate some nonproductive ideas, since they cannot pass scrutiny in a market with a modicum of efficiency.

The CAPM has shifted the burden of proof to the active manager.

The CAPM also helps active managers by distinguishing between the market and the residual component of return. Recall that this decomposition of return does not require any theory. It requires only good forecasts of beta. This can assist the manager's effort to control market risk; many active managers feel that they cannot accurately time the market and would prefer to maintain a portfolio beta close to 1. The decomposition of risk allows these managers to avoid taking active market positions.

The separation of return into market and residual components can help the active manager's research. There is no need to forecast the expected excess market return μ_M if you control beta. The manager can focus research on forecasting residual returns. The consensus expectations for the residual returns are zero; that's a convenient starting point. The CAPM provides consensus expected returns against which the manager can contrast his or her ideas.

The ideas behind the CAPM help the active manager to avoid the risk of market timing and to focus research on residual returns that have a consensus expectation of zero.

FORECASTS OF BETA AND EXPECTED MARKET RETURNS

The CAPM forecasts of expected return will be only as good as the forecasts of beta. There are a multitude of procedures for forecasting beta. The simplest involves using historical beta derived from an analysis of past returns. A slightly more complicated procedure invokes a bayesian adjustment to these historical betas. In Chap. 3, "Risk," we will discuss a more adaptive and forward-looking approach to forecasting risk in general and beta in particular.

We can estimate the expected excess market return μ_M from an analysis of historical returns. Notice that any beta-neutral policy would not require an accurate estimate of μ_M. With a portfolio beta equal to 1.0, the market excess return will not contribute to active return.

SUMMARY

This chapter has presented the capital asset pricing model (CAPM) and discussed its motivation, its implications, and its relevance for active managers. In a later chapter, we will discuss some of the theoretical shortcomings of the CAPM along with an alternative model of expected asset returns called the APT.

PROBLEMS

1. In December 1992, Sears had a predicted beta of 1.05 with respect to the S&P 500 index. If the S&P 500 index subsequently underperformed Treasury bills by 5.0 percent, what would be the expected excess return to Sears?

2. If the long-term expected excess return to the S&P 500 index is 7 percent per year, what is the expected excess return to Sears?

3. Assume that residual returns are uncorrelated across stocks. Stock A has a beta of 1.15 and a volatility of 35 percent. Stock B has a beta of 0.95 and a volatility of 33 percent. If the market volatility is 20 percent, what is the correlation of stock A with stock B? Which stock has higher residual volatility?

4. What set of expected returns would lead us to invest 100 percent in GE stock?

5. According to the CAPM, what is the expected residual return of an active manager?

CHAPTER NOTES

The CAPM was developed by Sharpe (1964). Treynor (1961), Lintner (1965), and Mossin (1966) were on roughly the same track in the same era.

There is no controversy over the logic that links the premises of the CAPM to its conclusions. There is, however, some discussion of the validity of the predictions that the CAPM gives us. General discussions of this point can be found in Mullins (1982) or in Sharpe and Alexander's text (1990). The recent publicity concerning the validity of the CAPM focused on the results of Fama and French (1992). For a discussion of their results, see Black (1993) and Grinold (1993). A more advanced treatment of the econometric issues involved in this issue can be found in Litzenberger and Huang (1988).

The technical appendix assumes some familiarity with efficient set theory. This can be found in the appendix to Roll (1977), Merton (1972), Ingersoll (1987), or Litzenberger and Huang (1988). The technical appendix also explores connections between expected returns and portfolios, a topic first investigated by Black (1972).

REFERENCES

Black, Fischer. "Capital Market Equilibrium with Restricted Borrowing." *Journal of Business*, vol. 45, July 1972, pp. 444–455.
———. "Estimating Expected Returns." *Financial Analysts Journal*, vol. 49, September/October 1993, pp. 36–38.
Fama, Eugene F., and Kenneth R. French. "The Cross-Section of Expected Stock Returns." *Journal of Finance*, vol. 47, no. 2, June 1992, pp. 427–465.
Grauer, R., and N. Hakansson. "Higher Return, Lower Risk: Historical Returns on Long-Run Actually Managed Portfolios of Stocks, Bonds, and Bills." *Financial Analysts Journal*, vol. 38, no. 2, March/April 1982, pp. 2–16.
Grinold, Richard C. "Is Beta Dead Again?" *Financial Analysts Journal*, vol. 49, July/August 1993, pp. 28–34.
Ingersoll, Jonathan E., Jr. *Theory of Financial Decision Making* (Savage, Md.: Rowman & Littlefield Publishers, Inc., 1987).
Lintner, John. "The Valuation of Risk Assets and the Selection of Risky Investments in Stock Portfolios and Capital Budgets." *Review of Economics and Statistics*, vol. 47, no. 1, February 1965, pp. 13–37.

————. "Security Prices, Risk, and Maximal Gains from Diversification." *Journal of Finance*, vol. 20, no. 4, December 1965, pp. 587–615.

Litzenberger, Robert H., and Chi-Fu Huang. *Foundations for Financial Economics* (New York: North-Holland, 1988).

Markowitz, H. M. *Portfolio Selection: Efficient Diversification of Investment.* Cowles Foundation Monograph 16 (New Haven, Conn.: Yale University Press, 1959).

Merton, Robert C. "An Analytical Derivation of the Efficient Portfolio." *Journal of Financial and Quantitative Analysis*, vol. 7, September 1972, pp. 1851–1872.

Mossin, Jan. "Equilibrium in a Capital Asset Market." *Econometrica*, vol. 34, no. 4, October 1966, pp. 768–783.

Mullins, D. W., Jr. "Does the Capital Asset Pricing Model Work?" *Harvard Business Review*, January–February 1982, pp. 105–114.

Roll, Richard. "A Critique of the Asset Pricing Theory's Tests." *Journal of Financial Economics*, March 1977, pp. 129–176.

Rosenberg, Barr. "Prediction of Common Stock Betas." *Journal of Portfolio Management*, vol. 12, no. 2, Winter 1985, pp. 5–14.

Rudd, Andrew, and Henry K. Clasing, Jr. *Modern Portfolio Theory*, 2d ed. (Orinda, Calif.: Andrew Rudd, 1988).

Sharpe, William F. "Capital Asset Prices: A Theory of Market Equilibrium under Conditions of Risk." *Journal of Finance*, vol. 19, no. 3, September 1964, pp. 425–442.

————. "The Sharpe Ratio." *Journal of Portfolio Management*, vol. 21, no. 1, Fall 1994, pp. 49–58.

Sharpe, William F., and Gordon J. Alexander. *Investments* (Englewood Cliffs, N.J.: Prentice-Hall, 1990).

Treynor, J. L. "Toward a Theory of the Market Value of Risky Assets." Unpublished manuscript, 1961.

TECHNICAL APPENDIX

This appendix details results of mean/variance analysis that are fundamental to the CAPM and, to a certain extent, the APT. It begins with mathematical notation and preliminary assumptions. It then introduces the machinery of "characteristic portfolios" defined by distinctive risk and return properties. This machinery will suffice to derive the results of CAPM, and will prove useful in later chapters as well.

Particular characteristic portfolios include portfolio C, the minimum-variance portfolio, and portfolio Q, the portfolio with the highest ratio of expected return to standard deviation of return (highest Sharpe ratio). The efficient frontier describes a set of characteristic portfolios, defined by minimum variance for each achievable level of return. The CAPM reduces to the proposition that portfolio Q is the market portfolio.

Mathematical Notation

For clarity, we will represent scalars in plain text, vectors as bold lowercase letters, and matrices as bold uppercase letters.

h = the vector of risky asset holdings, i.e., a portfolio's percentage weights in each asset

f = the vector of expected excess returns

μ = the vector of expected excess returns under the CAPM; i.e., the CAPM holds when **f** = **μ**.

V = the covariance matrix of excess returns for the risky assets (assumed nonsingular)

β = the vector of asset betas

e = the vector of ones (i.e., $e_n = 1$)

We define "risk" as the annual standard deviation of excess return.

Assumptions

We consider a single period with no rebalancing of the portfolio within the period. The underlying assumptions are:

A_1 A risk-free asset exists.

A_2 All first and second moments exist.

A_3 It is not possible to build a fully invested portfolio that has zero risk.

A_4 The expected excess return on portfolio C, the fully invested portfolio with minimum risk, is positive.

We are keeping score in nominal terms, so for a reasonably short period there should be an instrument whose return is certain (a U.S. Treasury bill, for example).

In later chapters we will dispense with requirement A_4, that the fully invested minimum-risk portfolio has a positive expected excess return. This certainly holds for any reasonable set of numbers; however, it is not strictly necessary for many of the results that appear in these technical appendixes. See the technical appendix of Chapter 7 for more on that topic.

Characteristic Portfolios

Assets have a multitude of attributes, such as betas, expected returns, earnings-to-price (E/P) ratios, capitalization, membership in an economic sector, and the like. In this appendix, we will associate a *characteristic portfolio* with each asset attribute.

The characteristic portfolio will uniquely capture the defining attribute. The characteristic portfolio machinery will allow us to connect attributes and portfolios, and to identify a portfolio's exposure to the attribute in terms of its covariance with the characteristic portfolio.

This process is reversible. We can start with a portfolio and find the attribute that this portfolio expresses most effectively.

Once we have established the relationship between the attributes and the portfolios, the CAPM becomes an economically motivated statement about the characteristic portfolio of the expected excess returns.

Let $\mathbf{a}^T = \{a_1, a_2, \dots, a_N\}$ be any vector of asset *attributes* or *characteristics*. The *exposure* of portfolio $\mathbf{h}_P$ to attribute $\mathbf{a}$ is simply $a_p = \sum_n a_n h_{P,n}$.

Proposition 1

1. For any attribute $a \neq 0$ there is a unique portfolio $\mathbf{h}_a$ that has minimum risk and unit exposure to a. The holdings of the characteristic portfolio $\mathbf{h}_a$, are

$$\mathbf{h}_a = \frac{\mathbf{V}^{-1}\mathbf{a}}{\mathbf{a}^T\mathbf{V}^{-1}\mathbf{a}} \qquad (2A.1)$$

Characteristic portfolios are not necessarily fully invested. They can include long and short positions and have significant leverage. Take the characteristic portfolio for earnings-to-price ratios. Since typical earnings-to-price ratios range roughly from 0.15 to 0, the characteristic portfolio will require leverage to generate a portfolio earnings-to-price ratio of 1. This leverage does not cause us problems, for two reasons. First, we typically analyze return per unit of risk, accounting for the leverage. Second, when it comes to building investable portfolios, we can always combine the benchmark with a small amount of the characteristic portfolio, effectively deleveraging it.

2. The variance of the characteristic portfolio $\mathbf{h}_a$ is given by

$$\sigma_a^2 = \mathbf{h}_a^T \mathbf{V} \mathbf{h}_a = \frac{1}{\mathbf{a}^T \mathbf{V}^{-1} \mathbf{a}} \qquad (2A.2)$$

3. The beta of all assets with respect to portfolio $\mathbf{h}_a$ is equal to $\mathbf{a}$:

$$\mathbf{a} = \frac{\mathbf{V} \mathbf{h}_a}{\sigma_a^2} \qquad (2A.3)$$

4. Consider two attributes a and d with characteristic portfolios $\mathbf{h}_a$ and $\mathbf{h}_d$. Let a_d and d_a be, respectively, the exposure of portfolio $\mathbf{h}_d$ to characteristic a and the exposure of portfolio $\mathbf{h}_a$ to characteristic d. The covariance of the characteristic portfolios satisfies

$$\sigma_{a,d} = a_d \sigma_a^2 = d_a \sigma_d^2 \qquad (2A.4)$$

5. If κ is a positive scalar, then the characteristic portfolio of κa is $\mathbf{h}_a / \kappa$. Because characteristic portfolios have unit exposure to the attribute, if we multiply the attribute by κ, we will need to divide the characteristic portfolio by κ to preserve unit exposure.

6. If characteristic a is a weighted combination of characteristics d and f, then the characteristic portfolio of a is a weighted combination of the characteristic portfolios of d and f; in particular, if $a = \kappa_d d + \kappa_f f$, then

$$\mathbf{h}_a = \left(\frac{\kappa_d \sigma_a^2}{\sigma_d^2} \right) \mathbf{h}_d + \left(\frac{\kappa_f \sigma_a^2}{\sigma_f^2} \right) \mathbf{h}_f \qquad (2A.5)$$

where

$$\frac{1}{\sigma_a^2} = \left(\frac{\kappa_d a_d}{\sigma_d^2} \right) + \left(\frac{\kappa_f a_f}{\sigma_f^2} \right) \qquad (2A.6)$$

Proof   We derive the holdings of the characteristic portfolio by solving the defining optimization problem. The portfolio is minimum risk, given the constraint that its exposure to characteristic a

equals 1. The first-order conditions for minimizing $\mathbf{h}^T\mathbf{Vh}$ subject to the constraint $\mathbf{h}^T\mathbf{a} = 1$ are

$$\mathbf{h}^T\mathbf{a} = 1 \tag{2A.7}$$

$$\mathbf{Vh} - \theta\mathbf{a} = 0 \tag{2A.8}$$

where θ is the Lagrange multiplier. Equation (2A.8) implies that $\mathbf{h}$ is proportional to $\mathbf{V}^{-1}\mathbf{a}$, with proportionality constant θ. We can then use Eq. (2A.7) to solve for θ. The results are

$$\mathbf{h}_a = \frac{\mathbf{V}^{-1}\mathbf{a}}{\mathbf{a}^T\mathbf{V}^{-1}\mathbf{a}} \tag{2A.9}$$

and

$$\theta = \frac{1}{\mathbf{a}^T\mathbf{V}^{-1}\mathbf{a}} \tag{2A.10}$$

This proves item 1.

We can verify item 2 using Eq. (2A.9) and the definition of portfolio variance. We can verify item 3 similarly, using the definition of $\boldsymbol{\beta}$ with respect to portfolio P as $\mathbf{Vh}_P/\sigma_P^2$.

For item (4), note that

$$\sigma_{ad} = \mathbf{h}_a^T\mathbf{Vh}_d \tag{2A.11}$$
$$= \{\mathbf{h}_a^T\mathbf{V}\}\mathbf{h}_d$$
$$= \{\sigma_a^2\mathbf{a}^T\}\mathbf{h}_d$$
$$= a_d\sigma_a^2$$

and

$$\sigma_{ad} = \mathbf{h}_a^T\mathbf{Vh}_d \tag{2A.12}$$
$$= \mathbf{h}_a^T\{\mathbf{Vh}_d\}$$
$$= \mathbf{h}_a^T\{\sigma_d^2\mathbf{d}\}$$
$$= d_a\sigma_d^2$$

Items 5 and 6 simply follow from substituting the result in 3 and clearing up the debris.

Examples

Portfolio C Suppose

$$\mathbf{e}^T = \{1, 1, \ldots, 1\} \tag{2A.13}$$

is the attribute. Every portfolio's exposure to $\mathbf{e}$, $(e_p = \sum_n h_{P,n})$ measures the extent of its investment. If $e_p = 1$, then the portfolio is fully invested. Portfolio C, the characteristic portfolio for attribute $\mathbf{e}$, is the minimum-risk fully invested portfolio:

$$\mathbf{h}_C = \frac{\mathbf{V}^{-1}\mathbf{e}}{\mathbf{e}^T\mathbf{V}^{-1}\mathbf{e}} \qquad (2A.14)$$

$$\sigma_C^2 = \mathbf{h}_C^T\mathbf{V}\mathbf{h}_C = \frac{1}{\mathbf{e}^T\mathbf{V}^{-1}\mathbf{e}} \qquad (2A.15)$$

$$\mathbf{e} = \frac{\mathbf{V}\mathbf{h}_C}{\sigma_C^2} \qquad (2A.16)$$

Equation (2A.16) demonstrates that every asset has a beta of 1 with respect to C.[9] In addition, for any portfolio P, we have

$$\sigma_{P,C} = e_p\sigma_C^2 \qquad (2A.17)$$

the covariance of any fully invested portfolio ($e_p = 1$) with portfolio C is σ_C^2.

Portfolio B   Suppose β is the attribute, where beta is defined by some benchmark portfolio B:

$$\beta = \frac{\mathbf{V}\mathbf{h}_B}{\sigma_B^2} \qquad (2A.18)$$

Then the benchmark is the characteristic portfolio of beta, i.e.,

$$\mathbf{h}_\beta = \frac{\mathbf{V}^{-1}\beta}{\beta^T\mathbf{V}^{-1}\beta} \qquad (2A.19)$$

$$= \mathbf{h}_B$$

---

[9] Here is some intuition behind this result. As we will learn in Chapter 3, each asset's marginal contribution to portfolio risk is proportional to its beta with respect to the portfolio. Since portfolio C is the minimum-risk portfolio, each asset must have identical marginal contribution to risk. Otherwise we could trade assets to reduce portfolio risk. So each asset has identical marginal contribution to risk, and hence identical beta. Since the beta of the portfolio with respect to itself must be 1, the value of those identical asset betas must be 1.

and

$$\sigma_B^2 = \mathbf{h}_B^T \mathbf{V} \mathbf{h}_B \qquad (2A.20)$$

$$= \frac{1}{\boldsymbol{\beta}^T \mathbf{V}^{-1} \boldsymbol{\beta}}$$

So the benchmark is the minimum-risk portfolio with a beta of 1. This makes sense intuitively. All $\beta = 1$ portfolios have the same systematic risk. Since the benchmark has zero residual risk, it has the minimum total risk of all $\beta = 1$ portfolios.

Using item 4 of the proposition, we see that the relationship between portfolios *B* and *C* is

$$\sigma_{B,C} = e_B \sigma_C^2 = \beta_C \sigma_B^2 \qquad (2A.21)$$

Portfolio q   The expected excess returns $\mathbf{f}$ have portfolio q (discussed below) as their characteristic portfolio.

Sharpe Ratio
For any risky portfolio P ($\sigma_P > 0$), the *Sharpe ratio* is defined as the expected excess return on portfolio P, f_P, divided by the risk of portfolio P:

$$\mathrm{SR}_P = \frac{f_P}{\sigma_P} \qquad (2A.22)$$

Proposition 2: Portfolio with the Maximum Sharpe Ratio
Let q be the characteristic portfolio of the expected excess returns f:

$$\mathbf{h}_q = \frac{\mathbf{V}^{-1}\mathbf{f}}{\mathbf{f}^T\mathbf{V}^{-1}\mathbf{f}} \qquad (2A.23)$$

Then

1. $$\mathrm{SR}_q = \max\{\mathrm{SR}_P | P\} = (\mathbf{f}^T\mathbf{V}^{-1}\mathbf{f})^{1/2} \qquad (2A.24)$$

2. $$f_q = 1 \qquad (2A.25)$$

$$\sigma_q^2 = \frac{1}{\mathbf{f}^T\mathbf{V}^{-1}\mathbf{f}} \qquad (2A.26)$$

3.
$$f = \frac{Vh_q}{\sigma_q^2} \qquad (2A.27)$$

$$= \left(\frac{Vh_q}{\sigma_q}\right)SR_q$$

4. If ρ_{Pq} is the correlation between portfolios P and q, then
$$SR_P = \rho_{Pq}SR_q \qquad (2A.28)$$

5. The fraction of q invested in risky assets is given by

$$e_q = \frac{f_C\sigma_q^2}{\sigma_C^2} \qquad (2A.29)$$

Proof For any portfolio h_P, the Sharpe ratio is $SR_P = f_P/\sigma_P$. For any positive constant κ, the portfolio with holdings κh_P will also have a Sharpe ratio equal to SR_P. Thus, in looking for the maximum Sharpe ratio, we can set the expected excess return to 1 and minimize risk. We then minimize h^TVh subject to the constraint that $h^Tf = 1$. This is just the problem we solved to get h_q, the characteristic portfolio of f.

Items 2 and 3 are just properties of the characteristic portfolio. For 4, premultiply 3 by h_P and divide by σ_P. This yields

$$SR_P = \frac{f_P}{\sigma_P} = \frac{h_P^T f}{\sigma_P} \qquad (2A.30)$$

$$= \sigma_{Pq}\left(\frac{f_q}{\sigma_q^2}\right)\left(\frac{1}{\sigma_P}\right)$$

or

$$SR_P = \left(\frac{\sigma_{Pq}}{\sigma_P\sigma_q}\right)\left(\frac{f_q}{\sigma_q}\right) = \rho_{Pq}SR_q \qquad (2A.31)$$

Part 5 follows from Eq. (2A.4):

$$\sigma_{q,C} = e_q\sigma_C^2 = f_C\sigma_q^2 \qquad (2A.32)$$

Portfolio A Define alpha as $\alpha = f - \beta\, f_B$. Let h_A be the characteristic portfolio for alpha, the minimum-risk portfolio with alpha of 100 percent. (Portfolio A will involve significant leverage.) According to Eq. (2A.5), we can express h_A in terms of h_B and h_q. From Eq. (2A.4), we see that the relationship between alpha and beta is

$\sigma_{B,A} = \alpha_B \sigma_A^2 = \beta_A \sigma_B^2$. However, $\alpha_B = 0$ by construction, and so portfolios A and B are uncorrelated, and $\beta_A = 0$.

In many cases, we will find it convenient to assume that there is a fully invested portfolio that explains expected excess returns. That will be the case if the expected excess return on portfolio C is positive. This is not an unreasonable assumption, and we will use it throughout the book. The next proposition details some of its consequences.

Proposition 3
Assume that $f_C > 0$.

1. Portfolio q is net long:

$$e_q > 0 \qquad (2A.33)$$

Let portfolio Q be the characteristic portfolio of $e_q \mathbf{f}$. Portfolio Q is fully invested, with holdings $\mathbf{h}_Q = \mathbf{h}_q/e_q$. In addition, $SR_Q = SR_q$, and for any portfolio P with a correlation $\rho_{P,Q}$ with portfolio Q, we have

$$SR_P = \rho_{P,Q} SR_Q \qquad (2A.34)$$

2.
$$\frac{f_C}{\sigma_C^2} = \frac{f_Q}{\sigma_Q^2} \qquad (2A.35)$$

$$\mathbf{f} = f_Q\left(\frac{\mathbf{V h}_Q}{\sigma_Q^2}\right) = f_Q \boldsymbol{\beta}_{\text{with respect to } Q} \qquad (2A.36)$$

Note that Eq. (2A.36) specifies exactly how portfolio Q "explains" expected returns.

3.
$$\beta_Q = \frac{f_B \sigma_Q^2}{f_Q \sigma_B^2} \qquad (2A.37)$$

4. If the benchmark is fully invested, $e_B = 1$, then

$$\beta_Q = \frac{\beta_C f_B}{f_C} \qquad (2A.38)$$

Proof   For part 1, note that $e_Q \sigma_C^2 = f_C \sigma_Q^2$ and $f_C > 0$ imply $e_q > 0$. From part 5 of proposition 1,

$$\mathbf{h}_Q = \frac{\mathbf{h}_q}{e_q} \qquad (2A.39)$$

$$= \frac{\mathbf{h}_q \sigma_C^2}{f_C \sigma_q^2}$$

The holdings in portfolio Q are a positive multiple of the holdings in q, and so their Sharpe ratios and correlations with other portfolios are the same.

For item 2, start with $\mathbf{f} = \mathbf{Vh}_q/\sigma_q^2$ and use $1/\sigma_q^2 = f_C/e_q\sigma_C^2$. This yields $\mathbf{f} = f_C(\mathbf{Vh}_Q/\sigma_C^2)$. If we multiply this by $\mathbf{h}_Q$, we get $f_C/\sigma_C^2 = f_Q/\sigma_Q^2$, and $\mathbf{f} = f_Q(\mathbf{Vh}_Q/\sigma_Q^2)$.

For item 3, premultiply Eq. (2A.27) by $\mathbf{h}_B$. This yields

$$f_B = \{\mathbf{h}_B^T\mathbf{Vh}_Q\}\left(\frac{f_Q}{\sigma_Q^2}\right) \qquad (2A.40)$$

$$= \left\{\frac{\mathbf{h}_B^T\mathbf{Vh}_Q}{\sigma_B^2}\right\}\left(\frac{\sigma_B^2 f_Q}{\sigma_Q^2}\right)$$

and so

$$f_B = \beta_Q\left(\frac{\sigma_B^2 f_Q}{\sigma_Q^2}\right) \qquad (2A.41)$$

which gives 3.

For item 4, note that $e_B = 1$ and $\sigma_{B,C} = e_B\sigma_C^2 = \beta_C\sigma_B^2$ imply that $\beta_C = \sigma_C^2/\sigma_B^2$. When this is combined with $f_C/\sigma_C^2 = f_Q/\sigma_Q^2$, we get 4.

Partial List of Characteristic Portfolios

Characteristic	Portfolio
$\mathbf{f}$	$\mathbf{h}_q$
$e_q\mathbf{f}$	$\mathbf{h}_Q$ (if $f_C > 0$)
$\boldsymbol{\beta}$	$\mathbf{h}_B$
$\mathbf{e}$	$\mathbf{h}_C$
$\boldsymbol{\alpha} = \mathbf{f} - \boldsymbol{\beta}f_B$	$\mathbf{h}_A$

We have built portfolios capturing the important characteristics for portfolio management. These portfolios will play significant roles as we further develop the theory. For example, if we want to build a portfolio based on our alphas, but with a beta of 1, full investment, and conforming to our preferences for risk and return, we will build a linear combination of portfolios A, B, and C.

The Efficient Frontier

Now focus on two characteristic fully invested portfolios: portfolio
C and portfolio Q. At this point we would like to introduce a set
of distinctive portfolios called the efficient frontier. Portfolio C and
portfolio Q are both elements of this set. In fact, we will see that
all efficient-frontier portfolios are weighted combinations of portfolio C and portfolio Q, so each element of the efficient-frontier is a
characteristic portfolio. The return and risk characteristics of efficient frontier portfolios are simply parameterized in terms of the
return and risk characteristics of portfolio C and portfolio Q.

A fully invested portfolio is *efficient* if it has minimum risk
among all portfolios with the same expected return. Efficient frontier portfolios solve the minimization problem

$$\text{Minimize } \frac{h^T V h}{2} \tag{2A.42}$$

subject to the full investment and expected excess return constraints
(but not a long-only constraint):

$$e^T h = 1 \tag{2A.43}$$

$$f^T h = f_P \tag{2A.44}$$

We can solve this minimization problem to find:

$$h_P = \left(\frac{f_Q - f_P}{f_Q - f_C}\right) h_C + \left(\frac{f_P - f_C}{f_Q - f_C}\right) h_Q \tag{2A.45}$$

where we have used the definitions of h_C and h_Q and have assumed
that $f \neq e$. So efficient frontier portfolios are weighted combinations
of portfolio C and portfolio Q.

Remember that the correspondence between characteristics
and portfolios is one-to-one. We can therefore solve for the characteristic a_P that underlies each efficient portfolio, using Eq. (2A.45)
and (2A.5). In each case, the characteristic is a linear combination
of e and $e_q f$, the characteristics underlying portfolios C and Q, respectively:

$$a_P = w_C e + w_Q e_q f \tag{2A.46}$$

$$= \frac{1}{\sigma_P^2(f_Q - f_C)} \{\sigma_C^2(f_Q - f_P)e + \sigma_Q^2(f_P - f_C)e_q f\}$$

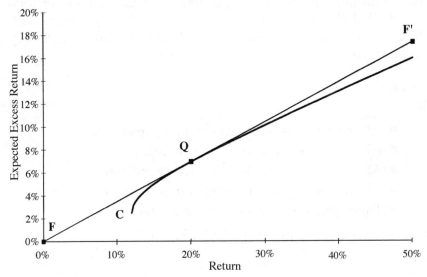

Figure 2A.1 The efficient frontier.

We can now use Eq. (2A.45) to solve for the variance of the efficient-frontier portfolios. We find

$$\sigma_P^2 = \sigma_C^2 + \kappa(f_P - f_C)^2 \qquad (2A..47)$$

with

$$\kappa = \frac{(\sigma_Q^2 - \sigma_C^2)}{(f_Q - f_C)^2} \qquad (2A.48)$$

We depict this relationship in Fig. 2A.1. In this figure, portfolio Q has a volatility of 20 percent and an expected excess return of 7 percent. Portfolio C has a volatility of 12 percent and, therefore, an expected excess return of 2.52 percent. The risk-free asset appears at the origin.

The Capital Asset Pricing Model

We establish the CAPM in two steps. We have already accomplished step 1, showing in Eq. (2A.36) that the vector of asset expected excess returns is proportional to the vector of asset betas with respect to portfolio Q. In step 2, we show that certain assumptions lead us to the conclusion that portfolio Q is the market portfolio M, i.e., that the market portfolio M is indeed the portfolio with the highest ratio of expected excess return to risk among all fully invested portfolios.

Theorem
If

- All investors have mean/variance preferences.
- All assets are included in the analysis.
- All investors know the expected excess returns.
- All investors agree on asset variances and covariances.
- There are no transactions costs or taxes.

then portfolio Q is equal to portfolio M, and

$$\mathbf{f} = \boldsymbol{\mu} = \boldsymbol{\beta}\mu_M \qquad (2A.49)$$

Proof   If all investors are free of transactions costs, have the same information, and choose portfolios in a mean/variance-efficient way, then each investor will choose a portfolio that is a mixture of Q and the risk-free portfolio F. That would place each investor somewhere along the line FQF' in Fig. 2A.1. Portfolios from F to Q combine the risk-free portfolio (lending) and portfolio Q. Portfolios from Q to F' represent a levered position (borrowing) in portfolio Q.

When we aggregate (add up, weighted by value invested) the portfolios of all investors, they must equal the market portfolio M, since the net supply of borrowing and lending must equal zero. The only way that the portfolios along FQF' can aggregate to a fully invested portfolio is to have that aggregate equal Q. The aggregate must equal M, and the aggregate must equal Q. Therefore $M = Q$.

EXERCISES

1. Show that $\beta_C = \sigma_C^2/\sigma_M^2$. Since portfolio C is the minimum-variance portfolio, this relationship implies that $\beta_C \leq 1$, with $\beta_C = 1$ only if the market is the minimum-variance portfolio.
2. Show that $f_Q = f_C + \sigma_C^2/(\kappa f_C)$; i.e., $\kappa = \sigma_C^2/(f_C(f_Q - f_C))$.

3. What is the "characteristic" associated with the MMI portfolio? How would you find it?

4. Prove that the fully invested portfolio that maximizes $f_P - \lambda\sigma_P^2$ has expected excess return $f^* = f_C + 1/(2\lambda\kappa)$.

5. Prove that portfolio Q is the optimal solution in Exercise 4 if $\lambda = f_C/(2\sigma_C^2) = f_Q/(2\sigma_Q^2)$.

6. Suppose portfolio T is on the fully invested efficient frontier. Prove Eq. (2A.45), i.e., that there exists a w_T such that $\mathbf{h}_T = w_T\mathbf{h}_C + (1 - w_T)\mathbf{h}_Q$.

7. If T is fully invested and efficient and $T \neq C$, prove that there exists a fully invested efficient portfolio T^* such that $\text{Cov}\{r_T, r_{T^*}\} = 0$.

8. For any $T \neq C$ on the efficient frontier and any fully invested portfolio P, show that we can write

$$E\{r_P\} = E\{r_{T^*}\} + E\{r_T - r_{T^*}\}\left(\frac{\text{Cov}\{r_P, r_T\}}{\text{Var}\{r_T\}}\right)$$

where T^* is the fully invested efficient portfolio that is uncorrelated with T.

9. If P is any fully invested portfolio, and T is the efficient fully invested efficient portfolio with the same expected returns as P, $\mu_P = \mu_T$, we can always write the returns to P as $r_P = r_C + \{r_T - r_C\} + \{r_P - r_T\}$. Prove that these three components of return are uncorrelated. We can interpret the risks associated with these three components as the cost of full investment, $\text{Var}\{r_C\}$; the cost of the extra expected return $\mu_P - \mu_C$, $\text{Var}\{r_T - r_C\}$; and the diversifiable cost, $\text{Var}\{r_P - r_T\}$.

APPLICATIONS EXERCISES[10]

For ease of calculation, focus on just MMI assets when considering these application exercises. The MMI is a share-weighted 20-stock

---

[10]Applications exercises will appear on occasion throughout the book. These are exercises that require access to applications tools, e.g., a risk model and an optimizer. Applications exercises often aim to demonstrate results in the book, not through mathematical proof, but through software "experiments."

index (you can consider it a portfolio with 100 shares of each stock). Also define the market as the capitalization-weighted MMI, or CAPMMI for short.

1. Restricting attention to MMI stocks, build the minimum-variance fully invested portfolio (portfolio C). What are the betas of the constituent stocks with respect to this portfolio? Verify Eq. (2A.16).

2. Build an efficient, fully invested portfolio with CAPM expected returns (proportional to betas with respect to the CAPMMI, which has an assumed expected excess return of 6 percent). Use a risk aversion of $\lambda = 6/\sigma_{mkt}^2$, where σ_{mkt}^2 is the risk of the CAPMMI.

   a. What are the beta and expected return to the portfolio?

   b. Compare this portfolio to the linear combination of portfolios C and B described in Eq. (2A.45). In this case, portfolio B is the CAPMMI.

CHAPTER 3

Risk

INTRODUCTION

In the previous chapter we presented the CAPM as a model of consensus expected return. Expected return is the protagonist in the drama of active management. Risk is the antagonist.

This section will present the definition of risk that is used throughout the book. The important lessons are:

- Risk is the standard deviation of return.
- Risks don't add.
- Many institutional investors care more about active and residual risk than about total risk.
- Active risk depends primarily on the size of the active position, not the size of the benchmark position.
- The cost of risk is proportional to variance.
- Risk models identify the important sources of risk and separate risk into components.

We start with our definition of risk.

DEFINING RISK

Risk is an abstract concept. An economist considers risk to be expressed in a person's preferences. What one individual perceives as risky may not be perceived as risky by another.[1]

---

[1]There is a vast literature on this subject. The books of Arrow, Raiffa, and Borch are a good introduction. See also Bernstein (1996) for a compelling argument that the understanding of risk was one of the key developments of modern civilization.

We need an operational and therefore universal and impersonal definition of risk. Institutional money managers are agents of pension fund trustees, who are themselves agents of the corporation and the beneficiaries of the fund. In that setting, we cannot hope to have a personal view of risk. For this reason, the risk measure we seek is what an economist might call a measure of uncertainty rather than of risk.

We need a symmetric view of risk. Institutional money managers are judged relative to a benchmark or relative to their peers. The money manager who does not hold a stock that goes up suffers as much as one who holds a larger than average amount of a stock that goes down.

We need a flexible definition of risk. Our definition of risk should apply both to individual stocks and to portfolios. We should be able to talk about realized risk in the past and to forecast risk over any future horizon.

We want to limit ourselves to a measure of risk that we can accurately forecast. Partly for this reason, we want a measure of risk that we can build up from assets to portfolios. We need not only the risk for each asset, but also the risk for every possible combination of assets into portfolios.

So our definition of risk must meet several criteria. At the same time, we have a choice of several potential risk measures. Let's review them.

To begin with, all definitions of risk arise fundamentally from the probability distributions of possible returns. This distribution describes the probability that the return will be between 1 and 1.01 percent, the probability of a return between 1.01 and 1.02 percent, etc. For example, Fig. 3.1 displays the empirical distribution of monthly returns for the Fidelity Magellan Fund, based on its performance from January 1973 to September 1994. According to this distribution, 26 percent of the Magellan Fund monthly returns fell between 2.5 and 7.5 percent.

The distribution of returns describes the probabilities of all possible outcomes. As a result, it is complicated and full of detail. It can answer all questions about returns and probabilities. It can be a forecast or a summary of realized returns. Conceptually, it applies to every fund type: equity, bond, or other. Unfortunately, the distribution of returns is too complicated and detailed in its

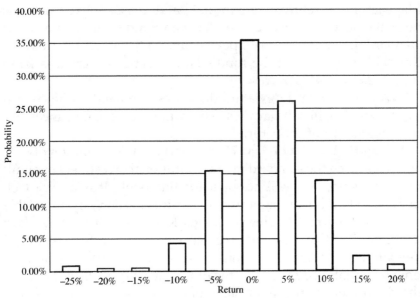

Figure 3.1 Magellan Fund. January 1973–September 1994.

entirety. Hence all our risk measure choices will attempt to capture in a single number the essentials of risk that are more fully described in the complete distribution. Because of this simplification, each definition of risk will have at least some shortcomings. Different measures may also have shortcomings based on difficulties of accurate estimation. As we will discuss later, by assuming a normal distribution, we can calculate all these risk measures as mathematical translations of the mean and standard deviation. But first we will discuss these alternatives without that assumption.

The *standard deviation* measures the spread of the distribution about its mean. Investors commonly refer to the standard deviation as the volatility. The variance is the square of the standard deviation. For our Magellan Fund example, the standard deviation of the monthly returns was 6.3 percent and the mean was 1.6 percent. If these returns were normally distributed, then two-thirds of the returns would lie within 6.3 percentage points of the mean, i.e., in the band between −4.7 and 7.9 percent. In fact, 73 percent of the

Magellan Fund returns were in that band, reasonably close to the normal distribution result. The Magellan Fund's annual mean and standard deviation were 19.2 percent and 21.8 percent, respectively. Roughly two-thirds of the fund's annual returns were in a band from -2.6% to 41 percent.

As the standard deviation decreases, the band within which most returns will fall narrows. The standard deviation measures the uncertainty of the returns.

Standard deviation was Harry Markowitz's definition of risk, and it has been the standard in the institutional investment community ever since. We will adopt it for this book. It is a very well understood and unambiguous statistic. It is particularly applicable to existing tools for building portfolios. Knowing just asset standard deviations and correlations, we can calculate portfolio standard deviations. Standard deviations tend to be relatively stable over time (especially compared to mean returns and other moments of the distribution), and financial economists have developed very powerful tools for accurately forecasting standard deviations.

But before we discuss the standard deviation in more detail, we will discuss some alternative definitions. Critics of the standard deviation point out that it measures the possibility of returns both above and below the mean. Most investors would define risk as involving small or negative returns (although short sellers have the opposite view). This has generated an alternative risk measure: *semivariance,* or *downside risk.*

Semivariance is defined in analogy to variance, but using only returns below the mean. If the returns are symmetric—i.e., the return is equally likely to be x percent above or x percent below the mean—then the semivariance is exactly one-half the variance. Authors differ in defining downside risk. One approach defines downside risk as the square root of the semivariance, in analogy to the relation between standard deviation and variance.

From January 1973 to September 1994, the Magellan Fund had a realized semivariance of 21.6, which was 55 percent of its variance of 39.5. According to Fig. 3.1, the distribution extended slightly farther to the left (negative returns) than to the right (positive returns), and so the semivariance was slightly more than half the variance.

A variant of this definition is *target semivariance*, a generalization of semivariance that focuses on returns below a target, instead of just below the mean.

Downside risk clearly answers the critics of standard deviation by focusing entirely on the undesirable returns. However, there are several problems with downside risk. First, its definition is not as unambiguous as that of standard deviation or variance, nor are its statistical properties as well known. Second, it is computationally challenging for large portfolio construction problems. Aggregating semivariance from assets to portfolios is extremely difficult to do well.[2]

Third, to the extent that investment returns are reasonably symmetric, most definitions of downside risk are simply proportional to standard deviation or variance and so contain no additional information. Active returns (relative to a benchmark) should be symmetric by construction.

To the extent that investment returns may not be symmetric, there are problems in forecasting downside risk. Return asymmetries are not stable over time, and so are very difficult to forecast.[3] Realized downside risk may not be a good forecast of future downside risk.

Moreover, we estimate downside risk with only half of the data, and so we lose statistical accuracy. This problem is accentuated for target semivariance, which often focuses even more on events in the "tail" of the distribution.

Shortfall probability is another risk definition, and one that is perhaps closely related to an intuitive conception of what risk is. The shortfall probability is the probability that the return will lie below some target amount. For example, the probability of a Magellan Fund monthly loss in excess of 10 percent was 3.4 percent.

Shortfall probability has the advantage of closely corresponding to an intuitive definition of risk. However, it faces the same problems as downside risk: ambiguity, poor statistical understand-

---

[2]The evidence cited in the section "How Do Risk Models Work?" asserts that it is impossible to do this well.
[3]The exception is for options or dynamic strategies like portfolio insurance, which have been engineered to exhibit asymmetries.

ing, difficulty of forecasting, and dependence on individual investor preferences.

Forecasting is a particularly thorny problem, and it is accentuated as the shortfall target becomes lower. At the extreme, probability forecasts for very large shortfalls are influenced by perhaps only one or two observations.

Value at risk is similar to shortfall probability. Where shortfall probability takes a target return and calculates the probability of returns falling below that, value at risk takes a target probability, e.g., the 1 percent or 5 percent lowest returns, and converts that probability to an associated return. For the Magellan Fund, the worst 1 percent of all returns exceeded a 20.8 percent loss. For a $1000 investment in the Magellan Fund, the value at risk was $208.

Value at risk is closely related to shortfall probability, and shares the same advantages and disadvantages.

Where does the normal distribution fit into this discussion of risk statistics? The normal distribution is a standard assumption in academic investment research and is a standard distribution throughout statistics. It is completely defined by its mean and standard deviation. Much research has shown that investment returns do not exactly follow normal distributions, but instead have wider distributions; i.e., the probability of extreme events is larger for real investments than a normal distribution would imply.

The above definitions of risk all attempt to capture the risk inherent in the "true" return distribution. An alternative approach would be to assume that returns are normally distributed. Then the mean and standard deviation immediately fix the other statistics: downside risk, semivariance, shortfall probability, and value at risk. Such an approach might robustly estimate the quantities that are of most interest to individual investors, using the most accurate estimates and a few reasonable assumptions.

More generally, this points out that the choice of how to define risk is separate from the choice of how to report risk. But any approach relying on the normal distribution would strongly motivate us to focus on standard deviation at the asset level, which we can aggregate to the portfolio level. Reporting a final number then as standard deviation or as some mathematical transformation of standard deviation is a matter of personal taste, rather than an influence on our choice of portfolio.

STANDARD DEVIATION

The definition of risk that meets our criteria of being universal, symmetric, flexible, and accurately forecastable is the standard deviation of return.[4] If R_P is a portfolio's total return (i.e., a number like 1.10 if the portfolio returned 10 percent), then the portfolio's standard deviation of return is denoted by $\sigma_P \equiv \mathrm{Std}\{R_P\}$. A portfolio's excess return r_P differs from the total return R_P by R_F (a number like 1.04 if Treasury bills return 4 percent), which we know at the beginning of the period. Hence the risk of the excess return is equal to the risk of the total return. We will typically quote this risk, or standard deviation of return, on a percent per year basis.

The standard deviation has some interesting characteristics. In particular, it does *not* have the portfolio property. The standard deviation of a portfolio is not the weighted average of the standard deviations of the constituents. Suppose the correlation between the returns of stocks 1 and 2 is ρ_{12}. If we have a portfolio of 50 percent stock 1 and 50 percent stock 2, then

$$\sigma_P = \sqrt{(0.5 \cdot \sigma_1)^2 + (0.5 \cdot \sigma_2)^2 + 2 \cdot (0.5 \cdot \sigma_1) \cdot (0.5 \cdot \sigma_2) \cdot \rho_{12}} \quad (3.1)$$

and

$$\sigma_P \leq 0.5 \cdot \sigma_1 + 0.5 \cdot \sigma_2 \quad (3.2)$$

with the equality in Eq. (3.2) holding only if the two stocks are perfectly correlated ($\rho_{12} = 1$). For risk, the whole is less than the sum of its parts. This is the key to portfolio diversification. Figure 3.2 shows a simple example.

The risk of a portfolio made up of IBM and General Electric is plotted against the fraction of GE stock in the portfolio. The curved line represents the risk of the portfolio; the straight line represents the risk that we would obtain if the returns on IBM and GE were perfectly correlated. As of December 1992, the risk of GE was 27.4 percent/year, the risk of IBM was 29.7 percent/year, and the two returns were 62.9 percent correlated. The difference between

---

[4]For active investors in options and dynamic strategies such as portfolio insurance, the standard deviation is not the perfect risk definition. Yet even in that case, the standard deviation plays an important role [see Kahn and Stefek (1996)].

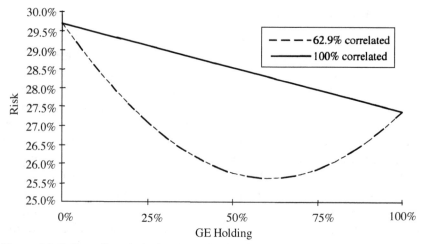

Figure 3.2 Fully invested GE/IBM portfolio.

the two lines is an indication of the benefit of diversification in reducing risk.

We can see the power of diversification in another example. Given a portfolio of N stocks, each with risk σ and uncorrelated returns, the risk of an equal-weighted portfolio of these stocks will be

$$\sigma_P = \frac{\sigma}{\sqrt{N}} \tag{3.3}$$

Note that the average risk is σ, while the portfolio risk is $\sigma/\sqrt{N}$.

For a more useful insight into diversification, now let us assume that the correlation between the returns of all pairs of stocks is equal to ρ. Then the risk of an equally weighted portfolio is

$$\sigma_P = \sigma \cdot \sqrt{\frac{1 + \rho \cdot (N - 1)}{N}} \tag{3.4}$$

In the limit that the portfolio contains a very large number of correlated stocks, this becomes

$$\sigma_P \rightarrow \sigma \cdot \sqrt{\rho} \tag{3.5}$$

To get a feel for this, consider the example of an equal-weighted portfolio of the 20 Major Market Index constituent stocks. In December 1992, these stocks had an average risk of 27.8 percent, while the equal-weighted portfolio has a risk of 20.4 percent. Equation (3.4) then implies an average correlation between these stocks of 0.52.

Risks don't add across stocks, and risks don't add across time. However, variance will add across time if the returns in one interval of time are uncorrelated with the returns in other intervals of time. The assumption is that returns are uncorrelated from period to period. The correlation of returns across time (called autocorrelation) is close to zero for most asset classes. This means that variances will grow with the length of the forecast horizon and the risk will grow with the square root of the forecast horizon. Thus a 5 percent annual active risk is equivalent to a 2.5 percent active risk over the first quarter or a 10 percent active risk over four years. Notice that the variance over the quarter, year, and four-year horizon (6.25, 25, and 100) remains proportional to the length of the horizon.

We use this relationship every time we "annualize" risk (i.e., standardize our risk numbers to an annual period). If we examine monthly returns to a stock and observe a monthly return standard deviation of $\sigma_{monthly}$, we convert this to annual risk through

$$\sigma_{annual} = \sqrt{12} \cdot \sigma_{monthly} \qquad (3.6)$$

Relative risk is important. If an investment manager is being compared to a performance benchmark, then the difference between the manager's portfolio's return r_P and the benchmark's return r_B is of crucial importance. We call this difference the active return r_{PA}. Correspondingly, we define the *active risk* ψ_P as the standard deviation of active return:

$$\psi_P = \text{Std}\{r_{PA}\} = \text{Std}\{r_P - r_B\} \qquad (3.7)$$

We sometimes call this active risk the *tracking error* of the portfolio, since it describes how well the portfolio can track the benchmark.

In Fig. 3.3, we consider a simple example. Suppose our benchmark is 40 percent IBM and 60 percent GE. The figure shows the active risk as a function of the holding of GE when the remainder

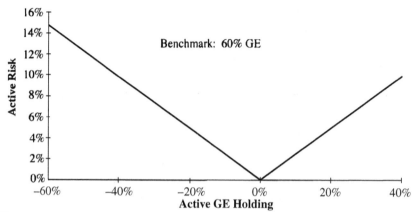

Figure 3.3 Fully invested GE/IBM portfolio.

of the portfolio is invested in IBM. The active position moves from +60 percent IBM and −60 percent GE at the left to −40 percent IBM and +40 percent GE at the right. Notice that the active holdings always add to zero.

There is a notion among investors that active risk is proportional to the capitalization of the asset. Thus, if the market weight for IBM is 4 percent, investors may set position limits of 2 percent on the low side and 6 percent on the high side, with the idea that this is a 50 percent over-weighting and a 50 percent underweighting. For another stock that is 0.6 percent of the benchmark, they may set position limits of 0.3 percent and 0.9 percent. So they limit the active exposure of IBM to ±2.0 percent, and that of the other stock to ±0.3 percent. But active risk depends on active exposure and stock risk. It does not depend on the benchmark holding of the stock. So while there may be cost and liquidity reasons for emphasizing larger stocks, it is not necessarily true that an active position of 1 percent in a large stock is less risky than an active position of 1 percent in a small stock.

Besides active risk, another relative measure of risk, residual risk, is also important. Residual risk is the risk of the return orthogonal to the systematic return. The residual risk of portfolio P relative to portfolio B is denoted by ω_P and defined by

$$\omega_P = \sqrt{\sigma_P^2 - \beta_P^2 \cdot \sigma_B^2} \qquad (3.8)$$

where

$$\beta_P = \frac{\text{Cov}\{r_P, r_B\}}{\text{Var}\{r_B\}} \qquad (3.9)$$

To provide a more intuitive understanding of total risk, residual risk, and beta at the asset level, we have calculated these numbers for large U.S. equities (the BARRA HICAP universe of roughly the largest 1200 stocks) using 60-month windows as of three widely varying dates: June 1980, June 1990, and December 1998. Table 3.1 presents a distribution of these numbers, where we have averaged over the distributions at the three dates.

So we can see that asset typical total risk numbers are 25 to 40 percent, typical residual risk numbers are 20 to 35 percent, and typical betas range from 0.80 to 1.35. For the risk numbers, the distributions varied very little from 1980 through 1998, with the exception of the 90th percentile (which increased for 1998). The betas varied a bit more over time, decreasing from 1980 through 1998. Note that the median beta need not equal 1. Only the capitalization-weighted beta will equal 1.

Variance is the square of standard deviation. In this book we will consistently use variance to measure the cost of risk. The cost of risk equates risk to an equivalent loss in expected return. In the context of active management, we will generally associate this cost with either active or residual risk. Figure 3.4 shows the cost of active risk based upon an active risk aversion of 0.1. With that level

T A B L E 3.1

Empirical Distribution of Risk Measures

Percentile	Total Risk (Percent)	Residual Risk (Percent)	Beta
90	50.8	45.0	1.67
75	40.1	34.3	1.36
50	30.6	25.1	1.08
25	24.6	19.6	0.79
10	20.4	16.4	0.52

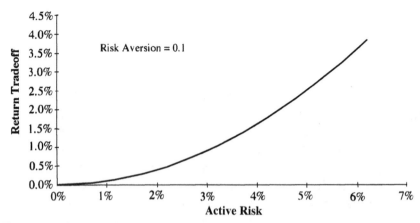

Figure 3.4 The cost of risk.

of active risk aversion, a 4 percent active risk translates into a
0.1 · (4 percent)^2 = 1.6 percent loss in expected return.

Now we turn our attention to models of stock risk.

ELEMENTARY RISK MODELS

The last section hinted at a significant problem in determining
portfolio risk. With two stocks in a portfolio, we need the volatility
of each, plus their correlation [see Eq. (3.1)]. For a 100-stock portfolio, we need 100 volatility estimates, plus the correlation of each
stock with every other stock (4950 correlations). More generally, as
the number of stocks N increases, the required number of correlations increases as $N(N - 1)/2$.

We can summarize all the required estimates by examining
the *covariance matrix* **V**:

$$V = \begin{bmatrix} \sigma_1^2 & \sigma_{12} & \cdots & \sigma_{1N} \\ \sigma_{12} & \sigma_2^2 & & \\ \vdots & & \ddots & \\ \sigma_{1N} & & & \sigma_N^2 \end{bmatrix} \qquad (3.10)$$

where we denote the covariance of r_i and r_j by σ_{ij}, and $\sigma_{ji} = \sigma_{ij}$.
The covariance matrix contains all the asset-level risk information
required to calculate portfolio-level risk. The goal of a risk model
is to accurately and efficiently forecast the covariance matrix. The

challenge arises because the covariance matrix contains so many independent quantities.

In this section, we consider three elementary stock risk models. The first is the single-factor diagonal model, which assigns each stock two components of risk: market risk and residual risk. The second is a model that assumes that all pairs of stocks have the same correlation. The third is a full covariance model based on historical returns.

The single-factor model of risk was an intellectual precursor to the CAPM, although the two models are distinct.[5] This model starts by analyzing returns as

$$r_n = \beta_n \cdot r_M + \theta_n \qquad (3.11)$$

where β_n is stock n's beta and θ_n is stock n's residual return. The single-factor risk model assumes that the residual returns θ_n are uncorrelated, and hence

$$\text{Cov}\{r_n, r_m\} = \beta_n \cdot \beta_m \cdot \sigma_M^2 \qquad (3.12)$$

and

$$\sigma_n^2 = \beta_n^2 \cdot \sigma_M^2 + \omega_n^2 \qquad (3.13)$$

Of course, residual returns are correlated. In fact, the market-weighted average of the residual returns is exactly zero:

$$\sum_n h_M(n) \cdot \theta_n = 0 \qquad (3.14)$$

Therefore, the residual correlation between stocks must be in general negative,[6] although we might expect a positive residual correlation among stocks in the same industry, e.g., large oil companies. Nevertheless this simple model of risk is attractive, since it isolates

---

[5]The CAPM is a model of expected returns. It assumes equilibrium, but not that all residual returns are uncorrelated. The single-factor risk model is not a model of expected returns. It assumes that all residual returns are uncorrelated, but not equilibrium. Sharpe described the single-factor model in his Ph.D. dissertation. He later developed the CAPM without requiring the assumptions of the single-factor model.

[6]We can see this most easily in a world of only two stocks with equal market capitalization. Equation (3.14) implies that $\theta_2 = -\theta_1$, the two residual returns are 100 percent negatively correlated. With hundreds of stocks in a market, the average negative correlation implied by Equation (3.14) is small.

market and residual risk and gives a conservative estimate, namely 0, of the residual covariance between stocks.

The second elementary risk model requires an estimate of each stock's risk σ_n and an average correlation ρ between stocks. That means that each covariance between any two stocks is

$$\text{Cov}\{r_n, r_m\} = \sigma_n \cdot \sigma_m \cdot \rho \qquad (3.15)$$

This second model has the virtue of simplicity and can be helpful in some "quick and dirty" applications. It ignores the subtle linkage between stocks in similar industries and firms with common attributes.

The third elementary model relies on historical variances and covariances. This procedure is neither robust nor reasonable. Historical models rely on data from T periods to estimate the N by N covariance matrix. If T is less than or equal to N, we can find active positions[7] that will appear riskless! So the historical approach requires $T > N$. For a monthly historical covariance matrix of S&P 500 stocks, this would require more than 40 years of data. And, even when T exceeds N, this historical procedure still has several problems:

- Circumventing the $T > N$ restriction requires short time periods, one day or one week, while the forecast horizon of the manager is generally one quarter or one year.
- Historical risk cannot deal with the changing nature of a company. Mergers and spinoffs cause problems.
- There is selection bias, as takeovers, LBOs, and failed companies are omitted.
- Sample bias will lead to some gross misestimates of covariance. A 500-asset covariance matrix contains 125,250 independent numbers. If 5 percent of these are poor estimates, we have 6262 poor estimates.

The reader will note limited enthusiasm for historical models of risk. We now turn to more structured models of stock risk.

---

[7]Mathematically, an N by N covariance matrix made up from T periods of returns will have rank equal to the minimum of N and $T - 1$. More intuitively, we can see the problem by comparing the number of observations to the number of quantities we wish to estimate. An N by N covariance matrix contains $N(N + 1)/2$ independent estimates. With N assets and T periods, we have NT observations. Requiring an absolute minimum of two observations per estimate (after all, we require at least two observations to estimate one standard deviation) implies that $T \geq N + 1$.

STRUCTURAL RISK MODELS[8]

In the previous section, we considered elementary risk models and found them either wanting or oversimplified. In this section, we look at structural multifactor risk models and trumpet their virtues.

The multiple-factor risk model is based on the notion that the return of a stock can be explained by a collection of common factors plus an idiosyncratic element that pertains to that particular stock. We can think of the common factors as forces that affect a group of stocks. These might be all the stocks in the banking industry, all stocks that are highly leveraged, all the smaller-capitalization stocks, etc. Below, we discuss possible types of factors in detail.

By identifying important factors, we can reduce the size of the problem. Instead of dealing with 6000 stocks (and 18,003,000 independent variances and covariances), we deal with 68 factors. The stocks change, the factors do not. The situation is much simpler when we focus on the smaller number of factors and allow the stocks to change their exposures to those factors.

A structural risk model begins by analyzing returns according to a simple linear structure with four components: the stock's excess returns, the stock's exposure to the factors, the attributed factor returns, and the specific returns. The structure is

$$r_n(t) = \sum_k X_{n,k}(t) \cdot b_k(t) + u_n(t) \qquad (3.16)$$

where $r_n(t)$ = *excess return* (return above the risk-free return) on stock n during the period from time t to time $t + 1$

$X_{n,k}(t)$ = *exposure* of asset n to factor k, estimated at time t. Exposures are frequently called *factor loadings*. For industry factors, the exposures are either 0 or 1, indicating whether the stock belongs to that industry or not.[9] For the other common factors, the exposures are standardized so that the average

---

[8]The authors have a history of interest in structural risk models, through their long association with BARRA.
[9]With adequate data, one can split large conglomerates into their components.

exposure over all stocks is 0, and the standard deviation across stocks is 1.

$b_k(t)$ = *factor return* to factor k during the period from time t to time $t + 1$.

$u_n(t)$ = stock n's *specific return* during the period from time t to time $t + 1$. This is the return that cannot be explained by the factors. It is sometimes called the *idiosyncratic return* to the stock: the return not explained by the model. However, the risk model will account for specific risk. Thus our risk predictions will explicitly consider the risk of u_n.

We have been very careful to define the time structure in this model. The exposures are known at time t, the beginning of the period. The asset returns, factor returns, and specific returns span the period from time t to time $t + 1$. In the rest of this chapter, we will suppress the explicit time variables.

We do not mean to convey any sense of causality in this model structure. The factors may or may not be the basic driving forces for security returns. In our view, they are merely dimensions along which to analyze risk.

We will now assume that the specific returns are not correlated with the factor returns and are not correlated with each other. With these assumptions and the return structure of Eq. (3.16), the risk structure is

$$V_{n,m} = \sum_{k_1,k_2 = 1}^{K} X_{n,k_1} \cdot F_{k_1,k_2} \cdot X_{m,k_2} + \Delta_{n,m} \qquad (3.17)$$

where $V_{n,m}$ = covariance of asset n with asset m. If $n = m$, this gives the variance of asset n

X_{n,k_1} = exposure of asset n to factor k_1, as defined above.

F_{k_1,k_2} = covariance of factor k_1 with factor k_2. If $k_1 = k_2$, this gives the variance of factor k_1.

$\Delta_{n,m}$ = specific covariance of asset n with asset m. We assume that all specific return correlations are zero, and so this term is zero unless $n = m$. In that case, this gives the specific variance of asset n.

CHOOSING THE FACTORS

The art of building multiple-factor risk models involves choosing appropriate factors. This search for factors is limited by only one key constraint: All factors must be a priori factors. That is, even though the factor returns are uncertain, the factor exposures must be known a priori, i.e. at the beginning of the period.

Within the constraint that the factors be a priori factors, a wide variety of factors are possible. We will attempt a rough classification scheme. To start, we can divide factors into three categories: responses to external influences, cross-sectional comparisons of asset attributes, and purely internal or statistical factors.[10] We will consider these in turn.

Responses to External Influences

One of the prevalent themes in the academic literature of financial economics is that there should be a demonstrable link between outside economic forces and the equity markets. The response factors are an attempt to capture that link. These factors include responses to return in the bond market (sometimes called bond beta), unexpected changes in inflation (inflation surprise), changes in oil prices, changes in exchange rates, changes in industrial production, and so on. These factors are sometimes called macrofactors. These measures can be powerful, but they suffer from three serious defects. The first is that we must estimate the response coefficient through regression analysis or some similar technique. A model with nine macrofactors covering 1000 stocks would require 1000 time series regressions each month, with each regression estimating nine response coefficients from perhaps 60 months of data. This leads to errors in the estimates, commonly called an error in variables problem.

The second drawback is that we base the estimate on behavior over a past period of generally 5 years. Even if this estimate is

---

[10]This classification scheme does not imply that investors can choose only one category of factors. For example, we have observed that factors based on responses to external influences do not add explanatory power to models built from factors based on cross-sectional comparisons of asset attributes. At least implicitly, the cross-sectional factors contain the response factors.

accurate in the statistical sense of capturing the true situation in the past, it may not be an accurate description of the current situation. In short, these response coefficients can be nonstationary. For example, the company may have changed its business practice by trying to control foreign exchange exposure.

Third, several of the macroeconomic data items are of poor quality, gathered by the government rather than observed in the market. This leads to inaccurate, delayed, and relatively infrequent observations.

Cross-Sectional Comparisons

These factors compare attributes of the stocks, with no link to the remainder of the economy. Cross-sectional attributes generally fall into two groups: fundamental and market. Fundamental attributes include ratios such as dividend yield and earnings yield, plus analysts' forecasts of future earnings per share. Market attributes include volatility over a past period, return over a past period, option implied volatility, share turnover, etc. To some extent, market attributes such as volatility and momentum may have the same difficulties (errors in variables, nonstationarity) that we described in the section above on the external response factors. Here, however, the factor interpretation is somewhat different. Take, for example, a momentum factor. Let's say this measures the price performance of the stock over the past 12 months. This factor is not intended as a forecast of continued success or of some mean reversion. It is merely a recognition that stocks that have been relatively successful (unsuccessful) over the past year will quite frequently behave in a common fashion. Sometimes the momentum will be reinforced, at other times it will be reversed, and at yet other times it will be irrelevant. We are accounting for the fact that in 5 or 6 months of the year, controlling for other attributes, previously successful stocks behave in a manner that is very different from that of previously unsuccessful stocks. We could say the same for stocks with high historical volatility, or other such factors. In our experience, these cross-sectional comparisons are quite powerful factors.

Statistical Factors

It is possible to amass returns data on a large number of stocks, turn the crank of a statistical meat grinder, and admire the factors produced by the machine: *factor ex machina*. This can be accomplished in an amazingly large number of ways: principal component analysis, maximum likelihood analysis, expectations maximization analysis. One can use a two-step approach by getting first the factors and then the exposures, simultaneously estimate both factors and exposures, or turn the problem on its head in the imaginative approach taken by Connor and Korajczyk (1988). We usually avoid statistical factors, because they are very difficult to interpret, and because the statistical estimation procedure is prone to discovering spurious correlations. These models also cannot capture factors whose exposures change over time. The statistical estimation machinery assumes and relies on each asset's constant exposure to each factor over the estimation period. For example, statistical models cannot capture momentum factors.

Given the many possible factors, we choose those which satisfy three criteria: They are incisive, intuitive, and interesting. Incisive factors distinguish returns. For example, if we look along the volatility axis, we will find that low-volatility stocks perform differently from high-volatility stocks at least three times per year. If we don't monitor our overall volatility exposure, then our returns can be upset with disturbing frequency.

Intuitive factors relate to interpretable and recognizable dimensions of the market. Credible stories define these factors. For example, size distinguishes the big companies at one end from the small companies at the other. Momentum separates the firms that have performed well from the firms that have done relatively poorly. Intuitive factors arise from recognizable investment themes. Factors in the U.S. equity market include industries, plus size, yield, value, success, volatility, growth, leverage, liquidity, and foreign currency sensitivity.

Interesting factors explain some part of performance. We can attribute a certain amount of return to each factor in each period. That factor might help explain exceptional return or beta or volatility. For example, stocks of large companies did well over a particular period. Or, high-volatility stocks are high-beta stocks.

Research leading to the appropriate factors, then, depends on both statistical techniques and investment intuition. Statistical techniques can identify the most incisive and interesting factors.

Investment intuition can help identify intuitive factors. Factors can have statistical significance or investment significance or both. Model research must take both forms of significance into account.

Given the above general discussion on choosing appropriate factors for a multiple-factor risk model, what typical factors do we choose? They fall into two broad categories: *industry factors* and *risk indices*. Industry factors measure the differing behavior of stocks in different industries. Risk indices measure the differing behavior of stocks across other, nonindustry dimensions.

INDUSTRY FACTORS

Industry groupings partition stocks into nonoverlapping classes. Industry groupings should satisfy several criteria:

- There should be a reasonable number of companies in each industry.
- There should be a reasonable fraction of capitalization in each industry.
- They should be in reasonable accord with the conventions and mindset of investors in that market.

For example, Table 3.2 shows the breakdown of a broad universe of over 11,000 U.S. stocks by BARRA industry group as of the end of August 1998.

Industry exposures are usually 0/1 variables: Stocks either are or are not in an industry. The market itself has unit exposure in total to the industries. Since large corporations can do business in several industries, we can extend the industry factors to account for membership in multiple industries. For example, for September 1998, BARRA's U.S. Equity risk model classified GE as 58 percent financial services, 20 percent heavy electrical equipment, 8 percent media, 7 percent medical products, and 7 percent property & casualty insurance.

RISK INDICES

Industries are not the only sources of stock risk. Risk indices measure the movements of stocks exposed to common investment

T A B L E 3.2

U.S. Equity Market Industry Breakdown: August 1998

Industry	Number of Firms	Percent of Market Capitalization
Mining & metals	216	0.77
Gold	122	0.25
Forest products and paper	112	1.04
Chemicals	288	2.99
Energy reserves & production	348	4.07
Oil refining	69	0.78
Oil services	84	1.04
Food & beverages	246	4.42
Alcohol	32	0.21
Tobacco	13	0.82
Home products	108	2.42
Grocery stores	53	0.66
Consumer durables	124	0.38
Motor vehicles & parts	141	1.79
Apparel & textiles	207	0.51
Clothing stores	72	0.59
Specialty retail	301	1.94
Department stores	33	2.24
Construction & real property	480	1.65
Publishing	142	0.91
Media	121	2.05
Hotels	89	0.38
Restaurants	182	0.69
Entertainment	139	1.28
Leisure	267	0.69
Environmental services	125	0.41
Heavy electrical equipment	98	0.70
Heavy machinery	50	0.42
Industrial parts	380	1.25
Electric utilities	100	2.62
Gas & water utilities	81	0.61
Railroads	33	0.63
Airlines	47	0.51
Trucking, shipping, air freight	116	0.34

Continued

T A B L E 3.2

(Continued)

Industry	Number of Firms	Percent of Market Capitalization
Medical providers & services	263	1.22
Medical products	442	2.91
Drugs	409	6.70
Electronic equipment	699	3.22
Semiconductors	196	1.94
Computer hardware, office equipment	388	4.62
Computer software	574	4.17
Defense & aerospace	95	1.55
Telephones	102	5.18
Wireless telecommunications	57	0.57
Information services	576	2.57
Industrial services	251	0.94
Life & health insurance	75	1.55
Property & casualty insurance	148	4.22
Banks	702	8.47
Thrifts	299	0.71
Securies & asset management	188	1.63
Financial services	534	5.80
Total	11,017	100.00

themes. Risk indices we have identified in the United States and other equity markets fall into these broad categories:

Volatility. Distinguishes stocks by their volatility. Assets that rank high in this dimension have been and are expected to be more volatile than average.

Momentum. Distinguishes stocks by recent performance.

Size. Distinguishes large stocks from small stocks.

Liquidity. Distinguishes stocks by how much their shares trade.

Growth. Distinguishes stocks by past and anticipated earnings growth.

Value. Distinguishes stocks by their fundamentals, in particular, ratios of earnings, dividends, cash flows, book value, sales, etc., to price: cheap versus expensive, relative to fundamentals.

Earnings volatility. Distinguishes stocks by their earnings volatility.

Financial leverage. Distinguishes firms by debt-to-equity ratio and exposure to interest-rate risk.

Any particular equity market can contain fewer or more risk indices, depending on its own idiosyncrasies.

Each broad category can typically contain several specific measurements of the category. We call these specific measurements *descriptors.* For instance, volatility measures might include recent daily return volatility, option-implied volatility, recent price range, and beta. Though descriptors in a category are typically correlated, each descriptor captures one aspect of the risk index. We construct risk index exposures by weighting the exposures of the descriptors within the risk index. We choose weights that maximize the explanatory and predictive power of the model. Relying on several different descriptors can also improve model robustness.

How do we quantify exposures to descriptors and risk indices? After all, the various categories involve different sets of natural units and ranges. To handle this, we rescale all raw exposure data:

$$x_{\text{normalized}} = \frac{x_{\text{raw}} - \langle x_{\text{raw}} \rangle}{\text{Std}[x_{\text{raw}}]} \tag{3.18}$$

where $\langle x_{\text{raw}} \rangle$ is the raw exposure value mean and $\text{Std}[x_{\text{raw}}]$ is the raw exposure value standard deviation, across the universe of assets. The result is that each risk index exposure has mean 0 and standard deviation 1. This standardization also facilitates the handling of outliers.

As an example of how this works, BARRA's U.S. Equity model assigns General Electric a size exposure of 1.90 for September 1998. This implies that, not surprisingly, General Electric lies significantly above average on the size dimension. For the same date, the model assigns Netscape a size exposure of -1.57. Netscape lies significantly below average on this dimension.

STRUCTURAL RISK MODEL COVARIANCE

The technical appendix discusses in detail how Eq. (3.16); the structural return equation, together with observed asset returns, leads to estimates of factor returns and specific returns. It also describes how those returns, estimated historically, lead to forecasts of the factor covariance matrix and the specific covariance matrix of Eq. (3.17). Here, we will assume that we have these covariance matrices and focus on the uses of a risk model.

THE USES OF A RISK MODEL

A model of risk has three broad uses. They involve the present, the future, and the past. We will describe them in turn, mainly focusing here on uses concerning the present. We will treat future and past risk in more detail in later chapters.

The Present: Current Portfolio Risk Analysis

The multiple-factor risk model analyzes current portfolio risk. It measures overall risk. More significantly, it decomposes that risk in several ways. This decomposition of risk identifies the important sources of risk in the portfolio and links those sources with aspirations for active return.

One way to divide the risk is to identify the market and residual components. An alternative is to look at risk relative to a benchmark and identify the active risk. A third way to divide the risk is between the model risk and the specific risk. The risk model can also perform marginal analysis: What assets are most and least diversifying in the portfolio, at the margin?

Risk analysis is important for both passive management and active management. Passive managers attempt to match the returns to a particular benchmark. Passive managers run index funds. However, depending on the benchmark, the manager's portfolio may not include all the stocks in the benchmark. For example, for a passive small-stock manager, transactions costs of holding the thousands of assets in a broad small-stock benchmark might be prohibitive. Current portfolio risk analysis can tell a passive manager the risk of his or her portfolio relative to the benchmark. This is the active risk, or tracking error. It is the volatility of the difference in return between the portfolio and the benchmark. Passive managers want minimum tracking error.

Of course, the focus of this book is active management. The goal of active managers is not to track their benchmarks as closely as possible, but rather to *outperform* those benchmarks. Still, risk analysis is important in active management, to focus active strategies. Active managers want to take on risk only along those dimensions where they believe they can outperform.

By suitably decomposing current portfolio risk, active managers can better understand the positioning of their portfolios. Risk analysis can tell active managers not only what their active risk is, but why and how to change it. Risk analysis can classify active bets into inherent bets, intentional bets, and incidental bets:

Inherent. An active manager who is trying to outperform a benchmark (or market) must bear the benchmark risk, i.e., the volatility of the benchmark itself. This risk is a constant part of the task, not under the portfolio manager's control.

Intentional. An active portfolio manager has identified stocks that she or he believes will do well and stocks that she or he believes will do poorly. In fact, the stocks with the highest expected returns should provide the highest marginal contributions to risk. This is welcome news; it tells the portfolio manager that the portfolio is consistent with his or her beliefs.

Incidental. These are unintentional side effects of the manager's active position. The manager has inadvertently created an active position on some factor that contributes significantly to marginal active risk. For example, a manager who builds a portfolio by screening on yield will have a large incidental bet on industries that have higher than average yields. Are these industry bets intentional or incidental? Incidental bets often arise through incremental portfolio management, where a sequence of stock-by-stock decisions, each plausible in isolation, leads to an accumulated incidental risk.

To understand portfolio risk characterization more concretely, consider the following example. Using the Major Market Index (MMI) as an investment portfolio, analyze its risk relative to the

S&P 500 as of the end of December 1992. The portfolio is shown in Table 3.3.

Comparing risk factor exposures versus the benchmark, this portfolio contains larger, less volatile stocks, with higher leverage and foreign income, and lower earnings variability: what you might expect from a portfolio of large stocks relative to a broader index. The portfolio also contains several industry bets.

The multiple-factor risk model forecasts 20.5 percent volatility for the portfolio and 20.1 percent volatility for the index. The portfolio tracking error is 4.2 percent. Assuming that active returns are normally distributed, the portfolio annual return will lie within 4.2 percentage points of the index annual return roughly two-thirds of the time. The model can forecast the portfolio's beta. Beta mea-

T A B L E 3.3

Stock	Shares	Percent Weight	Marginal Contribution to Active Risk
American Express	100	2.28	0.006
AT&T	100	4.68	−0.009
Chevron	100	6.37	0.040
Coca-Cola	100	3.84	0.029
Disney	100	3.94	0.018
Dow Chemicals	100	5.25	0.063
DuPont	100	4.32	0.041
Eastman Kodak	100	3.71	0.055
Exxon	100	5.61	0.047
General Electric	100	7.84	0.042
General Motors	100	2.96	0.046
IBM	100	4.62	0.074
International Paper	100	6.11	0.063
Johnson & Johnson	100	4.63	0.038
McDonalds	100	4.47	0.042
Merck	100	3.98	0.030
3M	100	9.23	0.057
Philip Morris	100	7.07	0.038
Procter & Gamble	100	4.92	0.040
Sears	100	4.17	0.010

sures the portfolio's inherent risk: its exposure to movements of the index. The MMI portfolio beta is 0.96. This implies that if the S&P 500 excess return were 100 basis points, we would expect the portfolio return to be 96 basis points.

As all economists know, life is led at the margin. The risk model will let us know the marginal impact on total, residual, or active risk of changes in portfolio exposures to factors or changes in stock holdings. The technical appendix provides mathematical details.

As an example, Table 3.3 also displays each asset's marginal contribution to active risk, the change in active risk given a 1 percent increase in the holdings of each stock. According to Table 3.3, increasing the holdings of American Express from 2.28 to 3.28 percent should increase the active risk by 0.6 basis point. Table 3.3 also shows AT&T—with the smallest (and in fact negative) marginal contribution to active risk—to be the most diversifying asset in the portfolio, and IBM—with the largest marginal contribution to active risk—to be the most concentrating asset in the portfolio.

The Future

A risk model helps in the design of future portfolios. Risk is one of the important design parameters in portfolio construction, which trades off expected return and risk. Chapter 14, "Portfolio Construction," will discuss this use of the risk model in some detail.

The Past

A risk model helps in evaluating the past performance of the portfolio. The risk model offers a decomposition of active return and allows for an attribution of risk to each category of return. Thus, the risks undertaken by the manager and the outcomes from taking those active positions will be clear. This allows the manager to determine which active bets have been rewarded and which have been penalized. There will be more on this topic in Chap. 17, "Performance Analysis."

HOW WELL DO RISK MODELS WORK?

We have chosen standard deviation as the definition of risk in part to facilitate aggregating risk from assets into portfolios. We have chosen the structural risk model methodology in order to accurately and efficiently forecast the required covariance matrix. Here we will describe some evidence that this methodology does perform as desired.

We will consider evidence from two studies. First, we will discuss a comparison of alternative forecasts of standard deviations: portfolio-based versus historical. The portfolio-based approach, aggregating from assets into portfolios, utilized structural risk models. Second, we will describe a comparison of historical forecasts of different risk measures: standard deviation versus alternatives. These alternative measures—e.g., downside risk—must forecast entirely on the basis of historical risk. These two levels of tests imply that we can forecast only standard deviations from historical data, and that portfolio-based forecasts of standard deviation surpass those historical estimates. We will not discuss comparisons of alternative structural risk models, but for more information, see Connor (1995) or Sheikh (1996).

The first study [Kahn (1997)] looked at 29 equity and bond mutual funds. For each fund, at a historical analysis date, the study generated two alternative forecasts of standard deviation: portfolio-based, using structural risk models, and historical, using the prior three-year standard deviation (from monthly returns). The study then analyzed each fund's performance over the subsequent year. The analysis period was 1993/1994. The study obviously was not exhaustive, as it analyzed only 29 funds, chosen based on the criteria of size, investor interest, and return patterns. The difficulty of obtaining fund holdings makes a comprehensive study of this type quite difficult.

The study analyzed how many funds experienced returns more than two standard deviations from the mean. With accurate risk forecasts, such returns should occur only about 5 percent of the time.

Using structural risk models and portfolio holdings to predict standard deviations, the study found zero three-sigma events and one two-sigma outcome (3 percent of observations); 76 percent of the observations were less than one sigma in magnitude. The historical risk results were not nearly as encouraging: there were one three-sigma outcome (3 percent of observations) and five two-sigma outcomes (17 percent of observations), and then 72 percent of the outcomes were less than one sigma in magnitude.

Of course, the portfolio-based forecasts could have outperformed the historical forecasts in this test by consistently overpredicting risk. Accurate risk forecasts should lead to few surprises, not zero surprises. However, subsequent analysis found no *statistically significant* evidence that either method over- or underpredicted risk on average.

A final test compared the two alternative forecasts to the standard deviation of the excess returns over the following year: the realized risk. The result: There was a much stronger relationship between portfolio-based forecasts and subsequent risk than between historical risk and subsequent risk.

The second study [Kahn and Stefek (1996)] compared the persistence of alternative risk measures (standard deviation, semivariance, target semivariance, shortfall probability) for 290 domestic equity mutual funds, 185 domestic bond mutual funds, and 1160 individual U.S. equities. In each case, the study looked at two consecutive five-year periods: January 1986 through December 1990 and January 1991 through December 1995 for the mutual funds; and September 1986 through August 1991 and September 1991 through August 1996 for the individual equity returns.

Because the alternative risk measures are in large part a function of the variance—for example, the semivariance is to first order just half the variance—the study explicitly examined the persistence of the information beyond that implied by the variance. So, for instance, it investigated the persistence of abnormal semivariance: semivariance minus half the variance. After all, the only reason to choose an alternative risk measure is for the information beyond variance that it contains.

The tests for persistence within each group of funds or assets simply regressed the risk measure in period 2 against the risk measure in period 1. Evidence of persistence includes high R^2 statistics for the regression and significant positive t statistics. The study tests whether higher- (lower-) risk portfolios in period 1 are also higher- (lower-) risk portfolios in period 2. We can use historical risk to forecast a future risk measure only if that risk measure persists.

To summarize the study results, standard deviation and variance exhibit very high persistence. The alternative risk measures exhibited no persistence beyond that implied by just the persistence of variance. It appears that we cannot forecast risk information beyond variance. Many other studies have shown that asset returns exhibit wide distributions, implying that we should be able to forecast something beyond variance (e.g., kurtosis). But this study investigates a different question; whether a portfolio with a wider distribution than average persists in exhibiting a wider distribution than average. This is the important question for portfolio selection, and the answer appears to be no.

Overall, these two studies confirm the important roles played by standard deviation and structural risk models in active management.

SUMMARY

Active management centers on the trade-off between expected returns and risk. This chapter has focused on risk. We have quantified risk as the standard deviation of annual returns, and the cost of risk as the variance of annual returns. Active managers care mainly about active and residual risk. Risk models, and structural risk models in particular, can provide insightful analysis by decomposing risk into total and active risk, market (or benchmark) and residual risk, model and specific risk; and by identifying inherent, intentional, and incidental bets. Risk models can analyze the present risks and bets in a portfolio, forecast future risk as part of the portfolio construction process, and analyze past risks to facilitate performance analysis. The evidence shows that structural risk models perform as desired.

PROBLEMS

1. If GE has an annual risk of 27.4 percent, what is the volatility of monthly GE returns?
2. Stock A has 25 percent risk, stock B has 50 percent risk, and their returns are 50 percent correlated. What fully invested portfolio of A and B has minimum total risk? (*Hint:* Try solving this graphically (e.g. in Excel), if you cannot determine the answer mathematically.)

3. What is the risk of an equal-weighted portfolio consisting of five stocks, each with 35 percent volatility and a 50 percent correlation with all other stocks? How does that decrease as the portfolio increases to 20 stocks or 100 stocks?

4. How do structural risk models help in estimating asset betas? How do these betas differ from those estimated from a 60-month beta regression?

REFERENCES

Arrow, Kenneth J. *Essays in the Theory of Risk-Bearing.* (Chicago: Markham Publishing Company, 1971).

Bernstein, Peter L. *Against the Gods: The Remarkable Story of Risk.* (New York: John Wiley & Sons, 1996).

Bollerslev, Tim, Ray Y. Chou, and Kenneth F. Kroner. "ARCH Modeling in Finance." *Journal of Econometrics,* vol. 52, 1992, pp. 5–59.

Borch, Karl H. *The Economics of Uncertainty.* (Princeton, N.J.: Princeton University Press, 1972).

Connor, Gregory. "The Three Types of Factor Models: A Comparison of Their Explanatory Power." *Financial Analysts Journal,* vol. 51, no. 3, May/June 1995, pp. 42–46.

Connor, Gregory, and Robert A. Korajczyk. "Risk and Return in an Equilibrium APT: Application of a New Test Methodology." *Journal of Financial Economics,* vol 21, no. 2, September 1988, pp. 255–289.

Engle, Robert F. "Autoregressive Conditional Heteroskedasticity with Estimates of the Variance of U.K. Inflation." *Econometrica,* vol. 50, 1982, pp. 987–1008.

Fama, Eugene, and James MacBeth. "Risk, Return, and Equilibrium: Empirical Tests." *Journal of Political Economy,* vol. 81, May–June 1973, pp. 607–636.

Grinold, Richard C., and Ronald N. Kahn. "Multiple Factor Models for Portfolio Risk." In *A Practitioner's Guide to Factor Models,* edited by John W. Peavy III. (Charlottesville, Va.: AIMR, 1994).

Jeffery, R. H. "A New Paradigm for Portfolio Risk." *Journal of Portfolio Management,* vol. 10, no. 1, Fall 1984, pp. 33–40.

Kahn, Ronald N. "Mutual Fund Risk." *BARRA Research Insights* (Berkeley, Calif.: BARRA, 1997).

Kahn, Ronald N., and Daniel Stefek. "Heat, Light, and Downside Risk." BARRA manuscript, 1996.

Kosmicke, R. "The Limited Relevance of Volatility to Risk." *Journal of Portfolio Management,* vol. 12, no. 1, Fall 1986, pp. 18–21.

Litterman, Robert. "Hot Spots and Hedges." *Journal of Portfolio Management,* December 1996, pp. 52–75.

Markowitz, H. M. *Portfolio Selection: Efficient Diversification of Investment.* Cowles Foundation Monograph 16 (New Haven, Conn.: Yale University Press, 1959).

Raiffa, H. *Decision Analysis: Introductory Lectures on Choices under Uncertainty* (Reading, Mass.: Addison-Wesley, 1968).

Rosenberg, B. "Extra-Market Components of Covariance in Security Markets." *Journal of Financial and Quantitative Analysis*, March 1974, pp. 263–274.

Rosenberg, B., and V. Marathe. "The Prediction of Investment Risk: Systematic and Residual Risk." *Proceedings of the Seminar on the Analysis of Security Prices*, (Chicago: University of Chicago Press), November 1975, pp. 85–224.

Rudd, Andrew, and Henry K. Clasing, Jr. *Modern Portfolio Theory* (Orinda, Calif.: Andrew Rudd, 1988), Chaps. 2 and 3.

Sharpe, William F. "A Simplified Model for Portfolio Analysis." *Management Science*, vol. 9, no. 1, January 1963, pp. 277–293.

Sheikh, Aamir. "BARRA's Risk Models." *BARRA Research Insights* (Berkeley, Calif.: BARRA, 1996).

TECHNICAL APPENDIX

We define the risk model in two parts. First, we model returns as

$$\mathbf{r} = \mathbf{X} \cdot \mathbf{b} + \mathbf{u} \tag{3A.1}$$

where $\mathbf{r}$ is an N vector of excess returns, $\mathbf{X}$ is an N by K matrix of factor exposures, $\mathbf{b}$ is a K vector of factor returns, and $\mathbf{u}$ is an N vector of specific returns.

We assume that

A1. The specific returns $\mathbf{u}$ are uncorrelated with the factor returns $\mathbf{b}$; i.e., $\text{Cov}\{u_n, b_k\} = 0$ for all n and k.

A2. The covariance of stock n's specific return u_n with stock m's specific return u_m is zero if $m \neq n$; i.e. $\text{Cov}\{u_n, u_m\} = 0$ if $m \neq n$.

With these assumptions, we can complete the definition of the risk model by expressing the N by N covariance matrix $\mathbf{V}$ of stock returns as

$$\mathbf{V} = \mathbf{X} \cdot \mathbf{F} \cdot \mathbf{X}^T + \mathbf{\Delta} \tag{3A.2}$$

where $\mathbf{F}$ is the K by K covariance matrix of the factor returns and $\mathbf{\Delta}$ is the N by N diagonal matrix of specific variance.

Model Estimation

Given exposures to the industry and risk index factors, we estimate factor returns via multiple regressions, using the Fama-MacBeth procedure (1973). The model is linear, and Eq. (3A.1) has the form of a multiple regression. We regress stock excess returns against factor exposures, choosing factor returns which minimize the (possibly weighted) sum of squared specific returns. In the United States, for example, BARRA uses a universe of 1500 of the largest companies, calculates their exposures from fundamental data, and runs one regression per month to estimate 65 factor returns from about 1500 observations. The R^2 statistic, which measures the explanatory power of the model, tends to average between 30 and 40 percent for models of monthly equity returns with roughly 1000 assets and 50 factors. Larger R^2 statistics tend to occur in months with larger market moves.

In this cross-sectional regression, which BARRA performs every period, the industry factors play the role of an intercept. The market as a whole has an exposure of 1 to the industries, and industry factor returns tend to pick up the market return. They are the more volatile factors in the model. The market has close to zero exposure to the risk indices, and risk index factor returns pick up extra-market returns. They are the less volatile factors in the market.

To efficiently estimate factor returns, we run generalized least squares (GLS) regressions, weighting each observed return by the inverse of its specific variance. In some models, we instead weight each observation by the square root of its market capitalization, which acts as a proxy for the inverse of its specific variance.[11]

While these cross-sectional regressions can involve more than 50 factors, the models do not suffer from multicollinearity. Most of the factors are industries (52 out of 65 in BARRA's U.S. Equity risk model in 1998), which are orthogonal. In addition, tests of variance inflation factors, which measure the inflation in estimate errors caused by multicollinearity, lie far below serious danger levels.

Factor Portfolios

This regression approach to estimating factor returns leads to an insightful interpretation of the factors. Weighted regression gym-

---

[11]Our research has shown that the square root is the appropriate power of market capitalization to mimic inverse specific variance. Larger companies have lower specific variance, and as company size doubles, specific variance shrinks by a factor of 0.7.

nastics lead to the following matrix expression for the estimated factor returns:

$$\mathbf{b} = (\mathbf{X}^T \cdot \mathbf{\Delta}^{-1} \cdot \mathbf{X})^{-1} \cdot \mathbf{X}^T \cdot \mathbf{\Delta}^{-1} \cdot \mathbf{r} \qquad (3A.3)$$

where $\mathbf{X}$ is the exposure matrix, $\mathbf{\Delta}^{-1}$ is the diagonal matrix of GLS regression weights, and $\mathbf{r}$ is the vector of excess returns. For each particular factor return, this is simply a weighted sum of excess returns:

$$b_k = \sum_{n=1}^{N} c_{k,n} \cdot r_n \qquad (3A.4)$$

In this form, we can interpret each factor return b_k as the return to a portfolio, with portfolio weights $c_{k,n}$. So factor returns are the returns to *factor portfolios*. The factor portfolio holdings are known a priori. The factor portfolio holdings ensure that the portfolio has unit exposure to the particular factor, zero exposure to every other factor, and minimum risk given those constraints.[12]

Factor portfolios resemble the characteristic portfolios introduced in the technical appendix to Chap. 2, except that they are multiple-factor in nature. That is, characteristic portfolios have unit exposure to their characteristic, but not necessarily zero exposure to a set of other factors.

There are two different interpretations of these portfolios. They are sometimes interpreted as *factor-mimicking portfolios*, because they mimic the behavior of some underlying basic factor. We interpret them more simply as portfolios that capture the specific effect we have defined through our exposures.

Factor portfolios typically contain both long and short positions. For example, the factor portfolio for the earnings-to-price factor in the U.S. market will have an earnings-to-price ratio one standard deviation above the market, while having zero exposure to all other factors. Zero exposure to an industry implies that the portfolio will hold some industry stocks long and others short,

---

[12]The only factor risk in a factor portfolio arises from the unit exposure to its factor, since all other factor exposures are zero. Hence the minimum-risk condition implies minimizing specific risk. The GLS weights in the regression ensure this.

with longs and shorts balancing. Factor portfolios are not investible portfolios, since, among other properties, these portfolios contain every single asset with some weight.

Factor Covariance Matrix

Once we have estimates of factor returns each period, we can estimate a factor covariance matrix: an estimate of all the factor variances and covariances. To effectively operate as a risk model, this factor covariance matrix should comprise our best forecast of future factor variances and covariances, over the investor's time horizon.

Forecasting covariance from a past history of factor returns is a subject worthy of a book in itself, and the details are beyond the scope of this effort. Basic techniques rely on weights over the past history and bayesian priors on covariance. More advanced techniques include forecasting variance conditional on recent events, as first suggested by Engle (1982). Such techniques assume that variance is constant only conditional on other variables. For a review of these ideas, see Bollerslev et al. (1992).

Specific Risk

To generate an asset-by-asset covariance matrix, we need not only the factor covariance matrix $\mathbf{F}$, but also the specific risk matrix $\mathbf{\Delta}$. Now, by definition, the model cannot explain a stock's specific return u_n. So the multiple-factor model can provide no insight into stock specific returns. However, for specific risk, we need to model specific return variance u_n^2 (assuming that mean specific return is zero).

In general, we model specific risk as[13]

$$u_n^2(t) = S(t)[1 + v_n(t)] \qquad (3A.5)$$

---

[13]To minimize the influence of outliers, we often model $|u_n|$ and not u_n^2. We then must correct for a systematic bias in modeling absolute deviation when we want to forecast standard deviation.

with

$$\left(\frac{1}{N}\right) \cdot \sum_{n=1}^{N} u_n^2(t) = S(t) \tag{3A.6}$$

and

$$\left(\frac{1}{N}\right) \cdot \sum_{n=1}^{N} v_n(t) = 0 \tag{3A.7}$$

So $S(t)$ measures the average specific variance across the universe of stocks, and v_n captures the cross-sectional variation in specific variance.

To forecast specific risk, we use a time series model for $S(t)$ and a linear multiple-factor model for $v_n(t)$. Models for $v_n(t)$ typically include some risk index factors, plus factors measuring recent squared specific returns. The time dependence in the model of $v_n(t)$ is captured by time variation in the exposures. We estimate model coefficients via one pooled regression over assets and time periods, with outliers trimmed.

Risk Analysis

A portfolio P is described by an N-element vector $\mathbf{h}_P$ that gives the portfolio's holdings of the N risky assets. The factor exposures of portfolio P are given by

$$\mathbf{x}_P = \mathbf{X}^T \cdot \mathbf{h}_P \tag{3A.8}$$

The variance of portfolio $\mathbf{P}$ is given by

$$\sigma_P^2 = \mathbf{x}_P^T \cdot \mathbf{F} \cdot \mathbf{x}_P + \mathbf{h}_P^T \cdot \mathbf{\Delta} \cdot \mathbf{h}_P \tag{3A.9}$$
$$= \mathbf{h}_P^T \cdot \mathbf{V} \cdot \mathbf{h}_P$$

A similar formula lets us calculate ψ_P, the active risk or tracking error. If $\mathbf{h}_B$ is the benchmark holdings vector, then we can define

$$\mathbf{h}_{PA} = \mathbf{h}_P - \mathbf{h}_B \tag{3A.10}$$

$$\mathbf{x}_{PA} = \mathbf{X}^T \cdot \mathbf{h}_{PA} \tag{3A.11}$$

and

$$\psi_P^2 = \mathbf{x}_{PA}^T \cdot \mathbf{F} \cdot \mathbf{x}_{PA} + \mathbf{h}_{PA}^T \cdot \boldsymbol{\Delta} \cdot \mathbf{h}_{PA} \qquad (3A.12)$$
$$= \mathbf{h}_{PA}^T \cdot \mathbf{V} \cdot \mathbf{h}_{PA}$$

Notice that we have separated both total and active risk into common-factor and specific components. This works because factor risks and specific risks are uncorrelated.

The decomposition of risk is more difficult if we want to separate market risk from residual risk. We must define beta first.

The N vector of stock betas relative to the benchmark $\mathbf{h}_B$ is defined by the equation

$$\boldsymbol{\beta} = \frac{\mathbf{V} \cdot \mathbf{h}_B}{\sigma_B^2} = \frac{\mathbf{X} \cdot \mathbf{F} \cdot \mathbf{x}_B + \boldsymbol{\Delta} \cdot \mathbf{h}_B}{\sigma_B^2} \qquad (3A.13)$$

If we define $\mathbf{b}$ and $\mathbf{d}$ as

$$\mathbf{b} = \frac{\mathbf{F} \cdot \mathbf{x}_B}{\sigma_B^2} \qquad (3A.14)$$

$$\mathbf{d} = \frac{\boldsymbol{\Delta} \cdot \mathbf{h}_B}{\sigma_B^2} \qquad (3A.15)$$

then we can write beta as

$$\boldsymbol{\beta} = \mathbf{X} \cdot \mathbf{b} + \mathbf{d} \qquad (3A.16)$$

So each asset's beta contains a factor contribution and a specific contribution. The specific contribution is zero for any asset not in the benchmark. In most cases, the industry factor contribution dominates beta.

The portfolio beta is

$$\beta_P = \mathbf{h}_P^T \cdot \boldsymbol{\beta} = \mathbf{x}_P^T \cdot \mathbf{b} + \mathbf{h}_P^T \cdot \mathbf{d} \qquad (3A.17)$$

A similar calculation yields the active beta.

The systematic and residual risk are then given respectively by the two terms

$$\sigma_P^2 = \beta_P^2 \cdot \sigma_B^2 + \omega_P^2 \qquad (3A.18)$$

where σ_P^2 is given by Eq. (3A.9) and β_P by Eq. (3A.17). It is possible to construct a residual covariance matrix

$$\mathbf{VR} = \mathbf{V} - \boldsymbol{\beta} \cdot \sigma_B^2 \cdot \boldsymbol{\beta}^T \qquad (3A.19)$$

Attribution of Risk

In some cases, it is possible to attribute a portion of risk to a single cause. We can separate market risk from residual risk, and we can separate common-factor risk from specific risk. In both cases, the two risk components are uncorrelated. When two sources of risk are correlated, then the covariance between them makes it difficult to allocate the risk. We will describe one approach, which first requires the introduction of marginal contributions to risk.

Marginal Contribution

Although total allocation of risk is difficult, we can examine the marginal effects of a change in the portfolio. This type of sensitivity analysis allows us to see what factors and assets have the largest impact on risk. The marginal impact on risk is measured by the partial derivative of the risk with respect to the asset holding. We will see in the technical appendix to Chap. 5 that marginal contributions to residual risk are directly proportional to alphas, with the constant of proportionality dependent on the information ratio.

We can compute marginal contributions for total risk, residual risk, and active risk. The N vector of marginal contributions to total risk is

$$\mathbf{MCTR} = \frac{\partial \sigma_P}{\partial \mathbf{h}_P^T} = \frac{\mathbf{V} \cdot \mathbf{h}_P}{\sigma_P} \qquad (3A.20)$$

The $\mathbf{MCTR}(n)$ is the partial derivative of σ_P with respect to $\mathbf{h}_P(n)$. We can think of it as the approximate change in portfolio risk given a 1 percent increase in the holding of asset n, financed by decreasing the cash account by 1 percent. Recall that the cash holding $\mathbf{h}_P(0)$ is given by $\mathbf{h}_P(0) = 1 - e_P$. To first order,

$$\Delta \sigma_P \approx \Delta \mathbf{h}_P^T \cdot \mathbf{MCTR} \qquad (3A.21)$$

In a similar way, we can define the marginal contribution to residual risk as

$$\mathbf{MCRR} = \frac{\mathbf{VR} \cdot \mathbf{h}_P}{\omega_P} = \frac{\mathbf{V} \cdot \mathbf{h}_{PR}}{\omega_P} \qquad (3A.22)$$

where $\mathbf{h}_{PR} = \mathbf{h}_P - \beta_P \cdot \mathbf{h}_B$ is the residual holdings vector for portfolio P.

Finally, the marginal contribution to active risk is given by

$$\mathbf{MCAR} = \frac{\mathbf{V} \cdot \mathbf{h}_{PA}}{\psi_P} \qquad (3A.23)$$

We can further decompose this marginal contribution to active risk into a market and a residual component.

$$\mathbf{MCAR} = \boldsymbol{\beta} \cdot k_1 + \mathbf{MCRR} \cdot k_2 \qquad (3A.24)$$

where

$$k_1 = \frac{\beta_{PA} \cdot \sigma_B^2}{\psi_P} \qquad (3A.25)$$

and

$$k_2 = \frac{\omega_P}{\psi_P} \qquad (3A.26)$$

We see that $0 \le k_2 \le 1$, and $k_2 = 1$ when $\beta_{PA} = 0$ and $k_1 = 0$.

Factor Marginal Contributions

Sometimes we wish to calculate sensitivities with respect to factor exposures instead of asset holdings. Let's think about what this means.

At the asset level, the marginal contributions capture the change in risk if we change the holding of just one asset, leaving all other assets unchanged.

At the factor level, the marginal contributions should capture the change in risk if we change the exposure to only one factor, leaving other factor exposures unchanged. To increase the portfolio's exposure to only factor k, we want to add a portfolio with exposure to factor k, and zero exposure to the other factors. A reasonable and well-defined choice is a factor portfolio. The factor portfolio has the proper exposures, and minimum risk given those exposures, so it is as close as we can come:

$$\mathbf{h}_{PA} \rightarrow \mathbf{h}_{PA} + \left[(\mathbf{X}^T \cdot \boldsymbol{\Delta}^{-1} \cdot \mathbf{X})^{-1} \cdot \mathbf{X}^T \cdot \boldsymbol{\Delta}^{-1} \right]^T \cdot \boldsymbol{\delta}_k \qquad (3A.27)$$

where $\left[(\mathbf{X}^T \cdot \boldsymbol{\Delta}^{-1} \cdot \mathbf{X})^{-1} \cdot \mathbf{X}^T \cdot \boldsymbol{\Delta}^{-1} \right]$ is the K by N vector of factor portfolios, and $\boldsymbol{\delta}_k$ is a K by 1 vector containing zeros except in the kth row, where it contains δ_k.

To find the effect on risk of adding this portfolio, we need only multiply the changes in each asset holding times the marginal contributions at the asset level. We present here only the calculation for marginal contribution to active risk:

$$\Delta\psi_P = \left[[(\mathbf{X}^T \cdot \mathbf{\Delta}^{-1} \cdot \mathbf{X})^{-1} \cdot \mathbf{X}^T \cdot \mathbf{\Delta}^{-1}]^T \cdot \mathbf{\delta}_k \right]^T \cdot \mathbf{MCAR} \quad (3A.28)$$

$$= \mathbf{\delta}_k^T \cdot (\mathbf{X}^T \cdot \mathbf{\Delta}^{-1} \cdot \mathbf{X})^{-1} \cdot \mathbf{X}^T \cdot \mathbf{\Delta}^{-1} \cdot \left(\frac{\mathbf{V} \cdot \mathbf{h}_{PA}}{\psi_P} \right)$$

We can simplify this result by using the factor decomposition of the covariance matrix. The result is

$$\frac{\Delta\psi_P}{\mathbf{\delta}_k^T} = \left(\frac{\mathbf{F} \cdot x_{PA}}{\psi_P} \right) + \left[\frac{(\mathbf{X}^T \cdot \mathbf{\Delta}^{-1} \cdot \mathbf{X})^{-1} \cdot x_{PA}}{\psi_P} \right] \quad (3A.29)$$

The first term above captures the change in factor risk due to changing the factor exposure. It resembles the form of the marginal contribution to active risk at the asset level [Eq. (3A.23)]. It would be the complete answer if we could change factor exposures while leaving asset holdings unchanged. The second term captures the change in specific risk due to changing the factor exposures using the actual factor portfolio. Remember that the factor portfolios have minimum specific risk among all portfolios with unit exposure to one factor and zero exposure to all other factors. Empirically, we find that the second term is much smaller than the first term.[14] Hence we typically make the reasonable approximation

$$\frac{\Delta\psi_P}{\mathbf{\delta}_k^T} \approx \left(\frac{\mathbf{F} \cdot x_{PA}}{\psi_P} \right) \quad (3A.30)$$

Sector Marginal Contributions

Having broached the subject of factor marginal contributions, we should also briefly mention sector marginal contributions. The idea is that we typically group industry factors into sectors. The sectors play no role in risk model estimation or risk calculation, but they

---

[14]The exception to this finding occurs with thin industry factors, i.e., industry factors with fewer than about 10 members. Thin industries suffer from large estimation errors. This is yet another reason to avoid them.

are convenient and intuitive constructs. So once we have determined how increases in industry exposures might affect risk, we may also want to know how an increase in sector exposure might affect risk.

This is a reasonable question. Unfortunately, its answer is ambiguous. When we calculated factor marginal contributions, we used a linear contribution of asset-level marginal contributions and relied on the relative unambiguousness of the factor portfolios. At the sector level, we want to calculate a linear combination of the industry factor marginal contributions, but the weights are less ambiguous now. We could increase the exposure to a sector by increasing only one particular industry in the section, increasing each industry the same amount, increasing each industry based on the portfolio industry weights, or increasing each industry based on the benchmark industry weights. One reasonable choice is to use the total (as opposed to active) industry weights from the portfolio. For example, consider a computer sector comprising two industries: software and hardware. If the portfolio contains only computer hardware manufacturers, then calculate computer sector marginal contributions based only on the hardware industry. If the portfolio's exposure to computers is 70 percent software and 30 percent hardware, use the 70/30 weights to calculate sector marginal contributions. In other words, assume that the investor would increase (or decrease) the exposure to computers in exactly the current proportions.

Clearly, the most important point about sector marginal contributions is to understand what calculation you need and what calculation you are receiving.

Attribution of Risk

We can use the marginal contributions to define a decomposition of risk. For concreteness, we will focus on a decomposition of active risk, but the ideas apply equally well to total or residual risk. First note the mathematical relationship

$$\mathbf{h}_{PA}^T \cdot \mathbf{MCAR} = \mathbf{h}_{PA}^T \cdot \left(\frac{\mathbf{V} \cdot \mathbf{h}_{PA}}{\psi_P} \right) = \psi_P \qquad (3A.31)$$

But Eq. (3A.31) implies an attribution of active risk. The amount of active risk ψ_P which we can attribute to asset n is $h_{PA}^T(n) \cdot MCAR(n)$. We can furthermore divide Equation (3A.31) by ψ_P, to give a *percentage* breakdown of active risk:

$$\frac{h_{PA}^T \cdot \mathbf{MCAR}}{\psi_P} = 1 \qquad (3A.32)$$

We can use Eq. (3A.32) to attribute to asset n a fraction $h_{PA}^T(n) \cdot MCAR(n)/\psi_P$ of the overall active risk.

How can we interpret this attribution scheme? In fact, the attributed returns are *relative* marginal contributions to active risk. Here is what we mean. As before, if we increase the holding in asset n,

$$\Delta\psi_P \approx \Delta h_{PA}(n) \cdot MCAR(n) \qquad (3A.33)$$

But we can rewrite this as

$$\Delta\psi_P \approx \left[\frac{\Delta h_{PA}(n)}{h_{PA}(n)}\right] \cdot h_{PA}(n) \cdot MCAR(n) \qquad (3A.34)$$

So the change in active risk depends on the relative change in the active holding of asset n, $\Delta h_{PA}(n)/h_{PA}(n)$, times the amount of active risk attributed to asset n. Hence we can interpret this amount of risk attributed to asset n as a relative marginal contribution, $RMCAR(n)$:

$$\mathbf{RMCAR} = \begin{bmatrix} h_{PA}(1) & \cdot & MCAR(1) \\ & \vdots & \\ h_{PA}(N) & \cdot & MCAR(N) \end{bmatrix} \qquad (3A.35)$$

and

$$\Delta\psi_P \approx \left[\left(\frac{\Delta h_{PA}(1)}{h_{PA}(1)}\right) \cdots \left(\frac{\Delta h_{PA}(N)}{h_{PA}(N)}\right)\right] \cdot \mathbf{RMCAR} \qquad (3A.36)$$

If we changed asset n's active holding from 1 percent to 1.01 percent, we could estimate the change in active risk as 0.01 times the $RMCAR$ for asset n.[15]

---

[15]There is another, more algebraic interpretation of these risk attributions. The difficult issue in attributing risk is how to handle the covariance terms. But covariances always arise in pairs (e.g., $2 \cdot \text{Cov}\{a,b\}$). This risk attribution scheme simply parcels one covariance term to each element (e.g., $1 \cdot \text{Cov}\{a,b\}$ to the risk of a and $1 \cdot \text{Cov}\{a,b\}$ to the risk of b).

Attribution to Factors

This is a straightforward extension of the previous ideas. Using the factor risk model, we have

$$\psi_P = \mathbf{x}_{PA}^T \cdot \mathbf{F} \cdot \mathbf{x}_{PA} + \mathbf{h}_{PA}^T \cdot \mathbf{\Delta} \cdot \mathbf{h}_{PA} \qquad (3A.37)$$

We can therefore define the factor marginal contributions, **FMCAR**, as

$$\mathbf{FMCAR} = \frac{\partial \psi_P}{\partial \mathbf{x}_{PA}^T} = \frac{\mathbf{F} \cdot \mathbf{x}_{PA}}{\psi_P} \qquad (3A.38)$$

But note that

$$\mathbf{x}_{PA}^T \cdot \mathbf{FMCAR} = \frac{\mathbf{h}_{PA}^T \cdot \mathbf{V} \cdot \mathbf{h}_{PA} - \mathbf{h}_{PA}^T \cdot \mathbf{\Delta} \cdot \mathbf{h}_{PA}}{\psi_P} \qquad (3A.39)$$

Hence, we can attribute active risk ψ to the factors and specific sources. We attribute $x_{PA}^T(j) \cdot FMCAR(j)$ to factor j, and $\mathbf{h}_{PA}^T \cdot \mathbf{\Delta} \cdot \mathbf{h}_{PA}/\psi_P$ overall to specific sources. Once again, we can interpret these attributions as *relative* marginal contributions.

Correlations and Market Volatility

As a final topic, we can illustrate one use of the simple one-factor model to understand the observed relationship between asset correlations and market volatility: Typically asset correlations increase as market volatility increases.

According to this simple model, the correlation between assets n and m is

$$\rho_{nm} = \frac{\beta_n \cdot \beta_m \cdot \sigma_M^2}{\sqrt{(\beta_n^2 \cdot \sigma_M^2 + \omega_n^2) \cdot (\beta_m^2 \cdot \sigma_M^2 + \omega_m^2)}} \qquad (3A.40)$$

The only contribution of the model is the simple form of the covariance in the numerator of Eq. (3A.40). But now let's assume that both assets have betas of 1, and identical residual risk. Then Eq. (3A.40) becomes

$$\rho_{nm} \to \frac{\sigma_M^2}{\sigma_M^2 + \omega^2} \qquad (3A.41)$$

We can now see that if residual risk is independent of market volatility, as market volatility increases, asset correlations increase. In periods of low market volatility, asset correlations will be relatively low.

Exercises

1. Show that:

$$\mathbf{h}_P^T \cdot \mathbf{MCTR} = \sigma_P$$

$$\mathbf{h}_P^T \cdot \mathbf{MCRR} = \omega_P$$

$$\mathbf{h}_{PA}^T \cdot \mathbf{MCAR} = \psi_P$$

2. Verify Eq. (3A.24).
3. Show that

$$\mathbf{h}_B^T \cdot \mathbf{MCRR} = 0$$

$$\mathbf{h}_B^T \cdot \mathbf{MCAR} = k_1$$

4. Using the single-factor model, assuming that every stock has equal residual risk ω_0, and considering equal-weighted portfolios to track the equal-weighted S&P 500, show that the residual risk of the N-stock portfolio will be

$$\omega_N^2 = \frac{\omega_0^2}{N}$$

What estimate does this provide of how well a 50-stock portfolio could track the S&P 500? Assume $\omega_0 = 25$ percent.

5. This is for prime-time players. Show that the inverse of $\mathbf{V}$ is given by

$$\mathbf{V}^{-1} = \mathbf{\Delta}^{-1} - \mathbf{\Delta}^{-1} \cdot \mathbf{X} \cdot \{\mathbf{X}^T \cdot \mathbf{\Delta}^{-1} \cdot \mathbf{X} + \mathbf{F}^{-1}\}^{-1} \cdot \mathbf{X}^T \cdot \mathbf{\Delta}^{-1}$$

As we will see in later chapters, portfolio construction problems typically involve inverting the covariance matrix. This useful relationship facilitates that computation by replacing the inversion of an N by N matrix with the inversion of K by K matrices, where $K \ll N$. Note that the inversion of N by N diagonal matrices is trivial.

Applications Problems

1. Calculate the average correlation between MMI assets. First, calculate the average volatility of each asset. Second, calculate the volatility of the equal-weighted portfolio of the assets. Use Eq. (3.4) to estimate the average correlation.

2. What are the average total risk, residual risk, and beta of the MMI assets (relative to the CAPMMI)?

3. Using MMI assets, construct a 20-stock portfolio to track the S&P 500. Compare the resulting tracking error to the answer to Exercise 4, where ω_0 is the average residual risk for MMI assets.

Exceptional Return, Benchmarks, and Value Added

INTRODUCTION

The CAPM provides consensus expected returns. A multiple-factor model can help to control risk. Consensus forecasts and risk control are available to all active managers. We need one more crucial ingredient in order to be effective: accurate forecasts of expected return. This chapter will discuss those forecasts of expected return and outline a procedure to transform those forecasts into portfolios.

The chapter is a gradual migration from theory to practice. In theory, we consider an all-embracing market consisting of all assets; in practice, there is a great degree of specialization, so we consider a benchmark with a limited number of assets. In theory, the investor is an individual concerned for his or her own needs; in practice, investment decisions are made by professionals who are one or more levels removed from the eventual beneficiary of those decisions. In theory, active management is a dubious undertaking; in practice, we must provide guidelines for the attempt. This chapter shows how theory is adapted to these institutional realities and the needs of the active manager.

The results of this chapter are as follows:

- The components of expected return are defined.
  Exceptional expected return is the difference between our forecasts and the consensus.
- Benchmark portfolios are a standard for the active manager.
- Active management value-added is expected exceptional return less a penalty for active variance.

- Management of total risk and return is distinct from management of active risk and return.
- Benchmark timing decisions are distinct from stock selection decisions.

This chapter sets out the ground rules used throughout the book. Those who don't like benchmarks should find some comfort in the notion that choosing the risk-free portfolio F as a benchmark puts one back in the traditional position of balancing expected return against total risk.

There are two things that this chapter *does not* do:

- Set up criteria for the proper choice of a benchmark for a specialist manager.
- Set a target for strategic asset allocation.

Strategic asset allocation establishes a benchmark for an entire pension fund. Strategic asset allocation is a vital question for the fund, for consultants, and for balanced mangers. We don't address that important question in this book.

BENCHMARKS

In many practical situations, an active manager will be asked to outperform a benchmark portfolio that cannot, in good conscience, be called "the market." Some would argue that this is always the case. Even that old standby, the S&P 500, represents only a fraction of the world's traded equities. If we toss in debt and real property, the S&P 500 will not look like a representative slice of the universe available to the institutional investor. For that reason, we are going to phase out the word *market* and shift to the word *benchmark*. The benchmark portfolio is also known by the aliases *bogey* and *normal* portfolio.

A benchmark portfolio is a consequence of institutional investment management. A trustee or sponsor generally hires several managers to invest the funds. These managers will typically specialize. So included among the managers will be a bond manager, an equity manager, an international manager, etc. The specialization can become finer.[1] The managers may specialize in passive equity strategies, growth stocks, value stocks, small-capitalization stocks, etc.

The sponsor should give all managers clear instructions regarding their responsibilities and any limitations on their actions. One of the best ways for an owner of funds to communicate those responsibilities is to specify a benchmark portfolio. For example, the benchmark for a U.S. international equity manager may be the Morgan Stanley Capital International EAFE index or the Financial Times EUROPAC index. The benchmark for a smaller-capitalization manager in the United States may be the Frank Russell 2000 index. The benchmark for an Australian manager of resource stocks may be a special index containing only the stocks in the Australian resource sector.

The manager's performance is judged relative to the performance of the benchmark. The manager's *active return* is the difference between the return on the manager's portfolio and the return on the benchmark portfolio.

The reader may feel that this practice has theoretical limitations. It undoubtedly does. However, it also has undeniable practical benefits. First, it allows investment managers to specialize and concentrate their expertise on a smaller collection of assets. The sponsors take charge of asset allocation. Second, it focuses the manager's attention on performance relative to the benchmark.

What guidelines can we provide for an institutional manager whose performance is judged relative to a benchmark? The manager's attention is directed toward the difference between the managed portfolio's returns and the benchmark portfolio's returns. The market portfolio is not specified and plays no direct role.

New Terminology

We have thrown out the market portfolio and are willing to work with a more ad hoc benchmark portfolio. At the same time, we don't want to abandon all the useful scaffolding that we had built up around the market.

---

[1]This specialization can be and has been carried to extremes. Each manager has a vested interest in creating a separate niche to avoid direct comparisons with other managers. This has led to a constant spawning of new styles.

The most important item to salvage is beta. As discussed in previous chapters, we can define beta outside of the CAPM context. If r_B is the excess return on the benchmark portfolio and r_n is the excess return on stock n, then we can define β_n as

$$r_n = \frac{\text{Cov}\{r_n, r_B\}}{\text{Var}\{r_B\}} \qquad (4.1)$$

We have robbed beta of its universal definition. Beta is no longer an absolute term. It is not beta with respect to *the market*, but beta with respect to *a benchmark*. Our notion of residual risk will also become relative. It is no longer residual to the market but residual to a benchmark.

The *active position* is the difference between the portfolio holdings and the benchmark holdings. The active holding in the risky assets is given by $\mathbf{h}_{PA}$,

$$\mathbf{h}_{PA} = \mathbf{h}_P - \mathbf{h}_B \qquad (4.2)$$

and the active cash holding is

$$\text{Active cash} = \mathbf{h}_P(0) - \mathbf{h}_B(0) = -\mathbf{e} \cdot \mathbf{h}_{PA} \qquad (4.3)$$

The *active variance* is the variance of the active position. If we let ψ_P be the active risk, we have

$$\psi_P^2 = \mathbf{h}_{PA}^T \cdot \mathbf{V} \cdot \mathbf{h}_{PA} \qquad (4.4)$$
$$= \sigma_P^2 + \sigma_B^2 - 2 \cdot \sigma_{P,B}$$

If we use our notion of beta relative to the benchmark and residual return θ_P relative to the benchmark, then we can write the active variance as

$$\psi_P^2 = \beta_{PA}^2 \cdot \sigma_B^2 + \omega_P^2 \qquad (4.5)$$

where β_P is the active beta (i.e., $\beta_P - 1$) and ω_P is the residual risk:

$$\text{Var}\{\theta_P\} \equiv \omega_P^2 \qquad (4.6)$$

Our definition of a benchmark will assist us in separating expected return into its component parts.

COMPONENTS OF EXPECTED RETURN

We can decompose expected return forecasts into four parts: a risk-free component (the time premium), a benchmark component (the risk premium), a benchmark timing component (exceptional benchmark return), and an alpha (expected residual return). If R_n is the total return on asset n, then we write

$$E\{R_n\} = 1 + i_F + \beta_n \cdot \mu_B + \beta_n \cdot \Delta f_B + \alpha_n \qquad (4.7)$$

We will now discuss each component and various combinations.

The Time Premium i_F

This is the return an investor receives for parting with the investment stake for a year. It is referred to as the time premium, i.e., the compensation for time. Since we know the return on a risk-free asset in advance, we can assign the time premium in advance.

The Risk Premium $\beta_n \cdot \mu_B$

We are borrowing from the CAPM here. The expected excess return on the benchmark, μ_B, is usually estimated by analysts as a very long run (70+ years) average (although other estimation methods are common). A number between 3 and 7 percent per annum is reasonable for most equity markets. Notice that low-beta assets will have lower risk premiums and high-beta assets will have greater risk premiums.

Exceptional Benchmark Return $\beta_n \cdot \Delta f_B$

The expected excess return on the benchmark μ_B cited above is based on very long run considerations. If you believe that the next year (or quarter, or month) will be quite different, then Δf_B is your measure of that difference between the expected excess return on the benchmark in the near future and the long-run expected excess return.

Alpha α_n

Alpha is the expected residual return, $\alpha_n = E\{\theta_n\}$.

Consider this breakdown of the -0.60% total return for the MMI portfolio over the month of December 1992, using the S&P 500 as a benchmark. Over this month, the forecast beta of the portfolio versus the S&P 500 was 0.96. Over this same month, the risk-free return was 26 basis points and the S&P 500 return was

131 basis points; we will assume an expected long-run excess
S&P 500 return of 50 basis points, so there was a benchmark surprise
of 55 basis points. Given this information, we can break down the
realized portfolio return as in Table 4.1.

We can combine these components of expected returns in various ways.

Consensus expected excess return $\beta_n \cdot \mu_B$. The consensus
expected excess return is the expected excess return
obtained if one accepts the benchmark as an ex ante
efficient portfolio with expected excess return μ_B. This set of
expected excess returns will cause us to choose our
portfolio to exactly match the benchmark portfolio.

Feeding these expected returns into an optimizer will
lead to combinations of the benchmark portfolio and cash,
with the cash fraction dependent on μ_B.

Expected excess return $f_n = \beta_n \cdot \mu_B + \beta_n \cdot \Delta f_B + \alpha_n$. The
expected excess return, denoted f_n, is made up of the risk
premium, the response to an exceptional benchmark
forecast, and the alpha.

Exceptional expected return $\beta_n \cdot \Delta f_B + \alpha_n$. The exceptional
expected return is the key to active management. The first
component, $\beta_n \cdot \Delta f_B$, measures benchmark timing,[2] and the
second component, α_n, measures stock selection.

T A B L E 4.1

MMI Return Breakdown: 12/92

Risk-free return	0.26%
Risk premium	0.48%
Exceptional benchmark return	0.53%
Alpha	−1.87%
Total return	−0.60%

[2]Note that the expected return $\beta_n \cdot \Delta f_B$ will generate a single bet for or against the
benchmark. The term *benchmark timing* more generally refers to this strategy over
time. By construction, $E\{\beta_n \cdot \Delta f_B\} = 0$ over time, so Δf_B will sometimes be positive
and sometimes be negative.

Starting with a list of expected returns $E\{R_n\}$, asset betas β_n, the weight of each asset in the benchmark $h_B(n)$, a risk-free rate i_F, and a long-run expected excess return on the benchmark μ_B, we can separate the expected returns into their component parts. The recipe is a simple and interesting spreadsheet exercise.

Step 1. Calculate the expected excess return on the benchmark.

$$f_B = \sum_n h_B(n) \cdot E\{R_n - (1 + i_F)\} \tag{4.8}$$

Step 2. The exceptional benchmark return is

$$\Delta f_B = f_B - \mu_B \tag{4.9}$$

Table 4.2 presents expected returns for MMI stocks in the United States, assuming a risk-free rate of 3.16 percent, an S&P 500 benchmark with an expected excess return of 6 percent, and historical alphas and betas over the 60-month period ending December 1992. The expected returns vary widely from stock to stock, much more than the betas vary. This happens because we are using historical alphas (which vary widely) to calculate expected returns.

Note that we have included cash and a benchmark composite in the list. Cash is the one asset that we are sure we can get right. The benchmark composite will have zero alpha, since there is by definition no residual return for the benchmark.

MANAGEMENT OF TOTAL RISK AND RETURN

The traditional (Markowitz-Sharpe) approach to modern portfolio theory is to consider the risk/expected return trade-offs available to the manager. In this section, we will follow that path. In the following sections, we will expand the risk/expected return framework to distinguish between benchmark and active risk.

The return/risk choices available with the consensus forecast are presented in Fig. 4.1. The horizontal axis measures portfolio risk and the vertical axis expected excess returns *using the consensus forecast* μ, which is $\beta \cdot \mu_B$. The hyperbola describes the combinations of expected excess return and risk that we can obtain with *fully*

T A B L E 4.2

Expected Returns for MMI Stocks

Stock	Alpha	Beta	Expected Return
American Express	−7.91%	1.21	2.53%
AT&T	3.47%	0.96	12.38%
Chevron	7.47%	0.45	13.32%
Coca-Cola	20.03%	1.00	29.19%
Disney	7.46%	1.24	18.05%
Dow Chemicals	−10.09%	1.11	−0.28%
DuPont	−0.43%	1.09	9.25%
Eastman Kodak	−9.04%	0.60	−2.29%
Exxon	4.51%	0.47	10.48%
General Electric	0.17%	1.31	11.20%
General Motors	−4.53%	0.90	4.01%
IBM	−19.04%	0.64	−12.04%
International Paper	−0.57%	1.16	9.46%
Johnson & Johnson	7.32%	1.15	17.40%
McDonalds	3.18%	1.07	12.77%
Merck	6.04%	1.09	15.73%
3M	0.47%	0.74	8.07%
Philip Morris	17.41%	0.97	26.38%
Procter & Gamble	8.05%	1.01	17.27%
Sears	−2.07%	1.04	7.32%
Cash	0.00%	0.00	3.16%
S&P 500	0.00%	1.00	9.16%

invested portfolios. The fully invested portfolio with the highest ratio of expected excess return to risk is the benchmark, B. There is no surprise here; consensus in implies consensus out.

Active management starts when the manager's forecasts differ from the consensus. If the manager has forecasts f of expected excess returns, then we have the risk/return choices shown in Fig. 4.2.

In Fig. 4.2, the benchmark is *not* on the efficient frontier. A fully invested portfolio Q that differs from B has the maximum ratio of f_P to σ_P. There are possibilities for doing better than B!

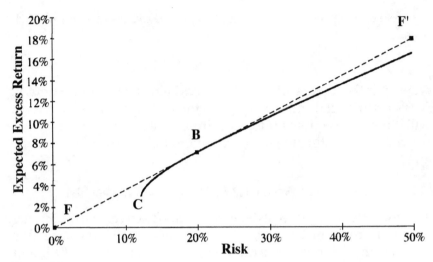

Figure 4.1

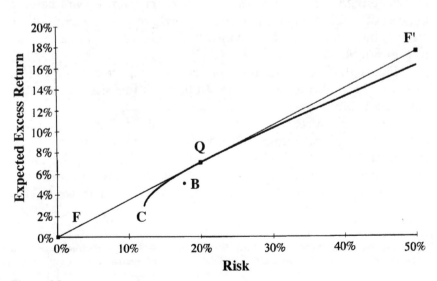

Figure 4.2

We can express the forecast of expected excess return for stock n as

$$f_n = \beta_n \cdot f_B + \alpha_n \qquad (4.10)$$

where f_B is the forecast of expected excess return for the benchmark, β_n is stock n's beta, and α_n is stock n's forecast alpha. These forecasts will differ from consensus forecasts to the extent that f_B differs from the consensus estimate μ_B and α_n differs from zero.

The Total Return/Total Risk Trade-Off

The portfolio we select will depend on our objective. The traditional approach uses a mean/variance criterion for portfolio choice.[3] We will call that criterion our *expected utility*, denote it as $U[P]$, and define it as

$$U[P] = f_P - \lambda_T \cdot \sigma_P^2 \qquad (4.11)$$

where f_P is the expected excess return and $\lambda_T \cdot \sigma_P^2$ is a penalty for risk. The parameter λ_T measures *aversion to total risk*, where total risk includes systematic risk (driven by the benchmark) and residual risk (from asset selection). Note that some authors have equivalently defined utility in terms of a risk acceptance parameter τ instead of a risk aversion parameter λ, where $\tau = 1/\lambda$. Still other authors have, for later mathematical convenience, used $\lambda/2$ instead of λ in Eq. (4.11).

Figure 4.3 shows the lines of constant expected utility $U[P]$. The trick is to find an eligible portfolio with the highest possible expected utility.

We can get a reasonable feel for the total risk aversion λ_T by trying some typical numbers. Consider a portfolio with a risk of 20 percent. If we think that the penalty for risk is on the order of one-half the expected excess return on the portfolio, then we anticipate a penalty of 3 or 4 percent. To get 3 percent, we would

---

[3]We can justify this in three ways: Returns are normally distributed, the investor has a quadratic utility function, or we are looking at the market over a relatively short period of time. The first two are in the Markowitz-Sharpe tradition. The third stems from the work of Merton on the approximation of general utility functions with quadratic utility functions over a short period of time.

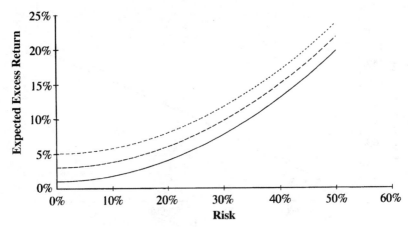

Figure 4.3 Constant expected utility lines.

use $\lambda_T = 0.0075$, since $3 = 0.0075 \cdot 400$. To get 4 percent, we would use $\lambda_T = 0.01$, since $4 = 0.01 \cdot 400$. As discussed in Chap. 3, λ_T is not dimensionless. In particular, it depends on whether we represent risk and return in percent or decimal, and whether we annualize.

There is a more scientific way to get a reasonable value for λ_T. Consider the case where we have no information, i.e., $\mathbf{f} = \boldsymbol{\mu}$, our forecasts are equal to the consensus. The expected benchmark excess return is μ_B, and the benchmark risk is σ_B. The level of total risk aversion that would lead[4] us to choose the benchmark portfolio is

$$\lambda_T = \frac{\mu_B}{2 \cdot \sigma_B^2} \tag{4.12}$$

If $\mu_B = 6$ percent and $\sigma_B = 20$ percent, then we find $\lambda_T = 0.0075$. If $\mu_B = 8$ percent and $\sigma_B = 16$ percent, we find $\lambda_T = 0.0156$.

---

[4]Consider the simple problem of mixing the benchmark portfolio B with the risk-free portfolio F. The expected excess return will be $\beta_P \cdot \mu_B$, where β_P is the fraction in the benchmark portfolio. The risk will be $\beta_P^2 \cdot \sigma_B^2$. The objective is

$$\beta_P \cdot \mu_B - \lambda_T \cdot \beta_P^2 \cdot \sigma_B^2$$

The first-order conditions are

$$\mu_B - 2 \cdot \lambda_T \cdot \beta_P \cdot \sigma_B^2 = 0$$

The optimal solution will be $\beta_P = 1$ when Eq. (4.12) holds.

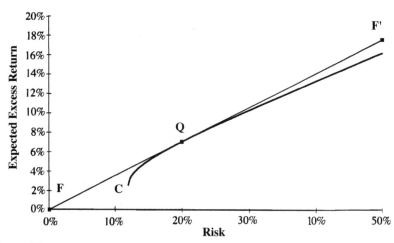

Figure 4.4

If we are willing to have cash in our portfolio, then we have the situation shown in Fig. 4.4. The efficient frontier consists of all the portfolios on the line from F through Q. The optimal portfolio, call it P, is the portfolio on the frontier with the highest risk-adjusted return.[5] Portfolio P will be a mixture of Q and F. The beta of P is

$$\beta_P = \frac{f_B}{2 \cdot \lambda_T \cdot \sigma_B^2} \qquad (4.13)$$

Using Eq. (4.12), and defining $\Delta f_B \equiv f_B - \mu_B$ to be the forecast of *exceptional* benchmark return, the beta of portfolio P becomes

$$\beta_P = 1 + \frac{\Delta f_B}{\mu_B} \qquad (4.14)$$

The active beta β_{PA}, the difference between β_P and 1, is the ratio of our forecast for benchmark exceptional return Δf_B to the consensus expected excess return on the benchmark μ_B.

---

[5]The holdings in P are given by

$$\mathbf{h}_P = \left(\frac{f_Q}{2 \cdot \lambda_T \cdot \sigma_Q^2}\right) \cdot \mathbf{h}_Q = \beta_P \cdot \mathbf{h}_B + \left(\frac{IR}{2 \cdot \lambda_T}\right) \cdot \mathbf{h}_A$$

where the information ratio IR measures the ratio of expected residual return to residual risk. Chapter 5 discusses it in detail. The technical appendix of Chap. 5 covers the characteristic portfolio of the alphas, portfolio A.

T A B L E   4.3

f_P	27.29%
σ_P	25.20%
β_P	1.05
α_P	20.99%
ω_P	13.78%

We will argue that this expected utility criterion will typically lead to portfolios that are too aggressive for institutional investment managers.[6]

Consider, for example, our expected return forecasts for the MMI stocks. Table 4.3 shows the attributes of the portfolio that we obtain using these stocks with a typical level of risk aversion ($\lambda = 0.0075$).

These portfolios are far too risky for the institutional manager. This is not due to the extravagant nature of the expected returns. The problem is not the total portfolio risk σ_P, it is the residual risk ω_P.

In total risk/return analysis, small levels of information lead to very high levels of residual risk.

In order to develop an objective that gives results that are more in line with institutional practice, we need to focus on the active component of return, and look at active risk/return trade-offs.

FOCUS ON VALUE-ADDED

In the previous section, we discovered that portfolio selection using an expected utility objective leads to levels of residual risk that are

---

[6]The optimal level of residual risk depends on the perceived quality of the manager's information. This is measured by the information ratio IR, a concept discussed in great detail in the next chapter. Optimistic estimates of the information ratio generally range from 0.5 to 1.0. The optimal level of residual risk is

$$\omega_P = \frac{IR}{2 \cdot \lambda_R}$$

A hopeful manager with an information ratio of 0.75 and total risk aversion of 0.01 would have 37.5 percent residual risk.

much higher than those observed among institutional portfolio managers. The root cause is our even-handed treatment of benchmark and active risk. There is actually a double standard—investment managers and pension plan sponsors are much more averse to the risk of deviation from the benchmark than they are averse to the risk of the benchmark.

Why are institutional money managers willing to accept the benchmark portfolio with 20 percent risk and loath to take on a portfolio with 21.00 percent risk if it contains 20 percent benchmark risk and 6.40 percent residual risk? The variance in the first case will be 400, and that in the second case will be $441 = (21\%)^2$. The difference in risk between 20 percent and 21 percent seems small.

Business Risk and Investment Risk

The explanation lies in the allocation of that risk. The owner of the funds, a pension fund or an endowment, bears the benchmark component of the risk. The owner of the funds assumed that risk when invested in that particular benchmark. The active manager, on the other hand, bears the responsibility for the residual risk.[7]

Let's say the benchmark is the S&P 500. Hundreds of managers are compared to the S&P 500. All of these managers will experience the same benchmark return. The S&P 500 is the tide that raises or lowers all boats. The managers cannot influence the tide. They will be separated by the residual returns. A high level of residual risk means that there is a large chance of being among the worst managers and a resulting possibility of termination. This is not a happy prospect, and so managers reduce their residual risk in order to avoid the business risk inherent in placing low in the table.

Fortunately, our view of risk and return allows us to accommodate this double standard for benchmark and residual risk.

In the technical appendix to this chapter, we will more rigorously derive the objective for the active manager, which splits risk and return into three parts, as described below.

---

[7]The active manager is, in fact, responsible for active risk. In the typical case of $\beta_p = 1$, residual risk equals active risk. If $\beta_p \neq 1$, the manager is responsible for both residual risk and active systematic risk.

Intrinsic, $f_B - \lambda_T \cdot \sigma_B^2$. This component arises from the risk and return of the benchmark. It is not under the manager's control. Note that we have used λ_T as aversion to total risk.

Timing, $\beta_{PA} \cdot \Delta f_B - \lambda_{BT} \cdot \beta_{PA}^2 \cdot \sigma_B^2$. This is the contribution from timing the benchmark. It is governed by the manager's active beta. Note the risk aversion λ_{BT} to the risk caused by benchmark timing.

Residual, $\alpha_P - \lambda_R \cdot \omega_P^2$. This is due to the manager's residual position. Here we have an aversion λ_R to the residual risk.

The last two parts of the objective measure the manager's ability to add value. The amount of *value added* is

$$\text{VA} = \{\beta_{PA} \cdot \Delta f_B - \lambda_{BT} \cdot \beta_{PA}^2 \cdot \sigma_B^2\} + \{\alpha_P - \lambda_R \cdot \omega_P^2\} \qquad (4.15)$$

The two components of the value-added objective are similar to the mean/variance utility objective that we considered in Eq. (4.11). In each component, there is an expected return term and a variance term. The risk aversion—λ_{BT} for benchmark timing and λ_R for residual risk—transforms the variance into a penalty deducted from the amount of expected returns. The value added is a risk-adjusted expected return that ignores any contribution of the benchmark to the risk and expected return.

The objective [Eq. (4.15)] splits the value added into value added by benchmark timing and value added by stock selection. We consider benchmark timing briefly in the section below, and in more detail in Chap. 19. We will consider stock selection in the next chapter.

BENCHMARK TIMING

Benchmark timing is the choice of an appropriate active beta, period by period. The bulk of this book will concentrate on the management of residual return. The exceptions are Chap. 18, "Asset Allocation," and Chap. 19, "Benchmark Timing."

We take this approach for four reasons:

- A majority of U.S. institutional managers and a growing minority of non-U.S. institutional managers do not use benchmark timing.

- It greatly simplifies the discussion. This will help the reader who accepts this premise or is at least willing to temporarily suspend disbelief.
- We may succeed. Recall the Russian proverb, "The man who chases two rabbits will catch neither."
- A more subtle reason, suggested in Chap. 6, "The Fundamental Law of Active Management," is that there is less chance of deriving substantial[8] value added through benchmark timing.

This separation of benchmark timing and stock selection is evident in Eq. (4.15). We can choose beta to maximize the first term in that equation. The optimal level of *active* beta will be

$$\beta_{PA} = \frac{\Delta f_B}{2 \cdot \lambda_{BT} \cdot \sigma_B^2} \qquad (4.16)$$

Very high levels of aversion to benchmark timing risk λ_{BT} will keep β_{PA} (and hence benchmark timing) close to zero. No benchmark forecast, i.e., $\Delta f_B = 0$, will also keep active beta equal to zero.

ACTIVE VERSUS RESIDUAL RETURNS

Our active management framework is quickly moving toward a focus on residual return and residual risk. How does this connect with the manager's goal of significant *active* return?

The residual return and risk are

$$\theta_P = r_P - \beta_P \cdot r_B \qquad (4.17)$$

$$\omega_P = \text{Std}\{\theta_P\} \qquad (4.18)$$

while the active return and risk are

$$r_{PA} = r_P - r_B = \theta_P + \beta_{PA} \cdot r_B \qquad (4.19)$$

$$\psi_P = \text{Std}\{r_{PA}\} = \sqrt{\omega_P^2 + \beta_{PA}^2 \cdot \sigma_B^2} \qquad (4.20)$$

---

[8]The reader is free to protest at this point. However, protests based on a single data point, such as "I knew a fellow who was in puts in October 1987" will not be allowed. To hint at the underlying argument, benchmark timing can clearly generate very large active returns in one particular period, just by luck. But this isn't the same as generating substantial *risk-adjusted* value added.

As long as the manager avoids benchmark timing and sets $\beta_P = 1$, active and residual returns (and risks) are identical. This is the case for most institutional equity managers, and for good reasons, which we will cover in Chap. 6. If the manager does engage in benchmark timing, then, as we can see in Eq. (4.19), the active return is the sum of the residual return and the benchmark timing return.

SUMMARY

Previous chapters have discussed consensus expected returns and risk. This chapter turns to the heart of active management: exceptional returns. In particular, it has focused on the components of exceptional returns and introduced the notion of a benchmark portfolio. The benchmark is determined by institutional considerations and can differ considerably from what is commonly considered the market portfolio.

We have looked at possible criteria for the active manager. The traditional criterion of maximizing expected utility does not appear to give results that are consistent with investment practice. The main reason for this is that the expected utility function approach fails to distinguish between sources of risk. But the client bears the benchmark risk, and the active manager bears the active risk of deviating from the benchmark.

In the appendix, we derive an objective that separates active risk into two components: active risk that is correlated with the benchmark, resulting from a choice of active beta (benchmark timing), and active residual risk that is uncorrelated with the benchmark and based on forecasts of residual return (alpha). A reader who has difficulty with this approach should realize that it is a generalization of the usual risk/expected return approach. If we take the risk-free asset, portfolio F, as the benchmark, then all return is residual return. If we equate the risk aversions for total risk, benchmark timing, and residual risk, i.e., $\lambda_T = \lambda_{BT} = \lambda_R$, then we are back in the traditional risk/expected return framework.

We turn to the management of residual return in the next chapter.

PROBLEMS

1. Assume a risk-free rate of 6 percent, a benchmark expected excess return of 6.5 percent, and a long-run benchmark expected excess return of 6 percent. Given that McDonald's has a beta of 1.07 and an expected total return of 15 percent, separate its expected return into
   Time premium
   Risk premium
   Exceptional benchmark return
   Alpha
   Consensus expected return
   Expected excess return
   Exceptional expected return
   What is the sum of the consensus expected return and the exceptional expected return?

2. Suppose the benchmark is not the market, and the CAPM holds. How will the CAPM expected returns split into the categories suggested in this chapter?

3. Given a benchmark risk of 20 percent and a portfolio risk of 21 percent, and assuming a portfolio beta of 1, what is the portfolio's residual risk? What is its active risk? How does this compare to the difference between the portfolio risk and the benchmark risk?

4. Investor A manages total return and risk $(f_P - \lambda_T \cdot \sigma_P^2)$, with risk aversion $\lambda_T = 0.0075$. Investor B manages residual risk and return $(\alpha_P - \lambda_R \cdot \omega_P^2)$, with risk aversion $\lambda_R = 0.075$ (moderate to aggressive). They each can choose between two portfolios:

$$f_1 = 10\%$$
$$\sigma_1 = 20.22\%$$
$$f_2 = 16\%$$
$$\sigma_2 = 25\%$$

Both portfolios have $\beta = 1$. Furthermore,

$$f_B = 6\%$$
$$\sigma_B = 20\%$$

Which portfolio will A prefer? Which portfolio will B prefer? (*Hint:* First calculate expected residual return and residual risk for the two portfolios.)

5. Assume that you are a mean/variance investor with total risk aversion of 0.0075. If a portfolio has an expected excess return of 6 percent and risk of 20 percent, what is your *certainty equivalent return,* the certain expected excess return that you would fairly trade for this portfolio?

REFERENCES

Jacobs, Bruce I., and Kenneth N. Levy. "Residual Risk: How Much Is Too Much?" *Journal of Portfolio Management*, vol. 22, no. 3, Spring 1996, pp. 10–16.

Markowitz, H. M. *Portfolio Selection: Efficient Diversification of Investment.* Cowles Foundation Monograph 16 (New Haven, Conn.: Yale University Press, 1959).

Merton, Robert C. "An Analytical Derivation of the Efficient Portfolio." *Journal of Financial and Quantitative Analysis*, vol. 7, September 1972, pp. 1851–1872.

Messmore, Tom. "Variance Drain." *Journal of Portfolio Management*, vol. 21, no. 4, Summer 1995, pp. 104–110.

Roll, Richard. "A Mean/Variance Analysis of Tracking Error." *Journal of Portfolio Management*, vol. 18, no. 4, Summer 1992, pp. 13–22.

Rosenberg, Barr. "How Active Should a Portfolio Be? The Risk-Reward Tradeoff." *Financial Analysts Journal*, vol. 35, no. 1, January/February 1979, pp. 49–62.

———. "Security Appraisal and Unsystematic Risk in Institutional Investment." *Proceedings of the Seminar on the Analysis of Security Prices,* (Chicago: University of Chicago Press), November 1976, pp. 171–237.

Rudd, Andrew. "Business Risk and Investment Risk." *Investment Management Review*, November/December 1987, pp. 19–27.

Rudd, Andrew, and Henry K. Clasing, Jr. *Modern Portfolio Theory,* 2d (Orinda, Calif.: Andrew Rudd, 1988).

Sharpe, William F. "Capital Asset Prices: A Theory of Market Equilibrium under Conditions of Risk." *Journal of Finance*, vol. 19, no. 3, September 1964, pp. 425–442.

TECHNICAL APPENDIX

In this appendix, we derive the objective for value-added management that we use throughout the book. The value-added objective looks at two sources of exceptional return and active risk. The sources are residual risk and benchmark timing.

An Objective for Value-Added Management

We begin by separating three items—a forecast of excess returns $\mathbf{f}$, the portfolio holdings $\mathbf{h}_P$, and the portfolio variance σ_P^2—into a benchmark and a residual (to the benchmark) component. Let $\mathbf{h}_{PR}$ represent portfolio P's residual holdings in the risky stocks. We have

$$\mathbf{h}_P = \beta_P \cdot \mathbf{h}_B + \mathbf{h}_{PR} \qquad (4A.1)$$

$$f_P = \beta_P \cdot f_B + \alpha_P \qquad (4A.2)$$

and $\qquad \sigma_P^2 = \beta_P^2 \cdot \sigma_B^2 + \omega_P^2 \qquad (4A.3)$

where the beta, β_P, is $\text{Cov}\{r_P r_B\}/\text{Var}\{r_B\}$, i.e., beta with respect to the benchmark.

We can decompose the expected excess return on portfolio P, f_P, into the sum of several items. If we recall that $\Delta f_B = f_B - \mu_B$ is the difference between our forecast of the benchmark's excess return and the long-run consensus, and that the portfolio beta $\beta_P = 1 + \beta_{PA}$, where β_{PA} is the *active beta*, Eq. (4A.2) leads to

$$f_P = f_B + \beta_{PA} \cdot f_B + \alpha_P \qquad (4A.4)$$

and $\qquad f_P = f_B + \beta_{PA} \cdot \mu_B + \beta_{PA} \cdot \Delta f_B + \alpha_P \qquad (4A.5)$

These expected excess return items are

1. f_B, expected benchmark excess return
2. $\beta_{PA} \cdot \mu_B$, return due to active beta and consensus forecast
3. $\beta_{PA} \cdot \Delta f_B$, return due to active beta and exceptional forecast
4. α_P, return due to stock alphas and stock selection

We can't do anything about item 1. Items 3 and 4 link our exceptional forecasts, Δf_B and α, with our active positions β_{PA} and $\mathbf{h}_{PR}$. Item 2 is curious. This is the effect on expected return of varying beta. Notice that item 2 contains no forecast information.

Starting with Eq. (4A.3), we can also split the portfolio's variance into several parts:

$$\sigma_P^2 = (1 + \beta_{PA})^2 \cdot \sigma_B^2 + \omega_P^2 \qquad (4A.6)$$

and $\qquad \sigma_P^2 = \sigma_B^2 + 2 \cdot \beta_{PA} \cdot \sigma_B^2 + \beta_{PA}^2 \cdot \sigma_B^2 + \omega_P^2 \qquad (4A.7)$

These variance items are, in turn,

5. σ_B^2, benchmark variance

6. $2 \cdot \beta_{PA} \cdot \sigma_B^2$, covariance due to active beta

7. $\beta_{PA}^2 \cdot \sigma_B^2$, variance due to active beta

8. ω_P^2, variance due to stock selection

Now consider a utility function which trades off exceptional return against risk. We start with a general utility function of the form $U = f - \lambda \cdot \sigma^2$ and apply the breakdowns of expected return and risk shown in items 1 through 8. Grouping together related return and risk items (1 and 5, 2 and 6, 3 and 7, 4 and 8), we generalize the usual approach by allowing *three* types of risk aversion, λ_T, λ_{BT} and λ_R for total, benchmark timing, and residual risk aversion. Items 5 and 6 contribute to total risk, item 7 to benchmark timing, and 8 to residual risk. The idea is to distinguish the *inherent risk* from owning the benchmark portfolio and the active risks the manager takes in trying to outperform by either benchmark timing or taking on residual risk.

We need to keep in mind why we are defining a utility function. It will lead us to choose a portfolio that maximizes that utility. So we will analyze terms based on their influence over our optimal portfolio.

The result of these manipulations is an overall utility function comprising the following elements:

9. $f_B - \lambda_T \cdot \sigma_B^2$, the benchmark component; it combines items 1 and 5. It is all forecast and no action (i.e., it has no influence on the optimal portfolio).

10. $\beta_{PA} \cdot \{\mu_B - 2 \cdot \lambda_T \cdot \sigma_B^2\}$, cross effects; it combines items 2 and 6. It includes action, but no forecast.

11. $\beta_{PA} \cdot \Delta f_B - \lambda_{BT} \cdot \beta_{PA}^2 \cdot \sigma_B^2$, benchmark timing; it combines items 3 and 7. It includes both forecast and action.

12. $\alpha_P - \lambda_R \cdot \omega_P^2$, stock selection; it combines items 4 and 8. It includes both forecast and action.

The first term, 9, is a constant and does not influence the active decision. It has no influence on our choice of optimal portfolio.

We will argue that the second term, 10, is zero regardless of the choice of β_{PA}. Item 10 does not depend on any forecast information; it is a permanent part of the objective that is not influenced by our investment insights. In addition, Eq. (4.12) implies that the expression in the curly brackets in 10 should be zero. Finally, imagine what would happen if our forecasts agreed with the consensus; i.e., if $\mathbf{f} = \boldsymbol{\mu}$. In that case, we would have $\Delta f_B = 0$ and $\alpha = 0$. The portfolio construction procedure should lead us to hold the benchmark; i.e., $\beta_{PA} = 0$, and $\omega_P = 0$. That will happen only if $\mu_B - 2 \cdot \lambda_T \cdot \sigma_B^2 = 0$.

After ignoring the constant term 9 and the zero term 10, we are left with the value-added objective:

$$VA[P] = \{\beta_{PA} \cdot \Delta f_B - \lambda_{BT} \cdot \beta_{PA}^2 \cdot \sigma_B^2\} + \{\alpha_P - \lambda_R \cdot \omega_P^2\} \quad (4A.8)$$

The objective of active management is to maximize this value added.

Exercise

1. Derive the benchmark timing result:

$$\beta_{PA} = \frac{\Delta f_B}{\mu_B}$$

Applications Exercises

1. Using a performance analysis software package, analyze the return on the MMI portfolio relative to an S&P 500 benchmark. Assume an expected excess return to the benchmark of 6 percent. What was the
   Time premium
   Realized risk premium
   Exceptional benchmark return
   Realized alpha

2. Examine the risk of the MMI portfolio relative to the S&P 500. Determine σ_{MMI}, $\sigma_{S\&P500}$, β_{MMI}, and ω_{MMI}.

CHAPTER 5

Residual Risk and Return: The Information Ratio

INTRODUCTION

The theory of investments is based on the premise that assets are fairly valued. This is reassuring for the financial economist and frustrating to the active manager. The active manager needs theoretical support. In the next four chapters we will provide a structure, if not a theory, for the active manager.

This chapter starts the process by building a strategic context for management of residual risk and return. Within that context, we will develop some concepts and rules of thumb that we find valuable in the evaluation and implementation of active strategies.

The reader is urged to *rise above the details*. Do not worry about transactions costs, restrictions on holdings, liquidity, short sales, or the source of the alphas. We will deal with those questions in later chapters. At this point, we should free ourselves from the clutter and look at active management from a strategic perspective. Later chapters on implementation will focus on the details and indicate how we might adjust our conclusions to take these important practical matters into consideration.

There is no prior theory. We must pull ourselves up by our bootstraps. Economists are good at this. Recall the parable of the engineer, the philosopher, and the economist stranded on a South Sea island with no tools, very little to eat on the island, and a large quantity of canned food. The engineer devises schemes for opening the cans by boiling them, dropping them on the rocks, etc. The philosopher ponders the trifling nature of food and the ultimate futility of life. The economist just sits and gazes out to sea. Suddenly, he jumps up and shouts, "I've got it! Assume you have a can opener."

The active manager's can opener is the assumption of success. The notion of success is captured and quantified by the information ratio. The information ratio says how good you think you are. The assumption of future success is used to open up other questions. If our insights are superior to those of other investors, then how we should use those insights?

We proceed with can opener and analysis. The results are insights, rules of thumb, and a formal procedure for managing residual risk and return. Some of the highlights are:

- The *information ratio* measures achievement ex post (looking backward) and connotes opportunity ex ante (looking forward).
- The information ratio defines the *residual frontier*, the opportunities available to the active manager.
- Each manager's information ratio and residual risk aversion determine his or her level of aggressiveness (residual risk).
- *Intuition* can lead to reasonable values for the information ratio and residual risk aversion.
- *Value added* depends on the manager's opportunities and aggressiveness.

The chapter starts with the definition of the information ratio, which is one of the book's central characters. In this chapter we use the information ratio in its ex ante (hope springs eternal) form. The ex ante information ratio is an indication of the opportunities available to the active manager; it determines the residual frontier. In Chap. 4 we defined an objective for the active manager that considers both risk and return. The main results of this chapter flow from the interaction of our opportunities (information ratio) with our objectives.

In Chap. 4 we showed that a manager could add value through either benchmark timing or stock selection. We postpone the discussion of benchmark timing to Chap. 19 and will concentrate on stock selection until that point. This means that we are concerned about the trade-off between residual risk and alpha. Recall that when portfolio beta is equal to 1, residual risk and active risk coincide.

A technical appendix considers the information ratio in merciless detail.

THE DEFINITION OF ALPHA

Looking forward (ex ante), alpha is a forecast of residual return. Looking backward (ex post), alpha is the average of the realized residual returns.

The term *alpha*, like the term *beta*, arises from the use of linear regression to break the return on a portfolio into a component that is perfectly correlated with the benchmark and an uncorrelated or residual component. If $r_P(t)$ are portfolio excess returns in periods $t = 1, 2, \ldots T$ and $r_B(t)$ are benchmark excess returns over those same periods, then the regression is

$$r_P(t) = \alpha_P + \beta_P \cdot r_B(t) + \epsilon_P(t) \tag{5.1}$$

The estimates of β_P and α_P obtained from the regression are the *realized* or *historical* beta and alpha. The residual returns for portfolio P are

$$\theta_P(t) = \alpha_P + \epsilon_P(t) \tag{5.2}$$

where α_P is the average residual return and $\epsilon_P(t)$ is the mean zero random component of residual return.

This chapter concentrates on forecast alphas. In Chap. 12, "Information Analysis," we'll learn how to evaluate the quality of the alpha forecasts. We'll consider realized alphas in Chap. 17, "Performance Analysis." Realized alphas are for keeping score. The job of the active manager is to score. To do that, we need good forecast alphas.

When we are looking to the future, alpha is a forecast of residual return. Let θ_n be the residual return on stock n. We have

$$\alpha_n = E\{\theta_n\} \tag{5.3}$$

Alpha has the portfolio property, since both residual returns and expectations have the portfolio property. Consider a simple case with two stocks whose alphas are α_1 and α_2. If we have a two-stock portfolio with holdings $h_P(1)$ in stock 1 and $h_P(2)$ in stock 2, then the alpha of the portfolio will be

$$\alpha_P = h_P(1) \cdot \alpha_1 + h_P(2) \cdot \alpha_2 \tag{5.4}$$

This is consistent with the notion that α_P is the forecast of expected residual return on the portfolio.

By definition, the benchmark portfolio will always have a residual return equal to 0; i.e., $\theta_B = 0$ with certainty. Therefore, the alpha of the benchmark portfolio must be 0; $\alpha_B = 0$. The requirement that $\alpha_B = 0$ is the restriction that the alphas be benchmark-neutral.

Recall that the risk-free portfolio also has a zero residual return, and so the alpha for cash α_F is always equal to 0. Thus any portfolio made up of a mixture of the benchmark and cash will have a zero alpha.

THE EX POST INFORMATION RATIO: A MEASURE OF ACHIEVEMENT

An *information ratio*,[1] denoted *IR*, is a ratio of (annualized) residual return to (annualized) residual risk. If we consider the information ratio for some realized residual return (ex post), we have realized residual return divided by the residual risk taken to obtain that return. Thus we may have an average of 2.3 percent residual return per year with residual risk of 3.45 percent. That is an information ratio of $2.3/3.45 = 0.67$.

A realized information ratio can (and frequently will) be negative. Don't forget that the information ratio of the benchmark must be exactly zero. If our residual return has averaged a poor -1.7 percent per year with the same residual risk level of 3.45 percent, then the realized information ratio is $(-1.7)/3.45 = -0.49$.

We will say more about ex post information ratios at the end of this chapter and in Chap. 17, "Performance Analysis." We offer one teaser: The ex-post information ratio is related to the t statistic one obtains for the alpha in the regression [Eq. (5.1)]. If the data in the regression cover Y years, then the information ratio is approximately the alpha's t statistic divided by the square root of Y.

---

[1]Treynor and Black (1973) refer to this quantity as the appraisal ratio.

THE EX ANTE INFORMATION RATIO: A MEASURE OF OPPORTUNITY

Now we look to the future. The information ratio is the expected level of annual residual return per unit of annual residual risk. There is an implication that information is being used efficiently. Thus, the more precise definition of the information ratio is the highest ratio of annual residual return to residual risk that the manager can obtain.

Let's begin with the analysis for a start-up investment manager with no track record. We will then compare results with some empirical observations.

We first need a plausible value for the information ratio. Recall that this is an assumed can opener. Don't get carried away—we are making this number up; we don't need to be terribly precise.

This new manager must develop target expectations for residual risk and return. The risk target is less controversial. We will assume that the manager is aiming for the 5 to 6 percent residual risk range. We will use 5.5 percent for concreteness.

Now what about the expected residual return target? The answer here involves a struggle between those two titans: hope and humility. A truly humble (no better than average) active manager would say zero. That's not good enough. You can't be an active manager with that much humility. A very hopeful manager, indeed a dreamer, might say 10 percent. This quixotic manager is confusing what is possible with what can be expected.

In the end, the manager must confront both hope and humility. Let's say the manager is assuming between 3 and 4 percent, or 3.5 percent, to pick a number.

Our ex ante information ratio is $3.5/5.5 = 0.64$. We have found our way to a sensible number. This analysis is intentionally vague. We don't care if the answer came out 0.63 or 0.65. This is not the time for spurious precision. Our analysis produced residual risk in the 5 to 6 percent range and expected (hoped-for) residual returns in the 3 to 4 percent range. In the extreme cases, we could have obtained an answer between $0.8 = 4/5$ and $0.5 = 3/6$.

So far, we have not revealed any empirically observed information ratios. The empirical results will vary somewhat by time period, by asset class, and by fee level. But overall, before-fee information ratios typically fall close to the distribution in Table 5.1.

T A B L E 5.1

Percentile	Information Ratio
90	1.0
75	0.5
50	0.0
25	−0.5
10	−1.0

A top-quartile manager has an information ratio of one-half. That's a good number to remember. Ex ante, investment managers should aspire to top-quartile status. Our analysis of a start-up investment manager's information ratio, which we estimated at 0.64, provided a reasonable ballpark estimate, consistent with Table 5.1.

Table 5.1 displays a symmetric distribution of information ratios, centered on zero. This is consistent with our fundamental understanding of active management as a zero-sum game.

Table 5.1 also implies that if IR = 0.5 is good, then IR = 1.0 is exceptional. We will further define IR = 0.75 as very good and use that simple classification scheme throughout the book. Later in this chapter, we will provide more details on empirical observations of information ratios, as well as on active returns and active risk.

We will now define the information ratio in a more formal manner. Given an alpha for each stock, any (random) portfolio P will have a portfolio alpha α_P and a portfolio residual risk ω_P. The *information ratio for portfolio P is*

$$\mathrm{IR}_P = \frac{\alpha_P}{\omega_P} \qquad (5.5)$$

Our personal "information ratio" is the maximum information ratio that we can attain over all possible portfolios:

$$\mathrm{IR} = \mathrm{Max}\{\mathrm{IR}_P | P\} \qquad (5.6)$$

So we measure our information ratio based on portfolios optimized to our alphas.

The notation IR hides the fact that the information ratio depends on the alphas. Indeed, one of the uses of the information ratio concept is to scale the alphas so that a reasonable value of IR is obtained through Eq. (5.6).

Our definition of the information ratio says that a manager who can get an expected residual return of 2 percent with 4 percent residual risk can also get an expected residual return of 3 percent with 6 percent residual risk. The ratio of risk to return stays constant and equal to the information ratio even as the level of risk changes. A small example will indicate that this is indeed the case.

We consider four stocks, cash, and a benchmark portfolio that is 25 percent in each of the stocks. Table 5.2 summarizes the situation. The alphas for both the benchmark portfolio (the weighted sum of the stock alphas) and cash are, of course, equal to zero. This is no accident.

The last four columns describe two possible portfolios, P and L. For each portfolio, we have shown the portfolio's total and active holdings. The active holdings are simply the portfolio holdings less the benchmark holdings. In portfolio P, we have positive active positions for the two stocks with positive alphas, and negative active positions for the stocks with negative alphas. Since the alpha for the benchmark is zero, we can calculate the alpha

T A B L E 5.2

Stock	Alpha	Bench-mark Weight	Portfolio P Total Weight	Portfolio P Active Weight	Portfolio L Total Weight	Portfolio L Active Weight
1	1.50%	25.00%	35.00%	10.00%	40.00%	15.00%
2	−2.00%	25.00%	10.00%	−15.00%	2.50%	−22.50%
3	1.75%	25.00%	40.00%	15.00%	47.50%	22.50%
4	−1.25%	25.00%	15.00%	−10.00%	10.00%	−15.00%
Bench-mark	0.00%					
Cash	0.00%					

for the portfolio using only the active holdings.[2] The alpha for portfolio P is

$$\alpha_P = (1.50\%) \cdot (0.10) + (-2.00\%) \cdot (-0.15)$$
$$+ (1.75\%) \cdot (0.15) + (-1.25\%) \cdot (-0.10) = 0.84$$

The risk of this active position is 2.04 percent.[3]

Notice that portfolio L is just a more aggressive version of portfolio P. This isn't clear when we look at the holdings in portfolio L, but it is obvious when we look at the active holdings. The active holdings of portfolio L are 50 percent greater than the active holdings of portfolio P. For stock 1, our active position goes from +10 percent to +15 percent. For stock 2, our active position goes from −15 percent to −22.5 percent. In both cases, the active position increases by 50 percent. This means that the alpha for portfolio L must be 50 percent larger as well, and that the active risk is also 50 percent higher.[4] If both the portfolio alpha and the residual risk increase by 50 percent, the ratio of the two will remain the same.

> **The information ratio is independent of the manager's level of aggressiveness.**

We will consistently assume that the information ratio is independent of the level of risk. This relationship eventually breaks down in real-world applications, because of constraints. So in Table 5.2, if there is a constraint on short selling, we have little additional room to bet against stock 2 beyond portfolio L. Chapter 15, "Long/Short Investing," expands on this idea, estimating a cost for the no short selling constraint based on the effective reduction in information ratio.

Although the information ratio is independent of the level of aggressiveness, it does depend on the time horizon. In order to

---

[2] The portfolio holdings are $\mathbf{h}_P = \mathbf{h}_B + \mathbf{h}_{PA}$, where $\mathbf{h}_B$ and $\mathbf{h}_{PA}$ are benchmark and active holdings. If $\boldsymbol{\alpha}$ is a vector of alphas, then $\boldsymbol{\alpha}^T \cdot \mathbf{h}_B = 0$ implies $\boldsymbol{\alpha}^T \cdot \mathbf{h}_P = \boldsymbol{\alpha}^T \cdot \mathbf{h}_{PA}$.

[3] Table 5.2 doesn't contain the information necessary to calculate this. But see Chap. 4 for the definition of active risk and the procedure for calculating active risk. If $\mathbf{V}$ is the covariance matrix, and $\mathbf{h}_P$ and $\mathbf{h}_B$ are the holdings in the managed and benchmark portfolios, respectively, then $\mathbf{h}_{PA} = \mathbf{h}_P - \mathbf{h}_B$ contains the active holdings and $\psi_P^2 = \mathbf{h}_{PA}^T \cdot \mathbf{V} \cdot \mathbf{h}_{PA}$ is the active variance.

[4] If the active holdings change from $\mathbf{h}_{PA}$ to $\phi \cdot \mathbf{h}_{PA}$, then the active risk changes from ψ_P to $\phi \cdot \psi_P = \sqrt{(\phi \cdot \mathbf{h}_{PA})^T \cdot \mathbf{V} \cdot (\phi \cdot \mathbf{h}_{PA})}$.

avoid confusion, we standardize by using a 1-year horizon. The reason is that expected returns and variances both tend to grow with the length of the horizon. Therefore risk, standard deviation, will grow as the square root of the horizon, and the ratio of expected return (growing with time) to risk (growing as the square root of time) will increase with the square root of time. That means that the quarterly information ratio is half as large as the annual information ratio. The monthly information ratio would be $1/\sqrt{12} = 0.288$ the size of the annual information ratio.

THE RESIDUAL FRONTIER: THE MANAGER'S OPPORTUNITY SET

The choices available to the active manager are easier to see if we look at the alpha versus residual risk trade-offs. The residual frontier will describe the opportunities available to the active manager. The ex ante information ratio determines the manager's residual frontier.

In Fig. 5.1 we have the residual frontier for an exceptional manager with an information ratio of 1. This residual frontier plots expected residual return α_p, against residual risk ω_p. The residual frontier is a straight line through the origin. Notice that portfolio Q is on the frontier. Portfolio Q is a solution to Eq. (5.6); i.e., IR $=$ IR$_Q$. Portfolio Q is not alone on the residual frontier. The

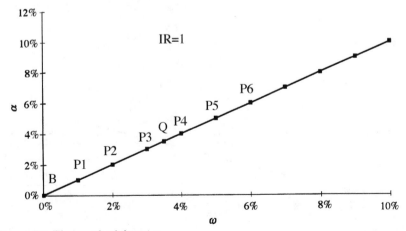

Figure 5.1 The residual frontier.

portfolios P_1, P_2, up to P_6 are also on the residual frontier. The manager can attain any expected residual return and residual risk combination below the frontier line. Portfolios P_1 through P_6 have (respectively) 1 percent to 6 percent expected residual return and residual risk.

The origin, designated B, represents the benchmark portfolio. The benchmark, by definition, has no residual return, and thus both α_B and ω_B are equal to zero. Likewise, the risk-free asset will reside at the origin, since the risk-free asset also has a zero residual return.

In Fig. 5.2 we show the residual frontiers of three different managers. The good manager has an information ratio of 0.5, the very good manager has an information ratio of 0.75, and the exceptional manager has an information ratio of 1.00.

We can see from Fig. 5.2 that the information ratio indicates opportunity. The manager with an information ratio of 0.75 has choices—portfolio P_1, for example—that are not available to the manager with an information ratio of 0.5. Similarly, the exceptional manager has opportunities—at point P_2, for example—that are not available to the very good manager. This doesn't mean that the very good manager cannot hold the stocks in portfolio P_2. It does mean that this very good manager's information will not lead him or her to that portfolio; it will, instead, lead this manager to a portfolio like P_1 that is on his or her residual frontier.

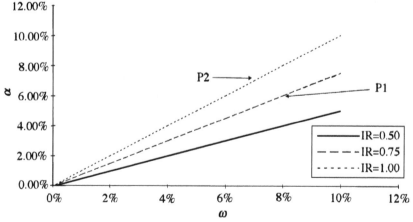

Figure 5.2 Opportunities.

Effectively, the information ratio defines a "budget constraint" for the active manager, as depicted graphically by the residual frontier:

$$\alpha_P = IR \cdot \omega_P \qquad (5.7)$$

At best (i.e., along the frontier), the manager can increase the expected residual return only through a corresponding increase in residual risk.

The appendix contains a wealth of technical detail about information ratios. We now turn our attention from the manager's opportunities to her or his objectives.

THE ACTIVE MANAGEMENT OBJECTIVE

The objective of active management (derived in Chap. 4) is to maximize the value added from residual return, where value added is measured as[5]

$$VA[P] = \alpha_P - \lambda_R \cdot \omega_P^2 \qquad (5.8)$$

This objective awards a credit for the expected residual return and a debit for residual risk. The parameter λ_R measures the aversion to residual risk; it transforms residual variance into a loss in alpha. In Fig. 5.3 we show the loss in alpha for different levels of residual risk. The three curves show high ($\lambda_R = 0.15$), moderate ($\lambda_R = 0.10$), and low ($\lambda_R = 0.05$) levels of residual risk aversion. In each case, the loss increases with the square of the residual risk ω_P. For a residual risk of $\omega_P = 5\%$, the losses are 3.75 percent, 2.5 percent, and 1.25 percent, respectively, for the high, moderate, and low levels of residual risk aversion.

The lines of equal value added, plotted as functions of expected residual return α_P and residual risk ω_P, are parabolas. In Fig. 5.4 we have plotted three such parabolas for value added of 2.5 percent, 1.4 percent, and 0.625 percent. These curves are of the form $\alpha_P = 2.5 + \lambda_R \cdot \omega_P^2$, $\alpha_P = 1.4 + \lambda_R \cdot \omega_P^2$, and $\alpha_P = 0.625 + \lambda_R \cdot \omega_P^2$. The figure shows the situation when we have a moderate level of residual

---

[5]We are ignoring benchmark timing, so active return equals residual return and active risk equals residual risk.

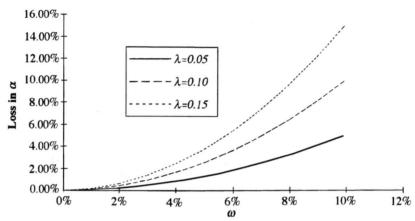

Figure 5.3 Loss in alpha.

risk aversion $\lambda_R = 0.10$. The three parabolas are parallel and increasing to the right. Every point along the top curve has a value added of 2.5 percent. The point {α = 2.5 percent, ω = 0 percent} and the point {α = 4.1 percent, ω = 4 percent} are on this curve. At the first point, with zero residual risk and an alpha of 2.5 percent, we have a value added of 2.5 percent. At the second point, the value added is still 2.5 percent, although we have risk. Thus, with ω = 4 percent and α = 4.1 percent, we have VA = $2.5 = 4.1 - (0.1) \cdot 4^2$.

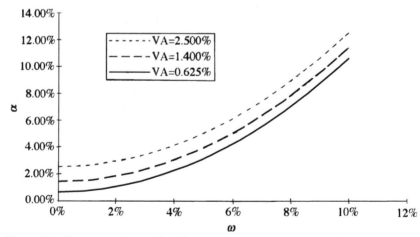

Figure 5.4 Constant value added lines.

We sometimes refer to the value added as the *certainty equivalent return*. Given a risk aversion λ_R, the investor will equate return α_P and risk ω_P with a certain return $\alpha_P - \lambda_R \cdot \omega_P^2$ to a (residual) risk-free investment.

PREFERENCES MEET OPPORTUNITIES

It is a basic tenet of economics that people prefer more to less. Our choices are limited by our opportunities. We have to choose in a manner that is consistent with our opportunities. The information ratio describes the opportunities open to the active manager. The active manager should explore those opportunities and choose the portfolio that maximizes value added.

Figure 5.5 shows the situation. The residual frontier corresponds to an information ratio of 0.75 and a residual risk aversion of $\lambda_R = 0.1$. Preferences are shown by the three preference curves, with risk-adjusted returns of 0.625 percent, 1.40 percent, and 2.5 percent, respectively.

We would like to have a risk-adjusted return of 2.5 percent. We can't do that well. The VA = 2.5 percent curve lies above the residual frontier. Life is a bit like that. We can achieve a risk-adjusted

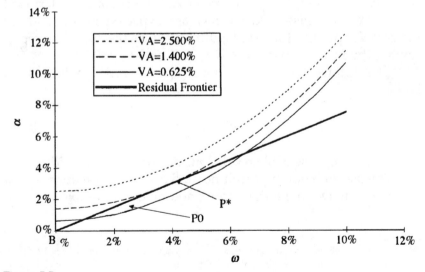

Figure 5.5

return of 0.625 percent. A value added of 0.625 percent is consistent with our opportunities; however, we can do better. Portfolio P_0 is in the opportunity set and is better than 0.625 percent.

The 1.40 percent curve is just right. The 1.4 percent value added curve is tangent to the residual frontier at portfolio P^*. We can't do any better, since every higher-value added line is outside the opportunity set. Therefore, portfolio P^* is our optimal choice.

AGGRESSIVENESS, OPPORTUNITY, AND RESIDUAL RISK AVERSION

The manager's information ratio and residual risk aversion determine a simple rule that links those concepts with the manager's optimal level of residual risk or aggressiveness. We can discover the rule through a more formal examination of the graphical analysis carried out in the last section.

The manager will want to choose a portfolio[6] on the residual frontier. The only question is the manager's level of aggressiveness. Using the "budget constraint" [Eq. (5.7)] in the manager's objective, Eq. (5.8), we find

$$VA[\omega_P] = \omega_P \cdot IR - \lambda_R \cdot \omega_P^2 \qquad (5.9)$$

Now we have completely parameterized the problem in terms of risk. As we increase risk, we increase expected return and we increase the penalty for risk. Figure 5.6 shows the situation, representing the median case with $IR = 0.75$ and $\lambda_R = 0.10$.

The optimal level of residual risk, ω^*, which maximizes VA $[\omega_P]$ is

$$\omega^* = \frac{IR}{2\lambda_R} \qquad (5.10)$$

This is certainly a sensible result. Our desired level of residual risk will increase with our opportunities and decrease with our residual risk aversion. Doubling the information ratio will double the opti-

---

[6]The formal problem is to maximize $\alpha - \lambda \cdot \omega^2$, subject to the constraint $\alpha/\omega \leq IR$. Since we know that the constraint will be binding at the optimal solution, we can use it to eliminate α from the objective.

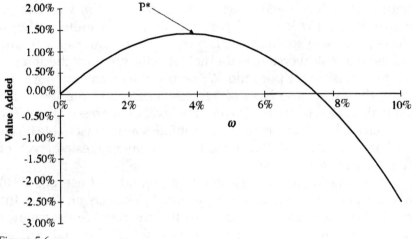

Figure 5.6

mal risk level. Doubling the risk aversion will halve the optimal risk level.

Table 5.3 shows how the residual risk will vary for reasonable values of the information ratio and residual risk aversion. The information ratio has three possible levels: 0.50 (good), 0.75 (very good), and 1.0 (exceptional). The residual risk aversion also has three possible levels: 0.05 (aggressive), 0.1 (moderate), and 0.15 (restrained).

The highest level of aggressiveness is 10 percent, corresponding to the low residual risk aversion ($\lambda_R = 0.05$) and the high information ratio (IR = 1.00). At the other corner, with fewer oppor-

T A B L E 5.3

Residual Risk

	Risk Aversion λ		
IR	Aggressive (0.05)	Moderate (0.10)	Restrained (0.15)
Exceptional (1.00)	10.00%	5.00%	3.33%
Very good (0.75)	7.50%	3.75%	2.50%
Good (0.50)	5.00%	2.50%	1.67%

tunities (IR = 0.50) and more restraint (λ_R = 0.15), we have an annual residual risk of 1.67 percent. Table 5.3 is quite useful; it allows a manager to link two alien concepts, the information ratio and residual risk aversion, to the more specific notion of the amount of residual risk in the portfolio. We see that the greater our opportunities, the higher the level of aggressiveness, and the lower the residual risk aversion, the greater the level of aggressiveness. The table also helps us calibrate our sensibilities as to reasonable levels of IR and λ_R. Equation (5.10) will tell us if any suggested levels of IR and λ_R are reasonable.

It is possible to turn the question around and use Eq. (5.10) to determine a reasonable level of residual risk aversion. Recall the information ratio analysis earlier in the chapter. We determined that the manager wanted 5.5 percent residual risk and had an information ratio of 0.64. We can rearrange Eq. (5.10) and extract an implied level of residual risk aversion:

$$\lambda_R = \frac{IR}{2 \cdot \omega^*} \tag{5.11}$$

For our example, we have $0.64/(2 \cdot 5.5) = 0.058$. The manager is aggressive, with risk aversion at the lower end of the spectrum.

VALUE ADDED: RISK-ADJUSTED RESIDUAL RETURN

We have located the optimal portfolio P^* at the point where the residual frontier is tangent to a preference line, and we have found a simple expression for the level of residual risk for the optimal portfolio. In this section, we will go one step further and determine the risk-adjusted residual return of the optimal portfolio P^*.

If we substitute the optimal level of residual risk [Eq. (5.10)] into Eq. (5.9), we find the relationship between the value added as measured by utility and the manager's opportunity as measured by the information ratio IR:

$$VA^* = VA[\omega^*] = \frac{IR^2}{4\lambda_R} = \frac{\omega^* \cdot IR}{2} \tag{5.12}$$

This says that the ability of the manager to add value increases as the *square* of the information ratio and decreases as the manager becomes more risk-averse. So a manager's information ratio determines his or her potential to add value.

Equation (5.12) states a critical result. Imagine we are risk-verse investors, with high λ_R. According to Equation (5.12), given our λ_R, we will maximize our value added by choosing the investment strategy (or manager) with the highest IR. But a very risk-tolerant investor will make exactly the same calculation. In fact, every investor seeks the strategy or manager with the highest information ratio. Different investors will differ only in how aggressively they implement the strategy.

The Information Ratio Is the Key to Active Management

Table 5.4 shows the value added for the same three choices of information ratio and residual risk aversion used in Table 5.3. In our best case, the value added is 5.00 percent per year. That is probably more than one could expect. In the worst case, the value added is 42 basis points per year. A good manager (IR = 0.50) with a conservative implementation (λ_R = 0.15, so ω^* = 1.66) will probably not add enough value to justify an active fee.

In our initial analysis of a manager's information ratio, we found IR = 0.64 and λ_R = 0.058, and so the value added is 1.77 percent per year.

THE β = 1 FRONTIER

How do our residual risk/return choices look in the total risk/ total return picture? The portfolios we will select (in the absence

T A B L E 5.4

Value Added

IR	Risk Aversion λ_R		
	Aggressive (0.05)	Moderate (0.10)	Restrained (0.15)
Exceptional (1.00)	5.00%	2.50%	1.67%
Very good (0.75)	2.81%	1.41%	0.94%
Good (0.50)	1.25%	0.63%	0.42%

of any benchmark timing) will lie along the $\beta = 1$ *frontier*. This is the set of all portfolios with beta equal to 1 that are efficient; i.e., they have the minimum risk for a specified level of expected return. They are not necessarily fully invested. We develop this concept more fully in the technical appendix.

Figure 5.7 compares different efficient frontiers. The efficient frontier is the straight line through F and Q. The efficient frontier for fully invested portfolios starts at C and runs through Q. The efficient frontier for portfolios with beta equal to 1 starts at the benchmark, B, and runs through P.

The benchmark is the minimum-risk portfolio with $\beta = 1$, since it has zero residual risk. All other $\beta = 1$ portfolios have the same systematic risk, but more residual risk.

A glance at Fig. 5.7 may make us rethink our value added objective. There are obviously portfolios that dominate the $\beta = 1$ frontier. However, these portfolios have a large amount of active risk, and therefore expose the manager to the business risk of poor *relative* performance.

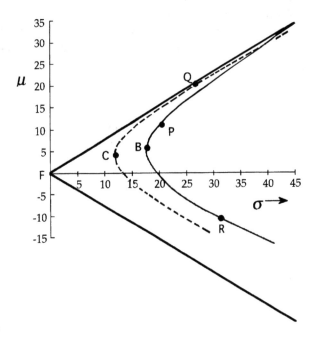

Figure 5.7

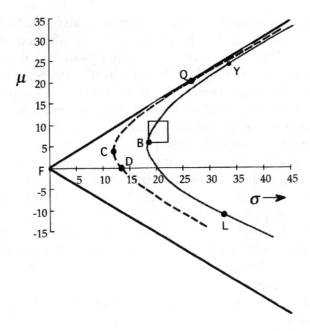

Figure 5.8

These two frontiers cross at the point along the fully invested frontier with β = 1. This crossing point will typically involve high levels of residual risk.

If we require our portfolios to satisfy a no active cash condition, then we have the situation shown in Fig. 5.8. The β = 1 no active cash frontier is the parabola centered on the benchmark portfolio B and passing through the portfolio Y. This efficient frontier combines the restriction to full investment (assuming that the benchmark is fully invested) with the β = 1 restriction. The opportunities without the no active cash restriction dominate those with the restriction. A constraint reduces our opportunities.

FORECAST ALPHAS DIRECTLY!

We have decided to manage relative to a benchmark and (at least until Chap. 19) to forgo benchmark timing. We have a need for alphas. We will discuss this topic at great length in the remainder of the book. However, we would like to show at this early stage that it isn't very hard to produce a rudimentary set of alphas with a small amount of work. One way to get these alphas is to start with expected returns and then go through the complicated procedure described in Chap. 4. An alternative is to skip the intermediate steps and forecast the alphas directly. In fact, one of the goals of developing the active management machinery is to avoid having to forecast several quantities (like the expected return to the benchmark) which probably will not ultimately influence our portfolio. Here, then, is a reasonable example of what we mean, converting a simple ranking of stocks into alpha forecasts. To start, sort the assets into five bins: strong buy, buy, hold, sell, and strong sell. Assign them respective alphas of 2.00 percent, 1.00 percent, 0.00 percent, −1.00 percent, and −2.00 percent. Then find the benchmark average alpha. If it is zero, we are finished. If it isn't zero (and there is no guarantee that it will be), modify the alphas by subtracting the benchmark average times the stock's beta from each original alpha.

These alphas will be benchmark-neutral. In the absence of constraints, they should lead[7] the manager to hold a portfolio with a beta of 1.00. One can imagine more and more elaborate variations on this theme. For example, we could classify stocks into economic sectors and then sort them into strong buy, buy, hold, sell, and strong sell bins.

This example illustrates two points. First, we need not forecast alphas with laserlike precision. We will see in Chap. 6, "The Fundamental Law of Active Management," that the accuracy of a successful forecaster of alphas is apt to be fairly low. Any procedure that keeps the process simple and moving in the correct direction will probably compensate for losses in accuracy in the second and third

---

[7]The manager's objective is to maximize $\mathbf{h}_{PA}^T \cdot \boldsymbol{\alpha} - \lambda_R \cdot \mathbf{h}_{PA}^T \cdot \mathbf{V} \cdot \mathbf{h}_{PA}$. In the absence of constraints, the optimal solution, call it $\mathbf{h}_{PA}^*$, will satisfy $\boldsymbol{\alpha} - 2 \cdot \lambda_R \cdot \mathbf{V} \cdot \mathbf{h}_{PA}^* = 0$. If we multiply these first-order conditions by the benchmark weights $\mathbf{h}_B$, and recall that $\mathbf{h}_B^T \cdot \mathbf{V} = \sigma_B^2 \cdot \boldsymbol{\beta}^T$ and $\alpha_B = 0$, we find

$$\mathbf{h}_B^T \cdot \boldsymbol{\alpha} = \alpha_B = 0$$
$$= 2 \cdot \lambda_R \cdot \mathbf{h}_B^T \cdot \mathbf{V} \cdot \mathbf{h}_{PA}^* = 2 \cdot \lambda_R \cdot \sigma_B^2 \cdot \boldsymbol{\beta}^T \cdot \mathbf{h}_{PA}^*$$
$$= 2 \cdot \lambda_R \cdot \sigma_B^2 \cdot \beta_{PA}^*$$

decimal places. Second, although it may be difficult to forecast alphas correctly, it is not difficult to forecast alphas directly.

EMPIRICAL OBSERVATIONS

This section looks in more detail at the empirical results concerning active manager information ratios and risk.

Earlier, we described the "generic" distribution of before-fee information ratios. This generic distribution seems to apply across many different asset classes, stocks to bonds to international. Here we will present some of the empirical observations underlying the generic result.

These results were produced and partly described in Kahn and Rudd (1995, 1997). They arise from analysis of active U.S. domestic equity and bond mutual funds and institutional portfolios. These empirical studies utilized style analysis, which we describe in Chap. 17, "Performance Analysis." Suffice it to say that this analysis allows us to estimate several empirical distributions of interest here. Table 5.5 briefly describes the data underlying the results that follow. The time periods involved are admittedly short, in part because style analysis requires an extensive in-sample period to determine a custom benchmark for each fund. The good news is that these are out-of-sample results. The bad news is that they do not cover an extensive time period.

The short time period will not bias the median estimates, but the large sample errors associated with the short time period will

T A B L E   5.5

Study	Number of Funds	Calculation Time Period
U.S. active equity mutual funds	300	January 1991–December 1993
U.S. active equity institutional portfolios	367	October 1995–December 1996
U.S. active bond mutual funds	195	April 1993–September 1994
U.S. active bond institutional portfolios	215	October 1995–December 1996

T A B L E 5.6

Information Ratios, U.S. Active Equity Investments

	Mutual Funds		Institutional Portfolios	
Percentile	Before Fees	After Fees	Before Fees	After Fees
90	1.33	1.08	1.25	1.01
75	0.78	0.58	0.63	0.48
50	0.32	0.12	−0.01	−0.15
25	−0.08	−0.33	−0.56	−0.72
10	−0.47	−0.72	−1.03	−1.25

broaden the distributions.[8] The problem is more severe for institutional portfolios, where we have only quarterly return data, and hence a smaller number of observations.

Tables 5.6 and 5.7 display empirical distributions of information ratios for equity and bond investors, respectively. These tables generally support the generic distribution of Table 5.1, especially considering that all empirical results will depend on time period, analysis methodology, etc.

T A B L E 5.7

Information Ratios, U.S. Active Bond Investments

	Mutual Funds		Institutional Portfolios	
Percentile	Before Fees	After Fees	Before Fees	After Fees
90	1.14	0.50	1.81	1.29
75	0.50	−0.22	0.89	0.38
50	−0.11	−0.86	0.01	−0.57
25	−0.61	−1.50	−0.62	−1.37
10	−1.22	−2.21	−1.50	−2.41

---

[8]In the extreme, imagine a sample of 300 funds, each with true IR = 0. We will observe a distribution of sample information ratios. It may well center on IR = 0, but that distribution will shrink toward zero only as we increase our observation period.

For equity investors, the empirical data show that top-quartile investors achieve information ratios of 0.63 to 0.78 before fees and 0.58 to 0.48 after fees. Given the standard errors for these results of roughly 0.05, and the fact that estimation errors tend to broaden the distribution, these empirical results are roughly consistent with Table 5.1.

The before-fee data on bond managers look roughly similar to the equity results, with top-quartile information ratios ranging from 0.50 to 0.89. The after-fee results differ strikingly from the equity manager results. For more on this phenomenon, see Kahn (1998).

Overall, given these empirical results, Table 5.1 appears to be a very good ex ante distribution of information ratios, before fees.

We can also look at distributions of active risk. Tables 5.8 and 5.9 show the distributions. Active managers should find this risk information useful: It helps define manager aggressiveness relative to the broad universe of active managers.

For equity managers, median active risk falls between 4 and 5 percent. Mutual fund risk resembles institutional portfolio risk, except at the low-risk end of the spectrum, where institutional managers offer lower-risk products.

For active domestic bond managers, the risk distributions vary between mutual funds and institutional portfolios, although both are well below the active equity risk distribution. Median active risk is 1.33 percent for bond mutual funds and only 0.61 percent for institutional bond portfolios.

T A B L E 5.8

Annual Active Risk, U.S. Active Equity
Investments

Percentile	Mutual Funds	Institutional Portfolios
90	9.87%	9.49%
75	7.00%	6.47%
50	4.76%	4.39%
25	3.66%	2.85%
10	2.90%	1.93%

T A B L E 5.9

Annual Active Risk, U.S. Active Bond Investments

Percentile	Mutual Funds	Institutional Portfolios
90	3.44%	1.89%
75	2.01%	0.98%
50	1.33%	0.61%
25	0.96%	0.41%
10	0.74%	0.26%

SUMMARY

We have built a simple framework for the management of residual risk and return. There are two key constructs in this framework:

- The information ratio as a measure of our opportunities
- The residual risk aversion as a measure of our willingness to exploit those opportunities

These two constructs determine our desired level of residual risk [Eq. (5.10)] and our ability to add value [Equation (5.12)]. In the next chapter, we will push this analysis further to uncover some of the structure that leads to the information ratio.

PROBLEMS

1. What is the information ratio of a passive manager?
2. What is the information ratio required to add a risk-adjusted return of 2.5 percent with a moderate risk aversion level of 0.10? What level of active risk would that require?
3. Starting with the universe of MMI stocks, we make the assumptions

   Q = MMI portfolio
   f_Q = 6%
   B = capitalization-weighted MMI portfolio

We calculate (as of January 1995) that

Portfolio	β with Respect to B	β with Respect to Q	σ
B	1.000	0.965	15.50%
Q	1.004	1.000	15.82%
C	0.865	0.831	14.42%

where portfolio C is the minimum-variance (fully invested) portfolio. For each portfolio (Q, B, and C), calculate f, α, ω, SR, and IR.

4. You have a residual risk aversion of $\lambda_R = 0.12$ and an information ratio of IR = 0.60. What is your optimal level of residual risk? What is your optimal value added?

5. Oops. In fact, your information ratio is really only IR = 0.30. How much value added have you lost by setting your residual risk level according to Problem 4 instead of at its correct optimal level?

6. You are an active manager with an information ratio of IR = 0.50 (top quartile) and a target level of residual risk of 4 percent. What residual risk aversion should lead to that level of risk?

REFERENCES

Ambachtsheer, Keith. "Where are the Customer's Alphas?" *Journal of Portfolio Management*, vol. 4, no. 1, Fall 1977, pp. 52–56.

Goodwin, Thomas H. "The Information Ratio." *Financial Analysts Journal*, vol. 54, no. 4, July/August 1998, pp. 34–43.

Kahn, Ronald N. "Bond Managers Need to Take More Risk." *Journal of Portfolio Management*, vol. 24, no. 3, Spring 1998, pp. 70–76.

Kahn, Ronald N., and Andrew Rudd. "Does Historical Performance Predict Future Performance?" *Financial Analysts Journal*, vol. 51, no. 6, November/December 1995, pp. 43–52.

———. "The Persistence of Equity Style Performance: Evidence from Mutual Fund Data." In *The Handbook of Equity Style Management*, 2d ed., edited by Daniel T. Coggin, Frank J. Fabozzi, and Robert Arnott (New Hope, PA: Frank J. Fabozzi Associates), 1997, pp. 257–267.

———. "The Persistence of Fixed Income Style Performance: Evidence from Mutual Fund Data." In *Managing Fixed Income Portfolios*, edited by Frank J. Fabozzi (New Hope, PA: Frank J. Fabozzi Associates), 1997, pp. 299–307.

Roll, Richard. "A Mean/Variance Analysis of Tracking Error." *Journal of Portfolio Management*, vol. 18, no. 4, Summer 1992, pp. 13–23.

Rosenberg, Barr. "Security Appraisal and Unsystematic Risk in Institutional Investment." *Proceedings of the Seminar on the Analysis of Security Prices* (Chicago: University of Chicago Press), November 1976, pp. 171–237.

Rudd, Andrew, and Henry K. Clasing, Jr. *Modern Portfolio Theory*, 2d ed.. (Orinda, Calif.: Andrew Rudd, 1988).

Sharpe, William F. "The Sharpe Ratio." *Journal of Portfolio Management*, vol. 21, no. 1, Fall 1994, pp. 49–59.

Treynor, Jack, and Fischer Black. "How to Use Security Analysis to Improve Portfolio Selection." *Journal of Business*, vol. 46, no. 1, January 1973, pp. 66–86.

TECHNICAL APPENDIX

The Characteristic Portfolio of Alpha

Our basic input is a vector of asset alphas: $\alpha = \{\alpha_1, \alpha_2, \ldots, \alpha_N\}$. The alpha for asset n is a forecast of asset n's expected residual return, where we define residual relative to the benchmark portfolio. Since the alphas are forecasts of residual return, both the benchmark and the risk-free asset will have alphas of zero; i.e., $\alpha_B = \alpha_F = 0$.

The characteristic portfolio of the alphas (see the appendix to Chap. 2) will exploit the information as efficiently as possible. Call portfolio A the characteristic portfolio of the alphas:

$$\mathbf{h}_A = \frac{\mathbf{V}^{-1} \cdot \alpha}{\alpha^T \cdot \mathbf{V}^{-1} \cdot \alpha} \tag{5A.1}$$

Portfolio A has an alpha of 1, $\mathbf{h}_A^T \cdot \alpha = 1$, and it has minimum risk among all portfolios with that property. The variance of portfolio A is

$$\sigma_A^2 = \mathbf{h}_A^T \cdot \mathbf{V} \cdot \mathbf{h}_A = \frac{1}{\alpha^T \cdot \mathbf{V}^{-1} \cdot \alpha} \tag{5A.2}$$

In addition, we can define alpha in terms of Portfolio A:

$$\alpha = \frac{\mathbf{V} \cdot \mathbf{h}_A}{\sigma_A^2} \tag{5A.3}$$

Information Ratios

For any portfolio P with $\omega_P > 0$, define IR_P as

$$IR_P = \frac{\alpha_P}{\omega_P} \tag{5A.4}$$

If $\omega_P = 0$, we set $IR_P = 0$. We call IR_P the *information ratio of portfolio P*. We define the information ratio IR as the largest possible value of IR_P given alphas $\{\alpha_n\}$, i.e.,

$$IR = \text{Max}\{IR_P|P\} \tag{5A.5}$$

In the technical appendix to Chap. 2, we identified portfolio Q as the fully invested portfolio with the maximum Sharpe ratio, the ratio of expected excess return per unit of risk. Portfolio Q maximizes f_P/σ_P over all portfolios P. In this appendix, we will establish a link between portfolio Q, portfolio A, and the information ratio.

Portfolio A has the following list of interesting properties.

Proposition 1

  1. Portfolio A has a zero beta; $\beta_A = \boldsymbol{\beta}^T \cdot \mathbf{h}_A = 0$. It therefore typically has long and short positions.
  2. Portfolio A has the maximum information ratio:

$$IR = IR_A = \sqrt{\boldsymbol{\alpha}^T \cdot \mathbf{V}^{-1} \cdot \boldsymbol{\alpha}} \geq IR_P \qquad \text{for all } P \tag{5A.6}$$

  3. Portfolio A has total and residual risk equal to 1 divided by IR:

$$\omega_A = \sigma_A = \frac{1}{IR} \tag{5A.7}$$

  4. Any portfolio P that can be written as

$$\mathbf{h}_P = \beta_P \cdot \mathbf{h}_B + \alpha_P \cdot \mathbf{h}_A \qquad \text{with } \alpha_P > 0 \tag{5A.8}$$

has $IR_P = IR$.

5. Portfolio Q is a mixture of the benchmark and portfolio A:

$$\mathbf{h}_Q = \beta_Q \cdot \mathbf{h}_B + \alpha_Q \cdot \mathbf{h}_A \qquad (5A.9)$$

where

$$\beta_Q = \frac{f_B \cdot \sigma_Q^2}{f_Q \cdot \sigma_B^2} \qquad (5A.10)$$

and

$$\alpha_Q = \frac{\sigma_Q^2}{f_Q \cdot \omega_A^2} \qquad (5A.11)$$

Therefore $IR_Q = IR$. The information ratio of portfolio Q equals that of portfolio A.

6. Total holdings in risky assets for Portfolio A are

$$e_A = \frac{\alpha_C \cdot \omega_A^2}{\sigma_C^2} . \qquad (5A.12)$$

7. Let θ_P be the residual return on any portfolio P. The information ratio of portfolio P is

$$IR_P = IR_Q \cdot Corr\{\theta_P, \theta_Q\} \qquad (5A.13)$$

8. The (maximum) information ratio is related to portfolio Q's (maximum) Sharpe ratio:

$$IR = \frac{\alpha_Q}{\omega_Q} = SR \cdot \left(\frac{\omega_Q}{\sigma_Q}\right) \qquad (5A.14)$$

9. We can represent alpha as

$$\alpha = IR \cdot \left(\frac{\mathbf{V} \cdot \mathbf{h}_A}{\omega_A}\right) = IR \cdot \mathbf{MCRR}_Q \qquad (5A.15)$$

Equation (5A.15) is an important result. It directly relates alphas to marginal contributions to residual risk, with the information ratio as the constant of proportionality. Thus, active managers should always check the marginal contributions to residual risk within their portfolios. For example, if they have an information ratio of 0.5, then half the marginal contributions should equal their alphas. This is a very useful check, especially on portfolios constructed by hand (as opposed to using an optimizer).

10. The Sharpe ratio of the benchmark is related to the maximal information ratio and Sharpe ratio:

$$SR_B^2 = SR^2 - IR^2 \qquad (5A.16)$$

Proof We verify the properties directly.

For item 1, recall from the appendix to Chap. 2 that since $\mathbf{h}_B$ is the characteristic portfolio of beta and $\mathbf{h}_A$ is the characteristic portfolio of alpha, we have $\sigma_{B,A} = \beta_A \cdot \sigma_B^2 = \alpha_B \cdot \sigma_A^2$. Thus $\alpha_B = 0$ implies $\beta_A = 0$. It isn't surprising that $\alpha_B = 0$. The characteristic portfolio for beta has minimum risk given $\beta = 1$. It has zero residual risk, and hence zero alpha. Portfolio A has minimum risk given $\alpha = 1$. Since it bets on residual returns, we would expect it to have minimum systematic risk, i.e., $\beta = 0$.

For item 2, consider any portfolio L with holdings $\mathbf{h}_L$. For any β_P and scalar $\kappa > 0$, we can construct another portfolio $\mathbf{P}$ with holdings

$$\mathbf{h}_P = \beta_P \cdot \mathbf{h}_B + \kappa \cdot (\mathbf{h}_L - \beta_L \cdot \mathbf{h}_B) \qquad (5A.17)$$

The residual holdings of P and L are proportional. Thus $\alpha_P = \kappa \cdot \alpha_L$ and $\omega_P = \kappa \cdot \omega_L$ and $IR_L = IR_P$. When looking for a portfolio with a maximum information ratio, we might as well restrict ourselves to portfolios with beta of 0 and alpha of 1. Portfolio A has minimum risk among all such portfolios; therefore A has the maximum information ratio.

We can verify item 3 using Eq. (5A.2) and (5A.6), and the fact that $\beta_A = 0$.

We can verify item 4 using Eq. (5A.17), with L equal to A and $\kappa = \alpha_P > 0$.

For item 5, write the expected excess returns as

$$\mathbf{f} = f_B \cdot \boldsymbol{\beta} + \boldsymbol{\alpha} = f_B \cdot \left(\frac{\mathbf{V} \cdot \mathbf{h}_B}{\sigma_B^2}\right) + \left(\frac{\mathbf{V} \cdot \mathbf{h}_A}{\sigma_A^2}\right) \qquad (5A.18)$$

and as

$$\mathbf{f} = f_Q \cdot \left(\frac{\mathbf{V} \cdot \mathbf{h}_Q}{\sigma_Q^2}\right) \qquad (5A.19)$$

since Q is proportional to the characteristic portfolio of $\mathbf{f}$. Equating Eqs. (5A.18) and (5A.19) and multiplying by $\mathbf{V}^{-1}$, leads to

$$\left(\frac{f_Q}{\sigma_Q^2}\right) \cdot \mathbf{h}_Q = \left(\frac{f_B}{\sigma_B^2}\right) \cdot \mathbf{h}_B + \left(\frac{1}{\sigma_A^2}\right) \cdot \mathbf{h}_A \qquad (5A.20)$$

Premultiplying by (σ_Q^2/f_Q), and recalling that $\sigma_A = \omega_A$, leads to

$$\mathbf{h}_Q = \left(\frac{f_B \cdot \sigma_Q^2}{f_Q \cdot \sigma_B^2}\right) \cdot \mathbf{h}_B + \left(\frac{\sigma_Q^2}{f_Q \cdot \omega_A^2}\right) \cdot \mathbf{h}_A \qquad (5A.21)$$

This verifies Eqs. (5A.9) through (5A.11), and item 4 tells us that $IR_Q = IR$.

We can verify item 6 by using the fact that portfolio C is the characteristic portfolio of $\mathbf{e}$, the vector of all ones. Hence we have $\sigma_{C,A} = e_A \cdot \sigma_C^2 = \alpha_C \cdot \sigma_A^2$.

To verify item 7, for any portfolio P, we can write

$$\alpha_P = \mathbf{h}_P^T \cdot \boldsymbol{\alpha} = \frac{\mathbf{h}_P^T \cdot \mathbf{V} \cdot \mathbf{h}_A}{\omega_A^2} = IR \cdot \left(\frac{\mathbf{h}_P^T \cdot \mathbf{V} \cdot \mathbf{h}_A}{\omega_A}\right) \qquad (5A.22)$$

Since portfolio A has a beta of 0, we can write

$$\mathbf{h}_P^T \cdot \mathbf{V} \cdot \mathbf{h}_A = Cov\{r_P, r_A\} = Cov\{\theta_P, \theta_A\} \qquad (5A.23)$$

where θ_P and θ_A are the residual returns on portfolios P and A. If we divide Eq. (5A.22) by the residual risk of portfolio P, ω_P, we find

$$\frac{\alpha_P}{\omega_P} = IR_P = IR \cdot \left(\frac{Cov\{\theta_P, \theta_A\}}{\omega_P \cdot \omega_A}\right) = IR \cdot Corr\{\theta_P, \theta_A\} \qquad (5A.24)$$

Notice that $\theta_Q = \alpha_Q \cdot \theta_A$, so the residual returns on portfolios A and Q are perfectly correlated, and thus $Corr\{\theta_B, \theta_A\} = Corr\{\theta_B, \theta_Q\}$.

For item 8, start with Eq. (5A.11) and divide both sides by α_Q. Then use the facts that $\omega_Q = \alpha_Q \cdot \omega_A$, $SR = f_Q/\sigma_Q$, and $IR = 1/\omega_A$.

We can prove the first part of item 9 by using Eq. (5A.3) and the fact that $IR = 1/\omega_A$. The marginal contribution to residual risk of asset n in portfolio Q is $Cov\{\theta_Q, \theta_n\}/\omega_Q$. However, the residual holdings of portfolio Q are $\alpha_Q \cdot \mathbf{h}_A$, and the residual risk of portfolio Q is $\omega_Q = \alpha_Q \cdot \omega_A$. Thus, $\mathbf{V} \cdot \mathbf{h}_A/\omega_A = MCRR_Q$.

To prove item 10, recall that $SR^2 = \mathbf{f}^T \cdot \mathbf{V}^{-1} \cdot \mathbf{f}$ and $\mathbf{f} = \boldsymbol{\beta} \cdot f_B + \boldsymbol{\alpha}$. Then use $\boldsymbol{\beta}^T \cdot \mathbf{V}^{-1} \cdot \boldsymbol{\alpha} = 0$, which is just $\beta_A = 0$, $IR^2 = \boldsymbol{\alpha}^T \cdot$

$\mathbf{V}^{-1} \cdot \boldsymbol{\alpha}$, and $\mathrm{SR}_B^2 = (f_B/\sigma_B)^2 = f_B^2 \cdot (\boldsymbol{\beta}^T \cdot \mathbf{V}^{-1} \cdot \boldsymbol{\beta})$. The last relationship follows since the benchmark is the characteristic portfolio of beta (see the appendix to Chap. 2).

Optimal Policy and Optimal Value Added

Portfolio A is key to the problem of finding an optimal residual position. Consider the problem

$$\mathrm{VA} = \mathrm{Max}\{\mathbf{h}_P^T \cdot \boldsymbol{\alpha} - \lambda_R \cdot \mathbf{h}_P^T \cdot \mathbf{VR} \cdot \mathbf{h}_P\} \qquad (5\mathrm{A}.25)$$

Proposition 2
The optimal solutions to Eqs. (5A.25) are given by

$$\mathbf{h}_P = \beta_P \cdot \mathbf{h}_B + \left(\frac{\mathrm{IR}}{2 \cdot \lambda_R \cdot \omega_A}\right) \cdot \mathbf{h}_A \qquad (5\mathrm{A}.26)$$

where β_P is *arbitrary*.

The value added by the optimal solution is

$$\mathrm{VA} = \frac{\mathrm{IR}^2}{4 \cdot \lambda_R} \qquad (5\mathrm{A}.27)$$

and the residual volatility of the optimal solution is

$$\omega_P = \frac{\mathrm{IR}}{2 \cdot \lambda_R} \qquad (5\mathrm{A}.28)$$

Proof The first-order conditions for the problem in Eq. (5A.25) are

$$\boldsymbol{\alpha} = 2 \cdot \lambda_R \cdot (\mathbf{V} - \boldsymbol{\beta} \cdot \sigma_B^2 \cdot \boldsymbol{\beta}^T) \cdot \mathbf{h}_P \qquad (5\mathrm{A}.29)$$

A solution is optimal if and only if $\mathbf{h}_P$ solves Eq. (5A.29). Let $\beta_P = \boldsymbol{\beta}^T \cdot \mathbf{h}_P$. This yields

$$\boldsymbol{\alpha} + 2 \cdot \lambda_R \cdot \boldsymbol{\beta} \cdot \sigma_B^2 \cdot \beta_P = 2 \cdot \lambda_R \cdot \mathbf{V} \cdot \mathbf{h}_P \qquad (5\mathrm{A}.30)$$

Now substitute for alpha using Eq. (5A.3) and for $\boldsymbol{\beta} \cdot \sigma_B^2$ with $\mathbf{V} \cdot \mathbf{h}_B$. The result is

$$\mathrm{IR} \cdot \left(\frac{\mathbf{V} \cdot \mathbf{h}_A}{\omega_A}\right) + 2 \cdot \lambda_R \cdot \beta_P \cdot \mathbf{V} \cdot \mathbf{h}_B = 2 \cdot \lambda_R \cdot \mathbf{V} \cdot \mathbf{h}_P \qquad (5\mathrm{A}.31)$$

Multiply Eq. (5A.31) by $\mathbf{V}^{-1}$, and divide by $2 \cdot \lambda_R$. This yields Eq.

(5A.26). Equation (5A.28) follows, since h_A/ω_A has residual volatility equal to 1. For Eq. (5A.27), substitute the optimal solution, Eq. (5A.26), in the objective and gather terms.

Notice that h_P will have beta equal to β_P, so we are consistent. It should be obvious that beta is irrelevant for the problem in Eq. (5A.26). The alphas are benchmark-neutral, so the alpha part of the objective in Eq. (5A.26) does not change as the portfolio's beta changes. Also, the residual risk is independent of the portfolio beta, and so ω_P will be independent of β_P as well.

The β = 1 Active Frontier

Our analysis to this point will let us specify the set of efficient portfolios that are constrained to have beta equal to 1, a fixed level of expected return, and minimal risk. These are interesting portfolios for institutional active managers. (There is a reason that we have relegated benchmark timing to the end of the book.) Since we will require beta equal to 1, the risk and expected return will be given by

$$\sigma_P^2 = \sigma_B^2 + \omega_P^2 \qquad (5A.32)$$

and
$$f_P = f_B + \alpha_P \qquad (5A.33)$$

The benchmark is the minimum-variance portfolio with beta equal to 1. The benchmark is the hinge in the $\beta = 1$ frontier in the same way that portfolio C is the hinge for the frontier of fully invested portfolios. To be on the $\beta = 1$ frontier, a portfolio must have a beta equal to 1 and a minimal amount of residual risk per unit of alpha. These will be portfolios on the alpha/residual risk efficient frontier, with ratios of alpha to residual risk equal to the information ratio. The residual variance is given by

$$\omega_P^2 = \frac{\alpha_P^2}{IR^2} \qquad (5A.34)$$

When we combine these last three equations, we have the equation for the $\beta = 1$ frontier:

$$\sigma_P^2 = \sigma_B^2 + \left(\frac{1}{IR^2}\right) \cdot (f_P - f_B)^2 \qquad (5A.35)$$

The Active Position Y: No Active Cash and No Active Beta

Portfolio A is the minimum-variance portfolio that has a unit exposure to alpha. However, it may turn out that portfolio A has a large positive or negative cash exposure. In active management, we often wish to move away from our benchmark and toward an efficient implementation of our alphas, while assuming no active cash position or active beta. But from item 6 of Proposition 1, we see that $e_A = 0$ if and only if $\alpha_C = 0$. Here we will introduce a new portfolio, portfolio Y, and discuss its properties. In the next section we will show that portfolio Y is the solution to the problem of optimizing our alphas subject to active cash and beta constraints.

To begin, define the residual holdings of portfolio C as

$$\mathbf{h}_{CR} = \mathbf{h}_C - \beta_C \cdot \mathbf{h}_B \qquad (5A.36)$$

Portfolio Y is a combination of portfolio A and portfolio CR:

$$\mathbf{h}_Y = \frac{\mathbf{h}_A}{\omega_A} - \left(\frac{IR_C}{IR}\right) \cdot \left(\frac{\mathbf{h}_{CR}}{\omega_C}\right) \qquad (5A.37)$$

Proposition 3
Portfolio Y has the following properties:

1. Portfolio Y has a zero beta; $\beta_Y = 0$.
2. Portfolio Y has total and residual variance

$$\omega_Y^2 = 1 - \left(\frac{IR_C}{IR}\right)^2 \qquad (5A.38)$$

3. Portfolio Y has an alpha given by

$$\alpha_Y = IR \cdot \left[1 - \left(\frac{IR_C}{IR}\right)^2\right] \qquad (5A.39)$$

4. Portfolio Y has a zero cash position: $e_Y = 0$. Note that Y is an *active* position. Property 4 guarantees that its long risky holdings exactly match its short risky holdings, and hence its cash position must be zero.

5. Portfolio Y has an information ratio

$$\mathrm{IR}_Y = \mathrm{IR} \cdot \sqrt{1 - \left(\frac{\mathrm{IR}_C}{\mathrm{IR}}\right)^2} = \mathrm{IR} \cdot \sqrt{1 - \mathrm{Corr}^2\{\theta_Q, \theta_C\}} \quad (5A.40)$$

Proof Item 1 follows because $\mathbf{h}_Y$ is a linear combination of two portfolios, each with zero beta.

To show item 2, calculate the variance of $\mathbf{h}_Y$ using Eq. (5A.37). To calculate the covariance of $\mathbf{h}_A$ and $\mathbf{h}_{CR}$, note that $\sigma_{C,A} = e_A \cdot \sigma_C^2 = \alpha_C \cdot \omega_A^2$, and that the covariance between $\mathbf{h}_{CR}$ and $\mathbf{h}_A$ is the same as the covariance between $\mathbf{h}_C$ and $\mathbf{h}_A$ since portfolio A is pure residual.

Item 3 follows by direct calculation starting with Eq. (5A.37).

To prove item 4, use $\mathbf{e}^T \cdot \mathbf{h}_{CR} = 1 - \beta_C \cdot e_B$ and $\omega_C^2 = \sigma_C^2 \cdot (1 - \beta_C \cdot e_B)$.

Item 5 is a direct result of items 2 and 3.

The Optimal No Active Beta and No Active Cash Portfolio

Portfolio Y is linked to the problem of finding an optimal residual position under the restrictions of no active beta and no active cash. The problem is

$$\mathrm{Max}\{\mathbf{h}_P^T \cdot \boldsymbol{\alpha} - \lambda_R \cdot \mathbf{h}_P^T \cdot \mathbf{VR} \cdot \mathbf{h}_P\} \quad (5A.41)$$

subject to $\boldsymbol{\beta}^T \cdot \mathbf{h}_P = 1$ and $\mathbf{e}^T \cdot \mathbf{h}_P = e_B$.

Proposition 4
The optimal solution of Eq. (5A.41) is

$$\mathbf{h}_P = \mathbf{h}_B + \left(\frac{\mathrm{IR}}{2 \cdot \lambda_R}\right) \cdot \mathbf{h}_Y \quad (5A.42)$$

Proof The constraints dictate that the optimal solution to the problem must be of the form $\mathbf{h}_P = \mathbf{h}_B + \mathbf{h}_{PR}$, where $\mathbf{h}_{PR}$ is a residual position with no active cash, i.e., $\mathbf{e}^T \cdot \mathbf{h}_{PR} = 0$. We will associate the rather strange Lagrange multipliers $2 \cdot \lambda_R \cdot \sigma_B^2 \cdot \phi$ and $2 \cdot \lambda_R \cdot \sigma_C^2 \cdot \pi$

with the beta and holdings constraints, respectively. The first-order conditions are the two constraints, plus

$$\boldsymbol{\alpha} + (2 \cdot \lambda_R \cdot \sigma_B^2 \cdot \phi) \cdot \boldsymbol{\beta} + (2 \cdot \lambda_R \cdot \sigma_C^2 \cdot \pi) \cdot \mathbf{e} = 2 \cdot \lambda_R \cdot \mathbf{VR} \cdot \mathbf{h}_{PR} \tag{5A.43}$$

In Eq. (5A.43), we can write $\boldsymbol{\alpha}$ as $\mathrm{IR}^2 \cdot \mathbf{V} \cdot \mathbf{h}_A$, $\sigma_B^2 \cdot \boldsymbol{\beta}$ as $\mathbf{V} \cdot \mathbf{h}_B$, and $\sigma_C^2 \cdot \mathbf{e}$ as $\mathbf{V} \cdot \mathbf{h}_C$. If we make those substitutions, multiply by $\mathbf{V}^{-1}$, and divide by $2 \cdot \lambda_R$, we find

$$\mathbf{h}_{PR} = \left(\frac{\mathrm{IR}^2}{2 \cdot \lambda_R} \right) \cdot \mathbf{h}_A + \phi \cdot \mathbf{h}_B + \pi \cdot \mathbf{h}_C \tag{5A.44}$$

The constraints on beta and total holdings along with $\omega_C^2 = \sigma_C^2 \cdot (1 - \beta_C \cdot e_B)$ allow us to solve for ϕ and π. The solutions are

$$\pi = \frac{-\alpha_C}{2 \cdot \lambda_R \cdot \omega_C^2} \tag{5A.45}$$

$$\phi = -\pi \cdot \beta_C \tag{5A.46}$$

When we combine these results, we find $\mathbf{h}_{PR} = (\mathrm{IR}/2 \cdot \lambda_R) \cdot \mathbf{h}_Y$, the desired result.

Thus far in this technical appendix, we have described key portfolios involved in managing residual risk and return, and have discussed how these affect our understanding of the information ratio. At this point, we turn to two more mundane properties of the information ratio: how it scales with investment time period and with the scale of the alphas.

Proposition 5

Consider a time period of length T years. If the residual return in any time interval is independent of the residual returns in other time intervals, and the residual returns have the same mean and standard deviation in all time intervals, then the ratio of the residual return over the period $[0,T]$ to the residual risk over the period $[0,T]$ will grow with the square root of T.

Proof Divide the period $[0,T]$ into K intervals of length $\Delta t = T/K$. Let $k = 1,2,\ldots,K$ index the intervals; interval k runs from time $(k - 1) \cdot \Delta t$ to $k \cdot \Delta t$. Let $\theta(k)$ be the residual return in interval k, and let $\theta = \sum_k \theta(k)$ be the residual return over $[0,T]$. The expected value of $\theta(k)$ is the same for all k—say, $\alpha = E\{\theta(k)\}$—and so

$$E\{\theta\} = E\left\{\sum_k \theta(k)\right\} = K \cdot E\{\theta(k)\} = K \cdot \alpha \qquad (5A.47)$$

The $\theta(k)$ have a constant variance, $\text{Var}\{\theta(k)\} = \omega^2$. Since the $\theta(k)$ are independent, we have

$$\text{Var}\{\theta\} = \text{Var}\left\{\sum_k \theta(k)\right\} = K \cdot \text{Var}\{\theta(k)\} = K \cdot \omega^2 \qquad (5A.48)$$

and $$\text{Std}\{\theta\} = \sqrt{K} \cdot \omega \qquad (5A.49)$$

Therefore, $$\frac{E\{\theta\}}{\text{Std}\{\theta\}} = \sqrt{K} \cdot \left(\frac{\alpha}{\omega}\right) = \sqrt{\frac{T}{\Delta t}} \cdot \left(\frac{\alpha}{\omega}\right) \qquad (5A.50)$$

which is the promised result. Note that the annual information ratio is $\sqrt{1/\Delta t} \cdot (\alpha/\omega)$

Proposition 6
The information ratio is linear in the input alphas.

Proof   Rescale α by a factor π in Eq. (5A.6). The resulting information ratio is $\pi \cdot \text{IR}$.

   We find this obvious result quite useful. One difficulty that arises in practice is the use of alphas that are so optimistic that they overwhelm any reasonable constraints on risk. The alphas usually need to be scaled down. Given a set of alphas, one could calculate (there are programs that do this) $\text{IR}_0 = \sqrt{\alpha^T \cdot V^{-1} \cdot \alpha}$. Suppose we find $\text{IR}_0 = 2.46$. We know from our common-sense discussion in this chapter that numbers like 0.75 are more reasonable. If we multiply the alphas by $\pi = 0.75/2.46$, then the information ratio for the scaled alphas will be 0.75. We could put these scaled alphas into an optimization program with a reasonable level of active risk aversion ($\lambda = 0.10$) and expect plausible results.

Exercises

1. Demonstrate that

$$\left(\frac{f_Q}{\sigma_Q}\right)^2 = \left(\frac{f_B}{\sigma_B}\right)^2 + IR^2$$

2. Demonstrate that

$$\beta_Q = \frac{\beta_C \cdot f_B}{\beta_C \cdot f_B + \alpha_C}$$

Note that $\beta_C = (\sigma_C/\sigma_B)^2$. In the absence of benchmark timing, i.e., if $f_B = \mu_B$, the alpha of portfolio C is the key to determining the beta of portfolio Q.

Applications Exercises

For these exercises, assume that

$$\text{Portfolio } B = \text{CAPMMI}$$

$$\text{Portfolio } Q = \text{MMI}$$

$$f_Q = 6 \text{ percent}$$

Applications Exercises 1, 2, and 3 are closely related to Problem 3 at the end of the main body of this chapter. The difference is that here you need to supply all the numbers.

1. What are the expected excess returns and residual returns for portfolios B, Q, and C?
2. What are the total and residual risks for portfolios B, Q, and C?
3. What are the Sharpe ratios and information ratios for portfolios B, Q, and C?
4. Demonstrate Eq. (5A.16).
5. Demonstrate the relationship shown in Exercise 2 above.

The Fundamental Law of Active Management

INTRODUCTION

In Chap. 5, the information ratio played the role of the "assumed can opener" for our investigation of active strategies. In this chapter, we will give that can opener more substance by finding the attributes of an investment strategy that will determine the information ratio.

The insights that we gain will be useful in guiding a research program and in enhancing the quality of an investment strategy. Major points in this chapter are:

- A strategy's breadth is the number of independent, active decisions available per year.
- The manager's skill, measured by the information coefficient, is the correlation between forecasts and results.
- The fundamental law of active management explains the information ratio in terms of breadth and skill.
- The additivity of the fundamental law allows for an attribution of value added to different components of a strategy.

THE FUNDAMENTAL LAW

The information ratio is a measure of a manager's opportunities. If we assume that the manager exploits those opportunities in a way that is mean/variance-efficient, then the value added by the manager will be proportional to the information ratio squared. As we saw in Chap. 5, all investors seek the strategies and managers with the highest information ratios. In this chapter, we investigate how to achieve high information ratios.

A simple and surprisingly general formula called the *fundamental law of active management* gives an approximation to the information ratio. We derive the result in the technical appendix. The law is based on two attributes of a strategy, breadth and skill. The breadth of a strategy is the number of independent investment decisions that are made each year, and the skill, represented by the information coefficient, measures the quality of those investment decisions. The formal definitions are as follows:

> BR is the strategy's *breadth*. Breadth is defined as the number of independent forecasts of exceptional return we make per year.
>
> IC is the manager's *information coefficient*. This measure of skill is the correlation of each forecast with the actual outcomes. We have assumed for convenience that IC is the same for all forecasts.

The law connects breadth and skill to the information ratio through the (approximately true) formula:

$$IR = IC \cdot \sqrt{BR} \qquad (6.1)$$

The approximation underlying Eq. (6.1) ignores the benefits of reducing risk that our forecasts provide. For relatively low values of IC (below 0.1), this reduction in risk is extremely small. We consider the assumptions behind the law in detail in a later section.

To increase the information ratio from 0.5 to 1.0, we need to either double our skill, increase our breadth by a factor of 4, or do some combination of the above.

In Chap. 5, we established a relationship [Eq. (5.10)] between the level of residual risk and the information ratio. With the aid of the fundamental law, we can express that relationship in terms of skill and breadth:

$$\omega^* = \frac{IR}{2\lambda_R} = \frac{IC \cdot \sqrt{BR}}{2\lambda_R} \qquad (6.2)$$

We see that the desired level of aggressiveness will increase directly with the skill level and as the square root of the breadth. The breadth allows for diversification among the active bets so that the overall level of aggressiveness ω^* can increase. The skill increases the possibility of success; thus, we are willing to incur more risk, since the gains appear to be larger.

The value a manager can add depends on the information ratio [Eq. (5.12)]. If we express the manager's ability to add value in terms of skill and breadth, we see

$$VA^* = \frac{IR^2}{4\lambda_R} = \frac{IC^2 \cdot BR}{4\lambda_R} \tag{6.3}$$

The value added by a strategy (the risk-adjusted return) will increase with the breadth and with the square of the skill level.

The fundamental law is designed to give us insight into active management. It isn't an operational tool. A manager needs to know the trade-offs between increasing the breadth of the strategy BR—by either covering more stocks or shortening the time horizons of the forecasts—and improving skill IC. Thus we can see that a 50 percent increase in the strategy breadth (with no diminution in skill) is equivalent to a 22 percent increase in skill (maintaining the same breadth). A quick calculation of this sort may be quite valuable before launching a major research project. Operationally, it will prove difficult in particular to estimate BR accurately, because of the requirement that the forecasts be independent.

Figure 6.1 shows the trade-offs between breadth and skill for two levels of the information ratio.

We can see the power of the law by making an assessment of three strategies. In each strategy, we want an information ratio of 0.50. Start with a market timer who has independent information about market returns each quarter. The market timer needs an information coefficient of 0.25, since $0.50 = 0.25 \cdot \sqrt{4}$. As an alternative, consider a stock selecter who follows 100 companies and revises the assessments each quarter. The stock selecter makes 400 bets per year; he needs an information coefficient of 0.025, since $0.50 = 0.025 \cdot \sqrt{400}$. As a third example, consider a specialist who follows two companies and revises her bets on each 200 times per year. The specialist will make 400 bets per year and require a skill level of 0.025. The stock selecter achieves breadth by looking

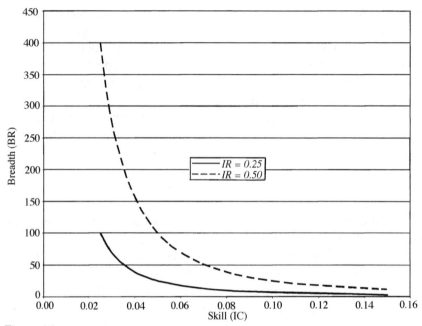

Figure 6.1

at a large number of companies intermittently, and the specialist achieves it by examining a small group of companies constantly. We can see from these examples that strategies with similar information ratios can differ radically in the requirements they place on the investor.

EXAMPLES

We can give three very straightforward examples of the law in action. First, consider a gambling example. Since we want to be successful active managers, we will play the role of the casino. Let's take a roulette game where bettors choose either red or black. The roulette wheel has 18 red spots, 18 black spots, and 1 green spot. Each of the 37 spots has probability 1/37 of being selected at each turn of the wheel. The green spot is our advantage.

If the bettor chooses black, the casino wins if the wheel stops on green or red. If the bettor chooses red, the casino wins if the wheel stops on green or black. Consider a $1.00 bet. The casino puts up a matching \$1.00; that's the casino's investment. The casino will end up with \$2.00 (a plus 100 percent return) with probability 19/37, and with zero (a minus 100 percent return) with probability 18/37. The casino's expected percentage return per \$1.00 bet is

$$\left(\frac{19}{37}\right) \cdot (100\%) + \left(\frac{18}{37}\right) \cdot (-100\%) = 2.7027\%$$

The standard deviation of the return on that single bet is 99.9634%.[1] If there is one bet of \$1.00 in a year, the information ratio for the casino will be 0.027038 = 2.7027/99.9634. In this case, our skill is 1/37 and our breadth is one. The formula predicts an information ratio of 0.027027. That's pretty close.

We can see the dramatic effect breadth has by operating like a real casino and having 1 million bets of \$1.00 in a year. Then the expected return will remain at 2.7027 percent, but the standard deviation drops to 0.09996 percent. This gives us an information ratio of 27.038. The formula predicts $(1/37) \cdot \sqrt{1,000,000} = 27.027$.

We could (American casinos do) add another green spot on the wheel and increase our advantage to 2/38. Then our expected return per bet will be 5.263 percent, and the standard deviation will be 99.861 percent. For 1 million plays per year, the expected return stays at 5.263 percent, and the standard deviation drops to 0.09986 percent. The information ratio is 52.70. The formula with IC = 2/38, and BR = 1,000,000 leads to an information ratio of 52.63. Owning a casino beats investment management hands down.

As a second example, consider the problem of forecasting semiannual residual returns on a collection of 200 stocks. We will designate the residual returns as θ_n. To make the calculations easier, we assume that

- The residual returns are independent across stocks.
- The residual returns have an expected value of zero.
- The standard deviation of the semiannual residual return is 17.32 percent—that's 24.49 percent annual for each stock.

---

[1]The variance is $(19/37) \cdot (100\% - 100\%/37)^2 + (18/37) \cdot (-100\% - 100\%/37)^2 = 9992.696\%^2$, and therefore the standard deviation is 99.9634.

Our information advantage is an ability to forecast the residual returns. The correlation between our forecasts and the subsequent residual returns is 0.0577. One way to picture our situation is to imagine the residual return itself as the sum of 300 independent terms for each stock, $\theta_{n,j}$ for $j = 1, 2, \ldots, 300$:

$$\theta_n = \sum_j \theta_{n,j} \qquad (6.4)$$

where each $\theta_{n,j}$ is equally likely to be $+1.00$ percent or -1.00 percent. Each $\theta_{n,j}$ will have a mean of 0 and standard deviation of 1.00 percent. The standard deviation of 300 of these added together will be $\sqrt{300} = 17.32$.

Our forecasting procedure tells us $\theta_{n,1}$ and leaves us in the dark about $\theta_{n,2}$ through $\theta_{n,300}$. The correlation of $\theta_{n,1}$ with θ_n will be 0.0577.[2] There are 300 equally important things that we might know about each stock, and we know only 1 of them. We don't know very much.

Since we are following 200 stocks, we will have 200 pieces of information twice a year, for a total of 400 per year. Our information coefficient, the correlation of $\theta_{n,1}$ and θ_n, is 0.0577. According to the fundamental law, the information ratio should be $0.0577 \cdot \sqrt{400} = 1.154$.

Can we fashion an investment strategy that will achieve an information ratio that high? In order to describe a portfolio strategy to exploit this information and calculate its attributes easily, we need a simplifying assumption. Assume that the benchmark portfolio is an equal-weighted portfolio of the 200 stocks (0.50 percent each). In each 6-month period, we expect to have about 100 stocks with a forecasted residual return for the quarter of $+1.00$ percent and 100 stocks with a forecasted residual return of -1.00 percent. This is akin to a buy list and a sell list. We will equal-weight the buy list (at 1.00 percent each), and not hold the sell list.

---

[2]The covariance of $\theta_{n,1}$ with θ_n is 1, since $\theta_{n,1}$ is uncorrelated with $\theta_{n,j}$ for $j \geq 2$. Since the standard deviations of $\theta_{n,1}$ and θ_n are 1.0 and 17.32, respectively, their correlation is 0.0577. (The correlation is the covariance divided by the two standard deviations. See Appendix C.)

The expected *active* return will be 1.00 percent per 6 months with an active standard deviation of 1.2227 percent per 6 months.[3] The 6-month information ratio is 0.8179. To calculate an annual information ratio, we multiply the 6-month information ratio by the square root of 2, to find $\sqrt{2} \cdot 0.8179 = 1.1566$. This is slightly greater than the 1.154 predicted by the formula, since the formula does not consider the slight reduction in uncertainty resulting from the knowledge of $\theta_{n,1}$.[4]

We can also consider a third example, to put the information coefficient in further context. Suppose we want to forecast the direction of the market each quarter. In this simple example, we care only about forecasting direction. We will model the market direction as a variable $x(t) = \pm 1$, where x has mean 0 and standard deviation 1. Our forecast is $y(t) = \pm 1$, also with mean 0 and standard deviation 1. Then the information coefficient—the correlation of $x(t)$ and $y(t)$—depends on the covariance of $x(t)$ and $y(t)$:

$$IC = \text{Cov}\{x(t),y(t)\} = \frac{1}{N} \cdot \sum_{t=1}^{N} x(t) \cdot y(t) \qquad (6.5)$$

where we observe N bets on market direction.

If we correctly forecast market direction $(x = y)$ N_1 times, and incorrectly forecast market direction $(x = -y)$ $N - N_1$ times, then the information coefficient is

$$IC = \frac{1}{N} \cdot [N_1 - (N - N_1)] = 2 \cdot \left(\frac{N_1}{N}\right) - 1 \qquad (6.6)$$

---

[3]The active holdings are 1/200 for 100 stocks and $-1/200$ for another 100 stocks. The expected active return is $100 \cdot (1/200) \cdot (1\%) + 100 \cdot (-1/200) \cdot (-1\%) = 1\%$. The residual variance of each asset (conditional on knowing $\theta_{n,1}$) is 299. The active variance of our position is $\sum_n (1/200)^2 \cdot 299 = \frac{299}{200} = (1.2227)^2$.

[4]We can go one step further with this example. In each half year, about 50 of the stocks will move from the buy list to the sell list, and another 50 will move from the sell list to the buy list. To implement the change will require about 50 percent turnover per 6 months, or 100 percent turnover per year. If round-trip transactions costs are 0.80 percent, then we lose 0.80 percent per year in transactions costs. The information ratio drops to 0.70, since the annual alpha net of costs is 1.21 percent and the annual residual risk stays at 1.729 percent.

Equation (6.6) provides some further intuition into the information coefficient. For example, we saw that an information coefficient of 0.0577 can lead to an information ratio above 1.0 (top decile, according to Chap. 5). Using Eq. (6.6), an IC = 0.0577 corresponds to correctly forecasting direction only 52.885 percent of the time—a small edge indeed.

These examples not only show the formula at work, but also show how little information one needs in order to be highly successful. In fact, an information coefficient of 0.02 between forecasted stock return and realized return over 200 stocks each quarter [with an implied accuracy of only 51 percent according to Eq. (6.6)] will produce a highly respectable information ratio of 0.56.

ADDITIVITY

The fundamental law is additive in the squared information ratios. Suppose there are two classes of stocks. In class 1 you have BR_1 stocks and a skill level of IC_1. Class 2 has BR_2 stocks and a skill level IC_2. The information ratio for the aggregate will be

$$IR^2 = BR_1 \cdot IC_1^2 + BR_2 \cdot IC_2^2 \tag{6.7}$$

assuming optimal implementation of the alphas across the combined set of stocks.[5] Notice that this is the sum of the squared information ratios for the first class and second class combined. Suppose the manager currently follows 200 stocks with semiannual forecasts; the breadth is 400. The information coefficient for these forecasts is 0.04. The information ratio will be $0.8 = 0.04 \cdot \sqrt{400}$. How would the information ratio and value added increase if the manager was to follow an additional 100 stocks (again with two forecasts per year) with information coefficient 0.03? The manager's value added will be proportional to $0.64 + (0.03)^2 \cdot 200 = 0.64 + 0.18 = 0.82$. There will be a 28 percent increase in the manager's ability to add value. The information ratio will increase from 0.8 to $0.906 = \sqrt{0.82}$.

---

[5]For example, if you index the second set of stocks, the combined information ratio will be only IR_1.

The additivity works along other dimensions as well. Suppose a manager follows 400 equities and takes a position on these on the average of once per year. The manager's information coefficient is 0.03. This yields an information ratio of $0.6 = 0.03 \cdot \sqrt{400}$. In addition, the manager makes a quarterly forecast on the market. The information coefficient for the market forecasts is 0.1. The information ratio for the market timing is $0.2 = 0.1 \cdot \sqrt{4}$. The overall information ratio will be the square root of the sum of the squared information ratios for stock selection and market timing: 0.63.

We can even carry this notion to an international portfolio. Figure 6.2 shows the breakdown of return on an international portfolio. The active return comes from three main sources: active currency positions, active allocations across countries, and active allocations within country markets.

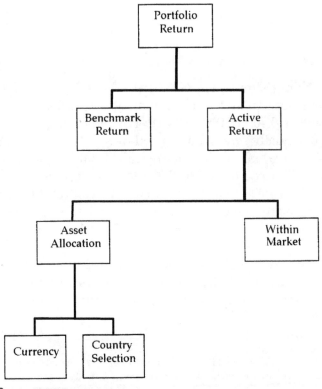

Figure 6.2

Assume that we are based in London, and that we invest in four countries: the United States, Japan, Germany, and the United Kingdom. There are three currency bets available to us;[6] we revise our currency position each quarter, and so we make 12 independent bets per year. We also make active bets across countries. These bet on the local elements of market return (separated from the currency component). We revise these market allocations each quarter. In addition we select stocks in each of the markets. We follow 400 stocks in the United States, 300 in Japan, 200 in the United Kingdom, and 100 in Germany. We revise our forecasts on these stocks once a year. Suppose our skill levels are IC_C for currency, IC_M for market allocation, and IC_{US}, IC_J, IC_{UK}, and IC_G for the national stocks. The overall information ratio will be

$$IR = \sqrt{IC_C^2 \cdot 12 + IC_M^2 \cdot 12 + IC_{US}^2 \cdot 400 + IC_J^2 \cdot 300 + IC_{UK}^2 \cdot 200 + IC_G^2 \cdot 100} \tag{6.8}$$

To make things simple, suppose that $IC_{US} = IC_J = IC_{UK} = IC_G = 0.02$. Then the squared information ratio contribution from the stocks will be $0.40 = 1000 \cdot (0.02)^2$. For the timing component to contribute equally, we would need $IC_C = IC_M = 0.129$, since $0.40 = 24 \cdot (0.129)^2$. Consider a more realistic (although still optimistic) information coefficient of 0.075 for the currency and market allocation decisions. That would make the contribution from currency and market allocation 0.135. The total squared information ratio would be $0.535 = 0.40 + 0.135$. The total information ratio is $0.73 = \sqrt{0.535}$.

The additivity holds across managers. In this case, we must assume that the allocation across the managers is optimal. Suppose a sponsor hires three equity managers with information ratios 0.75,

---

[6]With only one country, we would have no currency bet. Two countries would allow one currency bet, etc. The total active currency position must be zero.

0.50, and 0.30. Then the information ratio that the sponsor can obtain is 0.95,[7] since $(0.95)^2 = (0.75)^2 + (0.50)^2 + (0.30)^2$.

There are other applications of the law. Most notable is its use in scaling alphas; i.e., making sure that forecasts of exceptional stock returns are consistent with the manager's information ratio. That point will be discussed in Chap. 14, "Portfolio Construction."

ASSUMPTIONS

The law, like everything else, is based on assumptions that are not quite true. We'll discuss some of those assumptions later. However, the basic insight we can gain from the law is clear: It is important to play often (high BR) and to play well (high IC).

The forecasts should be independent. This means that forecast 2 should not be based on a source of information that is correlated

---

[7]Suppose manager n has information ratio IR_n and active risk ω_n. The sponsor's utility is

$$\sum_n y_n \cdot IR_n \cdot \omega_n - \lambda_{SA} \cdot \sum_n (y_n \cdot \omega_n)^2$$

assuming independent active risks and a sponsor's active risk aversion of λ_{SA}. The optimal allocation to manager n is

$$y_n^* = \frac{IR_n}{2\lambda_{SA} \cdot \omega_n}$$

The overall alpha will be

$$\alpha = \sum_n y_n^* \cdot \omega_n \cdot IR_n = \left(\frac{1}{2\lambda_{SA}}\right) \cdot \sum_n IR_n^2$$

The active variance will be

$$\omega^2 = \sum_n (y_n^* \cdot \omega_n)^2 = \left(\frac{1}{2\lambda_{SA}}\right)^2 \cdot \sum_n IR_n^2$$

and so the ratio of the alpha to the standard deviation will be

$$IR = \sqrt{\sum_n IR_n^2}$$

with the sources of forecast 1. For example, suppose that our first forecast is based on an assumption that growth stocks will do poorly, and our second is based on an assumption that high-yield stocks will do well. These pieces of information are not independent; growth stocks tend to have very low yields, and not many high-yield stocks would be called growth stocks. We've just picked out two ways to measure the same phenomenon. An example of independent forecasts is a quarterly adjustment of the portfolio's beta from 1.00 to either 1.05 or 0.95 as a market timing decision based on *new* information each quarter.

In a situation where analysts provide recommendations on a firm-by-firm basis, it is possible to check the level of dependence among these forecasts by first quantifying the recommendations and then regressing them against attributes of the firms. Analysts may like all the firms in a particular industry: Their stock picks are actually a single industry bet. All recommended stocks may have a high earnings yield: The analysts have made a single bet on earnings-to-price ratios. Finally, analysts may like all firms that have performed well in the last year; instead of a firm-by-firm bet, we have a single bet on the concept of momentum. More significantly, the residuals of the regression will actually be independent forecasts of individual stock return. Thus the regression analysis gives us the opportunity both to uncover consistent patterns in our recommendations and to remove them if we choose.

The same masking of dependence can occur over time. If you reassess your industry bets on the basis of new information each year, but rebalance your portfolios monthly, you shouldn't think that you make 12 industry bets per year. You just make the same bet 12 times.

We can see how dependence in the information sources will lower our overall skill level with a simple example. Consider the case where there are two sources of information. Separately, each has a level of skill IC; that is, the forecasts have a correlation of IC with the eventual returns. However, if the two information sources are dependent, then the information derived from the second source is not entirely new. Part of the second source's information will just reinforce what we knew from the first source, and part will be new or incremental information. We have to discover the value of the incremental information. As one can imagine, the greater the dependence between the two information sources, the lower the value of the incremental information. If γ is the correlation between the two information sources, then the skill level of the combined sources, IC(com), will be

$$IC(com) = IC \cdot \sqrt{\frac{2}{1 + \gamma}} \qquad (6.9)$$

If there is no correlation between sources ($\gamma = 0$), then $IC^2(com) = 2 \cdot IC^2$—the two sources will add in their ability to add value. As γ increases toward 1, the value of the second source diminishes.

For example, recall the case earlier in this chapter where the residual return θ_n on stock n was made up of 300 nuggets of return $\theta_{n,j}$ for $j = 1,2, \ldots , 300$. Suppose we have two information sources on the stocks. Source 1 knows $\theta_{n,1}$ and $\theta_{n,2}$ and source 2 knows $\theta_{n,2}$ and $\theta_{n,3}$. The information coefficient of each source is 0.0816. In this situation, the information coefficient of the combined sources will be 0.0942, since the information supplied by source 2 is correlated with that supplied by source 1; $\gamma = 0.5$. The formula gives $0.0816 \cdot \sqrt{2/1.5} = 0.0942$, which you can confirm by a direct calculation.

The law is based on the assumption that each of the BR active bets has the same level of skill. In fact, the manager will have greater skills in one area than another. We can see from the additivity principle, Eq. (6.7), that the square of the information ratio is the sum of the squares of the information ratios for the particular sources. Figure 6.3 demonstrates this phenomenon. If we order the information sources from highest skill level to lowest, then the total value added is just the area under the "skill" curve. Notice that the law assumes that the skill curve is horizontal; i.e., we replace the sum of the skill levels by an average skill level.

The strongest assumption behind the law is that the manager will accurately gauge the value of information and build portfolios that use that information in an optimal way. This requires insight and humility, a desirable combination that is not usually found in one individual.

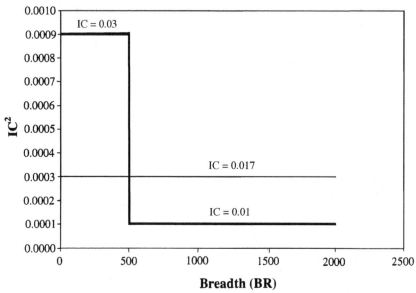

Figure 6.3

NOT THE LAW OF LARGE NUMBERS

A few investment professionals interpret the fundamental law of active management as a version of the statistical law of large numbers. This is a misinterpretation of one law or both. The law of large numbers says that sample averages for large samples will be very close to the true mean, and that our approximation of the true mean gets better and better as the sample gets larger.

The fundamental law says that more breadth is better if you can maintain the skill level. However, the law is just as valid with a breadth of 10 as with a breadth of 1000. The information ratio is still $IR = IC \cdot \sqrt{BR}$.

This confusion stems from the role of breadth. More breadth at the same skill level lets us diversify the residual risk. This is analogous to the role of large sample sizes in the law of large numbers, where the large sample size allows us to diversify the sampling error.

TESTS

The fundamental law is a guideline, not an operational tool. It is desirable that we have some faith in the law's ability to make reasonable predictions. We have conducted some tests of the law and found it to be excellent in its predictions.

The tests took the following form: Each year we supply alphas for BR stocks. The alphas are a mixture of the residual return on the stock over the next year and some random noise. The mixture can be set[8] so that the correlation of the forecasts with the residuals will be IC. That gives us a prediction of the information ratio that we should realize with these alphas.

The realized information ratios for optimal portfolios based on these forecasts are statistically indistinguishable from the forecasts of the fundamental law. When we then impose institutional constraints limiting short sales, the realized information ratios drop somewhat.

INVESTMENT STYLE

The law encourages managers to have an eclectic style. If a manager can find some independent source of information that will be of use, then he or she should exploit that information. It is the manager's need to present a clear picture of his or her style to clients that inhibits the manager from adopting an eclectic style. At the same time, the sponsor who hires a stable of managers has an incentive to diversify their styles in order to ensure that their bets are independent. The way investment management is currently organized in the United States, the managers prepare the distinct ingredients and the sponsor makes the stew.

SUMMARY

We have shown how the information ratio of an active manager can be explained by two components: the skill (IC) of the investment manager and the breadth (BR) of the strategy. These are related to the value added by the strategy by a simple formula [Eq. (6.3)].

---

[8]The forecast is

$$\alpha = IC \cdot [IC \cdot \theta + \omega \cdot \sqrt{1 - IC^2} \cdot z]$$

where z is a random number with mean 0 and variance 1. We see that $Var\{\alpha\} = IC^2 \cdot Var\{\theta\}$ and $Cov\{\alpha,\theta\} = IC^2 \cdot Var\{\theta\}$, and so $Corr\{\alpha,\theta\} = IC$.

Three main assumptions underlie this result. First and fore-most, we assumed that the manager has an accurate measure of his or her own skills and exploits information in an optimal way. Second, we assumed that the sources of information are indepen-dent; i.e., the manager doesn't bet twice on a repackaged form of the same information. Third, we assumed that the skill involved in forecasting each component, IC, is the same. The first assumption, call it competence or hypercompetence, is the most crucial. Invest-ment managers need a precise idea of what they know and, more significantly, what they don't know. Moreover, they need to know how to turn their ideas into portfolios and gain the benefits of their insights. The second two assumptions are merely simplifying approximations and can be mitigated by some of the devices men-tioned above.

The message is clear: you must play often and play well to win at the investment management game. It takes only a modest amount of skill to win as long as that skill is deployed frequently and across a large number of stocks.

PROBLEMS

1. Manager A is a stock picker. He follows 250 companies, making new forecasts each quarter. His forecasts are 2 percent correlated with subsequent residual returns. Manager B engages in tactical asset allocation, timing four equity styles (value, growth, large, small) every quarter. What must Manager B's skill level be to match Manager A's information ratio? What information ratio could a sponsor achieve by employing both managers, assuming that Manager B has a skill level of 8 percent?

2. A stock picker follows 500 stocks and updates his alphas every month. He has an $IC = 0.05$ and an $IR = 1.0$. How many bets does he make per year? How many independent bets does he make per year? What does this tell you about his alphas?

3. In the example involving residual returns θ_n composed of 300 elements $\theta_{n,j}$, an investment manager much choose between three research programs:

a. Follow 200 stocks each quarter and accurately forecast $\theta_{n,12}$ and $\theta_{n,15}$.

b. Follow 200 stocks each quarter and accurately forecast $\theta_{n,5}$ and $\theta_{n,105}$.

c. Follow 100 stocks each quarter and accurately forecast $\theta_{n,5}$, $\theta_{n,12}$, and $\theta_{n,105}$.

Compare the three programs, all assumed to be equally costly. Which would be most effective (highest value added)?

REFERENCES

Divecha, Arjun, and Richard C. Grinold. "Normal Portfolios: Issues for Sponsors, Managers and Consultants." *Financial Analysts Journal*, vol. 45, no. 2, 1989, pp. 7–13.

Ferguson, Robert. "Active Portfolio Management." *Financial Analysts Journal*, vol. 31, no. 3, 1975, pp. 63–72.

———. "The Trouble with Performance Measurement." *Journal of Portfolio Management*, vol. 12, no. 3, 1986.

Fisher, Lawrence. "Using Modern Portfolio Theory to Maintain an Efficiently Diversified Portfolio." *Financial Analysts Journal*, vol. 31, no. 3, 1975, pp. 73–85.

Grinold, Richard. "The Fundamental Law of Active Management." *Journal of Portfolio Management*, vol. 15, no. 3, 1989, pp. 30–37.

Jacobs, Bruce I., and Kenneth N. Levy. "The Law of One Alpha." *Journal of Portfolio Management*, vol. 21, no. 4, 1995, pp. 78–79.

Rosenberg, Barr. "Security Appraisal and Unsystematic Risk in Institutional Investment." *Proceedings of the Seminar on the Analysis of Security Prices* (Chicago: University of Chicago Press, November 1976), pp. 171–237.

Rudd, Andrew. "Business Risk and Investment Risk." *Investment Management Review*, November-December 1987, pp. 19–27.

Sharpe, William F. "Mutual Fund Performance." *Journal of Business*, vol. 39, no. 1, January 1966, pp. 66–86.

Treynor, Jack, and Fischer Black. "How to Use Security Analysis to Improve Portfolio Selection." *Journal of Business*, vol. 46, no. 1, 1973, pp. 66–86.

TECHNICAL APPENDIX

In this appendix we derive the fundamental law. The derivation includes three steps:

- Measuring the impact of the information on the means and variances of the returns

- Solution for the optimal policy
- Calculation and approximation of the information ratio

To facilitate the analysis, we will introduce orthogonal bases for both the residual returns and the information signals. We require these independent bases in order to isolate the independent bets driving the policy.

The Information Model

We can express the excess returns on the universe of N securities as

$$\mathbf{r} = \boldsymbol{\beta} \cdot r_B + \boldsymbol{\theta} \tag{6A.1}$$

where $\boldsymbol{\beta}$ = the asset's betas with respect to the benchmark
$\boldsymbol{\theta}$ = the residual returns
r_B = the excess return on the benchmark

We will model the residual returns $\boldsymbol{\theta}$ as

$$\boldsymbol{\theta} = \mathbf{A} \cdot \mathbf{x} \tag{6A.2}$$

where $\mathbf{x}$ = a vector of N uncorrelated standardized random variables, each with mean 0 and standard deviation 1
$\mathbf{A}$ = an N by N matrix equal to the square root of the residual covariance matrix of $\mathbf{r}$; i.e., $\mathbf{V} = \boldsymbol{\beta} \cdot \sigma_B^2 \cdot \boldsymbol{\beta}^T + \mathbf{A} \cdot \mathbf{A}^T$

Note that $\mathbf{A}$ has rank $N - 1$, since the benchmark holdings $\mathbf{h}_B$ will satisfy $\mathbf{A}^T \cdot \mathbf{h}_B = 0$.

If the residual returns are uncorrelated, then $\mathbf{A}$ is simply a diagonal matrix of residual risks. More generally, $\mathbf{A}$ linearly translates between the correlated residual returns and a set of uncorrelated movements.

Our information arrives as BR *signals* $\mathbf{z}$. With very little loss of generality, we can *assume* that these signals $\mathbf{z}$ have a joint normal distribution with mean 0 and standard deviation equal to 1. We write $\mathbf{z}$ as

$$\mathbf{z} = \mathbf{E} \cdot \mathbf{y} \tag{6A.3}$$
$$\mathbf{y} = \mathbf{J} \cdot \mathbf{z}^T$$

where $\mathbf{y}$ = a vector of BR uncorrelated random variables, each
            with mean 0 and standard deviation equal to 1
     $\mathbf{E}$ = the square root of the covariance matrix of $\mathbf{z}$; i.e.,
            $\mathrm{Var}\{\mathbf{z}\} = \mathbf{E} \cdot \mathbf{E}^T$
     $\mathbf{J}$ = the inverse of $\mathbf{E}$

So our signals may be correlated. The matrix $\mathbf{E}$, like the matrix
$\mathbf{A}$, translates to an equivalent set of uncorrelated signals. At one
extreme, our signals may contain stock-specific information. Then
$\mathbf{E}$ is the identity matrix. But for industry momentum signals, for
example, $\mathbf{E}$ may separate industry-specific information from sector
and marketwide information.

Let $\mathbf{Q} = \mathrm{Cov}\{\boldsymbol{\theta},\mathbf{z}\}$ be the N by BR covariance matrix between
the residual returns $\boldsymbol{\theta}$ and signals $\mathbf{z}$, and let $\mathbf{P} = \mathrm{Corr}\{\mathbf{x},\mathbf{y}\}$ be the
N by BR correlation matrix between the vectors $\mathbf{x}$ and $\mathbf{y}$. It follows
that $\mathbf{Q} = \mathbf{A} \cdot \mathbf{P} \cdot \mathbf{E}^T$. The items of interest to the active manager are
the mean and variance of $\boldsymbol{\theta}$ *conditional* on the signal $\mathbf{z}$. These are[9]

$$E\{\boldsymbol{\theta}|\mathbf{z}\} = \boldsymbol{\alpha}(\mathbf{z}) = \mathbf{A} \cdot \mathbf{P} \cdot \mathbf{J} \cdot \mathbf{z} \qquad (6\mathrm{A}.4)$$

$$\mathrm{Var}\{\boldsymbol{\theta}|\mathbf{z}\} = \mathbf{G} = \mathbf{A} \cdot (\mathbf{I} - \mathbf{P} \cdot \mathbf{P}^T) \cdot \mathbf{A}^T \qquad (6\mathrm{A}.5)$$

Note:

- The unconditional expectation of $\boldsymbol{\alpha}(\mathbf{z})$ is 0.
- The conditional variance of the residual returns is
  independent of the value of $\mathbf{z}$.
- The unconditional variance of the alphas is $\mathrm{Var}\{\boldsymbol{\alpha}(\mathbf{z})\} =$
  $\mathbf{A} \cdot \mathbf{P} \cdot \mathbf{P}^T \cdot \mathbf{A}^T$.

The Objective

The active manager's objective is to maximize the value added
through stock selection, as derived in Chap. 4. We are ignoring the
benchmark timing component, although that will reappear in a
later chapter devoted to benchmark timing.

---

[9]We will develop these ideas more fully in Chap. 10. For now, we simply note that Eqs.
(6A.4) and (6A.5) are based on best linear unbiased estimators. Equation (6A.4) is
closely related to the regression result. If we regress $\boldsymbol{\theta}$ against $\mathbf{z}$, i.e., $\theta_n = a + b \cdot$
$z_n + \epsilon_n$, then $E\{\theta_n \mid z_n\} = a + b \cdot z_n$. The regression coefficient b is $\mathrm{Cov}\{\theta,z\} \cdot$
$\mathrm{Var}^{-1}\{z\}$. Assuming $a = 0$ leads to Eq. (6A.4).

The objective is: Given **z**, choose a residual position (i.e., β = 0) **h*(z)** to solve the optimization problem

$$VA[z] = \text{Max}\{h^T \cdot \alpha(z) - \lambda \cdot h^T \cdot G \cdot h \,|\, z\} \qquad (6A.6)$$

This is the standard optimization, here conditional on particular information **z**. We will not impose the full investment condition, but rather the residual condition of zero beta.

The Optimal Active Position

The first-order conditions for the maximization problem, Eq. (6A.6), are

$$a(z) = 2\lambda \cdot G \cdot h^*(z) \qquad (6A.7)$$

or, using Eqs. (6A.4) and (6A.5),

$$A \cdot P \cdot J \cdot z = 2 \cdot \lambda \cdot A \cdot (I - P \cdot P^T) \cdot A^T \cdot h^*(z) \qquad (6A.8)$$

The additional restriction that **h*(z)** is a residual position, i.e., $\beta^T \cdot h^*(z) = 0$, will uniquely determine **h*(z)**.

With some manipulation, we find

$$A^T \cdot h^*(z) = \left(\frac{1}{2\lambda}\right) \cdot D \cdot P \cdot J \cdot z \qquad (6A.9)$$

with

$$D = (I - P \cdot P^T)^{-1} \qquad (6A.10)$$

We have derived the optimal holdings, conditional on **z**. From here, we will need to calculate the information ratio conditional on **z**, and then take the expectation over the distribution of possible values of **z**.

Calculation and Approximation of the Information Ratio

The optimal portfolio's alpha is

$$h^{*T}(z) \cdot \alpha(z) = \left(\frac{1}{2\lambda}\right) \cdot z^T \cdot J^T \cdot P^T \cdot D \cdot P \cdot J \cdot z \qquad (6A.11)$$

while the optimal portfolio's residual variance is

$$\mathbf{h}^{*T}(\mathbf{z}) \cdot \mathbf{G} \cdot \mathbf{h}^*(\mathbf{z}) = \left(\frac{1}{4\lambda^2}\right) \cdot \mathbf{z}^T \cdot \mathbf{J}^T \cdot \mathbf{P}^T \cdot \mathbf{D} \cdot \mathbf{P} \cdot \mathbf{J} \cdot \mathbf{z} \qquad (6A.12)$$

where the matrix calculations in Eqs. (6A.11) and (6A.12) are identical. Therefore, the squared information ratio *conditional* on the knowledge $\mathbf{z}$, will be

$$IR^2(\mathbf{z}) = \mathbf{z}^T \cdot \mathbf{J}^T \cdot \mathbf{P}^T \cdot \mathbf{D} \cdot \mathbf{P} \cdot \mathbf{J} \cdot \mathbf{z} \qquad (6A.13)$$
$$= \mathbf{y}^T \cdot (\mathbf{P}^T \cdot \mathbf{D} \cdot \mathbf{P}) \cdot \mathbf{y}$$

The unconditional squared information ratio is

$$IR^2 = E\{IR^2(\mathbf{z})\} = Tr\{\mathbf{P}^T \cdot \mathbf{D} \cdot \mathbf{P}\} \qquad (6A.14)$$

where $Tr\{\bullet\}$ is the trace (sum of the diagonal elements) and we have taken the expectation of the uncorrelated $N[0,1]$ random variables $\mathbf{y}$. (Note that $E\{y^2\} = 1$.)

We complete our analysis by approximating $Tr\{\mathbf{P}^T \cdot \mathbf{D} \cdot \mathbf{P}\}$. We can write $\mathbf{D}$ as

$$\mathbf{D} = \mathbf{I} + (\mathbf{P} \cdot \mathbf{P}^T) + (\mathbf{P} \cdot \mathbf{P}^T \cdot \mathbf{P} \cdot \mathbf{P}^T) + (\mathbf{P} \cdot \mathbf{P}^T \cdot \mathbf{P} \cdot \mathbf{P}^T \cdot \mathbf{P} \cdot \mathbf{P}^T) + \cdots$$
$$(6A.15)$$

so $\qquad \mathbf{P}^T \cdot \mathbf{D} \cdot \mathbf{P} = (\mathbf{P}^T \cdot \mathbf{P}) + (\mathbf{P}^T \cdot \mathbf{P} \cdot \mathbf{P}^T \cdot \mathbf{P}) + \cdots \qquad (6A.16)$

With typical correlations being extremely close to zero, and the most optimistic being close to 0.1, we can safely ignore all but the first term in Eq. (6A.16). In effect, we are ignoring the reduction in variance due to knowledge of $\mathbf{z}$. The trace of $\mathbf{P}^T \cdot \mathbf{P}$ is therefore

$$Tr\{\mathbf{P}^T \cdot \mathbf{D} \cdot \mathbf{P}\} \approx Tr\{\mathbf{P}^T \cdot \mathbf{P}\} = \sum_{n=1}^{N} \sum_{b=1}^{BR} \rho_{n,b}^2 \qquad (6A.17)$$

where we are summing the correlations between orthonormal basis elements $\mathbf{x}$ of the residual returns and independent signals $\mathbf{y}$ over all assets and signals.

To achieve the form of the fundamental law requires two more steps. First, sum the correlation of each signal with the basis elements, over the basis elements:

$$\zeta_b^2 = \sum_{n=1}^{N} \rho_{n,b}^2 \qquad (6A.18)$$

We then have that

$$\mathrm{IR}^2 = \sum_{b=1}^{\mathrm{BR}} \zeta_b^2 \qquad\qquad (6\mathrm{A}.19)$$

which already exhibits the additivity of the fundamental law. Finally, by assuming that all the signals have equal value,

$$\zeta_b^2 = \rho^2 = \mathrm{IC}^2 \qquad\qquad (6\mathrm{A}.20)$$

we find the desired result:

$$\mathrm{IR}^2 = \mathrm{BR} \cdot \mathrm{IC}^2 \qquad\qquad (6\mathrm{A}.21)$$

Exercises

For the following exercises, consider the following model of a stock picker's forecast monthly alphas:

$$\alpha_n = a \cdot \theta_n + b \cdot z_n$$

$$\mathrm{Std}\{\alpha_n\} = \mathrm{IC} \cdot \mathrm{Std}\{\theta_n\} = \frac{\mathrm{IC} \cdot \omega_n}{\sqrt{12}}$$

where α_n is the forecast residual return, θ_n is the subsequent realized residual return, and z_n is a random variable with mean 0 and standard deviation 1, uncorrelated with θ_n and with z_m ($m \neq n$).

1. Given that $a = \mathrm{IC}^2$, what coefficient b will ensure that

$$\mathrm{Std}\{\alpha_n\} = \mathrm{IC} \cdot \mathrm{Std}\{\theta_n\} = \frac{\mathrm{IC} \cdot \omega_n}{\sqrt{12}}$$

2. What is the manager's information coefficient in this model?

3. Assume that the model applies to the 500 stocks in the S&P 500, with $a = 0.0001$ and $\omega_n = 20$ percent. What is the information ratio of the model, according to the fundamental law?

4. Distinguish this model of alpha from the binary model introduced in the main part of the chapter.

Applications Exercises

Consider the performance of the MMI versus the S&P 500 over the past 5 years.

1. What are the active return and active risk of the MMI portfolio over this period? What is its information ratio (based on active risk and return)?

2. What is the t-statistic of the active return? How does it compare to the information ratio? Distinguish what the IR measures from what the t-statistic measures.

PART TWO

Expected Returns and Valuation

CHAPTER 7

Expected Returns and the Arbitrage Pricing Theory

INTRODUCTION

We have now completed our treatment of fundamentals. The next three chapters cover expected returns and valuation.

The arbitrage pricing theory (APT) is an interesting and powerful alternative to the CAPM for forecasting expected returns. This chapter describes the APT and emphasizes its implications for active managers. The conclusions are:

- The APT is a model of expected returns.
- Application of the APT is an art, not a science.
- The APT points the quantitative manager toward the relationship between factors and expected returns.
- APT factors can be defined in a multitude of ways. These may be fundamental, technical, or macro factors.
- The flexibility of the APT makes it inappropriate as a model for *consensus* expected returns, but an appropriate model for a *manager's* expected returns.
- The APT is a source of information to the active manager. It should be flexible. If all active managers shared the same information, it would be worthless.

The APT requires less stringent assumptions than the CAPM and produces similar results. This makes it sound as if the APT is a dominant theory. The difficulty is that the APT says that it is *possible* to forecast expected stock returns but it doesn't tell you *how* to do so. It has been called the "arbitrary" pricing theory for just this reason. The CAPM, in contrast, comes with a user's manual.

The APT states that each stock's expected excess return is determined by the stock's factor exposures. The link between the expected excess return and the stock factor exposures is described in Eq. (7.2). For each factor, there is a weight (called a factor forecast) such that the stock's expected excess return is the sum over all the factors of the stock's factor exposures times the factor forecasts.

The theory doesn't say what the factors are, how to calculate a stock's exposure to the factors, or what the weights should be in the linear combination. This is where science steps out and art steps in.

In discussing the APT, one should be careful to distinguish among

- Stories that *motivate* the APT. These usually involve basic economic forces that alter the relative valuation of stocks. The motivating stories may mislead some people into thinking that it is necessary for the APT to be based on exogenous macroeconomic factors. The applications described in this chapter indicate that this is not the case.
- Attempts to *implement* the APT. The APT is by nature arbitrary. Different individuals' attempts to implement it will take different forms. One should not confuse a particular implementation with the theory.
- The *theory*. The technical theory has evolved since its origins in the mid- to late 1970s. This chapter will provide an idiosyncratic view of the theory. Other ways to look at the APT are cited in the chapter notes.

This chapter will first detail some weaknesses of the CAPM that the APT was designed to correct. It will then describe the APT and its evolution as a theory. The final sections of this chapter will deal with the problem of implementation and give some examples of ways in which people either have tried or could try to implement APT models.

TROUBLE WITH THE CAPM

The CAPM is based on the notion that the market portfolio is not only mean/variance-efficient but, in fact, the fully invested portfolio with the highest ratio of expected excess return to volatility. In practice, the theory has been applied to say that common, broad-based stock indices are efficient: the S&P 500 in the United States, the FTA in the United Kingdom, and the TSE1 in Japan.

If we consider a broader notion of the market, including all bonds, international investments, and other assets such as precious metals, real property, etc., then we can see that the market consists of more than the local stock index. Even if the CAPM is true in some broader context of a worldwide portfolio, it cannot be valid in the restricted single-market world in which it is ordinarily applied. All of the other assumptions underlying the CAPM (mean/variance preferences, identical expectations of mean and variance, no taxes or transactions costs, no restrictions on stock positions, etc.) can be challenged, adding additional wounds. The most grievous of these is the CAPM requirement that all participants know every stock's expected excess return. This assumption should be viewed in the context of our quest to get a handle on the expected excess returns in the first place! Thus we would suspect that the CAPM can be only approximately true. It provides a guideline that should be neither ignored nor taken as gospel.

One dramatic episode that points out the weakness of the CAPM occurred for U.S. equities in 1983 and 1984, during a period characterized by a considerable drop in interest rates. The equities most adversely affected had high betas, and the equities most beneficially affected had low betas.

We can illustrate this episode by a simple experiment. In December 1982, take the stocks in the S&P 500, order them according to their predicted beta, and form ten portfolios, each with an equal amount of capitalization. Portfolio 1 has the lowest-beta stocks, portfolio 2 the next lowest group, and so on, with portfolio 10 holding the highest-beta stocks. Then follow the capitalization-weighted returns on these portfolios for the next 24 months. It turns out that over the out-of-sample period, the predicted betas were excellent forecasts of the realized betas. No problem here. In Fig. 7.1, we see the scatter diagram of predicted versus realized beta.

The regression line in Fig. 7.1 has a slope of 0.93, and the R^2 of this regression was 0.89. The prediction of beta was quite accurate.

The CAPM would say that the alpha of each portfolio should be zero. It didn't turn out that way. Not only were several of

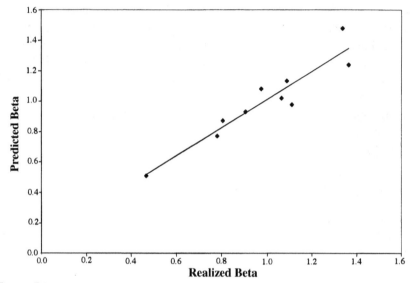

Figure 7.1

the alphas significantly different from zero, they were perversely related to the portfolio betas. The results are shown in the scatter diagram in Fig. 7.2.

Remember that we already checked our predictions of beta and found that they were quite accurate. The explanation for this event must lie elsewhere. Something, most likely changes in interest rates and changes in inflationary expectations, was making higher-beta stocks have negative residual returns and lower-beta stocks have higher residual returns.[1] This pattern was common throughout the early 1980s.

There are periods in which CAPM predictions of expected excess returns appear to have systematic defects.

This episodic evidence is meant to be suggestive, not to dash the CAPM once and for all. In fact, financial statisticians have

---

[1]This points out the hazards of benchmark timing by tilting the portfolio toward higher-beta stocks. The market was up considerably over this period; however, higher-beta stocks had relatively bad results. Benchmark timing with futures would have been much more effective, since it did not entail a residual bet on the high-beta stocks.

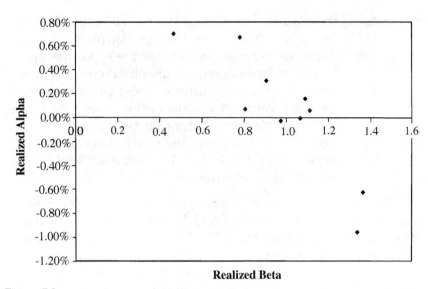

Figure 7.2

thrown considerable empirical sophistication into attempts to prove or disprove the validity of the CAPM, without coming to any hard-and-fast conclusions.[2] Those efforts should be enough to convince the investor to value the notion that the market plays a central—indeed, the most important—role in the formation of expected returns. However, the example should be enough to convince you that it is worthwhile to look for further explanations.

THE APT

The APT postulates a multiple-factor model of excess returns. It assumes that there are K factors such that the excess returns can be expressed as

$$r_n = \sum_{k=1}^{K} X_{n,k} \cdot b_k + u_n \tag{7.1}$$

[2]Most recently, Fama and French (1992) have attempted to discredit the CAPM, with considerable publicity. However, as described in Black (1993) and Grinold (1993), these results require careful scrutiny.

where $X_{n,k}$ = the *exposure of stock n to factor k*. The exposures are frequently called *factor loadings*. For practical purposes, we will assume that the exposures are known before the returns are observed.

b_k = the *factor return* for factor k. These factor returns are either attributed to the factors at the end of the period or observed during the period.

u_n = stock n's *specific return*, the return that cannot be explained by the factors. It is sometimes called the idiosyncratic return to the stock.

We impose very little structure[3] on the model. The astute reader will note that the APT model, Eq. (7.1), is identical in structure to the structural risk model, Eq. (3.16). However, the focus is now on expected returns, not risk.

The APT is about expected excess returns. The main result is that we can express expected excess returns in terms of the model's factor exposures. The APT formula for expected excess return is

$$f_n = E\{r_n\} = \sum_{k=1}^{K} X_{n,k} \cdot m_k \qquad (7.2)$$

where m_k is the *factor forecast* for factor k. The theory says that a correct factor forecast will exist. It doesn't say how to find it.

The APT maintains that the expected excess return on any stock is determined by that stock's factor exposures and the factor forecasts associated with those factors.

EXAMPLES

We can breathe some life into this formula by considering a few examples. The CAPM is the first example. For the CAPM, we have one factor, $K = 1$. The stock's exposure to that factor is the stock's beta; i.e., $X_{n,1} = \beta_n$. The expected return associated with the factor is $m_1 = E\{r_M\} = f_M$, the expected excess return on the market.

---

[3]We assume that the specific returns $u(n)$ are uncorrelated with the factor returns $b(k)$; i.e., $\text{Cov}\{b(k),u(n)\} = 0$. In most practical applications, we assume that the specific returns are uncorrelated with each other; i.e., $\text{Cov}\{u(n),u(m)\} = 0$ if $m \neq n$; however, we do not need this second assumption for the theory to hold.

The second example is more substantial. We first classify stocks by their industry membership, then look at four other attributes of the companies. These attributes are chosen for the purpose of example only. (Why these attributes, and why defined in just this way? That question reinforces the notion that the APT model will be in the eye of the model builder. It will be as much a matter of taste as anything else.) The four attributes selected are

- A forecast of earnings growth based on the IBES consensus forecast and past realized earnings growth
- Bond beta: the response of the stock to returns on an index of government bonds
- Size: the natural logarithm of equity capitalization
- Return on equity (ROE): earnings divided by book

The four attributes include a forecast (earnings growth), a macroeconomic characteristic (bond beta), a firm characteristic (size), and a fundamental data item (return on equity).

It is easier to make comparisons across factors if they are all expressed in the same fashion. One way to do this is to standardize the exposure by subtracting the market average from each attribute and dividing by the standard deviation. In that way, the average exposure will equal zero, roughly 66 percent of the stocks will have exposures running from -1 up to $+1$, and only 5 percent of the stocks will have exposures above $+2$ or below -2. Table 7.1 displays the primary industry, standardized exposures to these four factors, and predicted beta for the 20 stocks in the Major Market Index as of December 1992. Note that these exposures are standardized across a broad universe of over 1000 stocks, so, for example, the size factor exposures for the Major Market Index stocks are all positive.

The APT forecast is based on the factor forecasts for the four factors and a forecast for the chemical industry. The factor forecasts are 2.0 percent for growth, 2.5 percent for bond beta, -1.5 percent for size, and 0.0 percent for return on equity. (These forecasts are for illustration only.) We think that growth firms will do well, interest-rate-sensitive stocks (which are usually highly leveraged firms) will do well, smaller stocks will do well, and return on equity will be irrelevant. In addition, we forecast 8 percent for the chemical industry, and 6 percent for all other industries.

T A B L E 7.1

Stock	Industry	Growth	Bond β	Size	ROE	Beta
American Express	Financial services	0.17	-0.05	0.19	-0.28	1.16
AT&T	Telephones	-0.16	0.74	1.47	-0.59	0.84
Chevron	Energy reserves and production	-0.53	-0.24	0.83	-0.72	0.70
Coca-Cola	Food and beverage	-0.02	0.30	1.41	1.48	1.06
Disney	Entertainment	0.13	-0.86	0.71	0.42	1.13
Dow Chemical	Chemical	-0.64	-0.92	0.48	0.22	1.13
DuPont	Chemical	-0.10	-0.74	1.05	-0.41	0.93
Eastman Kodak	Leisure	-0.19	-0.30	0.39	-0.55	0.94
Exxon	Energy reserves and production	-0.67	0.03	1.67	-0.27	0.71
General Electric	Heavy electrical	-0.24	0.13	1.56	0.15	1.10
General Motors	Motor vehicles	2.74	-1.80	0.73	-1.24	1.25
IBM	Computer hardware	0.51	-0.62	1.16	-0.62	1.11
International Paper	Forest products and paper	-0.23	-1.08	0.01	-0.49	1.08
Johnson & Johnson	Medical products	-0.12	0.68	1.06	0.78	1.07
McDonalds	Restaurant	-0.16	0.28	0.55	0.24	1.06
Merck	Drugs	-0.04	0.46	1.37	2.28	1.10
3M	Chemical	-0.22	-0.69	0.78	0.20	0.91
Philip Morris	Tobacco	-0.01	0.30	1.60	1.22	1.02
Procter & Gamble	Home products	-0.32	0.80	1.12	0.41	1.05
Sears	Department stores	-0.34	-1.29	0.45	-0.69	1.10

T A B L E 7.2

Stock	Industry	APT	CAPM	APT-CAPM
American Express	Finance services	5.93%	6.96%	−1.03%
AT&T	Telephones	5.33%	5.04%	0.29%
Chevron	Energy reserves and production	3.10%	4.20%	−1.11%
Coca-Cola	Food and beverage	4.60%	6.36%	−1.77%
Disney	Entertainment	3.05%	6.78%	−3.74%
Dow Chemical	Chemical	3.70%	6.78%	−3.08%
DuPont	Chemical	4.38%	5.58%	−1.21%
Eastman Kodak	Leisure	4.29%	5.64%	−1.36%
Exxon	Energy reserves and production	2.23%	4.26%	−2.03%
General Electric	Heavy electrical	3.51%	6.60%	−3.10%
General Motors	Motor vehicles	5.89%	7.50%	−1.62%
IBM	Computer hardware	3.73%	6.66%	−2.93%
International Paper	Forest products and paper	2.83%	6.48%	−3.66%
Johnson & Johnson	Medical products	5.87%	6.42%	−0.55%
McDonalds	Restaurant	5.56%	6.36%	−0.81%
Merck	Drugs	5.02%	6.60%	−1.59%
3M	Chemical	4.67%	5.46%	−0.80%
Philip Morris	Tobacco	4.33%	6.12%	−1.79%
Procter & Gamble	Home products	5.68%	6.30%	−0.62%
Sears	Department stores	1.42%	6.60%	−5.18%

The CAPM forecast is for 6 percent expected market excess return.

We display the final stock forecasts in Table 7.2. Here we display the APT forecast, the CAPM forecast, and the residual APT forecast (the APT forecast less the CAPM forecast).

We can see from this example that whatever the use of an APT model in forecasting expected returns, it can make a great talking point. By putting in different expectations for the various factors, we could automatically generate mountains of research.

THE APT RATIONALE

The APT result follows from an arbitrage argument. What would happen if we had a returns model like Eq. (7.1), and the APT

relationship [Eq. (7.2)] *failed* to hold? We could find an active position with zero exposure to all of the factors[4] and expected excess
return of 1 percent. Since the active position has zero factor exposure, it has almost no risk, and so we can achieve 1 percent expected
excess return at low risk levels. We can therefore also add this
active position to any portfolio *P* and improve our performance
by increasing expected excess return with little additional risk.

Arbitrage means a certain gain at zero expense. In the case
described above, we have a nearly certain gain, since the expected
return is positive and the risk is very, very small. There is no
expense, since it is an active portfolio (zero net investment). We
call this second situation a quasi-arbitrage opportunity. If we rule
out these quasi-arbitrage opportunities, then the APT must hold.

How do we find the factor model that will do this wonderful
trick? The APT is silent on that question. However, a little old-
fashioned mean/standard deviation analysis can provide some
clues.

PORTFOLIO Q AND THE APT

The APT is marvelously flexible. We can concentrate on any desired
group of stocks.[5] Among any group of *N* stocks, there will be an
efficient frontier for portfolios made up of the *N* risky stocks. Figure
7.3 shows a typical frontier.

With each portfolio we can associate a *risk*, as measured by
the standard deviation of its returns, and a *reward*, as measured by
the expected excess return. Portfolio *Q* in Fig. 7.3 has the highest
reward-to-risk ratio (Sharpe ratio).

Knowledge of portfolio *Q* is sufficient to calculate all expected
returns.[6] Portfolio *Q* plays the same role as the market portfolio
does in the CAPM; in fact, the CAPM is another way of saying
that portfolio *Q* is the market portfolio.[7]

---

[4]This will typically imply net zero investment, unless the factor model does not have an
intercept. Even then, we have built a portfolio with almost no risk and 1 percent
expected excess return. We can combine this with the risk-free asset for a net zero
investment with an expected excess return and almost no risk.
[5]Contrast this with the CAPM, where coverage should, in theory, be universal.
[6]And vice versa. See Chap. 2 for more details.
[7]See the technical appendix to Chap. 2.

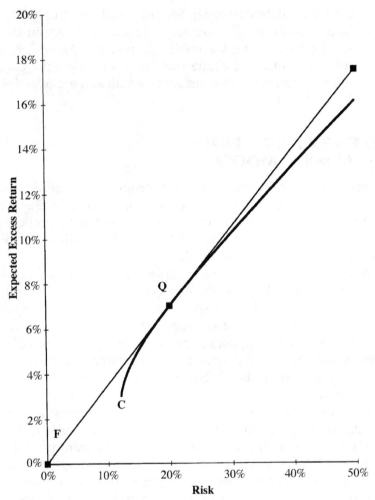

Figure 7.3

The expected excess return on any stock will be proportional to that stock's beta with respect to portfolio Q. We might assume that we can stop here. We cannot, since we don't know portfolio Q. However, all is not lost. We can learn something from portfolio Q.

We need to separate two issues at this point. The first is defining a qualified model, and the second is finding the correct set of factor forecasts. A multiple-factor model [as in Eq. (7.1)] is *qualified* if it is possible to find factor forecasts $m(k)$ such that Eq. (7.2) holds.

Once we have a qualified model, we still must come up with the correct factor forecasts $m(k)$. We argue in the next section that it should not be hard to find a qualified model. However, in the section following that, we argue that the ability to make correct factor forecasts requires both considerable skill and a model linked to investment intuition.

THE EASY PART: FINDING A QUALIFIED MODEL

This section describes the technical properties required for a multiple-factor model to qualify for successful APT implementation. The details are in the technical appendix. More significantly, we argue by example that we can fairly easily find qualified models. Let's start with the technical result.

A factor model of the type described in Eq. (7.1) is qualified, i.e., Eq. (7.2), will hold for some factor forecasts m_k, if and only if portfolio Q is *diversified with respect to that factor model*. Diversified with respect to the factor model means that among all portfolios with the same factor exposures as portfolio Q, portfolio Q has minimum risk. No other portfolio with the same factor exposures is less risky than portfolio Q. How do we translate this technical rule into practice?

A frontier portfolio like Q should be highly diversified in the conventional sense of the word. Portfolio Q will contain all the stocks, with no exceptionally large holdings. We want portfolio Q to be diversified with respect to the multiple-factor model. Common sense would say that any multiple-factor model that captures the important differential movements in the stocks will qualify. The arbitrary aspect of the APT can be a benefit as well as a drawback! It's a drawback in that we don't know exactly what to do; it's a benefit in that it suggests that there are reasonable steps that will possibly succeed.

We can check this idea by devising some surrogates for portfolio Q and seeing if they are diversified with respect to the BARRA U.S. Equity model. The BARRA model was constructed to help portfolio managers control risk, not to explain expected returns. However, it does attempt to capture those aspects of the market that cause some groups of stocks to behave differently from others.

T A B L E 7.3

Portfolio	Number of Assets	Unexplained Variance (%)
MMI	20	2.51
OEX	100	0.99
S&P 500	500	0.30
FR1000	1000	0.21
FR3000	3000	0.18
ALLUS	~6000	0.17

We find that well over 99 percent of the variance of highly diversified portfolios is captured by the factor component. Table 7.3 shows
the percentage of total risk that is not explained by the model for
several major U.S. equity indices as of December 1992. The ALLUS
portfolio includes approximately the 6000 largest U.S. companies,
which are followed by BARRA.

Table 7.3 indicates that portfolios are highly diversified with
respect to the BARRA model. It may be possible to find a portfolio
that has the same factor exposures as the Frank Russell 3000 index
and less risk. However, the two portfolios would have the same
factor risk (recall that they have the same factor exposures), and
so they can differ only in their specific risk. Since 99.82 percent of
the risk is explained by the factor component of return, there is
very little margin for improvement. We cannot find portfolios that
have the same factor exposures and substantially less risk, since
the amount of nonfactor risk is already negligible.

> Any factor model that is good at explaining the risk of a diversified
> portfolio should be (nearly) qualified as an APT model.

The exact specification of the factor model may not be important in qualifying a model. What is important is that the model
contain sufficient factors to capture movement in the important dimensions.

THE HARD PART: FACTOR FORECASTS

We have settled one part of the implementation question. Any
reasonably robust risk model in the form of Eq. (7.1) should qualify.

The next step is to find the amount of expected excess return, m_k in Eq. (7.2), to associate with each factor.

Forecasting the m_k is not easy just because we may have 1000 stocks and only 10 factors. If it were true that "fewer is better," then we could just concentrate on forecasting the returns to the bond market and the stock market. In fact, as the fundamental law of active management states, it is better to make more forecasts than fewer for a given level of skill. If we can forecast expected returns on 1000 stocks or 10 factors, then to retain the same value added, we need ten times more skill in forecasting the factor returns than in forecasting the stock returns.

The simplest approach to forecasting m_k is to calculate a history of factor returns and take their average. This is the forecast that would have worked best in the past—i.e., a backcast rather than a forecast. If we hope that the past average helps in the future, we are implicitly assuming an element of stationarity in the market. The APT does not provide any guarantees here. However, there is hope. One of the non-APT reasons to focus on factors is the knowledge that the factor relationship is more stable than the stock relationship. For example, it is probably more valuable to know how growth stocks have done in the past than to know the past returns of a particular stock that is currently classified as a growth stock. The problem is that the stock may not have been classified as a growth stock over the earlier period; the stock may have changed its stripes. However, the factor returns will give us some information on how it may perform in its current set of stripes!

Haugen and Baker (1996) have proposed an APT model whose factor forecasts rely simply on historical factor returns. Their factors roughly resemble the BARRA model, except that they replace more than 50 industries with 10 sectors, and they replace 13 risk indices with 40 descriptors.[8] Each factor forecast is then simply the trailing 12-month average of the factor returns. So they forecast the finance sector return, the IBES estimated earnings-to-price factor return, etc., as their past 12-month averages.

Model structure can be very helpful in developing good forecasts. As we'll see in the next section, APT models can be either purely statistical or structural. The factors have some meaning in

---

[8]This leads to collinearity, which the BARRA model attempts to avoid.

the structural model; they don't in a purely statistical model. In statistical models, we have very little latitude in forecasting the factor returns. In a structural model, with factors that are linked to specified characteristics of the stocks, factor forecasts can be interpreted as forecasts for stocks that share a similar characteristic. We can apply both common sense and alternative statistical procedures to check those forecasts.

Factor forecasts are easier if there is some explicit link between the factors and our intuition. Consider, for example, a "bond market beta" factor. This factor will show how the stock will react as bond prices (i.e., interest rates) change. A forecast for this factor is in fact a forecast for the bond market. This doesn't mean that forecasting future interest rates is easy. It means that the knowledge that you are, in fact, forecasting interest rates should make the task clearer.

A similar result would hold for a factor defined in terms of a stock's fundamentals. Consider a "growth" factor, with consensus growth expectations as the factor exposures. Now our forecast is an expression of our outlook for growth stocks. Once again, we haven't guaranteed that we can forecast the outlook for growth stocks correctly. We have simply made the task more explicit, and thus given ourselves a greater chance for success.

This suggests an opportunistic approach to building an APT model. We should take advantage of our conclusion that we can easily build qualified APT models. We should use factors that we have some ability to forecast. Suppose we are reasonably good at forecasting returns to gold, oil, bonds, yen, etc., and we have some skill at predicting economic fluctuations. We should work from our strengths and build an APT model based on those factors, then round out the model with some others (industry variables) to capture the bulk of the risk. There is no use building the world's greatest (most qualified) APT model if we cannot come up with the factor forecasts.

Factor forecasts are difficult. Structure should help.

The next section describes some approaches to building an APT model.

APPLICATIONS

We have tried to emphasize the flexible nature of the APT. There are many ways to build APT models. The arbitrary nature of the

APT leaves enormous room for creativity in implementation. Two equally well-informed scholars working independently will not come up with similar implementations. We've given six illustrations here. They fall into two catagories, structural and statistical.

Structural models postulate some relationships between specific variables. The variables can be macroeconomic (unanticipated inflation, change in interest rates, etc.), fundamental (growth in earnings, return on equity, market share), or market-related (beta, industry membership). All types of variables can be used in one model. Practitioners tend to prefer the structural models, since these models allow them to connect the factors with specific variables and therefore link their investment experience and intuition to the model.

Statistical models line up the returns data and turn a crank. Academics build APT models to test various hypotheses about market efficiency, the efficacy of the CAPM, etc. Academics tend to prefer the purely statistical models, since they can avoid putting their prejudgments into the model in that way.

There are a great many ways to build an APT model.

Structural Model 1: Given Exposures, Estimate Factor Returns

The BARRA model, described in detail in Chap. 3, "Risk," can function as an APT model. As we saw above, it qualifies with ease, and it is just as easy (i.e., not very) to forecast returns to the BARRA factors as to any others. The BARRA model takes the factor exposures as given based on current characteristics of the stocks, such as their earnings yield and relative size. The factor returns are estimates.

Structural Model 2: Given Factor Returns, Estimate Exposures

In this model, the factor returns are given. For example, take the factor returns as the return on the value-weighted NYSE, gold, a government bond index, a basket of foreign currencies, and a basket of traded commodities. Set the exposure of each stock to the NYSE equal to 1. For the other factors, determine the past exposure of the stock to the factor returns by regressing the difference between the stock return and the NYSE return on the returns of the other factors.

The factor forecasts are forecasts of the future values of the factor returns. Note that we hope that the estimated factor exposures are stable over time.

Structural Model 3: Combine Structural Models 1 and 2

This model is the inevitable hybrid of structural models 1 and 2: Start with some primitive factor definitions, estimate the stock's factor exposure as in structural model 2, then attribute returns to the factors as in structural model 1.

Statistical Model 1: Principal Components Analysis

Look at the returns of a collection of stocks, or portfolios of stocks, over many months—say 50 stocks over 200 months. Calculate the 50 by 50 matrix of realized covariance between these stocks over the 200 months. Do a principal components analysis of the 50 by 50 covariance matrix. Typically, one will find that the first 20 components will explain 90 percent or more of the risk. Call these 20 principal component returns the factors. These factors are purely statistical constructs. We might as well call them Dick, Jane, Spot, . . . or red, green, blue . . . .

The analysis will tell us the exposures of the 50 stocks to the factors. It will also give us the returns on those factors over the 200 months. The factor returns will be uncorrelated. We can determine the exposures to the factors of stocks that were not included in the original group by regressing the returns of the new stocks on the returns to the factors. The regression coefficients will measure the exposures to the factors; the fact that the factor returns are uncorrelated is useful at this stage. To implement this model, we need a forecast of the m_k. The obvious forecast is the historical average of the factor returns. It may be the only possible forecast: Since the factors are by construction abstract, it would be hard to justify a forecast that differed from the historical average.

Statistical Model 2: Maximum Likelihood Factor Analysis

Here we perform a massive maximum likelihood estimation, looking at Eq. (7.1) over 60 months. To make this possible, we assume that the stock's exposures $X_{n,k}$ are constant over the 5-year period. If we applied this to 500 stocks over 60 months and looked for 10 factors, we would be using $500 \cdot 60 = 30,000$ returns to estimate $500 \cdot 10 = 5000$ exposures and $60 \cdot 10 = 600$ factor returns.

Statistical Model 3: The Dual of Statistical Model 2

This is quite imaginative. A detailed description is difficult, but see Connor and Korajczyk (1988). When N stocks are observed over T time periods, N is usually much greater than T. Instead of analyzing the principal components of the N by N historical covariance matrix, we look at the T by T matrix of covariances. This analysis reverses the role of factor exposure and factor return!

SUMMARY

We have described the APT and talked about its relevance for active management. The APT is a powerful theory, but difficult to apply. The APT does not in any way relieve the active manager of the need for insight and skill. It is a framework that can help skilled and insightful active managers harness their abilities.

Problems

1. According to the APT, what are the expected values of the u_n in Eq. (7.1)? What is the corresponding relationship for the CAPM?
2. Work by Fama and French, and others, over the past decade has identified size and book-to-price ratios as two critical factors determining expected returns. How would you build an APT model based on those two factors? Would the model require additional factors?

3. In the example shown in Table 7.2, most of the CAPM forecasts exceed the APT forecasts. Why? Are APT forecasts required to match CAPM forecasts on average?

4. In an earnings-to-price tilt fund, the portfolio holdings consist (approximately) of the benchmark plus a multiple c times the earnings-to-price factor portfolio (which has unit exposure to earnings-to-price and zero exposure to all other factors). Thus, the tilt fund manager has an active exposure c to earnings-to-price. If the manager uses a constant multiple c over time, what does that imply about the manager's factor forecasts for earnings-to-price?

5. You have built an APT model based on industry, growth, bond beta, size, and return on equity (ROE). This month your factor forecasts are

Heavy electrical industry	6.0%
Growth	2.0%
Bond beta	−1.0%
Size	−0.5%
ROE	1.0%

These forecasts lead to a benchmark expected excess return of 6.0 percent. Given the following data for GE,

Industry	Heavy electrical
Growth	−0.24
Bond beta	0.13
Size	1.56
ROE	0.15
Beta	1.10

what is its alpha according to your model?

NOTES

In the early 1970s, Sharpe (1977) (the paper was written in 1973), Merton (1973), and Rosenberg (1974) advocated multiple-factor approaches to the CAPM. Their arguments were based on reasoning similar to that underlying the CAPM. The results were a multiple-beta form of the CAPM, identical in form to Eq. (7.2). In fact, an active money management product called a "yield tilt fund" was launched based on the notion that higher-yielding stocks had higher expected returns.

In the mid-1970s, Ross (1976) proposed a different way of looking at expected stock returns. Ross used the notion of arbitrage, which was the foundation of Black and Scholes's work on the valuation of options. In certain cases the mere ruling out of arbitrage opportunities is sufficient to produce an explicit formula for a stock's value. Later other authors, notably Connor (1984) and Huberman (1982), added additional assumptions and structure to produce the exact form of Eq. (7.2). Modern theoretical treatments of the APT reserve a role for the market portfolio. See Connor (1986) for a discussion.

Bower, Bower, and Logue (1984); Roll and Ross (1984); and Sharpe (1984) have expositions of the APT aimed at professionals. See also Rosenberg (1981) and Rudd and Rosenberg (1980) for a discussion of the CAPM and APT. The text by Sharpe and Alexander (1990) has an excellent discussion.

Applications of the APT are described in Roll and Ross (1979), Chen, Roll, and Ross (1986), Lehmann and Modest (1988), and Connor and Korajczyk (1986).

For a discussion of some of the econometric and statistical issues surrounding the APT, see Shanken (1982), Shanken (1985), and the articles cited in those papers.

Actual implementations of APT models are described by Roll and Ross; Chen, Roll, and Ross; Lehmann and Modest; Connor and Korajczyk, etc.

REFERENCES

Black, Fischer. "Estimating Expected Returns." *Financial Analysts Journal*, vol. 49, no. 5, 1993, pp. 36–38.

Bower, D. H., R. S. Bower, and D. E. Logue. "A Primer on Arbitrage Pricing Theory." *The Midland Journal of Corporate Finance*, vol. 2, no. 3, 1984, pp. 31-40.

Chamberlain, G., and M. Rothschild. "Arbitrage, Factor Structure, and Mean-Variance Analysis on Large Asset Markets." *Econometrica* vol. 51, no. 5, 1983, pp. 1281–1304.

Chen, N., R. Roll, and S. Ross. "Economic Forces and the Stock Market." *Journal of Business*, vol. 59, no. 3, 1986, pp. 383–404.

Connor, Gregory. "A Unified Beta Pricing Theory." *Journal of Economic Theory*, vol. 34, no. 1, 1984, pp. 13–31.

———. "Notes on the Arbitrage Pricing Theory." In *Frontiers of Financial Theory*, edited by G. Constantinides and S. Bhattacharya (Boston: Rowman and Littlefield, 1986).

Connor, Gregory, and Robert A. Korajczyk. "Performance Measurement with the Arbitrage Pricing Theory." Northwestern University working paper, 1986.

———. "Risk and Return in an Equilibrium APT: Application of a New Test Methodology." *Journal of Financial Economics* vol. 21, no. 2, 1988, pp. 255–290.

Fama, Eugene F., and Kenneth R. French. "The Cross-Section of Expected Stock Returns." *Journal of Finance*, vol 67, no. 2, 1992, pp. 427–465.

Grinold, R. "Is Beta Dead Again?" *Financial Analysts Journal*, vol 49, no. 4, 1993, pp. 28–34.

Haugen, Robert A., and Nardin L. Baker. "Commonality in the Determinants of Expected Stock Returns." *Journal of Financial Economics*, vol. 41, no. 3, 1996, pp. 401–439.

Huberman, G. "A Simple Approach to Arbitrage Pricing Theory." *Journal of Economic Theory*, vol. 28, 1982, pp. 183–191.

Lehmann, Bruce N., and David Modest. "The Empirical Foundations of the Arbitrage Pricing Theory." *Journal of Financial Economics*, vol. 21, no. 2, 1988, pp. 213–254.

Mayers, D., and E. M. Rice. "Measuring Portfolio Performance and the Empirical Content of Asset Pricing Models." *Journal of Financial Economics*, vol. 7, no. 2, 1979, pp. 3–28.

Merton, R. C. "An Intertemporal Capital Asset Pricing Model." *Econometrica*, vol. 41, no. 1, 1973, pp. 867–887.

Pfleiderer, P. "A Short Note on the Similarities and the Differences between the Capital Asset Pricing Model and the Arbitrage Pricing Theory." Stanford University Graduate School of Business working paper, 1983.

Roll, Richard. "A Critique of the Asset Pricing Theory's Tests." *Journal of Financial Economics*, vol. 4, no. 2, 1977, pp. 129–176.

Roll, Richard, and Stephen A. Ross. "An Empirical Investigation of the Arbitrage Pricing Theory." *Journal of Finance*, vol. 35, no. 5, 1979, pp. 1073–1103.

———. "The Arbitrage Pricing Theory Approach to Strategic Portfolio Planning." *Financial Analysts Journal*, vol. 40, no. 3, 1984, pp. 14–26.

Rosenberg, Barr. "Extra-Market Components of Covariance in Security Returns." *Journal of Financial and Quantitative Analysis*, vol. 9, no. 2, 1974, pp. 263–274.

———. "The Capital Asset Pricing Model and the Market Model." *Journal of Portfolio Management*, vol. 7, no. 2, 1981, pp. 5–16.

Ross, Stephen A. "The Arbitrage Theory of Capital Asset Pricing." *Journal of Economic Theory*, vol. 13, 1976, pp. 341–360.

Rudd, Andrew, and Henry K. Clasing, Jr. *Modern Portfolio Theory*, 2d ed. (Orinda, Calif.: Andrew Rudd, 1988).

Rudd, Andrew, and Barr Rosenberg. "The 'Market Model' in Investment Management." *Journal of Finance*, vol. 35, no. 2, 1980, pp. 597–607.

Shanken, J. "The Arbitrage Pricing Theory: Is It Testable?" *Journal of Finance,* vol. 37, no. 5, 1982, pp. 1129–1140.

———. "Multi-Beta CAPM or Equilibrium APT? A Reply to Dybvig and Ross." *Journal of Finance,* vol. 40, no. 4, 1985, pp. 1189–1196.

———. "The Current State of the Arbitrage Pricing Theory." *Journal of Finance,* vol. 47, no. 4, 1992, pp. 1569–1574.

Sharpe, William F. "Factor Models, CAPMs, and the APT." *Journal of Portfolio Management,* vol. 11, no. 1, 1984, pp. 21–25.

Sharpe, William F. "The Capital Asset Pricing Model: A 'Multi-Beta' Interpretation." In *Financial Decision Making under Uncertainty,* edited by Haim Levy and Marshall Sarant (New York: Academic Press, 1977).

Sharpe, William F., and Gordon J. Alexander. *Investments* (Englewood Cliffs, N.J.: Prentice-Hall, 1990).

TECHNICAL APPENDIX

This appendix contains

- A description of factor models of stock return
- A derivation of the APT in terms of factor models

Factor Models

A factor model represents excess returns as

$$\mathbf{r} = \mathbf{X} \cdot \mathbf{b} + \mathbf{u} \qquad (7A.1)$$

where $\mathbf{X}$ is the N by K matrix of stock exposures to the factors, $\mathbf{b}$ is the vector of K factor returns, and $\mathbf{u}$ is the specific return vector.

For any portfolio P with holdings $\mathbf{h}_p$ of the risky assets, the portfolio's *factor exposures* are

$$\mathbf{x}_p = \mathbf{X}^T \cdot \mathbf{h}_p \qquad (7A.2)$$

Recall that portfolio C is the fully invested portfolio with minimum variance and that portfolio Q is the fully invested portfolio that has the highest ratio of expected excess return to risk. In the technical appendix to Chap. 2, we established that the expected excess return on each asset is proportional to that asset's beta with respect to portfolio Q.

We assume that

- $f_C > 0$, and thus portfolio Q exists and $f_Q > 0$.

- The specific returns **u** are uncorrelated with the factor returns **b**.
- The factor exposures **X** are known with certainty at the start of the period.

With these assumptions, the N by N asset covariance matrix is

$$\mathbf{V} = \mathbf{X} \cdot \mathbf{F} \cdot \mathbf{X}^T + \mathbf{\Delta} \qquad (7A.3)$$

where **F** is the K by K covariance of the factors and **Δ** is an N by N matrix that gives the covariance of the specific returns. We usually assume that **Δ** is a diagonal matrix, although that is not necessary.

We refer to the *factor model* as (**X**, **F**, **Δ**). We say that a factor model *explains* expected excess returns **f** if we can express the vector of expected excess returns **f** as a linear combination of the factor exposures **X**. The model (**X**, **F**, **Δ**) explains expected excess returns if there is a K-element vector of factor forecasts **m** such that

$$\mathbf{f} = \mathbf{X} \cdot \mathbf{m} \qquad (7A.4)$$

Equation (7A.4) gives us an expression for **f**. In the appendix to Chap. 2, we derived another expression for **f** involving portfolio Q. Let's look for the link between these two expressions.

The N-element vector of stock covariances with respect to portfolio Q is

$$\mathbf{V} \cdot \mathbf{h}_Q = (\mathbf{X} \cdot \mathbf{F} \cdot \mathbf{X}^T + \mathbf{\Delta}) \cdot \mathbf{h}_Q \qquad (7A.5)$$

From Eq. (2A.36) (Proposition 3 in the technical appendix to Chap. 2), we know that the expected excess returns are

$$\mathbf{f} = f_Q \cdot \frac{\mathbf{V} \cdot \mathbf{h}_Q}{\sigma_Q^2} = \kappa_Q \cdot (\mathbf{X} \cdot \mathbf{F} \cdot \mathbf{X}^T + \mathbf{\Delta}) \cdot \mathbf{h}_Q \qquad (7A.6)$$

where

$$\kappa_Q = \frac{f_Q}{\sigma_Q^2} \qquad (7A.7)$$

Compare Eqs. (7A.4) and (7A.6). We are getting perilously close to the APT result. As an initial stab, we could write $\mathbf{m}^* = \kappa_Q \cdot \mathbf{F} \cdot \mathbf{X}^T \cdot \mathbf{h}_Q$. Then

$$\mathbf{f} = \mathbf{X} \cdot \mathbf{m}^* + \kappa_Q \cdot \mathbf{\Delta} \cdot \mathbf{h}_Q \qquad (7A.8)$$

One alternative is to ignore the second term and live with

a little imperfection. To attain perfection, however, we need one additional assumption. We show below that this assumption works *and* that we need to make it; i.e., this assumption is both necessary and sufficient. First a definition: A portfolio P is *diversified with respect to the factor model* (**X**, **F**, **Δ**) if portfolio P has minimal risk among all portfolios that have the same factor exposures as portfolio P; i.e., of all portfolios **h** with $\mathbf{X}^T \cdot \mathbf{h}_P = \mathbf{x}_P$, portfolio P has the least risk.

Our assumption is that portfolio Q is diversified with respect to the factor model (**X**, **F**, **Δ**).

Proposition 1 (APT)

The factor model (**X**, **F**, **Δ**) explains expected excess returns *if and only if* portfolio Q is diversified with respect to (**X**, **F**, **Δ**).

Proof Suppose first that portfolio Q is diversified with respect to (**X**, **F**, **Δ**). Now we can find the portfolio with exposures $\mathbf{x}_Q$ that has minimal risk by solving

$$\text{Minimize } \frac{(\mathbf{h}^T \cdot \mathbf{V} \cdot \mathbf{h})}{2}, \text{ subject to } \mathbf{X}^T \cdot \mathbf{h} = \mathbf{x}_Q \qquad (7A.9)$$

The first-order conditions for this problem are satisfied by the optimal solution **h*** and a K-element vector of Lagrange multipliers **π** that satisfy

$$\mathbf{V} \cdot \mathbf{h}^* - \mathbf{X} \cdot \boldsymbol{\pi} = 0 \qquad (7A.10)$$

$$\mathbf{X}^T \cdot \mathbf{h} = \mathbf{x}_Q \qquad (7A.11)$$

Since portfolio Q is diversified with respect to (**X**, **F**, **Δ**), then $\mathbf{h}_Q = \mathbf{h}^*$ is the optimal solution. Therefore

$$\mathbf{V} \cdot \mathbf{h}_Q = \mathbf{X} \cdot \boldsymbol{\pi} \qquad (7A.12)$$

Combining Eq. (7A.12) with Eqs. (7A.6), (7A.7), and (7A.4) leads to

$$\mathbf{m} = \kappa_Q \cdot \boldsymbol{\pi} \qquad (7A.13)$$

and the factor model (**X**, **F**, **Δ**) explains the expected excess returns.

For the converse, suppose that the factor model (**X**, **F**, **Δ**) explains the expected excess returns and that portfolio Q is *not* diversified with respect to (**X**, **F**, **Δ**). Then there exists a portfolio P with the same exposures as portfolio Q, i.e., $x_P = \mathbf{X}^T \cdot \mathbf{h}_P = x_Q$, and less risk than portfolio Q, i.e., $\sigma_P^2 < \sigma_Q^2$. However, we have $f_P = f_Q$, since the factor exposures determine the expected returns, and portfolios P and Q have identical factor exposures. So $\dfrac{f_P}{\sigma_P} > \dfrac{f_Q}{\sigma_Q}$.

Portfolio P cannot be all cash, since the expected excess return on cash is zero. Therefore portfolio P is a mixture of cash and a nonzero fraction of some fully invested portfolio P^*. It must be that $f_P/\sigma_P = f_{P^*}/\sigma_{P^*}$. Recall, however, that portfolio Q is the fully invested portfolio with the largest possible ratio of expected excess return to risk. This contradiction establishes the point: Portfolio Q must be diversified with respect to $(\mathbf{X}, \mathbf{F}, \boldsymbol{\Delta})$.

Exercises

1. A factor model contains an *intercept* if some weighted combination of the columns of $\mathbf{X}$ is equal to a vector of 1s. This will, of course, be true if one of the columns of $\mathbf{X}$ is a column of 1s. It will also be true if $\mathbf{X}$ contains a classification of stocks by industry or economic sector. The technical requirement for a model to have an intercept is that there exists a K-element vector $\mathbf{g}$ such that $\mathbf{e} = \mathbf{X} \cdot \mathbf{g}$. Assume that the model contains an intercept, and demonstrate that we can then determine the fraction of the portfolio invested in risky assets by looking only at the portfolio's factor exposures.

2. Show that a model that does not contain an intercept is indeed strange. In particular, show there will be a fully invested portfolio with zero exposures to all the factors—a portfolio P with $\mathbf{h}_P^T \cdot \mathbf{e} = 1$ (fully invested) and $x_P = \mathbf{X}^T \cdot \mathbf{h}_P = 0$ (zero exposure to each factor).

Applications Exercises

1. What is the percentage of unexplained variance in the CAPMMI portfolio? Does this portfolio qualify as highly diversified? How much would it be possible to lower the risk of the CAPMMI in a portfolio with identical factor exposures?

2. Assume an excess return forecast of 5 percent per year for a value factor, excess return of −1 percent per year for a size factor, and excess return forecasts of zero for all other factors. Using the CAPMMI as a benchmark, what MMI asset has the highest alpha? What is its value?

CHAPTER 8

Valuation in Theory

INTRODUCTION

Valuation is the central concept of active management. Active managers must believe that their assessment of value is better than the market or consensus assessment. In this chapter, we describe a basic theory of valuation. The following chapters will illustrate practical valuation procedures and any links that these might have with theory.

This chapter contains three important messages:

- The modern theory of valuation connects stock values to risk-adjusted expected cash flows.
- The theory is closely related to the theory of option pricing, and is consistent with the CAPM and the APT.
- Valuation (and misvaluation) is connected to expected returns.

THE MODERN THEORY OF VALUATION

The modern theory of asset valuation is general, esoteric, and worth studying. The theory provides a framework for judging more ad hoc and practical valuation methods.

We start with the important premise that a stock's value is derived from the cash flows an investor can obtain from owning the stock. These cash flows arise as dividends or as the future value

of the stock realized by selling the stock.[1] The key to the theory
will be discounting these uncertain cash flows back to the present.
This is the same task required for option pricing, and readers familiar with option pricing theory will recognize the similarities (which
we will make more explicit in the technical appendix).

Certain Cash Flows

In the simplest case, the investor will obtain a certain cash flow
$cf(t)$ at future time t. To make it even simpler, we assume a constant
risk-free interest rate that applies over all maturities. Let i_F be the
(annual) return on a risk-free investment. When interest rates are
6 percent annually, then $i_F = 0.06$. The present value of a promised
$1.00 in 1 year is $1/(1 + i_F)$. The promise of $1.00 in t years is $1/(1 + i_F)^t$ and the present value of $cf(t)$ dollars in t years is

$$p = \frac{cf(t)}{(1 + i_F)^t} \tag{8.1}$$

Equation (8.1) is the basis for valuing fixed-income instruments
with certain cash flows. Given a stream of cash flows, e.g., $cf(1)$ in
1 year, $cf(2)$ in 2 years, etc., the valuation formula becomes

$$p = \sum_{t=1}^{T} \frac{cf(t)}{(1 + i_F)^t} \tag{8.2}$$

For example, if we have a promise of 6 dollars in 1 year and 10
dollars in 3 years and $i_F = 0.06$, we find

$$p = \frac{6}{1.06} + \frac{10}{(1.06)^3} = 14.06 \tag{8.3}$$

Uncertain Cash Flows

Equation (8.1) fails when the cash flows are uncertain. Uncertainty
means that there is more than one possible value for the future

---

[1] If the stock is fairly valued, it doesn't matter whether we consider a sale in five years or
six months. In practice, it may matter, since the key to using the valuation scheme
is to find some future time when the stock will be fairly valued, and work
backward toward a current fair value.

cash flows. We need a way to describe those possibilities. We do this by listing the possible outcomes at time t and determining the probability of each outcome. This is easier said than done in practice, but remember, this is the theory chapter. Let's push on bravely and ask what we would do next if we could define both the possible future cash flows and the probability of each outcome.

We can index the possible outcomes at time t by s (for states). Let $\pi(t,s)$ be the probability of outcome s at time t, and let $cf(t,s)$ be the uncertain cash flow at time t in state s. The probabilities are nonnegative and sum to 1; i.e., $\sum_s \pi(t,s) = 1$ for every t.

As an example, consider a 1-month period, $t = 1/12$, and a stock currently valued at 50. In 1 month its value (sale price plus any dividend paid in the month) will be either $cf(t,1) = 49$ or $cf(t,2) = 53$. The outcomes are equally likely; $\pi(t,1) = \pi(t,2) = 0.5$. The risk-free interest over the year is 6 percent. The expected cash flow is 51, and the standard deviation is 2.

Given this information, how should we value these uncertain cash flows? The simplest and most tempting way is to generalize Eq. (8.1), replacing certain cash flows with *expected* cash flows:

$$E\{cf(t)\} = \sum_s \pi(t,s) \cdot cf(t,s) \qquad (8.4)$$

Unfortunately, this doesn't work. Expectations generally overestimate the stock's value. When the cash flows are uncertain, we usually find

$$p < \frac{E\{cf(t)\}}{(1 + i_F)^t} = \frac{\sum_s \pi(t,s) \cdot cf(t,s)}{(1 + i_F)^t} \qquad (8.5)$$

In our example, the discounted expected cash flows lead to a value of 50.75, but the current price is 50. The problem is that expected cash flows do not take account of risk. An instrument with an expected but uncertain cash flow of 51 should not have the same price as an instrument with a certain cash flow of 51. The two have the same expected cash flows, but one is certain and one is not. We must dig deeper to find a valuation formula.

THE VALUATION FORMULA

Before we present a valuation formula, we can list the properties that a reasonable formula should display. There are several.[2]

1. If all future cash flows are nonnegative, the value is nonnegative.
2. If we double (or triple or halve) the cash flows, the value should change in the same proportion.
3. If we add two sets of cash flows, the value of the total cash flow should be the sum of the values of each separately.
4. The valuation formula should reduce to Eq. (8.1) in the case of certain cash flows.
5. The formula should agree with the market value of securities.

Property 1 is certainly sensible; if we can't lose and we might gain, the opportunity should be worth something. Property 2 says that the price of six shares is six times the price of one share. Property 3 combined with property 2 says that our valuation rule works for portfolios. We can value each stock in the portfolio and know that the portfolio's value is simply the weighted sum of the values for each stock separately. Property 3 not only lets us combine stocks into portfolios, but also allows us to value each cash flow in a stream of cash flows separately. Thus we could value next quarter's dividend separately from the dividend the quarter following. The cash flows for the 3-month and 6-month dividends may be highly correlated, but that doesn't matter; the valuation formula should still get each right.

Property 3 also lets us see the flexibility of this valuation notion. Suppose we have a stock that pays a quarterly dividend and the next dividend occurs in 3 months. Rather than consider an indefinite sequence of dividends, we can always consider the stock as the promise of the next four dividends plus the price of

---

[2]We omit from this list the technical stipulation that if $\pi(t,s^*) = 0$ for some state s^* and $cf(t,s^*) = 1$, but $cf(t,s) = 0$ for $s \neq s^*$, the value of the cash flow must be zero. We attach no value to promised cash flows for outcomes that can't happen, e.g., a put option with an exercise price of -10.

the stock in 1 year. The price in 1 year is the final cash flow that we receive. The 1 year was arbitrary. We could have used the price in 1 month, before the first dividend, or in 2 years, after eight dividends. The valuation formula should give us the same answer no matter how we represent the cash flows!

Property 4 says that we can value a certain cash flow of any maturity. This is clearly a prerequisite to valuing uncertain cash flows of any maturity. Equation (8.1) is based on a constant interest rate. We can easily generalize it to allow for risk-free rates that depend on maturity.

Property 5 says that the valuation formula works. This is where the active manager and the economist part company. The active manager is interested in using the concept to find stocks for which the formula is *not* working. In practice, property 5 can be used to say that the valuation is correct on average or within certain groups. The active manager is free to look within those groups for under- and overpriced stocks.

We know the properties that we want. How do we get them?

RISK-ADJUSTED EXPECTATIONS

There are two ways to modify the right side of Eq. (8.5) in order to get a straightforward relationship like Eq. (8.1). One possibility is to introduce a risk-adjusted interest rate. Then we could discount the expected cash flows at the higher (one presumes) rate of interest and therefore lower their value. This seems like a good idea, and, as we'll see in the next chapter, it is used in practice. It is just a straightforward extension of the CAPM and the APT, which state

$$E\left\{\frac{\text{cf}(t)}{p}\right\} = 1 + i_F + \beta \cdot f_Q \qquad (8.6)$$

where cf(t) is the stock value in 1 year, and so

$$p = \frac{E\{\text{cf}(t)\}}{1 + i_F + \beta \cdot f_Q} \qquad (8.7)$$

Here the risk-adjusted interest rate is based on the asset's beta and the expected excess return to portfolio Q. The term $i_F + \beta \cdot f_Q$ is sometimes called the equity cost of capital.

While this risk-adjusted interest rate is simple and easy to understand, this valuation approach can break down. In particular, imagine a coin-toss security worth $100,000 (if heads) or $-$100,000 (if tails). The expected cash flow is zero. Any attempt to value this by adjusting the discount rate will still get zero.[3]

The modern theory of valuation employs the alternative modification of Eq. (8.5): risk-adjusted expectations $E^*\{cf(t)\}$. As we will see, this approach will go far beyond Eq. (8.7) in providing insight into valuation and unifying concepts from the CAPM, the APT, and options pricing. By introducing a unique risk-adjusted probability distribution, we will be able to consistently discount all adjusted expected cash flows at the same risk-free rate.

We obtain the risk adjustment by introducing value multiples[4] $v(t,s)$, so the modified expectation can be written as

$$E^*\{cf(t)\} = E\{v(t) \cdot cf(t)\} = \sum_s \pi(t,s) \cdot v(t,s) \cdot cf(t,s) \qquad (8.8)$$

where $v(t,s)$ is

- Positive
- With expected value 1
- A function of the return to portfolio Q and proportional to the total return on a portfolio S, the portfolio with minimum second moment of total return (see appendix)

In the technical appendix, we will show that these valuation multiples exist as long as there are no arbitrage opportunities in the valuation scheme. Arbitrage can occur if we can start with a nonpositive amount of money at $t = 0$ and have all outcomes nonnegative with at least one outcome positive.

---

[3]In Eq. (8.7), this situation leads to both the numerator and the denominator approaching zero. See Problem 3 for more details.

[4]Technically, $v(t,s)$ is a Radon-Nikodyn derivative, and $\pi^*(t,s) = v(t,s) \cdot \pi(t,s)$ is a Martingale equivalent measure.

With this definition of the risk-adjusted expectations, we obtain our valuation formula:

$$p = \sum_{t=1}^{T} \frac{E^* \{cf(t)\}}{(1 + i_F)^t} \tag{8.9}$$

All modern valuation theories, including option theory, the CAPM, and the APT, use valuation formulas that have the form of Eq. (8.9). The technical appendix will discuss this in more detail.

Let's check that Eq. (8.9) has the required valuation properties. Since $v(t)$ is positive, property 1 will hold: Nonnegative cash flows will lead to nonnegative risk-adjusted expectations $E^*\{cf(t)\}$ and, by Eq. (8.9), nonnegative values.

The valuation rule is linear, so properties 2 and 3 have to hold. That means that Eq. (8.9) has the portfolio property. If stock n has uncertain cash flows $cf_n(t)$, and the weight of stock n in portfolio P is h_{P_n}, then the portfolio's cash flow is $cf_P(t) = \sum_n h_{P_n} \cdot cf_n(t)$, and the value of portfolio P is

$$p = \sum_{t} \frac{E^* \{cf_P(t)\}}{(1 + i_F)^t} = \sum_{n} h_{P_n} \cdot p_n \tag{8.10}$$

where

$$p_n = \sum_{t} \frac{E^* \{cf_n(t)\}}{(1 + i_F)^t} \tag{8.11}$$

is the value of stock n valued in isolation.

If the cash flow $cf(t)$ is certain, then

$$E^*\{cf_n(t)\} = E\{v(t) \cdot cf(t)\} = cf(t) \cdot E\{v(t)\} = cf(t) \tag{8.12}$$

The first equality follows from the definition of E^*, the second equality because $cf(t)$ is certain, and the third equality because $v(t)$ has expected value of 1. This means that property 4 is true: Eq. (8.9) will agree with Eq. (8.1) when the cash flows are certain.

We hope that property 5 holds, at least on average. If property 5 held for all stocks, the active manager would not find any opportunities in the marketplace.

INTERPRETATIONS

The value multiples $v(t,s)$ help define a new set of probabilities $\pi^*(t,s) = \pi(t,s) \cdot v(t,s)$. The risk-adjusted expectation E^* uses the modified set of probabilities.

In the simple example used previously, the outcomes $cf(t,1) = 49$ and $cf(t,2) = 53$ are equally likely, $\pi(t,1) = \pi(t,2) = 0.5$, and the risk-free interest over the year is 6 percent, $i_F = 0.06$. We find (see the appendix) that $v(t,1) = 1.38$ and $v(t,2) = 0.62$. This is consistent with properties 1 through 5. The altered probabilities are $\pi^*(t,1) = 0.5 \cdot 1.38 = 0.69$ and $\pi^*(t,2) = 0.5 \cdot 0.62 = 0.31$. The valuation for the risky stock works out correctly:

$$50 = \frac{(0.69 \cdot 49 + 0.31 \cdot 53)}{(1.06)^{1/12}} \tag{8.13}$$

The Role of Covariance

The definition of covariance and the fact that $E\{v(t)\} = 1$, can be used to link the true and risk-adjusted expectations of $cf(t)$:

$$E^*\{cf(t)\} = Cov\{cf(t),v(t)\} + E\{cf(t)\} \tag{8.14}$$

Equations (8.5) and (8.9) imply that the covariance term will, in general, be negative; in our example, we have $E^*\{cf(t)\} = 50.24$ and $E\{cf(t)\} = 51$, and so the covariance term is -0.76. This is the explicit penalty for the risk. Its present value is -0.756.

An alternative interpretation of the valuation formula is that the value multiples modify the cash flows. The value multiples $v(t,s)$ change the cash flows by amplifying some, if $v(t,s) > 1$, and reducing others, if $v(t,s) < 1$. Since the value multiples have expected value equal to 1, they are on average unbiased. For our example, the rescaled cash flows are $67.62 = 1.38 \cdot 49$ and $32.86 = 0.62 \cdot 53$.

Suppose that $cf_M(t)$ is proportional to the total return on the market portfolio. Then, the negative covariance indicates that $v(t,s)$ will tend to be less than 1 when the market is doing better than its average (good times) and $v(t,s)$ will tend to be larger than 1.0 when the market is below its average. The expectations E^* makes the risk adjustment by placing a lower value on good-time cash flows as compared to bad-time cash flows. There is no great surprise here. This means that the marginal amount of cash flow is worth more when cash flow in general is scarce.

MARKET-DEPENDENT VALUATION

According to the modern theory of valuation, the key elements of Eq. (8.9), both the risk-free rate of interest and the value multipliers $v(t,s)$, are market-dependent and not stock-dependent. The only stock information needed is the potential cash flows $cf(t,s)$. We use the same $v(t,s)$ and the same i_F for all instruments: for IBM stock, for GM puts, or for the S&P 500 portfolio. This critical property arises in all modern asset valuation theories, including the CAPM and the APT, which assert that only systematic risks are priced.

The APT frames this issue in the context of arbitrage-free pricing: that assets with identical exposures to nondiversifiable risks should have identical returns. This notion of arbitrage-free pricing is critical to proving that the value multiples cannot depend on individual stock returns, but only on portfolio Q returns.

We have discovered a simple formula for the value of a stock providing a sequence of uncertain cash flows. The formula uses adjusted expectations of the cash flows and discounts those adjusted expectations at market rates of interest to obtain a present value for the stock. In some cases, such as option valuation and variants of the CAPM, explicit formulas allow us to calculate the modified cash flows. In other cases, such as the APT, these modified expectations exist, although we don't have specific information for calculating them.[5] The appendix includes examples of these applications.

VALUE AND EXPECTED RETURN

We can now link formulas for expected return, i.e., the CAPM and the APT, and the valuation formula just described. Consider a stock currently priced at $p(0)$, paying a dividend d at the end of 1 year, and with an uncertain price $p(1)$ at the end of the year. Assume

---

[5]If we knew the true APT factors, so that we could calculate portfolio Q or portfolio S, then we could calculate the modified cash flows.

that the stock is fairly valued now and will be fairly valued at the end of the year. If we sell the stock at the end of the year, the cash flow will be the dividend plus the sale price: cf(1) = d + $p(1)$. The valuation formula over one period is

$$p(0) = \frac{E^* \{d + p(1)\}}{(1 + i_F)} = \frac{E\{v(1) \cdot [d \cdot p(1)]\}}{(1 + i_F)} \qquad (8.15)$$

If $p(0) \neq 0$, then we can convert Eq. (8.15) to an expected return equation. Define total return $R = [d + p(1)]/p(0)$. Divide Eq. (8.15) by $p(0)$, and multiply by $1 + i_F$. Then recall that $E\{v(1)\} = 1$. The net result is

$$E\{R\} = (1 + i_F) - \text{Cov}\{v,R\} \qquad (8.16)$$

and

$$E^* \{R\} = (1 + i_F) = E\{v \cdot R\} \qquad (8.17)$$

Equation (8.16) says that the expected excess return on all stocks is determined by their covariance with v. This result is suspiciously close to the CAPM and the APT results, that the expected excess return on every stock is determined by its covariance with portfolio Q (which for the CAPM is the market). The technical appendix will show, in fact, that v is a function of the return to portfolio Q and proportional to the return to a portfolio S, which is a combination of the risk-free asset and portfolio Q. So we will relate Eq. (8.16) to the CAPM and the APT. And, not only can we derive Eq. (8.16) from Eq. (8.15), we can also derive Eq. (8.15) from Eq. (8.16). Our previously derived expected return formulas imply valuation as in Eq. (8.15).

Equation (8.17) also demonstrates that under the modified probabilities, the expected return on the risky investment is equal to the return on the risk-free investment. In fact, under the modified expectations, all stocks have (modified) expected returns equal to the risk-free return.

What if the market price and the model price don't agree? Suppose we start with an asset that has a market value $p(0,\text{mkt})$ that is not equal to zero and is not properly valued:

$$p(0,\text{mkt}) \neq \frac{E^* \{cf(1)\}}{1 + i_F} = p(0,\text{mdl}) \qquad (8.18)$$

Define κ and γ such that

$$\kappa = \frac{p(0,\text{mdl}) - p(0,\text{mkt})}{p(0,\text{mkt})} \qquad (8.19)$$

and

$$\gamma \cdot \kappa = \frac{p(1,\text{mdl}) - p(1,\text{mkt})}{p(1,\text{mkt}) + d} \qquad (8.20)$$

The parameter κ measures the extent of misvaluation of the stock; it is the percentage difference between the fitted and market prices at time 0. The parameter γ measures the persistence of the misvaluation: how long it will take for the market to learn what we know. Presumably $0 \leq \gamma \leq 1$. If this is a "slow idea," then γ will be close to 1.0; much of the mispricing will remain. If this is a "fast idea," then γ will be close to 0. We can think of $-0.69/\ln\{\gamma\}$ as the half-life of the misvaluation, the number of years it will take for half the misvaluation to disappear.

Equations (8.16), (8.19), and (8.20) yield[6]

$$E\{R\} = 1 + i_F - \text{Cov}\{v,R\} + \alpha \qquad (8.21)$$

where α is

$$\alpha = (1 + i_F) \cdot \left[\frac{\kappa \cdot (1 - \gamma)}{1 + \kappa \cdot \gamma} \right] \qquad (8.22)$$

Equation (8.22) breaks the expected return into what we would expect if the stock were fairly valued and a second term that corrects for the market's incorrect valuation of the stock. Notice that $\alpha = 0$ if either $\kappa = 0$ or $\gamma = 1$; it is no good if the world never learns that this stock is improperly valued. Also, if $\gamma = 0$, then $\alpha = (1 + i_F) \cdot \kappa$; we realize the full benefit, plus interest, over the period.

Table 8.1 shows the alphas we get for different levels of κ and γ. It assumes a 6 percent annual interest rate.

---

[6] Define R^* as the return to the fairly priced asset, and show that R is proportional to R^*. Equation (8.21) then follows directly from Eq. (8.16).

T A B L E 8.1

	γ				
κ	0.0	0.2	0.4	0.6	0.8
1%	1.06%	0.85%	0.63%	0.42%	0.21%
5%	5.30%	4.20%	3.12%	2.06%	1.02%
10%	10.60%	8.31%	6.12%	4.00%	1.96%
25%	26.50%	20.19%	14.45%	9.22%	4.42%
50%	53.00%	38.55%	26.50%	16.31%	7.57%

SUMMARY

The modern theory of valuation prices uncertain future cash flows by risk-adjusting the expected cash flows and discounting them to the present using the risk-free rate. This theory is consistent with the CAPM and APT models, which forecast expected returns; and in fact the risk-adjusting procedure is related to portfolio Q.

If the market doesn't currently price the asset fairly, then the asset's expected return comprises two components: the return expected if the asset were fairly priced, and a correction term based on the market price's approaching fair value.

PROBLEMS

1. In the simple stock example described in the text, value a European call option on the stock with a strike price of 50, maturing at the end of the 1-month period. The option cash flows at the end of the period are $Max\{0,p(t,s) - 50\}$, where $p(t,s)$ is the stock price at time t in state s.

2. Compare Eq. (8.16) to the CAPM result for expected returns, to relate v to r_Q. Impose the requirement that $E\{v\} = 1$ to determine v exactly as a function of r_Q.

3. Using the simple stock example in the text, price an instrument which pays $1 in state 1 [$cf(t,1) = 1$] and $-1 in state 2 [$cf(t,2) = -1$]. What is the expected return to

this asset? What is its beta with respect to the stock? How does this relate to the breakdown of Eq. (8.7)?

4. You believe that stock X is 25 percent undervalued, and that it will take 3.1 years for half of this misvaluation to disappear. What is your forecast for the alpha of stock X over the next year?

REFERENCES

Arrow, Kenneth J. *Essays in the Theory of Risk-Bearing* (Chicago: Markham Publishing Company, 1971).

Bar-Yosef, Sasson, and Hayne Leland. Risk Adjusted Discounting. University of California, Berkeley Research Program in Finance working paper #134, December 1982.

Black, Fischer, and Myron Scholes. "The Pricing of Options and Corporate Liabilities." *Journal of Political Economy*, vol. 81, no. 3, 1973, pp. 637–654.

Chamberlain, Gary, and M. Rothschild. "Arbitrage, Factor Structure and Mean-Variance Analysis on Large Asset Markets." *Econometrica*, vol 51, no. 5, 1983, pp. 1281–1304.

Cox, John C., and Mark Rubinstein. *Options Markets* (Englewood Cliffs, N.J.: Prentice-Hall, 1985).

Debreu, Gerard. *Theory of Value* (New York: John Wiley & Sons, 1959).

Garman, Mark B. "A General Theory of Asset Valuation under Diffusion State Processes." University of California, Berkeley Research Program in Finance working paper #50, 1976.

Garman, Mark B. "Towards a Semigroup Pricing Theory." *Journal of Finance*, vol. 40, no. 3, 1985, pp. 847–861.

Grinold, Richard C. "The Valuation of Dependent Securities in a Diffusion Process," University of California, Berkeley Research Program in Finance working paper #59, April 1977.

———. "Market Value Maximization and Markov Dynamic Programming." *Management Science*, vol. 29 no. 5, 1983, pp. 583–594.

———. "Ex-Ante Characterization of an Efficient Portfolio." University of California, Berkeley Research Program in Finance working paper #59, September 1987.

Harrison, Michael J., and David M. Kreps. "Martingales and Arbitrage in Multiperiod Securities Markets." *Journal of Economic Theory*, vol 20, 1979, pp. 381–408.

Hull, John. *Options, Futures, and Other Derivative Securities* (Englewood Cliffs, N.J.: Prentice-Hall, 1989).

Ohlson, James A. "A Synthesis of Security Valuation Theory and the Role of Dividends, Cash Flows, and Earnings." Columbia University working paper, April 1989.

Ross, Stephen. "Return, Risk, and Arbitrage." In *Risk and Return in Finance*, edited by I. Friend and J. Bicksler (Cambridge, Mass.: Ballinger, 1976).

Rubinstein, Mark. "The Valuation of Uncertain Income Streams and the Pricing of Options." *Bell Journal of Economics*, vol 7, 1976, pp. 407–425.

Sharpe, William F. "Capital Asset Prices: A Theory of Market Equilibrium under Conditions of Risk." *Journal of Finance*, vol. 19, no. 3, 1964, pp. 425–442.

Williams, John Burr. *The Theory of Investment Value* (Amsterdam: North-Holland Publishing Company, 1964).

Technical Appendix

This appendix derives some of the results used in the text. In particular,

- We derive the basic valuation result in the case of a finite number of outcomes.
- We illustrate the basic valuation result using option pricing.
- We apply the CAPM (or really mean/variance theory) to valuation.
- We introduce portfolio S as a more general portfolio approach to valuation.

Theory of Valuation

Consider a finite number of assets indexed by $n = 0, 1, \ldots, N$ over a finite number of periods T. Start at time $t = 0$, and observe the prices of the assets at times $t = 1, 2, \ldots, T$. The prices evolve along paths. The collection of paths determines the possible outcomes. At time $t = T$, we will know what path we have followed. At time $t = 0$, we know only the set of possible paths. At intermediate times, $0 < t < T$, we have partial knowledge of the eventual path we will follow.

Specifying the state of knowledge at each intermediate point in time determines the system. Knowledge is refined through time, as the collection of possible paths shrinks. At time t, we can be in one of $S(t)$ states, where a state indicates a collection of possible paths we might be following. As time moves on, this set of possible paths is reduced, until at time T we know what path we have been following. Figure 8A.1 illustrates a case in which there are 3 time periods and 11 possible paths.

We can make this more precise. At time $t \geq 1$ in state s, we will know the unique time $t - 1$ state that preceded state s; the

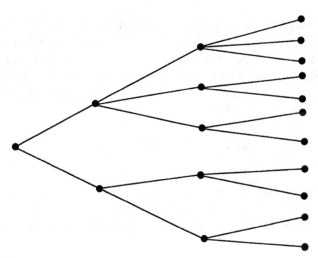

Figure 8A.1

predecessor is denoted $\phi(s,t)$. We will also know the possible *successors* to (s,t) at time $t + 1$. That collection of possible successors is denoted $\Omega(s,t)$. For every possible successor $z \in \Omega(s,t)$, we must have (s,t) as a predecessor; i.e., if $z \in \Omega(s,t)$, then $\phi(z,t+1) = s$. Similarly, if $z \notin \Omega(s,t)$, then $\phi(z,t+1) \neq s$. The set of all possible states at time t is denoted $\Phi(t)$.

We have probabilities $\pi\{s,t\}$ of being in state s at time t. We require only that these probabilities be positive.

Asset prices are given by $p_n(s,t)$, the price of asset n if state s occurs at time t. Since there is only one state at time $t = 0$, we have $p_n(1,0)$ as the initial prices.

One of the assets, call it asset $n = 0$, is risk-free. At time t in state s, a positive risk-free rate of interest $i_F(s,t)$ will prevail from time t until time $t + 1$. We start with $p_0(1,0) = 1$. At time $t + 1$, we have

$$p_0(z,t + 1) = [1 + i_F(s,t)] \cdot p_0(s,t) \qquad (8A.1)$$

for every $z \in \Omega(s,t)$. This assumption allows future rates of interest to be uncertain, although we will always know what rate of interest obtains over the next period.

To make life simple, we will ignore dividends. This means that we can assume either that all dividends are paid at time T or that $p_n(s,t)$ includes accumulated dividends.

An investment *strategy* is determined by the $N+1$–element vector $\mathbf{NS}(s,t) = \{NS_0(s,t), NS_1(s,t), \ldots, NS_N(s,t)\}$ for each state, time, and asset. It describes the number of shares of that asset in the portfolio at that state and held from time t to time $t + 1$. The value of the portfolio at time t in state s using strategy $\mathbf{NS}$ is denoted $W(s,t)$. The value $W(s,t)$ is

$$W(s,t) = \sum_{n=0}^{N} NS_n(s,t) \cdot p_n(s,t) \qquad (8A.2)$$

To conserve value, we impose a *self-financing* condition: The value of the portfolio at the end of period t-1 must exactly match the value of the portfolio at the start of period t. Mathematically, for $t \geq 1$ and $s \in \Phi(t)$,

$$W(s,t) = \sum_{n=0}^{N} NS_n(s,t) \cdot p_n(s,t) = \sum_{n=0}^{N} NS_n[\phi(s,t),t-1] \cdot p_n(s,t)$$

$$(8A.3)$$

The value of the portfolio before it is revised is the same as the value of the portfolio after it is revised.

An *arbitrage opportunity* is available if we can find an investment strategy that starts with a nonpositive amount of money, $W(1,0) \leq 0$; is guaranteed not to lose money, $W(s,t) \geq 0$ for $s \in \Phi(T)$; and makes money in at least one outcome, $\sum_{s \in \Phi(T)} W(s,T) > 0$.

Proposition 1

If there are no arbitrage opportunities, we can find positive valuation multiples $v(s,t) > 0$ such that for any asset $n = 0, 1, 2, \ldots, N$ and any time $t = 1, 2, \ldots, T$,

$$p_n(1,0) = \sum_{s \in \Phi(t)} \pi(s,t) \cdot v(s,t) \cdot \left\{ \frac{p_n(s,t)}{p_0(s,t)} \right\} \qquad (8A.4)$$

Proof   Consider the following linear program:

$$\text{Max}\left\{ \sum_{s \in \Phi(T)} W(s,T) \right\} \qquad (8A.5)$$

subject to

$$\sum_{n=0}^{N} \mathrm{NS}_n(1,0) \cdot p_n(1,0) \le 0 \qquad (8A.6)$$

$$-\sum_{n=0}^{N} \mathrm{NS}_n(s,t) \cdot p_n(s,t) + \sum_{n=0}^{N} \mathrm{NS}_n[\phi(s,t),t-1] \cdot p_n(s,t) = 0 \quad (8A.7)$$

for every $1 \le t < T$ and $s \in \Phi(t)$, and $\qquad (8A.8)$

$$-\sum_{n=0}^{N} \mathrm{NS}_n(s,T) \cdot p_n(s,T) + W(s,T) = 0$$

$$W(s,T) \ge 0 \qquad (8A.9)$$

for $s \in \Phi(T)$.

The linear program maximizes the sum of the end-period wealths across the possible states, subject to the constraints of initial wealth nonpositive [Eq. (8A.6)], self-financing strategies [Eq. (8A.7)], end-period wealth definition [Eq. (8A.8)], and nonnegative end-period wealth in each possible state [Eq. (8A.9)].

Given the constraints of initial wealth nonpositive and final wealth nonnegative, this linear program has a feasible solution: $\mathrm{NS}_n(s,t) = 0$ for all n, s, and t. By the no-arbitrage condition, this is an optimal solution as well; i.e., no solution will exhibit positive value for the objective.

The duality theorem of linear programming then implies that there will be an optimal solution $q(s,t)$ to the dual problem. The dual problem is

$$\mathrm{Min}\left\{\sum_{t=0}^{T} \sum_{s \in \Phi(t)} q(s,t)\right\} \qquad (8A.10)$$

subject to

$$-q(s,t) \cdot p_n(s,t) + \sum_{z \in \Omega(s,t)} q(z,t+1) \cdot p_n(z,t+1) = 0 \quad (8A.11)$$

for all $n = 0, \ldots, N$; $0 \leq t < T$; $s \in \Phi(t)$, and

$$q(1,0) \geq 0 \tag{8A.12}$$

$$q(s,T) \geq 1 \tag{8A.13}$$

for all $s \in \Phi(T)$.

Let $q(s,t)$ be an optimal dual solution. Equation (8A.13) guarantees that $q(s,T)$ are positive, and in fact greater than 1. We can further show, by successive applications of Eq. (8A.11), that each $q(s,t)$ is positive, using the risk-free asset:

$$q(s,t) = \{1 + i_F(s,t)\} \cdot \sum_{z \in \Omega(s,t)} q(z,t + 1) \tag{8A.14}$$

Define the conditional probabilities $\pi^*(z,t + 1 \mid s,t)$ by

$$\pi^*(z,t + 1 \mid s,t) = \begin{cases} \dfrac{1 + i_F(s,t)}{q(s,t)} \cdot q(z,t + 1) & \text{if } z \in \Omega(s,t) \\ 0 & \text{if } z \notin \Omega(s,t) \end{cases} \tag{8A.15}$$

This definition, along with Eq. (8A.11), leads to the intertemporal valuation formula

$$\left\{\frac{p_n(s,t)}{p_0(s,t)}\right\} = \sum_{z \in \Omega(s,t)} \pi^*(z,t + 1 \mid s,t) \cdot \left\{\frac{p_n(z,t + 1)}{p_0(z,t + 1)}\right\} \tag{8A.16}$$

This formula requires probabilities in states $(z,t+1)$ conditional on predecessor states (s,t). We would like to rewrite these in terms of unconditional probabilities, which we can derive starting with $\pi^*(1,0) = 1$. Then, using the laws of probability and the fact that state s at time $t+1$ has a unique predecessor $\phi(s,t+1)$ at time t,

$$\pi^*(s,t + 1) = \pi^*[s,t + 1 \mid \phi(s,t + 1),t] \cdot \pi^*[\phi(s,t + 1),t] \tag{8A.17}$$

The valuation multipliers are then

$$v(s,t) = \frac{\pi^*(s,t)}{\pi(s,t)} \tag{8A.18}$$

Repeated application of Eqs. (8A.16) through (8A.18) will demonstrate Proposition 1, Eq. (8A.4).[7,8]

Options Pricing

The most familiar context for the modern theory of valuation is in options pricing. Here is an example, which we also used in the main text of the chapter. Consider a single stock and a single 1-month period with two equally likely outcomes. The stock can go either up, the UP event, or down, the DN event. The risk-free asset increases in value from 1.00 to $R_F = (1 + i_F)^{1/12} = 1.00487$, corresponding to an annual interest rate of 6 percent. The stock's initial price is $p = 50$, and its final value is equally likely to be

---

[7]This proof demonstrates the existence but not the uniqueness of the valuation mulipliers. Only if we have a complete market will we have unique valuation multipliers. In a complete market, for any t, we will be able to devise a self-financing strategy that pays off 1 in state s and 0 in states $u \in S(t)$, $u \neq s$. Not only that, we will be able to determine the minimum initial input, $V^*(s,t)$, into a self-financing strategy necessary to produce $W(s,t) = 1$, $W(u,t) = 0$ for $u \in S(t)$, $u \neq s$. The term $V^*(s,t)$ will be positive because of the no-arbitrage condition, and

$$v(s,t) = \frac{\pi(s,t)}{V^*(s,t) \cdot p_0(s,t)}$$

[8]Proposition 1 required the absence of arbitrage opportunities. In practice, e.g., if we generate prices via Monte Carlo, the process may not be exactly arbitrage-free. However, we can trick the process into being arbitrage-free by assuming that the original probabilities are the Martingale probabilities and adjusting the original prices appropriately. To be exact, define $\delta_n(s,t)$ and adjusted prices $p_n^*(s,t)$:

$$\delta_n(s,t) = \left\{ \frac{\{1 + i_F(s,t)\} \cdot p_n^*(s,t)}{\sum_{z \in S(t)} \pi(z,t+1 \mid s,t) \cdot p_n(z,t+1)} \right\}$$

with

$$p_n^*(1,0) = p_n(1,0)$$

and

$$p_n^*(z,t+1) = \delta_n(s,t) \cdot p_n(z,t+1)$$

for $z \in \Omega(s,t)$.

With these adjusted prices, Eq. (8A.16) will hold using the original probabilities. Variations of this idea are used sometimes in options pricing theory.

$p_{UP} = 53$ or $p_{DN} = 49$. The outcomes UP and DN are equally likely: $\pi_{UP} = \pi_{DN} = 0.5$.

Now let's calculate the valuation measure in the UP and DN states. Following Eq. (8A.11), the dual linear program in this simple case is

$$q_0 - \{q_{UP} \cdot R_F + q_{DN} \cdot R_F\} = 0 \qquad (8A.19)$$

$$q_0 \cdot 50 - \{q_{UP} \cdot 53 + q_{DN} \cdot 49\} = 0 \qquad (8A.20)$$

with $q_0 \geq 0$ and $q_{UP}, q_{DN} \geq 1$. Solving for $v_{UP} = \left\{ \dfrac{q_{UP}}{q_0 \cdot \pi_{UP}} \right\}$, $v_{DN} = \left\{ \dfrac{q_{DN}}{q_0 \cdot \pi_{DN}} \right\}$, we find 0.62 and 1.38, respectively.

We can check that these valuation multiples correctly value both the risk-free asset and the stock. These multiples will be non-negative[9] as long as $\left\{ \dfrac{p_{UP}}{p} \right\} > \{1 + i_F\} > \left\{ \dfrac{p_{DN}}{p} \right\}$, and their expected value will always be 1.0.

Of course, options pricing theory was developed to price options, and given these valuation multiples, we can price any claim contingent on the stock price. For this simple case in particular, we can price options maturing at the end of the period, with payouts dependent on the ending stock value. The payout for a call option would have the form $\text{Max}[0, S(T) - K]$, where K is the strike price.

We can easily expand this framework to multiple periods. For a more substantial treatment, see the texts by Cox and Rubinstein and by Hull.

Connection with the CAPM and APT

The main body of the chapter discussed the connection between valuation and expected returns. We revisit that topic here. Let p_n be the initial value of stock n, d_n the dividends paid on the stock (at the end of the month), and p_n^* the final value. Let R_n, R_F, and R_Q be the total returns on the stock, the risk-free asset, and portfolio Q. The excess returns are r_n and r_Q. In the CAPM, portfolio Q is the market.

---

[9] If these conditions do not hold, then arbitrage opportunities exist.

Proposition 2

The valuation function v depends only on the return to portfolio Q, according to

$$v(s) = 1 - \kappa \cdot \{r_Q(s) - f_Q\} \tag{8A.21}$$

with

$$\kappa = \frac{f_Q}{\sigma_Q^2} \tag{8A.22}$$

Proof   Define the return on asset n with outcome s as

$$R_n(s) = \frac{p_n^*(s) + d_n(s)}{p_n} \tag{8A.23}$$

Since portfolio Q defines expected excess returns,

$$E\{R_n\} = R_F + \kappa \cdot \mathrm{Cov}\{r_n, r_Q\} \tag{8A.24}$$

The definition of covariance implies

$$\mathrm{Cov}\{r_n, r_Q\} = \mathrm{Cov}\{R_n, r_Q\} = E\{R_n \cdot (r_Q - E\{r_Q\})\} \tag{8A.25}$$

Now, Eq. (8A.25), in combination with Eqs. (8A.24) and (8A.21), leads to

$$p_n = \frac{E\{v(s) \cdot [p_n^*(s) + d_n(s)]\}}{1 + i_F} \tag{8A.26}$$

This is the desired result.

Notice that v depends only on portfolio Q's return. The expected value of v is 1 and, since $\kappa > 0$, v decreases as the market return increases. Reasonable estimates of κ are between 1.5 and 2.00; as an example, we'll choose 1.75. Hence v is negative if $r_Q > f_Q + 0.57$. If the expected annual excess return to the market was approximately 6 percent, this would be a 63 percent excess market return: more than a three standard deviation event. In fact, the largest two annual S&P 500 returns since 1926 have been a 54 percent return in 1933 and a 53 percent return in 1954.

Proposition 2 relates the valuation multipliers v to the excess return to portfolio Q. Alternatively, we can introduce a new portfolio, portfolio S, which also explains excess returns and whose total returns are directly proportional to the valuation multipliers. For the purpose of this technical appendix, portfolio S provides simply another view of excess returns and valuation. We introduce portfolio S because (although we will not make use of this property) it is also a more robust approach to excess returns and valuation than portfolio Q. We require very few assumptions to determine that portfolio S exists and explains excess returns. For example, while we require that the expected excess return to portfolio C be positive for the existence of portfolio Q, portfolio S exists and explains expected excess returns even without that assumption.

Portfolio S

We define a portfolio S as the portfolio containing both risky and riskless assets with the minimum second moment of total return. We will investigate the properties of portfolio S, including its relation to excess returns, portfolio Q, and the valuation multipliers.

The total return for any portfolio P is given by $R_P = 1 + i_F + r_P$. Portfolio S solves the problem

$$\text{Min}\{E\{R_P^2\}\} \tag{8A.27}$$

where portfolio P contains both risky and risk-free assets. The risk-free portfolio would give us second moment R_F^2. Portfolio S has even less.

Proposition 3[10]
For any portfolio P, we have

$$E\{r_P\} = \phi \cdot \text{Cov}\{r_P, r_S\} \tag{8A.28}$$

---

[10]This proposition is actually true much more generally. We can let R_S and R_P be the returns to strategies involving rebalancing, option replication, etc. Given a stochastic risk-free rate, and R_F the return to the strategy that rolls over the risk-free investment, we find

$$E\{R_P - R_F\} = R_F + \phi \cdot \text{Cov}\{R_P - R_F, R_S\}$$

where

$$\phi = \frac{-1}{E\{R_S\}}$$

as in the main text of the appendix.

where

$$\phi = \frac{-1}{E\{1 + i_F + r_S\}} = \frac{f_S}{\sigma_S^2} \qquad (8A.29)$$

Proof Consider a portfolio $P(w)$ with fraction $(1 - w)$ invested in portfolio S and fraction w invested in portfolio P. The total return on this mixture will be

$$R_P(w) = R_S + w \cdot \{R_P - R_S\} \qquad (8A.30)$$

Define $g_P(w)$ as the expected second moment of the return on the mixture:

$$g_P(w) = E\{R_P^2(w)\} = E\{R_S^2\} + 2 \cdot w \cdot E\{R_S \cdot (R_P \qquad (8A.31)$$
$$- R_S)\} + w^2 \cdot E\{(R_P - R_S)^2\}$$

Since R_S is the portfolio that has minimum second moment, the derivative of $g_P(w)$ at $w = 0$ must be zero. Hence

$$E\{R_S \cdot (R_P - R_S)\} = 0 \qquad (8A.32)$$

for any portfolio P. We can expand this to

$$Cov\{r_P, r_S\} + E\{R_P\} \cdot E\{R_S\} = E\{R_S^2\} \qquad (8A.33)$$

Equation (8A.33) holds for any portfolio P, including the risk-free portfolio F, and so

$$E\{R_F\} \cdot E\{R_S\} = E\{R_S^2\} \qquad (8A.34)$$

Combining Eqs. (8A.33) and (8A.34) leads to Proposition 3, Eq. (8A.28).

Proposition 3 demonstrated the connection between portfolio S and expected returns. We also know the connection between portfolio Q and expected returns. And so, there is a link between portfolio S and portfolio Q.

Proposition 4
If

- Portfolio S solves Eq. (8A.27)

- Portfolio Q is the fully invested portfolio with maximum Sharpe ratio[11]

then portfolio S is a mixture of portfolio F and portfolio Q:

$$R_S = R_F + w_Q \cdot \{R_Q - R_F\} \qquad (8A.35)$$

where

$$w_Q = \frac{-\text{SR}_Q \cdot \{1 + i_F\}}{\sigma_Q \cdot \{1 + \text{SR}_Q^2\}} \qquad (8A.36)$$

Proof   Given an arbitrary starting fully invested portfolio P, consider a portfolio $P(w)$ composed of a fraction w invested in portfolio P and a fraction $(1 - w)$ invested in portfolio F. Its total return is

$$R_P(w) = R_F + w \cdot \{R_P - R_F\} \qquad (8A.37)$$

Now choose w to minimize the expected second moment, $E\{R_P^2(w_P)\}$, of the return. The optimal w is

$$w_P = \frac{-\text{SR}_P \cdot \{1 + i_F\}}{\sigma_P \cdot \{1 + \text{SR}_P^2\}} \qquad (8A.38)$$

with associated optimal expected second moment

$$E\{R_P^2(w_P)\} = \frac{(1 + i_F)^2}{1 + \text{SR}_P^2} \qquad (8A.39)$$

As long as SR_P is not zero, we can do better than just the risk-free portfolio. In fact, the larger SR_P is in absolute value, the better we can do. We achieve the minimum second moment over all portfolios (risky plus risk-free) by choosing the fully invested portfolio P that maximizes SR_P^2: portfolio Q. This proves Proposition 4, Eq. (8A.35).

Our final task is to express the valuation multiples in terms of portfolio S.

---

[11]We are making the familiar assumption that portfolio C has positive expected excess return, and so portfolio Q—the fully invested portfolio that explains expected excess returns—exists.

Proposition 5
The valuation multiples are

$$v = \frac{R_S}{E\{R_S\}} \qquad (8A.40)$$

Proof Combining Proposition 3 [Eq. (8A.28)], which explains expected excess returns using portfolio S, and Proposition 2 [Eq. (8A.21)], which expresses the valuation multiples in terms of portfolio Q, we can derive

$$p_n = \frac{E\{(p_n^* + d_n) \cdot v\}}{R_F} \qquad (8A.41)$$

where

$$v = 1 - \phi \cdot (R_S - E\{R_S\}) \qquad (8A.42)$$

Since $\phi = -1/E\{R_S\}$, this simplifies to Proposition 5, Eq. (8A.40).

Exercises

1. Using the definitions from the technical appendix to Chap. 2, what is the characteristic associated with portfolio S?
2. Show that the portfolio S holdings in risky assets satisfy

$$\mathbf{V} \cdot \mathbf{h}_S = -E\{R_S\} \cdot \mathbf{f}$$

3. Show that portfolio S exists even if $f_C < 0$, and that if $f_C = 0$, then portfolio S will consist of 100 percent cash plus offsetting long and short positions in risky assets.
4. Prove the portfolio S analog of Proposition 1 in the technical appendix of Chap. 7, i.e., that the factor model $(\mathbf{X}, \mathbf{F}, \mathbf{\Delta})$ explains expected excess returns if and only if portfolio S is diversified with respect to $(\mathbf{X}, \mathbf{F}, \mathbf{\Delta})$.

Applications Exercises

1. If portfolio Q is the MMI and $\mu_Q = 6$ percent, what is portfolio S? Use Proposition 4 of the technical appendix, which expresses portfolio S in terms of portfolio Q.

2. Using the result from the first applications exercise, what is the valuation multiple in the state defined by $r_Q = 5$ percent? Use Proposition 5 of the technical appendix. If interest rates are 6 percent, what is the value of an option which pays $1 in 1 year only in the state defined by $r_Q = 5$ percent? Assume that the probability of that state occurring is 50 percent.

CHAPTER 9

Valuation in Practice

INTRODUCTION

The previous chapter investigated the theory of valuation. That theory has proved useful in valuing options, futures, and other derivative instruments, but has yet to be used for the valuation of equities. In this chapter, we will look at some of the quantitative methods that have been used for equity valuation. These will be ad hoc, although they will have some vague connection with theory. The reader should not be surprised that the chapter does not describe a "right" way to value stocks. We described the theoretically correct approach in the previous chapter. This chapter is evidence of our inability to make the theoretically correct scheme operational. We have to turn to more ad hoc schemes.

The reader should keep the humility principle in mind: The marketplace may be right and you may be wrong. The reader should also keep the fundamental law of active management in mind: You don't have to be right much more than 50 percent of the time to add value! With these modest goals in mind we shall commence.

Insights included in this chapter are:

- The basic theory of corporate finance provides ground rules for acceptable valuation models.
- The standard valuation model is the dividend discount model, which focuses on dividends, earnings, and growth. Dividend discount models are only as good as their growth forecasts.

- Comparative valuation models price attributes of a firm.
- Returns-based analysis focuses directly on the ultimate goal of valuation models: forecasting exceptional returns. Returns-based analysis is related to APT models.

The goal is to find assets that are unfairly valued by the market, hoping that the market will eventually correct itself. This requires some insight. Quantitative methods can help to focus that insight and use it efficiently, but they are not a substitute for insight.

CORPORATE FINANCE

The modern theory of corporate finance is based on the notion of market efficiency. Modigliani and Miller showed the power of market efficiency in their classic studies demonstrating that

- Dividend policy influences only the scheduling of cash flows received by the shareholder. It is a "pay you now or pay you later" arrangement. Dividend policy doesn't affect the total value of the payments.
- A firm's financing policy does not affect the total value of the firm. Financing policy will keep the total value of the firm's liabilities constant.

These ideas were extremely controversial at first, but they have stood up for decades and are at least partially responsible for the authors' Nobel prizes. Active managers with market inefficiency in their veins can read these two precepts as: "Dividend and financing policy aren't very important." Any valuation method that hinges on some magic associated with dividends or debt financing may be dangerous.

The economic value of a firm comes from its profitable activities. If the firm can transform inputs it buys for $1.00 into outputs it sells 3 months later for $1.45, then the firm can profit. If the firm can find additional projects that create value, then the firm can grow. This ability to generate profits and to make those profits grow is at the heart of attempts at valuing the firm. Much of the confusion about the Modigliani and Miller results arises from two issues: taxes and a failure to separate the operations of the firm from its financing activities.

Let's ignore taxes for the moment. The failure to separate operations from financial decisions is quite natural. A firm borrows because it has capital expenditures that are needed to support future growth. A firm increases its dividend because its operations have been successful and future success is anticipated. We want to separate the operational considerations (the new plant, the successful product, etc.) from the financial. The new plant could have been financed from either retained earnings (reduced dividends), sale of new equity, or issuance of new debt. The benefits of the successful product launch could be used to retire debt, kept as retained earnings, or distributed as dividends. With the aid of the Modigliani and Miller principles, we can consider the firm's equity value as stemming from two sources: operational value and financial value:

$$\text{Stock value} = \text{financial value} + \text{operational value} \quad (9.1)$$

In a simple context, the financial value is the difference between the firm's capital surplus and its debt. The capital surplus is any money left after we have paid dividends and interest (if any) and paid for new investments that are needed in order to grow or sustain the operational side of the business.

The operational value is derived from the revenue from operations (excluding interest), less the cost of those operations (labor, materials, and support, but not interest expense), and less the capital costs of maintaining and augmenting the capital stock (plant, machines, research, etc.).

As an example, think of two firms operating side by side. The widget side of the business builds widgets, sells widgets, and invests in new and better widget-making equipment. The financing side of the business pays interest, pays dividends, retains earnings, issues (or repurchases) shares, and issues (or repurchases) bonds. If the financial side of the business is net long (retained earnings plus paid-in capital exceeds debt), then it invests the balance at the risk-free rate. If the financing side is net short, then it pays interest on the difference between the equity account and the bond account.

As Modigliani and Miller point out, value is created on the widget side of the business. The financial side of the business moves money through time and allocates shares of the operational value between stock- and bondholders. A debt incurred today implies a sequence of interest payments in the future. The present value of those interest payments is equal to the present value of the debt.

Figure 9.1 shows the flows into and out of our prototype firm. On the first level, we have the operating company. We call its output the cash flow. The cash flow is an input to the financial company. As we can see, the financial company pays dividends, pays interest if there is a debt position, collects interest on the capital surplus (if any), and either issues or repurchases dept and equity.

Figure 9.1 might be called the world according to Modigliani and Miller. It is a conceptually useful way to look at the firm. Unfortunately, accountants don't share this view. Accounting information is based on the aggregate of the operational and financial sides of the firm. By adjusting dividend and debt policy, it is possible to manipulate not only dividends and debt/equity ratios, but earnings per share (EPS), the growth in EPS, earnings-to-price ratios, and book-to-price ratios.

The reader should keep these Modigliani and Miller principles in mind in conjuring up and evaluating valuation schemes. Most of those schemes start with the notion of dividends. We'll start there too.

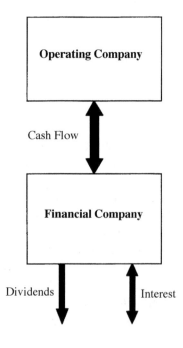

Figure 9.1

THE DIVIDEND DISCOUNT MODEL

John Burr Williams, in his classic *Theory of Investment Value*, anticipated much of modern financial theory. In particular, Williams stressed the role of dividends as a determinant of value in an early version of the dividend discount model. An investor is paid for an investment either through dividends or through the sale of the asset. The sale price is based on the market's assessment of the firm's ability to pay future dividends.

Other variables such as earnings may be important in valuing a firm, but their importance is derived from their ability to predict the future flow of dividends to the investor. So high current earnings may signal the firm's ability to increase dividends, and low current earnings signal a possible future decrease in dividends, or at least delays in future increases.

This emphasis on dividends appears to clash with the Modigliani and Miller principle on dividend policy. This is not really the case. You can read the Modigliani and Miller principle as "pay me now or pay me later." What Modigliani and Miller say is that the firm is free to schedule the payment of the dividends to the investor in any way it likes. The scheduling will not (or should not) affect the market's perception of the value of the firm.

The emphasis on dividends may also appear jarring to today's U.S. equity investors, conditioned to focus almost exclusively on price appreciation, almost to the point of disdaining current dividends. This wasn't always the case. In the 1950s and earlier, dividend yields exceeded bond yields. Equities are riskier than bonds, so investors required added incentives to purchase equities, according to the logic then. Even now, high-yield bonds follow this trend.

Certainty

If $p(0)$ is the price of the firm at time 0, i_F is the per-period interest rate, and $d(t)$ is the certain dividend to be paid at time t, then both Williams and our theoretical valuation formula would say that

$$p(0) = \frac{d(1)}{(1 + i_F)} + \frac{d(2)}{(1 + i_F)^2} + \cdots + \frac{d(t)}{(1 + i_F)^t} + \cdots \qquad (9.2)$$

Modigliani and Miller interpret this equation as both a valuation formula (i.e., a definition of $p(0)$) and a constraint on dividend policy [i.e., increasing $d(1)$ by 1 dollar and decreasing $d(2)$ by $(1 + i_F)$ dollars will preserve the total value of the firm]. As we saw in the preceding chapter, uncertainty complicates the analysis.

Uncertainty

We can capture uncertainty in the future dividends with a risk-adjusted discount rate[1] y called the dividend discount rate.

$$p(0) = \frac{d(1)}{(1 + y)} + \frac{d(2)}{(1 + y)^2} + \cdots + \frac{d(t)}{(1 + y)^t} + \cdots = \sum_t \frac{d(t)}{(1 + y)^t}$$

(9.3)

Equation (9.3) can serve as either a net present value formula or an internal rate of return formula. In the net present value application, we take the sequence of dividends $d(t)$ and the dividend discount rate y as given, and solve for the price $p(0)$. Any discrepancy between the model price $p(0)$ and the market price would imply an opportunity for exceptional return.

In the internal rate of return calculation, we take the sequence of dividends $d(t)$ and the price $p(0)$ as given, and solve for the dividend discount rate y. This internal rate of return—an expected total rate of return given the dividends and the price—may also imply an opportunity for exceptional return if it differs from the consensus expected total return $i_F + \beta \cdot f_B$. Later, we will return to these two approaches and the connection between dividend discount models and expected returns. We now confront the biggest challenge presented by Eq. (9.3): the specification of the dividend stream $d(t)$. To start, we will consider the constant-growth model.

---

[1]Recall that in the previous chapter, we showed that the theoretically pure approach is to keep the discount rates equal to the risk-free rate and "risk-adjust" the anticipated cash flows.

The Constant-Growth Dividend Discount Model

The constant-growth, or Gordon-Shapiro, dividend discount model assumes that dividends grow at a constant rate g. In other words,

$$d(t) = d(1) \cdot (1 + g)^{t-1} \tag{9.4}$$

Substituting Eq. (9.4) into Eq. (9.3) and applying some algebra, we find the simplified formula

$$p(0) = \frac{d(1)}{(y - g)} \tag{9.5}$$

This is the fundamental result of the constant-growth dividend discount model. Given a dividend $d(1)$ and a growth rate g, the stock price increases as the dividend discount rate decreases, and vice versa. Low prices imply high dividend discount rates, and high prices imply low dividend discount rates or high growth rates.

We will now consider another approach that leads to the same destination and provides further insight into Eq. (9.5). We can split the return on a stock into two parts, the dividend yield and the capital appreciation:

$$i_F + r = \frac{d}{p} + \xi = \frac{[d + (\tilde{p} - p)]}{p} \tag{9.6}$$

where p = the price of the stock at the beginning of the period
$\quad\quad\ \tilde{p}$ = the price of the stock at the end of the period
$\quad\quad\ d$ = the dividend paid in the period (assumed to be paid at the end)
$\quad\quad i_F$ = the risk-free rate of interest
$\quad\quad\ r$ = the excess return
$\quad\quad\ \xi$ = the uncertain amount of capital appreciation

Let $g = E\{\xi\}$ be the expected rate of capital appreciation, $f = E\{r\}$ be the expected excess return, and $y = i_F + f$ be the expected total rate of return. Taking expected values, Eq. (9.6) becomes

$$i_F + f = \frac{d}{p} + g = y \tag{9.7}$$

We are assuming that the dividend is known or that d represents the expected dividend. We are also assuming that the expected total rate of return *over the period*, $i_F + f$, equals the internal rate of return y, which is the (constant) average return calculated *over the entire future stream of dividends.*

Solving Eq. (9.7) for the price leads back to the constant-growth dividend discount model result:

$$p = \frac{d}{(y - g)} \tag{9.8}$$

Equations (9.5) and (9.8) imply that the expected rate of capital appreciation is identical to the expected rate of dividend growth. So far, this is something of a tautology, since we have, in fact, defined g to make this work. But we will next introduce a model for growth g, to show that we can equate it to the expected rate of capital appreciation.

MODELING GROWTH

We can use a simple model to show that the expected rate of capital appreciation equals the growth in the company's earnings per share and the growth in the company's dividends. Let

$e(t)$ = earnings in period t
$d(t)$ = dividends paid out at the end of period t
κ = company's payout ratio
$I(t)$ = amount reinvested
ρ = return on reinvested earnings

and assume that the payout ratio κ and reinvestment rate of return ρ remain constant. In particular, assume that \$1 of investment produces an expected perpetual stream of ρ dollars per period. Then, earnings either flow into dividends or are reinvested:

$$e(t) = d(t) + I(t) \tag{9.9}$$

The dividends constitute a fraction κ of the earnings:

$$d(t) = \kappa \cdot e(t) \tag{9.10}$$

The reinvested earnings constitute the remaining fraction $(1 - \kappa)$ of the earnings:

$$I(t) = (1 - \kappa) \cdot e(t) \tag{9.11}$$

And, since reinvestment produces returns ρ, we can determine $e(t + 1)$ based on $e(t)$ and the fraction reinvested:

$$e(t + 1) = [1 + (1 - \kappa) \cdot \rho] \cdot e(t) \qquad (9.12)$$

Equation (9.12) simply states that next year's earnings equal this year's earnings plus an increase due to the return on the portion of this year's earnings that was reinvested (the increase in equity).

Of course, $e(t)$ and $e(t + 1)$ lead to the growth rate:

$$e(t + 1) = (1 + g) \cdot e(t) \qquad (9.13)$$

Therefore

$$g = (1 - \kappa) \cdot \rho \qquad (9.14)$$

and, as desired,

$$d(t) = d(1) \cdot (1 + g)^{t-1} \qquad (9.15)$$

The payout ratio is constant, and hence dividends are proportional to earnings. Therefore, the dividend growth rate [in Eq. (9.15)] is also the earnings growth rate [in Eq. (9.13)]. Moreover, this growth rate is determined by both the reinvestment rate $1 - \kappa$ (a measure of opportunity) and the average return on reinvested capital ρ [from Eq. (9.14)]. This average return on invested capital is, in turn, linked to the return on equity. Suppose $b(t)$ is the book value at time t, and we start with $e(1) = \rho \cdot b(0)$; then book value will grow at rate g as well, and ρ will be the constant return on equity: $e(t) = \rho \cdot b(t - 1)$.

Multiple Stocks

The more general form of the dividend discount model for multiple stocks indexed by $n = 1, 2, \ldots N$ is

$$p_n(0) = \sum_t \frac{d_n(t)}{(1 + y_n)^t} \qquad (9.16)$$

The multiple-stock version of Eq. (9.7) becomes

$$\frac{d_n}{p_n} + g_n = i_F + f_n = y_n \qquad (9.17)$$

We can give this analysis some teeth by combining it with the consensus expected returns. The expected return f_n includes both consensus expected returns[2] and alphas: $f_n = \beta_n \cdot f_B + \alpha_n$. Substituting into Eq. (9.17), we see that

$$\frac{d_n}{p_n} + g_n = i_F + \beta_n \cdot f_B + \alpha_n = y_n \qquad (9.18)$$

We illustrate this relationship in Fig. 9.2, for a 4 percent risk-free rate, a 6 percent expected excess return on the benchmark, and an asset beta of 1.2. If the asset's yield is 2.5 percent, then it will be fairly priced, $\alpha_n = 0$, if the expected rate of capital appreciation is 8.7 percent.

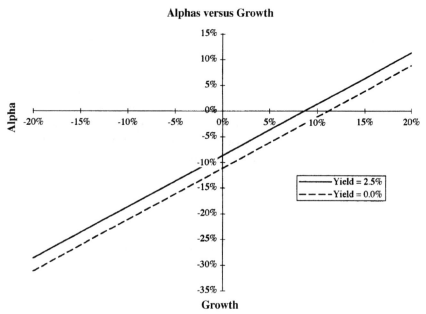

Figure 9.2

---

[2]Here we will assume that the expected benchmark return f_B matches the long-run consensus expected benchmark return μ_B; i.e., we are assuming no benchmark timing.

If we solve Eq. (9.18) for alpha, then we have a simple model for expected exceptional return in terms of yield, risk (as measured by beta), and growth:

$$\alpha_n = \left(\frac{d_n}{p_n} - i_F\right) + (g_n - \beta_n \cdot f_B) \qquad (9.19)$$

This formula points out the most important insight we must keep in mind while using a dividend discount model:

The Golden Rule of the Dividend Discount Model: _g_ in, _g_ out.

Each additional 1 percent of growth adds 1 percent to the alpha. The alphas that come out of the dividend discount model are as good as (or as bad as) the growth estimates that go in. If it's garbage in, then it's garbage out.

Implied Growth Rates

We can use Eq. (9.19) in a novel way: starting with the presumption that the assets are fairly priced, and determining the growth rates necessary to fairly price the assets. We call these the _implied growth rates:_

$$g_n^* = (i_F + \beta_n \cdot f_B) - \frac{d_n}{p_n} \qquad (9.20)$$

We know the risk-free rate i_F, and we can estimate the beta and the yield with reasonable accuracy. We can also make a reasonable estimate of the expected excess return on the market f_B.

The implied growth rates are handy in several ways. First they provide a rational feel for what growth rates should be, and help to point out consistent biases in analysts' estimates, either within sectors or across all stocks. Second, the implied growth rates can identify companies whose prices reflect unrealistic growth prospects.

For example, in Table 9.1 we have listed the Major Market Index stocks along with their yield, 60-month historical beta, and implied growth rates as of December 1992. The table assumes an expected excess return on the Major Market Index, f_B, of 6 percent and uses the risk-free rate (3-month Treasury bills) of 3.1 percent, which was the rate at the end of December 1992.

T A B L E 9.1

Stock	Yield	Beta	Implied Growth Rate
American Express	4.00%	1.21	6.36%
AT&T	2.60%	0.96	6.26%
Chevron	4.70%	0.45	1.10%
Coca-Cola	1.30%	1.00	7.80%
Disney	0.50%	1.24	10.04%
Dow Chemical	4.50%	1.11	5.26%
DuPont	3.70%	1.09	5.94%
Eastman Kodak	4.90%	0.60	1.80%
Exxon	4.70%	0.47	1.22%
General Electric	2.90%	1.31	8.06%
General Motors	2.50%	0.90	6.00%
IBM	9.60%	0.64	−2.66%
International Paper	2.50%	1.16	7.56%
Johnson & Johnson	1.80%	1.15	8.20%
McDonalds	0.80%	1.07	8.72%
Merck	2.30%	1.09	7.34%
3M	3.20%	0.74	4.34%
Philip Morris	3.40%	0.97	5.52%
Procter & Gamble	2.10%	1.01	7.06%
Sears	4.40%	1.04	4.94%

We can see that reasonable growth rates average about 5.5 percent and that the standard deviation of growth rates in the Major Market Index is 3.1 percent. One of the difficulties in using a dividend discount model is implicit in the Golden Rule: The growth inputs can be wildly unrealistic. They tend to be too large in general, since Wall Street research (which drives the consensus) is interested in selling stocks, and positive bullish outlooks help to sell stocks.

Dealing with Unrealistic Growth Rates

We can treat this problem of unrealistic growth estimates in three ways. The first is a direct approach:

1. Group stocks into sectors.

2. Calculate the implied growth rate for each stock in the sector.

3. Modify the growth forecasts so that they have the same mean and standard deviation as the implied growth rates in each sector.

This approach linearly transforms the growth estimate g_n to

$$g_n' = a + b \cdot g_n \qquad (9.21)$$

where we choose a and b to match the mean and standard deviation of the implied growth rates g_n^*. The result is

$$g_n' = \text{Mean}\{g^*\} + \left(\frac{\text{Std}\{g^*\}}{\text{Std}\{g\}}\right) \cdot (g_n - \text{Mean}\{g^*\}) \qquad (9.22)$$

where we calculate the mean and standard deviation cross-sectionally over stocks in the sector. The revised growth estimates are the sector average implied growth rate plus a term proportional to the difference between the initial growth estimates and that sector average implied growth rate.

Table 9.2 shows the results of this approach for the stocks in the Major Market Index, using the 5-year historical earnings-per-share growth rates (as of December 1992) as inputs. In this table, we have treated all these stocks as one sector. Table 9.2 also shows the alphas from Eq. (9.19), based on the modified growth inputs.

One possible difficulty with this approach is that it may delete valuable sector timing information. Remember that the implied growth rates assume zero alphas, so this scheme will move the sector alphas toward zero.[3] If you have no sector timing ability, then this is not a problem, but if you are trying to time sectors, you must account for sector alphas when generating target mean growth rates for each sector.

The second approach to dealing with unrealistic growth estimates is a variant of the first approach which can, in principle,

[3]Issues of coverage and capitalization weighting keep the sector alphas from exactly equaling zero after this procedure.

T A B L E 9.2

Stock	Growth Forecast	Modified Forecast	Alpha
American Express	−3.20%	4.90%	−1.46%
AT&T	−19.21%	2.21%	−4.05%
Chevron	3.18%	4.91%	3.81%
Coca-Cola	19.31%	8.68%	0.88%
Disney	12.18%	7.49%	−2.55%
Dow Chemicals	−23.22%	1.54%	−3.72%
DuPont	−7.46%	4.19%	−1.75%
Eastman Kodak	−37.51%	−0.86%	−2.66%
Exxon	3.32%	6.00%	4.78%
General Electric	16.14%	8.15%	0.09%
General Motors	4.72%	6.23%	0.23%
IBM	−32.53%	−0.03%	2.63%
International Paper	−10.86%	3.62%	−3.94%
Johnson & Johnson	15.27%	8.01%	−0.19%
McDonalds	12.09%	7.47%	−1.25%
Merck	22.95%	9.30%	1.96%
3M	4.48%	6.19%	1.85%
Philip Morris	22.92%	9.29%	3.77%
Procter & Gamble	23.30%	9.35%	2.29%
Sears	−7.96%	4.10%	−0.84%
Mean	0.58%	5.54%	-0.01%
Standard deviation	18.40%	3.09%	2.70%

account for the investor's skill in predicting growth. As we will discover in Chap. 10, a basic linear forecasting result is

$$g_n' = g_n^* + c \cdot (g_n - g_n^*) \tag{9.23}$$

Unlike in Eq. (9.22), we start with the stock's implied growth rate, not the sector average, and shift away from it based on comparing the initial growth forecast to the *stock's* implied growth rate.

Furthermore, as we will learn in Chap. 10, the constant c depends in part on the investor's skill in predicting growth, where we measure skill using the correlation between forecast and realized growth rates. With no skill, we set c to zero. We leave the details to Chap. 10.

A third, more conventional and more elaborate, approach to getting realistic growth inputs is the three-stage dividend discount model.

THE THREE-STAGE DIVIDEND DISCOUNT MODEL

The three-stage dividend discount model is built on the premise that we may have some insights about a company's prospects over the short run (1 to 4 years), but we have little long-range information. Therefore, we should use something like the implied growth rate for the company (or the sector) as the long-run value, and interpolate between the long and the short.

The idea stems from the initial dividend discount formula [Eq. (9.3)], which would naturally lead one to distinguish between long-range and short-range growth rates.

The three-stage dividend discount model is complicated. The reader who is uninterested in the details can skip to the next subsection, where we comment (negatively) on the net effect of the three-stage approach.

There are several ways to build a three-stage dividend discount model. What follows is typical, and we don't believe that different model structures give materially different results. The required inputs include the following:

T_1, T_2 = times which define the stages—stage 1 runs from 0 to T_1, stage 2 from T_1 to T_2, and stage 3 from T_2 onward

g_{IN} = the short-term (0 to T_1) forecast growth in earnings per share

g_{EQ} = the long-range or equilibrium (T_2 onward) forecast growth in earnings per share

κ_0 = the current (0 to T_1) payout ratio

κ_{EQ} = the long-run (T_2 onwards) payout ratio

$EPS(1)$ = the forecast of next year's earnings per share

y_{EQ} = the equilibrium expected rate of return, $i_F + \beta \cdot f_B$

We input the short-term and long-term growth forecasts. For the growth during the intermediate period, we linearly interpolate:

$$g(t) = g_{\text{IN}} \cdot \left(\frac{T_2 - t}{T_2 - T_1}\right) + g_{\text{EQ}} \cdot \left(\frac{t - T_1}{T_2 - T_1}\right) \qquad (9.24)$$

for $T_1 \le t \le T_2$. We similarly interpolate the payout ratios $\kappa(t)$. Then the earnings per share and dividend paths will be

$$\text{EPS}(t) = [1 + g(t)] \cdot \text{EPS}(t - 1) \qquad (9.25)$$

$$d(t) = \kappa(t) \cdot \text{EPS}(t) \qquad (9.26)$$

We now proceed by first finding a time T_2 value of the company, and then focusing on the current value of the company. At time T_2, we can value the company using the equilibrium growth and dividend discount rates:

$$p(T_2) = \frac{d(T_2 + 1)}{[y_{\text{EQ}} - g_{\text{EQ}}]} \qquad (9.27)$$

Then we can solve for the dividend discount rate y that discounts to the current price $p(0)$:

$$p(0) = \sum_{t=1}^{T_2} \frac{d(t)}{(1 + y)^t} + \frac{p(T_2)}{(1 + y)^{T_2}} \qquad (9.28)$$

The Three-Stage Dividend Discount Model Evaluated

The entire three-stage dividend discount procedure is motivated by the tension between a short-run growth rate g_{IN} and a long-run rate g_{EQ}. In spirit, it is just another approach to adjusting g_{IN} toward g_{EQ} and applying Eq. (9.3). A cynical view would even be that this is an elaborate (and confusing) way to smooth the growth inputs. It is important to remember that the three-stage dividend discount

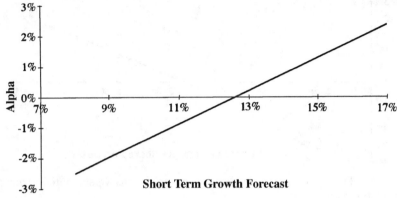

Figure 9.3 Three stage dividend discount model. Alpha versus short term growth forecast.

model is not magic. It cannot transform bad growth forecasts into good growth forecasts. The golden rule still applies.

To understand this better, consider the following example. We will set up a typical three-stage dividend discount model[4] and use it to estimate internal rates of return and alphas (by subtracting $i_F + \beta \cdot f_B$). Figure 9.3 illustrates the almost linear relationship between g_{IN} and alpha. In this case, the implied growth rate is 12.62 percent, and each additional 1 percent of growth adds 0.54 percent to the alpha. The golden rule has been modified slightly, to say "g in, $0.54 \cdot (g - 12.62$ percent) out."

We can apply the same analysis to observe the sensitivity of alpha to the initial earnings per share forecast. Figure 9.4 illustrates the result. The relationship between the initial earnings per share forecast and the alpha is slightly nonlinear; however, 30 basis points of alpha for each $0.20 of earnings per share is a reasonable guide.

---

[4]The parameters are 5 and 15 years for the stage times, 0.0 for the short-run payout, and 0.3 for the long-run payout. The long-run expected market excess return was 5.5 percent, the stock's beta was 1.2, and the risk-free rate was 4 percent. This means that the stock's long-run fair expected return was 10.60 percent. The first year's EPS number was $4.80, and the market price was $50.00.

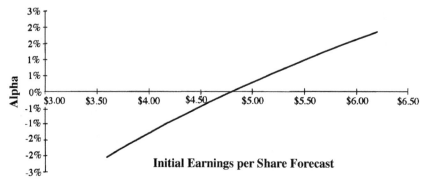

Figure 9.4 Three stage dividend discount model. Alpha versus initial earnings per share forecast.

DIVIDEND DISCOUNT MODELS AND RETURNS

To use a dividend discount model in the context of active portfolio management, the information in the model must be converted into forecasts of exceptional return. There are two standard approaches, based on calculating either internal rates of return or net present values. These approaches differ in their assumption of the horizon over which any misvaluation will disappear.

In the internal rate of return mode, we use the stream of dividends and the current market price as inputs, and solve for the internal rate of return y which matches the dividends to the market price. We then obtain asset alphas in two steps: first aggregate the rates of returns y_n to estimate the predicted benchmark excess return f_B,

$$f_B = y_B - i_F = \sum_n y_n \cdot h_{B,n} - i_F \qquad (9.29)$$

and then convert the internal rates of return to expected residual returns:

$$\alpha_n = y_n - (i_F + \beta_n \cdot f_B) \qquad (9.30)$$

The underlying assumption is that the misvaluation of the asset will persist; i.e., after 1 year, the proper discount rate will still be

y_n and not the "fair" rate $i_F + \beta_n \cdot f_B$. To see this, we can verify, using Eq. (9.3), that the expected total rate of return for the asset will be y_n, if we assume that y_n remains constant. Mathematically,

$$\left[\frac{p_n(1) + d_n(1) - p_n(0)}{p_n(0)} \right] = y_n \qquad (9.31)$$

assuming

$$p_n(1) = \sum_{t=2} \frac{d_n(t)}{(1 + y_n)^{t-1}} \qquad (9.32)$$

The expected price in 1 year is simply the dividend stream from year 2 on, discounted at the same internal rate of return y_n. The alphas from Eq. (9.27) presume that the mispricing will persist indefinitely, and that one will continue to reap the benefits.

In the net present value mode, we take the stream of dividends and a fair discount rate $y_n = i_F + \beta_n \cdot f_B$ as inputs, and solve for the fair market price as we would for a net present value calculation. We then compare this price to the current market price, to determine the degree of overvaluation or undervaluation. To convert these "pricing errors" into alphas, we could use the following two-step process. First we adjust f_B (and hence y_n) so that the aggregate fair market value of all the assets equals the aggregate current market value of the assets. Second, assuming that the pricing error disappears after 1 year, we define alpha as

$$\alpha_n^* = \left[\frac{p_n(0,\text{model}) - p_n(0,\text{market})}{p_n(0,\text{market})} \right] \cdot (1 + i_F + \beta_n \cdot f_B) \qquad (9.33)$$

or approximately as[5]

$$\alpha_n^* \approx \left[\frac{p_n(0,\text{model}) - p_n(0,\text{market})}{p_n(0,\text{market})} \right] \qquad (9.34)$$

The alpha forecast in Eq. (9.33) presumes that all of the misvaluation

---

[5]For monthly alpha forecasts, Eqs. (9.33) and (9.34) differ by about a factor of 1.01.

will disappear in 1 year. In fact, we derive Eq. (9.33) by defining alpha using

$$i_F + \beta_n \cdot f_B + \alpha_n^* = \left[\frac{p_n(1) + d_n(1) - p_n(0,\text{market})}{p_n(0,\text{market})} \right] \quad (9.35)$$

and assuming

$$p_n(1) = \sum_{t=2} \frac{d_n(t)}{(1 + i_F + \beta_n \cdot f_B)^{t-1}} \quad (9.36)$$

i.e., the end-of-year price is the net present value of the future stream of dividends, discounted at the fair rate $i_F + \beta_n \cdot f_B$.

Beneficial Side Effects
of Dividend Discount Models

Beyond their possible value in forecasting exceptional returns, dividend discount models also have some beneficial institutional side effects. The dividend discount model is a process. Used properly, it entails keeping records and viewing all assets on an equal footing. Hence, it can identify the judgmental input to a portfolio. We can compare the portfolio that the dividend discount model would have purchased with the actual portfolio, and attribute the difference to judgmental overrides and implementation costs (trading, etc.). In the longer run, this process can lead to evaluation and improvement of the inputs.

On the downside, total devotion to the dividend discount model as the only appoach to valuation is a form of tunnel vision. In the remainder of this chapter we will consider some other practical approaches to valuation.

COMPARATIVE VALUATION

The theoretical valuation formula of Chap. 8 and the dividend discount model look to future dividends as the source of value. There is an alternative, which involves looking at the current characteristics of a company and asking if that company is fairly valued relative to other companies with similar characteristics. The most obvious and simple example compares companies solely on the basis of current price-earnings ratios. *The Wall Street Journal* provides these numbers every day. A second example is the rules of thumb quoted by investment bankers: "Consulting firms sell for two times revenues," "Asset management firms sell for 5 percent of assets," etc.

These examples are familiar, unidimensional (and possibly static) approaches to valuation based on current attributes. Comparative valuation, as we will describe it, is a more systematic and sophisticated (multidimensional) application of this idea: pricing by comparison with analogous companies, or as a function of sales and/or earnings multiples. We will *motivate*[6] this approach using the dividend discount model as a starting point.

The "clean surplus" equation of accounting[7] connects a company's dividends, earnings, and book value according to

$$b(t) = b(t-1) + e(t) - d(t) \tag{9.37}$$

where we measure the book values $b(t-1)$ and $b(t)$ at the beginning and end of period t (running from $t-1$ to time t), the earnings $e(t)$ accrue during period t, and the company pays the dividend $d(t)$ at the end.

We can use the dividend discount rate y to split earnings into two parts: required and exceptional:

$$e(t) = y \cdot b(t-1) + e^*(t) \tag{9.38}$$

Anticipating that these exceptional earnings $e^*(t)$ will die out gradually leads to

$$e^*(t+1) = \delta \cdot e^*(t) + \text{noise} \tag{9.39}$$

where $\delta < 1$. Now combine Eqs. (9.37), (9.38), and (9.39) to estimate the *expected* dividend, which is what the dividend discount model requires:

$$d(1) = (1+y) \cdot b(0) + e^*(1) - b(1) \tag{9.40}$$
$$d(2) = (1+y) \cdot b(1) + \delta \cdot e^*(1) - b(2)$$
$$d(t) = (1+y) \cdot b(t-1) + \delta^{t-1} e^*(1) - b(t)$$

---

[6]In this case, "motivate" will involve a set of assumptions and logic leading to a formula, rather than any rigorous derivation. We will then use the formula in an empirical way.
[7]See Ohlson (1989) for an in-depth discussion.

Now substitute this expected dividend stream into the dividend discount model [Eq. (9.3)] to find (after some manipulation)

$$p(0) = b(0) + \left(\frac{e^*(1)}{1 + y - \delta}\right) \tag{9.41}$$

$$= \left(\frac{1 - \delta}{1 + y - \delta}\right) \cdot b(0) + \left(\frac{1}{1 + y - \delta}\right) \cdot e(1)$$

Equation (9.41) expresses the current price as a linear combination of anticipated earnings $e(1)$ and current book value $b(0)$. The coefficients are company-specific and depend on the dividend discount rate and the persistence of exceptional earnings.

This particular derivation is motivation for a more general application. In the general case, we would like to explain today's price $p(0)$ in terms of several characteristics: earnings, book, anticipated earnings, cash flow, dividends, sales, debt, etc. The idea is to use a cross-sectional comparison of similar companies and thus isolate those that are overpriced or underpriced.

For example, suppose we wished to apply the ideas contained in Eq. (9.41) to a group of similar medium-sized electrical utilities. We are looking for coefficients c_1 and c_2 to fit

$$p_n(0) = c_1 \cdot b_n(0) + c_2 \cdot e_n(1) + \epsilon_n \tag{9.42}$$

Starting from Eq. (9.41), the idea is that for these similar companies, the coefficients should be identical, and so the pricing error ϵ_n will identify misvaluations. The exact procedure for implementing Eq. (9.42) could vary, from an ordinary least-squares (OLS) regression, to a generalized least squares (GLS) regression that takes into account company prices, to a pooled cross-sectional and longitudinal regression that looks at the relationship across time and across assets.

In general, the goal of comparative valuation is to estimate a relationship

$$\frac{\text{Market}}{\text{price}} = \frac{\text{fitted}}{\text{price}} + \text{error} \tag{9.43}$$

where the fitted price depends upon a variety of company characteristics. Equation (9.43) leads to an exceptional return forecast of

$$\alpha = -\frac{\text{error}}{\substack{\text{market} \\ \text{price}}} = \frac{\substack{\text{fitted} \\ \text{price}} - \substack{\text{market} \\ \text{price}}}{\substack{\text{market} \\ \text{price}}} \qquad (9.44)$$

presuming that the fitted price is more accurate than the market price, and that the asset will move to the fitted price over the horizon of the alpha.

We can provide an arbitrage interpretation of this comparative analysis. Suppose we split the companies into two groups: the overvalued companies (with market price exceeding fitted price) and the undervalued companies (with market price less than fitted price). We can then construct a portfolio of the overvalued companies and a portfolio of the undervalued companies with identical attributes: e.g., the same sales, the same debt, and the same earnings. This creates two megacompanies—call them OV and UV, respectively—that are alike in all important attributes. However, we can purchase megacompany UV more cheaply than megacompany OV. Two "identical" companies selling for different prices is an arbitrage opportunity.

This comparative valuation procedure requires only current and forecast information, e.g., current book value and anticipated earnings, and thus is independent of the past. It is not an extrapolation of historical data. It also is a high-tech way of mimicking the investment banking valuation procedures, which are typically grounded on multiples of sales and earnings. The hope is that the set of characteristics in the model completely determines company valuations.

If the model omits some important attribute, the valuation may be misleading: The pricing errors may measure just the missing component, not an actual misvaluation. One example of a missing factor might be brand value. If we ignored brand name value and applied comparative valuation to a consumer goods sector, we might find some companies that were overvalued on average over time. This might not be an opportunity to sell, but rather the appearance of brand value. One way to account for this would be to compare current overvaluation or undervaluation to historical average valuations.

Comparative valuation is quite flexible in practice. We can build separate valuation models for banks, mining and extraction companies, industrials, electric utilities, etc. This can help us focus on comparability within groups of similar companies.

RETURNS-BASED ANALYSIS

The linear valuation model described above can serve as a useful introduction to returns-based analysis. The valuation model made a link between a purported percentage pricing error (the difference between the fitted and the current price divided by the current price) and the future residual return. Why not attack the problem directly and try to fit the price in a way that best forecasts residual returns? Suppose company n has attributes (earnings, dividends, book, sales, etc.) $A_{n,k}(t)$ at time t. We might try the following model to directly explain residual returns using these attributes:

$$\theta_n(t) = \sum_k A_{n,k}(t) \cdot g_k(t) + \epsilon_n(t) \tag{9.45}$$

Equation (9.45) is one example of returns-based analysis. A more typical returns-based analysis works with excess returns $r_n(t)$ rather than the residual returns $\theta_n(t)$, and uses risk control factors to separate residual and benchmark returns. Its basic form is similar to Eq. (9.45):

$$r_n(t) = \sum_{k=1} X_{n,k}(t) \cdot b_k(t) + u_n(t) \tag{9.46}$$

but here the company exposures $X_{n,k}(t)$ include both the attributes $A_{n,k}(t)$ and the risk control factors.

Equation (9.46) has the form of an APT model, as discussed in Chap. 7. At the same time, Eq. (9.46) may be somewhat more flexible. According to Chap. 7, we can fairly easily find qualified APT models—any factor model that can explain the returns to a diversified portfolio should probably do. But Eq. (9.46) could include all the APT model factors as risk factors, plus a new signal to forecast specific returns from that APT model. The APT theory doesn't allow forecasting of specific returns. But we are now in the ad hoc, empirical, nonefficient world of active management. We have the flexibility to forecast specific returns [although in Eq. (9.46) we express that forecast as another factor].

There are three important points to note concerning the use of the linear model [Eq. (9.46)] to forecast returns. First, in a true GLS regression, the factor return $b_k(t)$ is the return on a *factor portfolio* with unit exposure to factor k, zero exposure to the other factors, and minimum risk. If we know the exposures $X_{n,k}(t)$ at the start of the period, even without knowing the returns $r_n(t)$, we can determine the holdings in the factor portfolio at the start of the period necessary to achieve the factor return $b_k(t)$.

Second, the equations *aggregate*. In particular, looking at the benchmark return,

$$r_B(t) = \sum_k x_{B,k}(t) \cdot b_k(t) + u_B(t) \qquad (9.47)$$

where
$$x_{B,k}(t) = \sum_n h_{B,n}(t) \cdot X_{n,k}(t) \qquad (9.48)$$

We will utilize this linear aggregation property to help separate residual from benchmark returns.

Third, when estimated using least-squares regression, the linear model [Eq. (9.46)] can be unduly influenced by outliers. One rule of thumb is to pull in all outliers in the $X_{n,k}(t)$ to ± 3 standard deviations about the mean. This will help avoid having all the explanatory power arise out of only one or two (possibly suspect) observations.

The simplest approach to separating residual from benchmark returns is to model the residual returns directly, as in Eq. (9.45).

Even then, we should be careful. The aggregate equation for the benchmark is

$$\theta_B(t) = \sum_k a_{B,k}(t) \cdot g_k(t) + \epsilon_B(t) \qquad (9.49)$$

where
$$a_{B,k}(t) = \sum_n h_{B,n}(t) \cdot A_{n,k}(t) \qquad (9.50)$$

Since $\theta_B(t) \equiv 0$, we should adjust[8] the variables $A_{n,k}(t)$ so that $a_{B,k}(t) = 0$.

In the more typical situation where we are modeling excess returns, to separate benchmark from residual returns, we must include one or more variables that will pick up the benchmark return. The simplest approach is to include predicted beta as a risk control factor, and make sure that all other characteristics have a benchmark-weighted average of zero. The factor return associated with predicted beta will tend to pick up the benchmark return, leaving the other factors to describe residual returns. A more complicated procedure is to include a group of industry or sector variables as risk control factors. The factor returns associated with these industry or sector variables will pick up the benchmark effect.[9] These industry or sector assignments add up to an intercept term in the regression. To separate bench-

---

[8]If $Z_{n,k}(t)$ is the raw description of the exposure of asset n to attribute k at time t, and

$$z_{B,k}(t) = \sum_n h_{B,n}(t) \cdot Z_{n,k}(t)$$

is the benchmark exposure to attribute k at time t, then replace $Z_{n,k}(t)$ with

$$A_{n,k}(t) = Z_{n,k}(t) - z_{B,k}(t)$$

If the beta of asset n is $\beta_n(t)$, then a slight variant is to replace $Z_{n,k}(t)$ with

$$A_{n,k}(t) = Z_{n,k}(t) - \beta_n(t) \cdot z_{B,k}(t)$$

[9]The remaining factor portfolio returns may still be correlated with the benchmark, even if the benchmark's exposure to the factor is zero. For example, factors associated with volatility (even after adjusting for market neutrality) tend to exhibit strong positive correlation with the market.

mark from residual returns, the choice[10] is between a beta and an intercept term.

Using Returns-Based Analysis

Once set up, returns-based analysis examines past returns and attributes those returns to firm characteristics. The active manager starts the process by searching for appropriate characteristics. Some characteristics might directly explain residual returns—for example, alpha forecasts from dividend discount models or comparative valuation models. Other characteristics include reversal effects (e.g., last month's realized residual returns), momentum effects (e.g., the past 12 months' realized returns), earnings surprise effects, or particular accounting variables possibly connected with exceptional returns.[11] In this case, the hope is that the factor returns $b_k(t)$ associated with these characteristics exhibit consistent positive returns.

Alternatively, the manager could choose characteristics associated with investment themes, sometimes in favor and sometimes not—for example, growth forecasts or company size. Then the associated factor returns $b_k(t)$ would not consistently exhibit positive returns, but the manager would hope to forecast the sign and magnitude of these returns. For example, how will growth stocks or small-capitalization stocks perform relative to the market as a

---

[10]A word of caution if you try to include both betas and an intercept (or sectors or industries). There will be no problem with the factor portfolios that have benchmark-neutral attributes. Those factor portfolios will have both a zero beta and zero net investment. The difficulty is that the benchmark return will be spread between the beta factor and the intercept. We can avoid this confusion by introducing an equivalent regression. Suppose $Z_{n,k}(t)$ is the allocation of company n to sector k and:

$$z_{B,k}(t) = \sum_{n=1} h_{B,n}(t) \cdot Z_{n,k}(t)$$

is the benchmark exposure to sector k at time t. If we substitute

$$X_{n,k}(t) = Z_{n,k}(t) - \beta_n(t) \cdot z_{B,k}(t)$$

for $Z_{n,k}(t)$, we can interpret the factor portfolio returns as the residual (the factor portfolio's beta will be zero) return on sector k when we control for the other variables. The returns to the benchmark-neutral factors will not change.

[11]For examples, see Ou and Penman (1989) and Lev and Thiagarajan (1993).

whole? These forecasts might rely on extrapolations of past factor returns, e.g., using moving averages. More sophisticated forecasting might use economic indicators such as long and short interest rates, changes in interest rates, corporate bond spreads, or average dividend yields versus interest rates.

Sometimes the manager may wish to forecast factor returns even for characteristics that generally exhibit consistent positive factor returns. For example, the BARRA Success factor in the United States, a momentum factor, generally exhibits positive returns. However, these returns are often negative in the month of January.[12] Managers who wish to bet on momentum should take into account (forecast) this January effect.

Managers can of course combine these different types of signals, forecasting factor returns for investment themes as well as using company-level valuation models. The relative emphasis will depend on the information ratios associated with these various efforts. Chapter 12, "Information Analysis," and Chap. 17, "Performance Analysis," describe this research and evaluation effort in more detail. Chapters 10 and 11, which cover forecasting, will greatly expand on the technical issues surrounding forecasting of returns. The notes section of this chapter includes a list of popular investment signals.

SUMMARY

This chapter began with a discussion of corporate finance, to motivate the development of valuation models based on appropriate corporate attributes. It then discussed dividend discount models in considerable detail, especially the critical issues of dealing with growth and expected future dividend payments, and converting information from the dividend discount model into exceptional return forecasts. The chapter went on to empirically expand the dividend discount concept with comparative valuation models, less rigorous in principle but more flexible in practice. The chapter ended with a discussion of returns-based analysis—which focuses

---

[12]We attribute this to investors' tendency to "window dress" portfolios by keeping winners for the year-end and selling losers in December, and to accelerate capital losses (take them in December) and postpone capital gains (take them in January).

directly on forecasts of exceptional return— and alternative empirical approaches that are available.

NOTES

Given the nature of active management, we can't provide recipes for finding superior information. Hence, this chapter has focused on structure and methodology. But we can provide some indication of what types of information U.S. equity investors have found useful in the past. According to an annual survey of institutional investors conducted by Merrill Lynch, these factors, attributes, and models include

- EPS variability
- Return on equity
- Foreign exposure
- Beta
- Price/earnings ratios
- Price/sales ratios
- Size
- Earnings estimate revisions
- Neglect
- Rating revision
- Dividend yield
- EPS momentum
- Projected growth
- Low price
- Duration
- Relative strength
- EPS torpedo
- Earnings estimation dispersion
- Debt/equity ratio
- EPS surprise
- DDM
- Price/cash flow ratios
- Price/book ratios

Most investors responding to the survey relied on five to seven of these factors. See Bernstein (1998) for details.

PROBLEMS

1. According to Modigliani and Miller (and ignoring tax effects), how would the value of a firm change if it borrowed money to repurchase outstanding common stock, greatly increasing its leverage? What if it changed its payout ratio?

2. Discuss the problem of growth forecasts in the context of the constant-growth dividend discount model [Eq. (9.5)]. How would you reconcile the growth forecasts with the implied growth forecasts for AT&T in Tables 9.1 and 9.2?

3. Stock X has a beta of 1.20 and pays no dividend. If the risk-free rate is 6 percent and the expected excess market return is 6 percent, what is stock X's implied growth rate?

4. You are a manager who believes that book-to-price (B/P), earnings-to-price (E/P), and beta are the three variables that determine stock value. Given monthly B/P, E/P, and beta values for 500 stocks, how could you implement your strategy (a) using comparative valuation? (b) using returns-based analysis?

5. A stock trading with a P/E ratio of 15 has a payout ratio of 0.5 and an expected return of 12 percent. What is its growth rate, according to the constant-growth DDM?

REFERENCES

Bernstein, Peter L. "Off the Average." *Journal of Portfolio Management*, vol. 24, no. 1, 1997, p. 3.

Bernstein, Richard. "Quantitative Viewpoint: 1998 Institutional Factor Survey." *Merrill Lynch Quantitative Publication*, Nov. 25, 1998.

Brennan, Michael J. "Stripping the S&P 500 Index." *Financial Analysts Journal*, vol. 54, no. 1, 1998, pp. 12–22.

Chugh, Lal C., and Joseph W. Meador. "The Stock Valuation Process: The Analyst's View." *Financial Analysts Journal*, vol. 40, no. 6, 1984, pp. 41–48.

Durand, David. "Afterthoughts on a Controversy with Modigliani and Miller, plus Thoughts on Growth and the Cost of Capital." *Financial Management*, vol. 18, no. 2, 1989, pp. 12–18.

Fama, Eugene F., and Kenneth R. French. "Taxes, Financing Decisions, and Firm Value." *Journal of Finance*, vol. 53, no. 3, 1998, pp. 819–843.

Fouse, William. "Risk and Liquidity: The Keys to Stock Price Behavior." *Financial Analysts Journal*, vol. 32, no. 3, 1976, pp. 35–45.

———. "Risk and Liquidity Revisited." *Financial Analysts Journal*, vol. 33, no. 1, 1977, pp. 40–45.

Gordon, Myron J. *The Investment, Financing, and Valuation of the Corporation* (Homewood, Ill.: Richard D. Irwin, 1962).

Gordon, Myron J., and E. Shapiro. "Capital Equipment Analysis: The Required Rate of Profit." *Management Science*, vol. 3, October 1956, pp. 102–110.

Grant, James L. "Foundations of EVA for Investment Managers." *Journal of Portfolio Management*, vol. 23, no. 1, 1996, pp. 41–48.

Jacobs, Bruce I., and Kenneth N. Levy. "Disentangling Equity Return Opportunities: New Insights and Investment Opportunities." *Financial Analysts Journal*, vol. 44, no. 3, 1988, pp. 18–44.

———. "Forecasting the Size Effect." *Financial Analysts Journal*, vol 45, no. 3, 1989, pp. 38–54.

Lev, Baruch, and S. Ramu Thiagarajan. "Fundamental Information Analysis." *Journal of Accounting Research*, vol. 31, no. 2, 1993, pp. 190–215.

Modigliani, Franco, and Merton H. Miller. "Dividend Policy, Growth, and the Valuation of Shares." *Journal of Business*, vol 34, no. 4, 1961, pp. 411–433.

Ohlson, James A. "Accounting Earnings, Book Value, and Dividends: The Theory of the Clean Surplus Equation (Part I)." Columbia University working paper, January 1989.

Ou, Jane, and Stephen Penman. "Financial Statement Analysis and the Prediction of Stock Returns." *Journal of Accounting and Economics*, vol. 11, no. 4, November 1989, pp. 295–329.

Rosenberg, Barr, Kenneth Reid, and Ronald Lanstein. "Persuasive Evidence of Market Inefficiency." *Journal of Portfolio Management*, vol. 11, no. 3, 1985, pp. 9–17.

Rozeff, Michael S. "The Three-Phase Dividend Discount Model and the ROPE Model." *Journal of Portfolio Management*, vol. 16, no. 2, 1989, pp. 36–42.

Sharpe, William F., and Gordon J. Alexander. *Investments* (Englewood Cliffs, N.J.: Prentice-Hall, 1990).

Wilcox, Jarrod W. "The P/B-ROE Valuation Model." *Financial Analysts Journal*, vol. 40, no. 1, 1984, pp. 58–66.

Williams, John Burr. *The Theory of Investment Value* (Amsterdam: North-Holland Publishing Company, 1964).

TECHNICAL APPENDIX

This technical appendix will discuss how to handle nonlinear models and fractiles in the (linear) returns-based framework. The idea will be to capture the nonlinearities in the *exposures* to linearly estimated factors. We can even make these exposures bench-mark-neutral.

Let's start with an example. Suppose you think that the relationship between earnings yield and return is not linear. Here is one approach to testing that hypothesis. Divide the assets into three categories, high earnings yield, low earnings yield, and average earnings yield,[13] and consider two earnings yield variables, high yield and average yield. So the model is

$$\theta_n = X_{n,high} \cdot b_{high} + X_{n,ave} \cdot b_{ave} \qquad (9A.1)$$

The high-earnings-yield assets have $X_{n,high} = 1$ and $X_{n,ave} = 0$. The average-earnings-yield assets have $X_{n,high} = 0$ and $X_{n,ave} = 1$. We can determine the exposures of the low-yield assets by imposing benchmark neutrality. Assuming that each group has equal capitalization, the condition $\theta_B = 0$ leads to

$$b_{low} = -(b_{high} + b_{ave}) \qquad (9A.2)$$

So for the low-yield assets, we must have $X_{n,high} = -1$ and $X_{n,ave} = -1$.

Once we estimate the factor returns, we can determine whether there exist any nonlinearities. For example, one sign of a nonlinear effect would be the return to the high-yield assets relative to the average assets differing significantly from the return of the low-yield assets relative to the average assets.

We can clearly extend this approach to quartiles, quintiles, or deciles. In fact, this returns-based fractile analysis has the advantage of allowing for controls. We can make sure that each fractile portfolio is sector- and/or benchmark-neutral, and perhaps neutral on some other dimension that we believe may be confounding the effect.

Other methods for analyzing nonlinear effects also exist. Let's start with an attribute $X_{n,1}$ that is benchmark-neutral: $\sum_n h_{B,n} \cdot X_{n,1} = 0$. We wish to analyze nonlinearities while still ensuring

---

[13]The choice of three categories is arbitrary, and mainly done for ease of explanation. If we considered four categories, this would be quartile analysis. As in quartile analysis, we also have a choice in how to form the group: equal number in each group or equal capitalization in each group.

benchmark neutrality. A simple approach is to include a new variable:

$$X_{n,2} = X_{n,1}^2 - \sum_n h_{B,n} \cdot X_{n,1}^2 \qquad (9A.3)$$

The squared exposure has the disadvantage of placing undue emphasis on outliers. Other alternatives would include using the absolute value of $X_{n,1}$, the square root of the absolute value of $X_{n,1}$, or the $\text{Max}\{0, X_{n,1}\}$, in each case benchmark-neutralized as in Eq. (9A.3). Each of these would reduce the nonlinear effect for the more extreme positive and negative values of $X_{n,1}$.

Exercise

1. You forecast an alpha of 2 percent for stocks that have E/P above the benchmark average *and* IBES growth above the benchmark average. On average, what must your alpha forecasts be for stocks that do not satisfy these two criteria? If you assume an alpha of zero for stocks which have either above-average E/P or above-average IBES growth, but not both, what is your average alpha for stocks with E/P and IBES growth both below average?

Applications Exercise

1. Use appropriate software (e.g. BARRA's Aegis and Alphabuilder products) to determine the current dividend-to-price ratio, dividend growth, and beta (with respect to the CAPMMI) for GE and Coke. Using these data, a risk-free rate of 6 percent, and expected benchmark excess return of 6 percent, what are the prices implied by the constant-growth DDM? What is the dividend discount rate? Estimate alphas for GE and Coke using both methods described in the section "Dividend Discount Models and Returns."

PART THREE

Information Processing

CHAPTER 10

Forecasting Basics

INTRODUCTION

We have completed our discussion of expected returns and valuation. We now move on to the third major section of the book: information processing. We now assume some source of alpha information. In this section, we tackle a critical problem: how to efficiently analyze and process that information. We will spend two chapters looking forward: describing how to turn information into alphas. We will then look backward, with a chapter on information analysis. The last chapter in this section will look forward and backward, covering the information horizon.

Active management is forecasting. The consensus forecasts of expected returns, efficiently implemented, lead to the market or benchmark portfolio. Active managers earn their title by investing in portfolios that differ from their benchmark. As long as they claim to be efficiently investing based on their information, they are at least implicitly forecasting expected returns.

Forecasting is too large a topic to deal with adequately in this book. Instead, we will give the reader some insight into how forecasting techniques can refine raw information and turn it into alphas and forecasts of exceptional return. Earnings estimates, measures of price momentum, and brokers' buy recommendations are pieces of raw information. This chapter and the next will discuss how to turn such raw information into forecasts of exceptional return.

These two chapters on forecasting and the following chapters on information analysis and the information horizon are all closely linked. In this chapter, we will try to deal with terminology and gather some insights. In the next chapter, "Advanced Forecasting," we will apply those insights to some standard real-world issues faced by most active institutional investment managers. In Chap. 12, "Information Analysis," we will show how we can *evaluate* the ability of a variable or a combination of variables to predict returns. In Chap. 13, "The Information Horizon," we will focus specifically on the critical time component of information, using the tools developed in the previous chapters.

The main insights gained in this chapter are the following:

- Active management is forecasting.
- The unconditional or naïve forecast is the consensus expected return. The conditional or informed forecast is dependent on the information source. Historical averages make poor unconditional forecasts.
- A basic forecasting formula connects the naïve and informed forecasts, and handles single and multiple sources of information.
- The refined forecast has the form volatility · IC · score.
- Forecasts of return have negligible effect on forecasts of risk.

NAÏVE, RAW, AND REFINED FORECASTS

Here we will introduce several types of forecasts, and establish a link between our forecasts and returns via the basic forecasting formula. The *naïve* forecast is the consensus expected return. It is the informationless (or uninformed) forecast. The naïve forecast leads to the benchmark holdings.

The *raw* forecast contains the active manager's information in raw form: an earnings estimate, a buy or sell recommendation, etc. The raw forecast can come in a variety of units and scales, and is not directly a forecast of exceptional return.

The basic forecasting formula transforms raw forecasts into *refined* forecasts. The outputs of the formula are forecasts in the form (and units) of exceptional returns, adjusted for the information content of the raw forecast. The formula (which we derive in the appendix) is[1]

$$E\{r|g\} = E\{r\} + \text{Cov}\{r,g\} \cdot \text{Var}^{-1}\{g\} \cdot (g - E\{g\}) \qquad (10.1)$$

where r = excess return vector (N assets)
  g = raw forecast vector (K forecasts)
  $E\{r\}$ = naïve (consensus) forecast
  $E\{g\}$ = expected forecast
  $E\{r \mid g\}$ = informed expected return: the expected return conditional on g

At its core, Eq. (10.1) relates forecasts that differ from their expected levels to forecasts of returns that differ from their expected levels. In fact, we will define the *refined* forecast as the change in expected return due to observing g:

$$\phi \equiv E\{r \mid g\} - E\{r\} = \text{Cov}\{r,g\} \cdot \text{Var}^{-1}\{g\} \cdot (g - E\{g\}) \quad (10.2)$$

This is the exceptional return referred to in previous chapters. It can include both residual return forecasts and benchmark timing. And, given a benchmark portfolio B, the naïve (consensus) forecast is

$$E\{r\} = \beta \cdot \mu_B \qquad (10.3)$$

where we define betas relative to the benchmark and μ_B is the consensus expected excess return of the benchmark. Historical average returns are a poor alternative to these consensus expected returns for the active manager. As discussed in Chap. 2, historical average returns have very large sample errors, and are inappropriate for new or changing stocks. More importantly, Eq. (10.3) provides consensus returns leading to the benchmark.

An equivalent way to think about the basic forecasting formula is to apply it directly to the residual returns θ. Then, instead of Eq. (10.3), we have the equivalent result

$$E\{\theta\} = 0 \qquad (10.4)$$

---

[1]We are using the notation for conditional expectation $E\{r|g\}$ somewhat loosely.

the consensus expected residual returns are 0, and

$$\alpha = \text{Cov}\{\boldsymbol{\theta}, \mathbf{g}\} \cdot \text{Var}^{-1}\{\mathbf{g}\} \cdot (\mathbf{g} - E\{\mathbf{g}\}) \qquad (10.5)$$

In the next sections we will explore the meaning and use of the basic forecasting formula.

REFINING RAW INFORMATION: ONE ASSET AND ONE FORECAST

Let's start with the simplest case—one asset and one forecast—and look at it in two ways. First, we will use the pedagogical tool of the binary model, which we introduced in Chap. 6. Here we will see exactly the processes generating returns and forecasts. Second, we will use regression analysis, where we will not see the underlying processes. Fortunately, these two approaches to the same problem lead us to roughly the same conclusion. This mutual confirmation will reinforce our trust in the formula for refining information. As a side benefit, we will extract a forecasting rule of thumb that will prove useful in countless situations.

In the binary model, we presume that we understand the processes generating returns and forecasts. Suppose we are forecasting return over one quarter; the expected excess return over the quarter is $E\{r\} = 1.5$ percent, and the quarterly volatility is 9 percent. That is equivalent to an annual expected excess return of 6 percent and an annual volatility of 18 percent.

We can write the return we are forecasting as

$$r = 1.5 + \theta_1 + \theta_2 + \cdots + \theta_{81} \qquad (10.6)$$

where 1.5 is the certain expected return, and the 81 random elements θ_i capture the uncertain component of the return. The θ_i are independent and equally likely to achieve $+1$ or -1; thus, each θ_i has expectation 0 and variance 1. The variance of r is 81, corresponding to the desired 9 percent per quarter volatility. We can think of the variables θ_1 through θ_{81} as unit bundles of uncertainty. The random component in the return is the sum of these 81 simple components. We cannot observe the values of the individual θ_i; we can only observe the sum, r.

We observe the return at the end of an investment period, but we must forecast at the beginning of the period. In our example, the forecast, g, has an expected value of 2 percent and a standard deviation of 4 percent. We can model the forecast in a manner similar to the return:

$$g = 2.0 + \theta_1 + \theta_2 + \theta_3 + \eta_1 + \eta_2 + \cdots + \eta_{13} \quad (10.7)$$

The variables θ_1 through θ_3 are elements of the return r. The forecaster actually knows something about part of the return, and knows it at the beginning of the period. The components η_1 through η_{13} are additional bundles of uncertainty in the forecast. They have nothing to do with the return. The forecast is a combination of useful and useless information. The η_j are independent of each other and independent of the θ_i. Each η_j can achieve $+1$ or -1 with equal probability. We can think of the θ_i as bits of signal and the η_j as bits of noise. The forecaster gets 16 unit bundles of information; 3 are signal, 13 are noise. Alas, the forecaster sees only the sum and cannot sort out the signal from the noise.

The covariance of g and r is simply the number of elements of return that they have in common. In this case, $\mathrm{Cov}\{r,g\} = 3$ (θ_1 through θ_3). The correlation between g and r is the skill level or IC:

$$\mathrm{IC} = \mathrm{Corr}\{r,g\} = \frac{\mathrm{Cov}\{r,g\}}{\mathrm{Std}\{r\} \cdot \mathrm{Std}\{g\}} = \frac{3}{9 \cdot 4} = 0.0833 \quad (10.8)$$

We obtain the best linear estimate of the return conditional on knowledge of g by using Eq. (10.1). Focusing now on the refined forecast, for the case of a single asset and a single forecast, we can express this as

$$\phi = \mathrm{Std}\{r\} \cdot \mathrm{Corr}\{r,g\} \cdot \left(\frac{g - E\{g\}}{\mathrm{Std}\{g\}}\right) \quad (10.9)$$

In this particular case, we have

$$\phi = 9 \cdot 0.0833 \cdot \left(\frac{g - 2}{4}\right) \quad (10.10)$$

THE FORECASTING RULE OF THUMB

In the case of one asset and one forecast, we refine the forecast by

- Standardizing the raw forecast by subtracting the expected forecast and dividing by the standard deviation of the forecasts. We call that standardized version of the raw forecast a *score* or *z score*.

■ Scaling the score to account for the skill level of the forecaster (the IC) and the volatility of the return we are attempting to forecast.

Equation (10.9) leads to the forecasting rule of thumb:

$$\text{Refined forecast} = \text{volatility} \cdot \text{IC} \cdot \text{score} \qquad (10.11)$$

With this rule of thumb, we can gain insight into the forecasting process and derive refined forecasts in unstructured situations. In our example, we have a (quarterly) volatility of 9 percent and an IC of 0.0833. The refined forecast will be $0.75 = 0.0833 \cdot 9$ times the score (the standardized raw forecast). If the scores are normally distributed, then our refined forecast will be between -0.75 and $+0.75$ percent two quarters out of three. The refined forecast will be outside the range $\{-1.50 \text{ percent}, +1.50 \text{ percent}\}$ one quarter in twenty.

The forecasting rule of thumb [Eq. (10.11)] also shows the correct behavior in the limiting case of no forecasting skill. If the IC $= 0$, then the refined forecasts are all zero, as they should be in this case.

We will find the same rule of thumb if we use regression analysis instead of the binary model. In the binary model, we presumed that we knew the structure generating the returns and the forecasts. In reality, we are in the dark and must make inferences from available data, or guess based on experience and intuition. Given the data, we will refine the raw forecasts using regression analysis.

Consider a time series of forecasts $g(t)$ and subsequent returns $r(t)$ over a sample of T periods. Let m_r and m_g be the sample averages for r and g, and let $\text{Var}\{r\}$, $\text{Var}\{g\}$, and $\text{Cov}\{r,g\}$ be the sample variances and covariances. We will use the time series regression

$$r(t) = c_0 + c_1 \cdot g(t) + \epsilon(t) \qquad (10.12)$$

as our refining tool. The least-squares estimates of c_1 and c_0 are

$$c_1 = \frac{\text{Cov}\{r,g\}}{\text{Var}\{g\}} = \frac{\text{Std}\{r\} \cdot \text{Corr}\{r,g\}}{\text{Std}\{g\}} \qquad (10.13)$$

$$c_0 = m_r - c_1 \cdot m_g \qquad (10.14)$$

Defining the score as

$$z(t) = \frac{g(t) - m_g}{\text{Std}\{g\}} \tag{10.15}$$

and using the regression results and the definition of refined forecast, we find

$$\phi = \text{Std}\{r\} \cdot \text{Corr}\{r,g\} \cdot z(T + 1) \tag{10.16}$$
$$= \text{volatility} \cdot \text{IC} \cdot \text{score}$$

This is identical to the result in the binary model, except that we are now using the sample history to estimate the IC and the volatility of r and to standardize the raw forecast.[2]

So both the binary model and the regression analysis lead to the same forecasting rule of thumb: The refined forecast of exceptional return has the form volatility $\cdot$ IC $\cdot$ score. For a given signal, the volatility and IC components will be constant, and the score will distinguish this forecast for the asset from previous forecasts for the asset.

Forecasts have the form volatility $\cdot$ IC $\cdot$ score.

Intuition

This refinement process—converting raw forecasts into refined forecasts—controls for three factors: expectations, skill, and volatility. The score calculation controls for expectations by the subtraction of the unconditional expected raw forecast. We can illustrate the intuition here with an example: earnings surprise. An earnings surprise model forecasts alphas based on how reported earnings compare to prior expectations. When earnings just match expectations, the stock price doesn't move. More generally, we expect exceptional price movement only when the raw information doesn't match consensus expectations.

---

[2]As we have noted earlier, our estimates of the means of the returns m_r generally contain a great deal of sample error. The sample errors affect the parameter $c_0 = m_r - c_1 \cdot m_g$. If we have a strong prior reason to believe that the unconditional expected return is equal to m, then we can replace the estimate of the coefficient c_0 by $c_0^* = m - c_1 \cdot m_g$. A Bayesian analysis would start with a prior that the mean is $m \pm d$ and then mix in the sample evidence.

The refinement process controls for skill through the IC term. If IC = 0, the raw forecast contains no useful information, and we set the refined forecast of exceptional return to zero.

Finally, the refinement process controls for volatility. Note first that in the volatility · IC · score construction, the IC and score terms are dimensionless. The volatility term provides the dimensions of return. Also note that given a skill level and two stocks with the same score, the higher-volatility stock receives the higher alpha. Perhaps a utility stock and an Internet stock both appear on a broker's buy list. We expect both stocks to rise. The Internet stock (presumably the more volatile) should rise more.

As we will discuss in the next chapter, the forecasting rule of thumb can also hold for a cross-sectional forecast of exceptional returns, so the score is what distinguishes one stock from another. The average and standard deviation of the time series of scores for a particular stock over time should be close to 0 and 1, respectively. The average and standard deviation of the scores over many stocks at one point in time should also be close to 0 and 1, respectively.

Table 10.1 illustrates the rule of thumb for the Major Market Index as of December 1992. We have used an IC level of 0.09 and used a random number generator to sample the scores from a standard normal distribution.

REFINING FORECASTS: ONE ASSET AND TWO FORECASTS

Let's go back to the binary model and assume we are forecasting the same excess return r with the forecast g from before and a new raw forecast g':

$$g' = 0.5 + \theta_3 + \theta_4 + \theta_5 + \theta_6 + \eta_{10} + \eta_{11} + \cdots \qquad (10.17)$$
$$+ \eta_{30}$$

Forecasts g and g' share one element of signal (θ_3) and four elements of noise ($\eta_{10}, \eta_{11}, \eta_{12},$ and η_{13}). Forecast g' has 25 units of uncertainty; thus Var$\{g'\}$ = 25. Forecast g' contains four elements of signal ($\theta_3, \theta_4, \theta_5, \theta_6$); thus Cov$\{r,g'\}$ = 4. The correlation of r and g' (IC$_{g'}$) is Corr$\{r,g'\}$ = $4/(9 \cdot 5)$ = 0.089. Forecast g' has five bits of information in common with forecast g ($\theta_3, \eta_{10}, \eta_{11}, \eta_{12},$ and η_{13}), and thus Cov$\{g,g'\}$ = 5.

T A B L E 10.1

MMI Stock	Residual Volatility	Score	Alpha
American Express	23.26%	0.35	0.73%
AT&T	15.89%	0.71	1.01%
Chevron	20.44%	−0.25	−0.45%
Coca-Cola	18.92%	−0.48	−0.82%
Disney	19.17%	0.36	0.62%
Dow Chemical	16.93%	−0.77	−1.17%
DuPont	17.29%	1.58	2.47%
Exxon	21.13%	0.00	−0.01%
General Electric	14.42%	0.77	1.01%
General Motors	23.46%	1.98	4.17%
IBM	30.32%	−0.67	−1.84%
International Paper	19.83%	−0.03	−0.05%
Johnson & Johnson	18.97%	−1.77	−3.02%
Kodak	19.20%	−0.06	−0.10%
McDonalds	20.54%	−0.45	−0.82%
Merck	20.43%	0.74	1.36%
3M	13.41%	0.35	0.42%
Procter & Gamble	16.29%	−2.32	−3.40%
Philip Morris	20.17%	−0.89	−1.62%
Sears	22.33%	0.85	1.70%

We now have enough information to use Eq. (10.1). If we were using only g' in this example, we would find

$$\phi = 9 \cdot (0.089) \cdot \left(\frac{g' - 0.5}{5}\right) = (0.16) \cdot (g' - 0.5) \quad (10.18)$$

but combining g and g', we find

$$\phi = (0.1467) \cdot (g - 2.0) + (0.1307) \cdot (g' - 0.5) \quad (10.19)$$

with an IC for the refined combined forecast of 0.1090.

In the case of one asset and two forecasts, we can actually calculate an explicit general result (and rule of thumb):

$$\phi = \text{Std}\{r\} \cdot IC_g^* \cdot z_g + \text{Std}\{r\} \cdot IC_{g'}^* \cdot z_{g'} \quad (10.20)$$

The revised skill levels IC_g^* and $IC_{g'}^*$ take into account the correlation between the forecasts. If $\rho_{gg'}$ is the correlation between forecasts g and g', then:

$$IC_g^* = \frac{IC_g - \rho_{gg'} \cdot IC_{g'}}{1 - \rho_{gg'}^2} \tag{10.21}$$

$$IC_{g'}^* = \frac{IC_{g'} - \rho_{gg'} \cdot IC_g}{1 - \rho_{gg'}^2} \tag{10.22}$$

If the forecasts are uncorrelated, the combined forecast reduces to the sum of the refined forecasts for g and g'. If the forecasts are completely correlated ($\rho_{gg'} = 1$), then Eqs. (10.21) and (10.22) break down (remember that $IC_g = IC_{g'}$ in that case). The second forecast adds nothing.

We could equivalently repackage the scores instead of the ICs. The idea would be to create orthogonal linear combinations of the original scores. In the two-signal example here,

$$z_g^* = \frac{z_g + z_{g'}}{\sqrt{2 \cdot (1 + \rho_{gg'})}} \tag{10.23}$$

and

$$z_{g'}^* = \frac{z_g - z_{g'}}{\sqrt{2 \cdot (1 - \rho_{gg'})}} \tag{10.24}$$

They would exhibit revised ICs

$$IC_g^{**} = \frac{IC_g + IC_{g'}}{\sqrt{2 \cdot (1 + \rho_{gg'})}} \tag{10.25}$$

and

$$IC_{g'}^{**} = \frac{IC_g - IC_{g'}}{\sqrt{2 \cdot (1 - \rho_{gg'})}} \tag{10.26}$$

Since the repackaged scores are uncorrelated, combining them reduces to simple addition.

We can also show that in the two-signal case the IC of the combined forecast is

$$IC_{combined} = \sqrt{\frac{IC_g^2 + IC_{g'}^2 - 2 \cdot \rho_{gg'} \cdot IC_g \cdot IC_{g'}}{1 - \rho_{gg'}^2}} \tag{10.27}$$

If the forecasts are uncorrelated, the square of the combined IC is the sum of the squares of the two component ICs.

We can repeat the two-forecast, one-asset example with regression analysis. The time series regression is now

$$r(t) = c_0 + c_1 \cdot g(t) + c_2 \cdot g'(t) + \epsilon(t) \tag{10.28}$$

and our refined forecast will be

$$\phi = c_1 \cdot [g(T + 1) - m_g] + c_2 \cdot [g'(T + 1) - m_{g'}] \tag{10.29}$$

In our example, with a sufficiently long history (T is very large), we would estimate c_1 close to 0.1467 and c_2 close to 0.1307.

The case of one asset and more than two signals involves more complicated algebra (see the appendix for details). But we can provide some suggestion of what the refinement process does in those cases. Imagine, for example, three signals, each with the same IC. What if the first two signals are highly correlated, but are uncorrelated with the third signal? If all three signals were uncorrelated, we would equal-weight them (simply add the separately refined forecasts). But the refinement process will account for the correlations by halving the ICs of the two correlated signals. Effectively, we will count the uncorrelated signal equally with the sum of the two correlated signals. The general mathematical result captures this intuitive idea, while accounting for all possible intercorrelations.

REFINING FORECASTS: MULTIPLE ASSETS AND MULTIPLE FORECASTS

With multiple assets and multiple forecasts, it is more difficult to apply the basic forecast rule. This is because we lack sufficient data and insight to uncover the required structure. With two forecasts g and g' on each of 500 stocks, the covariance matrix of g and g' is 1000 by 1000, and the covariance of the returns and g and g' is a 500 by 1000 matrix. We will treat this topic in the next chapter, although this chapter includes some simple examples.

EXAMPLES

Now we will consider several practical and less structured examples that rely heavily on our volatility $\cdot$ IC $\cdot$ score rule of thumb for producing a refined forecast of exceptional return. We are assuming that estimates of residual volatility are available. In the absence of sufficient historical information to decide on the IC of the raw forecasts, use these vague but tested guidelines: A good forecaster has IC = 0.05, a great forecaster has IC = 0.10, and a world-class forecaster has IC = 0.15. An IC higher than 0.20 usually signals a faulty backtest or imminent investigation for insider dealing.

A Tip

Consider that most ad hoc of all situations, the stock tip.[3] Let's say the stock in question has typical residual volatility of 20 percent. To change the subjective stock tip into a forecast of residual return, we need the IC and the score. For the IC, look to the track record of the source: If the source is great, set IC = 0.1; if the source is good, IC = 0.05; and if the source is a waste of time, then IC = 0. For the score, we can give a run-of-the-mill tip (very positive) a 1.0 and a very, very positive tip a 2.0. Table 10.2 shows the spectrum of possibilities and the ability to transform some unstructured qualitative information into a more useful quantitative form.

Up/Down Forecast

In a major investment firm, the most notorious and accurate forecaster was a fellow named Charlie. For years, as portfolio managers filed into work, Charlie greeted them with the enthusiastic words: "Market's going up today!" Charlie was right two-thirds of the

T A B L E 10.2

IC	Very Positive (Score = 1)	Very, Very Positive (Score = 2)
Great 0.10	2.0%	4.0%
Good 0.05	1.0%	2.0%
No information 0.00	0.0%	0.0%

_____

[3]Andrew Rudd suggested this example.

time. Of course, Charlie's forecasts weren't very valuable, since the market should on average go up, and two-thirds is about the historical average. The value in the forecast comes from separating up days from down days.

Suppose the expected annual market return is 6 percent with annual risk of 18 percent, corresponding to an expected monthly return of 0.50 percent with a monthly standard deviation of 5.20 percent. We can represent monthly up/down forecasts as $Raw(t) = +1$ for up and $Raw(t) = -1$ for down. If the raw forecasts are consistent with the returns, i.e., two-thirds are $+1$, then the mean and standard deviation of the raw scores will be $1/3$ and 0.9428, respectively. The standardized scores are 0.707 and -1.414. Given an IC (correlating the forecasts with the returns), we find that Refined $= 0.50 + (5.20) \cdot IC \cdot (0.707)$ for an up forecast and Refined $= 0.50 - (5.20) \cdot IC \cdot (1.414)$ for a down forecast. With moderate skill (IC $= 0.075$), the forecasts are 0.78 percent for an up market and -0.05 percent for a down market. The asymmetry follows because, in the absence of any information, we expect an up market with a 0.50 percent return.

Buy and Sell Recommendations

A more structured example involves a buy and sell list. In this case, we give a score of $+1.0$ to the buys and a score of -1.0 to the sells. If we apply this to the Major Market Index stocks, with a random choice of buy and sell and an IC of 0.09, we see the alphas shown in Table 10.3. The rule gives higher alphas to the more volatile stocks. If we ignored the rule and gave an alpha of $+1$ percent to the buy stocks and an alpha of -1 percent to the sell stocks, then an optimizer would select those buy stocks with the lowest residual risk.

Fractiles

Some managers group their assets into deciles or quintiles or quartiles. This is a refinement of the buy/sell idea, which partitions the assets into two groups. If assets have a raw score of 1 through 10 depending on their decile membership, we can turn these into standardized scores by subtracting the average (perhaps value-

T A B L E   10.3

MMI Stock	Residual Volatility	View	Score	Alpha
American Express	23.26%	Sell	−1	−2.09%
AT&T	15.89%	Buy	1	1.43%
Chevron	20.44%	Buy	1	1.84%
Coca-Cola	18.92%	Sell	−1	−1.70%
Disney	19.17%	Sell	−1	−1.73%
Dow Chemical	16.93%	Buy	1	1.52%
DuPont	17.92%	Buy	1	1.56%
Exxon	21.13%	Sell	−1	−1.90%
General Electric	14.42%	Sell	−1	−1.30%
General Motors	23.46%	Buy	1	2.11%
IBM	30.32%	Buy	1	2.73%
International Paper	19.83%	Sell	−1	−1.78%
Johnson & Johnson	18.97%	Buy	1	1.71%
Kodak	19.20%	Buy	1	1.73%
McDonalds	20.54%	Buy	1	1.85%
Merck	20.43%	Sell	−1	−1.84%
3M	13.41%	Sell	−1	−1.21%
Procter & Gamble	16.29%	Sell	−1	−1.47%
Philip Morris	20.17%	Buy	1	1.82%
Sears	22.33%	Sell	−1	−2.01%

weighted) raw score and dividing by the standard deviation of the raw scores.

Rankings

A ranking is similar to a fractile grouping except that there is only one asset in each group. We can look at the rankings, say 1 through 762, as raw scores. First, check to see if the asset ranked 1 is the best or the worst! Then we can, using various degrees of sophistication, transform those rankings into standardized scores.

The Forecast Horizon: New and Old Forecasts

Suppose that we generate a raw forecast each month and that these forecasts are useful in predicting returns for the next 2 months. In this case, the forecast frequency (how often the forecasts arrive) is 1 month and the forecast horizon (the horizon over which the forecasts have predictive power) is 2 months. How do we operate in this situation? As we will show in Chap. 13, the answer is to treat the old forecast as a separate source of information and apply the basic forecasting formula.

FORECASTING AND RISK

Suppose the correlation between the S&P 500 and the MIDCAP has been 0.95 over the past 10 years, but new information leads to a forecast that the S&P 500 will do poorly in the next quarter and the MIDCAP will do well. The temptation is to replace the historical correlation, 0.95, with a negative correlation, since we believe that S&P 500 and MIDCAP returns will move in opposite directions.

This temptation is incorrect. This line of thought confounds the notion of conditional means (i.e., the expected return on the S&P 500 taking into consideration the research) and the notion of conditional covariance (i.e., how the research should influence forecasts of variance and covariance).

It is surprising to note that forecasts of returns have negligible effect on forecasts of volatility and correlation. It is even more surprising to note that what little effect there is has *nothing* to do with the *forecast* and *everything* to do with the *skill of the forecaster*. Thus, in our example, we would adjust the risk forecast in the same way even if the forecast were for the S&P 500 to do well and the MIDCAP to do poorly! This welcome news makes life easier. We can concentrate on the expected return part of the problem and not worry about the risk part.

This result arises because risk measures uncertainty in the return. A skillful forecaster can reduce the amount of uncertainty in the return, and a perfect forecaster reduces the uncertainty to zero (the returns can still vary from month to month, but only exactly according to forecast). For any forecaster, however, the size of the remaining uncertainty in the return stays the same, independent of any particular forecast. And, given typical skill levels, the reduction in risk due to the skill of the forecaster is minimal.

T A B L E 10.4

IC	σ_{POST}
0.00	18.00
0.05	17.98
0.10	17.91
0.15	17.80
0.25	17.43
0.95	5.62
1.00	0.00

Let σ_{PRIOR} and σ_{POST} be estimates of volatility without forecast information and with forecast information. The formula[4] relating these is

$$\sigma_{POST} = \sigma_{PRIOR} \cdot \sqrt{1 - IC^2} \qquad (10.30)$$

Table 10.4 shows how a preforecast volatility of $\sigma_{PRIOR} = 18$ percent (annual) would change depending on the IC of the researcher. Reasonable levels of the IC (from 0 to 0.15) have very little effect on the volatility forecasts.

So much for the volatility forecasts. What about the correlations? The calculation is more complicated, but the general result will be the same. Consider the simplest case of two assets and two forecasts. We now have four balls in the air. We will call the assets S&P 500 (*L* for large) and MIDCAP (*M* for medium). The task is to determine how the correlation between the medium and large stock returns will be changed by our research. This will require some notation. Suppose that the correlation between the medium and large stock returns is ρ_{ML} (in our example, $\rho_{ML} = 0.95$). The term IC_M captures the correlation between the forecasts for the MIDCAP and the subsequent MIDCAP returns. A typical (optimis-

---

[4]The basic variance forecasting formula is

$$Var\{r|g\} = Var\{r\} - Cov\{r,g\} \cdot Var^{-1}\{g\} \cdot Cov\{g,r\}$$

This leads to Eq. (10.30). This formula is discussed in Proposition 2 of the technical appendix.

tic) number is 0.1. The term IC_L is the correlation between the large stock (S&P 500) forecasts and the subsequent S&P 500 returns—again, typically 0.1 or smaller.

We will assume that the correlation between the forecasts is also ρ_{ML}. We also have to specify the cross-correlations between the MIDCAP forecasts and the S&P 500 return and between the S&P 500 forecasts and the MIDCAP return. For simplicity, we will assume that these are zero.[5]

Under those reasonable assumptions, we find the following formula for the revised correlation:

$$\rho^*_{ML} = \rho_{ML} \cdot \left[\frac{1 - IC_M \cdot IC_L}{\sqrt{(1 - IC_M^2) \cdot (1 - IC_L^2)}} \right] \qquad (10.31)$$

At first, this appears to be a formidable equation. However, if $IC_M = IC_L$, then the naïve correlation forecast is unchanged. A little analysis will show that the correlation changes very little when the information coefficients are in the 0 to 0.15 range. Once again, the revised correlation depends only on our skill at forecasting and not on the forecast.

What can we conclude? The researcher who tries to forecast returns over the near horizon should ignore the slight impact of those forecasts on the volatility and correlation estimates for the assets. Asset allocators in particular should take note of this. Many asset allocators are seduced by the possibility of forecasting volatility and correlation along with returns. They believe that the market has changed and is obeying a new reality. The same force responsible for the exceptional returns is also changing the covariance structure. This is easier to imagine than to establish. There is some evidence of "regime changes" in short-run currency volatilities and correlations, however, in general there is more stability than instability in asset volatilities and correlations.

---

[5]It might be slightly more clever to say that the MIDCAP forecast gives us some insight (through IC_M) into future MIDCAP returns, and that future MIDCAP returns give us insight (through ρ_{ML}) into future S&P 500 returns. That would lead us to correlations of $IC_M \cdot \rho_{ML}$ between the MIDCAP forecast and the S&P 500 return, and of $IC_L \cdot \rho_{ML}$ between the S&P 500 forecast and the MIDCAP return.

ADVANCED TECHNIQUES

Up to this point, we have concentrated on simple techniques like counting in the binary model or linear regression. There are a host of more sophisticated forecasting procedures. As a general rule, increasing levels of sophistication carry both additional power and a larger chance that you may lose control of the process: The investment insights become submerged, the technique takes over, and you lose sight of the statistical significance of the results. If the technique is in control of you rather than the other way around, then you should probably look for more basic and more stable tools.

A guiding principle is to move from the simple to the more complicated; master the simple cases, understand the shortcomings, and then move to more complicated situations and techniques. Also, when using sophisticated techniques, always run two specific tests to make sure they are working correctly. First, see how they work when you feed in random data. Successful predictions from random data indicate a problem. Second, feed in simulated data where you know the underlying relationship. Does the sophisticated technique find it? Many sophisticated techniques do not come with associated statistical tests. Fortunately, modern computers, combined with the bootstrapping methodology, allow you to run your own statistical tests.

Here we will present several specific advanced techniques. In the next chapter, "Advanced Forecasting," we come back to the basic methodology, but apply it to more complex, real-world situations.

Time Series Analysis

This is a world unto itself, with its own jargon and notation. The textbook of Box and Jenkins (1976) is standard, as is the more recent treatment by Lütkepohl (1991). The litany of models is:

AR(q). Autoregressive: The time t value of a variable, $r(t)$, depends on a weighted sum of the varible's past q values $\{r(t\text{-}1), r(t\text{-}2), \ldots, r(t\text{-}q)\}$ plus some random input, $e(t)$:

$$r(t) = a_0 + a_1 \cdot r(t-1) + \cdots + a_q \cdot r(t-q) + e(t)$$

MA(p). Moving average: The time t value of a variable is the weighted average of a sum of $p + 1$ random (independent) inputs $e(t)$, $e(t - 1)$, ..., $e(t - p)$:

$$r(t) = e(t) + c_1 \cdot e(t - 1) + \cdots + c_p \cdot e(t - p) + c_0$$

ARMA(q,p). Autoregressive moving average. You guessed it, a combination of AR(q) and MA(p).

ARIMA. ARMA applied to first differences; i.e., instead of looking at returns, look at the changes in returns.

VARMA. ARMA applied to more than one variable at a time: vector ARMA. The method predicts K returns using J possible explanatory variables along with their lagged values.

ARCH, GARCH, etc.

ARCH stands for autoregressive conditional heteroskedasticity, and GARCH for Generalized ARCH. Typically, the goal of these models is to forecast volatility (and sometimes correlations). Robert Engle developed this technique. For a review of applications in finance, see the article by Bollerslev, Chou, and Kroner (1992).

The ARCH and GARCH methods apply when volatility changes in some predictable fashion; e.g., periods of high volatility tend to follow large negative or positive returns. The standard GARCH model of volatility posits the following structure: Three factors influence current volatility. First, even changing volatility exhibits a long-run average. Second, mean reversion will tend to move current volatility toward that long-run average. Third, recent returns can shock volatility away from the long-run average. These are basic time series concepts applied to volatility instead of return.

More advanced GARCH models allow for the differing influence of large negative and large positive recent returns. We often observe that stock market volatility increases on downturns, but decreases as the market rises.

ARCH and related nonlinear techniques are most useful when a limited number of returns are under consideration; i.e., they are more appropriate for asset allocation than for stock selection. In risk models, these techniques can enhance the forecast covariance matrix by improving the forecast of market or systematic risk. The idea is to extract the most important single factor, and then apply this advanced technique to that one time series. ARCH techniques are most pronounced when the investment horizon is short—days rather than the longer investment horizon of months or years. Finally, ARCH techniques can be extremely useful in strategies that have a strong option component, because better volatility forecasts lead directly to better option prices.

Kalman Filters

Kalman filters are closely linked to Bayesian analysis. Our fundamental forecasting law is a simple example. We start with a prior mean and variance for the returns and then adapt that mean and variance conditional on some new information. Kalman filters work in the same manner, although their working is often obscured by electrical engineering/optimal control jargon. See Bryson and Ho (1969), chap. 12, for an introduction to Kalman filters and an exploration of the links with Bayesian analysis when the random variables are normally distributed. See the paper of Diderrich (1985) for a link between Kalman filters and Goldberger-Theil estimators in regression analysis.

Chaos

Chaos theory concerns unstable and nonlinear phenomena. In the investment context, it has come to mean the discovery and use of nonlinear models of return and volatility. We would like to distinguish between random phenomena and predictable phenomena that are generated in a deterministic but highly nonlinear way. These can appear to be the same thing.

A typical example is the random-number generator. Computers generate random numbers in a totally reproducible way, but the numbers appear to be random. The forecaster using chaos theory starts with the output of the random-number generator and tries to reverse-engineer the nonlinear rules that are used to produce its outputs. This is not an easy task.

Another example of chaos is the tent map. Given an initial number $x(0)$ between 0 and 1, we generate the next number with

$$x(t) = \text{Min}\{2 \cdot x(t-1), 2 - 2 \cdot x(t-1)\} \qquad (10.32)$$

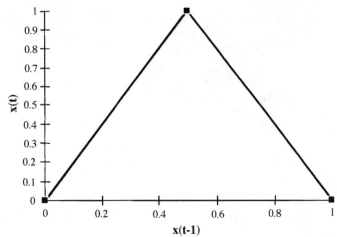

Figure 10.1

If $x(t)$ gets stuck on 0, choose $x(t+1)$ at random. This rule will produce a sequence of numbers that looks very much like a sequence of randomly distributed numbers between 0 and 1. However, if we look in two dimensions at the pairs $\{x(t-1),x(t)\}$, we see that they all lie on the tent-shaped line in Fig. 10.1. For a true sequence of random numbers, the pairs $\{x(t-1),x(t)\}$ would fill up the entire square in two dimensions.

To apply chaos theory to forecasting, take the residuals from the forecasting rules and look at these two-, three-, and higher-dimension pictures for evidence of a nonlinear relationship like the tent map. If there is such evidence, strengthen the model by trying to capture that relationship. See the paper by Hsieh (1995) for an excellent application of this idea and some interesting modeling techniques.

Neural Nets[6]

In the past few years, application of neural nets to various problems across the spectrum of the investment world has gained wide pub-

---

[6]Hertz, Krogh, and Palmer (1991) is a standard reference.

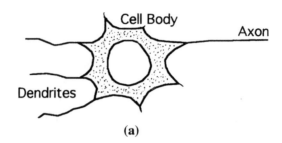

(a)

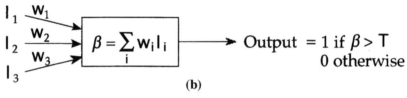

(b)

Figure 10.2

licity. Hornik, Stinchcombe, and White (1988) have shown that neural nets can approximate almost any conceivable function. In problems involving high signal-to-noise ratios, neural nets have proved to be a powerful analytic tool. In problems involving low signal-to-noise ratios, in particular forecasting exceptional returns, the applicability of neural nets is far from certain.[7]

Neural nets are a model of computation inspired by biological neural circuitry (see Fig. 10.2). Each artificial neuron weights several input signals to determine its output signal nonlinearly. Typically, as the weighted input signal exceeds some threshold T, the output quickly varies from 0 to 1. A neural network is an assembly of these artificial neurons, with, for example, a layer of input neurons feeding into an inner (hidden) layer of neurons that feeds into an output layer (Fig. 10.3).

Neural nets can solve very general problems, but they are not very intuitive. Unlike more standard computer programs, neural nets do not have the problem solution built into them from the

---

[7]See Kahn and Basu (1994).

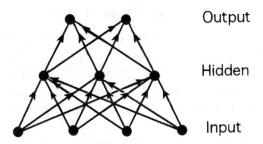

Output

Hidden

Input

Figure 10.3

ground up. Instead, they are taught how to solve the problem by training them with a particular set of data. The neural net is trained (its internal coefficients estimated) to optimally match inputs with desired outputs. Therefore, neural nets are very dependent on the data used for training.

Neural nets have been applied to many areas of research and finance. All of these fall into two general categories, which we can illustrate by example. We characterize the first category by the problem of modeling bond ratings. Here we wish to apply neural net technology to predict bond ratings from underlying company financial data. Effectively, we are reverse-engineering the process implemented by Moody's and S&P. We can characterize this problem by its nonlinear relation between the financial data and the ratings, its relative stability over time, and its high signal-to-noise ratio. We can illustrate the second general category by the application of neural nets to forecasting returns. Here we wish to use neural nets to predict asset returns from underlying financial and economic data and past returns. We can characterize this problem by its nonlinear relation between explanatory variables and observed returns, its relative instability over time, and its low signal-to-noise ratio.

Neural nets have worked well for the first type of problem, characterized by nonlinearities, stable relationships, and high signal-to-noise ratios. As for the second type of problem, many financial researchers have applied neural nets here, with many claims of success. However, definitive and statistically significant proof of success is still lacking.

Genetic Algorithms[8]

Genetic algorithms are a heuristic optimization method motivated by a loose analogy to the process of biological evolution. Species evolve through survival of the fittest; each generation begets the next through a mixture of mating, mutation, and training. The overall population thus evolves in a semirandom manner toward greater fitness.

The computational analogy is optimizing a function of several variables, where each combination of the variables defines an "individual" and the function to be maximized is the "fitness" criterion.

We choose a random initial "population" and evaluate the fitness of each individual member; then we create each successive generation by combining the fittest members of its prior generation. We repeat this last step until we converge to a best solution. A strong element of randomness in the "evolution" step allows wide exploration of possible solutions. For instance, we can randomly combine elements of the fitter solutions or randomly alter some elements of a fit solution—we label these "mating" and "mutation," respectively.

One area where we have applied genetic algorithms is the paring problem, e.g., find the best 50-stock portfolio to track the S&P 500. A standard quadratic optimizer can find the optimal portfolio weights for a given list of 50 stocks to track the S&P 500. The tricky part is to search through the possible lists of 50 names. The combinatorics involved guarantee that we can't exactly solve this problem.

BARRA and others have developed heuristic approaches to this problem. After considerable research efforts (~6 person-months), they have developed methods which quickly (a few seconds on a 1998 PC) find reasonable answers. As an alternative, they coded a genetic algorithm in a weekend; it found similarly good answers to this problem after about 48 hours of CPU time on a similarly powered machine. So for this type of problem, genetic algorithms are quite attractive as one-time solutions. They are perhaps less attractive for use in industrial-strength commercial software.

---

[8]Holland (1975) is a standard reference.

In the realm of forecasting, we often search for the signal with maximum information ratio. Imagine instead a "population" of possible signals, initially chosen at random, which we then "evolve" using the criterion of maximum information ratio.

Since genetic algorithms are effectively able (in successful applications) to "learn" the characteristics of the fittest solutions, they require less coding than analytic techniques, and they run faster than an explicit examination of all possible solutions.

SUMMARY

Active management is forecasting. We can use a basic forecasting formula to adjust forecast returns away from the consensus, based on how far the raw forecasts differ from the consensus and on the information content of the raw forecasts. We capture this basic result in the forecasting rule of thumb: The exceptional return forecast takes on the form volatility · IC · score. The chapter has applied these relationships in several specific examples.

The next chapter will move on to some more complicated situations, especially those involving multiple assets and cross-sectional forecasts.

PROBLEMS

1. Assume that residual returns are uncorrelated, and that we will use an optimizer to maximize risk-adjusted residual return. Using the data in Table 10.3, what asset will the optimizer choose as the largest positive active holding? How would that change if we had assigned $\alpha = 1$ for buys and $\alpha = -1$ for sells? *Hint:* At optimality, assuming uncorrelated residual returns, the optimal active holdings are

$$h_n = \frac{\alpha_n}{2 \cdot \lambda_R \cdot \omega_n^2}$$

2. For the situation described in Problem 1, show that using the forecasting rule of thumb, we assume equal risk for each asset. What happens if we just use $\alpha = 1$ for buys and $\alpha = -1$ for sells?

3. Use the basic forecasting formula [Eq. (10.1)] to derive Eq. (10.20), the refined forecast in the case of one asset and two forecasts.

4. In the case of two forecasts [Eq. (10.20)], what is the variance of the combined forecast? What is its covariance with the return? Verify explicitly that the combination of g and g' in the example leads to an IC of 0.1090. Compare this to the result from Eq. (10.23).

5. You are using a neural net to forecast returns to one stock. The net inputs include fundamental accounting data, analysts' forecasts, and past returns. The net combines these nonlinearly. How would the forecasting rule of thumb change under these circumstances?

REFERENCES

Bickel, P. J., and K. A. Doksum. *Mathematical Statistics* (San Francisco: Holden Day, 1977), pp. 127–129.

Black, Fisher, and Robert Litterman, "Global Asset Allocation with Equities, Bonds, and Currencies." *Fixed Income Research*, Goldman, Sachs & Co., New York, October 1991.

Bollerslev, T., R. Y. Chou, and K. F. Kroner. "ARCH Modeling in Finance." *Journal of Econometrics*, vol. 52, no. 1, April 1992, pp. 5–59.

Box, George E. P., and Gwilym M. Jenkins. *Time Series Analysis: Forecasting and Control* (San Francisco: Holden-Day, 1976).

Bryson, A. E., and Y. C. Ho. *Applied Optimal Control.* (Waltham, MA: Blaisdell, 1969).

Chopra, Vijay Kumar, and Patricia Lin. "Improving Financial Forecasting: Combining Data with Intuition." *Journal of Portfolio Management*, vol. 22, no. 3, 1996, pp. 97–105.

Diderrich, G. T. "The Kalman Filter from the Perspective of Goldberger-Theil Estimators." *The American Statistician*, vol. 39, no. 3, 1985, pp. 193–198.

Grinold, Richard C. "Alpha Is Volatility Times IC Times Score, or Real Alphas Don't Get Eaten." *Journal of Portfolio Management*, vol. 20, no. 4, 1994, pp. 9–16.

Hertz, J., A. Krogh, and Richard G. Palmer. *Introduction to the Theory of Neural Computation* (Redwood City, Calif.: Addison-Wesley, 1991).

Holland, John H. *Adaptation in Natural and Artificial Systems* (Ann Arbor: University of Michigan Press, 1975).

Hornik, K., M. Stinchcombe, and H. White. "Multi-layer Feedforward Networks Are Universal Approximators." Working paper, University of California, San Diego, June 1988.

Hsieh, D. A. "Chaos and Nonlinear Dynamics: Application to Financial Markets." *Journal of Finance*, vol. 46, no. 5, 1991, pp. 1839–1877.

————. "Nonlinear Dynamics in Financial Markets: Evidence and Implications." *Financial Analysts Journal*, vol. 51, no. 4, 1995, pp. 55–62.

Johnson, N. L., and S. Kotz. *Distributions in Statistics: Continuous Multivariate Distributions* (New York: John Wiley & Sons, 1972), pp. 40–41.

Kahn, Ronald N., and Archan Basu. "Neural Nets and Fixed Income Strategies." *BARRA Newsletter*, Fall 1994.

Lütkepohl, H. *Introduction to Multiple Time Series Analysis* (New York: Springer-Verlag, 1991).

Rao, C. R. *Linear Statistical Inference and Its Application*, 2d ed. (New York: John Wiley & Sons, 1973), pp. 314–333.

Searle, S. R. *Linear Models* (New York: John Wiley & Sons, 1971), pp. 88–89.

Theil, Henri. *Principles of Econometrics* (New York: John Wiley & Sons, 1971), pp. 122–123.

TECHNICAL APPENDIX

This appendix will cover two technical topics: deriving the basic forecasting formula, along with some related technical results, and analyzing specific examples from the main text of the chapter.

The Basic Forecasting Formula

We will now show that the basic forecasting formula provides the linear unbiased estimate with minimum mean squared error. Most statistics books discuss this topic under the name of either *minimum variance unbiased estimates* (m.v.u.e.) or *best linear unbiased estimates* (b.l.u.e.),[9] and deal with the case where $\text{Var}\{g\}$, $E\{g\}$, and $\text{Cov}\{r,g\}$ are unknown.

Let's start with the estimate:

$$\hat{\mathbf{r}} = E\{\mathbf{r}\} + \text{Cov}\{\mathbf{r,g}\} \cdot \text{Var}^{-1}\{\mathbf{g}\} \cdot (\mathbf{g} - E\{\mathbf{g}\}) \qquad (10\text{A}.1)$$

Proposition 1

$\hat{\mathbf{r}}$ is

1. An unbiased estimate of $\mathbf{r}$
2. The estimate of $\mathbf{r}$ that has the smallest mean squared error among all *linear* estimates of $\mathbf{r}$

---

[9]See Bickel and Doksum (1977), pp. 127–129; Theil (1977), pp. 122–123; and Rao (1973), pp. 314–333.

Proof A general linear estimate can be written as

$$\mathbf{r}(\mathbf{g};\mathbf{b},\mathbf{A}) = \mathbf{b} + \mathbf{A} \cdot \mathbf{g} \qquad (10A.2)$$

The estimation error is $\mathbf{q} = \mathbf{r} - \mathbf{r}(\mathbf{g};\mathbf{b},\mathbf{A})$, and the mean squared error is

$$\text{MSE}\{\mathbf{b},\mathbf{A}\} = E\{\mathbf{q}^T \cdot \mathbf{q}\} = E\left\{\sum_n q_n^2\right\} \qquad (10A.3)$$

To minimize the mean squared error, we take the derivative of $\text{MSE}\{\mathbf{b},\mathbf{A}\}$ with respect to each of the N elements of $\mathbf{b}$ and each of the $N \cdot K$ elements of $\mathbf{A}$ and set them equal to 0.

Setting the derivative with respect to b_n equal to 0 yields

$$b_n = E\{r_n\} - \sum_{k=1}^{K} A_{n,k} \cdot E\{g_k\} \qquad (10A.4)$$

This result, along with Eq. (10A.2), demonstrates that the expected error is 0, i.e., the linear estimate that minimizes mean squared error is unbiased. We can therefore restrict our attention to linear estimates of the form

$$\mathbf{r}(\mathbf{g};\mathbf{b},\mathbf{A}) = E\{\mathbf{r}\} + \mathbf{A} \cdot (\mathbf{g} - E\{\mathbf{g}\}) \qquad (10A.5)$$

For convenience, let us introduce the notation $\mathbf{s} = \mathbf{g} - E\{\mathbf{g}\}$ and $\mathbf{p} = \mathbf{r} - E\{\mathbf{r}\}$. With this notation, we have $\mathbf{q} = \mathbf{p} - \mathbf{A} \cdot \mathbf{s}$, and so $E\{\mathbf{g}\} = 0$ and

$$\text{MSE}\{\mathbf{A}\} = E\{\mathbf{p}^T \cdot \mathbf{p}\} - 2 \cdot E\{\mathbf{p}^T \cdot \mathbf{A} \cdot \mathbf{s}\} + E\{\mathbf{s}^T \cdot \mathbf{A}^T \cdot \mathbf{A} \cdot \mathbf{s}\} \quad (10A.6)$$

Taking the derivative of the mean squared error with respect to the element $A_{n,k}$ leads to

$$E\{q_n,s_k\} = \text{Cov}\{q_n,s_k\} = E\left\{\left(p_n - \sum_{j=1}^{K} A_{n,j} \cdot s_j\right) \cdot s_k\right\} \quad (10A.7)$$

According to Eq. (10A.7), the errors in our estimate are uncorrelated with the raw forecasts. If **q** and **s** are correlated, we are leaving some information on the table; we should exploit any correlation to further reduce the mean squared error.

In matrix notation, Eq. (10A.7) becomes

$$E\{q \cdot s^T\} = Cov\{r,g\} - A \cdot Var\{g\} = 0 \qquad (10A.8)$$

$$A = Cov\{r,g\} \cdot Var^{-1}\{g\} \qquad (10A.9)$$

Equations (10A.9) and (10A.5) now demonstrate that $\hat{r}$ is the linear estimate with minimum mean squared error.

The linear estimate $\hat{r}$ has additional properties if **r** and **g** have a joint normal distribution.

Proposition 2

If {r,g} have a normal distribution, then

1. $\hat{r}$ is the maximum likelihood estimate of **r** given **g**.
2. $\hat{r} = E\{r|g\}$ is the conditional expectation of **r** given **g**.
3. $Var\{r|g\} = Var\{r\} - Cov\{r,g\} \cdot Var^{-1}\{g\} \cdot Cov\{g,r\}$ is the conditional variance of **r** given **g**.
4. $\hat{r}$ has minimum mean squared error among all unbiased estimates, whether they are linear or not.

Proof   The covariance of **r** and **g** is

$$V = \begin{cases} Var\{r\} & Cov\{r,g\} \\ Cov\{g,r\} & Var\{g\} \end{cases} \qquad (10A.10)$$

and the inverse covariance matrix is

$$V^{-1} = Q = \begin{cases} Q\{r\} & Q\{r,g\} \\ Q\{g,r\} & Q\{g\} \end{cases} \qquad (10A.11)$$

Given an observation {p,s} and the normal distribution assumption, the likelihood of that observation is

$$L = \frac{\exp\left\{-\dfrac{(p^T,s^T) \cdot Q \cdot (p,s)}{2}\right\}}{\sqrt{(2\pi)^{N+K} \det[Q]}} \qquad (10A.12)$$

Maximizing the log likelihood function is therefore equivalent to minimizing

$$\mathbf{p}^T \cdot \mathbf{Q}\{\mathbf{r}\} \cdot \mathbf{p} + 2 \cdot \mathbf{p}^T \cdot \mathbf{Q}\{\mathbf{r},\mathbf{g}\} \cdot \mathbf{s} + \mathbf{s}^T \cdot \mathbf{Q}\{\mathbf{g}\} \cdot \mathbf{s} \quad (10A.13)$$

If we fix $\mathbf{s}$ and choose $\mathbf{p}$ to minimize Eq. (10A.13), the optimal $\mathbf{p}^*$ is

$$\mathbf{p}^* = -\mathbf{Q}^{-1}\{\mathbf{r}\} \cdot \mathbf{Q}\{\mathbf{r},\mathbf{g}\} \cdot \mathbf{s} \quad (10A.14)$$

However, since $\mathbf{Q}$ is the inverse of $\mathbf{V}$, we can use Eqs. (10A.10) and (10A.11) to show that

$$\mathrm{Cov}\{\mathbf{r},\mathbf{g}\} \cdot \mathrm{Var}^{-1}\{\mathbf{g}\} = -\mathbf{Q}^{-1}\{\mathbf{r}\} \cdot \mathbf{Q}\{\mathbf{r},\mathbf{g}\} \quad (10A.15)$$

Equations (10A.14) and (10A.15) establish item 1.

Items 2 and 3 are standard properties of the multinormal distribution.[10] Note that

$$\mathbf{Q}^{-1}\{\mathbf{r}\} = \mathrm{Var}\{\mathbf{r}\} - \mathrm{Cov}\{\mathbf{r},\mathbf{g}\} \cdot \mathrm{Var}^{-1}\{\mathbf{g}\} \cdot \mathrm{Cov}\{\mathbf{g},\mathbf{r}\} \quad (10A.16)$$

Item 4 involves some statistical theory. There is a covariance matrix, called the Cramer-Rao lower bound, such that the covariance of any *unbiased* estimate of $\mathbf{r}$ will be greater than or equal to the Cramer-Rao lower bound.[11] In the case of normal random variables, one can show that $\mathrm{Var}\{\mathbf{r}|\mathbf{g}\}$ equals the Cramer-Rao lower bound, and thus it is the minimum-variance unbiased estimate without adding the restriction that the estimate must be linear.

Technical Treatment of Examples

We have now proved the basic forecasting formula and discussed some further technical results. The remainder of the appendix will discuss some specific examples from the main text concerning multiple forecasts for an asset.

Let's consider the case of one asset with K forecasts:

$$\mathbf{g} = [g_1, \ldots, g_K] \quad (10A.17)$$

---

[10]See Johnson and Kotz (1972), pp. 40–41.
[11]See Rao (1973) or Searle (1971).

$$\text{and } \text{Var}\{\mathbf{g}\} = \begin{bmatrix} \text{Std}\{g_1\} & & 0 \\ & \ddots & \\ 0 & & \text{Std}\{g_K\} \end{bmatrix} \tag{10A.18}$$

$$\cdot \, \boldsymbol{\rho}_g \cdot \begin{bmatrix} \text{Std}\{g_1\} & & 0 \\ & \ddots & \\ 0 & & \text{Std}\{g_K\} \end{bmatrix}$$

Now the covariance matrix between the return and these K signals will involve K information coefficients:

$$\text{Cov}\{\mathbf{r},\mathbf{g}\} = \omega \cdot [IC_1 \dots IC_K] \cdot \begin{bmatrix} \text{Std}\{g_1\} & & 0 \\ & \ddots & \\ 0 & & \text{Std}\{g_K\} \end{bmatrix} \tag{10A.19}$$

We can now substitute Eqs. (10A.18) and (10A.19) into the basic forecasting formula [Eq. (10.2)], to find

$$\phi = \text{Cov}\{\mathbf{r},\mathbf{g}\} \cdot \text{Var}^{-1}\{\mathbf{g}\} \cdot (\mathbf{g} - E\{\mathbf{g}\}) \tag{10A.20}$$

$$= \omega \cdot [IC_1 \dots IC_K] \cdot \boldsymbol{\rho}_g^{-1} \cdot \begin{bmatrix} \dfrac{1}{\text{Std}\{g_1\}} & & 0 \\ & \ddots & \\ 0 & & \dfrac{1}{\text{Std}\{g_K\}} \end{bmatrix} \cdot \begin{bmatrix} g_1 - E\{g_1\} \\ \vdots \\ g_K - E\{g_K\} \end{bmatrix}$$

Using our definition of scores, $\mathbf{z}$, we can simplify this to

$$\phi = \omega \cdot [IC_1 \dots IC_K] \cdot \boldsymbol{\rho}_g^{-1} \cdot \begin{bmatrix} z_1 \\ \vdots \\ z_K \end{bmatrix} \tag{10A.21}$$

$$= \omega \cdot IC^T \cdot \boldsymbol{\rho}_g^{-1} \cdot \mathbf{z}$$

where
$$z_j \equiv \frac{g_j - E\{g_j\}}{\text{Std}\{g_j\}} \tag{10A.22}$$

Furthermore, we can use Eq. (10A.21) to calculate the variance

of the combined signal, its covariance with the return, and hence
its combined information coefficient:

$$IC_{combined} = \sqrt{IC^T \cdot \rho_g^{-1} \cdot IC} \qquad (10A.23)$$

Equations (10A.21) and (10A.23) are the general results. If
$K = 1$, then $\rho_g = 1$, and these reduce to the standard volatility $\cdot$ IC $\cdot$
score. If $K = 2$, then

$$\rho_g = \begin{bmatrix} 1 & \rho_{12} \\ \rho_{12} & 1 \end{bmatrix} \qquad (10A.24)$$

$$\rho_g^{-1} = \left(\frac{1}{1 - \rho_{12}^2}\right) \cdot \begin{bmatrix} 1 & -\rho_{12} \\ -\rho_{12} & 1 \end{bmatrix} \qquad (10A.25)$$

and $\quad \phi = \omega \cdot \left(\frac{IC_1 - \rho_{12} \cdot IC_2}{1 - \rho_{12}^2}\right) \cdot z_1 + \omega \cdot \left(\frac{IC_2 - \rho_{12} \cdot IC_1}{1 - \rho_{12}^2}\right) \cdot z_2$

$$(10A.26)$$

which is basically Eq. (10.20) in the main text. We can similarly
show that Eq. (10A.23) reduces to Eq. (10.23) when $K = 2$.
If $K = 3$, we need to invert:

$$\rho_g = \begin{bmatrix} 1 & \rho_{12} & \rho_{13} \\ \rho_{12} & 1 & \rho_{23} \\ \rho_{13} & \rho_{23} & 1 \end{bmatrix} \qquad (10A.27)$$

For any number of forecasts, the key is to invert the matrix ρ_g. Note
that for any number of forecasts, Eq. (10A.21) always leads to
refined forecasts of the form

$$\phi = \omega \cdot \sum_j IC_j' \cdot z_j \qquad (10A.28)$$

The refined forecast is always a linear combination of the scores.
The goal of this methodology is simply to determine the weights
(the adjusted information coefficients) in that linear combination.

Exercise

1. Using Eq. (10A.21), what is the variance of the combined forecast? What is its covariance with the return? Remember that the combined forecast is simply a linear combination of signals. We know the volatilities and correlations of all the signals, and we know the correlation of each signal with the return.

   Verify Eq. (10A.23) for the IC of the combined forecast. Demonstrate that when $K = 2$, it reduces to Eq. (10.27) in the main text of the chapter.

CHAPTER 11

Advanced Forecasting

INTRODUCTION

Chapter 10 covered forecasting basics, especially the insight that refined alphas control for volatility, skill, and expectations. In the context of a single asset, Chapter 10 also examined how to combine multiple signals, and even briefly presented some choices of advanced and nonlinear methodologies.

Chapter 10 has provided much of the insight into forecasting. But it hasn't covered the standard case facing institutional managers: multiple assets. This chapter will mainly focus on that important practical topic. It will also cover the particular case of factor forecasts, and some ideas about dealing with uncertain information coefficients.

Highlights will include the following:

- The single-asset methodology also applies to multiple assets.
- A complication occurs when we have cross-sectional and not time series scores. In many cases, we need not multiply cross-sectional scores by volatility.
- If you have information and you forecast some factor returns, do not set other factor forecasts to zero.
- Uncertainty in the IC will lead to shrinkage in the alpha.

We begin with the discussion of multiple assets.

MULTIPLE ASSETS

The standard situation for an institutional manager involves multiple assets: choosing a portfolio that will outperform the benchmark. The chapters in Part 1, "Foundations," discussed exactly this case.

First, we must point out that the basic forecasting formula, Eq. (10.1), applies in the case of multiple assets and multiple signals:

$$E\{\mathbf{r}|\mathbf{g}\} = E\{\mathbf{r}\} + \text{Cov}\{\mathbf{r,g}\} \cdot \text{Var}^{-1}\{\mathbf{g}\} \cdot (\mathbf{g} - E\{\mathbf{g}\}) \qquad (11.1)$$

In Eq. (11.1), we can treat both $\mathbf{r}$ and $\mathbf{g}$ as vectors of length N and K, respectively, where K/N measures the number of signals per asset. In the case of one signal per asset, the technical appendix will show that the forecasting rule of thumb still applies for each asset n:

$$\phi_n = \omega_n \cdot \text{IC} \cdot z_{\text{TS},n} \qquad (11.2)$$

We are assuming that the signal has the same information coefficient across all assets.

We have also introduced the subscript "TS" to explicitly label the score as a time series score. The time series of scores for asset n, $z_{\text{TS},n}$, has mean 0 and standard deviation 1. This is the definition of score that we discussed in Chap. 10. We will contrast these scores with cross-sectional scores, $z_{\text{CS},n}$.

Unfortunately, Eq. (11.2) doesn't describe the typical situation facing a manager: a numerical forecast for each stock at a given time. We do not have N time series scores; rather, we can calculate one set of cross-sectional scores. Cross-sectional scores have mean 0 and standard deviation 1 across N stocks at one time. We want time series scores. We have cross-sectional scores. How do we proceed?

CROSS-SECTIONAL SCORES

The time series score $z_{\text{TS},n}$ depends not only on the current signal, $g_n(t)$, but also on the time series average and the standard deviation of g_n:

$$z_{\text{TS},n}(t) = \frac{g_n(t) - E_{\text{TS}}\{g_n\}}{\text{Std}_{\text{TS}}\{g_n\}} \qquad (11.3)$$

But if we can calculate only a cross-sectional set of $\{g_n\}$ (i.e., g_n

for $n = 1, 2, \ldots N$ at one time t), we can calculate only cross-sectional scores:

$$z_{CS,n}(t) = \frac{g_n(t) - E_{CS}\{g_n(t)\}}{Std_{CS}\{g_n(t)\}} \qquad (11.4)$$

How can we move from the cross-sectional scores we can easily observe to the time series scores required for Eq. (11.2)?

For simplicity, let's assume that the mean forecast over time is 0 for each stock, and that the IC for each stock is the same and that forecasts are uncorrected across stocks. We will then analyze two cases. In Case 1, the time series standard deviation of the signal is the same for each asset. In Case 2, the time series standard deviations of the signals are proportional to stock volatility. For example, if stock A is twice as volatile as stock B, its raw signal $g_A(t)$ will be twice as volatile as $g_B(t)$.

Case 1: Identical Time Series Signal Volatilities

In case 1, we are assuming that

$$Std_{TS}\{g_n\} = c_1 \qquad (11.5)$$

where c_1 is independent of n. In this case, we can estimate c_1 via time series or cross-sectional analysis. We can estimate c_1 from a time series of scores chosen from a distribution with standard deviation c_1. Alternatively, we can estimate c_1 by choosing cross-sectionally from a set of distributions, each with mean 0 and standard deviation c_1. In other words, if the time series standard deviations are identical, then time series scores equal cross-sectional scores:

$$z_{TS,n} = \frac{g_n}{Std_{TS}\{g_n\}} = \frac{g_n}{c_1} = \frac{g_n}{Std_{CS}\{g_n\}} \qquad (11.6)$$

$$\alpha_n = \omega_n \cdot IC \cdot z_{CS,n} \qquad (11.7)$$

Case 2: Time Series Signal Volatilities Proportional to Asset Volatilities

In case 2, we assume that time series standard deviations depend on asset volatilities:

$$Std_{TS}\{g_n\} = c_2 \cdot \omega_n \qquad (11.8)$$

Once again, we assume that all time series means are 0. But starting with Eq. (11.8), we can estimate the constant c_2 by observing that

$$c_2 = \text{Std}_{TS} \left\{ \frac{g_n}{\omega_n} \right\} \tag{11.9}$$

By assumption, the coefficient c_2 is independent of n. But in that case, we can equivalently estimate it from time series or cross-sectional data, assuming forecasts are uncorrelated across assets:

$$c_2 = \text{Std}_{CS} \left\{ \frac{g_n}{\omega_n} \right\} \tag{11.10}$$

With this cross-sectional estimate of c_2 and with Eq. (11.8), we can restate the basic result, Eq. (11.2), as

$$\phi_n = \omega_n \cdot \text{IC} \cdot \left(\frac{g_n}{c_2 \cdot \omega_n} \right) \tag{11.11}$$

$$\phi_n = \text{IC} \cdot \left(\frac{g_n}{\text{Std}_{CS} \left\{ \frac{g_n}{\omega_n} \right\}} \right) \tag{11.12}$$

To rewrite this explicitly in terms of cross-sectional scores,

$$\phi_n = \text{IC} \cdot \left(\frac{\text{Std}_{CS}\{g_n\}}{\text{Std}_{CS} \left\{ \frac{g_n}{\omega_n} \right\}} \right) \cdot \left(\frac{g_n}{\text{Std}_{CS}\{g_n\}} \right) \tag{11.13}$$

But the second term on the right-hand side of Eq. (11.13) is just a number, independent of n. We will call it c_g. Hence

$$\phi_n = \text{IC} \cdot c_g \cdot z_{CS,n} \tag{11.14}$$

So if the time series signal volatilities are proportional to asset volatilities, then the refined forecasts are proportional to cross-sectional scores and independent of volatility. In case 2, forecasts still equal volatility $\cdot$ IC $\cdot$ score, but this is proportional to IC $\cdot$ cross-sectional score. The constant of proportionality c_g, can vary by signal.

Empirical Evidence

It appears that the question of how to refine cross-sectional signals depends critically on how time series signal volatilities vary from stock to stock. In the previous section, we analyzed two extremes: independent of stock volatility and proportional to stock volatility.

Here we will examine several specific signals along two particular dimensions. First, we will simply observe how the time series signal volatilities depend on asset volatilities. Second, we will compare the performance of the alphas refined according to Eqs. (11.7) and (11.14). We hope to find empirical results consistent with our analysis. (For another approach to empirically testing alpha scaling, see the technical appendix.)

We will examine six U.S. equity signals commercially available from BARRA:

Dividend discount model (DDM)

Estimate change

Estimate revision

Relative strength

Residual reversal

Sector momentum

The dividend discount model provides internal rates of return from a three-stage model, as outlined in Chap. 9. The estimate change signal is the 1-month change in consensus estimated annual earnings,[1] divided by current price. The estimate revision signal combines the 1-month change in consensus estimated annual earnings with the 1-month stock return (to help account for stocks whose prices have already reacted to the change in consensus). The relative strength signal combines each stock's return over the past 13 months with its return over the past month [i.e., it attempts to capture momentum over roughly the past year, and it controls for short-term (1-month) reversal effects]. The residual reversal signal uses 1-month returns, residual to industry and risk index

---

[1]This is based on a weighted combination of estimated earnings in fiscal years 1 and 2. The weights depend on where the current date stands in the fiscal year. At the beginning of fiscal year 1, all the weight is on fiscal year 1. As the year progresses, the model places more and more weight on fiscal year 2.

effects. The sector momentum signal is the 1-month return to capitalization-weighted sector portfolios. Each stock in the sector receives the same signal.

BARRA provides these signals as monthly cross-sectional scores. The sector momentum signal stands out in this group as the only signal on which many assets receive the same score.

In the first empirical test, we simply calculated 60-month time series signal volatilities for roughly the largest 1200 U.S. stocks (the BARRA HICAP universe) as of December 1994. We then ran the following cross-sectional regression:

$$\text{Std}_{\text{TS}}\{g_n\} = a + b \cdot \omega_n + \epsilon_n \tag{11.15}$$

This regression will test whether the time series signal volatilities vary from stock to stock by residual volatility. Most importantly, we want to know the R^2 statistic for the regression, and also the t statistic for the estimated coefficient b. We find the results given in Table 11.1.

For all the signals except sector momentum, we see a very strong positive linear relationship between time series signal volatilities and asset residual volatilities. This implies that we need *not* rescale these cross-sectional scores by volatility when estimating expected exceptional return.

We tested this idea by calculating expected exceptional returns using both Eq. 11.7 and Eq. 11.14. We will describe the test methodology in detail in Chap. 12. For each method, we built optimal portfo-

T A B L E   11.1

Model	R^2	t statistic (b)
DDM	0.37	19.3
Estimate change	0.34	18.0
Estimate revision	0.31	17.0
Relative strength	0.72	54.3
Residual reversal	0.77	62.2
Sector momentum	0.01	−3.8

T A B L E 11.2

Model	Information Ratio		
	$IC \cdot z_{cs}$	$\omega_n \cdot IC \cdot z_{cs}$	R^2
DDM	1.31	1.19	0.37
Estimate change	1.92	1.87	0.34
Estimate revision	3.55	3.32	0.31
Relative strength	1.93	1.93	0.72
Residual reversal	2.51	2.18	0.77
Sector momentum	1.91	2.10	0.01

lios based on the refined signal, and looked at information ratios from backtests.[2] Table 11.2 contains the results.

The evidence in Table 11.2 is completely consistent with the evidence from Table 11.1. Five of the models (all but sector momentum) exhibit a strong relationship between signal volatility and asset residual volatility. And in each case, the cross-sectional scores [the correct refined signals according to Eq. (11.14)] match or outperform those scores multiplied by residual volatility.

In the one case in which signal volatilities did not vary with asset volatilities, sector momentum, the cross-sectional scores multiplied by volatility [the correct refined signals according to Eq. (11.7)] outperformed the cross-sectional scores alone.

The empirical evidence supports the previous analysis. Given cross-sectional scores, the critical question is whether signal volatilities vary with asset volatilities. The refining process always multiplies time series scores by volatility. This does not always imply multiplying cross-sectional scores by volatility.

Forecasts have the form volatility · IC · score. Sometimes this is simply proportional to IC · cross-sectional score.

---

[2]In this test, we industry-neutralized all but the sector momentum signal. Hence each signal is defined relative to its industry. Industry-neutralizing sector momentum would set it to zero.

WHY NOT FORECAST CROSS-SECTIONAL ALPHAS DIRECTLY?

We built up our entire forecasting methodology in Chap.10 from time series analysis. We have now spent considerable effort adapting that methodology to the more standard application involving cross-sectional scores. Why don't we just apply the forecasting methodology directly to the cross-sectional information? Can't we simply discard all the time series machinery and focus directly on cross-sectional behavior?

In the simple case where we have N asset returns and N signals, all at one time, Eq. (11.1) reduces to

$$\phi_n = \text{IC} \cdot \text{Std}_{CS}\{\theta_n\} \cdot z_{CS,n} \tag{11.16}$$

where $\text{Std}_{CS}\{\theta_n\}$ is the *cross-sectional* volatility of the residual returns. For any given time t, it is just a constant. For all practical purposes, Eq. (11.16) is equivalent to Eq. (11.14).

That result may be reassuring, but the analysis is overly simplistic. Estimating expected exceptional returns from only one cross-sectional panel of data is fraught with problems. In one month, industries will probably explain much of the cross-sectional variation in returns. The next month, the same will be true, but the industries will be different. This month, Internet stocks. Next month, health care. The following month, banks. The refining process must, of necessity, analyze both time series and cross-sectional information. We need to know what we can consistently forecast over time.

In general, we must use both time series and cross-sectional data in Eq. (11.1). We have chosen to attack the time series problem first, and then add the complexity of cross-sectional data. As we will see, the fully general case is too complex to handle exactly. We must apply structure to tackle it.

MULTIPLE FORECASTS FOR EACH OF *N* STOCKS

In Chap. 10, we explicitly handled the case of two forecasts for one asset, and also described mathematically how to handle multiple forecasts for an asset.

With some simplifying assumptions, the results from Chap. 10 apply in the case of multiple assets, asset by asset. The simplifying assumptions are fairly restrictive. Each information source j has an information coefficient vector $\mathbf{IC}_j$. The elements of $\mathbf{IC}_j$ describe the information coefficient asset by asset. For each information source, a correlation matrix $\boldsymbol{\rho}_j$ describes the signal correlations across assets. The simplifying assumptions state that

$$IC_j(n) = IC_j \qquad\qquad (11.17)$$

$$\boldsymbol{\rho}_j = \boldsymbol{\rho} \qquad\qquad (11.18)$$

Information source j exhibits the same information coefficient for all assets, and the correlation of its signal across assets matches the correlation of every other information source's signal across assets. Furthermore, we must assume that the correlation between every g_{in} and g_{jn} is just ρ_{ij}, a constant describing the correlation between signals i and j. With these simplifying assumptions, we can apply the results of Chap. 10, asset by asset. We still must remember that the Chap. 10 results depend on time series scores and not cross-sectional scores.

The technical appendix provides some further insight into handling the general case of multiple forecasts for multiple assets. If we are unwilling to accept the assumptions above, we need to supply an alternative structure.

FACTOR FORECASTS

One standard way to apply structure to the case of multiple assets is through a factor model. In particular, the arbitrage pricing theory (APT) states that all return forecasts must assume the form

$$E\{\mathbf{r}\} = \mathbf{X} \cdot \mathbf{m} \qquad\qquad (11.19)$$

where

$$\mathbf{r} = \mathbf{X} \cdot \mathbf{b} + \mathbf{u} \qquad\qquad (11.20)$$

and

$$\mathbf{m} = E\{\mathbf{b}\} \qquad\qquad (11.20)$$

Typically, the problem of forecasting hundreds, if not thousands, of asset returns reduces to a problem of forecasting a handful of factor returns. Many institutional managers apply just such methods, as we saw in Chap 7.

In the typical case, some of the APT factors immediately suggest factor forecasts. For example, some factors may generate consistent returns month after month. We always want portfolios that *tilt* toward these factors. Other factors may require timing, i.e., their returns vary from positive to negative, with no implied tilt direction.

We have observed many investment managers, therefore, face the following problem: They can forecast one or a few factors, but they have no information (in their opinion) about the other factors. Should they set the other factor forecasts to zero?

We can apply the basic forecasting formula to solve this problem. Let's assume that we have a signal g_1 to forecast b_1. We know how to refine g_1 to forecast b_1. What should we expect for the other factors?

Using the basic forecasting formula,

$$E\{b_j|g_1\} = E\{b_j\} + \text{Cov}\{b_j,g_1\} \cdot \text{Var}^{-1}\{g_1\} \cdot (g_1 - E\{g_1\}) \qquad (11.22)$$

How do we calculate the covariance and correlation of b_j and g_1? Let's begin by assuming that g_1 contains some information about b_1, plus noise:

$$g_1 = \text{IC}^2 \cdot b_1 + \text{IC} \cdot \sqrt{1 - \text{IC}^2} \cdot \omega_1 \cdot Z \qquad (11.23)$$

where Z has mean 0 and standard deviation 1 and is uncorrelated with b_1 (and all other b_j). Using Eq. (11.22), we can calculate

$$\text{Cov}\{b_j,g_1\} = \text{IC}^2 \cdot \text{Cov}\{b_j,b_1\} \qquad (11.24)$$
$$= \text{IC}^2 \cdot \rho_{1j} \cdot \omega_j \cdot \omega_1$$

Substituting this back into Eq. (11.22), and assuming that $E\{b_j\} = 0$, we find

$$E\{b_j|g_1\} = \text{IC} \cdot \rho_{1j} \cdot \omega_j \cdot \left(\frac{g_1 - E\{g_1\}}{\text{Std}\{g_1\}} \right) \qquad (11.25)$$
$$= \text{IC} \cdot \rho_{1j} \cdot \omega_j \cdot z_1$$

According to Eq. (11.25), if we forecast $E\{b_1|g_1\} \neq 0$, we should not set $E\{b_j|g_1\} = 0$.

T A B L E 11.3

Strategy	IR
A	3.26
B	3.42
C	1.57

We have empirically tested Eq. (11.25) in the following case. We used the BARRA U.S. Equity model (version 2), and assumed that we had explicit information only for the book-to-price (B/P) factor. We then looked at three variants of a B/P strategy:

A. Bet only on B/P.

B. Use the information about B/P to also bet on other risk indices.

C. Use B/P information to bet only on other factors.

Case C is rather perverse, but an interesting empirical test of the idea. Using data for the 5-year period from May 1990 through April 1995, we found the results in Table 11.3.

We can observe from Table 11.3 that using the information about b_1 to bet on b_j improves the performance of the signal. We can also observe that even perverse strategy C, using information about b_1 to bet on factors other than b_1, exhibits a high information ratio. We would also expect the squared information ratio for strategy B to roughly match the sum of the squared information ratios for strategies A and C. This is true.

UNCERTAIN INFORMATION COEFFICIENTS

This and the previous chapter have discussed how to refine raw signals based on expectations, volatility, and skill, with skill measured by the information coefficient. We have also discussed how to combine signals with differing information coefficients.

A common practical problem, however, involves uncertainty in the information coefficients themselves, and how this should influence the refined signals. For example, how should we combine two signals with equal estimated IC if one has much higher estimation errors? We would expect to weight the signal with the more certain IC more heavily. None of our machinery so far implies that answer, however. In fact, it isn't obvious how to account for IC estimation errors in our framework.

This is because our methodology so far has explicitly ignored this problem. Achieving algebraic results requires assuming that we know something. In our analysis so far, we have assumed that we know the ICs.

Fortunately, some modest tweaking of our Bayesian methodology can handle the case of uncertain ICs. We will explicitly handle the case of one signal, but will discuss the more general result.

We will use regression methodology to analyze the problem. We are attempting to forecast residual returns $\theta(t)$ with signal $g(t)$. We will refine the signal via regression:

$$\theta(t) = a + b \cdot g(t) + \epsilon_\theta(t) \tag{11.26}$$

For this analysis, we will assume that $\theta(t)$ and $g(t)$ both have mean 0. Hence

$$a = 0 \tag{11.27}$$

$$b = \frac{\text{Cov}\{\theta,g\}}{\text{Var}\{g\}} = \frac{\displaystyle\sum_{t=1}^{T} \theta(t) \cdot g(t)}{\displaystyle\sum_{t=1}^{T} g^2(t)} \tag{11.28}$$

We will handle uncertainty in the estimated IC by adding a prior, $\hat{b}$, to the regression, Eq. (11.26). We now have

$$\begin{bmatrix} \theta(1) \\ \vdots \\ \theta(T) \\ \hat{b} \end{bmatrix} = \begin{bmatrix} g(1) \\ \vdots \\ g(T) \\ 1 \end{bmatrix} \cdot b' + \begin{bmatrix} \epsilon_\theta(1) \\ \vdots \\ \epsilon_\theta(T) \\ \epsilon_b \end{bmatrix} \tag{11.29}$$

where we will weight the observations of $\theta(t)$ by $1/\omega_\theta^2$, and the prior by $1/\omega_b^2$, where ω_θ is the standard deviation of $\epsilon_\theta(t)$ and ω_b is the standard deviation of ϵ_b.

Equation (11.29) displays a useful mathematical trick. We can add a prior as an additional "observation" in the standard regression. With the above weights, this corresponds to a maximum likelihood analysis, with the likelihood of each residual return observation being combined with the likelihood of the observed coefficient, given the prior.

Solving this regression for the adjusted coefficient b' leads to

$$b' = \frac{(1/\omega_\theta^2) \cdot \displaystyle\sum_{t=1}^{T} \theta(t) \cdot g(t) + (\hat{b}/\omega_b^2)}{(1/\omega_\theta^2) \cdot \displaystyle\sum_{t=1}^{T} g^2(t) + (1/\omega_b^2)} \qquad (11.30)$$

We will use a prior of $\hat{b} = 0$. The technical appendix will show [following Connor (1997)] that Eq. (11.30) then reduces to

$$b' = \left[\frac{1}{1 + (1/[T \cdot E\{R^2/(1 - R^2)\}])} \right] \cdot b \qquad (11.31)$$

which involves the expected R^2 statistic from the (no prior) regression. Since this R^2 statistic should equal IC^2, and hence be quite small, we can approximate Eq. (11.31) as

$$b' \approx \left(\frac{1}{1 + \left[\dfrac{1}{(T \cdot IC^2)} \right]} \right) \cdot b \qquad (11.32)$$

Equation (11.32) describes a shrinkage of the original estimate b to account for uncertainty. With a large number of observations T or a high information coefficient, we remain close to the naïve estimate b. But with fewer periods, or with lower information coefficients, we shrink closer to zero. Table 11.4 shows the shrinkage as a function of IC and months of observation T. The shrinkage is quite significant even for very good signals observed over long periods of time. For poor signals, the adjusted coefficient shrinks to zero (the prior).

Note that Eq (11.31) applies the Bayesian shrinkage to the regression coefficient b, not directly to the IC. As we will show in the technical appendix, uncertainty in the IC will typically dominate overall uncertainty in the regression coefficient.

T A B L E 11.4

Months	Information Coefficient		
	0.00	0.05	0.10
36	0.00	0.08	0.26
60	0.00	0.13	0.38
90	0.00	0.18	0.47
120	0.00	0.23	0.55
240	0.00	0.38	0.71

What about the case of multiple signals? The same Bayesian shrinkage applies, but with the marginal R^2 statistics replacing the total R^2 statistic in Eq. (11.31). With multiple signals, these marginal R^2 statistics attribute the total R^2 to the signals. Each signal's marginal R^2 equals the total R^2 minus the R^2 achieved with that coefficient set to zero. These marginal R^2 statistics sum to the total R^2 statistic. This methodology places a premium on parsimony. A new signal with small marginal explanatory power will experience substantial shrinkage.

SUMMARY

This chapter began with the foundations built in Chap. 10—how to refine forecasts for one asset—and grappled with the typical and more complicated cases of multiple assets and uncertainties in estimated ICs. The basic forecasting formula applies to multiple assets, but typically requires so many separate estimates that it demands additional structure. Investment managers often rely on cross-sectional scores. In many cases, refined exceptional returns are directly proportional to cross-sectional scores.

When forecasting factor returns (e.g., in APT models), use your available information to forecast all the factors.

The greater the uncertainty in our estimated IC, the more we will shrink the IC toward zero.

PROBLEMS

1. Signal 1 and signal 2 have equal IC, and both exhibit signal volatilities proportional to asset volatilities. Do the two signals receive equal weight in the forecast exceptional return?

2. What IR would you naïvely expect if you combined strategies A and C in Table 11.3? Why might the observed answer differ from the naïve result?

3. How much should you shrink coefficient b, connecting raw signals and realized returns, estimated with $R^2 = 0.05$ after 120 months?

REFERENCES

Black, Fisher, and Robert Litterman. "Global Asset Allocation with Equities, Bonds, and Currencies." *Fixed Income Research*, Goldman, Sachs & Co., New York, October 1991.

Connor, Gregory. "Sensible Return Forecasting for Portfolio Management." *Financial Analysts Journal*, vol. 53, no. 5, 1997, pp. 44–51.

Grinold, Richard C. "Alpha Is Volatility Times IC Times Score, or Real Alphas Don't Get Eaten." *Journal of Portfolio Management*, vol. 20, no. 4, 1994, pp. 9–16.

Kahn, Ronald. "Alpha Analytics." BARRA Equity Research Seminar, Pebble Beach, Calif., June 1995.

TECHNICAL APPENDIX

In this appendix, we examine in more detail the analysis of forecasts for multiple assets, discuss an alternative method for testing volatility scaling, and treat in more detail the case of uncertain information coefficients.

One Forecast for Each of *N* Assets

Consider the case with $K = N$ forecasts, one forecast g_n for each asset return r_n. We will make the assumption that the IC is the same for each forecast:

$$\text{Cov}\{r_n, g_n\} = \text{IC} \cdot \omega_n \cdot \text{Std}_{\text{TS}}\{g_n\} \tag{11A.1}$$

What about the covariance of r_n with g_m? We will assume that r_n is correlated with g_m only through g_n, i.e.,

$$\text{Cov}\{r_n, g_m\} = IC \cdot \omega_n \cdot \rho_{nm} \cdot \text{Std}_{TS}\{g_m\} \qquad (11A.2)$$

where ρ_{nm} measures the correlation of g_n and g_m. In matrix notation,

$$\text{Cov}\{\mathbf{r}, \mathbf{g}\} = IC \cdot \boldsymbol{\omega} \cdot \boldsymbol{\rho} \cdot \mathbf{Std} \qquad (11A.3)$$

$$\text{Var}\{\mathbf{g}\} = \mathbf{Std} \cdot \boldsymbol{\rho} \cdot \mathbf{Std} \qquad (11A.4)$$

where $\boldsymbol{\omega}$ and $\mathbf{Std}$ are diagonal matrices with $\{\omega_n\}$ and $\{\text{Std}[g_n]\}$, respectively, on the diagonal. Substituting this into the basic forecasting formula [Eq. (11.1)], we find

$$\boldsymbol{\phi} = IC \cdot \boldsymbol{\omega} \cdot \mathbf{Std}^{-1} \cdot (\mathbf{g} - E\{\mathbf{g}\}) \qquad (11A.5)$$

Hence, each forecast takes on the form

$$\phi_n = IC \cdot \omega_n \cdot \left(\frac{g_n - E\{g_n\}}{\text{Std}_{TS}[g_n]} \right) \qquad (11A.6)$$

Two Forecasts for Each of N Assets

Next, consider the case where $K = 2N$. Now $\mathbf{g} = \{\mathbf{g}_1, \mathbf{g}_2\}$, with two raw forecasts for each stock. We will make the simplifying assumptions

$$\text{Var}\{\mathbf{g}\} = \mathbf{Std} \cdot \begin{bmatrix} \boldsymbol{\rho} & \rho_{12} \cdot \boldsymbol{\rho} \\ \rho_{12} \cdot \boldsymbol{\rho} & \boldsymbol{\rho} \end{bmatrix} \cdot \mathbf{Std} \qquad (11A.7)$$

$$\text{Cov}\{\mathbf{r}, \mathbf{g}\} = \boldsymbol{\omega} \cdot [IC_1 \cdot \mathbf{I} \quad IC_2 \cdot \mathbf{I}] \cdot \begin{bmatrix} \boldsymbol{\rho} & 0 \\ 0 & \boldsymbol{\rho} \end{bmatrix} \cdot \mathbf{Std} \qquad (11A.8)$$

Thus the correlation matrix for the $\mathbf{g}_1$ is identical to the correlation matrix for the $\mathbf{g}_2$. The correlation between every g_{1n} and g_{2n} is described by the scalar constant ρ_{12}. The correlation between every g_{1n} and r_n is described by the scalar constant IC_1, and the correlation between every g_{2n} and r_n is described by the scalar constant IC_2.

We can substitute Eqs. (11A.7) and (11A.8) into the basic forecasting formula, to find

$$\boldsymbol{\phi} = \boldsymbol{\omega} \cdot \left[\left(\frac{IC_1 - \rho_{12} \cdot IC_2}{1 - \rho_{12}^2} \right) \cdot \mathbf{I} \quad \left(\frac{IC_2 - \rho_{12} \cdot IC_1}{1 - \rho_{12}^2} \right) \cdot \mathbf{I} \right] \qquad (11A.9)$$

$$\cdot \mathbf{Std}^{-1} \cdot [\mathbf{g} - E\{\mathbf{g}\}]$$

Once again the refined exceptional forecast takes on the form volatility $\cdot$ IC $\cdot$ score. In this case, we adjust the information coefficients based on the correlation between the forecasts $\mathbf{g}_1$ and $\mathbf{g}_2$.

Multiple Forecasts for Each of N Assets

The general case is easier to understand if we transform the raw forecasts $\mathbf{g}$ into a set of uncorrelated (orthogonal) forecasts $\mathbf{y}$. We can always write

$$\text{Var}\{\mathbf{g}\} = \mathbf{H}^T \cdot \mathbf{H} \tag{11A.10}$$

$$\mathbf{y} \equiv (\mathbf{H}^T)^{-1} \cdot [\mathbf{g} - E\{\mathbf{g}\}] \tag{11A.11}$$

where the $\mathbf{y}$ are standardized and uncorrelated raw forecasts: $E\{\mathbf{y}\} = 0$, $\text{Var}\{\mathbf{y}\} = \mathbf{I}$. We can also show that

$$\text{Cov}\{\mathbf{r,g}\} = \text{Cov}\{\mathbf{r,y}\} \cdot \mathbf{H} \tag{11A.12}$$

and so

$$\boldsymbol{\phi} = \boldsymbol{\omega} \cdot \text{Corr}\{\mathbf{r,y}\} \cdot \mathbf{y} \tag{11A.13}$$

Thus the general result, that the refined forecast has the form volatility $\cdot$ IC $\cdot$ score, still holds, although in the general case it involves transformed scores $\mathbf{y}$ and an IC matrix $\text{Corr}\{\mathbf{r,y}\}$. To go beyond this result, we need to impose more structure on this correlation matrix.[3]

Testing Alpha Scaling

A separate approach to testing whether we have appropriately scaled alphas by volatility is to look at the amount of risk we take per asset. Assuming uncorrrelated residual risks,

$$h_{\text{PA}}^{*}(n) = \frac{\alpha_n}{2 \cdot \lambda_R \cdot \omega_n^2} \tag{11A.14}$$

---

[3]Here is an alternative empirical procedure for combining K forecasts for each of N assets. First estimate K factor portfolio returns, one for each forecast for the N assets. Each factor portfolio should control exposure to the other $K - 1$ factors. Then choose an optimal set of K weights to maximize the information ratio of the portfolio of factor portfolios. Use these to determine the weights on the K forecasts for each of the N assets.

Using the forecasting rule of thumb,

$$h_{PA}^*(n) = \frac{IC \cdot z_n}{2 \cdot \lambda_R \cdot \omega_n} \tag{11A.15}$$

and the portfolio risk becomes

$$\omega_P^2 = \left(\frac{IC}{2 \cdot \lambda_R}\right)^2 \cdot \sum_n z_n^2 \tag{11A.16}$$

Equation (11A.16) implies that we *expect* equal risk contributions from each asset, since $E\{z^2\} = 1$ for each asset. So, for example, we could define buckets of equal numbers of assets, based on volatility, and calculate the contribution to residual variance from each bucket. Each bucket should contain a sufficient number of assets to control the sampling error around $E\{z^2\}$.

If different buckets exhibit different contributions to risk, then either the volatility scaling is incorrect or we have imposed different information coefficients for different buckets.

This method also applies to buckets defined on the basis of other attributes.

Uncertain ICs

The main text of the chapter analyzed how to shrink estimated ICs based on their estimation error. The technique actually focused on the regression coefficient b:

$$\theta(t) = a + b \cdot g(t) + \epsilon(t) \tag{11A.17}$$

where
$$b = \frac{\text{Cov}\{\theta,g\}}{\text{Var}\{g\}} = \frac{IC \cdot \omega}{\text{Std}\{g\}} \tag{11A.18}$$

and not directly on the IC. However, we will show that the estimation error in the IC dominates the overall estimation error in b. Hence it is reasonable to assume that we are applying the Bayesian shrinkage to the IC.

Given Eq. (11A.18), how do estimation errors influence our estimate of b? Using Δ to denote uncertainties in the variables,

$$\Delta b = \Delta IC \cdot \frac{\omega}{Std\{g\}} + \Delta\omega \cdot \frac{IC}{Std\{g\}} - \frac{IC \cdot \omega}{Var\{g\}} \Delta Std\{g\} \quad (11A.19)$$

$$\frac{\Delta b}{b} = \frac{\Delta IC}{IC} + \frac{\Delta\omega}{\omega} - \frac{\Delta Std\{g\}}{Std\{g\}} \quad (11A.20)$$

Hence

$$Var\left\{\frac{\Delta b}{b}\right\} = Var\left\{\frac{\Delta IC}{IC}\right\} + Var\left\{\frac{\Delta\omega}{\omega}\right\} \quad (11A.21)$$

$$+ Var\left\{\frac{\Delta Std\{g\}}{Std\{g\}}\right\} + covariances$$

We can analyze Eq. (11A.21) in more detail if we assume that

1. The errors are uncorrelated (so the covariance terms disappear).
2. We have large sample sizes.
3. All errors are normally distributed.

We can then use the results for standard error variances for sample standard deviations and correlations:

$$Var\{\Delta\sigma\} = \frac{\sigma^2}{2N} \quad (11A.22)$$

$$Var\{\Delta\rho\} = \frac{(1 - \rho^2)^2}{N} \quad (11A.23)$$

Substituting these results in Eq. (11A.21), assuming $IC << 1$, and simplifying leads to

$$Var\left\{\frac{\Delta b}{b}\right\} = \frac{1}{IC^2 \cdot T} + \frac{1}{T} \quad (11A.24)$$

where T measures the number of months of observations. The first term on the right-hand side of Eq. (11A.24) is the contribution from uncertainty in the IC. The second term is the contribution from uncertainty in ω and $Std\{g\}$. Since $IC << 1$, the error in the IC dominates the error in the regression coefficient.

Exercises

1. We are following N assets but have a forecast only for
   asset 1 (N assets, $K = 1$). Should we set all other
   forecasts equal to their consensus values ($\phi_n = 0$, $n =
   2, \ldots, N$)? How should the N forecasts differ from their
   consensus values based on this one forecast?

2. Compare the result from Exercise 1 to the CAPM result
   for a forecast of exceptional market return. Black and
   Litterman have pursued these ideas in the context of
   international asset allocation in their international CAPM
   model.

3. How could you connect the best linear unbiased estimate
   combining K forecasts for each of N assets to an
   approach estimating factor portfolios for each of the K
   forecasts and then optimally combining those factor
   portfolios to maximize the overall information ratio?

Application Exercise

1. Compute the coefficient c_g for at least two signals. This
   requires a cross-sectional set of signals and residual
   volatilities. If the signals had equal ICs, what does this
   imply about their relative weighting?

CHAPTER 12

Information Analysis

INTRODUCTION

Information is the vital input into any active management strategy. Information separates active management from passive management. Information, properly applied, allows active managers to outperform their informationless benchmarks.

Information analysis is the science of evaluating information content and refining information to build portfolios. Information analysis works for managers who have a nonquantitative process and for managers who have a quantitative investment process—the only requirement is that there is a process.

Information is a rather fuzzy concept. Information analysis begins by transforming information into something concrete: investment portfolios. Then it analyzes the performance of those portfolios to determine the value of the information. Information analysis can work with something as simple as an analyst's buy and sell recommendations. Or it can work with alpha forecasts for a broad universe of stocks. Information analysis is not concerned with the intuition or process used to generate stock recommendations, only with the recommendations themselves.

Information analysis can be precise. It can determine whether information is valuable on the upside, the downside, or both. It can determine whether information is valuable over short horizons or long horizons. It can determine whether information is adding value to your investment process.

Information analysis occurs before backtesting in the investment process. Information analysis looks at the unfettered value

315

of signals. Backtesting then takes those signals that have been identified as containing information and develops investable strategies. Backtesting looks not only at information content, but also at turnover, tradability, and transactions costs.

This chapter will focus very explicitly on information analysis. It will present a unified treatment of information analysis, with both theoretical discussions and concrete examples. Information analysis is a broad subject. This chapter will cover the general approach, but will also recommend a specific approach to best analyze investment information. The key insights in the chapter are as follows:

- Information analysis is a two-step process.
- Step 1 is to turn information into portfolios.
- Step 2 is to analyze the performance of those portfolios.
- Event studies provide analysis when information arrives episodically.

The chapter will describe how and where information appears in the active management process, and then introduce and discuss in detail the two-step process of information analysis. We will include some discussion of performance analysis, but a more in-depth treatment of that subject will appear in Chap. 17. We will treat event studies of episodic information as a special topic. The chapter will end by describing the pitfalls of information analysis. Information analysis is a tool, and, as with a hammer, one must distinguish between thumb and nail.

INFORMATION AND ACTIVE MANAGEMENT

Where and how does information arise in active management? Active managers, as opposed to passive managers, apply information to achieve superior returns relative to a benchmark. Passive managers simply try to replicate the performance of the benchmark. They have no information.

Active managers use information to predict the future exceptional return on a group of stocks. The emphasis is on predicting *alpha*, or residual return: beta-adjusted return relative to a benchmark. We want to know what stocks will do better than average and what stocks will do worse, on a risk-adjusted basis.

So, when we talk about information in the context of active management, we are really talking about alpha predictors. For any set of data pertaining to stocks, we can ask: Do these data help predict alphas? We will even call this set of data a *predictor*.

In general, any predictor is made up of signal plus noise. The signal is linked with future stock returns. The noise masks the signal and makes the task of information analysis both difficult and exciting. Random numbers contain no signal, only noise. Information analysis is an effort to find the signal-to-noise ratio.

A predictor will cover a number of time periods and a number of stocks in each time period. The information at the beginning of period t is a data item for each stock. The data item can be as simple as +1 for all stocks on a recommended buy list and −1 for all stocks on a sell list. On the other hand, the data item can be a precise alpha: 2.15 percent for one stock, −3.72 percent for another, etc. Other predictors might be scores. Crude scores can be a grouping of stocks into categories, a more refined version of the buy and sell idea. Other scores might be a ranking of the stocks along some dimension. Notice that it is possible to start with alphas and produce a ranking. It is also possible to start with a ranking and produce other scores, such as 4 for the stocks in the highest quartile, down to 1 for the stocks in the lowest quartile.

The predictors can be publicly available information, such as consensus earnings forecasts, or they can be derived data, such as a change in consensus earnings forecasts. Predictors are limited only by availability and imagination.

We can classify information along the following dimensions:

- Primary or processed
- Judgmental or impartial
- Ordinal or cardinal
- Historical, contemporary, or forecast

Primary information is information in its most basic form. Usually information is processed to some extent. An example would be a firm's short-term liabilities as a primary piece of information, and the ratio of those liabilities to short-term assets as a processed piece of information. Just because information is processed doesn't mean that it is necessarily better. It may be a poorer predictor of returns.

Judgmental information comes with significant human input. It is, by its nature, irreproducible. Expectations data from a single expert or a panel of experts is an example.

With ordinal data, assets are classified into groups and some indication of the order of preference of one group over the other is provided. The buy, sell, hold classification is an example of ordinal data. With cardinal information, a number is associated with each asset, with some importance associated with the numerical values.

We can categorize information as historical, contemporary, or forecast. Average earnings over the past three years is historical information; the most recent earnings is current information; and forecast future earnings is forecast information.

In this chapter, we will use the example of book-to-price data in the United States to generate return predictors according to various standard schemes. For instance, we can generate a buy list and a sell list by ranking all stocks according to book-to-price ratios and placing the top half on the buy list and the bottom half on the sell list. The purpose of this and other examples is not to suggest novel new strategies, but simply to illustrate information analysis techniques.

Underlying the book-to-price examples will be the hypothesis that book-to-price ratios contain information concerning future stock returns, and, in particular, that high-book-to-price stocks will outperform low-book-to-price stocks. Is this hypothesis true? How much information is contained in book-to-price ratios? We will apply information analysis and find out.

INFORMATION ANALYSIS

Information analysis is a two-step process:

Step 1: Turn predictions into portfolios.
Step 2: Evaluate the performance of those portfolios.

In step 1, the information is transformed into a concrete object: a portfolio. In step 2, the performance of the portfolio is then analyzed.

Information analysis is flexible. There are a great many ways to turn predictions into portfolios and a great many ways to evaluate performance. We will explore many of these alternatives below.

STEP 1: INFORMATION INTO PORTFOLIOS

Let's start with step 1, turning predictions into portfolios. Since we have predictions for each time period, we will generate portfolios for each time period.[1] There are a great many ways to generate portfolios from predictions, and the procedure selected could depend on the type of prediction. Here are six possibilities. For each case, we have listed the general idea, and then discussed how to apply this to data concerning book-to-price ratios. Later we will analyze the performance of these portfolios.

▪ *Procedure 1.* With buy and sell recommendations, we could equal- (or value-) weight the buy group and the sell group.

Using book-to-price ratios, we can generate the buy and sell lists, as described above, by first ranking stocks by book-to-price and then putting the top half on the buy list and the bottom half on the sell list.

▪ *Procedure 2.* With scores, we can build a portfolio for each score by equal- (or value-) weighting within each score category.

We can generate scores from book-to-price ratios by ranking stocks by book-to-price ratio, as before, and then, for example, giving the top fifth of the list (by number or capitalization) a score of 5, the next fifth a score of 4, down to the bottom fifth, with a score of 1. This is simply dividing stocks into quintiles by book-to-price.

▪ *Procedure 3.* With straight alphas, we can split the stocks into two groups, one group with higher than average alphas and one group with lower than average alphas. Then we can weight the stocks in each group by how far their alpha exceeds (or lies below) the average. This is an elaboration of procedure 1.

One way to generate alphas from book-to-price ratios is to assume that they are linearly related to the book-to-price ratios. So

---

[1]The choice of time period may affect information analysis. As a general comment, the investment time period should match the information time period. Portfolios based on daily information—information that changes daily and influences daily returns—should be regenerated each day. Portfolios based on quarterly information—information that changes quarterly and influences quarterly returns—should be regenerated each quarter. Chapter 13, "The Information Horizon," will treat this topic in detail.

we can weight each asset in our buy and sell list by how far its book-to-price ratio lies above or below the average.

- *Procedure 4.* With straight alphas, we can rank the assets according to alpha, then group the assets into quintiles (or deciles or quartiles or halves) and equal- (or value-) weight within each group. This is an elaboration of procedure 2.

For alphas linearly related to book-to-price ratios, this is a straightforward extension of procedure 3.

- *Procedure 5.* With any numerical score, we can build a factor portfolio that bets on the prediction and does not make a market bet. The factor portfolio consists of a long portfolio and a short portfolio. The long and short portfolios have equal value and equal beta, but the long portfolio will have a unit bet on the prediction, relative to the short portfolio. Given these constraints, the long portfolio will track the short portfolio as closely as possible.

For book-to-price data, we can build long and short portfolios with equal value and beta, with the long portfolio exhibiting a book-to-price ratio one standard deviation above that of the short portfolio, and designed so that the long portfolio will track the short portfolio as closely as possible.

- *Procedure 6.* With any numerical score, we can build a factor portfolio, consisting of a long and a short portfolio, designed so that the long and short portfolios are matched on a set of prespecified control variables. For example, we could make sure the long and short portfolios match on industry, sector, or small-capitalization stock exposures. This is a more elaborate form of procedure 5, where we controlled only for beta (as a measure of exposure to market risk). Using the book-to-price data, this is an extension of procedure 5.

The general idea should be clear. We are trying to establish some sort of relative performance. In each case, we will produce two or more portfolios. In the first, third, fifth and sixth procedures, we will have a long and a short portfolio. The long bets on the information; the short bets against it. In procedure 2, we have a portfolio for each score, and in procedure 4, we have a portfolio for each quintile.

Procedures 5 and 6 are more elaborate and "quantitative" than the first four procedures. They require more sophisticated technology, which we describe in detail in the technical appendix. However, the basic inputs—the information being analyzed—

needn't be based on a quantitative strategy. Numerical scores derived by any method will work.

While procedures 5 and 6 are more elaborate, they also isolate the information contained in the data more precisely. These procedures build portfolios based solely on new information in the data, controlling for other important factors in the market.

Because they set up a controlled experiment, we recommend procedure 5 or procedure 6 as the best approach for analyzing the information contained in any numerical scores.

To be explicit about step 1, let's apply some of these procedures in two separate examples based on book-to-price ratios from January 1988 through December 1992.

For Example A, we will build portfolios according to procedure 2. Every month we will rank assets in the S&P 500 by book-to-price ratio, and then divide them into quintiles, defined so that each quintile has equal capitalization. We will turn these quintiles into portfolios by capitalization-weighting the assets in each quintile.

For Example B, we will build portfolios according to procedure 5. Every month we will build two portfolios, a long portfolio and a short portfolio. The two portfolios will have equal value and beta. The long portfolio will exhibit a book-to-price ratio one standard deviation above that of the short portfolio. And given these constraints, the long portfolio will track the short portfolio as closely as possible. What can these examples tell us about the investment information contained in book-to-price ratios?

STEP 2: PERFORMANCE EVALUATION

We have turned the data into two or more portfolios. Now we must evaluate the performance of those portfolios.[2] The general topic of performance analysis is a complicated one, and we will discuss it in detail in Chap. 17. Here we will simply present several approaches and summary statistics, including the information ratio and information coefficient.

---

[2]This step, performance analysis, is very sensitive to errors in asset prices. A mistake in the price one month can appear (mistakenly) to be an opportunity. If the data error is fixed in the following month, it will appear as if the pricing error corrected itself over the month: an opportunity realized.

The simplest form of performance analysis is just to calculate the cumulative returns on the portfolios and the benchmark, and plot them. Some summary statistics, like the means and standard deviations of the returns, can augment this analysis.

Figure 12.1 illustrates this basic analysis for Example A. It shows the cumulative active return on each of the five quintile portfolios. These results are interesting. From January 1988 through the beginning of 1989, the portfolios perform approximately in ranked order. The highest-book-to-price-quintile portfolio has the highest cumulative return, and the lowest-book-to-price-quintile portfolio has almost the lowest cumulative return. However, the situation changed dramatically in 1989 through 1990. Book-to-price ratios are standard "value" measures, and value stocks underperformed growth stocks in this period. And, over the entire five-year analysis period, the lowest-book-to-price-quintile portfolio has the highest cumulative return, with the highest-quintile portfolio in a distant second place. Still, we constructed the quintile portfolios based only on book-to-price ratios, without controlling for other factors. The quintiles may contain incidental bets that muddy the analysis.

Figure 12.2 shows the cumulative returns for the long, short, and net (long minus short) portfolios for Example B. It tells a slightly different story from Fig. 12.1. Here too the long portfolio, which bets on book-to-price, is the best performer over the early period, but the short portfolio, which bets against book-to-price, catches up by 1990. However, unlike the bottom-quintile portfolio from Example A, the short portfolio is not ultimately the best performer.

The net portfolio has a forecast beta of zero, and we can see that its returns appear uncorrelated with the market. The net bet on book-to-price works well until early 1989, and then disappears through 1990 and 1991. It begins to work again in 1992. Comparing Figs. 12.1 and 12.2, different approaches for constructing portfolios from the same basic information lead to different observed performance and different estimates of information content.

t Statistics, Information Ratios, and Information Coefficients

So far, we have discussed only the simplest form of performance analysis: looking at the returns. More sophisticated analyses go

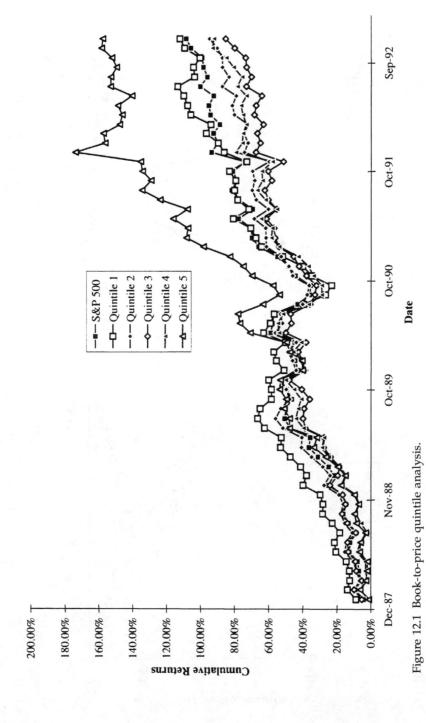

Figure 12.1 Book-to-price quintile analysis.

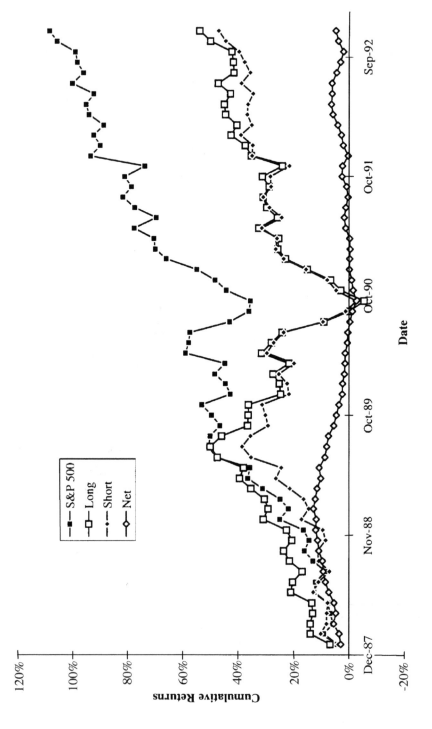

Figure 12.2 Factor portfolio analysis.

beyond this to investigate statistical significance, value added, and skill, as measured by t statistics, information ratios, and information coefficients. All are related.

We start with regression analysis on the portfolio returns, regressing the excess portfolio returns against the excess benchmark returns, to separate the portfolio return into two components, one benchmark-related and the other non-benchmark-related:

$$r(t) = \alpha + \beta \cdot r_B(t) + \epsilon(t) \qquad (12.1)$$

This regression will estimate the portfolio's alpha and beta, and will evaluate, via the t statistic, whether the alpha is significantly different from zero.

The t statistic for the portfolio's alpha is

$$t\text{-stat} = \frac{\alpha}{SE(\alpha)} \qquad (12.2)$$

simply the ratio of the estimated alpha to the standard error of the estimate. This statistic measures whether the alpha differs significantly from zero. Assuming that alphas are normally distributed, if the t statistic exceeds 2, then the probability that simple luck generated these returns is less than 5 percent.

Applying regression analysis to Example A, we find the results shown in Table 12.1. This analysis corroborates the visual results from Fig. 12.1. Only the highest- and lowest-quintile portfolios outperformed the S&P 500, and only they exhibit positive alphas. Unfortunately, none of the alphas are significant at the 95 percent confidence level, according to the t statistics. The analysis of beta

T A B L E   12.1

Quintile	Alpha	t Alpha	Beta	t Beta
Highest	0.03%	0.14	1.02	16.05
High	−0.06%	−0.05	0.92	28.14
Mid	−0.14%	−0.97	0.92	24.76
Low	−0.15%	−1.10	1.04	28.86
Lowest	0.31%	1.15	1.12	16.35

T A B L E 12.2

Portfolio	Alpha	t Alpha	Beta	t Beta
Long	−0.02%	−0.10	1.08	18.43
Short	−0.11%	−0.76	1.08	29.94
Net	0.08%	0.59	0.00	0.04

shows that the quintiles differed significantly in their exposure to the market.

Applying regression analysis to Example B, we find the results shown in Table 12.2. This analysis is consistent with Fig. 12.2.* The alphas for both long and short portfolios are negative, with the net portfolio exhibiting zero beta and net positive alpha. None of the alphas are significant at the 95 percent confidence level.

So far, this analysis has focused only on *t* statistics. What about information ratios? As we have discussed in previous chapters, the information ratio is the best single statistic for capturing the potential for value added from active management. In Examples A and B, we observe the information ratios shown in Table 12.3.

T A B L E 12.3

Portfolio	Information Ratio
Example A	
Highest quintile	0.06
High quintile	−0.21
Mid quintile	−0.45
Low quintile	−0.51
Lowest quintile	0.53
Example B	
Long portfolio	−0.05
Short portfolio	−0.35
Net portfolio	0.27

---

*Note that Fig. 12.2 contains cumulative *excess* returns for the Long, Short, and Net portfolios, but cumulative *total* returns for the S&P 500. Cumulative excess returns for the S&P 500 would look more consistent with the estimated alphas and betas in Table 12.2.

The highest information ratio appears for the lowest-quintile portfolio. The next best information ratio appears for the net portfolio, which explicitly hedges out any market bets.

The t statistic and the information ratio are closely related. The t statistic is the ratio of alpha to its standard error. The information ratio is the ratio of annual alpha to its annual risk. If we observe returns over a period of T years, the information ratio is approximately the t statistic divided by the square root of the number of years of observation:

$$IR \approx \frac{t\text{-stat}}{\sqrt{T}} \qquad (12.3)$$

This relationship becomes more exact as the number of observations increases.

Do not let this close mathematical relationship obscure the fundamental distinction between the two ratios. The t statistic measures the statistical significance of the return; the information ratio captures the risk-reward trade-off of the strategy and the manager's value added. An information ratio of 0.5 observed over 5 years may be statistically more significant than an information ratio of 0.5 observed over 1 year, but their value added will be equal.[3] The distinction between the t statistic and the information ratio arises because we define value added based on risk over a particular horizon, in this case 1 year.

The third statistic of interest is the information coefficient. This correlation between forecast and realized alphas is a critical component in determining the information ratio, according to the fundamental law of active management, and is a critical input for refining alphas and combining signals, as described in Chaps. 10 and 11.

In the context of information analysis, the information coefficient is the correlation between our data and realized alphas. If the data item is all noise and no signal, the information coefficient is

---

[3]In fact, the standard error of the information ratio is (approximately) inversely related to the number of years over which we observe the returns:

$$SE[IR] \approx \frac{1}{\sqrt{Y}}$$

For more details, see Chap. 17.

0. If the data item is all signal and no noise, the information coefficient is 1. If there is a perverse relationship between the data item and the subsequent alpha, the information coefficient can be negative. The information coefficient must lie between +1 and −1.

Going back to our example, the information coefficient of the book-to-price signals over the period January 1988 through December 1992 is 0.01.

As we saw in Chap. 6, the information coefficient is related to the information ratio by the fundamental law of active management:

$$IR \approx IC \cdot \sqrt{BR} \qquad (12.4)$$

where BR measures the breadth of the information, the number of independent bets per year which the information will allow. In our example, given an information ratio of 0.27 and an information coefficient of 0.01, we can back out that the book-to-price information allows a little over 700 independent bets per year. Since the information covers 500 assets 12 times per year, it generates 6000 information items per year. Evidently not all are independent. As a practical matter, the parameter BR is more difficult to measure than either the information ratio or the information coefficient.

Advanced Topics in Performance Analysis

The subject of performance analysis is quite broad, and we will cover it in detail in Chap. 17. Still, it is worth briefly mentioning some advanced topics that pertain to analyzing information.

The first topic concerns portfolio turnover. Our two-step process has been to turn information into portfolios and then analyze the performance of those portfolios. Since we have the portfolios, we can also investigate their turnover. In fact, given transactions costs, turnover will directly affect performance. Turnover becomes important as we move from information analysis to backtesting and development of investable strategies.

Other topics concern more detailed levels of analysis that our approach allows. For instance, when we build long and short portfolios to bet for and against the information, we can also observe whether our information better predicts upside or downside alphas.

Beyond upside and downside information, we can also investigate whether the data contain information pertaining to up markets or down markets. How well do the portfolios perform in periods when the market is rising and in periods when the market is falling?

Finally, some advanced topics involve the connection between performance analysis and the step of turning information into portfolios. We can investigate the importance of controlling for other variables: industries, size, etc. We can construct portfolios with different controls, and analyze the performance in each case.

EVENT STUDIES

So far, our analysis of information has assumed that our information arrives regularly—e.g., every month for every asset in our investment universe. This facilitates building monthly portfolios and then observing their performance. Some information doesn't arrive in neat cross-sectional packages. Some information-laden events occur at different times for different assets. We need a methodology for analyzing these sources of information: the event study.

Where cross-sectional information analysis looks at all the information arriving at a date, event studies look at information arriving with a type of event. Only our imagination and the existence of relevant data will limit possible event studies. Examples of events we could analyze include

- An earnings announcement
- A new CEO
- A change in dividend
- A stock split

Three types of variables play a role in event studies: a description of the event, asset returns after the event, and conditioning variables from before the event. Often, the description of the event is a 0/1 variable: The event happened or it didn't. This is the case, for example, if a company hires a new CEO. Other events warrant a more complicated description. For example, studies of earnings announcements use the "earnings surprise" as the relevant variable. This is the announced earnings less consensus forecasts, divided by the dispersion of analysts' forecasts or some other measure of the uncertainty in earnings. As a second example, we could use the change in yield to describe a dividend change event.

Next, we need the asset's return after the event. This requires special care, because event studies analyze events at different times. They must avoid confounding calendar time with the time measured relative to the event, by extracting the distortions that arise because the events occurred at separate calendar times. For example, stock ABC increased dividends from \$1.65 to \$1.70 on August 6, 1999, and stock XYZ reduced dividends from \$0.95 to \$0.80 on September 5, 1996. In both cases, we want to look at the performance of the stock in the month, quarter, and year subsequent to the event. But the market after September 5, 1996, might have differed radically from the market after August 6, 1999. Hence, event studies typically use asset residual returns after the event.[4]

Finally, we may wish to use additional conditioning variables characterizing the firm at the time of the event. Starting with the above list of example events, here are some possible characterizations:

- An earnings announcement
  -Surprise in the previous quarter
- A new CEO
  -From the inside or outside
  -Predecessor's fate: retired, fired or departed?
- A change in dividend
  -Company leverage
- A stock split
  -Percent of institutional ownership
  -Has there been a change in leadership?

How to Do an Event Study

In the generic case, we start with $n = 1, 2, \ldots, N$ events; residual returns cumulated from period 1 to period j following each event, $\theta_n(1,j)$; the residual risk estimate over the period, $\omega_n(1,j)$; and condi-

---

[4]For even more control over market conditions, we could use asset-specific returns (net of the market and other common factors).

tioning variables X_{nk}, where $k = 1, 2, \ldots, K$ indexes the different conditioning variables for each event n.

Once we have compiled and organized all this information, the event study takes the form of a regression:

$$\frac{\theta_n(1,j)}{\omega_n(1,j)} = b_0(1,j) + \sum_k X_{nk} \cdot b_k(1,j) + \epsilon_n(1,j) \qquad (12.5)$$

Once we have implemented the event study as a regression, we can apply the usual statistical analysis. We obviously care about the significance of the explanatory variables.

We will also be interested in how the coefficients change with distance from the event, even separating the future returns into segments. If we are counting trading days, we could look at performance by week: $\theta_n(1,5)$, $\theta_n(6,10)$, etc. To analyze performance in, e.g., the second week, run the regression

$$\frac{\theta_n(6,10)}{\omega_n(6,10)} = b_0(6,10) + \sum_k X_{nk} \cdot b_k(6,10) + \epsilon_n(6,10) \qquad (12.6)$$

Note that in these event study regressions, the dependent variable (the left-hand side of the equation) has ex ante mean 0 and standard deviation 1, and the in-sample estimate of the IC of the signal is $\sqrt{R^2}$ from the regression.

From Event Study to Alpha

Given the analysis above and an event that just occurred, the forecast alpha over the next j periods is

$$\alpha_n(1,j) = \omega_n(1,j) \cdot \left[b_0(1,j) + \sum_k X_{nk} \cdot b_k(1,j) \right] \qquad (12.7)$$

If the event occurred j_1 periods earlier, the forecast alpha is

$$\alpha_n(1,j) = \omega_n(1,j) \cdot \left[b_0(j_1, j + j_1) + \sum_k X_{nk} \cdot b_k(j_1, j + j_1) \right] \qquad (12.8)$$

Equations (12.7) and (12.8) are consistent with the volatility $\cdot$ IC $\cdot$ score rule of thumb. The first term, $\omega_n(1,j)$, is the volatility. The fitted part of the regression, $b_0(1,j) + \sum_k X_{nk} \cdot b_k(1,j)$, will be of the order of IC $\cdot$ score, since we made the dependent variable have ex ante mean 0 and standard deviation 1.

Relationship to Cross-sectional Studies

The results from an event study do not translate directly into an ex ante information ratio, as cross-sectional results do. We could, of course, calculate both an ex ante and an ex post information ratio using the alphas described above.

But we can also use a simple model to derive some insight into the relationship between our event study results and information ratios. Three factors are important to this relationship: the rate at which events occur, the ability to forecast future returns, and the decay rate of that forecasting ability.

Our simple model will first assume that the number of trading days between events has a geometric distribution. The probability that an event will occur in any given day is p. The probability that the next event occurs in j days is $p \cdot (1 - p)^{j-1}$. This just accounts for the probability that the event doesn't occur for $j - 1$ days, and then occurs 1 day. The expected number of days between events is $1/p$.

The model will then account for forecasting ability with the information coefficient. The information coefficient for the first day after the event is IC(1).

Finally, the model will account for the decay in forecasting ability as we move away from the event. This is the information horizon, which we treat in depth in Chap. 13. For now, we will simply assume that the information coefficient decays exponentially over time. For j days after the event,

$$\text{IC}(j) = \text{IC}(1) \cdot \gamma^{j-1} \qquad (12.9)$$

Sometimes we have a better sense of a half-life than of a decay constant. We can easily convert from one to the other. The half-life in days is simply $\log\{0.5\}/\log\{\gamma\}$.

With this information, and assuming J trading days per year and an investment universe of N roughly similar assets, the model estimates the annual information coefficient,

$$IC(J) = IC(1) \cdot \frac{(1 - \gamma^J)}{(1 - \gamma) \cdot \sqrt{J}} \tag{12.10}$$

and the information ratio,

$$IR = IC(J) \cdot \sqrt{\frac{p \cdot N}{1 - (1 - p) \cdot \gamma^2}} \tag{12.11}$$

The technical appendix provides the details. Note that combining Eq. (12.11) with the fundamental law of active management implies a measure of the breadth of the event information. Effectively, we are receiving fresh information on N^* assets, where

$$N^* \equiv \frac{p \cdot N}{1 - (1 - p) \cdot \gamma^2} \tag{12.12}$$

Equation (12.12) captures the essence of the process. If p is large (close to 1), events happen every day and $N^* \approx N$. But what if p is small? If our event is the appointment of a new CEO, which might occur every 7 years or so, then $p = 0.00056$. For such rare events, the effective breadth is

$$N^* \approx \frac{p \cdot N}{1 - \gamma^2} \tag{12.13}$$

Assuming an annual information coefficient of 0.04 and 1000 assets, Fig. 12.3 shows how the information ratio depends on the number of events per year and the half-life of the information.

THE PITFALLS OF INFORMATION ANALYSIS

Information analysis is a powerful tool. If we can use information analysis to evaluate the investment value of a set of raw data, we can also use it to refine those data. If this is done correctly, we are separating wheat from chaff. If it is done incorrectly, we are data mining.

Data mining can fool an analyst into believing that information exists when it does not. Data mining can lead managers to bet on

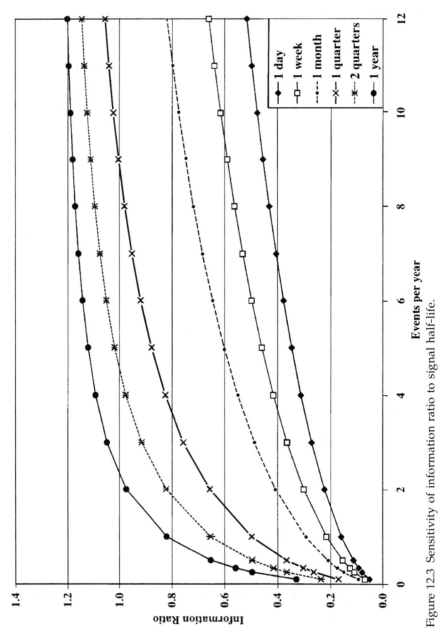

Figure 12.3 Sensitivity of information ratio to signal half-life.

information that doesn't exist. Data mining is the bane of information analysis.

Data Mining Is Easy

Why is it that so many ideas look great in backtests and disappoint upon implementation? Backtesters always have 95 percent confidence in their results, so why are investors disappointed far more than 5 percent of the time? It turns out to be surprisingly easy to search through historical data and find patterns that don't really exist.

To understand why data mining is easy, we must first understand the statistics of coincidence. Let's begin with some noninvestment examples. Then we will move on to investment research.

Several years ago, Evelyn Adams won the New Jersey state lottery twice in 4 months. Newspapers put the odds of that happening at 17 trillion to 1, an incredibly improbable event. A few months later, two Harvard statisticians, Percy Diaconis and Frederick Mosteller, showed that a double win in the lottery is not a particularly improbable event. They estimated the odds at 30 to 1. What explains the enormous discrepancy in these two probabilities?

It turns out that the odds of Evelyn Adams's winning the lottery twice are in fact 17 trillion to 1. But that result is presumably of interest only to her immediate family. The odds of someone, somewhere, winning two lotteries—given the millions of people entering lotteries every day—are only 30 to 1. If it wasn't Evelyn Adams, it could have been someone else.

Coincidences appear improbable only when viewed from a narrow perspective. When viewed from the correct (broad) perspective, coincidences are no longer so improbable. Let's consider another noninvestment example: Norman Bloom, arguably the world's greatest data miner.

Norman Bloom died a few years ago in the midst of his quest to prove the existence of God through baseball statistics and the Dow Jones average. He argued that "BOTH INSTRUMENTS are in effect GREAT LABORATORY EXPERIMENTS wherein GREAT AMOUNTS OF RECORDED DATA ARE COLLECTED, AND PUBLISHED" (capitalization Bloom's). As but one example of his thousands of analyses of baseball, he argued that the fact that George

Brett, the Kansas City third baseman, hit his third home run in the third game of the playoffs, to tie the score 3–3, could not be a coincidence—it must prove the existence of God. In the investment arena, he argued that the Dow's 13 crossings of the 1000 line in 1976 mirrored the 13 colonies which united in 1776—which also could not be a coincidence. (He pointed out, too, that the 12th crossing occurred on his birthday, deftly combining message and messenger.) He never took into account the enormous volume of data—in fact, the entire New York Public Library's worth—he searched through to find these coincidences. His focus was narrow, not broad.

With Bloom's passing, the title of world's greatest living data miner has been left open. Recently, however, Michael Drosnin, author of *The Bible Code,* seems to have filled it.[5]

The importance of perspective for understanding the statistics of coincidence was perhaps best summarized by, of all people, Marcel Proust—who often showed keen mathematical intuition:

> The number of pawns on the human chessboard being less than the number of combinations that they are capable of forming, in a theater from which all the people we know and might have expected to find are absent, there turns up one whom we never imagined that we should see again and who appears so opportunely that the coincidence seems to us providential, although, no doubt, some other coincidence would have occurred in its stead had we not been in that place but in some other, where other desires would have been born and another old acquaintance forthcoming to help us satisfy them.[6]

Investment Research

Investment research involves exactly the same statistics and the same issues of perspective. The typical investment data mining example involves t statistics gathered from backtesting strategies.

---

[5]For a review of *The Bible Code,* see Kahn (1998).
[6]*The Guermantes Way, Cities of the Plain,* vol. 2 of *Remembrance of Things Past* C.K. Scott Moncrieff and Terance Kilmartin, translators, (New York: Vintage Books, 1982), p. 178.

The narrow perspective says, "After 19 false starts, this 20th invest-ment strategy finally works. It has a t statistic of 2."

But the broad perspective on this situation is quite different. In fact, given 20 informationless strategies, the probability of finding at least one with a t statistic of 2 is 64 percent. The narrow perspec-tive substantially inflates our confidence in the results. When the situation is viewed from the proper perspective, confidence in the results decreases accordingly.[7]

Fortunately, four guidelines can help keep information analy-sis from turning into data mining: intuition, restraint, sensibleness, and out-of-sample testing.

First, intuition must guide the search for information before the backtest begins. Intuition should not be driven strictly by data. Ideally, it should arise from a general understanding of the forces governing investment returns and the economy as a whole. The book-to-price strategy satisfies the criterion of intuition. The infor-mation tells us which stocks provide book value cheaply. Of course, intuition is a necessary but not a sufficient criterion for finding valuable information. Some information is already widely known by market participants and fairly priced in the market. On the other hand, nonintuitive information that appears valuable in this analysis usually fails upon implementation. Sunspots, skirt lengths, and Super Bowl victories can appear valuable over carefully chosen historical periods, but are completely nonintuitive. Data mining can easily find such accidental correlations. They do not translate into successful implementations.

Second, restraint should govern the backtesting process. Statis-tical analysis shows that, given enough trials of valueless informa-tion, one incarnation (usually the last one analyzed) will look good. After 20 tests of worthless information, 1 should look significant at the 95 percent confidence level. In principle, researchers should map out possible information variations before the testing begins. There are many possible variations of the book-to-price informa-tion. We can use current price or price contemporaneous with the book value accounting information. We can try stock sectors, to find where the relationship works best. With each variation, the

---

[7]For a detailed analysis of these pitfalls, see Kahn (1990).

information drifts further from intuition, pushed along by the particular historical data.

Third, performance should be sensible. The information that deserves most scrutiny is that which appears to perform too well. Only about 10 percent of observed realized information ratios lie above 1. Carefully and skeptically examine information ratios above 2 that arise in information analysis. The book-to-price data in our example are straightforward, publicly available information. In the fairly efficient U.S. market, an information ratio above 2 for such information should not be believed. Information ratios far above 2 signal mistakes in the analysis, not phenomenal insight.

Fourth, out-of-sample testing can serve as a quantitative check on data mining. Valueless information honed to perfection on one set of historical data should reveal its true nature when tested on a second set of historical data. Book-to-price ratios tuned using 1980 to 1985 monthly returns must also outperform in 1986. Book-to-price ratios tuned using January, March, May, July, September, and November monthly returns must also outperform in February, April, June, August, October, and December. Out-of-sample testing helps ensure that the information not only describes historical returns, but predicts future returns.

SUMMARY

This chapter has presented a thorough discussion of information analysis. Information analysis proceeds in two steps. First, information is transformed into investment portfolios. Second, the performance of those portfolios is analyzed. To quantify that performance—and the value of the information being analyzed—the information ratio most succinctly measures the potential investment value added contained in the information.

PROBLEMS

1. What problems can arise in using scores instead of alphas in information analysis? Where in the analysis would these problems show up?

2. What do you conclude from the information analysis presented concerning book-to-price ratios in the United States?

3. Why might we see misleading results if we looked only at the relative performance of top- and bottom-quintile portfolios instead of looking at factor portfolio performance?

4. The probability of observing a $|t$ statistic$| > 2$, using random data, is only 5 percent. Hence our confidence in the estimate is 95 percent. Show that the probability of observing at least one $|t$ statistic$| > 2$ with 20 regressions on independent sets of random data is 64 percent.

5. Show that the standard error of the information ratio is approximately $1/\sqrt{T}$, where T is the number of years of observation. Assume that you can measure the standard deviation of returns with perfect accuracy, so that all the error is in the estimate of the mean. Remember that the standard error of an estimated mean is $1/\sqrt{N}$, where N is the number of observations.

6. You wish to analyze the value of corporate insider stock transactions. Should you analyze these using the standard cross-sectional methodology or an event study? If you use an event study, what conditioning variables will you consider?

7. Haugen and Baker (1996) have proposed an APT model in which expected factor returns are simply based on past 12-month moving averages. Applying this idea to the BARRA U.S. Equity model from January 1974 through March 1996 leads to an information ratio of 1.79. Applying this idea only to the risk indices in the model (using consensus expected returns for industries) leads to an information ratio of 1.26. What information ratio would you expect to find from applying this model to industries only? If the full application exhibits an information coefficient of 0.05, what is the implied breadth of the strategy?

8. A current get-rich-quick Web site guarantees that over the next 3 months, at least three stocks mentioned on the site will exhibit annualized returns of at least 300 percent. Assuming that all stock returns are independent, normally distributed, and with expected annual returns

of 12 percent and risk of 35 percent, (*a*) what is the probability that over one quarter at least 3 stocks out of 500 exhibit annualized returns of at least 300%? (*b*) How many stocks must the Web site include for this probability to be 50 percent? (*c*) Identify at least two real-world deviations from the above assumptions, and discuss how they would affect the calculated probabilities.

NOTES

The science of information analysis began in the 1970s with work by Treynor and Black (1973), Hodges and Brealey (1973), Ambachtsheer (1974), Rosenberg (1976), and Ambachtsheer and Farrell (1979). These authors all investigated the role of active management in investing: Its ability to add value and measures for determining this. Treynor and Black and Hodges and Brealey were the first to examine the role of security analysis and active management within the context of the capital asset pricing model. They investigated what is required if active management is to outperform the market, and identified the importance of correlations between return forecasts and outcomes among these requirements. Ambachtsheer, alone and with Farrell, provided further insights into the active management process and turning information into investments. He also coined the term "information coefficient," or IC, to describe this correlation between forecasts of residual returns (alphas) and subsequent realizations. Rosenberg investigated the active management process and measures of its performance as part of his analysis of the optimal amount of active management for institutional investors.

REFERENCES

Ambachtsheer, Keith P. "Profit Potential in an 'Almost Efficient' Market." *Journal of Portfolio Management,* vol. 1, no. 1, 1974, pp. 84–87.

———. "Where Are the Customers' Alphas?" *Journal of Portfolio Management,* vol. 4, no. 1, 1977, pp. 52–56.

Ambachtsheer, Keith P., and James L. Farrell Jr. "Can Active Management Add Value?" *Financial Analysts Journal,* vol. 35, no. 6, 1979, pp. 39–47.

Drosnin, Michael. *The Bible Code* (New York: Simon & Schuster, 1997).

Frankfurter, George M., and Elton G. McGoun. "The Event Study: Is It Either?" *Journal of Investing,* vol. 4, no. 2, 1995, pp. 8–16.

Grinold, Richard C. "The Fundamental Law of Active Management." *Journal of Portfolio Management*, vol. 15, no. 3, 1989, pp. 30–37.

Grinold, Richard C., and Ronald N. Kahn. "Information Analysis." *Journal of Portfolio Management*, vol. 18, no. 3, 1992, pp. 14–21.

Haugen, Robert A., and Nardin L. Baker. "Commonality in the Determinants of Expected Stock Returns." *Journal of Financial Economics*, vol. 41, no. 3, 1996, pp. 401–439.

Hodges, S. D., and R. A. Brealey. "Portfolio Selection in a Dynamic and Uncertain World." *Financial Analysts Journal*, vol. 29, no. 2, 1973, pp. 50–65.

Kahn, Ronald N. "What Practitioners Need to Know about Backtesting." *Financial Analysts Journal*, vol. 46, no. 4, 1990, pp. 17–20.

———. "Three Classic Errors in Statistics from Baseball to Investment Research." *Financial Analysts Journal*, vol. 53, no. 5, 1997, pp. 6–8.

———. "Book Review: *The Bible Code.*" *Horizon: The BARRA Newsletter*, Winter 1998.

Kritzman, Mark P. "What Practitioners Need to Know about Event Studies." *Financial Analysts Journal*, vol. 50, no. 6, 1994, pp. 17–20.

Proust, Marcel. The Guermantes Way, Cities of the Plain, vol. 2 of *Remembrance of Things Past*, translated by C.K. Scott Moncrieff and Terence Kilmartin (New York: Vintage Books, 1982), p. 178.

Rosenberg, Barr. "Security Appraisal and Unsystematic Risk in Institutional Investment." *Proceedings of the Seminar on the Analysis of Security Prices* (Chicago: University of Chicago Press, 1976), pp. 171–237.

Salinger, Michael. "Standard Errors in Event Studies." *Journal of Financial and Quantitative Analysis*, vol. 27, no. 1, 1992, pp. 39–53.

Treynor, Jack, and Fischer Black. "How to Use Security Analysis to Improve Portfolio Selection." *Journal of Business*, vol. 46, no. 1, 1973, pp. 68–86.

TECHNICAL APPENDIX

This technical appendix will discuss mathematically the more controlled quantitative approaches to constructing portfolios to efficiently bet on a particular information item $\mathbf{a}$, while controlling for risk. It will also detail the model used to connect event studies to cross-sectional studies.

Information-Efficient Portfolios

Basically, this is just an optimization problem. We want to choose the minimum-risk portfolio $\mathbf{h}_a$ subject to a set of constraints:

$$\text{Minimize} \quad \mathbf{h}^T \cdot \mathbf{V} \cdot \mathbf{h} \qquad (12A.1)$$

$$\text{Subject to} \quad \mathbf{h}^T \cdot \mathbf{a} = 1 \qquad (12A.2)$$

$$\text{and} \quad \mathbf{h}^T \cdot \mathbf{Z} = 0 \qquad (12A.3)$$

If we ignore the constraints, $\mathbf{z}$, in Eq. (12A.3), then the solution to this problem is the characteristic portfolio for $\mathbf{a}$. Constraints we could add include

- $\mathbf{h}^T \cdot \boldsymbol{\beta} = 0$ (zero beta)
- $\mathbf{h}^T \cdot \mathbf{e} = 0$ (zero net investment)
- $\mathbf{h}^T \cdot \mathbf{X} = 0$ (zero exposure to risk model factors)

Long and Short Portfolios

The portfolio $\mathbf{h}_a$ will include long and short positions:

$$\mathbf{h}_a = \mathbf{h}_{aL} - \mathbf{h}_{aS} \qquad (12A.4)$$

where $\mathbf{h}_{aL}$ and $\mathbf{h}_{aS}$ are defined such that their holdings are all non-negative:

$$h_{aL,n} = \text{Max}\{0, h_{a,n}\} \qquad (12A.5)$$

$$h_{aS,n} = \text{Max}\{0, -h_{a,n}\} \qquad (12A.6)$$

If we add the net zero investment constraint, then the long and short portfolios will exactly balance.

We see from Eq. (12A.4) that $\text{Var}\{\mathbf{h}_a\}$ is identical to $\text{Var}\{\mathbf{h}_{aL} - \mathbf{h}_{aS}\}$, and so minimizing the variance of $\mathbf{h}_a$ subject to constraints is the same as minimizing the tracking of $\mathbf{h}_{aL}$ versus $\mathbf{h}_{aS}$ subject to the same constraints.

We can separately monitor the performance of $\mathbf{h}_{aL}$ and $\mathbf{h}_{aS}$ to observe whether $\mathbf{a}$ contains upside and/or downside information, respectively.

Relation to Regression

This factor portfolio approach is related to the regression approach to estimating factor returns. Given excess returns $\mathbf{r}$, information $\mathbf{a}$, and exposures $\mathbf{X}$, we can estimate factor returns:

$$\mathbf{r} = \mathbf{Y} \cdot \mathbf{b} + \boldsymbol{\epsilon} \qquad (12A.7)$$

where $\mathbf{Y}$ is an $N \times (J + 1)$ matrix whose first J columns contain $\mathbf{X}$

and whose last column contains **a**. Estimating **b** with weights **W** (stored as a diagonal $N \times N$ matrix) leads to

$$\mathbf{b} = (\mathbf{Y}^T \cdot \mathbf{W} \cdot \mathbf{Y})^{-1} \cdot \mathbf{Y}^T \cdot \mathbf{W} \cdot \mathbf{r} \qquad (12A.8)$$

the estimates which minimize $\boldsymbol{\epsilon}^T \cdot \mathbf{W} \cdot \boldsymbol{\epsilon}$. These estimates are linear combinations of the asset returns; hence, we can rewrite this as

$$\mathbf{b} = \mathbf{H}^T \cdot \mathbf{r} \qquad (12A.9)$$

where $\qquad \mathbf{H}^T = (\mathbf{Y}^T \cdot \mathbf{W} \cdot \mathbf{Y})^{-1} \cdot \mathbf{Y}^T \cdot \mathbf{W} \qquad (12A.10)$

is the $(J + 1) \times N$ matrix of factor portfolio holdings. Note that

$$\mathbf{H}^T \cdot \mathbf{Y} = \mathbf{I} \qquad (12A.11)$$

so each factor portfolio has unit exposure to its particular factor and zero exposure to all other factors.

The portfolio $\mathbf{h}_{J+1}$, the last column of the matrix **H**, has return b_a, the estimated return in Eq. (12A.9) corresponding to information **a**. Where $\mathbf{h}_a$ is the minimum-risk portfolio with $\mathbf{h}^T \cdot \mathbf{a} = 1$ and subject to various constraints, $\mathbf{h}_{J+1}$ is the portfolio with minimum $\boldsymbol{\epsilon}^T \cdot \mathbf{W} \cdot \boldsymbol{\epsilon}$ with $\mathbf{h}^T \cdot \mathbf{a} = 1$ and subject to various constraints.

Event Studies and Cross-sectional Studies

The main text stated results [Eqs. (12.10) and (12.11)] connecting information coefficients from event studies, along with event rates and information horizons, to cross-sectional information ratios. We derive those results here.

First we derive the annual information coefficient IC(J), given the one-day information coefficient IC(1). (We assume J trading days in the year.) The one-day information coefficient states that the correlation between our signal and the one-day residual return is IC(1):

$$\text{Corr}\{z(0),\theta(1)\} = \text{IC}(1) \qquad (12A.12)$$

With no loss of generality, we can assume that our signal has standard deviation 1. Hence, the covariance of the signal with the one-day residual return is

$$\text{Cov}\{z(0),\theta(1)\} = \omega(1) \cdot \text{IC}(1) \qquad (12A.13)$$

We have assumed that our information coefficient decays with decay constant γ. Hence, the covariance of our signal with the residual return on day J is

$$\text{Cov}\{z(0),\theta(J)\} = \omega(1) \cdot \text{IC}(1) \cdot \gamma^{J-1} \qquad (12A.14)$$

To derive the annual information coefficient, we first need the covariance of our signal with the annual residual return, which is the sum of the J daily residual returns:

$$\text{Cov}\left\{z(0), \sum_{j=1}^{J} \theta(j)\right\} = \omega(1) \cdot \text{IC}(1) \cdot \sum_{j=1}^{J} \gamma^{j-1} \qquad (12A.15)$$

We can sum this geometric series to find

$$\text{Cov}\left\{z(0), \sum_{j=1}^{J} \theta(j)\right\} = \omega(1) \cdot \text{IC}(1) \cdot \left(\frac{1 - \gamma^{J}}{1 - \gamma}\right) \qquad (12A.16)$$

The annual information coefficient is simply the correlation associated with this covariance. We need only divide by the annual residual volatility:

$$\text{IC}(J) = \text{IC}(1) \cdot \frac{(1 - \gamma^{J})}{(1 - \gamma) \cdot \sqrt{J}} \qquad (12A.17)$$

This is Eq. (12.10) from the main text.

Next we need to derive the result for the information ratio. The annualized alpha, assuming that the event has just occurred, is

$$\alpha(0) = \text{IC}(J) \cdot \omega \cdot z \qquad (12A.18)$$

But if the information arrived j days ago, the alpha is

$$\alpha(j) = \text{IC}(J) \cdot \omega \cdot z \cdot \gamma^{j-1} \qquad (12A.19)$$

The information ratio for a given set of alphas is simply $\sqrt{\alpha^{T} \cdot V^{-1} \cdot \alpha}$. [See, for example, Eq. (5A.6).] We will calculate the square of the information ratio by taking the expectation of the square of this result over the distribution of possible signals z. We will assume uncorrelated residual returns. We must account for the fact that, cross-sectionally, different assets will have different event delays. So we must calculate

$$IR^2 = E\left\{\sum_{n=1}^{N}\left[\frac{IC(J) \cdot \omega_n \cdot z_n \cdot \gamma^{j_n - 1}}{\omega_n}\right]^2\right\} \tag{12A.20}$$

We can simplify this somewhat, to

$$IR^2 = \left[\frac{IC(J)}{\gamma}\right]^2 \cdot E\left\{\sum_{n=1}^{N}(z_n \cdot \gamma^{j_n})^2\right\} \tag{12A.21}$$

We must make further assumptions to estimate the expectation in Eq. (12A.21). First, we assume the same expectation for each asset n:

$$E\left\{\sum_{n=1}^{N}(z_n \cdot \gamma^{j_n})^2\right\} = N \cdot E\{(z \cdot \gamma^j)^2\} \tag{12A.22}$$

Second, we assume that we can separate the two terms in the expectation. So effectively, for any value of j, we will take the expectation of z^2, since the score shouldn't depend on the value of j:

$$E\{(z \cdot \gamma^j)^2\} = E\{z^2\} \cdot E\{\gamma^{2j}\} = E\{\gamma^{2j}\} \tag{12A.23}$$

We must calculate one last expectation. Here we know the distribution of event arrival times. Hence

$$E\{\gamma^{2j}\} = \sum_{j=1}^{\infty} \gamma^{2j} \cdot p \cdot (1 - p)^j \tag{12A.24}$$

We can once again apply results concerning the summation of geometric series. We find

$$E\{\gamma^{2j}\} = \frac{p \cdot \gamma^2}{1 - (1 - p) \cdot \gamma^2} \tag{12A.25}$$

Combining Eqs. (12A.21) through (12A.23) and (12A.25) leads to the final result:

$$IR = IC(J) \cdot \sqrt{\frac{p \cdot N}{1 - (1 - p) \cdot \gamma^2}} \tag{12A.26}$$

This is Eq. (12.11) from the main text.

CHAPTER 13

The Information Horizon

INTRODUCTION

There is a time dimension to information. Information arrives at different rates and is valuable over longer or shorter periods. For most signals, the arrival rate is fixed. The shelf life (or information horizon) is the main focus of interest. Is this a fast signal that fades in 3 or 4 days, or is it a slow signal that retains its value over the next year? The latest is not necessarily the greatest. In some cases, a mix of old and new information is more valuable than just the latest information.

Chapters 10 and 11 developed a methodology for processing information and described how to optimally combine sources of information. Chapter 12 presented an approach to analyzing the information content of signals. Chapter 13 will rely on both methodologies to tackle the special topic of the information horizon.

We will begin by applying information analysis at the "macro" level: looking at returns to multiasset strategies. These may be based on one or several sources of information, possibly but not necessarily optimally combined. The goal is to determine the information horizon, and whether the strategy is effectively using the information in a temporal sense, i.e., whether any time average or time difference of the information could improve performance. This analysis has the advantage of requiring only the returns, not a detailed knowledge of the inner workings of the strategy.

At the "micro" level, we will apply the methodology of Chap. 10 to the special case of optimal mixing of old and new signals.

The in-depth analysis of simple cases provides insight into the phenomena we observe in more complicated and realistic cases. These micro results echo the macro results.

Insights in this chapter include the following:

- The information horizon should be defined as the half-life of the information's forecasting ability.
- A strategy's horizon is an intrinsic property. Time averages or time differences can change performance, but they will not change the horizon.
- Lagged signals or scores and past returns can improve investment performance.

MACROANALYSIS OF THE INFORMATION HORIZON

A natural definition of the information horizon, or shelf life, of a strategy is the decay rate of the information ratio. What does it cost us if a procrastinating investment committee forces a 1-month delay in implementing the recommendations? We use the May 1 portfolio in June, the June 1 portfolio in July, and so forth. What if there is a 2-month delay? Or a 6-month delay? In general, delays will lead to a reduction in the strategy's potential as measured by its information ratio. A reasonable measure of the decay rate is the *half-life*, the time it takes for the information ratio to drop to one-half of its value when implemented with immediacy. In practice, this means that we approximate the decay in the information ratio as an exponential where a certain fraction of the information is lost in each period.

The half-life is a remarkably robust characteristic of the strategy. Attempts to improve the signal using its temporal dimensions may improve performance, but they will have little or no effect on the strategy's half-life!

In Fig. 13.1, we see a gradual decay in the strategy's realized information ratio as we delay implementation for more and more months. The half-life is 1.2 years.

The ability to add value is proportional to the square of the information ratio. Thus the half-life for adding value is one-half that of the information ratio. In the case illustrated in Fig. 13.1, we

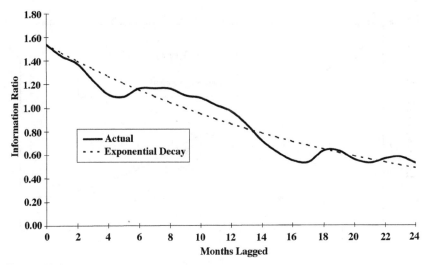

Figure 13.1

have a half-life of 0.6 year for value added as opposed to 1.2 years for the information ratio. This is a long-horizon strategy. We can delay implementation of the recommended trades for more than 6 months and still realize 50 percent of the value added.

Figure 13.2 shows a strategy with a very short half-life.

The interplay of information and time is as subtle as the interplay of food and time. "Fresh is best" is a good rule but not universally accurate: Vegetables and baked goods are best when fresh, fruit needs to ripen; wine and cheese improve with age, and sherry is best as a blend of several vintages. Is the information sherry, vegetables, or wine?

We can see if there is any value in the old information with a thought experiment. Suppose there are two investment managers, Manager Now and Manager Later. Manager Now employs an excellent strategy, with an information ratio of 1.5. Manager Later's research consists of sifting through Manager Now's trash to find a listing of last month's portfolio. Thus Manager Later follows the same strategy as Manager Now, but with the portfolios 1 month behind. Manager Later has an information ratio of 1.20. Both managers have an active risk level of 4 percent.

Should we hire Manager Now, Manager Later, or a mix of Now and Later? This decision hinges on the correlation of the active

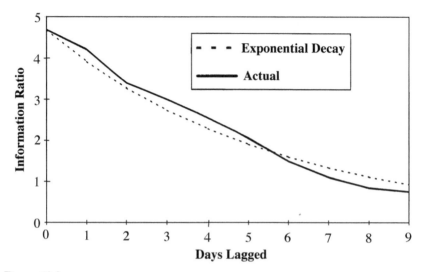

Figure 13.2

returns. If the correlation between Manager Now's and Manager Later's active returns is less than $0.80 = 1.2/1.5$, the decay rate of the information ratio, then we can add value by hiring both Now and Later. If the correlation is more than 0.80, we want to hedge Manager Now's performance by going short manager Later. Figure 13.3 shows the mix of Now and Later that we would want as a function of the correlation between their active returns. At a correlation of 0.7 between the active returns of Managers Now and Later, the best mix is 18.5 percent to Manager Later and 81.5 percent to Manager Now. If we presume a correlation of 0.85 in the active returns of Managers Now and Later, then the optimal mix is a 118.5 percent long position with Manager Now offset by an 18.5 percent short position with Manager Later.

We will show in the technical appendix that given a decay rate of γ and a correlation of ρ, the optimal weight on Now is

$$w^{*}_{\text{Now}} = \frac{\gamma + x}{\gamma + 1} \tag{13.1}$$

where

$$x \equiv \frac{1 - \gamma}{1 - \rho} \tag{13.2}$$

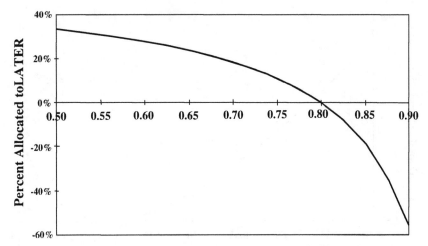

Correlation of LATER's active return with NOW's active return

Figure 13.3

Figure 13.4 shows the change in the overall information ratio that results from combining Managers Now and Later. We see that there is no gain if the active return correlation is 0.8 and that there are modest gains if the active return correlation strays above or below that key level. The algebraic result here is

$$\text{IR}^* = \text{IR}_{\text{Now}} \cdot \frac{(\gamma + x) + \gamma \cdot (1 - x)}{\sqrt{(\gamma + x)^2 + (1 - x)^2 + 2 \cdot (\gamma + x) \cdot (1 - x) \cdot \rho}} \tag{13.3}$$

We will show more generally in the technical appendix that the optimal combination of past portfolios mixes them so that the correlation between the time t and the time $t - 1$ portfolios equals the decay rate of the information ratio. For example, if the l-period lagged information ratio is $\text{IR}_l = \gamma^l \cdot \text{IR}_0$ and the portfolios at each time t are denoted $\mathbf{h}(t), \mathbf{h}(t - 1), \ldots, \mathbf{h}(t - l), \ldots$, then the combination with the best information ratio will be

$$\mathbf{h}^*(t) = \sum_{l=0}^{\infty} \gamma^l \cdot [\mathbf{h}(t - l) - \rho \cdot \mathbf{h}(t - l - 1)] \tag{13.4}$$

$$= [\mathbf{h}(t) - \rho \cdot \mathbf{h}(t - 1)] + \gamma \cdot \mathbf{h}^*(t - 1)$$

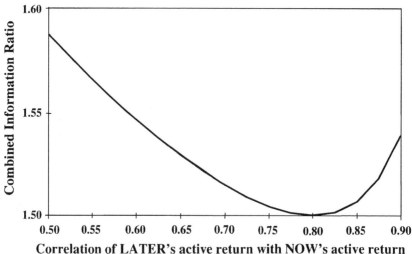

Figure 13.4

The correlation of active returns for the holdings $\mathbf{h}^*(t)$ and $\mathbf{h}^*(t-1)$ will be γ. Note that $\mathbf{h}^*$ is a weighted average of innovations, with $\mathbf{h}(t-l) - \rho \cdot \mathbf{h}(t-l-1)$ capturing the new information in $\mathbf{h}(t-l)$.[1]

This application of information analysis can quickly help a manager determine if she or he is leaving any information on the table, since a real manager can easily combine managers Now and Later merely by combining the most recently recommended portfolio with the portfolio recommended in the previous period. For example, if the active return correlation is 0.5, then a mix of 33 percent of the lagged portfolio and 67 percent of the current portfolio would produce an information ratio of 1.59. Combining the portfolios is combining the outputs of the investment management process. If there is a process where it is possible to link inputs with outputs, then we could also proceed by mixing the lagged inputs and the current inputs in the same 33 percent and 67 percent ratios.

---

[1] If you regress $\theta(t-l)$ on $\theta(t-l-1)$, the coefficient on $\theta(t-l-1)$ should be ρ, since $\omega(t-l) = \omega(t-l-1)$. Hence Eq. (13.4) effectively represents the residuals from such a regression.

This optimal mix of Now and Later will improve performance *although it will not change the horizon.* If we make an optimal mixture of the old portfolios, the information ratio will increase, but the horizon (half-life) of the resulting strategy will be exactly the same as the horizon of the original strategy.

MICROANALYSIS OF THE INFORMATION HORIZON

We will now apply our information processing methodology to analyzing the information horizon at the micro level. We will focus on the case of one asset, or, more precisely, one time series.[2] This asset has return $r(0,\Delta t)$ over a period between time 0 and time Δt. For convenience, we assume that the expected return is 0. The volatility of the return is σ times the square root of Δt. We assume, in general, that the asset returns are uncorrelated.

Information arrives periodically, in bundles that we'll call scores, at time intervals of length Δt—perhaps an hour, a day, a week, a month, a quarter, or a year. These scores have mean 0 and standard deviation 1, as described in Chap. 10.

The special information contained in the scores may allow us to predict the return $r(0,\Delta t)$. This prediction, or alpha, depends on the arrival rate and shelf life of that information.

In the simplest case, "just-in-time" signals, the signal is of value in forecasting return during the interval until the next one arrives, but it is of no value in forecasting the return in subsequent periods. For example, a signal that arrives on April 30 helps in forecasting the May return but is of no use for June, July, etc. The next signal, which arrives May 31, helps with the June return.

Let $IC(\Delta t)$ be the correlation of the score with the return over the period $\{0,\Delta t\}$. Given a score $s(0)$, the standardized signal at time 0, the conditional expectation of $r(0,\Delta t)$ is

$$\alpha(\Delta t) = (\sigma \cdot \sqrt{\Delta t}) \cdot IC(\Delta t) \cdot s(0) \qquad (13.5)$$

---

[2] The point is that our results apply to a single asset, or a factor return, or a portfolio long stocks and short bonds.

The information coefficient IC(Δt) is a measure of forecast accuracy over the period. The first goal is to determine the value of the information. Here we will use the information ratio. We can use the fundamental law of active management to determine the information ratio as a function of the forecast interval:

$$IR^2 = [IC(\Delta t)]^2 \cdot \left(\frac{1}{\Delta t}\right) \qquad\qquad (13.6)$$

where we measure the breadth BR as simply the inverse of the period, i.e., $1/\Delta t$. For example, a signal that arrives once per month has a breadth of 12. We can see immediately that there is a trade-off between the arrival rate, captured by Δt, and the accuracy, captured by IC(Δt).

Two-Period Shelf Life

In the simplest case described above, we had "just-in-time" information. The interarrival time Δt matched the shelf life Δt. Now we'll consider cases where the interarrival time is shorter than the shelf life.[3] In particular, we receive scores each period, and a score's shelf life is two periods long. The April 30 score predicts the returns for May and June. The May 31 score predicts the returns for June and July. We can measure the IC of the score on a period-by-period basis. The term IC_1 measures the correlation between the score and the first period's return, and the term IC_2 measures the correlation between the score and the second period's return. The information coefficient $IC_{1\&2}$ is the correlation between the score and the two-period return. The relation between these information coefficients is

$$IC_{1\&2} = \frac{IC_1 + IC_2}{\sqrt{2}} \qquad\qquad (13.7)$$

---

[3]It is possible, although less interesting, to have the interarrival time exceed the shelf life. An example is earnings surprise for international companies; the information arrives once a year, and its value has generally expired long before the next year's earnings announcement.

For example, a correlation of $IC_1 = 0.15$ for the first period's return and $IC_2 = 0.075$ for the second period's return would imply a correlation of $IC_{1\&2} = (0.15 + 0.075)/\sqrt{2} = 0.159$ for the two periods. We are blessed with a longer shelf life. It remains to see how we handle this blessing.

We want to make a one-period forecast based on the most recent score, $s(0)$, and the previous score, $s(-\Delta t)$. In the monthly example, we combine the April 30 score and the May 31 score to produce a forecast for June. The critical variable in producing a best forecast will be the correlation ρ between $s(0)$ and $s(-\Delta t)$.

In Chap. 10, we derived how to optimally combine two separate signals. That result applies here as well, with the second signal being simply the lag of the first signal:

$$\alpha(\Delta t) = \sigma \cdot \sqrt{\Delta t} \cdot \{IC_1^* \cdot s(0) + IC_2^* \cdot s(-\Delta t)\} \qquad (13.8)$$

The modified information coefficients IC_1^* and IC_2^* correct for the correlation between the signals:

$$IC_1^* = \frac{IC_1 - \rho \cdot IC_2}{1 - \rho^2} \qquad (13.9)$$

$$IC_2^* = \frac{IC_2 - \rho \cdot IC_1}{1 - \rho^2} \qquad (13.10)$$

The IC of the combined signal is

$$IC^* = \sqrt{\frac{IC_1^2 + IC_2^2 - 2 \cdot IC_1 \cdot IC_2 \cdot \rho}{1 - \rho^2}} \qquad (13.11)$$

Figure 13.5 shows how the modified information coefficients change as the correlation between the signals varies, assuming $IC_1 = 0.15$ and $IC_2 = 0.075$.

The combined forecast dominates using either the first or the second score in isolation. Figure 13.6 demonstrates this for our example.

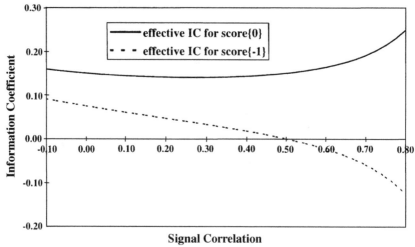

Figure 13.5

The lagged score, $s(-\Delta t)$, can help improve the forecast in one of two ways:

- *Diversification*, as a second predictor of the return $r(0,\Delta t)$
- *Hedging*, as a way of reducing the noise in $s(0)$

The scores are part truth and part noise. The truth portion is perfectly correlated with future return. The noise component is uncorrelated with future return. By adding a fraction of the previous score to the current score, we can reinforce the known facts and diversify the noise. This is a good idea if $IC_2 > \rho \cdot IC_1$, i.e., when there is a relatively strong remaining signal and relatively low correlation. The alternative is to subtract a fraction of the second score from the first. This loses some signal, but if the scores are strongly correlated, it will hedge the noise. Hedging is the most beneficial path to follow if $IC_2 < \rho \cdot IC_1$, i.e., when there is a relatively weak signal and strong correlation. In the intermediate case, when $IC_2 = \rho \cdot IC_1$, then $IC_1^* = IC_1$ and $IC_2^* = 0$. In effect, we ignore the previous score.[4] We can see this critical point in Figs. 13.5 and 13.6

---

[4]There are, of course, cases where $IC_2 > IC_1$ (as opposed to just $IC_2 > \rho \cdot IC_1$). The correlation with period 2 is actually stronger than the correlation with period 1. In this case, one would be advised to look into autocorrelation of the return.

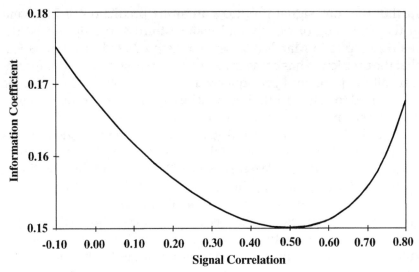

Figure 13.6

where the correlation reaches 0.5, exactly the ratio of the information coefficients.

This result for optimally combining new and old information closely matches our results from the macroanalysis. In fact, Figs. 13.5 and 13.6 from the microanalysis resemble Figs. 13.3 and 13.4 from the macroanalysis. This is quite reassuring. We will now see, however, that we can drill considerably deeper in microanalysis.

HAS THE ALPHA BEEN REALIZED?

Prior to the 1967 Arab-Israeli war, then private citizen Richard Nixon predicted that

1. There would not be a war.
2. If a war started, it would be a long war.

The war started within days, making Mr. Nixon's first prediction no longer operative. When the war was over a week later, the second prediction went nonoperative. You don't receive such dramatic and immediate feedback when you're predicting asset returns.

Suppose that we have, as above, alphas arriving each month that are useful in predicting returns over the next 2 months. Suppose further that our signal produces an alpha prediction of 2 percent at the beginning of March, and make a third supposition that the realized alpha in March is 2 percent, as predicted. It would seem that the prediction has come true and we can ignore the old information; all the juice has been squeezed out of it. Not so! Many people find it hard to believe, but they may be right for the wrong reasons.[5] That 2 percent return may have been incidental.

To deal with this possibility, we can use the previous period's return, $r(-\Delta t,0)$ as another possible variable in the prediction of next period's return, $r(0,\Delta t)$. We turn $r(-\Delta t,0)$ into a score by dividing it by its standard deviation; the score is $r(-\Delta t,0)/(\sigma \cdot \sqrt{\Delta t})$.

We now have three predictors of $r(0,\Delta t)$: $s(0)$, $s(-\Delta t)$, and $r(-\Delta t,0)/(\sigma \cdot \sqrt{\Delta t})$. When there is no serial correlation in the returns and no correlation between past returns and current scores, the rule for adapting to the observed return changes the previous score and is thus called "settling old scores." The settled score[6] is

$$s^*(-\Delta t) = s(-\Delta t) - \frac{IC_1 \cdot r(-\Delta t,0)}{\sigma \cdot \sqrt{\Delta t}} \qquad (13.12)$$

The "correction" in the previous score, the term $IC_1 \cdot r(-\Delta t,0)/(\sigma \cdot \sqrt{\Delta t})$, is the part of the score that has been used up. The greater the ability to predict, the more we discount from the score.

In general, the settling score effect is small, since the impact depends on the product of IC_1 and IC_2^*. However, there can be a considerable effect in extreme situations. For example, consider an asset allocation model with a stock minus bond score of -2.16 on October 1, 1987. The October return was a 6.5 standard deviation event; i.e., $r(-\Delta t,0)/(\sigma \cdot \sqrt{\Delta t}) = -6.5$. With a first period $IC_1 = 0.15$, the corrected score is $s^*(-1) = -1.18$. This is an extraordinary change reflecting the extraordinary event. In a typical month with, say, a 1 standard deviation event in the return, we would make a small change of 0.15 to the score.

---

[5]On the other hand, people are always willing to believe that if they were wrong, it was for the right reasons.

[6]Technically, Eq. (13.12) does not describe a score, because it has a standard deviation not equal to 1. Dividing by $1 - IC_1^2$ will correct this problem. However, we prefer to use Eq. (13.12) in the form given.

In this analysis, we have ignored some complicating features. For example, if returns are autocorrelated, past returns play a double role by settling old scores, as described above, and bringing information about next period's return. It also often happens that past returns have an impact on future scores. The causality flows from return to score, as well as from score to return. With a momentum signal, higher past returns generally mean higher future scores. With a value signal, large past returns tend to imply lower future scores.[7] The microanalysis methodology can handle both of these situations. The technical appendix treats one special case, using the binary model.

GRADUAL DECLINE IN THE VALUE OF THE INFORMATION

The one- and two-period models described above are easy to analyze but lack realism. A more sensible information model is one of gradual decline in forecasting power. The information coefficient decays as we move more and more periods away from the arrival of the information. A score available at time June 30 has a correlation with July return of IC. The correlation with August return is IC · δ. In general, the correlation with return in month $n + 1$ is IC · δ^n. We can relate this continuous decay to the half-life:

$$\delta = \left(\frac{1}{2}\right)^{\Delta t/\mathrm{HL}} \tag{13.13}$$

or
$$\mathrm{HL} = \frac{-\Delta t \cdot \ln\{2\}}{\ln\{\delta\}} \tag{13.14}$$

Figure 13.7 shows a gradual attrition of the information's power. In this case, monthly intervals, the half-life is one quarter; HL = 0.25, δ = 0.7937. We can see the exponential decay in the monthly

---

[7]One way to eliminate this problem is to design a new score that is the residual of the old scores regressed against the prior returns. This procedure extracts the component explained by prior returns and isolates the component uncorrelated with prior returns.

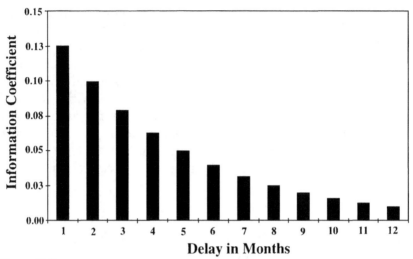

Figure 13.7

information coefficient over time.[8] As the score and the return move farther apart, the information coefficient decreases.

A different cut at this is to look at the correlation of the signal with returns over longer and longer periods. Instead of lagging the scores, we can lead the returns. We can examine the correlation of a monthly score with the monthly return, 2-month return, quarterly return, annual return, etc.

What will influence the information coefficient for longer and longer return horizons? On the positive side, the longer return horizons should more completely reflect the signal's information. On the negative side, increasing volatility, $\sigma \cdot \sqrt{t}$, accompanies the longer time periods. We will show in the technical appendix that the correlation of the returns with the signal over longer and longer periods is

$$IC(0,t) = \text{Corr}\{r(0,t),s(0)\} = IC \cdot \sqrt{\frac{\Delta t}{t}} \cdot \frac{1 - \delta^{t/\Delta t}}{1 - \delta} \qquad (13.15)$$

where the IC in Eq. (13.15) is the information coefficient over the

---

[8]Measuring the IC each period ahead has the benefit of avoiding double counting by using the dreaded "overlapping intervals."

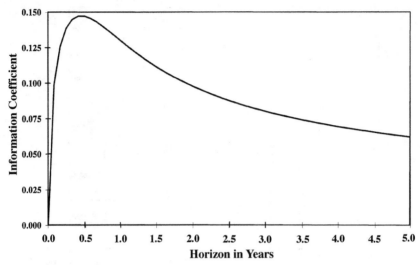

Figure 13.8

initial period of length Δt. Figure 13.8 illustrates this relationship. The signal has its highest predictive power when the horizon is about twice the half-life of the signal.[9]

As the signals arrive, we can use the most recent, or we can attempt to combine new and old in order to get a more powerful forecast. The ability to improve will still hinge on two parameters:

- The decay factor δ
- The correlation ρ between the adjacent scores

If $\delta = \rho$, then the most recent score has all the information that we need. If $\delta > \rho$, we can diversify by using past scores to reinforce the information. Finally, if $\delta < \rho$, we can use past signals to hedge the noise in the most recent signal. This is a message we've seen before, in the macroanalysis and in the two-period case.

To use the information in an optimal way, mix the past signals so that the new mix has an autocorrelation equal to δ. The recipe is

$$s^*(0) = \sum_{m=0} \delta^m \cdot \{s(-m \cdot \Delta t) - \rho \cdot s[-(m-1) \cdot \Delta t]\} \quad (13.16)$$

$$= s(0) - \rho \cdot s(-\Delta t) + \delta \cdot s^*(-\Delta t)$$

---

[9]The function $(1 - e^{-x})/\sqrt{x}$ has a maximum value of 0.6382 at $x = 1.257$.

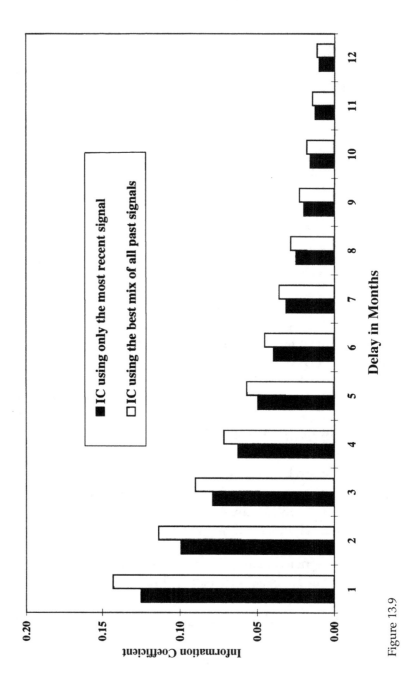

Figure 13.9

This is effectively the same result we saw in Eq. (13.4). This optimally repackaged information will have the same half-life as the original information. For example, in Fig. 13.9 we show the original and repacked information coefficients. The half-life is one quarter, and the correlation between signals is 0.5.

SUMMARY

The information horizon (half-life) is a critical characteristic of a signal or strategy. The horizon can help us see if we are using information efficiently in a temporal sense. Macroanalysis can fairly easily tell you if your strategy is temporally efficient. Microanalysis provides insight into how this works, and can handle many important cases. Past information—signals and returns—can help the current forecast.

NOTES

Investment horizon is a term generally used in a strategic sense for either the individual or the institutional investor. The horizon metaphor is apt for an institutional investor, since an ongoing institution's investment horizon will continually precede the institution into the future. The long view is used to set a strategic asset allocation and investment policy.

In the individual investor's case, the horizon metaphor is not particularly appropriate; there is no receding horizon. We have an uncertain, but finite, term until retirement and another, also uncertain, interval until death. This is one of life's cruel jokes. Samuelson (1994) has more to say in this regard.

For another, more technical horizon topic, see Goetzmann and Edwards (1994) and Ferguson and Simaan (1996). They tackle the question of horizon as it relates to a single-period portfolio mean/variance optimization. The questions are: How long a period should we consider? and, Does it matter? This analysis hinges on the interaction between the compounding nature of returns and the additive nature of a buy and hold portfolio. It can get complicated, and it does. Some of the difficulty goes away when you consider multiperiod investing or continuous rebalancing. If you assume lognormal returns, continuous rebalancing, and a power utility function for cumulative return at the horizon, the portfolio selected will be independent of the horizon. See Merton (1990), pp. 137–145.

PROBLEMS

1. Your research has identified a monthly signal with IR = 1. You notice that delaying its implementation by one quarter reduces the IR to 0.75. What is the signal's half-life? What is the half-life of the value added?
2. In further researching the signal in Problem 1, you discover that the correlation of active returns to this signal and this signal implemented 1 month late is 0.75. What is the optimal combination of current and lagged portfolios?
3. You forecast α = 2 percent for a stock with ω = 25 percent, based on a signal with IC = 0.05. Suddenly the stock moves, with θ = 10 percent. How should you adjust your alpha? Is it now positive or negative?

REFERENCES

Atkins, Allen B., and Edward A. Dyl. "Transactions Costs and Holding Periods for Common Stocks." *Journal of Finance,* vol. 52, no. 1, 1997, pp. 309–325.

Ferguson, Robert, and Yusif Simaan. "Portfolio Composition and the Investment Horizon Revisited." *Journal of Portfolio Management,* vol. 22, no. 4, 1996, pp. 62–68.

Goetzmann, William N., and F. R. Edwards. "Short Horizon Inputs and Long Horizon Portfolio Choice." *Journal of Portfolio Management,* vol. 20, no. 4, 1994, pp. 76–81.

Grinold, Richard C. "Alpha Is Volatility Times IC Times Score," *Journal of Portfolio Management,* vol. 20, no. 4, 1994, pp. 9–16.

———. "The Information Horizon." *Journal of Portfolio Management,* vol. 24, no. 1, 1997, pp. 57–67.

Merton, Robert C. *Continuous Time Finance,* (Cambridge, MA: Blackwell, 1990).

Samuelson, Paul A. "The Long Term Case for Equities." *Journal of Portfolio Management,* vol. 21, no. 1, 1994, pp. 15–24.

TECHNICAL APPENDIX

We will use this technical appendix to derive several results presented in the main text. We will show that mixtures of past strategies cannot change the half-life of the strategy. We will analyze the optimal mixture of past strategies. We will show how the correlation of a signal with returns of varying horizons depends on that horizon. Finally, we include an explicit optimal combination of current and past signals and past returns, in the context of the binary model.

Mixtures of Past Strategies

Let's start with some basic notation. We will need to explicitly keep track of lagged information:

$\mathbf{h}_{PA}(j)$ = active portfolio lagged j periods
$\theta(j)$ = return to the j-lag active portfolio[10]
$IR(j)$ = information ratio for the j-lag portfolio

We will further make the assumptions that

$$\mathbf{h}_{PA}^T(j) \cdot \mathbf{V} \cdot \mathbf{h}_{PA}(j) = \omega^2 \qquad (13A.1)$$

$$\mathbf{h}_{PA}^T(j) \cdot \mathbf{V} \cdot \mathbf{h}_{PA}(k) = \omega^2 \cdot \rho(|j - k|) \qquad (13A.2)$$

The first assumption is not remarkable. It just says that any old active position will have the same active risk as any other. Note that this implies that any decay in the information ratio over time must arise solely as a result of decay in the alpha:

$$IR(j) = \gamma^j \cdot IR(0) = \frac{\alpha(j)}{\omega} \qquad (13A.3)$$

The second assumption is stronger. It says that the covariance between lagged positions depends only on the time interval between them. Note that this is weaker than saying that there is a single parameter ρ such that $\rho(|j - k|) = \rho^{|j - k|}$.

We define a mixture of past strategies using weights $y(j)$, $j = 0, 1, 2, \ldots$. This mixture of past strategies will have an information ratio $IR^*(0)$. But we can also lag this mixture strategy, giving rise to a new sequence of lagged information ratios $IR^*(j)$, $j = 0, 1, 2, \ldots$.

---

[10]We are assuming here that the portfolio beta is 1, and so active returns equal residual returns.

Proposition

If the strategy information ratios decay exponentially [as in Eq. (13A.3)], then any mixture strategy will exhibit information ratios which also decay exponentially, at the same rate:

$$IR^*(j) = \gamma^j \cdot IR^*(0) \tag{13A.4}$$

Proof The active holdings for the j-lag mixture strategy are

$$\mathbf{h}^*(j) = \sum_{k=0} y(k) \cdot \mathbf{h}(j + k) \tag{13A.5}$$

with active returns

$$\theta^*(j) = \sum_{k=0} y(k) \cdot \theta(j + k) \tag{13A.6}$$

Our first step is to show that, while the risk of the mixture strategy does not generally equal the risk of the underlying strategy, the dependence on lag is the same. In fact, the risk of the mixture strategy is independent of lag.

The risk of the lagged mixture strategy is

$$\text{Var}\{\theta^*(j)\} = \text{Var}\left\{\sum_{k=0} y(k) \cdot \theta(j + k)\right\} \tag{13A.7}$$

$$= \sum_k \sum_m y(k) \cdot \text{Cov}\{\theta(j + k), \theta(j + m)\} \cdot y(m)$$

But our assumptions, Eqs. (13A.1) and (13A.2), guarantee that

$$\text{Cov}\{\theta(j + k), \theta(j + m)\} = \text{Cov}\{\theta(k), \theta(m)\} \tag{13A.8}$$

Hence
$$\text{Var}\{\theta^*(j)\} = \text{Var}\{\theta^*(0)\} = (\omega^*)^2 \tag{13A.9}$$

So the decay in the information ratio for the mixture strategy must depend entirely on the decay in the alpha for the mixture strategy. We can now show that this decays at the same rate as the alpha for as the underlying strategy.

The information ratio for the unlagged mixture strategy is

$$IR^*(0) = \frac{\alpha^*(0)}{\omega^*} = \frac{\displaystyle\sum_{k=0} \alpha(k) \cdot y(k)}{\omega^*} \tag{13A.10}$$

But we can relate these alphas to information ratios:

$$IR^*(0) = \frac{\sum_{k=0} \omega \cdot IR(k) \cdot y(k)}{\omega^*} \qquad (13A.11)$$

The information ratio for the lagged mixture strategy is

$$IR^*(j) = \frac{\alpha^*(j)}{\omega^*} = \frac{\sum_{k=0} \alpha(j+k) \cdot y(k)}{\omega^*} \qquad (13A.12)$$

We can relate this too to the information ratios:

$$IR^*(j) = \frac{\sum_{k=0} \omega \cdot IR(j+k) \cdot y(k)}{\omega^*} \qquad (13A.13)$$

Finally, we can simply calculate the ratio of lagged to unlagged information ratios for the mixture strategy. Using Eqs. (13A.11) and (13A.13), this becomes

$$\frac{IR^*(j)}{IR^*(0)} = \frac{\sum_{k=0} IR(j+k) \cdot y(k)}{\sum_{k=0} IR(k) \cdot y(k)} \qquad (13A.14)$$

But using Eq. (13A.3), this becomes the desired result:

$$\frac{IR^*(j)}{IR^*(0)} = \gamma^j \qquad (13A.15)$$

While we will not explicitly demonstrate this, the correlation structure of lags of a mixture strategy retains the structure exhibited by lags of the underlying strategy, namely, that the correlation depends only on the separation between the two lags of the mixture strategy.

Optimal Strategy Mixtures

The main text presented two sets of results concerning optimal strategy mixtures. First, it presented the optimal mix of Now and Later, the current and lagged portfolios. It then stated a more general result, that optimal strategies should exhibit a correlation structure matched to the decay of the information. We will calculate both results here. We begin with the combination of Now and Later.

Our goal is to combine current and past portfolios so as to maximize the resulting information ratio. We characterize the current portfolio with statistics α_{Now}, ω, and IR_{Now}, and the lagged portfolio with statistics α_{Later}, ω, and IR_{Later}. Note that the current and lagged portfolios exhibit the same risk. We will also assume a correlation ρ between current and lagged active returns, and a decay factor γ between current and lagged information ratios. Using w_{Now} to express the weight on the current portfolio, the combined alpha is

$$\alpha_p = w_{Now} \cdot \alpha_{Now} + (1 - w_{Now}) \cdot \alpha_{Later} \qquad (13A.16)$$
$$= \omega \cdot IR_{Now} \cdot [w_{Now} + (1 - w_{Now}) \cdot \gamma]$$

Here we have explicitly used the decay factor to express the information ratio of the lagged portfolio. We can express the risk of the combined portfolio as

$$\omega_p^2 = w_{Now}^2 \cdot \omega^2 + (1 - w_{Now})^2 \cdot \omega^2 + 2 \cdot w_{Now} \cdot (1 - w_{Now}) \cdot \omega^2 \cdot \rho$$
$$= \omega^2 \cdot [w_{Now}^2 + (1 - w_{Now})^2 + 2 \cdot w_{Now} \cdot (1 - w_{Now}) \cdot \rho]$$
$$(13A.17)$$

We can put this all together and express the combined information ratio as

$$\left(\frac{IR_p}{IR_{Now}} \right)^2 = \frac{[w_{Now} + (1 - w_{Now}) \cdot \gamma]^2}{w_{Now}^2 + (1 - w_{Now})^2 + 2 \cdot w_{Now} \cdot (1 - w_{Now}) \cdot \rho}$$
$$(13A.18)$$

To maximize the combined information ratio, we need to take the derivative of Eq. (13A.18) with respect to w_{NOW}, and set it equal to zero. The procedure is algebraically messy, but straightforward. The result is

$$w_{Now}^* = \frac{\gamma + x}{\gamma + 1} \qquad (13A.19)$$

where

$$x \equiv \frac{1 - \gamma}{1 - \rho} \qquad (13A.20)$$

as stated in the main text. Furthermore, we can take Eq. (13A.19) and substitute it back into Eq. (13A.18) to determine the maximum information ratio achieved. The result is

$$IR^* = IR_{Now} \cdot \frac{(\gamma + x) + \gamma \cdot (1 - x)}{\sqrt{(\gamma + x)^2 + (1 - x)^2 + 2 \cdot (\gamma + x) \cdot (1 - x) \cdot \rho}}$$

$$(13A.21)$$

General Optimality Condition

We will now treat the general optimality condition quoted in the main text. We will use the notation introduced at the beginning of this appendix. In this general case, we want to minimize the variance of the mixture strategy, subject to the constraint that the alpha remains constant (i.e., equal to the alpha of the current underlying strategy). Mathematically,

$$\text{Min}\left\{ \text{Var}\left\{ \sum_{j=0}^{\infty} y(j) \cdot \theta(j) \right\} \right\}$$

$$(13A.22)$$

subject to the constraint

$$\sum_{j=0}^{\infty} y(j) \cdot \omega \cdot IR(j) = \alpha(0) = \omega \cdot IR(0)$$

$$(13A.23)$$

Note that the problem is feasible, since the case $\{y(0) = 1; y(i) = 0, i \neq 0\}$ satisfies the constraint. Using a Lagrange multiplier, we can rewrite the minimization problem as

$$\text{Min}\left\{ \text{Var}\left\{ \sum_{j=0}^{\infty} y(j) \cdot \theta(j) \right\} + c \cdot \left[\sum_{j=0}^{\infty} y(j) \cdot IR(j) - IR(0) \right] \right\} \quad (13A.24)$$

The first-order conditions are

$$2 \cdot \text{Cov}\left\{ \theta(j), \sum_{k=0}^{\infty} y(k) \cdot \theta(k) \right\} + c \cdot IR(j) = 0 \quad (13A.25)$$

plus the constraint. Note that Eq. (13A.25) represents a set of equations, one for each lag j. Now, to solve for the Lagrange multiplier

c, we can multiply the equation for each lag j by the weight $y(j)$, and sum them. The covariance term becomes

$$\sum_{j=0}^{\infty} 2 \cdot y(j) \cdot \text{Cov}\left\{\theta(j), \sum_{k=0}^{\infty} y(k) \cdot \theta(k)\right\} \tag{13A.26}$$

$$= 2 \cdot \text{Var}\left\{\sum_{k=0}^{\infty} y(k) \cdot \theta(k)\right\} = 2 \cdot (\omega^*)^2$$

The information ratio term becomes

$$\sum_{j=0}^{\infty} c \cdot y(j) \cdot \text{IR}(j) = c \cdot \text{IR}(0) \tag{13A.27}$$

Putting this together, we find that the term c is

$$c = \frac{-2 \cdot (\omega^*)^2}{\text{IR}(0)} \tag{13A.28}$$

and the covariance relationship (first-order condition) becomes

$$\text{Cov}\{\theta(j), \theta^*(0)\} = \frac{(\omega^*)^2 \cdot \text{IR}(j)}{\text{IR}(0)} \tag{13A.29}$$

Here we have used the notation θ^* for the active return to the mixture strategy.

In this scheme, the mixture strategy has a higher information ratio than the underlying strategy specifically because it has lower risk. We have constrained the alpha to remain constant. Hence the ratio of $\text{IR}(0)$ to $\text{IR}^*(0)$ is just the ratio of ω^* to ω. So we can rewrite Eq. (13A.29) as

$$\text{Cov}\{\theta(j), \theta^*(0)\} = \frac{\omega \cdot \omega^* \cdot \text{IR}(j)}{\text{IR}^*(0)} \tag{13A.30}$$

This is close to the answer we are seeking. We now have the covariance structure between the underlying strategy and the optimal mixed strategy. We want the covariance structure between the optimal strategy and its lags. We can calculate this easily. The lagged optimal strategy active return is

$$\theta^*(k) = \sum_{j=0}^{\infty} y(j) \cdot \theta(j + k) \tag{13A.31}$$

We can calculate the covariance of this with $\theta^*(0)$. Using Eq. (13A.30) and the definition of $IR^*(k)$, this becomes

$$\text{Cov}\{\theta^*(k),\theta^*(0)\} = \frac{(\omega^*)^2 \cdot IR^*(k)}{IR^*(0)} \qquad (13A.32)$$

This directly reduces to the result we want:

$$\text{Corr}\{\theta^*(k),\theta^*(0)\} = \frac{IR^*(k)}{IR^*(0)} \qquad (13A.33)$$

that the correlation between lagged optimal mixes falls off as the information ratio falls off between the lagged optimal mixes. In particular, focusing on just one lag, the information ratio decays by δ, and we have devised the optimal mix so that the correlation between the current and lagged optimal mix is also δ, according to Eq. (13A.33).

The result in Eq. (13A.33) plus the previous result [Eq. (13A.9)] that all lags of mixture strategies maintain the same risk allows us to directly verify Eq. (13.4). The optimal current mixture holdings are just γ times the lagged mixture holdings, plus the innovation in the current strategy. We can verify that the innovation term is uncorrelated with the lagged mixture strategy.

Return/Signal Correlations as a Function of Horizon

The main text states results concerning the correlation of a score with returns of increasing horizons, in the case where the information decays by a factor of δ each period. We derive the result here. We measure the return horizon as variable t, the sum of several periods of length Δt. The correlation of our score with returns over periods of length Δt out in the future decays by a factor of δ each period. The goal here is to sum up these effects for a return over a period from 0 to t. We need to calculate

$$\text{Corr}\{r(0,t),s(0)\} = \frac{\text{Cov}\{r(0,t),s(0)\}}{\text{Std}\{r(0,t)\}} \qquad (13A.34)$$

Remember that the standard deviation of the score is 1. We can expand $r(0,t)$ into a sum of returns over periods Δt:

$$\text{Corr}\{r(0,t),s(0)\} = \frac{\text{Cov}\left\{\displaystyle\sum_{j=1}^{t/\Delta t} r[(j-1)\cdot \Delta t, j\cdot \Delta t], s(0)\right\}}{\text{Std}\left\{\displaystyle\sum_{j=1}^{t/\Delta t} r[(j-1)\cdot \Delta t, j\cdot \Delta t]\right\}} \qquad (13\text{A}.35)$$

Now we can use the decay relationship and an assumed orthogonality in returns over different periods to simplify this to

$$\text{Corr}\{r(0,t),s(0)\} = \frac{\text{IC}\cdot \omega \cdot \sqrt{\Delta t}\cdot (1 + \delta + \delta^2 + \cdots + \delta^{(t/\Delta t)-1})}{\omega \cdot \sqrt{t}} \qquad (13\text{A}.36)$$

We can sum this finite power series to find

$$\text{Corr}\{r(0,t),s(0)\} = \text{IC}\cdot \sqrt{\frac{\Delta t}{t}}\cdot \frac{1 - \delta^{t/\Delta t}}{1 - \delta} \qquad (13\text{A}.37)$$

the result quoted in the main text.

Optimal Mixing of Current and Past Signal and Past Return

Finally, we include an explicit analysis combining current and past signals and the past return, using the binary model.

Suppose we forecast the residual return each month, and that forecast contains information about the residual returns in the next 2 months. Assume that the expected residual return is 0 and the monthly volatility is 6 percent (annual 20.78 percent). In period t, we have

$$r(t) = \sum_{j=1}^{36} \theta_j(t) \qquad (13\text{A}.38)$$

The forecasts have zero mean and a 4 percent standard deviation:

$$g(t) = \theta_1(t) + \theta_2(t) + \theta_3(t) + \theta_3(t+1) + \theta_4(t+1) \qquad (13\text{A}.39)$$
$$+ \eta_1(t) + \cdots + \eta_7(t) + \eta_1(t-1) + \cdots + \eta_4(t-1)$$

The forecast $g(t)$, available at the beginning of period t, has four components:

- Three signals about return in the coming period: $\{\theta_1(t), \theta_2(t), \theta_3(t)\}$
- Two signals about return in the following period: $\{\theta_3(t + 1), \theta_4(t + 1)\}$
- Seven elements of new noise: $\{\eta_1(t), \eta_2(t), \ldots, \eta_7(t)\}$
- Four echoes of old noise: $\{\eta(t - 1), \eta_2(t - 1), \ldots, \eta_4(t - 1)\}$

Of course, we observe only the sum of the elements in these four groups.

In forecasting the residual return in period t, both the current forecast and the previous forecast will be of use. The covariance of the most recent forecast with the return is 3, the covariance of the previous forecast with the return is 2, and the covariance between $g(t)$ and $g(t - 1)$ is 5, since they share one element of signal and four elements of noise. The basic forecasting rule therefore leads to

$$E\{r(t) \mid g(t), g(t - 1)\} = (0.1645) \cdot g(t) + (0.0736) \cdot g(t - 1) \quad (13A.40)$$

The IC of this refined forecast with the return is 0.1334. Note that the IC of $g(t)$ alone is 0.125 and the IC of $g(t - 1)$ is 0.0833.

We can actually do slightly better by adding a source of information that we have available: last period's residual return $r(t - 1)$. The covariance of $g(t - 1)$ and $r(t - 1)$ is 3. In this model, $r(t - 1)$ is not correlated with $g(t)$ or $r(t)$, so $r(t - 1)$ itself is useless as a predictor of $r(t)$. However, $r(t - 1)$ combined with $g(t)$ and $g(t - 1)$ is (oh, so slightly) useful. Working through the basic forecasting formula again, we now find

$$E\{r(t) \mid g(t), g(t - 1), r(t - 1)\} \quad (13A.41)$$
$$= (0.1641) \cdot g(t) + (0.0749) \cdot g(t - 1) - (0.0062) \cdot r(t - 1)$$

and the IC of the refined forecast is now 0.1335.

When the forecast horizon is shorter than the information horizon, treat the older forecasts like forecasts from a different source. Past realized returns may also improve the forecast.

Exercises

1. Show that any mixture strategy obeys the same correlation structure we have assumed for the underlying strategies. Namely, show that

$$\text{Corr}\{\theta^*(j), \theta^*(k)\} = \rho^*(|j - k|)$$

2. Show that the optimal combination of Now and Later leads to a mixture strategy with the correlation of the mixture and its first lag equal to the decay factor γ.

PART FOUR

Implementation

Portfolio Construction

INTRODUCTION

Implementation is the efficient translation of research into portfolios. Implementation is not glamorous, but it is important. Good implementation can't help poor research, but poor implementation can foil good research. A manager with excellent information and faulty implementation can snatch defeat from the jaws of victory.

Implementation includes both portfolio construction, the subject of this chapter (and to some extent the next chapter), and trading, a subject of Chap. 16. This chapter will take a manager's investment constraints (e.g., no short sales) as given and build the best possible portfolio subject to those limitations. It will assume the standard objective: maximizing active returns minus an active risk penalty. The next chapter will focus specifically on the very standard no short sales constraint and its surprisingly significant impact. This chapter will also take transactions costs as just an input to the portfolio construction problem. Chapter 16 will focus more on how to estimate transactions costs and methods for reducing them.

Portfolio construction requires several inputs: the current portfolio, alphas, covariance estimates, transactions cost estimates, and an active risk aversion. Of these inputs, we can measure only the current portfolio with near certainty. The alphas, covariances, and transactions cost estimates are all subject to error. The alphas are often unreasonable and subject to hidden biases. The covariances and transactions costs are noisy estimates; we hope that they are unbiased, but we know that they are not measured with certainty. Even risk aversion is not certain. Most active managers will have a target level of active risk that we must make consistent with an active risk aversion.

Implementation schemes must address two questions. First, what portfolio would we choose given inputs (alpha, covariance, active risk aversion, and transactions costs) known without error? Second, what procedures can we use to make the portfolio construction process robust in the presence of unreasonable and noisy inputs? How do you handle perfect data, and how do you handle less than perfect data?

How to handle perfect data is the easier dilemna. With no transactions costs, the goal is to maximize value added within any limitations on the manager's behavior imposed by the client. Transactions costs make the problem more difficult. We must be careful to compare transactions costs incurred at a point in time with returns and risk realized over a period of time.

This chapter will mainly focus on the second question, how to handle less than perfect data. Many of the procedures used in portfolio construction are, in fact, indirect methods of coping with noisy data. With that point of view, we hope to make portfolio construction more efficient by directly attacking the problem of imperfect or "noisy" inputs.

Several points emerge in this chapter:

- Implementation schemes are, in part, safeguards against poor research.
- With alpha analysis, the alphas can be adjusted so that they are in line with the manager's desires for risk control and anticipated sources of value added.
- Portfolio construction techniques include screening, stratified sampling, linear programming, and quadratic programming. Given sufficiently accurate risk estimates, the quadratic programming technique most consistently achieves high value added.
- For most active institutional portfolio managers, building portfolios using alternative risk measures greatly increases the effort (and the chance of error) without greatly affecting the result.

- Managers running separate accounts for multiple clients can control dispersion, but cannot eliminate it.

Let's start with the relationship between the most important input, alpha, and the output, the revised portfolio.

ALPHAS AND PORTFOLIO CONSTRUCTION

Active management should be easy with the right alphas. Sometimes it isn't. Most active managers construct portfolios subject to certain constraints, agreed upon with the client. For example, most institutional portfolio managers do not take short positions and limit the amount of cash in the portfolio. Others may restrict asset coverage because of requirements concerning liquidity, self-dealing, and so on. These limits can make the portfolio less efficient, but they are hard to avoid.

Managers often add their own restrictions to the process. A manager may require that the portfolio be neutral across economic sectors or industries. The manager may limit individual stock positions to ensure diversification of the active bets. The manager may want to avoid any position based on a forecast of the benchmark portfolio's performance. Managers often use such restrictions to make portfolio construction more robust.

There is another way to reach the same final portfolio: simply adjust the inputs. We can always replace a very sophisticated (i.e., complicated) portfolio construction procedure that leads to active holdings $\mathbf{h}_{PA}^*$, active risk ψ_P^*, and an ex ante information ratio IR with a direct unconstrained mean/variance optimization using a modified set of alphas and the appropriate level of risk aversion.[1] The modified alphas are

$$\boldsymbol{\alpha}' = \left(\frac{\text{IR}}{\psi_P^*}\right) \cdot \mathbf{V} \cdot \mathbf{h}_{PA}^* \tag{14.1}$$

---

[1] The simple procedure maximizes $\mathbf{h}_{PA}^T \cdot \boldsymbol{\alpha}' - \lambda_A' \cdot \mathbf{h}_{PA}^T \cdot \mathbf{V} \cdot \mathbf{h}_{PA}$. The first-order conditions for this problem are $\boldsymbol{\alpha}' = 2 \cdot \lambda_A' \cdot \mathbf{V} \cdot \mathbf{h}_{PA}^*$. Equations (14.1) and (14.2) ensure that $\mathbf{h}_{PA}$ will satisfy the first-order conditions. Note that we are explicitly focusing portfolio construction on active return and risk, instead of residual return and risk. Without benchmark timing, these perspectives are identical.

and the appropriate active risk aversion is

$$\lambda_A' = \frac{\text{IR}}{2 \cdot \psi_P^*} \qquad (14.2)$$

Table 14.1 illustrates this for Major Market Index stocks as of December 1992. We assign each stock an alpha (chosen randomly in this example), and first run an unconstrained optimization of risk-adjusted active return (relative to the Major Market Index) using an active risk aversion of 0.0833. Table 14.1 shows the result. The unconstrained optimization sells American Express and Coca-Cola short, and invests almost 18 percent of the portfolio in 3M. We then add constraints; we disallow short sales and require that portfolio holdings cannot exceed benchmark holdings by more than

T A B L E   14.1

Stock	Index Weight	Alpha	Optimal Holding	Constrained Optimal Holding	Modified Alpha
American Express	2.28%	−3.44%	−0.54%	0.00%	−1.14%
AT&T	4.68%	1.38%	6.39%	6.18%	0.30%
Chevron	6.37%	0.56%	7.41%	7.05%	0.11%
Coca-Cola	3.84%	−2.93%	−2.22%	0.00%	−0.78%
Disney	3.94%	1.77%	5.79%	5.85%	0.60%
Dow Chemical	5.25%	0.36%	5.78%	6.07%	0.22%
DuPont	4.32%	−1.50%	1.54%	1.67%	−0.65%
Eastman Kodak	3.72%	0.81%	4.07%	4.22%	0.14%
Exxon	5.60%	−0.10%	4.57%	4.39%	−0.19%
General Electric	7.84%	−2.80%	0.53%	0.92%	−1.10%
General Motors	2.96%	−2.50%	1.93%	1.96%	−0.52%
IBM	4.62%	−2.44%	3.24%	3.54%	−0.51%
International Paper	6.11%	−0.37%	5.73%	6.15%	0.01%
Johnson & Johnson	4.63%	2.34%	7.67%	7.71%	0.66%
McDonalds	4.47%	0.86%	5.07%	4.98%	0.14%
Merck	3.98%	0.80%	4.72%	4.78%	0.20%
3M	9.23%	3.98%	17.95%	14.23%	0.91%
Philip Morris	7.07%	0.71%	7.82%	7.81%	0.12%
Procter & Gamble	4.92%	1.83%	6.99%	6.96%	0.44%
Sears	4.17%	0.69%	5.57%	5.54%	0.35%

5 percent. This result is also displayed in Table 14.1. The optimal portfolio no longer holds American Express or Coca-Cola at all, and the holding of 3M moves to exactly 5 percent above the benchmark holding. The other positions also adjust.

This constrained optimization corresponds to an unconstrained optimization using the same active risk aversion of 0.0833 and the modified alphas displayed in the last column of Table 14.1. We derive these using Eqs. (14.1) and (14.2). These modified alphas are pulled in toward zero relative to the original alphas, as we would expect, since the constraints moved the optimal portfolio closer to the benchmark. The original alphas have a standard deviation of 2.00 percent, while the modified alphas have a standard deviation of 0.57 percent.

We can replace any portfolio construction process, regardless of its sophistication, by a process that first refines the alphas and then uses a simple unconstrained mean/variance optimization to determine the active positions.

This is not an argument against complicated implementation schemes. It simply focuses our attention on a reason for the complexity. If the implementation scheme is, in part, a safeguard against unrealistic or unreasonable inputs, perhaps we can, more fruitfully, address this problem directly. A direct attack calls for either refining the alphas (preprocessing) or designing implementation procedures that explicitly recognize the procedure's role as an "input moderator." The next section discusses preprocessing of alphas.

ALPHA ANALYSIS

We can greatly simplify the implementation procedure if we ensure that our alphas are consistent with our beliefs and goals. Here we will outline some procedures for refining alphas that can simplify the implementation procedure, and explicitly link our refinement in the alphas to the desired properties of the resulting portfolios. We begin with the standard data screening procedures of scaling and trimming.[2]

---

[2]Because of their simplicity, we treat scaling and trimming first. However, when we implement alpha analysis, we impose scaling and trimming as the final step in the process.

Scale the Alphas

Alphas have a natural structure, as we discussed in the forecasting rule of thumb in Chap. 10: α = volatility · IC · score. This structure includes a natural scale for the alphas. We expect the information coefficient (IC) and residual risk (volatility) for a set of alphas to be approximately constant, with the score having mean 0 and standard deviation 1 across the set. Hence the alphas should have mean 0 and standard deviation, or *scale*, of Std{α} ~ volatility · IC.[3] An information coefficient of 0.05 and a typical residual risk of 30 percent would lead to an alpha scale of 1.5 percent. In this case, the mean alpha would be 0, with roughly two-thirds of the stocks having alphas between −1.5 percent and +1.5 percent and roughly 5 percent of the stocks having alphas larger than +3.0 percent or less than −3.0 percent. In Table 14.1, the original alphas have a standard deviation of 2.00 percent and the modified alphas have a standard deviation of 0.57 percent. This implies that the constraints in that example effectively shrank the IC by 62 percent, a significant reduction. There is value in noting this explicitly, rather than hiding it under a rug of optimizer constraints.

The scale of the alphas will depend on the information coefficient of the manager. If the alphas input to portfolio construction do not have the proper scale, then rescale them.

Trim Alpha Outliers

The second refinement of the alphas is to trim extreme values. Very large positive or negative alphas can have undue influence. Closely examine all stocks with alphas greater in magnitude than, say, three times the scale of the alphas. A detailed analysis may show that some of these alphas depend upon questionable data and should

---

[3]There is a related approach to determining the correct scale that uses the information ratio instead of the information coefficient. This approach calculates the information ratio implied by the alphas and scales them, if necessary, to match the manager's ex ante information ratio. The information ratio implied by the alphas is $IR_0 = \sqrt{\alpha^T \cdot V^{-1} \cdot \alpha}$. We can calculate this quickly by running an optimization with unrestricted cash holdings, no constraints, no limitations on asset holdings, and an active risk aversion of 0.5. The optimal active portfolio is $h_{PA}^* = V^{-1} \cdot \alpha$, and the optimal portfolio alpha is $(IR_0)^2$. If IR is the desired ex ante information ratio, we can rescale the alphas by a factor (IR/IR_0).

be ignored (set to zero), while others may appear genuine. Pull in these remaining genuine alphas to three times scale in magnitude.

A second and more extreme approach to trimming alphas is to force[4] them into a normal distribution with benchmark alpha equal to 0 and the required scale factor. Such an approach is extreme because it typically utilizes only the ranking information in the alphas and ignores the size of the alphas. After such a transformation, you must recheck benchmark neutrality and scaling.

Neutralization

Beyond scaling and trimming, we can remove biases or undesirable bets from our alphas. We call this process *neutralization*. It has implications, not surprisingly, in terms of both alphas and portfolios.

Benchmark neutralization means that the benchmark has 0 alpha. If our initial alphas imply an alpha for the benchmark, the neutralization process recenters the alphas to remove the benchmark alpha. From the portfolio perspective, benchmark neutralization means that the optimal portfolio will have a beta of 1, i.e., the portfolio will not make any bet on the benchmark.

Neutralization is a sophisticated procedure, but it isn't uniquely defined. As the technical appendix will demonstrate, we can achieve even benchmark neutrality in more than one way. This is easy to see from the portfolio perspective: We can choose many different portfolios to hedge out any active beta.

As a general principle, we should consider a priori how to neutralize our alphas. The choices will include benchmark, cash, industry, and factor neutralization. Do our alphas contain any information distinguishing one industry from another? If not, then industry-neutralize. The a priori approach works better than simply trying all possibilities and choosing the best performer.

---

[4]Suppose that $h_{B,n}$ is the benchmark weight for asset n. Assume for convenience that the assets are ordered so that $\alpha_1 \leq \alpha_2 \leq \alpha_3$, etc. Then define $p_1 = 0.5 \cdot h_{B,1}$ and for $n \geq 2$, $p_n = p_{n-1} + 0.5 \cdot (h_{B,n-1} + h_{B,n})$. We have $0 < p_1 < p_2 < \cdots < p_{N-1} < p_N < 1$. Find the normal variate z_n that satisfies $p_n = \Phi\{z_n\}$, where Φ is the cumulative normal distribution. We can use the z variables as alphas, after adjustments for location and scale.

Benchmark- and Cash-Neutral Alphas

The first and simplest neutralization is to make the alphas benchmark-neutral. By definition, the benchmark portfolio has 0 alpha, although the benchmark may experience exceptional return. Setting the benchmark alpha to 0 ensures that the alphas are benchmark-neutral and avoids benchmark timing.

In the same spirit, we may also want to make the alphas cash-neutral; i.e., the alphas will not lead to any active cash position. It is possible (see Exercise 11 in the technical appendix) to make the alphas both cash- and benchmark-neutral.

Table 14.2 displays the modified alphas from Table 14.1 and shows how they change when we make them benchmark-neutral. In this example, the benchmark alpha is only 1.6 basis points, so

T A B L E 14.2

Stock	Beta	Modified Alpha	Modified Benchmark-Neutral Alpha
American Express	1.21	−1.14%	−1.16%
AT&T	0.96	0.30%	0.29%
Chevron	0.46	0.11%	0.10%
Coca Cola	0.96	−0.78%	−0.79%
Disney	1.23	0.60%	0.58%
Dow Chemical	1.13	0.22%	0.20%
DuPont	1.09	−0.65%	−0.67%
Eastman Kodak	0.60	0.14%	0.13%
Exxon	0.46	−0.19%	−0.20%
General Electric	1.30	−1.10%	−1.12%
General Motors	0.90	−0.52%	−0.53%
IBM	0.64	−0.51%	−0.52%
International Paper	1.18	0.01%	−0.01%
Johnson & Johnson	1.13	0.66%	0.64%
McDonalds	1.06	0.14%	0.12%
Merck	1.06	0.20%	0.18%
3M	0.74	0.91%	0.90%
Philip Morris	0.94	0.12%	0.10%
Procter & Gamble	1.00	0.44%	0.42%
Sears	1.05	0.35%	0.33%

subtracting $\beta_n \cdot \alpha_B$ from each modified alpha does not change the alpha very much. We have shifted the alpha of the benchmark Major Market Index from 1.6 basis points to 0. This small change in alpha is consistent with the observation that the optimal portfolio before benchmark neutralizing had a beta very close to 1.

Risk-Factor-Neutral Alphas

The multiple-factor approach to portfolio analysis separates return along several dimensions. A manager can identify each of those dimensions as either a source of risk or a source of value added. By this definition, the manager does not have any ability to forecast the risk factors. Therefore, he or she should neutralize the alphas against the risk factors. The neutralized alphas will include only information on the factors the manager can forecast, along with specific asset information. Once neutralized, the alphas of the risk factors will be 0.

For example, a manager can ensure that her portfolios contain no active bets on industries or on a size factor. Here is one simple approach to making alphas industry-neutral: Calculate the (capitalization-weighted) alpha for each industry, then subtract the industry average alpha from each alpha in that industry.

The technical appendix presents a more detailed account of alpha analysis in the context of a multiple-factor model. We can modify the alphas to achieve desired active common-factor positions and to isolate the part of the alpha that does not influence the common-factor positions.

TRANSACTIONS COSTS

Up to this point, the struggle has been between alpha and active risk. Any klutz can juggle two rubber chickens. The juggling becomes complicated when the third chicken enters the performance. In portfolio construction, that third rubber chicken is *transactions costs*, the cost of moving from one portfolio to another. It has been said that accurate estimation of transactions costs is just as important as accurate forecasts of exceptional return. That is an overstatement,[5] but it does point out the crucial role transactions costs play.

In addition to complicating the portfolio construction problem, transactions costs have their own inherent difficulties. We will see that transactions costs force greater precision on our estimates of alpha. We will also confront the complication of comparing transactions costs at a point in time with returns and risk which occur over an investment horizon. The more difficult issues of what determines transactions costs, how to measure them, and how to avoid them, we postpone until Chap. 16.

When we consider only alphas and active risk in the portfolio construction process, we can offset any problem in setting the scale of the alphas by increasing or decreasing the active risk aversion. Finding the correct trade-off between alpha and active risk is a one-dimensional problem. By turning a single knob, we can find the right balance. Transactions costs make this a two-dimensional problem. The trade-off between alpha and active risk remains, but now there is a new trade-off between the alpha and the transactions costs. We therefore must be precise in our choice of scale, to correctly trade off between the hypothetical alphas and the inevitable transactions costs.

The objective in portfolio construction is to maximize risk-adjusted annual active return. Rebalancing incurs transactions costs at that point in time. To contrast transactions costs incurred at that time with alphas and active risk expected over the next year requires a rule to allocate the transactions costs over the one-year period. We must amortize the transactions costs to compare them to the annual rate of gain from the alpha and the annual rate of loss from the active risk. The rate of amortization will depend on the anticipated holding period.

An example will illustrate this point. We will assume perfect certainty and a risk free rate of zero; and we will start and end invested in cash. Stock 1's current price is $100. The price of stock 1 will increase to $102 in the next 6 months and then remain at

---

[5]Perfect information regarding returns is much more valuable than perfect information regarding transactions costs. The returns are much less certain than the transactions costs. Accurate estimation of returns reduces uncertainty much more than accurate estimation of transactions costs.

$102. Stock 2's current price is also $100. The price of stock 2 will increase to $108 over the next 24 months and then remain at $108. The cost of buying and selling each stock is $0.75. The annual alpha for both stock 1 and stock 2 is 4 percent. To contrast the two situations more clearly, let's assume that in 6 months, and again in 12 months and in 18 months, we can find another stock like stock 1.

The sequence of 6-month purchases of stock 1 and its successors will each net a $2.00 profit before transactions costs. There will be transactions costs (recall that we start and end with cash) of $0.75, $1.50, $1.50, $1.50, and $0.75 at 0, 6, 12, 18, and 24 months, respectively. The total trading cost is $6, the gain on the shares is $8, the profit over 2 years is $2, and the annual percentage return is 1 percent.

With stock 2, over the 2-year period we will incur costs of $0.75 at 0 and 24 months. The total cost is $1.50, the gain is $8, the profit is $6.50, and the annual percentage return is 3.25 percent.

With the series of stock 1 trades, we realize an annual alpha of 4 percent and an annualized transactions cost of 3 percent. With the single deal in stock 2, we realize an annual alpha of 4 percent and an annualized transactions cost of 0.75 percent. For a 6-month holding period, we double the round-trip transactions cost to get the annual transactions cost, and for a 24-month holding period, we halve the round-trip transactions cost to get the annual transactions cost. There's a general rule here:

> **The annualized transactions cost is the round-trip cost divided by the holding period in years.**

Chapter 16, "Transactions Costs, Turnover, and Trading," will deal with the issues concerning the estimation and control of transactions costs. For the remainder of this chapter, we will assume that we know the cost for each anticipated trade.

PRACTICAL DETAILS

Before proceeding further in our analysis of portfolio construction, we should review some practical details concerning this process. First, how do we choose a risk aversion parameter?

We briefly discussed this problem in Chap. 5. There we found an optimality relationship between the information ratio, the risk aversion, and the optimal active risk. Repeating that result here, translated from residual to active return and risk,

$$\lambda_A = \frac{IR}{2 \cdot \psi_P} \qquad (14.3)$$

The point is that we have more intuition about our information ratio and our desired amount of active risk. Hence, we can use Eq. (14.3) to back out an appropriate risk aversion. If our information ratio is 0.5, and we desire 5 percent active risk, we should choose an active risk aversion of 0.05. Note that we must be careful to verify that our optimizer is using percents and not decimals.

A second practical matter concerns aversion to specific as opposed to common-factor risk. Several commercial optimizers utilize this decomposition of risk to allow differing aversions to these different sources of risk:

$$U = \alpha_P - (\lambda_{A,CF} \cdot \psi_{P,CF}^2 + \lambda_{A,SP} \cdot \psi_{P,SP}^2) \qquad (14.4)$$

An obvious reaction here is, "Risk is risk, why would I want to avoid one source of risk more than another?" This is a useful sentiment to keep in mind, but there are at least two reasons to consider implementing a higher aversion to specific risk. First, since specific risk arises from bets on specific assets, a high aversion to specific risk reduces bets on any one stock. In particular, this will reduce the size of your bets on the (to be determined) biggest losers. Second, for managers of multiple portfolios, aversion to specific risk can help reduce dispersion. This will push all those portfolios toward holding the same names.

The final practical details we will cover here concern alpha coverage. First, what happens if we forecast returns on stocks that are not in the benchmark? We can always handle that by expanding the benchmark to include those stocks, albeit with zero weight. This keeps stock n in the benchmark, but with no weight in determining the benchmark return or risk. Any position in stock n will be an active position, with active risk correctly handled.

What about the related problem, a lack of forecast returns for stocks in the benchmark? Chapter 11 provided a sophisticated approach to inferring alphas for some factors, based on the alphas for other factors. We could apply the same approach in this case. For stock-specific alphas, we can use the following approach.

Let N_1 represent the collection of stocks with forecasts, and N_0 the stocks without forecasts. The value-weighted fraction of stocks with forecasts is

$$H\{N_1\} = \sum_{n \in N_1} h_{B,n} \qquad (14.5)$$

The average alpha for group N_1 is

$$\alpha\{N_1\} = \frac{\sum_{n \in N_1} h_{B,n} \cdot \alpha_n}{H\{N_1\}} \qquad (14.6)$$

To round out the set of forecasts, set $\alpha_n^* = \alpha_n - \alpha\{N_1\}$ for stocks in N_1 and $\alpha_n^* = 0$ for stocks in N_0. These alphas are benchmark-neutral. Moreover, the stocks we did not cover will have a zero, and therefore neutral, forecast.

PORTFOLIO REVISIONS

How often should you revise your portfolio? Whenever you receive new information. That's the short answer. If a manager knows how to make the correct trade-off between expected active return, active risk, and transactions costs, frequent revision will not present a problem. If the manager has human failings, and is not sure of his or her ability to correctly specify the alphas, the active risk, and the transactions costs, then the manager may resort to less frequent revision as a safeguard.

Consider the unfortunate manager who underestimates transactions costs, makes large changes in alpha estimates very frequently, and revises his portfolio daily. This manager will churn the portfolio and suffer higher than expected transactions costs and lower than expected alpha. A crude but effective cure is to revise the portfolio less frequently.

More generally, even with accurate transactions costs estimates, as the horizon of the forecast alphas decreases, we expect them to contain larger amounts of noise. The returns themselves become noisier with shorter horizons. Rebalancing for very short horizons would involve frequent reactions to noise, not signal. But the transactions costs stay the same, whether we are reacting to signal or noise.

This trade-off between alpha, risk, and costs is difficult to analyze because of the inherent importance of the horizon. We expect to realize the alpha over some horizon. We must therefore amortize the transactions costs over that horizon.

We can capture the impact of new information, and decide whether to trade, by comparing the marginal contribution to value added for stock n, MCVA_n, to the transactions costs. The marginal contribution to value added shows how value added, as measured by risk-adjusted alpha, changes as the holding of the stock is increases, with an offsetting decrease in the cash position. As our holding in stock n increases, α_n measures the effect on portfolio alpha. The change in value added also depends upon the impact (at the margin) on active risk of adding more of stock n. The stock's marginal contribution to active risk, MCAR_n, measures the rate at which active risk changes as we add more of stock n. The loss in value added due to changes in the level of active risk will be proportional to MCAR_n. Stock n's marginal contribution to value added depends on its alpha and marginal contribution to active risk, in particular:

$$\mathrm{MCVA}_n = \alpha_n - 2 \cdot \lambda_A \cdot \psi \cdot \mathrm{MCAR}_n \qquad (14.7)$$

Let PC_n be the purchase cost and SC_n the sales cost for stock n. For purposes of illustration, we take $\mathrm{PC}_n = 0.50$ percent and $\mathrm{SC}_n = 0.75$ percent. If the current portfolio is optimal,[6] then the marginal contribution to value added for stock n should be less than the purchase cost. If it exceeded the purchase cost, say at 0.80 percent, then a purchase of stock n would yield a net benefit of 0.80 percent $-$ 0.50 percent $=$ 0.30 percent. Similarly the marginal contribution to value added must be greater than the negative of the sales cost. If it were -1.30 percent, then we could decrease our holding of stock n and save 1.30 percent at the margin. The cost would be the 0.75 percent transactions cost, for a net benefit of 1.30 percent $-$ 0.75 percent $=$ 0.55 percent.

---

[6]Assuming no limitations on holdings, no limitations on the cash position, and no additional constraints. Aficionados will realize that this analysis becomes more complicated, but not essentially different, if we include these additional constraints.

This observation allows us to put a band around the alpha for each stock. As long as the alpha stays within that band, the portfolio will remain optimal, and we should not react to new information. The bandwidth is the total of the sale plus purchase costs, 0.50 percent + 0.75 percent = 1.25 percent in our example. If we just purchased a stock, its marginal contribution to value added will equal its purchase cost. We are at the upper end of the band. Any increase in alpha would lead to further purchases. The alpha would have to decrease by 1.25 percent before we would consider selling the stock. The situation before new information arrives is

$$-SC_n \leq MCVA_n \leq PC_n \tag{14.8}$$

or, using Eq. (14.7),

$$2 \cdot \lambda_A \cdot \psi \cdot MCAR_n - SC_n \leq \alpha_n \leq PC_n + 2 \cdot \lambda_A \cdot \psi \cdot MCAR_n \tag{14.9}$$

This analysis has simplified the problem by subsuming the amortization horizon into the costs SC and PC. To fully treat the issue of when to rebalance requires analyzing the dynamic problem involving alphas, risks, and costs over time. There are some useful results from this general treatment, in the very simple case of one or two assets.

Leland (1996) solves the asset allocation problem of rebalancing around an optimal stock/bond allocation. Let's assume that the optimal allocation is 60/40. Assuming linear transactions costs and a utility function penalizing active variance (relative to the optimal allocation) and transactions costs *over time*, Leland shows that the optimal strategy involves a no-trade region around the 60/40 allocation. If the portfolio moves outside that region, the optimal strategy is to trade back to the boundary. Trading only to the boundary, not to the target allocation, cuts the turnover and transactions costs roughly in half, with effectively no change in risk over time. The size of the no-trade region depends on the transactions costs, the risk aversion, and the expected return and risk of stocks and bonds. Obviously, changing the size of the no-trade region will change the turnover for the strategy.

This result concerns a problem that is much simpler than our general active portfolio management problem: The solved problem

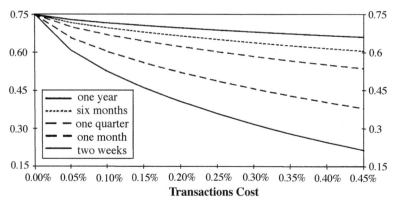

Figure 14.1 After-cost information ratio for various half-lives.

is one-dimensional and does not involve the flow of information (the target allocation is static). Still, it is useful in motivating rebalancing rules driven not purely by the passage of time (e.g., monthly or quarterly rebalancing), but rather by the portfolio's falling outside certain boundaries.

Another approach to the dynamic problem utilizes information horizon analysis, introduced in Chap. 13. Here we apply trading rules like Eq. (14.9) in the dynamic case of trading one position only, over an indefinite future,[7] with information characterized by an information horizon. Figure 14.1 shows how the after-cost information ratio declines as a function of both the (one-way) cost and the half-life of the signals. Two effects are at work. First, when we trade, we pay the costs. Second, and more subtle, the transactions costs makes us less eager; we lose by intimidation.

TECHNIQUES FOR PORTFOLIO CONSTRUCTION

There are as many techniques for portfolio construction as there are managers. Each manager adds a special twist. Despite this personalized nature of portfolio construction techniques, there are

---

[7]There is a pleasant symmetry in this approach. Conventional portfolio optimization considers lots of assets in a one-period framework; we are considering one-asset (position) in a multiple-period framework.

four generic classes of procedures that cover the vast majority of institutional portfolio management applications:[8]

- Screens
- Stratification
- Linear programming
- Quadratic programming

Before we examine these procedures in depth, we should recall our criteria. We are interested in high alpha, low active risk, and low transactions costs. Our figure of merit is value added less transactions costs:

$$\alpha_P - \lambda_A \cdot \psi_P^2 - TC \qquad (14.10)$$

We will see how each of these procedures deals with these three aspects of portfolio construction.

SCREENS

Screens are simple. Here is a screen recipe for building a portfolio from scratch:

1. Rank the stocks by alpha.
2. Choose the first 50 stocks (for example).
3. Equal-weight (or capitalization-weight) the stocks.

We can also use screens for rebalancing. Suppose we have alphas on 200 stocks (the followed list). Divide the stocks into three categories: the top 40, the next 60, and the remaining 100. Put any stock in the top 40 on the buy list, any stock in the bottom 100 on the sell list, and any stock in the middle 60 on the hold list. Starting with the current 50-stock portfolio, buy any stocks that are on the buy list but not in the portfolio. Then sell any assets that are in

---

[8]The techniques we review successfully handle monthly or quarterly rebalancing of portfolios of up to 1000 assets and asset universes that can exceed 10,000 for international investing. Later, we will discuss nonlinear programming and stochastic optimization, whose applications are generally limited to asset allocation schemes involving few (less than 25) asset classes and long planning horizons.

the portfolio and on the sell list. We can adjust the numbers 40, 60, and 100 to regulate turnover.

Screens have several attractive features. There is beauty in simplicity. The screen is easy to understand, with a clear link between cause (membership on a buy, sell, or hold list) and effect (membership in the portfolio). The screen is easy to computerize; it might be that mythical computer project that can be completed in two days! The screen is robust. Notice that it depends solely on ranking. Wild estimates of positive or negative alphas will not alter the result.

The screen enhances alphas by concentrating the portfolio in the high-alpha stocks. It strives for risk control by including a sufficient number of stocks (50 in the example) and by weighting them to avoid concentration in any single stock. Transactions costs are limited by controlling turnover through judicious choice of the size of the buy, sell, and hold lists.

Screens also have several shortcomings. They ignore all information in the alphas apart from the rankings. They do not protect against biases in the alphas. If all the utility stocks happen to be low in the alpha rankings, the portfolio will not include any utility stocks. Risk control is fragmentary at best. In our consulting experience, we have come across portfolios produced by screens that were considerably more risky than their managers had imagined. In spite of these significant shortcomings, screens are a very popular portfolio construction technique.

Stratification

Stratification is glorified screening. The term *stratification* comes from statistics. In statistics, stratification guards against sample bias by making sure that the sample population is representative of the total population as it is broken down into distinct subpopulations. The term is used very loosely in portfolio construction. When a portfolio manager says he uses stratified sampling, he wants the listener to (1) be impressed and (2) ask no further questions.

The key to stratification is splitting the list of followed stocks into categories. These categories are generally exclusive. The idea is to obtain risk control by making sure that the portfolio has a representative holding in each category. As a typical example, let's suppose that we classify stocks into 10 economic sectors and also classify the stocks in each sector by size: big, medium, and small. Thus, we classify all stocks into 30 categories based on economic sector and size. We also know the benchmark weight in each of the 30 categories.

To construct a portfolio, we mimic the screening exercise within each category. We rank the stocks by alpha and place them into buy, hold, and sell groups within each category in a way that will keep the turnover reasonable. We then weight the stocks so that the portfolio's weight in each category matches the benchmark's weight in that category. Stratification ensures that the portfolio matches the benchmark along these important dimensions.

The stratification scheme has the same benefits as screening, plus some. It is robust. Improving upon screening, it ignores any biases in the alphas across categories. It is somewhat transparent and easy to code. It has the same mechanism as screening for controlling turnover.

Stratification retains some of the shortcomings of a screen. It ignores some information, and does not consider slightly over-weighting one category and underweighting another. Often, little substantive research underlies the selection of the categories, and so risk control is rudimentary. Chosen well, the categories can lead to reasonable risk control. If some important risk dimensions are excluded, risk control will fail.

Linear Programming

A linear program (LP) is space-age stratification. The linear pro-gramming approach[9] characterizes stocks along dimensions of risk, e.g., industry, size, volatility, and beta. The linear program does not require that these dimensions distinctly and exclusively parti-tion the stocks. We can characterize stocks along all of these dimen-sions. The linear program will then attempt to build portfolios that are reasonably close to the benchmark portfolio in all of the dimensions used for risk control.

---

[9]A linear program is a useful tool for a variety of portfolio management applications. The application described here is but one of those applications.

It is also possible to set up a linear program with explicit transactions costs, a limit on turnover, and upper and lower position limits on each stock. The objective of the linear program is to maximize the portfolio's alpha less transactions costs, while remaining close to the benchmark portfolio in the risk control dimensions.

The linear program takes all the information about alpha into account and controls risk by keeping the characteristics of the portfolio close to the characteristics of the benchmark. However, the linear program has difficulty producing portfolios with a prespecified number of stocks. Also, the risk-control characteristics should not work at cross purposes with the alphas. For example, if the alphas tell you to shade the portfolio toward smaller stocks at some times and toward larger stocks at other times, you should not control risk on the size dimension.

Quadratic Programming

Quadratic programming (QP) is the ultimate[10] in portfolio construction. The quadratic program explicitly considers each of the three elements in our figure of merit: alpha, risk, and transactions costs. In addition, since a quadratic program includes a linear program as a special case, it can include all the constraints and limitations one finds in a linear program. This should be the best of all worlds. Alas, nothing is perfect.

One of the main themes of this chapter is dealing with less than perfect data. The quadratic program requires a great many more inputs than the other portfolio construction techniques. More inputs mean more noise. Does the benefit of explicitly considering risk outweigh the cost of introducing additional noise? A universe of 500 stocks will require 500 volatility estimates and 124,750 correlation estimates.[11] There are ample opportunities to make mistakes. It is a fear of garbage in, garbage out that deters managers from using a quadratic program.

---

[10]Given our criterion of portfolio alpha minus a penalty for active risk and less transactions costs.

[11]Chapter 3 discusses how to accurately approach this problem.

This fear is warranted. A lack of precision in the estimate of correlations is an inconvenience in the ordinary estimation of portfolio risk. For the most part, the estimation errors will cancel out. It is an obstacle in optimization. In optimization, the portfolio is selected to, among other things, have a low level of active risk. Because the optimizer tries to lower active risk, it will take advantage of opportunities that appear in the noisy estimates of covariance but are not present in reality.

An example can illustrate the point. Suppose we consider a simple cash versus market trade-off. Let ζ be the actual volatility of the market and σ our perceived volatility. If VA* is the optimal value added that we can obtain with the correct risk estimate ζ, then the loss[12] we obtain with the estimate σ is

$$\text{Loss} = \text{VA*} \cdot \left[1 - \left(\frac{\zeta}{\sigma} \right)^2 \right]^2 \qquad (14.11)$$

Figure 14.2 shows the percentage loss, Loss/VA*, as a function of the estimated market risk, assuming that the true market risk is 17

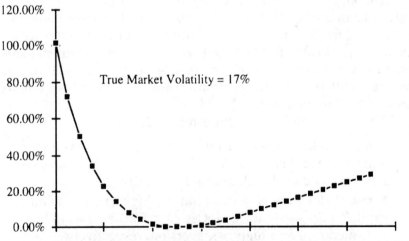

Figure 14.2 Estimated market volatility.

---

[12]The technical appendix derives a more general version of this result.

percent. In this example, market volatility estimates within 1 percent of the true market volatility will not hurt value added very much, but as estimation error begin to exceed 3 percent, the effect on value added becomes significant, especially if the error is an underestimate of volatility. In fact, an underestimate of 12 percent market volatility (5 percent below the "true" volatility) leads to a negative value added.

There are two lessons here. The first is that errors in the estimates of covariance lead to inefficient implementation. The second, which is more positive and, indeed, more important, is that it is vital to have good estimates of covariance. Rather than abandon the attempt, try to do a good job.

TESTS OF PORTFOLIO CONSTRUCTION METHODS

We can test the effectiveness of these portfolio construction procedures by putting them on an equal footing and judging the performance of their outputs. In this case, we will input identical alphas to four procedures, described below, and ignore transactions costs.[13]

The alphas are great. They include the actual returns to the 500 stocks in the S&P 500 over the next year plus noise, combined so that the correlation of the alphas with the returns (the information coefficient) is 0.1. The fundamental law of active management therefore predicts[14] an information ratio of 2.24. So not only will we feed the same alphas into each portfolio construction method, but we know what the final result should be.

The four portfolio construction techniques are

Screen I. Take the N stocks with the highest alphas and equal-weight them. Use $N = 50$, 100, and 150 for low, medium, and high risk aversion, respectively.

Screen II. Take the N stocks with the highest alphas and capitalization-weight them. Use $N = 50$, 100, and 150 for low, medium, and high risk aversion, respectively.

---

[13]For more details, see Muller (1993). We ignore transactions costs to simplify the test.
[14]The information coefficient of 0.1 and the breadth of 500 leads to IR = $0.1 \cdot \sqrt{500} =$ 2.24.

Strat. Take the *J* stocks with the highest alphas in each of the BARRA 55 industry categories. Use *J* = 1, 2, and 3 for low, medium, and high risk aversion portfolios, which will have 55, 110, and 165 stocks, respectively.

QP. Choose portfolios which maximize value added, assuming low, medium, and high risk aversion parameters. Use full investment and no short sales constraints, and constrain each position to constitute no more than 10 percent of the entire portfolio.

Portfolios were constructed in January 1984 and rebalanced in January 1985, January 1986, and May 1987, with portfolio performance tracked over the subsequent year. Table 14.3 contains the results.

Table 14.3 displays each portfolio's ex post information ratio. In this test, the quadratic programming approach clearly led to consistently the highest ex post information ratios. On average,

T A B L E 14.3

Date	Risk Aversion	Screen I	Screen II	Strat	QP
January 1984	High	1.10	1.30	0.63	2.16
	Medium	0.95	2.24	0.64	1.89
	Low	0.73	1.31	0.69	1.75
January 1985	High	0.78	1.47	1.98	0.98
	Medium	0.74	−0.53	1.29	1.68
	Low	0.50	−0.15	0.83	1.49
January 1986	High	1.17	0.91	0.69	2.08
	Medium	0.69	0.98	0.33	2.29
	Low	0.60	0.99	0.51	2.51
May 1987	High	1.43	2.04	2.82	2.14
	Medium	1.01	1.48	2.60	1.76
	Low	0.66	1.17	2.17	1.82
Average		0.86	1.10	1.27	1.88
Standard deviation		0.27	0.79	0.89	0.40
Maximum		1.43	2.24	2.82	2.51
Minimum		0.50	−0.53	0.33	0.98

Source: Peter Muller, "Empirical Tests of Biases in Equity Portfolio Optimization," in *Financial Optimization*, edited by Stavros A. Zenios (Cambridge: Cambridge University Press, 1993), Table 4-4.

it surpassed all the other techniques, and it exhibited consistent performance around that average. A stratified portfolio had the single highest ex post information ratio, but no consistency over time. The screening methods in general do not methodically control for risk, and Table 14.3 shows that one of the screened portfolios even experienced negative returns during one period.

Recall that the ex ante target for the information ratio was 2.24. None of the methods achieved that target, although the quadratic program came closest on average. Part of the reason for the shortfall is the constraints imposed on the optimizer. We calculated the target information ratio ignoring constraints. As we have seen, constraints can effectively reduce the information coefficient and hence the information ratio.

ALTERNATIVES TO MEAN/ VARIANCE OPTIMIZATION

In Chap. 3, we discussed alternatives to standard deviation as risk measurements. These included semivariance, downside risk, and shortfall probability. We reviewed the alternatives and chose standard deviation as the best overall risk measure. We return to the issue again here, since our portfolio construction objective expresses our utility, which may in fact depend on alternative measures of risk. But as two research efforts show, even if your personal preferences depend on alternative risk measures, mean/variance analysis will produce equivalent or better portfolios. We present the research conclusions here, and cite the works in the bibliography.

Kahn and Stefek (1996) focus on the forward-looking nature of portfolio construction. The utility function includes forecasts of future risk. Mean/variance analysis, as typically applied in asset selection, relies on sophisticated modeling techniques to accurately forecast risk. Chapter 3 discusses in detail both the advantages of structural risk models and their superior performance.

Forecasting of alternative risk measures must rely on historical returns–based analysis. Kahn and Stefek show that higher moments of asset and asset class return distributions exhibit very little predictability, especially where it is important for portfolio construction. Return kurtosis is predictable, in the sense that most return distributions exhibit positive kurtosis ("fat tails") most of the time.

The ranking of assets or asset classes by kurtosis exhibits very little predictability. The only exception is options, where return asymmetries are engineered into the payoff pattern.

The empirical result is that most alternative risk forecasts reduce to a standard deviation forecast plus noise, with even the standard deviation forecast based only on history. According to this research, even investors with preferences defined by alternative risk measures are better served by mean/variance analysis.[15]

Grinold (1999) takes a different approach to the same problem, in the specific case of asset allocation. First, he adjusts returns-based analysis to the institutional context: benchmark-aware investing with typical portfolios close to the benchmark. This is the same approach we have applied to mean/variance analysis in this book. Then he compares mean/variance and returns-based analysis, assuming that the benchmark holds no options and that all options are fairly priced.

The result is that portfolios constructed using returns-based analysis are very close to mean/variance portfolios, although they require much more effort to construct. Furthermore, managers using this approach very seldom buy options. If options are fairly priced relative to the underlying asset class, then optimization will pursue the alphas directly through the asset class, not indirectly through the options.

So Kahn and Stefek argue the asset selection case for mean/variance, and Grinold argues the asset allocation case for mean/variance. Furthermore, Grinold shows why institutional investors, with their aversion to benchmark risk, will seldom purchase options—the only type of asset requiring analysis beyond mean/variance.

As a final observation, though, some active institutional investors do buy options. We argue that they do so typically to evade restrictions on leverage or short selling, or because of liquidity

---

[15]The case of investors in options and dynamic strategies like portfolio insurance is a bit trickier, but also handled in the paper. There the conclusion is to apply mean/variance analysis to the active asset selection strategy, and to overlay an options-based strategy based on alternative risk measures. But see Grinold (1999), who shows that under reasonable assumptions, even with alternative risk measures, most institutional investors will not use such strategies.

concerns. Only in the case of currency options do we see much evidence of investors choosing options explicitly for their distributions. Many managers have a great aversion to currency losses, and options can provide downside protection. We still advocate using mean/variance analysis generally and, if necessary, treating currency options as a special case.

DISPERSION

Dispersion plagues every manager running separate accounts for multiple clients. Each account sees the same alphas, benchmark, and investment process. The cash flows and history differ, however, and the portfolios are not identical. Hence, portfolio returns are not identical.

We will define *dispersion* as the difference between the maximum return and minimum return for these separate account portfolios. If the holdings in each account are identical, dispersion will disappear. If transactions costs were zero, dispersion would disappear. Dispersion is a measure of how an individual client's portfolio may differ from the manager's reported composite returns. Dispersion is, at the least, a client support problem for investment managers.

In practice, dispersion can be enormous. We once observed five investors in a particular manager's strategy, in separate accounts, incur dispersion of 23 percent over a year. The manager's overall dispersion may have been even larger. This was just the dispersion involving these five clients. In another case, with another manager, one client outperformed the S&P 500 by 15 percent while another underperformed by 9 percent, in the same year. At that level, dispersion is much more than a client support problem.

We can classify dispersion by its various sources. The first type of dispersion is client-driven. Portfolios differ because individual clients impose different constraints. One pension fund may restrict investment in its company stock. Another may not allow the use of futures contracts. These client-initiated constraints lead to dispersion, but they are completely beyond the manager's control.

But managers can control other forms of dispersion. Often, dispersion arises through a lack of attention. Separate accounts exhibit different betas and different factor exposures through lack of attention. Managers should control this form of dispersion.

On the other hand, separate accounts with the same factor exposures and betas can still exhibit dispersion because of owning different assets. Often the cost of holding exactly the same assets in each account will exceed any benefit from reducing dispersion.

In fact, because of transactions costs, some dispersion is optimal. If transactions costs were zero, rebalancing all the separate accounts so that they hold exactly the same assets in the same proportions would have no cost. Dispersion would disappear, at no cost to investors. With transactions costs, however, managers can achieve zero dispersion only with increased transactions costs. Managers should reduce dispersion only until further reduction would substantially lower returns on average because much higher transactions costs would be incurred.

Example

To understand dispersion better, let's look at a concrete example. In this example, the manager runs an existing portfolio and receives cash to form a new portfolio investing in the same strategy. So at one point in time, the manager is both rebalancing the existing portfolio and constructing the new portfolio. The rebalanced portfolio holdings will reflect both new and old information. With zero transactions costs, the manager would rebalance to the new optimum. Given an existing portfolio, though, he rebalances only where the new information more than overcomes the transactions costs, as in Eq. (14.9).

This trade-off does not affect the new portfolio in the same way. The manager starts from cash, and while he would still like to minimize transactions costs, he assumes a fairly high transactions cost for the initial portfolio construction. For this example, we'll assume that the new portfolio he builds is optimal and reflects entirely the manager's new information.

Clearly there will be dispersion between the existing portfolio and the new portfolio. There are two methods by which the manager could reduce dispersion to zero. He could invest the new portfolio in the rebalanced existing portfolio. This sacrifices returns, since the new portfolio will reflect both new and old information instead of just new information. The other choice is to invest the composite in the new optimum. But this would require paying excess transactions costs. By treating the existing portfolio and the new portfolio separately, the manager accepts some level of dispersion in order to achieve higher average returns. Furthermore, he can hope that this dispersion will decrease over time.

Characterizing Dispersion

We will now perform some static analysis to understand the causes of dispersion. First, consider dispersion caused by different betas or factor exposures. If the separate account betas range from 0.9 to 1.1 and the market return is 35 percent one year, then the dispersion would be 7 percent based just on the differing betas. This range of betas is quite large for an efficient, quantitatively run optimal process, and yet it doesn't come close to explaining some of the extreme war stories.

Now let's consider static analysis of managed dispersion—where the manager has matched factor exposures but not assets across all accounts—to try to understand the magnitude of the effect. In this simple model, we will consider N portfolios, all equally weighted with identical factor exposures. Each portfolio contains 100 stocks, and out of that 100 stocks, M stocks appear in all the portfolios and $100 - M$ stocks are unique to the particular portfolio. Furthermore, every stock has identical specific risk of 20 percent. Figure 14.3 displays the results, assuming normal distributions.

We can use the model to show that dispersion will depend on the number of stocks the portfolios have in common, the overall levels of specific risk, and the overall number of portfolios under management.

Managing Dispersion

We have seen how some level of dispersion is optimal and have discussed why dispersion arises. The next question is whether dispersion decreases over time: Do dispersed portfolios converge, and how fast? In general, convergence will depend on the type

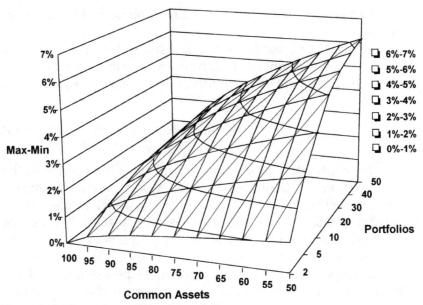

Figure 14.3 Dispersion: 100 stock portfolios.

of alphas in the strategy, the transactions costs, and possibly the portfolio construction methodology.

If alphas and risk stay absolutely constant over time, then dispersion will never disappear. There will always be a transactions cost barrier. An exact matching of portfolios will never pay. Furthermore, we can show (see the technical appendix) that the remaining tracking error is bounded based on the transactions costs and the manager's risk aversion:

$$\psi^2 \le \frac{TC}{2 \cdot \lambda_A} \qquad (14.12)$$

where TC measures the cost of trading from the initial portfolio to the zero transactions cost optimal portfolio (which we will refer to as portfolio Q), and we are measuring tracking error *and* risk aversion relative to portfolio Q. With very high risk aversion, all portfolios must be close to one another. But the higher the transactions costs, the more tracking error there is. Given intermediate risk aversion of $\lambda_A = 0.10$ and round-trip transactions costs of 2 percent, and assuming that moving from the initial portfolio to portfolio Q involves 10 percent turnover, Eq. (14.12) implies tracking error of 1 percent.

Since tracking error is bounded, dispersion is also bounded. Dispersion is proportional to tracking error, with the constant of proportionality dependent on the number of portfolios being managed:

$$E\{r_{PA,\max} - r_{PA,\min}\} = 2 \cdot \Phi^{-1}\left\{\left(\frac{1}{2}\right)^{1/N}\right\} \cdot \psi \qquad (14.13)$$

where this constant of proportionality involves the inverse of the cumulative normal distribution function Φ, and ψ is the tracking error of each portfolio relative to the composite (see the technical appendix for details). Figure 14.3 displays this function. For a given tracking error, more portfolios lead to more dispersion because more portfolios will further probe the extremes of the return distribution.

If the alphas and risk vary over time—the usual case—then convergence will occur. We can show that with changing alphas and risk each period, the portfolios will either maintain or, more typically, decrease the amount of dispersion. Over time, the process inexorably leads to convergence, because each separate account portfolio is chasing the same moving target. These general arguments do not, however, imply any particular time scale.

As an empirical example, we looked at five U.S. equity portfolios in a strategy with alphas based on book-to-price ratios and stock-specific alphas. Roughly two-thirds of the strategy's value came from the book-to-price factor tilt, with one-third arising from the stock-specific alphas. We started these five portfolios in January 1992 with 100 names in each portfolio, but not the same 100 names in each portfolio. Each portfolio had roughly 3 percent tracking error relative to the S&P 500. We analyzed the initial level of dispersion and then looked at how that changed over time. We used a consistent alpha generation process and standard mean/variance optimization with uniform transactions costs. To understand convergence and transactions costs, we looked at behavior as we changed the overall level of transactions costs.

What we found was a steady decrease in average tracking error (relative to the composite) and dispersion, with the smallest dispersion exhibited when we assumed the lowest transactions costs. Figure 14.4 displays the results. So even though our starting portfolios

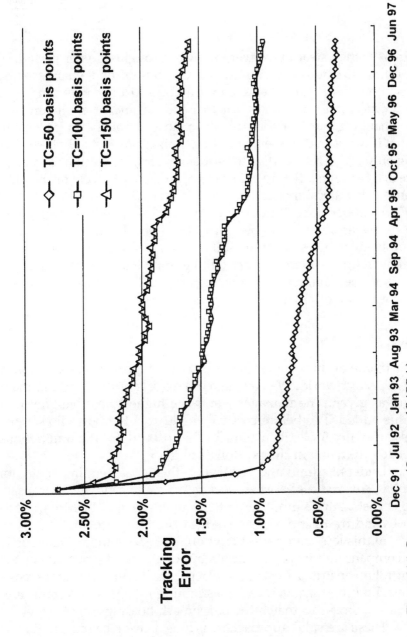

Figure 14.4 Convergence. (*Courtesy of BARRA.*)

differed, they steadily converged over a roughly 5-year period. In real-life situations, client-initiated constraints and client-specific cash flows will act to keep separate accounts from converging.

One final question is whether we can increase convergence by changing our portfolio construction technology. In particular, what if we used dual-benchmark optimization? Instead of penalizing only active risk relative to the benchmark, we would also penalize active risk relative to either the composite portfolio or the optimum calculated ignoring transactions costs.

Dual-benchmark optimization can clearly reduce dispersion, but only at an undesirable price. Dual-benchmark optimization simply introduces the trade-off we analyzed earlier: dispersion versus return. Unless you are willing to give up return in order to lower dispersion, do not implement the dual-benchmark optimization approach to managing dispersion.

SUMMARY

The theme of this chapter has been portfolio construction in a less than perfect world. We have taken the goals of the portfolio manager as given. The manager wants the highest possible after-cost value added. The before-cost value added is the portfolio's alpha less a penalty for active variance. The costs are for the transactions needed to maintain the portfolio's alpha.

Understanding and achieving this goal requires data on alphas, covariances between stock returns, and estimates of transactions costs. Alpha inputs are often unrealistic and biased. Covariances and transactions costs are measured imperfectly.

In this less than perfect environment, the standard reaction is to compensate for flawed inputs by regulating the outputs of the portfolio construction process: placing limits on active stock positions, limiting turnover, and constraining holdings in certain categories of stocks to match the benchmark holdings.

These are valid approaches, as long as we recognize that their purpose is to compensate for faulty inputs. We prefer a direct attack on the causes. Treat flaws in the alpha inputs with alpha analysis: Remove biases, trim outlandish values, and scale alphas in line with expectations for value added. This strengthens the link between research and portfolio construction. Then seek out the best possible estimates of risk and transactions costs. As appropriate, use a powerful portfolio construction tool with as few added constraints as possible.

Near the end of the chapter, we returned to the topic of alternative risk measures and alternatives to mean/variance optimization. For most active institutional managers (especially those who do not invest in options and optionlike dynamic strategies such as portfolio insurance), alternatives to mean/variance analysis greatly complicate portfolio construction without improving results. At the stock selection level, results may be much worse.

Finally, we analyzed the very practical issue of dispersion among separately managed accounts. We saw that managers can control dispersion—especially that driven by differing factor exposures—but should not reduce it to zero.

PROBLEMS

1. Table 14.1 shows both alphas used in a constrained optimization and the modified alphas which, in an unconstrained optimization, lead to the same holdings. Comparing these two sets of alphas can help in estimating the loss in value added caused by the constraints. How? What is that loss in this example? The next chapter will discuss this in more detail.

2. Discuss how restrictions on short sales are both a barrier to a manager's effective use of information and a safeguard against poor information.

3. Lisa is a value manager who chooses stocks based on their price/earnings ratios. What biases would you expect to see in her alphas? How should she construct portfolios based on these alphas, in order to bet only on specific asset returns?

4. You are a benchmark timer who in backtests can add 50 basis points of risk-adjusted value added. You forecast 14 percent benchmark volatility, the recent average, but unfortunately benchmark volatility turns out to be 17 percent. How much value can you add, given this misestimation of benchmark volatility?

5. You manage 20 separate accounts using the same investment process. Each portfolio holds about 100 names, with 90 names appearing in all the accounts and 10 names unique to the particular account. Roughly how much dispersion should you expect to see?

REFERENCES

Chopra, Vijay K., and William T. Ziemba. "The Effects of Errors in Means, Variances, and Covariances on Optimal Portfolio Choice." *Journal of Portfolio Management*, vol. 19, no. 2, 1993, pp. 6–11.

Connor, Gregory, and Hayne Leland. "Cash Management for Index Tracking." *Financial Analysts Journal*, vol. 51, no. 6, 1995, pp. 75–80.

Grinold, Richard C. "The Information Horizon." *Journal of Portfolio Management*, vol. 24, no. 1, 1997, pp. 57–67.

———. "Mean-Variance and Scenario-Based Approaches to Portfolio Selection." *Journal of Portfolio Management*, vol. 25, no. 2, Winter 1999, pp. 10–22.

Jorion, Philippe. "Portfolio Optimization in Practice." *Financial Analysts Journal*, vol. 48, no. 1, 1992, pp. 68–74.

Kahn, Ronald N. "Managing Dispersion." BARRA Equity Research Seminar, Pebble Beach, Calif., June 1997.

Kahn, Ronald N., and Daniel Stefek. "Heat, Light, and Downside Risk." *BARRA Preprint*, December 1996.

Leland, Hayne. *Optimal Asset Rebalancing in the Presence of Transactions Costs.* University of California Research Program in Finance, Publication 261, October 1996.

Michaud, Richard. "The Markowitz Optimization Enigma: Is 'Optimized' Optimal?" *Financial Analysts Journal*, vol. 45, no. 1, 1989, pp. 31–42.

Muller, Peter. "Empirical Tests of Biases in Equity Portfolio Optimization." In *Financial Optimization*, edited by Stavros A. Zenios (Cambridge: Cambridge University Press, 1993), pp. 80–98.

Rohweder, Herold C. "Implementing Stock Selection Ideas: Does Tracking Error Optimization Do Any Good?" *Journal of Portfolio Management*, vol. 24, no. 3, 1998, pp. 49–59.

Rudd, Andrew. "Optimal Selection of Passive Portfolios." *Financial Management*, vol. 9, no. 1, 1980, pp. 57–66.

Rudd, Andrew, and Barr Rosenberg. "Realistic Portfolio Optimization." *TIMS Study in the Management Sciences*, vol. 11, 1979, pp. 21–46.

Stevens, Guy V. G. "On the Inverse of the Covariance Matrix in Portfolio Analysis." *Journal of Finance*, vol. 53, no. 5, 1998, pp. 1821–1827.

TECHNICAL APPENDIX

This appendix covers three topics: alpha analysis, in particular how to neutralize alphas against various factor biases; the loss of value added due to errors in the estimated covariance matrix; and dispersion.

Alpha Analysis

Our goal in this section is to separate alphas into common-factor components and specific components, and correspondingly to define active portfolio positions arising from these distinct components. This will involve considerable algebra, but the result will allow us to carefully control our alphas: to neutralize particular factor alphas and even to input factor alphas designed to achieve target active factor exposures.

We will analyze stock alphas in the context of a multiple-factor model with N stocks and K factors:

$$\mathbf{r} = \mathbf{X} \cdot \mathbf{b} + \mathbf{u} \qquad (14A.1)$$

We make the usual assumptions that $\mathbf{b}$ and $\mathbf{u}$ are uncorrelated, and that the components of $\mathbf{u}$ are uncorrelated. The model has the covariance structure

$$\mathbf{V} = \mathbf{X} \cdot \mathbf{F} \cdot \mathbf{X}^T + \mathbf{\Delta} \qquad (14A.2)$$

The unconstrained portfolio construction procedure leads to an active position $\mathbf{h}_{PA}^*$ determined by the first-order conditions:

$$\frac{\boldsymbol{\alpha}}{2 \cdot \lambda_A} = \mathbf{V} \cdot \mathbf{h}_{PA}^* = \mathbf{X} \cdot \mathbf{F} \cdot \mathbf{x}_{PA}^* + \mathbf{\Delta} \cdot \mathbf{h}_{PA}^* \qquad (14A.3)$$

where $\mathbf{x}_{PA}^* = \mathbf{X}^T \cdot \mathbf{h}_{PA}^*$ is the active factor position.

We now want to separate $\boldsymbol{\alpha}$ into a common-factor component $\boldsymbol{\alpha}_{CF}$ and a specific component $\boldsymbol{\alpha}_{SP}$, and similarly separate $\mathbf{h}_{PA}^*$ into common-factor holdings $\mathbf{h}_{CF}$ and specific holdings $\mathbf{h}_{SP}$. We will eventually see that each component will separately satisfy Eq. (14A.3), with the common-factor alpha component leading to the common-factor active positions and the specific alpha component leading to the specific active positions and containing zero active factor positions.

Equation (14A.3) uniquely determines the optimal active holdings $\mathbf{h}_{PA}^*$ and optimal active factor exposures $\mathbf{x}_{PA}^*$. However, it does not uniquely determine a separation of $\mathbf{h}_{PA}^*$ into $\mathbf{h}_{CF}$ and $\mathbf{h}_{SP}$: There are an infinite number of portfolios with active factor exposures

x_{PA}^*. We can uniquely define the separation if we stipulate that h_{CF} is the minimum-risk portfolio with factor exposures x_{PA}^*.

Let H be the K by N matrix with factor portfolios as rows. The matrix H is

$$H = (X^T \cdot \Delta^{-1} \cdot X)^{-1} \cdot X^T \cdot \Delta^{-1} \qquad (14A.4)$$

Note that $H \cdot X = I$; each factor portfolio has unit exposure to its factor and zero exposure to all the other factors. Also remember that each factor portfolio has minimum risk, given its factor exposures.

Then, starting with the uniquely defined x_{PA}^* and our definition of h_{CF} as the minimum-risk portfolio with these factor exposures, we find

$$h_{CF} = H^T \cdot x_{PA}^* \qquad (14A.5)$$

Knowing that h_{CF} and h_{SP} add up to h_{PA}^*, and applying additional algebra, we find that

$$h_{SP} = \Delta^{-1} \cdot [I - X \cdot H] \cdot \left(\frac{\alpha}{2 \cdot \lambda_A}\right) \qquad (14A.6)$$

Exercise 1 at the end of this appendix asks the reader to demonstrate Eq. (14A.5), i.e., that, as defined, h_{CF} does lead to the minimum-risk portfolio with factor exposures x_{PA}^*. Exercise 2 asks the reader to demonstrate that h_{SP} does not contain any common-factor exposures, i.e., that $X^T \cdot h_{SP} = 0$.

The separation of the optimal holdings into common-factor and specific holdings has been the hard part of our task. With this behind us, the easier part is to separate α into a common-factor component α_{CF} and a specific component α_{SP}. These are

$$\alpha_{CF} = X \cdot H \cdot \alpha \qquad (14A.7)$$

and

$$\alpha_{SP} = \alpha - \alpha_{CF} = [I - X \cdot H] \cdot \alpha \qquad (14A.8)$$

Notice that $H \cdot \alpha$ is the alpha of each of the K factor portfolios. Call $\alpha_F = H \cdot \alpha$ the *factor alphas*. Then $X \cdot \alpha_F$ maps those factor alphas back onto the assets.

So we have separated both the optimal active holdings and the alphas into common-factor and specific pieces. We can also check the correspondence between common-factor alphas and common-factor holdings, and between specific alphas and specific holdings. According to Eq. (14A.3), the optimal active common-factor exposures are

$$\mathbf{x}_{PA}^* = \mathbf{X}^T \cdot \mathbf{V}^{-1} \cdot \left(\frac{\boldsymbol{\alpha}}{2 \cdot \lambda_A}\right) \qquad (14A.9)$$

Exercises 4, 5, and 6 help to show that just using $\boldsymbol{\alpha}_{CF}$ will lead to active holdings $\mathbf{h}_{CF}$ and common-factor exposures $\mathbf{x}_{PA}^*$, and that $\boldsymbol{\alpha}_{SP}$ will lead to active holdings $\mathbf{h}_{SP}$ and common-factor exposures of zero.

How can we use this glut of algebra? Suppose we believe that our alphas contain valuable information only for specific stock selection. Instead of relying on any factor forecasts inadvertently contained in our alphas, we have defined a target active position $\mathbf{x}_{PAT}^*$ for the common factors. To achieve this target, we can replace the original alpha $\boldsymbol{\alpha}$ with $\boldsymbol{\alpha}'$, where

$$\boldsymbol{\alpha}' = 2 \cdot \lambda_A \cdot \mathbf{V} \cdot \mathbf{H}^T \cdot \mathbf{x}_{PAT} + \boldsymbol{\alpha}_{SP} \qquad (14A.10)$$

The first term on the right-hand side of Eq. (14A.10) replaces $\boldsymbol{\alpha}_{CF}$ and will result in an active common-factor exposure of $\mathbf{x}_{PAT}^*$. The second term on the right-hand side of Eq. (14A.10) does not affect the common-factor positions and preserves the pure stock selection information from the original set of alphas.

The columns of the N by K matrix $\mathbf{V} \cdot \mathbf{H}^T$ are of particular interest. Column k of $\mathbf{V} \cdot \mathbf{H}^T$ leads to an active factor position that is positive for factor k and zero for all other factors. This insight can provide us with pinpoint control over the factors. Let's say we partition the factors so that $\mathbf{x} = \{\mathbf{y}, \mathbf{z}\}$, where we are willing to take an active position on the $\mathbf{y}$ factors and no active position on the $\mathbf{z}$ factors. Then we could set

$$\mathbf{x}_{PAT}^* = \{\mathbf{y}_{PAT}^*, 0\} \qquad (14A.11)$$

where $\mathbf{y}_{PA}^*$ is the y component of $\mathbf{x}_{PA}^*$. This would result in no active position on the $\mathbf{z}$ factors. If we wanted no active positions on any of the factors, we could set $\mathbf{x}_{PAT} = 0$.

Optimization and Data Errors

We now turn to the second topic of this technical appendix: the erosion in value added due to inaccuracies in our estimated covariance matrix.

Consider a situation where the true covariance matrix is $\mathbf{V}$, but the manager uses a covariance matrix $\mathbf{U} \neq \mathbf{V}$. To simplify matters, assume that the manager imposes no constraints. Using Eq. (14A.3), the manager then will choose optimal active positions

$$\mathbf{h}_{PA}^* = \mathbf{U}^{-1} \cdot \left(\frac{\alpha}{2 \cdot \lambda_A}\right) \qquad (14A.12)$$

Using $\mathbf{V}$ and $\mathbf{h}_{PA}^*$, the value added (risk-adjusted return) for the manager will be VA_U^*:

$$VA_U^* = \alpha^T \cdot \mathbf{h}_{PA}^* - \lambda_A \cdot \mathbf{h}_{PA}^{*T} \cdot \mathbf{V} \cdot \mathbf{h}_{PA}^* \qquad (14A.13)$$

If the manager had known the true covariance matrix, the active position would have been

$$\mathbf{h}_{PA}^{**} = \mathbf{V}^{-1} \cdot \left(\frac{\alpha}{2 \cdot \lambda_A}\right) \qquad (14A.14)$$

with value added VA_V^*:

$$VA_V^* = \alpha^T \cdot \mathbf{h}_{PA}^{**} - \lambda_A \cdot \mathbf{h}_{PA}^{**T} \cdot \mathbf{V} \cdot \mathbf{h}_{PA}^{**} \qquad (14A.15)$$

The loss in value added is just the difference between VA_V^* and VA_U^*. Using Eqs. (14A.12) and (14A.14), this becomes

$$\text{Loss} = \left(\frac{1}{4 \cdot \lambda_A}\right) \cdot \alpha^T \cdot [\mathbf{V}^{-1} - 2 \cdot \mathbf{U}^{-1} + \mathbf{U}^{-1} \cdot \mathbf{V} \cdot \mathbf{U}^{-1}] \cdot \alpha \qquad (14A.16)$$

where we have defined the loss as a positive quantity (i.e., the amount lost). You can see that if $\mathbf{U} = \mathbf{V}$, this term becomes zero.

Dispersion

Here we derive two results stated in the main text. First, we derive a bound on tracking error in the presence of transactions costs. Start with initial portfolio I and zero transactions cost optimal portfolio Q, which we will treat as a benchmark. To find an optimal solution, portfolio P, we will trade off tracking error relative to portfolio Q against the transactions costs of moving from portfolio I to portfolio P:

$$\text{Max}\left\{\begin{array}{c} -\lambda_A \cdot \mathbf{h}_{PA}^T \cdot \mathbf{V} \cdot \mathbf{h}_{PA} \\ -\text{Max}\{0, \mathbf{h}_{PA}^T - \mathbf{h}_{IA}^T\} \cdot \mathbf{PC} - \text{Max}\{0, \mathbf{h}_{IA}^T - \mathbf{h}_{PA}^T\} \cdot \mathbf{SC} \end{array}\right\} \quad (14A.17)$$

where $\mathbf{PC}$ is a vector of purchase costs, $\mathbf{SC}$ is a vector of sell costs, the inner maximum functions look element by element to determine whether we are purchasing or selling, and we have defined the active portfolio relative to portfolio Q. This optimization includes alphas implicitly, in portfolio Q.

At optimality,

$$-2 \cdot \lambda_A \cdot \mathbf{V} \cdot \mathbf{h}_{PA} - \mathbf{PC}' - \mathbf{SC}' = 0 \quad (14A.18)$$

where the elements of $\mathbf{PC}'$ match those of $\mathbf{PC}$ only if at optimality $h_{PA}(n) > h_{IA}(n)$ and are zero otherwise. We similarly define the elements of $\mathbf{SC}'$ based on whether we are selling the asset.

If we multiply Eq. (14A.18) by $\mathbf{h}_{PA}^T$, we find

$$-2 \cdot \lambda_A \cdot \psi_P^2 = \mathbf{h}_{PA}^T \cdot \mathbf{PC}' + \mathbf{h}_{PA}^T \cdot \mathbf{SC}' \quad (14A.19)$$

Now focus on an asset n that we purchased, $h_P(n) > h_I(n)$. For this asset, we expect $h_Q(n) \geq h_P(n)$, i.e., if it were not for transactions costs, we would have purchased even more and moved all the way from $h_I(n)$ to $h_Q(n)$. Therefore,

$$\mathbf{h}_{PA}^T \cdot \mathbf{PC}' \leq 0 \quad (14A.20)$$

and, once again for purchased assets,

$$h_Q(n) - h_I(n) \geq h_Q(n) - h_P(n) \quad (14A.21)$$

Similar arguments hold for sold assets. If we define

$$\text{TC} = (\mathbf{h}_Q^T - \mathbf{h}_I^T) \cdot \mathbf{PC}' + (\mathbf{h}_I^T - \mathbf{h}_Q^T) \cdot \mathbf{SC}' \quad (14A.22)$$

then Eqs. (14A.20), (14A.21), and (14A.19) imply

$$\psi_P^2 \leq \frac{\text{TC}}{2 \cdot \lambda_A} \quad (14A.23)$$

This is the result in the main text.

The other dispersion result we want to derive here concerns the expected dispersion for N portfolios, each with tracking error of ψ relative to a composite portfolio. Assuming that active returns r_{PA} relative to the composite are independent and normally distributed with mean 0 and standard deviation ψ, the probability of observing an active return less than some $r_{PA,max}$ is

$$\text{Prob}\{r_{PA} < r_{PA,max}\} = \Phi\left\{\frac{r_{PA}}{\psi}\right\} \qquad (14A.24)$$

The probability of observing N independent active returns, each less than $r_{PA,max}$, is

$$\text{Prob}\{\{r_{PA}(j)|j = 1, N\} < r_{PA,max}\} = \Phi^N\left\{\frac{r_{PA}}{\psi}\right\} \qquad (14A.25)$$

We can therefore solve for the expected (median) $r_{PA,max}$ as

$$\text{Prob}\{\{r_{PA}(j)|j = 1, N\} < E\{r_{PA,max}\}\} = \frac{1}{2} \qquad (14A.26)$$

or

$$E\{r_{PA,max}\} = \Phi^{-1}\left\{\left(\frac{1}{2}\right)^{1/N}\right\} \cdot \psi \qquad (14A.27)$$

Assuming symmetry, we will find a similar result for the expected minimum. Hence

$$E\{r_{PA,max} - r_{PA,min}\} = 2 \cdot \Phi^{-1}\left\{\left(\frac{1}{2}\right)^{1/N}\right\} \cdot \psi \qquad (14A.28)$$

as reported in the main text.

Exercises

1. Show that the minimum-risk portfolio with factor exposures x_P is given by $h_P = H^T \cdot x_P$, where H is defined in Eq. (14A.4). Recall that a portfolio is diversified with respect to the factor model (X,F,Δ), diversified for short, if it has minimum risk among all portfolios with the same factor exposures. This result says that all diversified portfolios are made up of a weighted combination of the factor portfolios.

2. Show that the optimal specific asset holdings h_{SP}, defined in Eq. (14A.6), have zero exposure to all the factors, i.e., $X^T \cdot h_{SP} = 0$.

3. Establish the following: If the benchmark portfolio is diversified and the alphas are benchmark-neutral, then both α_{CF} and α_{SP} are benchmark-neutral.

4. Establish the identities

$$X^T \cdot V^{-1} \cdot X \cdot H = X^T \cdot V^{-1} \qquad (14A.29)$$

$$X^T \cdot V^{-1} = F^{-1} \cdot [F^{-1} + X^T \cdot \Delta^{-1} \cdot X]^{-1} \cdot X^T \cdot \Delta^{-1} \qquad (14A.30)$$

Hint: Recall Exercise 5 in the technical appendix of Chap. 3.

5. Establish the identity

$$V \cdot H^T = X \cdot [F + (X^T \cdot \Delta^{-1} \cdot X)^{-1}] \qquad (14A.31)$$

6. Show that the common-factor component of alpha leads to the common-factor holdings, i.e., $2 \cdot \lambda_A \cdot V \cdot h_{CF} = \alpha_{CF}$, and that the specific component of alpha leads to the specific holdings, i.e., $2 \cdot \lambda_A \cdot V \cdot h_{SP} = \alpha_{SP}$. This implies the identities

$$V \cdot H^T \cdot X^T \cdot V^{-1} = X \cdot H \qquad (14A.32)$$

and $\quad (V \cdot \Delta^{-1} - I) \cdot (I - X \cdot H) = 0 \qquad (14A.33)$

7. This exercise invokes regression to separate the components of alpha. Show that we can calculate the factor alphas α_F using a weighted regression, $\alpha = X \cdot \alpha_F + \epsilon$, with weights inversely proportional to specific variance. The residual of this regression, i.e., ϵ, will equal α_{SP}.

8. Suppose we wish to constrain the common-factor exposures to satisfy $Q \cdot x = p$, where Q is a J by K matrix of rank J. This could constrain some factor exposures and leave others unconstrained. Let p^* be the result using the original alpha and an unconstrained optimization, i.e., $Q \cdot x_{PA}^* = p^*$. Show that the revised alpha

$$\alpha^+ = \alpha - 2 \cdot \lambda_A \cdot X \cdot Q^T$$
$$\cdot [Q \cdot X^T \cdot V^{-1} \cdot X \cdot Q^T]^{-1} \cdot (p^* - p)$$

will result in a portfolio that satisfies the constraints.

9. Consider the optimization

$$\text{Maximize } \{h^T \cdot \alpha - \lambda_A \cdot h^T \cdot V \cdot h\}$$

subject to the inequality constraints

$$b \leq A \cdot h \leq d$$

Show that any modified α^+, where α^+ satisfies

$$2 \cdot \lambda_A \cdot b \leq A \cdot V^{-1} \cdot \alpha^+ \leq 2 \cdot \lambda_A \cdot d$$

will produce a portfolio that satisfies the inequality constraints. How would you choose α^+?

10. Input alphas are *cash-neutral* if they lead to an active cash position of zero. Show that alphas are cash-neutral if and only if $h_C^T \cdot \alpha = 0$, where h_C is the fully invested portfolio with minimum risk.

11. To make the alphas both benchmark- and cash-neutral, modify them as follows:

$$\alpha^+ = \alpha - c_B \cdot V \cdot h_B - c_C \cdot V \cdot h_C$$

Choose the constants c_B and c_C to ensure benchmark neutrality, $h_B^T \cdot \alpha^+ = 0$, and cash neutrality, $h_C^T \cdot \alpha^+ = 0$. Why?

Applications Exercises

For these exercises, you will need alphas from a dividend discount model for all MMI stocks. (Alternatively, you could use alphas from some other valuation model, but it would be useful to have some intuition for these sources of alphas.)

1. Generate the unconstrained optimal portfolio using moderate active risk aversion of $\lambda_A = 0.10$ and the CAPMMI as benchmark. What is the optimal portfolio beta? What are the factor exposures of the optimal portfolio? Discuss any concerns over these factor exposures.

2. Now industry-neutralize the alphas and reoptimize. What are the new factor exposures? Compare the benefits of this portfolio to the previous optimal portfolio. How would you justify an argument that the first portfolio should outperform the second?

Long/Short Investing

INTRODUCTION

U.S. institutions have invested using long/short strategies since at least the late 1980s. These strategies have generated controversy, and, over time, increasing acceptance as a worthwhile innovation. Long/short strategies offer a distinct advantage over long-only strategies: the potential for more efficient use of information, particularly but not exclusively downside information.

This chapter will analyze several important aspects of long/short strategies and, by implication, some important and poorly understood aspects of long-only strategies. We will define long/short strategies and briefly introduce their advantages and the controversies surrounding these advantages. We will then analyze in detail the increased efficiency offered by long/short strategies and the subtle but pervasive effects of the long-only constraint. This analysis is therefore important to all managers—not just those offering long/short strategies. We will later discuss the appeal of long/short strategies and some empirical observations. The chapter ends with the usual notes, references, and technical appendix.

The main results of this chapter include the following:

- The benefits of long/short investing arise from the loosening of the (surprisingly important) long-only constraint.
- Long/short implementations offer the most improvement over long-only implementations when the universe of assets is large, the assets' volatility is low, and the strategy has high active risk.

- The long-only constraint tends to induce biases, particularly toward small stocks. Surprisingly, it can limit the ability to completely act on upside information, by not allowing short positions that could finance long positions.

In this chapter, we will define long/short strategies specifically as equity market–neutral strategies. These strategies have betas of 0 and equal long and short positions. Some databases group these strategies in the more general category of "hedge fund." However the hedge fund category can include almost any strategy that allows short positions. We will focus much more specifically on equity strategies managed according to the principles of this book, and with zero beta and zero net investment.

Long/short investing refers to a method for implementing active management ideas. We can implement any strategy as long/short or long-only. Long/short investing is general. It does not refer to a particular source of information.

Now, every long-only portfolio has an associated active portfolio with zero net investment and often zero beta. Therefore, every long-only portfolio has an associated long/short portfolio. But the long-only constraint has a significant impact on this associated long/short portfolio. Long/short strategies provide for more opportunities—particularly in the size of short positions in smaller stocks (assuming a capitalization-weighted benchmark).

Long/short strategies are becoming increasingly popular. According to *Pensions and Investments* (May 18, 1998), 30 investment management firms offer market-neutral strategies, up from the 21 investment management firms one year earlier.

Market-neutral strategies are something of a "phantom" strategy. The *Pensions and Investments* list does not include many large investment management firms that offer market-neutral strategies. It also appears to underreport the assets invested for some of the firms listed. Market-neutral strategies short stocks, a strategy frowned upon by some owners of funds. This apparently leads to enhanced discretion by the managers. But this is only part of the controversy.

THE CONTROVERSY

Proponents of long/short investing offer several arguments in its favor. One simple argument depends on diversification. A long/short implementation includes effectively a long portfolio and a short portfolio. If each of these portfolios separately has an information ratio of IR, and the two portfolios are uncorrelated, then the combined strategy, just through diversification, should exhibit an information ratio of IR · $\sqrt{2}$. The problem with this argument is that it applies just as well to the active portfolio associated with any long-only portfolio. So this argument can't be the justification for long/short investing.

A second argument for long/short investing claims that the complete dominance of long-only investing has preserved short-side inefficiencies, and hence the short side may offer higher alphas than the long side.

The third and most important argument for long/short investing is the enhanced efficiency that results from the loosening of the long-only constraint. The critical issue for long/short investing isn't diversification, but rather constraints.

These arguments in favor of long/short investing have generated considerable controversy. The first argument, based on diversification, is misleading if not simply incorrect. Not surprisingly, it has attracted considerable attack. The second argument is difficult to prove and brings up the issue of the high implementation costs associated with shorting stocks. The third argument is the critical issue, with implications for both long/short and long-only investors.

THE SURPRISING IMPACT OF THE LONG-ONLY CONSTRAINT

We are interested in the costs imposed by the most widespread institutional constraint—the restriction on short sales—or, equivalently, the benefits of easing that constraint. We will ignore transactions costs and all other constraints, and focus our attention on how this constraint affects the active frontier: the trade-off between exceptional return α and risk ω.

Let's start with a simple market that has N assets and an equal-weighted benchmark. We presume in addition that all assets have identical residual risk ω and that residual returns are uncorrelated. This model opens a small window and allows us to view the workings of the long-only constraint.

Let α_n be the expected residual return on asset n and λ_R the residual risk aversion. In this setup, assuming that we want zero active beta, the active position for asset n is

$$h_n = \frac{\alpha_n}{2 \cdot \lambda_R \cdot \omega^2} \tag{15.1}$$

The overall residual (and active) risk ψ_P is

$$\psi_P^2 = \frac{1}{4 \cdot \lambda_R^2 \cdot \omega^2} \cdot \sum_{n=1}^{N} \alpha_n^2 \tag{15.2}$$

We know from Chap. 10 that alphas have the form $\alpha_n = \omega \cdot (IR/\sqrt{N}) \cdot z_n$, where z_n is a score with mean 0 and standard deviation 1, and we have invoked the fundamental law of active management to write the information coefficient in terms of the information ratio and the number of assets. Hence, the active positions and portfolio active risk become

$$h_n = \frac{IR \cdot z_n}{2 \cdot \lambda_R \cdot \omega \cdot \sqrt{N}} \tag{15.3}$$

$$\psi_P = \frac{IR}{2 \cdot \lambda_R} \cdot \sqrt{\frac{1}{N} \sum_{n=1}^{N} z_n^2} \approx \frac{IR}{2 \cdot \lambda_R} \tag{15.4}$$

We can use Eqs. (15.3) and (15.4) to link the active position with the desired level of active risk ψ_P, the stock's residual risk ω, and the square root of the number of assets $\sqrt{N}$:

$$h_n = \frac{\psi_P \cdot z_n}{\sqrt{N} \cdot \omega} \tag{15.5}$$

The limitation on short sales becomes binding when the active position plus the benchmark holding is negative. For an equal-weighted benchmark, this occurs when

$$z_n \leq -\frac{\omega}{\sqrt{N} \cdot \psi_P} \tag{15.6}$$

Figure 15.1 shows this information boundary as a function of the number of stocks for different levels of active risk.

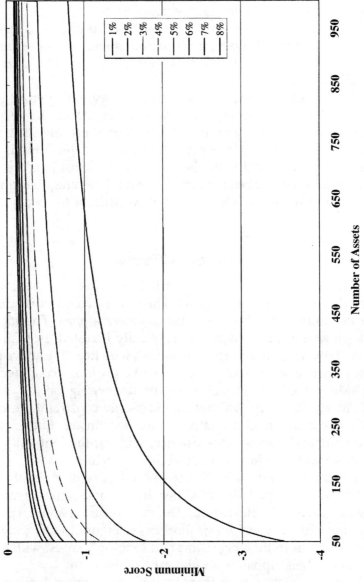

Figure 15.1 Sensitivity to portfolio active risk.

Information is wasted if the z score falls below the minimum level. The higher the minimum level, the more information we are likely to leave on the table. As an example, if we consider a strategy with 500 stocks, active risk of 5 percent, and typical residual risk of 25 percent, we will waste information whenever our score falls below -0.22. This will happen 41 percent of the time, assuming normally distributed scores.

This rough analysis indicates that an aggressive strategy involving a large number of lower-volatility assets should reap the largest benefits from easing the restriction on short sales. The more aggressive the strategy, the more likely it is to hit bounds. The lower the asset volatility, the larger the active positions we take. The more assets in the benchmark, the lower the average benchmark holding, and the more likely it is that we will hit the boundary.

Indirect Effects

In a long-only optimization, the restriction against short selling has both a direct and an indirect effect. The direct effect, studied above, is to preclude exploiting the most negative alphas. The indirect effect grows out of the desire to stay fully invested. In that case, we must finance positive active positions with negative active positions. Hence, a scarcity of negative active positions can affect the long side as well: Overweights require underweights.

Put another way, without the long-only constraint we could take larger underweights relative to our benchmark. But since underweights and overweights balance, without the long-only constraint we will take larger overweights as well.

We can illustrate this "knock-on" effect with a simple case. We start with an equal-weighted benchmark and generate random alphas for each of the 1000 assets. Then we construct optimal portfolios in the long-only and long/short cases. Figure 15.2 displays the active positions in the long/short and long-only cases, with assets ordered by their alphas from highest to lowest.

In the long/short case, there is a rough symmetry between the positive and negative active positions. The long-only case essentially assigns all assets after the first 300 the same negative alpha. We expected that the long-only portfolio would less efficiently handle neg-

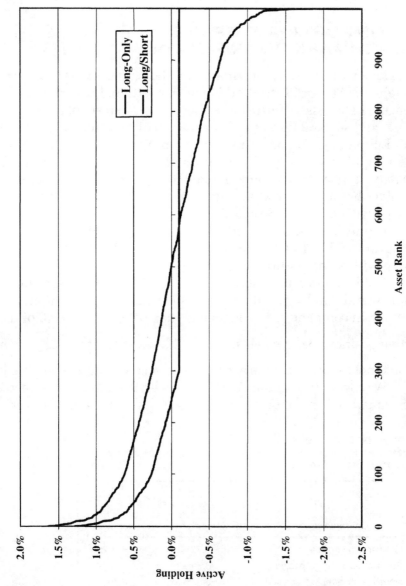

Figure 15.2 Long/short and long-only active positions: equal weighted benchmark.

ative alphas than the long/short portfolio. More surprisingly, Fig. 15.2 shows that it also less efficiently handles the positive alphas.

THE IMPORTANCE OF THE BENCHMARK DISTRIBUTION

This knock-on effect is more dramatic if the benchmark is not equal-weighted. We can illustrate this with an extreme case where the benchmark consists of 101 stocks. Stock 1 is 99 percent of the benchmark, and stocks 2 through 101 are each 0.01 percent: Gulliver and 100 Lilliputians. To make this even simpler, suppose that 50 of the Lilliputians have positive alphas of 3.73 percent and 50 have negative alphas of the same magnitude. We consider two cases: Gulliver has a positive alpha, again 3.73 percent, and Gulliver has a negative alpha, -3.73 percent.

In the long/short world, the capitalization of the stocks is irrelevant. Table 15.1 displays the active positions of the stocks, along with some portfolio characteristics:

Gulliver does not merit special consideration in the long/short world. Gulliver, Ltd., receives the same active position as a Lilliputian company with a similar alpha. Note that since all of the active positions are smaller than $\frac{1}{101}$, the no-short-sale restriction would not be binding if the benchmark assets were equal-weighted.

We encounter significant difficulty with the highly imbalanced benchmark when we disallow short sales. In that case, it makes a

T A B L E 15.1

Long/Short Results

Characteristic	α (Gulliver)	
	Positive	Negative
Gulliver active position	0.79%	−0.79%
Positive stock active position	0.79%	0.80%
Negative stock active position	−0.80%	−0.79%
Portfolio alpha	3.00%	3.00%
Portfolio active risk	2.00%	2.00%

T A B L E 15.2

Long-Only Results

Characteristic	α (Gulliver)	
	Positive	Negative
Gulliver active position	0.01%	−1.55%
Positive stock active position	0.01%	0.04%
Negative stock active position	−0.01%	−0.01%
Portfolio alpha	0.04%	0.15%
Portfolio active risk	0.02%	0.39%

great deal of difference whether Gulliver's alpha is positive or negative. With a negative alpha, we assume a very large negative active position (−1.55 percent) that allows us to finance the over-weightings of the Lilliputians with positive alphas.[1] But when Gulliver has a positive alpha, we can achieve only tiny active positions, both long and short. Table 15.2 displays the results.

The Gulliver example illustrates another problem: the potential for a significant size imbalance. The shortage of negative active positions causes relatively larger underweighting decisions on the higher-capitalization stocks. If the alpha on Gulliver had a 50/50 chance of being a positive or negative 3.73 percent, the average active holding of Gulliver would be −0.77 percent.

Capitalization-Weighted Benchmarks

The Gulliver example shows that the distribution of capitalization in the benchmark is an important determinant of the potential for

---

[1]There is an alternative approach:

- Relax the condition that the net overweight must equal the net underweight.
- Use a short cash position (leverage!) to finance the overweights.
- Sell the benchmark forward to cover the added benchmark exposure.

In the Gulliver model, this procedure allows us to achieve an alpha of 1.53 percent with an active risk of 1.42 percent. The negative cash position is 39 percent of the portfolio's unlevered value.

adding value in a long-only strategy. To calculate the benefits of long/short investing in realistic environments, we will need a model of the capitalization distribution. This requires a short detour.

We will use Lorenz curves to measure distributions of capitalization. To construct them, we must

- Calculate benchmark weight as a fraction of total capitalization.
- Order the assets from highest to lowest weight.
- Calculate the cumulative weight of the first n assets, as n moves from largest to smallest.

The Lorenz curve plots the series of cumulative weights. It starts at 0 and increases in a concave fashion until it reaches 1. If all assets have the same capitalization, it is a straight line.

Figure 15.3 shows Lorenz curves for the Frank Russell 1000 index, an equal-weighted portfolio, and a model portfolio designed (as we will describe below) to resemble the Frank Russell 1000 index.

One summary statistic for the Lorenz curve is the *Gini coefficient*, which is twice the area under the curve less the area under the equal-weighted curve. Gini coefficients must range between 0 (for equal-weighted benchmarks) and 1 (for single-asset benchmarks). So we can draw Lorenz curves for benchmarks with any arbitrary distribution of capitalization, and summarize any distribution with a Gini coefficient. To progress further, we must assume a specific form for the distribution of capitalization.

A Capitalization Model

We will assume that the distribution of capitalization is log-normal. Here is a one-parameter model that will produce such a distribution.

First, we order the N assets by capitalization, from largest ($n = 1$) to smallest ($n = N$). Define

$$p_n \equiv 1 - \left\{ \frac{1}{2 \cdot N} + \frac{n-1}{N} \right\} \tag{15.7}$$

These values look like probabilities. They start close to 1 and move toward 0 as the capitalization decreases. Next, we calculate a nor-

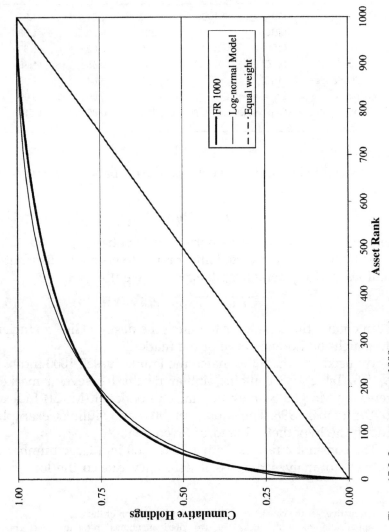

Figure 15.3 Lorenz curves: 1000 assets.

T A B L E 15.3

Country	Index	Assets	Gini	Constant c
U.S.	Frank Russell 1000	1000	0.71	1.55
U.S.	MSCI	381	0.66	1.38
U.K.	MSCI	135	0.63	1.30
Japan	MSCI	308	0.65	1.35
The Netherlands	MSCI	23	0.64	1.38
Freedonia	Equal weight	101	0.00	0.00
Freedonia	Cap weight	101	0.98	11.15

mally distributed quantity y_n such that the probability of observing y_n is p_n:

$$p_n = \Phi\{y_n\} \tag{15.8}$$

where $\Phi\{\ \}$ is the cumulative normal distribution.

So far, we have converted linear ranks to normally distributed quantities y_n. To generate capitalizations, we use

$$CAP_n = Exp\{c \cdot y_n\} \tag{15.9}$$

We can choose the constant c to match the desired Gini coefficient or to match the Lorenz curve of the market.[2]

We used this model to match the Frank Russell 1000 Index in Fig. 15.3. Table 15.3 contains similar results for several markets covered by Morgan Stanley Capital International (MSCI) Indexes as of September 1998. The equal-weighted and Gulliver examples reside in the hypothetical land of Freedonia.[3]

The constant c ranges from 1.30 to 1.60 in a large number of countries. To analyze the loss in efficiency due to the long-only

---

[2]As an alternative, set the constant c to the standard deviation of the log of the capitalization of all the stocks. The two criteria mentioned in the text place greater emphasis on fitting the larger-capitalization stocks.

[3]Freedonia appeared in the 1933 Marx Brothers movie *Duck Soup*. During a 1994 Balkan eruption, when asked if the United States should intervene in Freedonia, several U.S. congressmen laughed, several stated that it would require further study, and several more were in favor of intervention if Freedonia continued its policy of ethnic cleansing.

constraint, we will use the value 1.55. This stems from a feeling that the MSCI indices necessarily trim out a great many of the smaller stocks in a market. The Freedonia rows show an equal and a very unequal benchmark for comparison purposes.

Armed with this one-parameter model of the distribution of capitalization, we are ready to derive our rough estimates of the potential benefits of long/short investing.

An Estimate of the Benefits of Long/Short Investing

We cannot derive any analytical expression for the loss in efficiency due to the long-only constraint, since the problem contains an inequality constraint. But we can obtain a rough estimate of the magnitude of the impact with a computer simulation. As our previous simple analysis showed, the important variables in the simulation include the number of assets and the desired level of active risk. We considered 50, 100, 250, 500, and 1000 assets, with desired risk levels* from 1 to 8 percent by 1 percent increments, and from there to 20 percent by 2 percent increments.

For each of the 5 levels of assets and the 14 desired risk levels, we solved 900 randomly generated long-only optimizations. For each case, we assumed uncorrelated residual returns, identical residual risks of 25 percent, a full investment constraint, and an information ratio of 1.5. We ignored transactions costs and all other constraints. We generated alphas using

$$\alpha_n = \omega \cdot \left(\frac{IR}{\sqrt{N}}\right) \cdot z_n \qquad (15.10)$$

Figure 15.4 shows the active efficient frontier: the alpha per unit of active risk.

We can roughly estimate the efficient frontiers in Fig. 15.4 as

$$\alpha(\omega,N) = 100 \cdot IR \cdot \left\{ \frac{\{1 + \omega/100\}^{1 - \gamma(N)} - 1}{1 - \gamma(N)} \right\} \qquad (15.11)$$

---

[4]We used Eq. (15.4) to convert desired risk levels to risk aversions. We required extremely high levels of *desired* risk, since the long-only constraint severely hampers our ability to take risks.

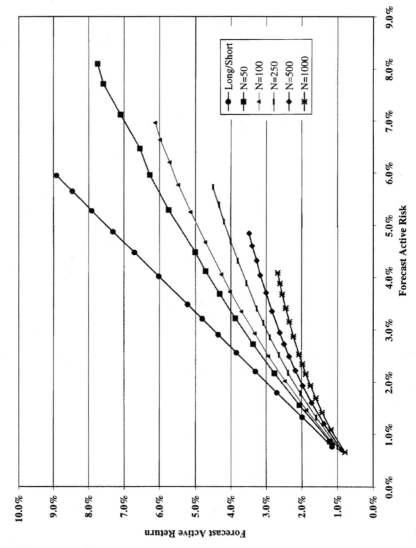

Figure 15.4

where $\qquad\qquad \gamma(N) = \{53 + N\}^{0.57} \qquad\qquad$ (15.12)

and, as elsewhere in the book, we measure α and ω in percent.

As anticipated, with the information ratio held constant, long-only implementations become less and less effective, the greater the number of assets. We can also see that higher desired active risk lowers efficiency. In fact, we can define an information ratio (and information coefficient) *shrinkage factor* as

$$\text{Shinkage} = \left[\frac{\alpha(\omega,N)/\omega}{\text{IR}}\right] \qquad (15.13)$$

$$= \left(\frac{100}{\omega}\right) \cdot \left\{\frac{\{1 + \omega/100\}^{1 - \gamma(N)} - 1}{1 - \gamma(N)}\right\}$$

Figure 15.5 illustrates the dependence of shrinkage on risk and the number of assets. For typical U.S. equity strategies—500 assets and 4.5 percent risk—the shrinkage is 49 percent according to Eq. (15.13),

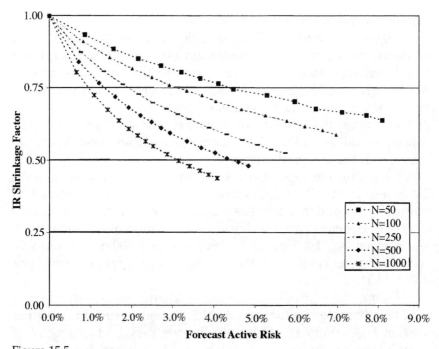

Figure 15.5

which agrees with Fig. 15.5. The long-only constraint has enormous impact: It cuts information ratios for typical strategies in half!

Equation (15.13) also allows us to quantify the appeal of enhanced indexing strategies, i.e., low-active-risk strategies. The shrinkage factor is 71 percent for a long-only strategy following 500 assets with only 2 percent active risk. At this lower level of risk, we lose only 29 percent of our original information ratio.

At high levels of active risk, long/short implementations can have a significant advantage over long-only implementations. At low levels of active risk, this advantage disappears. And, given the higher implementation costs of long/short strategies (e.g. the uptick rule, costs of borrowing), at very low levels of active risk, long-only implementations may offer an advantage.

With a large number of assets and the long-only constraint, it is difficult to achieve higher levels of active risk. Using Eq. (15.11), we can derive an empirical analog of Eq. (15.4):

$$\lambda_R = \frac{IR}{2 \cdot \omega \cdot (1 + \omega/100)^\gamma} \tag{15.14}$$

See the technical appendix for details.

Figures 15.4 and 15.5 illustrate efficient frontiers under several assumptions: an inherent information ratio of 1.5, a log-normal size distribution constant $c = 1.55$, and identical and uncorrelated residual risks of 25 percent. We have analyzed the sensitivities of the empirical results to these assumptions.

Changing the inherent information ratio does not affect our conclusions at all. As Eq. (15.11) implies, the efficient frontier simply scales with the information ratio.

Changing the log-normal size distribution constant through the range from 1.2 to 1.6, a wider range than we observed in examining several markets, has a very minor impact. Lower coefficients are closer to equal weighting, so the long-only constraint is less restrictive. At 4.5 percent active risk and 500 assets, though, as we vary this coefficient, the shrinkage factor ranges only from 0.49 to 0.51.

Figure 15.6 shows how our results change with asset residual risk. Our base-case assumption of 25 percent is very close to the median U.S. equity residual risk. But we may be focusing on a more narrow universe. As asset residual risk increases, we can achieve more risk with smaller active positions, making the long-

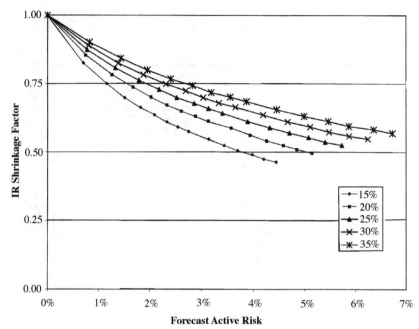

Figure 15.6 Sensitivity to asset residual risk.

only constraint less binding. At the extremely low level of 15 percent, the long-only constraint has very high impact. In the more reasonable range of 20 to 35 percent, the shrinkage factor at 4.5 percent risk and 250 assets ranges from 65 to 54 percent.

We can also analyze the assumption that every asset has equal residual risk. Given an average residual risk of 25 percent, and assuming 500 assets, we analyzed possible correlations between size (as measured by the log of capitalization) and the log of residual risk. We expect a negative correlation: Larger stocks tend to exhibit lower residual risk. Looking at large U.S. equities (the BARRA HICAP universe of roughly the largest 1200 stocks), this correlation has varied from roughly −0.51 to −0.57 over the past 25 years.

Figure 15.7 shows the frontier as we vary that correlation from 0 to −0.6. With a correlation of 0, we found a shrinkage factor of 49 percent at 4.5 percent active risk. With a correlation of −0.6, the situation improves, to a shrinkage factor of 0.63.

Finally, Fig. 15.8 displays the size bias that we anticipated. Figure 15.8 shows the result for various correlations between size and the log of residual risk, though the correlation does not signifi-

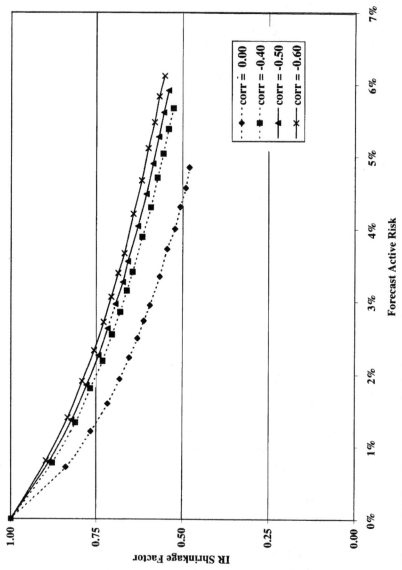

Figure 15.7 Sensitivity to size/volatility correlations.

436

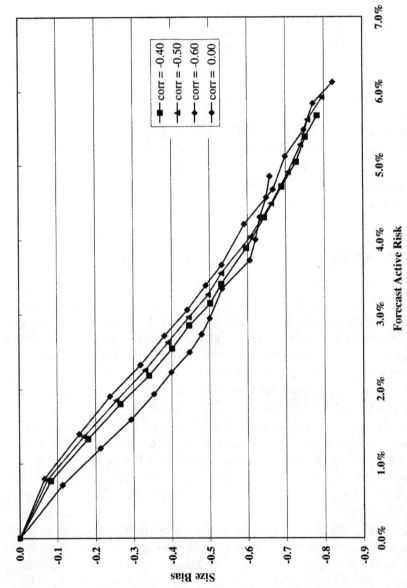

Figure 15.8 Size bias sensitivity to size/volatility correlations.

cantly change the result. We have measured size as log of capitalization, standardized to mean 0 and standard deviation 1. So an active size exposure of -0.3 means that the active portfolio has an average size exposure 0.3 standard deviation below the benchmark.

These size biases are significant. Figure 15.8 implies that a typical manager following 500 stocks and targeting 4.5 percent risk will exhibit a size exposure of -0.65. In the United States, from October 1997 through September 1998, the size factor in the BARRA U.S. equity model exhibited a return of 1.5 percent: Large stocks outperformed small stocks. This would have generated a 98-basis-point loss, just due to this incidental size bet. From September 1988 through September 1998, the same size factor experienced a cumulative gain of 3.61 percent, generating a loss of 2.35 percent over that 10-year period.

THE APPEAL OF LONG/SHORT INVESTING

Who should offer long/short strategies? Who should invest in them? Clearly, long/short strategies are a "pure" active management bet. The consensus expected return to long/short strategies is zero, since they have betas of zero. Put another way, the consensus investor does not invest in long/short strategies. Therefore, the most skillful active managers should offer long/short strategies. It allows them the freedom to implement their superior information most efficiently.

Long/short strategies offer no way to hide behind a benchmark. A long-only manager delivering 15 percent while the benchmark delivers 20 percent is arguably in a better position than a long/short manager losing 5 percent. While this isn't an intrinsic benefit of long-only strategies, it can be a practical benefit for investment managers.

Long/short strategies also offer investment managers the freedom to trade only on their superior information. They can build a long/short market-neutral portfolio using only utility stocks, if that is where they add value. They have no reason to buy stocks just because they are benchmark members. Both the long and the short sides of the portfolio may have large active risk relative to the S&P 500—just not to each other.

For investors, long/short strategies offer the most benefit to those investors who are best able to identify skillful managers. Given that, long/short strategies are quite appealing because of the (engineered) low correlation with equity market benchmarks. Long/short strategies can, in this way, successfully compete against bonds.

Long/short investing also offers the appeal of easy alpha portability. Futures contracts can move active return from one benchmark to another. If we start with a strategy managed relative to the S&P 500, and sell S&P 500 futures and buy FTSE 100 futures, we will transfer the alpha to the FTSE 100. In a conventional long-only strategy, this transfer requires an extra effort. It is not the natural thing to do. A long/short strategy places the notion of a portable alpha on center stage. With a long/short strategy, we start with the pure active return, and must chose a benchmark. The potential for transfer is thrust upon us.

Finally, long/short investing offers the possibility of more targeted active management fees. Long-only portfolios contain, to a large extent, the benchmark stocks. Long-only investors pay active fees for that passive core.[5] Long/short investors pay explicitly for the active holdings.

EMPIRICAL OBSERVATIONS

Here we wish to present preliminary observations on long/short strategies. These strategies do not have a sufficiently long track record to definitively compare their performance to that of long-only strategies. But we can begin to understand especially their risk profile, and observe at least initially their performance record.

These results are based on the performance of 14 U.S. long/short strategies with histories of varying lengths, but all in the 1990s, ending in March 1998.[6] These 14 strategies are those of large, sophisticated quantitative managers. Most of these managers are

---

[5]See Freeman (1997).
[6]See Kahn and Rudd (1998).

T A B L E   15.4

Percentile	History (Months)	Volatility	Beta	S&P 500 Correlation	IR
90	96	10.90%	0.10	0.23	1.45
75	86	6.22%	0.06	0.15	1.23
50	72	5.50%	0.02	0.04	1.00
25	50	4.12%	−0.03	−0.07	0.69
10	28	3.62%	−0.16	−0.20	0.44

BARRA clients. Table 15.4 shows the relevant observations. It is important to keep in mind the small and potentially nonrepresentative sample behind these data.

First, note that the risk levels here do not substantially differ from the typical active risk levels displayed in Table 5.8.[7] So, at least based on these 14 sophisticated implementations, long/short strategies do not exhibit substantially higher levels of risk than long-only strategies.

Second, according to Table 15.4, these strategies achieved market neutrality. They exhibit realized betas and market correlations very close to zero. In fact, the highest observed correlations corresponded to managers with the shortest track records. There is no statistical evidence that any of these strategies had true betas different from zero, and the realized numbers are all quite small. This (admittedly limited) sample refutes the argument that achieving market neutrality is difficult.

Third, at least in this historical period, these long/short strategies *as a group* exhibited remarkable performance. The performance results of 14 strategies over a particular market period do not prove that long/short implementations will boost information ratios, but they do help explain the increasing popularity of these strategies.

---

[7]The standard error of the mean risk level for these long/short strategies is 0.64 percent. So while the medians displayed here exceed those in Table 5.8, the difference is not significant at the 95 percent confidence level.

SUMMARY

Long/short investing is an increasingly popular approach to implementing active strategies. Long/short strategies offer the potential to more efficiently implement superior information. Because the long-only constraint is an inequality constraint, and because its impact depends on the distribution of benchmark holdings, we cannot derive many detailed analytical results on exact differences in efficiency. However, both simple models and detailed simulations show that the benefits of long/short investing can be significant, particularly when the universe of assets is large, the assets' volatility is low, and the strategy has high active risk.

From the opposite perspective, long-only managers should understand the surprising and significant impact of the long-only constraint on their portfolios. Among the surprises: This constraint induces a significant negative size bias, and it constrains long positions.

Empirical observations on long/short investing are preliminary, but should certainly inspire further interest and investigation.

NOTES

The debate over long/short investing has been contentious, and even acrimonious. In part, the controversy arose because the initial arguments in favor of long/short investing relied on diversification, as we discussed first. That simple argument is misleading in several ways.

The first serious criticism of long/short investing was by Michaud (1993). From there the debate moved to Arnott and Leinweber (1994), Michaud (1994), Jacobs and Levy (1995), and a conference of the Institute for Quantitative Research in Finance (the "Q Group"), "Long/Short Strategies in Equity and Fixed Income," at La Quinta, California, in October 1995. Jacobs and Levy (1996), Freeman (1997), Jacobs, Levy, and Starer (1998), and Levin (1998) have subsequently published further detailed analyses of aspects of long/short investing.

More recent work has looked at how long/short strategies fit into overall pension plans [Brush (1997)] and the performance of long/short managers [Kahn and Rudd (1998)].

PROBLEMS

1. Jill manages a long-only technology sector fund. Joe manages a risk-controlled, broadly diversified core equity fund. Both have information ratios of 0.5. Which would experience a larger boost in information ratio by implementing his or her strategy as a long/short portfolio? Under what circumstances would Jill come out ahead? What about Joe?

2. You have a strategy with an information ratio of 0.5, following 250 stocks. You invest long-only, with active risk of 4 percent. Approximately what alpha should you expect? Convert this to the shrinkage in skill (measured by the information coefficient) induced by the long-only constraint.

3. How could you mitigate the negative size bias induced by the long-only constraint?

REFERENCES

Arnott, Robert D., and David J. Leinweber. "Long-Short Strategies Reassessed." *Financial Analysts Journal,* vol. 50, no. 5, 1994, pp. 76–78.

Brush, John S. "Comparisons and Combinations of Long and Long/Short Strategies." *Financial Analysts Journal,* vol. 53, no. 3, 1997, pp. 81–89.

Dadachanji, Naozer. "Market Neutral Long/Short Strategies: The Perception versus the Reality." Presentation at the Q-Group Conference, La Quinta, Calif, October 1995.

Freeman, John D. "Investment Deadweight and the Advantages of Long/Short Portfolio Management." *VBA Journal,* September 1997, pp. 11–14.

Jacobs, Bruce I. "The Long and Short on Long/Short." *Journal of Investing,* vol. 6, no. 1, Spring 1997, Presentation at the Q-Group Conference, La Quinta, Calif, October 1995.

Jacobs, Bruce I., and Kenneth N. Levy. "More on Long-Short Strategies." *Financial Analysts Journal,* vol. 51, no. 2, 1995, pp. 88–90.

———. "20 Myths about Long-Short." *Financial Analysts Journal,* vol. 52, no. 5, 1996, pp. 81–85.

Jacobs, Bruce I., Kenneth N. Levy, and David Starer. "On the Optimality of Long-Short Strategies." *Financial Analysts Journal,* vol. 54, no. 2, 1998, pp. 40–51.

Kahn, Ronald N., and Andrew Rudd. "What's the Market for Market Neutral?" *BARRA Preprint,* June 1998.

Levin, Asriel. "Long/Short Investing—Who, Why, and How." In *Enhanced Index Strategies for the Multi-Manager Portfolio,* edited by Brian Bruce (New York: Institutional Investor, Inc., 1998).

Michaud, Richard O. "Are Long-Short Equity Strategies Superior?" *Financial Analysts Journal*, vol. 49, no. 6, 1993, pp.44–49. Presentation at the Q-Group Conference, La Quinta, Calif, October 1995.

Michaud, Richard O. "Reply to Arnott and Leinweber." *Financial Analysts Journal*, vol. 50, no. 5, 1994, pp. 78–80.

Pensions and Investments, May 18, 1998, and May 12, 1997, articles on market-neutral strategies.

TECHNICAL APPENDIX

We will present the derivation of Eq. (15.14), the risk aversion required to achieve a given level of risk.

We express utility in terms of risk as

$$U = \alpha(\omega) - \lambda_R \cdot \omega^2 \qquad (15A.1)$$

Using Eq. (15.11), this becomes

$$U = 100 \cdot IR \cdot \left\{ \frac{\{1 + \omega/100\}^{1 - \gamma(N)} - 1}{1 - \gamma(N)} \right\} - \lambda_R \cdot \omega^2 \qquad (15A.2)$$

We solve for the optimal level of risk by taking the derivative of U with respect to ω and setting the result equal to zero. We find

$$IR \cdot \left\{ 1 + \frac{\omega}{100} \right\}^{-\gamma(N)} = 2 \cdot \lambda_R \cdot \omega \qquad (15A.3)$$

This leads directly to Eq. (15.14).

Transactions Costs, Turnover, and Trading

INTRODUCTION

Transactions costs, turnover, and trading are the details involved in moving your current portfolio to your target portfolio.[1] These details are important. Studies show that, on average, active U.S. equity managers underperform the S&P 500 by 1 to 2 percent per year,[2] and, as Jack Treynor has argued, that average underperformance can only be due to transactions costs. Given that typical institutional managers seek to add only 2 to 3 percent active return (and charge ~0.5 percent for the effort), this is a significant obstacle.

Transactions costs often appear to be unimportant. Who cares about a 1 or 2 or even 5 percent cost if you expect the stock to double? Unfortunately, expectations are often wrong. At the end of the year, your performance is the net result of your winners and losers. But winner or loser, you still pay transactions costs. They can be the investment management version of death by a thousand cuts. A top-quartile manager with an information ratio of 0.5 may lose roughly half her returns because of transactions costs. They are important.

---

[1] In fact, they should influence your choice of target portfolio.

[2] A 1992 study by Lakonishok, Shleifer, and Vishny measured equal-weighted underperformance of 1.3 percent and capitalization-weighted underperformance of 2.6 percent relative to the S&P 500 for 341 U.S. equity managers over the period 1983 through 1989. A 1995 study by Malkiel looked at active equity mutual funds from 1982 to 1991. Interestingly, the naïve analysis showed an average underperformance relative to the S&P 500 of only 43 basis points, but after accounting for survivorship bias (including funds which existed but disappeared prior to 1991), the average underperformance increased to 1.83 percent.

Chapter 14 dealt with transactions costs as an input to the portfolio construction exercise. Now we will deal with transactions costs and turnover more broadly (how they arise), more concretely (how to estimate them), and more strategically (how to reduce these costs while preserving as much of the strategy's value added as possible). We will attack the strategic issue in two ways: reducing transactions costs by reducing turnover while retaining as much of the value added as possible, and reducing transactions costs through optimal trading.

Basic insights we will cover in this chapter include the following:

- Transactions costs increase with trade size and the desire for quick execution, which help to identify the manager as an informed trader and require increased inventory risk by the liquidity supplier.
- Transactions costs are difficult to measure. At the same time, accurate estimates of transactions costs, especially distinctions in transactions costs among different stock trades, can significantly affect realized value added.
- Transactions costs lower value added, but you can often achieve at least 75 percent of the value added with only half the turnover (and half the transactions costs). You can do better by distinguishing stocks by their transactions costs.
- Trading is itself a portfolio optimization problem, distinct from the portfolio construction problem. Optimal trading can lower transactions costs, though at the expense of additional short-term risk.
- There are several options for trade implementation, with rules of thumb on which to use when.

Turnover occurs whenever we construct or rebalance a portfolio, motivated by new information (new alphas) or risk control. Transactions costs are the penalty we pay for transacting. Transactions costs have several components: commissions, the bid/ask spread, market impact, and opportunity cost. Commissions are the charge per share paid to the broker for executing the trade. These tend to be the smallest component of the transactions costs, and the easiest to measure. The bid/ask (or bid/offer) spread is the difference between the highest bid and the lowest offer for the stock; it measures the loss from buying a share of stock (at the offer) and then immediately selling it (at the bid). The bid/ask spread is approximately the cost of trading one share of stock.[3]

Market impact is the cost of trading additional shares of stock.[4] To buy one share of stock, you need only pay the offer price. To buy 100,000 shares of stock, you may have to pay much more than the offer price. The 100,000-share price must be discovered through trading. It is not known a priori. Market impact is hard to measure because it is the cost of trading many shares relative to the cost of trading one share, and you cannot run a controlled experiment and trade both many shares and one share under identical conditions. Market impact is the financial analog of the Heisenberg uncertainty principle. Every trade alters the market.

MARKET MICROSTRUCTURE

The field of market microstructure studies the details of how markets work and transactions occur, in order to understand transactions costs, especially bid/ask spreads and market impact. This is a field of current active research that as yet lacks a single complete and widely accepted model. There is no CAPM or Black-Scholes model of trading. However, there are at least two ideas from this field that can illuminate the source of transactions costs.

When a portfolio manager trades, he or she must go to the marketplace to find someone to trade with. That other person, possibly a specialist on the New York Stock Exchange or a market maker on NASDAQ, will trade ("provide liquidity"), but for a price. Often this liquidity supplier's only business is providing short-term liquidity, i.e., he or she is not a long-term investor in the market.

Several considerations determine what price the liquidity supplier will charge (and *can* charge—after all, providing liquidity is a competitive business). First, the liquidity supplier would like to know why the manager is trading. In particular, does the manager

---

[3]You can never be certain of this cost until you actually trade.
[4]Some authors include the bid/ask spread in market impact, given that it is a market phenomenon (as opposed to commissions and taxes).

possess any unique nonpublic information that will soon change the stock price? Is the manager an "informed trader"? If so, the liquidity supplier would want to trade at the price the stock will reach once the information is public. Typically, though, the liquidity supplier can't tell if the manager has valuable information, has worthless information, or is trading only for risk control purposes. He or she can only guess at the value of the manager's information by the volume and urgency of the proposed trade. The larger and more urgent the trade, the more likely it is that the manager is informed, and the higher the price concession the liquidity supplier will demand. Market impact increases with trading volume.

A second consideration influencing transactions costs is inventory risk. Even without informed traders, market impact would still exist. Liquidity suppliers have no intention of holding positions in inventory for long periods of time. When the liquidity supplier trades, her or his goal is to hold the position in inventory only until an opposing trade comes along. Every minute before that opposing trade appears adds to the risk. The liquidity supplier has a risk/return trade-off, and will demand a price concession (return) to compensate for this inventory risk. The calculation of this risk involves several factors, but certainly the larger the trade size, the longer the period that the position is expected to remain in inventory, and hence the larger the inventory risk and the larger the market impact. Market impact increases with trading volume.

The theory of market microstructure can provide basic insights into the sources of transactions costs. The details of how these influences combine to produce the costs observed or inferred in actual markets is still under investigation and is beyond the scope of this book. However, we will utilize some of these basic insights throughout the chapter.

ANALYZING AND ESTIMATING TRANSACTIONS COSTS

Analyzing and estimating transactions costs is both difficult and important. Market impact is especially difficult to estimate because, as we have discussed, it is so difficult to measure.

Estimating transactions costs is important because accurate estimates can significantly affect realized value added, by helping the manager choose which stocks to trade when constraining turnover, and by helping him or her decide when to trade when scheduling trades to limit market impact.

This endeavor is sufficiently important that analytics vendors like BARRA and several broker/dealers now provide transactions cost estimation services.

Ideally, we would like to estimate expected transactions costs for each stock based on the manager's style and possible range of trade volumes. The theory of market microstructure says that transactions costs can depend on manager style, principally because of differences in trading speed. Managers who trade more aggressively (more quickly) should experience higher transactions costs.

Wayne Wagner (1993) has documented this effect, and illustrated the connection between information and transactions costs, by plotting transactions costs versus short-term return (gross of transactions costs) for a set of 20 managers. The most aggressive information trader was able to realize very large short-term returns, but they were offset by very large transactions costs. The slowest traders often even experienced negative short-term returns, but with small or even negative transactions costs. (To achieve negative transactions costs, they provided liquidity to others.)

Estimation of expected transactions costs requires measurement and analysis of past transactions costs. The best place to start is with the manager's past record of transactions and the powerful "implementation shortfall" approach to measuring the overall cost of trading.[5] The idea is to compare the returns to a paper portfolio with the returns to the actual portfolio. The paper portfolio is the manager's desired portfolio, executed as soon as he or she has devised it, without any transactions costs. Differences in returns to these two portfolios will arise as a result of commissions, the bid/ask spread, and market impact, as well as the opportunity costs of trades that were never executed. For example, some trades never execute because the trader keeps waiting for a good price while the stock keeps moving away. Wayne Wagner has estimated that such opportunity costs often dominate all transactions costs.

---

[5]Jack Treynor first suggested the approach, and Andre Perold later embellished it.

Many services that currently provide ex post transactions cost analysis do not use the implementation shortfall approach, because it involves considerable record keeping. They use simpler methods, such as comparing execution prices against the volume-weighted average price (VWAP) over the day. Such an approach measures market impact extremely crudely and misses opportunity costs completely. The method simply ignores trade orders that don't execute. And, as a performance benchmark, traders can easily game VWAP: They can arrange to look good by that measure.

The most difficult approach to transactions cost analysis is to directly research market tick-by-tick data. Both the previously described methods began with a particular manager's trades. When analyzing tick-by-tick data, we do not even know whether each trade was buyer- or seller-initiated. We must use rules to infer (inexactly) that information. For example, if a trade executes at the offer price or above, we might assume that it is buyer-initiated.

The tick-by-tick data are also full of surprising events—very large trades occurring with no price impact. But the record is never complete. Did the price move before the trade, in anticipation of its size? Did the trade of that size occur only because the trader knew beforehand that existing limit orders contained the necessary liquidity? Researchers refer to this as *censored*, or biased, data. The tick-by-tick data show trades, not orders placed, and certainly not orders not placed because the cost would be too high. Realized costs will underestimate expected costs.

There are several other problems with tick-by-tick trade data. The data set is enormous, generating significant data management challenges. But in spite of all these data, we only rarely observe some assets trading. These thinly traded assets are often the most costly to trade. So this record is missing information about the assets whose costs we often care about most.

Finally, tick-by-tick data are very noisy, because of discrete prices, nonsynchronous reporting of trades and quotes, and data errors.

All of these challenges affect not only the estimation of market impact but also the testing of models forecasting market impact. Clearly, building an accurate, industrial-strength transactions cost model is a very significant undertaking.

One approach to transactions costs which has proven fruitful, models costs based on inventory risk. The inventory risk model estimates market impact based on a liquidity supplier's risk of facilitating the trade. Here heuristically is how that works. First, given a proposed trade of size V_{trade}, the estimated time before a sufficient number of opposing trades appears in the market to clear out the liquidity supplier's net inventory in the stock is

$$\tau_{clear} \propto \frac{V_{trade}}{\overline{V}_{daily}} \tag{16.1}$$

where $\overline{V}_{daily}$ is the average daily volume (or forecast daily volume) in the stock. Equation (16.1) states that if you want to trade one day's volume, the liquidity supplier's estimated time to clear will be on the order of one day, and so on.

This time to clear implies an inventory risk, based on the stock's volatility:

$$\sigma_{inventory} = \sigma \cdot \sqrt{\frac{\tau_{clear}}{250}} \tag{16.2}$$

where Eq. (16.2) converts the stock's annual volatility σ to a volatility over the appropriate horizon. Equation (16.2) assumes that we measure τ_{clear} in days, and that a year contains 250 trading days.

The final step in the model assumes that the liquidity supplier demands a return (price concession or market impact) proportional to this inventory risk:

$$\frac{\Delta P}{P} = c \cdot \sigma_{inventory} \tag{16.3}$$

where c is the risk/return trade-off, and we measure return relative to the bid price for a seller-initiated trade and relative to the offer for a buyer-initiated trade. Since there exists some competition between liquidity suppliers, the market will help set the constant c.

For a seller-initiated trade, the transactions cost will include not only the price concession from the offer to the bid, but an additional concession below the bid price, depending on the size of the trade. The argument for the buyer-initiated trade is similar.

Combining Eqs. (16.1) through (16.3), adding commissions, and converting to units of return, leads to

$$\text{Cost} = \text{commisson} + \left(\frac{\text{bid / ask spread}}{\text{price}}\right) + c_{\text{tc}} \cdot \sqrt{\frac{V_{\text{trade}}}{V_{\text{daily}}}} \quad (16.4)$$

where c_{tc} includes the stock's volatility, a risk/return trade-off, and the conversion from annual to daily units.

In general, this approach and Eq. (16.4) are consistent with a trading rule of thumb that it costs roughly one day's volatility to trade one day's volume. This rule of thumb implies that $c_{\text{tc}} \sim O\{\sigma/\sqrt{250}\}$.

One consequence of this inventory risk approach is that market impact should increase as the square root of the amount traded. This agrees remarkably well with the empirical work of Loeb (1983)].[6] Because the total trading cost depends on the cost per share times the number of shares traded, it increases as the 3/2 power of the amount traded.

Loeb, a passive manager at Wells Fargo Investment Advisors, collected bids on different size blocks of stock. Figure 16.1 displays his results against a square root function. His observed dependence of cost on trade size clearly follows the square root pattern (plus fixed costs at low volume).

There are several ways to forecast transactions costs, starting with Eq. (16.4). A simple approach is to choose c_{tc} such that trades of typical size experience about 2 percent round-trip transactions costs, or to develop a better estimate based on analysis of the manager's past transactions. If your optimizer requires that transactions costs be expressed as a piecewise linear or quadratic function of trade size, then approximate Eq. (16.4) appropriately, in the region of expected trade sizes.

But the above approach leaves much on the table. This inventory risk approach can support more elaborate structural models,

---

[6]Researchers at BARRA, especially Nicolo Torre and Mark Ferrari, are responsible for identifying the square root dependence of the Loeb data. They have also used empirical methods to find the best-fitting exponent (square root corresponds to 1/2) in the dependence of market impact on trade volume. The square root provides the best fit. See BARRA (1997) for details.

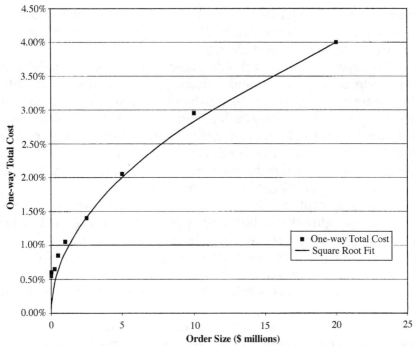

Figure 16.1

which can provide more dynamic and accurate estimates.[7] They can also provide more industrial-strength estimates: As we have seen, pure empirical approaches face many problems as a result of poor data quality; poor coverage, especially of illiquid and new assets; and poor timeliness. A structural attack can separate out easier-to-measure elements, facilitate extensions to all assets, benefit from cross-sectional estimation, impose reasonable behavior, and generally limit problems.

The inventory risk approach suggests a certain structure. It depends on a forecast of inventory risk and an estimate of the liquidity supplier's charge per unit of risk.

Chapter 3 presented structural models of risk. A structural model of inventory risk involves an estimate of asset risk and also estimates of the time to clear. To estimate both these quantities, the

---

[7]See BARRA (1997).

market impact model developed by BARRA relies on submodels to estimate asset volatility, trading volume and intensity (trade size and trade frequency), and elasticity.

By separating out each component, the BARRA model can apply appropriate insight and technology. We may have difficulty discerning patterns within the tick-by-tick market impact data. But we can apply our previous understanding of structural risk models to estimate asset risk. We can apply insights into trading volume and intensity which often hold across most stocks. For example, all stock trading exhibits higher volume at the open and close, and low volume in the vicinity of certain holidays.

Elasticity captures the dependence of buy versus sell orders on price. Imagine that a liquidity supplier fills a large sell order and demands a price concession. The trade price moves below the bid, and the supplier's inventory now has a positive position. But the low price will attract other buyers. Elasticity measures how the number of buyers versus sellers changes as we move away from an equilibrium price.

The BARRA market impact model uses the distribution of trade frequency, trade size, and elasticity to estimate time to clear, given any particular desired trade size. This time to clear, combined with estimated risk, leads to the inventory risk forecast. The final step uses a liquidity supplier's price of risk to convert inventory risk into an expected price concession. The BARRA model estimates this price of risk separately for buy orders and sell orders, and for exchange-traded and over-the-counter stocks.

As well as developing their model, BARRA researchers have also developed latent-variables methods for testing the accuracy of such models, given the problems with tick-by-tick data. For details, see BARRA (1997).

TURNOVER, TRANSACTIONS COSTS, AND VALUE ADDED

We now wish to go beyond the simple observation that transactions costs drag down performance, to see how much value added we can retain if we limit a strategy's turnover. We've all heard about the extremely promising strategy that unfortunately requires 80 percent turnover per month. Don't dismiss that policy out of hand. We may be able to add considerable value with the strategy if we restrict turnover to 40 percent, 20 percent, or even 10 percent per month.

We shall build a simple framework for analyzing the effects of transactions costs and turnover to help us understand the trade-off between value added and turnover. This framework will provide a lower bound on the amount of value added achievable with limited turnover, and also clarify the link between transactions costs and turnover. It will also provide a powerful argument for the importance of accurately distinguishing stocks based on their transactions costs.

For any portfolio P, consider value added

$$VA_P = \alpha_P - \lambda_A \cdot \psi_P^2 \qquad (16.5)$$

where ψ_P is the portfolio's active risk relative to the benchmark B. The manager starts with an initial portfolio I that has value added VA_I. We will limit the portfolios that we can choose to a choice set[8] CS. Portfolio Q is the portfolio in CS with the highest possible value added. We will assume for now that portfolio I is also in CS, but later relax that assumption. The increase in value added as we move from portfolio I to portfolio Q is

$$\Delta VA_Q = VA_Q - VA_I \qquad (16.6)$$

Now let TO_P represent the amount of turnover needed to move from portfolio I to portfolio P. As a preliminary, let us define turnover, since there are several possible choices. If $\mathbf{h}_P$ is the initial portfolio and $\mathbf{h}_P^*$ is the revised portfolio, then the purchase turnover is

$$TO_P = \sum_n \text{Max}\{0, h_{P,n}^* - h_{P,n}\} \qquad (16.7)$$

and the sales turnover is

$$TO_S = \sum_n \text{Max}\{0, h_{P,n} - h_{P,n}^*\} \qquad (16.8)$$

These purchase and sales turnover statistics do not include changes

---

[8]We are allowing for constraints that limit our choices, such as full investment in risky assets, portfolio beta equal to 1, no short sales, etc. The choice set CS is restricted to be closed and convex. We will consider two cases explicitly: CS defined by equality constraints and CS defined by inequality constraints.

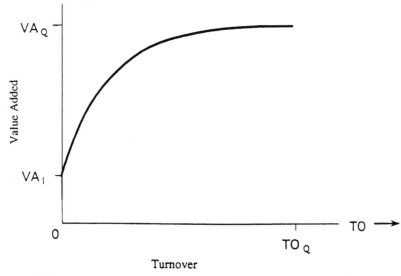

Figure 16.2

in cash position. One reasonable definition of turnover, which we will adopt, is

$$TO = Min\{TO_P, TO_S\} \qquad (16.9)$$

Turnover is the minimum of purchase and sales turnover. With no change in cash position, purchase turnover will equal sales turnover. This turnover definition accommodates contributions and withdrawals by not including them in the turnover formula.

The turnover required to move from portfolio I to portfolio Q is TO_Q. If we restrict turnover to be less than TO_Q, we will be giving up some value added in order to reduce cost. Let VA(TO) be the maximum amount of value added if turnover is less than or equal to TO. Figure 16.2 shows a typical situation. The frontier VA(TO) increases from VA_I to VA_Q. The concave[9] shape of the curve

---

[9]The concavity of VA(TO) follows from the value added function's being concave in the holdings h_P, the turnover function's being convex in h_P, and the choice set CS's being convex. The fact that VA(TO) is nondecreasing follows from common sense; i.e., a larger amount of turnover will let you do at least as well. The frontier will be made up of quadratic segments (piecewise quadratic) when the choice set is described by linear inequalities.

indicates a decreasing marginal return for each additional amount of turnover that we allow.

A Lower Bound

As the technical appendix will show in detail, when we assume that CS is defined by linear equality constraints (e.g., constraining the level of cash or the portfolio beta to equal specific targets) and includes portfolio I, we can obtain a quadratic *lower* bound on potential value added:

$$\text{VA(TO)} \geq \text{VA}_I + \Delta\text{VA}_Q \cdot \left[2 \cdot \left(\frac{\text{TO}}{\text{TO}_Q}\right) - \left(\frac{\text{TO}}{\text{TO}_Q}\right)^2 \right] \qquad (16.10)$$

Underlying this result is a very simple strategy, prorating a fraction TO/TO_Q of each trade needed to move from the initial portfolio I to the optimal portfolio Q. This strategy leads to a portfolio that is in CS, has turnover equal to TO, and meets the lower bound in Eq. (16.10).

We can express the sentiment of Eq. (16.10) in the value added/turnover rule of thumb:

> **You can achieve at least 75 percent of the (incremental) value added with 50 percent of the turnover.**

This result sounds even better in terms of an effective information ratio, since the value added is proportional to the square of the information ratio (at optimality). It implies that a strategy can retain at least 87 percent of its information ratio with half the turnover.[10]

The Value of Scheduling Trades

We can exceed the lower bound in Eq. (16.10) by judicious scheduling of trades, executing the most attractive opportunities first. For example, suppose there are only four assets. As we move from portfolio I to portfolio Q, we purchase 10 percent in assets 1 and

---

[10]The implication is loose for two reasons. First, we derived the relationship between value added and information ratio at optimality, assuming no constraints (e.g., on turnover). Second, in this chapter we have derived a relationship between turnover and *incremental* value added.

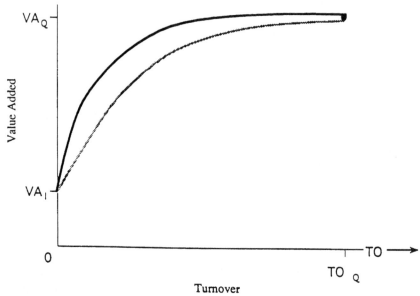

Figure 16.3

2 and sell 10 percent of our holdings in assets 3 and 4. Turnover is 20 percent. Suppose the alphas for the four assets are 5 percent, 3 percent, −3 percent, and −5 percent, respectively. Then buying 1 and selling 4 has a bigger impact on alpha than swapping 2 for 3. If we have restricted turnover to 10 percent, we could make an 8 percent trade of stock 1 for stock 4 and a 2 percent trade of 2 for 3 rather than doing 5 percent in each trade.

Figure 16.3 illustrates the situation. The solid line shows the frontier; the dotted line shows the lower bound. The maximum opportunity for exceeding the bound occurs for turnover somewhere between 0 and 100 percent of TO_Q.

Transactions Costs

The simplest assumption we can make about transactions costs is that round-trip costs are the same for all assets. Let TC be that level of costs. We wish to choose a portfolio P in CS that will maximize

$$VA_P - TC \cdot TO \tag{16.11}$$

Figure 16.4 illustrates the solution to this problem. Let SLOPE(TO) represent the slope of the value-added/turnover frontier when the

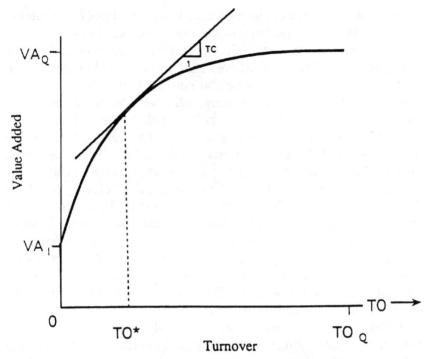

Figure 16.4

level of turnover is TO. Since the frontier is increasing and concave, SLOPE(TO) is positive and decreasing. The incremental gain from each additional amount of turnover is decreasing, so the slope of the frontier SLOPE(TO) will decrease to zero as TO increases to TO_Q. SLOPE(TO) represents the marginal gain in value added from additional transactions, and TC represents the marginal cost of additional transactions. The optimal level of turnover will occur where marginal cost equals marginal value added, i.e., where SLOPE(TO*) = TC.

As long as the transactions cost is positive and less than SLOPE(0), we can find a level of turnover TO* such that SLOPE(TO*) = TC. If TC > SLOPE(0), it is not worthwhile to transact at all, and the best solution is to stick with portfolio I.

Implied Transactions Costs

The slope of the value-added/turnover frontier can be interpreted as a transactions cost. We can reverse the logic and link any level of turnover to a transactions cost; e.g., a turnover level of 20 percent corresponds to a round-trip transactions cost of 2.46 percent.

Transactions costs contain observable components, such as commissions and spreads, as well as the unobservable market impact. Because managers cannot be sure that they have a precise measure of transactions costs, they will often seek to control those costs by establishing an ad hoc policy such as "no more than 20 percent turnover per quarter." The insight that relates the slope of the value-added/turnover frontier to the level of transactions costs provides an opportunity to analyze that cost control policy. One can fix the level of turnover at the required level TO_R and then find the slope, $SLOPE(TO_R)$, of the frontier at TO_R. Our ad hoc policy is consistent with an assumption that the general level of round-trip transactions costs is equal to $SLOPE(TO_R)$. If we have a notion that round-trip costs are around 2 percent, and we find that $SLOPE(TO_R)$ is about 4.5 percent, then something is awry. We can make three possible adjustments to get things back into harmony. One, we can increase our estimate of the round-trip costs from 2 percent. Two, we can increase the allowed level of turnover TO_R, since we are giving up more marginal value added (4.5 percent) than it is costing us to trade (2.0 percent). Three, we can reduce our estimates of our ability to add value by scaling our alphas back toward zero. A combination of these adjustments—a little give from all sides—would be fine as well. This type of analysis serves as a reality check on our policy and the overall investment process.

An Example

Consider the following example, using the S&P 100 stocks as a starting universe and the S&P 100 as the benchmark. We generated alphas[11] for the 100 stocks, centering and scaling so that they were benchmark-neutral, and also so that portfolio Q would have an alpha of 3.2 percent and an active risk of 4 percent when we used $\lambda_A = 0.1$. The initial portfolio contained 20 randomly chosen stocks, equal-weighted, with an alpha of 0.07 percent and an active risk of 5.29 percent, typical of a situation when a manager takes over an existing account.

---

[11]We produced 100 samples from the standard normal distribution.

T A B L E   16.1

Percentage of TO$_Q$	Value Added			Percentage of VA$_Q$	Implied Transactions Cost
	Lower Bound	Excess	Total		
0.0	−2.73	0.00	−2.73	0.0%	
10.0	−1.91	0.87	−1.03	39.2%	8.66%
20.0	−1.17	1.00	−0.18	59.0%	5.12%
30.0	−0.52	0.88	0.36	71.4%	3.40%
40.0	0.04	0.70	0.74	80.2%	2.50%
50.0	0.52	0.51	1.03	86.8%	1.90%
60.0	0.91	0.34	1.24	91.8%	1.43%
70.0	1.21	0.19	1.40	95.5%	1.02%
80.0	1.43	0.09	1.51	98.0%	0.67%
90.0	1.56	0.02	1.58	99.5%	0.33%
100.0	1.60	0.00	1.60	100.0%	0.00%

Table 16.1 displays the results, including the value added separated into two parts: the lower bound and the excess above the bound. The excess is the benefit we get from scheduling the best trades first. Table 16.1 also displays the implied transactions costs. We see that reasonable levels of round-trip costs (about 2 percent) do not call for large amounts of turnover, and that very low or high restrictions on turnover correspond to unrealistic levels of transactions costs.

Note that the value of being able to pick off the best trades (the difference between the lower bound and the actual fraction of value added) is largest when turnover is 20 percent of the level required to move to portfolio Q. In this case, the rule of thumb is conservative: We achieve 87 percent of the value-added for 50 percent of the turnover.[12]

---

[12]It is possible to make up a two-stock example where the lower bound on the frontier would be exact. Common sense indicates that with more stocks and a reasonable distribution of alphas, there is considerable room to add value by plucking the best opportunities.

Generalizing the Result

We made three assumptions in deriving these results: (1) the initial portfolio was in CS, (2) CS was described by linear equalities, and (3) all round-trip transactions costs are the same. We will reconsider these in turn.

If portfolio I is not in the choice set, then we can think of the portfolio construction problem as being a two-step process. In step 1, we find the portfolio J in the choice set such that the turnover in moving from portfolio I to portfolio J is minimal. The value added in moving[13] from portfolio I to portfolio J is not a consideration, so we may have $VA_I \geq VA_J$ or $VA_I < VA_J$. The turnover required to move from I to J is TO_J. The lower bound in Eq. (16.10) will still apply, although we start from portfolio J rather than portfolio I.

This situation can demonstrate the costs of adding constraints. What if portfolio I were not in CS, and we were limiting turnover to 10 percent per month? If the first 4 percent of the turnover is required to move the portfolio back into the choice set, then we have only 6 percent to take advantage of our new alphas.

If the choice set CS is described by inequality constraints, such as a restriction on short selling and upper limits on the individual asset holdings, then the analysis becomes more complicated. However, the value-added/turnover frontier VA(TO) will have the same increasing and concave slope that we see in Fig. 16.2. There will be a quadratic lower bound on VA(TO); however, that lower bound[14] is not as strong as the lower bound we obtain in the case with only equality constraints. You are not guaranteed three-quarters of the value added for one-half the turnover. Nevertheless, in our experience, 75 percent is still a reasonable lower bound.

So far, we have made the assumption that all round-trip transactions costs are the same. It is *good news* for the portfolio manager if the transactions costs differ (and she or he can forecast the difference). Recall that the difference between the lower bound and the value-added/turnover frontier stemmed from our ability to

---

[13]In a formal sense we are defining $VA_P = \alpha_P - \lambda_A \cdot \psi_P^2$ if $P \in$ CS and $VA_P = -\infty$ if $P \in$
     CS. This means that VA(TO) $= -\infty$ if TO $<$ TO_J.
[14]See the appendix for justification.

adroitly schedule the most value-enhancing trades first. Our ability to discriminate adds value. Differences in transactions costs further enhance our ability to discriminate.

We have analyzed this effect in our example. We began with the implied transactions costs at 1.90 percent for 50 percent of TO_Q. We then set the transactions costs to 75 percent of that, or 1.42 percent, for half of the stocks, and raised the transactions costs for the other stocks to 2.26 percent, so that transactions costs remained constant at 50 percent of TO_Q. Taking into account these differing costs when optimizing barely affected portfolio alphas or risk, but did reduce transactions costs by about 30 percent.

> **Accurate forecasts of the cost of trading can generate significant savings when used as part of the portfolio rebalancing process.**

The better our model of transactions costs, the better our ability to discriminate among stocks. In the example above, we distinguished stocks by their linear costs. More elaborate models can distinguish them on the basis of more accurate, dynamic, and non-linear costs.

Clearly we have seen promise in the approach of lowering transactions costs by lowering turnover while retaining much of the value added. Naïve versions of this can preserve 75 percent of the value added with 50 percent of the turnover, and clever versions, utilizing differences in asset alphas and asset transactions costs, can well exceed the naïve result. We now move on to a second approach to reducing transactions costs: optimal trading.

TRADING AS A PORTFOLIO OPTIMIZATION PROBLEM

Trading is a portfolio optimization problem, but not the portfolio construction problem we have discussed at length. Imagine that you have already completed the portfolio construction (or rebalancing) problem. You own a current portfolio, and you desire the output from the portfolio construction problem. You trade to move from your current portfolio to your desired portfolio. Scheduling these trades—what stock to trade first, second, etc.—over an allowed trading period is a portfolio optimization problem. The goal is to maximize trading utility:

$$\text{Utility} = \alpha_{\text{short}} - \lambda_S \cdot \psi_{\text{short}}^2 - \text{MI} \qquad (16.12)$$

defined as short-term alpha minus a short-term risk adjustment, minus market impact. This trading utility function swaps reduced market impact for increased short-term risk. We distinguish short-term alphas and risk from investment-horizon alphas and risk (discussed elsewhere in this book), because stock returns over hourly or daily horizons often behave quite differently from stock returns over monthly or quarterly horizons.

In portfolio construction, the goal is a target portfolio. In trading, the goal is a set of intermediate portfolios held at different times, starting with the current portfolio now, and ending with the target portfolio a short time later.

The benchmark for trading is immediate execution, and we measure return and risk relative to that benchmark in Eq. (16.12). The problem with quick execution, as discussed earlier, is that it increases market impact. Market impact costs increase with trade volume and speed.

What's the intuition about how risk, market impact, and alphas will affect trade scheduling? Risk considerations should keep the trade schedule close to the benchmark, i.e., push for quick execution. Market-impact considerations will tend to lead to even spacing of trades. Alphas will push for early or late execution.

An Example

The details of how to implement this optimal trading process—for example, how to model market impact as a function of how fast you trade—are beyond both the scope of this book and the state of the art of the investment management industry. However, it's useful to present a very simple example of the idea. Even this simple example, though, involves sophisticated mathematics that is relegated to the technical appendix.

Consider the trading process at its most basic: You have cash, and you want to buy one stock. You think the stock will go up. You want to buy soon, before the stock rises. But to avoid market impact, you are willing to be patient and assume some risk of missing the stock rise. What is your optimal trading strategy?

Here are the details. Start with cash amount M. After T days, you want to be fully invested in stock S, with expected return f and risk σ. The benchmark is immediate execution.

We need to quantify the return, risk, and transactions costs for the implemented portfolio relative to the benchmark. For this simple example, we can completely characterize the implemented portfolio at time t by the fractional holding of the stock $h(t)$. Assume that you can trade at any time and at any speed, so long as you are fully invested by day T. We then seek the optimal $h(t)$ at each time over the next T days. The cash position of the implemented portfolio is simply $1 - h(t)$. The active portfolio stock position relative to the benchmark is $h(t) - 1$, since the benchmark is fully invested. The implemented portfolio will have $h(0) = 0$ and $h(T) = 1$. Initially the portfolio is entirely cash, and at the end of T days the portfolio is fully invested in stock S.

Over the next T days, the cumulative portfolio active return will be

$$\alpha_{\text{short}} = \int_0^T dt\{ f \cdot [h(t) - 1]\} \tag{16.13}$$

This integrates (or sums up) the active return over each small period dt to calculate the total active return over the period of T days.

Similarly, the cumulative active risk of the implemented portfolio will be

$$\psi_{\text{short}}^2 = \int_0^T dt\{\sigma^2 \cdot [h(t) - 1]^2\} \tag{16.14}$$

Once again, this cumulative active risk integrates (or sums up) active risk contributions over each period dt of the full T-day trading period. This active risk involves the active portfolio position and the stock return risk.

Finally, we must treat cumulative transactions costs. For the example, we will focus specifically on market impact, the only interesting transactions costs in terms of influence on trading strategy.[15] We will model the cumulative active market impact as

$$\text{MI} = \int_0^T dt\{c \cdot \dot{h}^2(t)\} \tag{16.15}$$

with

$$\dot{h}(t) \equiv \frac{dh(t)}{dt} \tag{16.16}$$

Equation (16.15) models market impact as simply proportional to the square of the stock accumulation rate. The faster the portfolio holding changes, the larger the market impact.

This simple model ignores any memory effects—a big assumption, but only if trades are a significant fraction of daily volume. According to this, the market doesn't remember what you traded yesterday, it just sees what you are trading this instant. Still, the total market impact over the T-day trading period is the integral (or sum) of the market impact over each subperiod dt.

The technical appendix describes how to analytically solve for the $h(t)$ which maximizes Eq. (16.12). Here we will illustrate a graphical solution for different parameter choices. Three different elements influence the solution: return, risk, and market impact. We are looking at short horizons, and typically the risk and market impact components will dominate the expected returns components.[16] Assuming that the expected return is small, we still have two distinct cases: risk aversion dominates market impact, and market impact dominates risk. Figure 16.5 illustrates these two cases, using $T = 5$ days. When market impact dominates risk aversion, the optimal schedule is to evenly space trades, even though the benchmark is immediate execution. When risk dominates market impact, the optimal schedule will closely track the immediate execution benchmark. Within two days (40 percent of the period), the portfolio's stock position reaches 75 percent of its target.

---

[15]We can include other transactions costs (commissions and taxes) in our forecasts of stock returns, but they will not influence our trade schedule, since they are the same, no matter what the schedule.

[16]Risk scales with the square root of time, while expected return scales linearly with time. As the period shrinks, risk will increasingly dominate return.

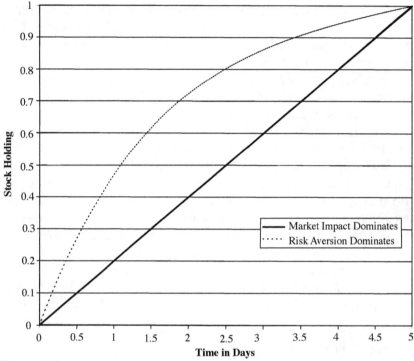

Figure 16.5

TRADE IMPLEMENTATION

After devising a trading strategy, either through the optimization described above or through some more ad hoc approach, the next step is actual trading. You can implement trades as market orders or as limit orders.[17]

Market orders are orders to trade a certain volume at the current market's best price. Limit orders are orders to trade a certain volume at a certain price. Limit orders trade off price impact against certainty of execution. Market orders can significantly move prices, but they will execute. Limit orders will execute at the limit price, *if* they execute (they may not).

---

[17]The choices for trade implementation are actually much more numerous. They include crossing networks, alternative stock exchanges, and principal bid transactions. Treatment of these alternatives lies beyond the scope of this book.

There is a current debate over the value of using limit orders in trading. Many argue that placing limit orders provides free options to the marketplace. For example, placing a limit order to buy at a price P constitutes offering to buy the stock at P, even if the stock is rapidly moving to 80 percent of P. Your only protection is the ability to cancel the order as the price begins to move.

Trading portfolios of limit orders has additional problems. For example, in a large market move, all the sell limit orders may execute while none of the buy orders execute. This will add market risk to the portfolio.

Given these concerns about limit orders, plus the typical portfolio manager's eagerness to complete the trades (implement the new alphas), the general rule is to use limit orders sparingly, mainly for the stocks with the highest anticipated market impact, and with limit prices set very close to the existing market prices.

The opposite side of the debate is that limit orders let value managers sell liquidity and earn the liquidity provider's profit. The appropriate order type may depend on the manager's style.

SUMMARY

We have discussed transactions costs, turnover, and trading, with a strategic focus on reducing the impact of transactions costs on performance. After discussing the origins of transactions costs and how they rise with trade volume and urgency, we focused on the question of analyzing and estimating transactions costs. This is difficult because measuring transactions costs is difficult, but it can significantly affect realized value added, as the rest of the chapter discussed. The most accurate analysis of transactions costs uses the implementation shortfall: comparing the actual portfolio with a paper portfolio implemented with no transactions costs.

We discussed the inventory risk approach to modeling market impact. This leads to behavior matching market observations, especially the dependence of price impact on the square root of volume traded. It also leads to practical forecasts of market impact, ranging from the fairly simple to the more complex structural market impact models.

One approach to reducing transactions costs is to reduce turnover while retaining value added. We developed a lower bound on value added as a function of turnover, and verified the rule of thumb that restricting turnover to one-half the level of turnover if there is no restriction on turnover will result in at least three-quarters of the value added. We can exceed that bound through our ability to skim off the most valuable trades first, and by accounting for differences in transactions costs between stocks. We also saw that the slope of the value-added/turnover frontier implies a level of round-trip transactions costs.

We then looked at the trading process directly, to see that trading itself is a portfolio optimization problem, distinct from portfolio construction. Optimal trading can reduce transactions costs, trading reduced market impact for additional short-term risk. Choices for trade implementation include market orders and limit orders. The disadvantages of limit orders make them most appropriate for the highest market impact stocks, with limit prices close to market prices.

PROBLEMS

1. Imagine that you are a stock trader, and that a portfolio manager plans to measure your trading prowess by comparing your execution prices with volume-weighted average prices. How would you attempt to look as good as possible by this measure? Would this always coincide with the best interests of the manager?

2. Why is it more difficult to beat the bound in Eq. (16.10) with a portfolio of only 2 stocks than with a portfolio of 100 stocks?

3. A strategy can achieve 200 basis points of value added with 200 percent annual turnover. How much value-added should it achieve with 100 percent annual turnover? How much turnover is required in order to achieve 100 basis points of value added?

4. How would the presence of memory effects in market impact change the trade optimization results displayed in Fig. 16.5?

5. In Fig. 16.5, why does high risk aversion lead to quick trading?

REFERENCES

Angel, James J., Gary L. Gastineau, and Clifford J. Webber. "Reducing the Market Impact of Large Stock Trades." *Journal of Portfolio Management,* vol. 24, no. 1, 1997, pp. 69–76.

Atkins, Allen B., and Edward A. Dyl. "Transactions Costs and Holding Periods for Common Stocks." *Journal of Finance,* vol. 52, no. 1, 1997, pp. 309–325.

BARRA, *Market Impact Model Handbook* (Berkeley, Calif.: BARRA, 1997).

Chan, Louis K. C., and Josef Lakonishok. "The Behavior of Stock Prices around Institutional Trades." *Journal of Finance,* vol. 50, no. 4, 1995, pp. 1147–1174.

———. "Institutional Equity Trading Costs: NYSE versus NASDAQ." *Journal of Finance,* vol. 52, no. 2, 1997, pp. 713–735.

Ellis, Charles D. "The Loser's Game." *Financial Analysts Journal,* vol. 31, no. 4, 1975, pp. 19–26.

Grinold, Richard C., and Mark Stuckelman. "The Value-Added/Turnover Frontier." *Journal of Portfolio Management,* vol. 19, no. 4, 1993, pp. 8–17.

Handa, Puneet, and Robert A. Schwartz. "Limit Order Trading." *Journal of Finance,* vol. 51, no. 5, 1996, pp. 1835–1861.

Kahn, Ronald N. "How the Execution of Trades Is Best Operationalized." In *Execution Techniques, True Trading Costs, and the Microstructure of Markets,* edited by Katrina F. Sherrerd (Charlottesville, Va.: AIMR 1993).

Keim, Donald B., and Ananth Madhavan. "The Cost of Institutional Equity Trades." *Financial Analysts Journal,* vol. 54, no. 4, 1998, pp. 50–69.

Lakonishok, Josef, Andre Shleifer, and Robert W. Vishny. "Study of U.S. Equity Money Manager Performance." Brookings Institute Study, 1992.

Loeb, Thomas F. "Trading Costs: The Critical Link between Investment Information and Results." *Financial Analysts Journal,* vol. 39, no. 3, 1983, pp. 39–44.

Malkiel, Burton. "Returns from Investing in Equity Mutual Funds 1971 to 1991." *Journal of Finance,* vol. 50, no. 2, 1995, pp. 549–572.

Modest, David. "What Have We Learned about Trading Costs? An Empirical Retrospective." Berkeley Program in Finance Seminar, March 1993.

Perold, Andre. "The Implementation Shortfall: Paper versus Reality." *Journal of Portfolio Management,* vol 14, no. 3, 1988, pp. 4–9.

Pogue, G. A. "An Extension of the Markowitz Portfolio Selection Model to Include Variable Transactions Costs, Short Sales, Leverage Policies and Taxes." *Journal of Finance,* vol. 45, no. 5, 1970, pp. 1005–1027.

Rudd, Andrew, and Barr Rosenberg.. "Realistic Portfolio Optimization." In *Portfolio Theory—Studies in Management Science,* vol. 11, edited by E. J. Elton and M. J. Gruber (Amsterdam: North Holland Press, 1979).

Schreiner, J. "Portfolio Revision: A Turnover-Constrained Approach." *Financial Management,* vol. 9, no. 1, 1980, pp. 67–75.

Treynor, Jack L. "The Only Game in Town." *Financial Analysts Journal,* vol. 27, no. 2, 1971, pp. 12–22.

———. "Types and Motivations of Market Participants." In *Execution Techniques, True Trading Costs, and the Microstructure of Markets,* edited by Katrina F. Sherrerd (Charlottesville, Va.: AIMR, 1993).

———. "The Invisible Costs of Trading." *Journal of Portfolio Management*, vol. 21, no. 1, 1994, pp. 71–78.

Wagner, Wayne H. (Ed.). *A Complete Guide to Securities Transactions: Controlling Costs and Enhancing Performance* (New York: Wiley, 1988).

———. "Defining and Measuring Trading Costs." In *Execution Techniques, True Trading Costs, and the Microstructure of Markets*, edited by Katrina F. Sherrerd (Charlottesville, Va.: AIMR, 1993).

Wagner, Wayne H., and Michael Banks. "Increasing Portfolio Effectiveness via Transaction Cost Management." *Journal of Portfolio Management*, vol. 19, no. 1, 1992, pp. 6–11.

Wagner, Wayne H., and Evan Schulman. "Passive Trading: Point and Counterpoint." *Journal of Portfolio Management*, vol. 20, no. 3, 1994, pp. 25–29.

TECHNICAL APPENDIX

This technical appendix will cover two topics: the bound on value added versus turnover, and the solution to the example trading optimization problem.

We begin by proving the bound on value added versus turnover for the cases of linear inequality and equality constraints. Eq. (16.10) corresponds exactly to the case of linear equality constraints.

Inequality Case, CS = $\{h | A \cdot h \leq b\}$

Portfolio Q is optimal for the problem Max$\{VA_P | h_P \in CS\}$. This means that we can find nonnegative Lagrange multipliers $\pi \geq 0$ such that

$$\alpha - 2 \cdot \lambda_A \cdot V \cdot (h_Q - h_B) - A^T \cdot \pi = 0 \qquad \pi \geq 0 \quad (16A.1)$$

and $$A \cdot h_Q \leq b \qquad \pi^T \cdot A \cdot h_Q = \pi^T \cdot b \qquad (16A.2)$$

Since $h_I \in CS$, we have $b - A \cdot h_I \geq 0$ and $\pi \geq 0$, so

$$\pi^T \cdot (b - A \cdot h_I) = \kappa \geq 0 \quad \text{or} \quad \pi^T \cdot A \cdot h_I = \pi^T \cdot b - \kappa \quad (16A.3)$$

If we premultiply Eq. (16A.1) by $(h_I - h_Q)$ and use Eqs. (16A.2) and (16A.3), we find that

$$-2 \cdot \lambda_A \cdot (h_I^T - h_Q^T) \cdot V \cdot (h_Q - h_B) = \alpha_Q - \alpha_I - \kappa \quad (16A.4)$$

Now consider the family of solutions as we move directly from portfolio I to portfolio Q:

$$\mathbf{h} = \mathbf{h}_I + \delta \cdot (\mathbf{h}_Q - \mathbf{h}_I) = \mathbf{h}_Q + (1 - \delta) \cdot (\mathbf{h}_I - \mathbf{h}_Q) \quad (16A.5)$$
$$= \mathbf{h}_Q - (1 - \delta) \cdot \mathbf{h}_T$$

where we have introduced the trade portfolio $\mathbf{h}_T$. These solutions are all in CS as long as $0 \le \delta \le 1$. The solutions have value added

$$\begin{aligned} \text{VA}\{\delta\} = \ & \alpha_Q + (1 - \delta) \cdot (\alpha_I - \alpha_Q) \\ & - \lambda_A \cdot [\psi_Q^2 + 2 \cdot (1 - \delta) \cdot (\mathbf{h}_I^T \\ & - \mathbf{h}_Q^T) \cdot \mathbf{V} \cdot (\mathbf{h}_Q^T - \mathbf{h}_B^T) + (1 - \delta)^2 \cdot \sigma_T^2] \end{aligned} \quad (16A.6)$$

where σ_T is the risk of $\mathbf{h}_T$. If we use Eq. (16A.4), then Eq. (16A.6) simplifies to

$$\text{VA}\{\delta\} = \text{VA}_Q - (1 - \delta) \cdot \kappa - \lambda_A \cdot (1 - \delta)^2 \cdot \sigma_T^2 \quad (16A.7)$$

Since $\text{VA}(0) = \text{VA}_I$, $\text{VA}(1) = \text{VA}_Q$, and $\Delta\text{VA}_Q = \text{VA}_Q - \text{VA}_I$, we have

$$\kappa = \Delta\text{VA}_Q - \lambda_A \cdot \sigma_T^2 \ge 0 \quad (16A.8)$$

Thus Eq. (16A.7) simplifies further to

$$\text{VA}\{\delta\} = \text{VA}_I + \Delta\text{VA}_Q \cdot (2 \cdot a \cdot \delta - b \cdot \delta^2) \quad (16A.9)$$

where
$$a = \frac{\lambda_A \cdot \sigma_T^2 + \kappa/2}{\lambda_A \cdot \sigma_T^2 + \kappa} \le 1 \quad (16A.10)$$

and
$$b = \frac{\lambda_A \cdot \sigma_T^2}{\lambda_A \cdot \sigma_T^2 + \kappa} \le a \le 1 \quad (16A.11)$$

The slope of $\text{VA}(\delta)$, Eq. (16A.9), is $2 \cdot \Delta\text{VA}_Q \cdot (a - b \cdot \delta)$, which is positive for $0 \le \delta < 1$ and decreases to κ as δ approaches 1.

Equality Case, CS = {h|A · h = b}

The analysis is as before, except that π in Eq. (16A.1) is unrestricted in sign. Therefore $\kappa = 0$ and, from Eq. (16A.8), $\Delta\text{VA}_Q = \lambda_A \cdot \sigma_T^2$. Thus Eq. (16A.9) simplifies to

$$\text{VA}\{\delta\} = \text{VA}_I + \Delta\text{VA}_Q \cdot [2 \cdot \delta - \delta^2] \quad (16A.12)$$

Trade Optimization

We will now describe how to solve analytically for the trading strategy $h(t)$ which maximizes utility in the simple example

$$\text{Utility} = \alpha_{\text{short}} - \lambda_S \cdot \psi^2_{\text{short}} - \text{MI} \tag{16A.13}$$

Schematically, we can represent the utility as

$$U = \int_0^T dt \cdot u(h,\dot{h}) \tag{16A.14}$$

At the optimal solution, the variation of this utility will be zero:

$$\delta U = \int_0^T dt \cdot \left\{ \frac{\partial u}{\partial h} \delta h + \frac{\partial u}{\partial \dot{h}} \delta \dot{h} \right\} = 0 \tag{16A.15}$$

Integrating the second term by parts (and remembering that the variation is zero at the fixed endpoints of the integral),

$$\delta U = \int_0^T dt \cdot \left\{ \frac{\partial u}{\partial h} - \frac{d}{dt}\left(\frac{\partial u}{\partial \dot{h}}\right) \right\} \delta h = 0 \tag{16A.16}$$

Thus we can maximize U by choosing $h(t)$ which satisfies

$$\frac{\partial u}{\partial h} - \frac{d}{dt}\left(\frac{\partial u}{\partial \dot{h}}\right) = 0 \tag{16A.17}$$

Applying this to the particular utility function [Eq. (16A.13)], the portfolio holding must satisfy the second-order ordinary differential equation

$$f - 2 \cdot \lambda_S \cdot \sigma^2 \cdot (h - 1) + 2 \cdot c \cdot \ddot{h} = 0 \tag{16A.18}$$

plus the boundary conditions $h(0) = 0$ and $h(T) = 1$. Defining relative parameters

$$s \equiv \frac{f}{2 \cdot c} \tag{16A.19}$$

$$g^2 \equiv \frac{\lambda_S \cdot \sigma^2}{c} \tag{16A.20}$$

and rearranging terms, Eq. (16A.18) becomes

$$\ddot{h} - g^2 \cdot h = -s - g^2 \tag{16A.21}$$

Applying standard mathematical techniques to Eq. (16A.21), we find that the optimal solution $h(t)$ is

$$h(t) = \left\{ \frac{-\dfrac{s}{g^2} + (1 + s/g^2) \cdot \cosh(g \cdot T)}{\sinh(g \cdot T)} \right\} \cdot \sinh(g \cdot t) \tag{16A.22}$$

$$- \left(1 + \frac{s}{g^2}\right) \cdot [\cosh(g \cdot t) - 1]$$

We can characterize various regimes for the solution $h(t)$ by looking at some dimensionless quantities which enter into the optimal $h(t)$:

$$(g \cdot T)^2 = \frac{\lambda_S \cdot \sigma^2 \cdot T^2}{c} \tag{16A.23}$$

R1. $(g \cdot T)^2 \gg 1$. Risk aversion dominates over market impact.
R2. $(g \cdot T)^2 \ll 1$. Market impact dominates over risk aversion.

$$s \cdot T^2 = \frac{f \cdot T^2}{2 \cdot c} \tag{16A.24}$$

R3. $s \cdot T^2 \gg 1$. Alpha is positive and dominant over market impact.
R4. $s \cdot T^2 \ll -1$. Alpha is negative and dominant over market impact.

$$\frac{s}{g^2} = \frac{f}{2 \cdot \lambda_S \cdot \sigma^2} \tag{16A.25}$$

R5. $|s/g^2| \gg 1$. Alpha (positive or negative) dominates risk aversion.
R6. $|s/g^2| \ll 1$. Risk aversion dominates over alpha.

If we assume that the alpha is zero, so that the coefficient $s = 0$ above, then it's interesting to see the limiting behavior of Eq. (16A.22) in regimes R1 and R2. When market impact dominates over risk, $h(t)$ follows a straight-line path from 0 to 1. The result is uniform trading. If, on the other hand, risk dominates over market impact, $h(t)$ exponentially approaches 1:

$$h(t) \rightarrow 1 - \text{Exp}\{-g \cdot t\} \qquad (16A.26)$$

Exercise

1. Assuming zero alpha, derive the limit of Eq. (16A.22) when market impact dominates over risk. Also show that in the limit that risk dominates over market impact, the optimal trade schedule reduces to an exponential, as in Eq. (16A.26).

Applications Exercises

Use alphas from a residual reversal model to build an optimal portfolio of MMI stocks. The initial portfolio is the MMI, and the benchmark is the CAPMMI. Use a risk aversion of 0.075 and the typical institutional constraints: full investment, no short sales.

1. What is the value added of the MMI? What is the value added of the optimal portfolio? What is the incremental value added?
2. What is the turnover in moving from the MMI to the optimal portfolio?
3. Now build a portfolio exactly halfway between the MMI and the optimal portfolio:

$$\mathbf{h}_P = \frac{\mathbf{h}_{\text{MMI}} + \mathbf{h}_{\text{optimal}}}{2}$$

   What is the turnover in moving from the MMI to this intermediate portfolio? What is its value added? Compare the incremental value added of this portfolio over the MMI to that of the optimal portfolio over the MMI. Verify Eq. (16.10).

CHAPTER 17

Performance Analysis

INTRODUCTION

Are you winning or losing? Why? Performance measurement will answer the first question and can help to answer the second. A sophisticated performance analysis system can provide valuable feedback for an active manager. The manager can tie his or her decisions to outcomes and identify success, failure, and possible improvements.

Performance analysis has evolved from the days when the performance goals were vague, if not primitive:

"Don't steal any money!"

"Don't lose any money!"

"Do a good job!"

"Do as well as I could at the bank!"

"Beat the market!"

"Justify your active management fee!"

The goal of performance analysis is to distinguish skilled from unskilled investment managers. Simple cross-sectional comparisons of returns can distinguish winners from losers. Time series analysis of the returns can start to separate skill from luck, by measuring return *and risk*. Time series analysis of returns and portfolio holdings can go the farthest toward analyzing where the manager has skill: what bets have paid off and what bets haven't. The manager's skill ex post should lie along dimensions promised ex ante.

The drive for sophisticated performance analysis systems has come from the owners of funds. Investment managers have, on the whole, fought an unsuccessful rear-guard action against the advance of performance analysis. This is understandable: The truly poor managers are afraid, the unlucky managers will be unjustly condemned, and the new managers have no track record. Only the skilled (or lucky) managers are enthusiastic.

Of course, these owners of funds make several key assumptions in using performance analysis: that skillful active management is possible; that skill is an inherent quality that persists over time; that statistically abnormal returns are a measure of skill; and that skillful managers identified in one period will show up as skillful in the next period. The evidence here is mixed, as we will discuss in this chapter and Chap. 20.

Performance analysis is useful not only for fund owners, but also for investment managers, who can use performance analysis to monitor and improve the investment process. The manager can make sure that the active positions in the portfolio are compensated, and that there have been no unnecessary risks in the portfolio.

Performance analysis can, ex post, help the manager avoid two major pitfalls in implementing an active strategy. The first is *incidental risk:* Managers may like growth stocks, for example, without being aware that growth stocks are concentrated in certain industry groups and concentrated in the group of stocks with higher volatility. The second pitfall is *incremental decision making.* A portfolio based on a sequence of individual asset decisions, each of them wise on the surface, can soon become much more risky than the portfolio manager intended. Risk analysis can diagnose these problems ex ante. Performance analysis can identify them ex post.

The lessons of this chapter are:

- The goal of performance analysis is to separate skill from luck. Cross-sectional comparisons are not up to this job.
- Returns-based performance analysis is the simplest method for analyzing both return and risk, and distinguishing skill from luck.
- Portfolio-based performance analysis is the most sophisticated approach to distinguishing skill and luck along many different dimensions.

- Performance analysis is most valuable to the sponsor (client) when there is an ex ante agreement on the manager's goals and an indication of how the manager intends to meet those goals.
- Performance analysis is valuable to the manager in that it lets the manager see which active management decisions are compensated and which are not.

SKILL AND LUCK

The fundamental goal of performance analysis is to separate skill from luck. But, how do you tell them apart? In a population of 1000 investment managers, about 5 percent, or 50, should have exceptional performance by chance alone. None of the successful managers will admit to being lucky; all of the unsuccessful managers will cite bad luck.

We present a facetious analysis of the market in Fig. 17.1. We have divided the managers along the dimensions of skill and luck. Those with both skill and luck are blessed. They deserve to thrive,

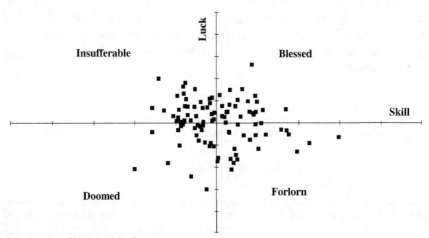

Figure 17.1 Skill and luck.

and they will. Those with neither skill nor luck are doomed. Natural selection is cruel but just. But what about the two other categories? Those managers with skill but no luck are forlorn. Their historical performance will not reflect their true skill. And, finally, there is the fourth category. These managers have luck without skill. We call them the insufferable. Most managers can easily think of someone else they believe is in this category.

Fortunately or unfortunately, we observe only the combination of skill and luck. Both the blessed and the insufferable will show up with positive return histories. The challenge is to separate the two groups.

The simple existence of positive returns does not prove skill. Almost half of all roulette players achieve positive returns each spin of the wheel, but over time they all lose. The existence of *very large* positive returns also does not prove skill. How much risk was taken on in generating that return? Performance analysis will involve comparing ex post returns to ex ante risk in a statistically rigorous way.

Chapter 12 included brief mentions of the standard error of the information ratio. The approximate result is

$$\text{SE\{IR\}} \approx \frac{1}{\sqrt{Y}} \tag{17.1}$$

where Y measures the number of *years* of observation.[1] The number of years enters because we define the information ratio as an annualized statistic. Equation (17.1) implies that to determine with 95 percent confidence (t statistic $= 2$) that a manager belongs in the top quartile (IR $= 0.5$) will require 16 years of observations.[2] It is a fact of investment management life that proof of investment prowess will remain elusive.

---

[1]This assumes that all the error arises from the estimated mean residual return. If we also account for the error arising from the estimated residual risk, we find

$$\text{SE\{IR\}} = \frac{1}{\sqrt{Y}} \cdot \sqrt{1 + \left(\frac{\text{IR}^2 \cdot \Delta t}{2}\right)}$$

where Δt is, e.g., $1/12$ if we observe monthly returns. See Problem 3 for more details.
[2]See Problem 4 for a discussion of why changing the information ratio from an annualized number to a monthly number does not improve our ability to statistically verify investment performance.

We can view the basic predicament from another angle. What if you are truly a top quartile manager, with an information ratio of 0.5? What is the probability that your monthly, quarterly, annual returns are positive? Figure 17.2 shows the result as the horizon varies. Over one month, you have only a 56% chance of positive realized alpha. Over a 5-year horizon, this rises to 87%. This implies that over the standard 5-year horizon, 13% of skilled managers will have negative realized alphas. Given the horizons for careers, and for ideas in the investment business, luck will always play a role.

The efficient markets hypothesis suggests that active managers have no skill. In its strong form, the hypothesis states that all currently known information is already reflected in security prices. Since all information is already in the prices, no additional information is available to active managers to use in generating exceptional returns. Active returns are completely random. The semistrong version states that all publicly available information is already reflected in security prices. Active management skill is really insider trading! The weak form of the hypothesis claims only that all previous price-based information is contained in current prices. This rules out technical analysis as skilled active management, but would allow for skillful active management based on fundamental and economic analysis.

There have also been many academic studies of active managers' performance. These studies have focused on three related questions:

- Does the average active manager outperform the benchmark?
- Do the top managers have skill?
- Does positive performance persist from period to period?

Chapter 20 will review these questions in more detail. The initial studies of mutual funds showed that the average manager underperformed the benchmark, in proportion to fund expenses, and that performance did not persist from period to period. Some recent studies have shown that the average manager matches the benchmark net of fees, that top managers do have statistically significant skill, and that positive performance may persist. Other studies have found no evidence for persistence of performance. The conclusion of all these conflicting studies is that even if performance does

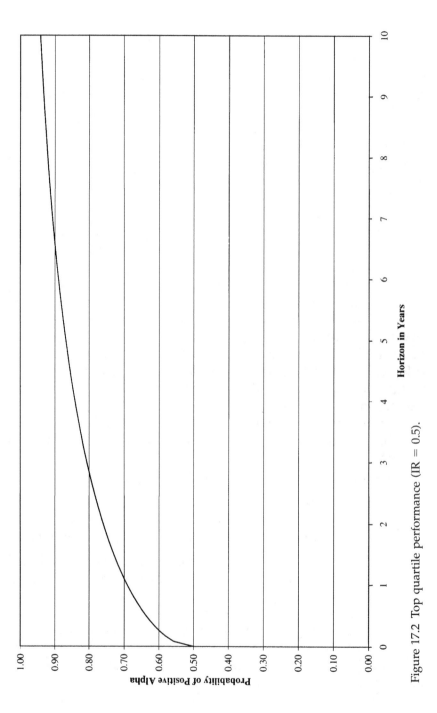

Figure 17.2 Top quartile performance (IR = 0.5).

persist, it certainly doesn't persist at any impressively high rate. Do 52 percent or 57 percent of winners repeat, and is this statistically significant?

DEFINING RETURNS

We begin our in-depth discussion of performance analysis by defining returns—this may seem obvious, but there are several definitions. Should we use compound returns or average returns, arithmetic returns or logarithmic returns? Compound returns have the benefit of providing an accurate measure of the value of the ending portfolio.[3] Arithmetic returns provide the benefit of using a linear model of returns across periods. We can see these points with an example. Let $R_P(t)$ be the portfolio's total return in period t, and let $R_B(t)$ and $R_F(t)$ be the total return on the benchmark and the risk-free asset. The compound total return on portfolio P over periods 1 through T, $R_P(1,T)$, is the product

$$R_P(1,T) = R_P(1) \cdot R_P(2) \cdot R_P(3) \cdots R_P(T) = \prod_{t=1}^{T} R_P(t) \quad (17.2)$$

The *geometric average return* for portfolio P, g_P, is the rate of return per period that would give the same cumulative return:

$$(1 + g_P)^T = \prod_{t=1}^{T} R_P(t) \quad (17.3)$$

The *average log return* z_P is

$$e^{z_P \cdot T} = \prod_{t=1}^{T} R_P(t) \quad (17.4)$$

or

$$z_P = \left(\frac{1}{T}\right) \cdot \sum_{t=1}^{T} \ln\{R_P(t)\} \quad (17.5)$$

---

[3]This is true unless the portfolio has experienced cash inflows and outflows. Even in that case, however, the industry standard approach to performance analysis is to equally weight each period's return, without accounting for differing portfolio values in different periods.

The geometric average return is compounded annually, while the average log return is compounded continuously. Finally, the (arithmetic) *average return a_P* is

$$1 + a_P = \left(\frac{1}{T}\right) \cdot \sum_{t=1}^{T} R_P(t) \qquad (17.6)$$

It is always[4] true that $z_P \leq g_P \leq a_P$. This does not necessarily say that one measure is better to use than the others. It does indicate that consistency is important, to make sure we are not comparing apples and oranges.

These issues become even more important when we attribute each period's return to different sources, and then aggregate all the sources over time. To cumulate returns, we need to account for cross products. We discuss one approach to this in the technical appendix.

CROSS-SECTIONAL COMPARISONS

The simplest type of performance analysis is a table that ranks active managers by the total performance of their fund over some period. Table 17.1 illustrates a typical table, showing median performance, key percentiles, and the performance of a diversified and widely followed index (the S&P 500), for a universe of institutional equity portfolios covered by the Plan Sponsor Network (PSN) over the period January 1988 through December 1992. These cross-sectional comparisons can provide a useful feel for the range of

---

[4]First, $z_P = \ln\{1 + g_P\} < g_P$ by the convexity of the logarithm function. We have a useful approximation $z_P = \ln\{1 + g_P\} \approx g_P - 0.5 \cdot g_P^2$. Again, by the convexity of the logarithm function,

$$\left(\frac{1}{T}\right) \cdot \sum_{t=1}^{T} \ln\{R_P(t)\} = \ln\{1 + g_P\}$$

$$\leq \ln\left\{\left(\frac{1}{T}\right) \cdot \sum_{t=1}^{T} R_P(t)\right\}$$

$$= \ln\{1 + a_P\}$$

so $g_P \leq a_P$. Finally, we have an approximation (exact for log normal) that $1 + a_P \approx \{1 + g_P\} \cdot \exp\{0.5 \cdot \sigma_P^2\}$, where σ_P^2 is the variance of $\ln\{R_P(t)\}$. This reduces to $a_P \approx g_P + 0.5 \cdot \sigma_P^2$.

T A B L E   17.1

Percentile	Annualized Return, 1988–1992
5th	23.57%
25th	18.97%
Median	16.31%
75th	14.50%
95th	10.92%
S&P 500	15.80%

performance numbers over a period; however, they have four drawbacks:

- They typically do not represent the complete population of institutional investment managers. Table 17.1 includes only those institutional equity portfolios that began no later than 1983, still existed in 1993, and are covered in the PSN database.
- These cross-sectional comparisons usually contain survivorship bias, which is increasingly severe the longer the horizon. Table 17.1 does not include firms that went out of business between 1983 and 1993.
- These cross-sectional comparisons ignore the fact that some of the reporting managers are managing $150 million portfolios, while others are managing $15 billion portfolios. The rule is one man, one vote—not one dollar, one vote.
- Cross-sectional comparisons do not adjust for risk. The top performer may have taken large risks and been lucky. We cannot untangle luck and skill in this comparison.

Figure 17.3 shows the impact of using a cross-sectional snapshot. Compare two managers, A and B. Over a 5-year period, Manager A has achieved a cumulative return 16 percent above the benchmark, while Manager B has outperformed by almost 20 percent. Based on this rather limited set of information, most people would prefer B to A, since B has clearly done better over the 5-year period.

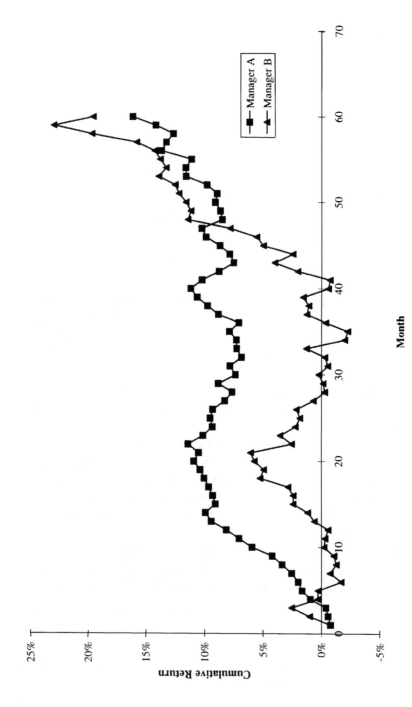

Figure 17.3 Cumulative return comparison.

Figure 17.3, however, shows the time paths that A and B followed over the 5-year period. After seeing Fig. 17.3, most observers prefer A to B, since A obviously incurred much less risk than B in getting to the current position.[5] If you had stopped the clock at most earlier times in the 5-year period, A would have been ahead.

Performance analysis must account for both return and risk.

RETURNS-BASED PERFORMANCE ANALYSIS: BASIC

The development of the CAPM and the notion of market efficiency in the 1960s encouraged academics to consider the problems of performance analysis. The CAPM maintained that consistent exceptional returns by one manager were unlikely. The academics devised tests to see if their theories were true, and the by-products of these tests are performance analysis techniques. These techniques analyze time series of returns. One approach, first proposed by Jensen (1968), separates returns into systematic and residual components, and then analyzes the statistical significance of the residual component. According to the CAPM, the residual return should be zero, and positive deviations from zero signify positive performance.

The CAPM also states that the market portfolio has the highest Sharpe ratio (ratio of excess return to risk), and Sharpe (1970) proposed performance analysis based on comparing Sharpe ratios. We will discuss the Jensen approach first, and then the Sharpe approach.

Returns Regression

Basic returns-based performance analysis according to Jensen involves regressing the time series of portfolio excess returns against benchmark excess returns, as discussed in Chap. 12.

---

[5]Manager A has realized an information ratio of 1.0 over this period, while Manager B has realized an information ratio of 0.7.

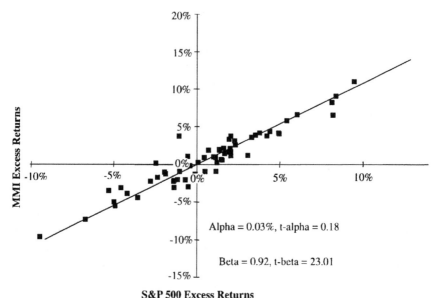

Figure 17.4 Returns regression.

Figure 17.4 shows the scatter diagram of excess returns to the Major Market Index portfolio and the S&P 500, together with a regression line, over the period from January 1988 through December 1992. The estimated coefficients in the regression are the portfolio's realized alpha and beta:

$$r_p(t) = \alpha_p + \beta_p \cdot r_B(t) + \epsilon_p(t) \tag{17.7}$$

Alpha appears in the diagram as the intercept of the regression line with the vertical axis. Beta is the slope of the regression line. For the above example, $\alpha_p = 0.03$ percent per month and $\beta_p = 0.92$. The regression divides the portfolio's excess return into the benchmark component, $\beta_p \cdot r_B(t)$, and the residual component, $\theta_p(t) = \alpha_p + \epsilon_p(t)$. Note that in this example, the residual return is quite different from the active return, because the active beta is -0.08. While the alpha is 3 basis points per month, the average active return is -4 basis points per month.

The CAPM suggests that alpha should be zero. The regression analysis provides us with confidence intervals for our estimates of alpha and beta. The t statistic for the alpha provides a rough test of the alpha's statistical significance. A rule of thumb is that a t statistic of 2 or more indicates that the performance of the portfolio is due to skill rather than luck. The probability of observing such a large alpha by chance is only 5 percent, assuming normal distributions.

The t statistic for the alpha is approximately

$$t_P \approx \left(\frac{\alpha_P}{\omega_P}\right) \cdot \sqrt{T} \qquad (17.8)$$

where α_P and ω_P are not annualized and T is the number of observations (periods). The t statistic measures whether α_P differs significantly from zero, and a significant t statistic requires a large α_P relative to its standard deviation, as well as many observations. For the example above, the t statistic for the estimated α_P is only 0.36, not statistically distinct from zero.

Chapter 12 has already discussed t statistics and their relation to information ratios and information coefficients. The t statistic measures the statistical significance of the return. The information ratio measures the ratio of annual return to risk, and is related to investment value added. Though closely related mathematically, they are fundamentally different quantities. The t statistic measures statistical significance and skill. The information ratio measures realized value added, whether it is statistically significant or not. While Jensen focused on alphas and t statistics, information ratios, given their relationship to value added, are also important for performance analysis.

The basic alternative to the Jensen approach is to compare Sharpe ratios for the portfolio and the benchmark. A portfolio with

$$\frac{\bar{r}_P}{\sigma_P} > \frac{\bar{r}_B}{\sigma_B} \qquad (17.9)$$

where $\bar{r}$ denotes mean excess return over the period, has demonstrated positive performance. Once again, we can analyze the statistical significance of this relationship. Assuming that the standard errors in our estimates of the mean returns $\bar{r}_P$ and $\bar{r}_B$ dominate the errors in our estimates of σ_P and σ_B, the standard error of each Sharpe ratio is approximately $1/\sqrt{N}$, where N is the number of observations. Hence a statistically significant (95 percent confidence level) demonstration of skill occurs when[6]

$$\left(\frac{\bar{r}_P}{\sigma_P} - \frac{\bar{r}_B}{\sigma_B}\right) > 2 \cdot \sqrt{\frac{2}{N}} \qquad (17.10)$$

Dybvig and Ross (1985) have shown[7] that superior performance according to Sharpe implies positive Jensen alphas, but that positive Jensen alphas do not imply positive performance according to Sharpe.

RETURNS-BASED PERFORMANCE ANALYSIS: ADVANCED

There are several refinements of the returns-only regression-based performance analysis. Some are statistical in nature. They refine the statistical tests. Examples of statistical refinements include Bayesian corrections and adjustments for heteroskedasticity and autocorrelations. Other refinements stem from financial theory. They attempt to extract additional information from the time series of returns. Examples of financial refinements include analyzing benchmark timing, using a priori betas, analyzing value added, controlling for public information, style analysis, and controlling for size and value. The last three refinements are controversial, in that they all argue that managers should receive credit only for returns beyond those available through various levels of public information. These proposals raise the bar on an already difficult enterprise.

Bayesian Correction

The first statistical refinement is a Bayesian correction. The Bayesian correction allows us to use our prior knowledge about the distribution of alphas and betas across managers. For example, imagine that we know that the prior distribution of monthly alphas has

---

[6] If the standard error of each term is $1/\sqrt{N}$, and the errors are uncorrelated, then the standard error of the difference is approximately $\sqrt{2/N}$.
[7] They provide analytic results and do not deal with issues of statistical significance.

mean 0 and standard deviation of 12.5 basis points per month. We then expect an alpha of 0, and would be "surprised" (a two-standard-deviation event) if the alpha were more than ± 3.00 percent per year (25 basis points per month). We can apply similar logic to the observed betas. The Bayesian analysis allows one to take this prior information into consideration in making judgments about the "true" values of α_P and β_P. For more information about this topic, see Vasicek (1973).

Heteroskedasticity

One of the assumptions underlying the regression model is that the error terms $\epsilon_P(t)$ have the same standard deviation for each t. We can employ various schemes to guard against failure of that assumption. We call this heteroskedasticity in the regression game.

Autocorrelation

A third statistical problem is autocorrelation. We assume that the error terms $\epsilon_P(t)$ are uncorrelated. If there is significant autocorrelation, then we can make an adjustment. This arises, for example, if we examine returns on overlapping periods.

Benchmark Timing

One financially based refinement to the regression model is a benchmark timing component. The expanded model is

$$r_P(t) = \alpha_P + \beta_P \cdot r_B(t) + \gamma_P \cdot \text{Max}\{0, r_B(t)\} + \epsilon_P(t) \qquad (17.11)$$

We include the variable γ_P to determine whether the manager has any benchmark timing skill. The model includes a "down-market" beta, β_P, and an "up-market" beta, $\beta_P + \gamma_P$. If γ_P is significantly positive, then we say that there is evidence of timing skill; benchmark exposure is significantly different in up and down cases. Figure 17.5 indicates how β_P, α_P, and γ_P relate to performance.

In our example of the Major Market Index portfolio versus the S&P 500 portfolio, not surprisingly, there is no evidence of benchmark timing ability. Over the period from January 1988

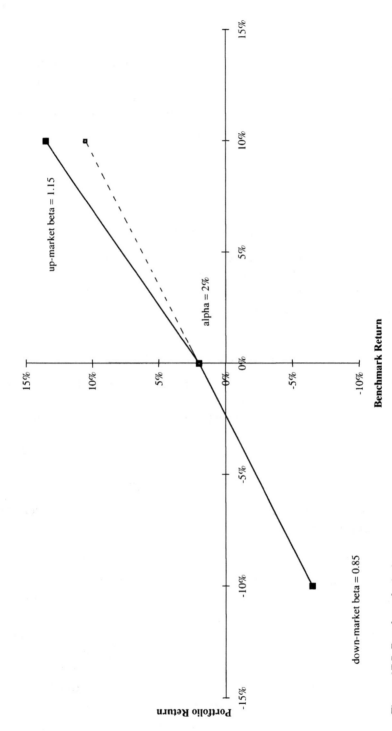

Figure 17.5 Benchmark timing.

through December 1992, $\beta_P = 0.95$ and $\gamma_P = -0.05$. The coefficient γ_P is not statistically distinct from zero, with a t statistic of only -0.41.

There is a longer discussion of the performance measurement aspects of benchmark timing in Chap. 19. See also the paper by Henriksson and Merton (1981).

A Priori Beta Estimates

Another embellishment of returns-based analysis is improved estimation of the beta. This can take the form of using a beta that is estimated before the fact. As we will discuss in Chap. 19, this can help in avoiding spurious correlations between the portfolio returns and benchmark returns. In the example of the Major Market Index portfolio versus the S&P 500 from 1988 through 1992, this can make a difference. While the realized beta was 0.92, the monthly forecast beta over the period ranged from 0.98 to 1.03. Changing from realized to forecast beta changes the portfolio's alpha from 3 basis points per month to -4 basis points per month.

Value Added

A different approach to analyzing the pattern of returns is to use the concept of value added and ideas from the theory of valuation (Chap. 8). The idea is to look at the pattern of portfolio excess returns and market excess returns. Suppose we have $T = 60$ months of returns, $\{r_P(t), r_B(t), r_F(t)\}$ for $t = 1, 2, \ldots, T$. We can think of a deal that says, "In the future the returns will equal $\{r_P(t), r_B(t), r_F(t)\}$ with probability $1/T$." How much would you pay for the opportunity to get the portfolio return under those conditions? You would pay one unit to get the risk-free or market returns; i.e., they are priced fairly. If the portfolio performs very well, you might be willing to pay 1.027 to get the portfolio returns. In that case, we say that the value added is 2.7 percent. If you were willing to pay only 0.974, then there would be a loss in value of 2.6 percent. The appendix shows how this analysis might be carried out.

Controlling for Public Information

Ferson and Schadt (1996) and Ferson and Warther (1996) have argued that the standard regression [Eq. (17.7)] doesn't properly condition for different market environments. They claim two things: first, that public information on dividend yields and interest rates can usefully predict market conditions, and second, that managers earn their living through nonpublic information. As a result, they adjust the basic CAPM regression to condition for public information. For example, they suggest the regression

$$r_P(t) = \alpha_P + \beta \cdot r_B(t) + \beta_y \cdot [r_B(t) \cdot y(t-1)] \tag{17.12}$$
$$+ \beta_i \cdot [r_B(t) \cdot i_F(t-1)] + \epsilon_P(t)$$

Equation (17.12) basically allows for beta varying with economic conditions, as modeled linearly through the market dividend yield $y(t)$ and the risk-free rate $i_F(t)$. Many managers would argue, with some justification, that Eq. (17.12) penalizes them by including ex post insight into the relationship between yields, interest rates, and market conditions.

Style Analysis

So far, all the advances discussed in returns-based performance analysis still rely on a prespecified benchmark, typically a standard index like the S&P 500. Sharpe (1992) proposed style analysis to customize a benchmark for each manager's returns, in order to measure the manager's contribution more exactly.

Style analysis attempts to extract as much information as possible from the time series of portfolio returns without requiring the portfolio holdings. Like the factor model approach, style analysis assumes that portfolio returns have the form

$$r_P(t) = \sum_{j=1}^{J} h_{Pj} \cdot r_j(t) + u_P(t) \tag{17.13}$$

where the $\{r_j(t)\}$ are returns to J *styles*, the h_{Pj} measure the portfolio's holdings of those styles, and $u_P(t)$ is the *selection return*, the portion of the return which style cannot explain. Here the styles typically allocate portfolio returns along the dimensions of value versus growth, large versus small capitalization, domestic versus international, and equities versus bonds. In addition to the returns to the portfolio of interest, the estimation approach also requires returns to portfolios that capture those styles.

We estimate holdings h_{Pj} via a quadratic program:

$$\text{Min}\{\text{Var}\{u_P(t)\}\} \qquad (17.14)$$

subject to $\qquad \sum_{j=1}^{J} h_{Pj} = 1 \qquad (17.15)$

and $\qquad h_{Pj} \geq 0 | j = 1, J \qquad (17.16)$

This differs from regression in two key ways. First, the holdings must be nonnegative and sum to 1. Second, the procedure minimizes the *variance* of the selection returns, not $\sum_{t=1}^{T} u_P^2(t)$. The objective does not penalize large mean selection returns—as regression would do—but only variance about that mean.

Style analysis requires only the time series of portfolio returns and the returns to a set of style indices. The result is a top-down attribution of the portfolio returns to style and selection. According to style analysis, the style holdings define the type of manager, and the selection returns distinguish among managers. Managers can demonstrate skill by producing large selection returns. We can calculate manager information ratios using the mean and standard deviation of the managers' selection returns.

In general, we can use style analysis to (1) identify manager style, (2) analyze performance, and (3) analyze risk. The first application, identifying manager style, is controversial. Several researchers [e.g., Lobosco and DiBartolomeo (1997) and Christopherson and Sabin (1998)] have pointed out the large standard errors associated with the estimated weights, driven in part by the significant correlation between the style indices. But this application, by itself, is of limited use. Identifying manager style usually requires no fancy machinery. Managers publicize their styles, and a peek at their portfolios can usually verify the claim.

Style-based performance analysis may also be inaccurate, although it is usually an improvement over the basic returns-based methodologies. It is an excellent tool for large studies of manager performance. Inaccuracies tend to cancel out from one manager to another in the large sample, and accurate and timely information on portfolio holdings is unavailable.

Risk analysis could use style analysis to identify portfolio exposures to style indices. Risk prediction would follow from these exposures, a style index covariance matrix, and an estimate of selection risk (based on historical selection returns). We could assume selection returns uncorrelated across managers. Once again, this would improve on risk prediction based only on beta, but would fall far short of the structural models we discussed in Chap. 3.

Controlling for Size and Value

Fama and French (1993) have proposed a performance analysis methodology very similar in spirit to Sharpe's style analysis. Their approach to performance uses the regression

$$r_P(t) = \alpha_P + \beta \cdot r_B(t) + \beta_S \cdot \text{SMB}(t) + \beta_V \cdot \text{HML}(t) + \epsilon_P(t) \quad (17.17)$$

This looks like a standard CAPM regression with two additional terms. The return SMB(t) ("small minus big") is the return to a portfolio long small-capitalization stocks and short large-capitalization stocks. The return HML(t) ("high minus low") is the return to a portfolio long high-book-to-price stocks and short low-book-to-price stocks. So Sharpe uses a quadratic programming approach and indices split along size and value (book-to-price) dimensions. Fama and French control along the same dimensions and use standard regression.

How do they build their two portfolio return series? First, each June, they identify the median capitalization for New York Stock Exchange (NYSE) stocks. They use that median to classify all stocks (including AMEX and NASDAQ stocks) as S (for small) or B (for big).

Second, using end-of-year data, they sort all stocks by book-to-price ratios. They classify the bottom 30 percent as L (for low), the middle 40 percent as M (for medium), and the top 30 percent as H (for high). These two splits lead to six portfolios: S/L, S/M, S/H, B/L, B/M, and B/H.

They then calculate capitalization-weighted returns to each of the six portfolios.

Finally, they define SMB(t) as the difference between the simple average of S/L, S/M, and S/H and the simple average of B/L, B/M, and B/H. Effectively, SMB(t) is the return on a net zero investment portfolio that is long small-capitalization stocks and short large-capitalization stocks, with long and short sides having roughly equal book-to-price ratios.

Similarly, they define HML(t) as the difference between the average of S/H and B/H and the average of S/L and B/L. Once again, this is the return on a net zero investment portfolio that is long high-book-to-price stocks and short low-book-to-price stocks, with long and short sides having roughly equal market capitalizations.

Carhart (1997) has extended this approach by also controlling for past 1-year momentum.

PORTFOLIO-BASED PERFORMANCE ANALYSIS

Returns-based analysis is a top-down approach to attributing returns to components, ex post, and statistically analyzing the manager's added value. At its simplest, the attribution is between systematic and residual returns, with managers given credit only for achieved residual returns. Style analysis is similar in approach, attributing returns to several style classes and giving managers credit only for the remaining selection returns. Returns-based performance analysis schemes typically allocate part of the returns to systematic or style components and give managers credit only for the remainder.

Portfolio-based performance analysis is a bottom-up approach, attributing returns to many components based on the ex ante portfolio holdings and then giving managers credit for returns along many of these components. This allows the analysis not only of whether the manager has added value, but of whether he or she has added value along dimensions agreed upon ex ante. Is he a skillful value manager? Does her value added arise from stock selection, beyond any bets on factors? Portfolio-based performance analysis can reveal this. In contrast to returns-based performance analysis, performance-based analysis schemes can attribute returns to several components of possible manager skill.

The returns-only analysis works without the full information available for performance analysis. We can say much more if we look at the actual portfolios held by the managers. In fact, two additional items of information can help in the analysis of performance:

- The portfolio holdings over time
- The goals and strategy of the manager

The analysis proceeds in two steps: performance attribution and performance analysis. Performance attribution focuses on a single period, attributing the return to several components. Performance analysis then focuses on the time series of returns attributed to each component. Based on statistical analysis, where (if anywhere) does the manager exhibit skill and add value?

Performance Attribution

Performance attribution looks at portfolio returns over a single period and attributes them to factors. The underlying principle is the multiple-factor model, first discussed in Chap. 3:

$$r_P(t) = \sum_j x_{Pj}(t) \cdot b_j(t) + u_P(t) \tag{17.18}$$

Examining returns ex post, we know the portfolio's exposures $x_{Pj}(t)$ at the beginning of the period, as well as the portfolio's realized return $r_P(t)$ and the estimated factor returns over the period. The return attributed to factor j is

$$r_{Pj}(t) = x_{Pj}(t) \cdot b_j(t) \tag{17.19}$$

The portfolio's specific return is $u_P(t)$.

We are free to choose factors as described in Chap. 3, and in fact we typically run performance attribution using the same risk-model factors. However, we are not in principle limited to the same factors as are in our risk model. In general, just as in the returns-based analysis, we want to choose some factors for risk control and others as sources of return. The risk control factors are typically industry or market factors, although later we can analyze skill in picking industries.

The return factors can include typical investment themes such as value or momentum. In building risk models, we always use ex ante factors: that is, those based on information known at the beginning of the period. For return attribution, we could also consider ex post factors: that is, those based on information known only at the end of the period. For example, we could use a factor based on IBES earnings forecasts available at the end of the period. We could interpret returns attributed to this factor as evidence of the manager's skill in forecasting IBES earnings projections.

Beyond the manager's returns attributed to factors will remain the specific return to the portfolio. A manager's ability to pick individual stocks, after controlling for the factors, will appear in this term. We call this term *specific asset selection.*

We typically think of the specific return as the component of return which cross-sectional factors cannot explain. That view suggests that we simply lump the portfolio's specific return all together. But for an individual strategy, some attributions of specific return may also make sense. If our strategy depends on analyst information, we may want to group specific returns by analyst. We think our auto industry analyst adds value. If this is true, we should see a positive contribution from auto-stock specific asset selection. Similarly, the specific returns can tell us if our strategy works better in some sectors than in others. This term doesn't tell us whether we have successfully picked one sector over another, it tells us whether we can pick stocks more accurately in one sector than in another.

Note that we have many choices as to how to attribute returns. We can choose the factors for attribution. We can attribute specific returns. We can even attribute part of our returns to the constraints in our portfolio construction process (e.g., we lost 32 basis points of performance last year as a result of our optimizer constraints).[8] Performance attribution is not a uniquely defined process. Commercially available performance analysis products choose widely applicable attribution schemes. Customized systems have no such limitations.

---

[8]For example, with linear equality constraints, $\mathbf{h}^T \cdot \mathbf{A} = 0$, and Lagrange multipliers $-\boldsymbol{\pi}$, the first-order conditions are

$$\alpha = 2 \cdot \lambda_A \cdot \mathbf{V} \cdot \mathbf{h}_{PA} + \boldsymbol{\pi} \cdot \mathbf{A} = 0$$

This effectively partitions the alpha between the portfolio and the constraints. For more details, see Grinold and Easton (1998).

We can apply performance attribution to total returns, active returns, and even active residual returns. For active returns, the analysis is exactly the same, but we work with active portfolio holdings and returns:

$$r_{PA}(t) = \sum_j x_{PAj}(t) \cdot b_j(t) + u_{PA}(t) \tag{17.20}$$

To break down active returns into systematic and residual, remember that we can define residual exposures as

$$x_{PARj} = x_{PAj} - \beta_{PA} \cdot x_{Bj} \tag{17.21}$$

where we simply subtract the active beta times the benchmark's exposure from the active exposure, and residual holdings similarly as

$$h_{PARn} = h_{PAn} - \beta_{PA} \cdot h_{Bn} \tag{17.22}$$

Substituting these into Eq. (17.20), and remembering that $u_{PA} = \sum_n h_{PAn} \cdot u_n$, we find

$$r_{PA}(t) = \beta_{PA} \cdot r_B(t) + \sum_j x_{PARj}(t) \cdot b_j(t) + u_{PAR}(t) \tag{17.23}$$

Equation (17.23) will allow a very detailed analysis of the sources of active returns relative to the benchmark.

As an example of performance attribution, consider the analysis of the Major Market Index portfolio versus an S&P 500 benchmark over the period January 1988 through December 1992. For now, focus on the returns over January 1988. Using the BARRA U.S. Equity model (version 2), the factor exposures are shown in Table 17.2.

Table 17.2 illustrates the attributed active return. Table 17.3 summarizes the attribution between systematic and residual this month. The active beta of the Major Market Index versus the S&P 500 is only 0.02, and so the active residual component is very

T A B L E   17.2

Factor	Active Exposure	Attributed Return
Variability in markets	−0.10	−0.02%
Success	0.14	−0.47%
Size	0.69	0.10%
Trading activity	0.04	0.02%
Growth	−0.14	−0.10%
Earnings-to-price ratio	−0.07	−0.04%
Book-to-price ratio	−0.11	−0.06%
Earnings variability	−0.23	0.10%
Financial leverage	−0.04	−0.03%
Foreign income	0.62	−0.02%
Labor intensity	0.06	0.02%
Yield	0.00	0.00%
Low capitalization	0.00	0.00%
Aluminum	−0.57%	0.02%
Iron and steel	0.13%	0.01%
Precious metals	−0.31%	0.04%
Miscellaneous mining and metals	−0.61%	−0.03%
Coal and uranium	0.32%	−0.03%
International oil	2.53%	0.24%
Domestic petroleum reserves	0.92%	0.08%
Foreign petroleum reserves	0.00%	0.00%
Oil refining and distribution	−0.54%	−0.04%
Oil services	−0.91%	−0.09%
Forest products	0.42%	−0.01%
Paper	2.64%	−0.18%
Agriculture and food	−1.76%	−0.08%
Beverages	1.66%	−0.05%
Liquor	−0.52%	−0.01%
Tobacco	2.86%	0.19%
Construction	−0.01%	0.00%
Chemicals	5.59%	0.11%
Tire and rubber	−0.22%	0.00%
Containers	−0.22%	0.01%
Producer goods	−2.32%	−0.08%
Pollution control	−0.78%	−0.02%

T A B L E 17.2

(Continued)

Factor	Active Exposure	Attributed Return
Electronics	−1.52%	0.04%
Aerospace	−1.96%	−0.08%
Business machines	1.59%	−0.01%
Soaps and housewares	4.19%	0.25%
Cosmetics	−0.55%	−0.03%
Apparel, textiles	−0.32%	−0.01%
Photographic, optical	2.76%	−0.12%
Consumer durables	−0.44%	−0.02%
Motor vehicles	1.70%	0.06%
Leisure, luxury	−0.37%	−0.01%
Health care	3.14%	0.11%
Drugs and medicine	10.45%	1.01%
Publishing	−2.21%	−0.01%
Media	−1.29%	−0.08%
Hotels and restaurants	−1.86%	−0.09%
Trucking, freight	−0.21%	−0.01%
Railroads, transit	−1.30%	−0.07%
Air transport	−0.69%	−0.01%
Transport by water	−0.06%	0.00%
Retail food	−0.72%	−0.03%
Other retail	−2.95%	−0.26%
Telephone, telegraph	−5.24%	−0.43%
Electric utilities	−4.39%	−0.34%
Gas utilities	−1.04%	−0.05%
Banks	−1.96%	−0.14%
Thrift institutions	−0.09%	−0.01%
Miscellaneous finance	1.19%	0.06%
Life insurance	−0.82%	−0.06%
Other insurance	−1.11%	−0.06%
Real property	−0.22%	0.00%
Mortgage financing	0.00%	0.00%
Services	−2.09%	−0.04%
Miscellaneous	0.14%	0.01%
Total attributed active return		−0.84%

T A B L E 17.3

Component		Attributed Return
Active systematic		0.06%
Active residual		−4.88%
Common factor	−0.75%	
Specific	−4.13%	
Active total		−4.82%

close to the active component. Comparing Tables 17.2 and 17.3, the active common-factor component is −0.84 percent and the active residual common-factor component is −0.75 percent.

Performance Analysis

Performance analysis begins with the attributed returns each period, and looks at the statistical significance and value added of the attributed return series. As before, this analysis will rely on t statistics and information ratios to determine statistical significance and value added.

For concreteness, consider the attribution defined in Eq. (17.23), with active returns separated into systematic and residual, and active residual returns further attributed to common factors and specific returns.

Start with the time series of active systematic returns. Most straightforward is a simple analysis of the mean return and its t statistic. However, according to the CAPM, we expect a positive return here if the active beta is positive on average. Hence, we will go one additional step and separate this time series into three components: one arising from the average active beta and the expected benchmark return, one arising from the average active beta and the deviation of realized benchmark return from its expectation, and the third from benchmark timing—deviations of the active beta from its mean. The first component, based on the average active beta and the expected benchmark return, is not a component of active management.

The total active systematic return over time is

$$\text{Active systematic} = \sum_t \beta_{PA}(t) \cdot r_B(t) \tag{17.24}$$

$$= \sum_t [\bar{\beta}_{PA} + \delta\beta_{PA}(t)] \cdot [\mu_B + (\bar{r}_B - \mu_B) + \delta r_B(t)]$$

$$= \sum_t \bar{\beta}_{PA} \cdot \mu_B + \sum_t \bar{\beta}_{PA} \cdot (\bar{r}_B - \mu_B)$$

$$+ \sum_t \delta\beta_{PA}(t) \cdot \delta r_B(t)$$

$$\text{Expected active beta return} = \sum_t \bar{\beta}_{PA} \cdot \mu_B \tag{17.25}$$

$$\text{Active beta surprise} = \sum_t \bar{\beta}_{PA} \cdot (\bar{r}_B - \mu_B) \tag{17.26}$$

$$\text{Active benchmark timing return} = \sum_t \delta\beta_{PA}(t) \cdot \delta r_B(t) \tag{17.27}$$

In Eqs. (17.24) through (17.27), $\bar{\beta}_{PA}$ is the average active beta, $\bar{r}_B$ is the average benchmark excess return over the period, and μ_B is the long-run expected benchmark excess return.

The analysis of the time series of attributed factor returns and specific returns is more straightforward.[9] We can examine each series for its mean, t statistic, and information ratio. For these, we need not only the mean returns, but also the risk for each factor. We can base risk on the realized standard deviation of the time series or on the ex ante forecast risk. The technical appendix describes an innovative approach which combines the two risk estimates, weighting realized risk more heavily the more observations there are in the analysis period.

Performance analysis, just like performance attribution, is not uniquely defined. The scheme outlined here is simply a reasonable approach to distinguishing the various sources of typical strategy returns. It will sometimes prove useful to customize a performance

---

[9]Of course, we can apply the same time series analysis to the factor returns that we applied to the systematic returns. In particular, we can separate each attributed factor return into two components, one based on the average active exposure and the other based on the timing of that exposure about its average.

T A B L E   17.4

Elements of Active Management	Annualized Active Contributions			
	Return	Risk	IR	*t* statistic
Systematic active returns				
Active beta surprise	0.02%	0.16%	0.23	0.51
Active benchmark timing	0.03%	0.19%	0.13	0.28
Total	0.06%	0.25%	0.24	0.54
Residual active returns				
Industry factors	0.27%	1.88%	0.12	0.26
Risk index factors	−0.97%	2.25%	−0.36	−0.81
Specific	0.12%	3.23%	0.01	0.02
Total	−0.58%	4.21%	−0.14	−0.30
Total active returns	−0.52%	4.22%	−0.12	−0.27

analysis scheme to a particular strategy, in order to isolate more precisely its sources of value added.

Table 17.4 summarizes this analysis for the example of the Major Market Index portfolio versus the S&P 500 benchmark.[10] Not surprisingly, given this example, Table 17.4 exhibits no strong demonstrations of skill or value added.

Now that we have analyzed each source of risk in turn, we can identify the best and worst policies followed by the manager: those time series which have achieved the highest and lowest returns on average. Here is where the manager's predefined goals and strategies should shine through. Stock pickers should see specific asset selection as one of their best strategies. Value managers should see value factors as their best strategies. Ex ante strategies that are inconsistent with best policy analysis can signal to the owner of the funds that the active manager has deviated in strategy and can signal to the manager that the strategy isn't doing what he or she expects it to do.

Table 17.5 displays the best and worst policies for the example Major Market Index portfolio versus the S&P 500 benchmark. Previ-

---

[10]The technical appendix includes a discussion of how we calculate annualized active contributions—in particular, how we deal with the issue of cumulating attributed returns.

T A B L E   17.5

Policy	Annualized Active Return
Five best policies	
Foreign income	0.44%
International oil	0.36%
Drugs, medicine	0.33%
Tobacco	0.22%
Health care (nondrug)	0.18%
Five worst policies	
Size	−1.24%
Photographic, optical	−0.48%
Business machines	−0.40%
Paper	−0.37%
Telephone, telegraph	−0.32%

ous analysis showed that the example included no demonstration of skill or value added, and comparing Table 17.5 to Table 17.2, we can see that the best and worst policies simply correspond to the largest-magnitude active exposures.

SUMMARY

The goal of performance analysis is to separate skill from luck. The more information available, the better the analysis. Using a simple cross section of returns to differentiate managers is insufficient. A time series of returns to managers and benchmarks can separate skill from luck. The most accurate performance analysis utilizes information on portfolio holdings and returns over time, to not only separate skill from luck, but also identify where the manager has skill.

NOTES

The science of performance analysis began in the 1960s with the seminal academic work of Sharpe (1966, 1970), Jensen (1968), and Treynor (1965). They used the CAPM as a starting point for developing the returns-based methodology described in this chapter. Their goal was to test market efficiency and analyze manager performance, a topic we will cover in Chap. 20.

Since then, many other academics have developed performance analysis methodologies, often motivated by the desire to further test market efficiency and manager performance. Some advances have come from application of clever statistical insights to the CAPM framework. Other refinements have followed new developments in finance theory. For example, Fama and French (1993) have proposed a new scheme which explicitly controls for size and book-to-market effects.

Most often, the academic treatments have focused on returns-based analysis, although Daniel, Grinblatt, Titman, and Wermers (1997) control for size, book-to-price, and momentum at the asset level (using quintile portfolios) and then aggregate specific returns up to the portfolio level.

Most of these new academic developments are contained within the practitioner-developed portfolio-based analysis methodology described in this chapter.

REFERENCES

Beckers, Stan. "Manager Skill and Investment Performance: How Strong Is the Link?" *Journal of Portfolio Management*, vol. 23, no. 4, 1997, pp. 9–23.

Carhart, Mark M. "On Persistence in Mutual Fund Performance." *Journal of Finance*, vol. 52, no. 1, 1997, pp. 57–82.

Christopherson, Jon A., and Frank C. Sabin. "How Effective Is the Effective Mix?" *Journal of Investment Consulting*, vol. 1, no. 1, 1998, pp. 39–50.

Daniel, Kent, Mark Grinblatt, Sheridan Titman, and Russ Wermers. "Measuring Mutual Fund Performance with Characteristic-based Benchmarks." *Journal of Finance*, vol. 52, no. 3, 1997, pp. 1035–1058.

DeBartolomeo, Dan, and Erik Witkowski. "Mutual Fund Misclassification: Evidence Based on Style Analysis." *Financial Analysts Journal*, vol. 53, no. 5, 1997, pp. 32–43.

Dybvig, Philip H., and Stephen A. Ross. "The Analytics of Performance Measurement Using a Security Market Line." *Journal of Finance*, vol 40, no. 2, 1985, pp. 401–416.

Fama, Eugene F., and Kenneth R. French. "Common Risk Factors in the Returns on Stocks and Bonds." *Journal of Financial Economics*, vol. 33, no. 1, 1993, pp. 3–56.

Ferson, Wayne E., and Rudi W. Schadt. "Measuring Fund Strategy and Performance in Changing Economic Conditions." *Journal of Finance*, vol. 51, no. 2, 1996, pp. 425–461.

Ferson, Wayne E., and Vincent A. Warther. "Evaluating Fund Performance in a Dynamic Market." *Financial Analysts Journal*, vol. 52, no. 6, 1996, pp. 20–28.

Grinold, Richard C., and Kelly K. Easton. "Attribution of Performance and Holdings." In *Worldwide Asset and Liability Modeling,* edited by William T. Ziemba and John M. Mulvey (Cambridge, England: Cambridge University Press, 1998), pp. 87–113.

Henriksson, Roy D., and Robert C. Merton. "On Market Timing and Investment Performance II. Statistical Procedures for Evaluating Forecasting Skills." *Journal of Business,* vol 54, no. 4, 1981, pp. 513–533.

Ippolito, Richard A. "On Studies of Mutual Fund Performance 1962–1991," *Financial Analysts Journal,* vol. 49, no. 1, 1993, pp. 42–50.

Jensen, Michael C. "The Performance of Mutual Funds in the Period 1945–1964." *Journal of Finance,* vol. 23, no. 2, 1968, pp. 389–416.

Jones, Frank J., and Ronald N. Kahn. "Stock Portfolio Attribution Analysis." In *The Handbook of Portfolio Management,* edited by Frank J. Fabozzi (New Hope, PA: Frank J. Fabozzi Associates, 1998), pp. 695–707.

Lehmann, B., and D. Modest. "Mutual Fund Performance Evaluation: A Comparison of Benchmarks and Benchmark Comparisons." *Journal of Finance,* vol. 42, no. 2, 1987, pp. 233–265.

Lobosco, Angelo, and Dan DiBartolomeo. "Approximating the Confidence Intervals for Sharpe Style Weights." *Financial Analysts Journal,* vol. 53, no. 4, 1997, pp. 80–85.

Modigliani, Franco, and Leah Modigliani. "Risk-Adjusted Performance." *Journal of Portfolio Management,* vol. 23, no. 2, 1997, pp. 45–54.

Rudd, Andrew, and Henry K. Clasing, Jr. *Modern Portfolio Theory,* 2nd ed. (Orinda, Calif.: Andrew Rudd, 1988).

Sharpe, William F. "Mutual Fund Performance." *Journal of Business,* vol 39, no. 1, 1966, pp. 119–138.

———. *Portfolio Theory and Capital Markets* (New York: McGraw-Hill, 1970).

———. "Asset Allocation: Management Style and Performance Measurement." *Journal of Portfolio Management,* vol . 18, no. 2, 1992, pp. 7–19.

Treynor, Jack L. "How to Rate Management of Investment Funds." *Harvard Business Review,* vol. 43, no. 1, January–February 1965, pp. 63–75.

Treynor, Jack L., and Fischer Black. "Portfolio Selection Using Spectal Information under the Assumptions of the Diagonal Model with Mean Variance Portfolio Objectives and Without Constraints." In *Mathematical Models in Investment and Finance* edited by G. P. Szego and K. Shell (Amsterdam: North-Holland 1972).

Vasicek, Oldrich A. "A Note on Using Cross-Sectional Information in Bayesian Estimation of Security Betas." *Journal of Finance,* vol. 28, no. 5, 1973, pp. 1233–1239.

PROBLEMS

1. Joe has been managing a portfolio over the past year. Performance analysis shows that he has realized an information ratio of 1 and a t statistic of 1 over this period. He argues that information ratios are what matter for value added, and so who cares about t statistics? Is he correct? What can you say about Joe's performance?

2. Jane has managed a portfolio for the past 25 years, realizing a t statistic of 2 and an information ratio of 0.4. She argues that her t statistic proves her skill. Compare her skill and added value to Joe's.

3. Prove the more exact result for the standard error of the information ratio,

$$\text{SE}\{\text{IR}\} = \frac{1}{\sqrt{Y}} \cdot \sqrt{1 + \left(\frac{\text{IR}^2 \cdot \Delta t}{2}\right)}$$

Assume that errors in the mean and standard deviation of the residual returns are uncorrelated, and use the normal distribution result:

$$\text{SE}[\omega] = \frac{\omega}{\sqrt{2 \cdot N}}$$

for a sample standard deviation from N observations.

4. Show that changing the information ratio from an annualized to a monthly statistic does not improve our ability to measure investment performance. It will still require a 16-year track record to demonstrate top-quartile performance with 95 percent confidence. First calculate the standard error of a monthly IR. Second, convert a top-quartile IR of 0.5 to its monthly equivalent. Finally, calculate the required time period to achieve a t statistic of 2.

5. Using Table 17.2, identify the largest active risk index and industry exposures and the largest risk index and industry attributed returns for the Major Market Index versus the S&P 500 from January 1988 to December 1992. Must the largest attributed returns always correspond to the largest active exposures?

6. Given portfolio returns of {5 percent, 10 percent, −10 percent} and benchmark returns of {1 percent, 5 percent, 10 percent}, what is the cumulative active return over this period? What are the cumulative returns to the portfolio and benchmark?

7. Why should portfolio-based performance analysis be more accurate than returns-based performance analysis?

8. How much statistical confidence would you have in an information ratio of 1 measured over 1 year? How many years of performance data would you need in order to measure an information ratio of 1 with 95 percent confidence?

9. Show that a portfolio Sharpe ratio above the benchmark Sharpe ratio implies a positive alpha for the portfolio, but that a positive alpha does not necessarily imply a Sharpe ratio above the benchmark Sharpe ratio.

TECHNICAL APPENDIX

We will discuss three technical topics in this appendix: how to cumulate attributed returns, how to combine forecast and realized risk numbers for performance analysis, and a valuation-based approach to performance analysis.

Cumulating Attributed Returns

We will investigate two issues here: cumulating active returns and cumulating more generally attributed returns. Let $R_P(t)$ be the portfolio's total return in period t, and let $R_B(t)$ and $R_F(t)$ be the total return on the benchmark and the risk-free asset. The compound total return on portfolio P over periods 1 through T, $R_P(1,T)$, is the product

$$R_P(1,T) = R_P(1) \cdot R_P(2) \cdot R_P(3) \cdots R_P(T) = \prod_{t=1}^{T} R_P(t) \quad (17A.1)$$

Similarly, we calculate the cumulative benchmark return as

$$R_B(1,T) = R_B(1) \cdot R_B(2) \cdot R_B(3) \cdots R_B(T) = \prod_{t=1}^{T} R_B(t) \quad (17A.2)$$

Hence the active cumulative return must be

$$R_{PA}(1,T) \equiv R_P(1,T) - R_B(1,T) \quad (17A.3)$$

Note that we do not calculate active cumulative returns by somehow cumulating the period-by-period active returns. For example,

$$R_{PA}(1, T) \quad (17A.4)$$
$$\neq [1 + R_P(1) - R_B(1)] \cdot [1 + R_P(2) - R_B(2)] \cdots [1 + R_P(T) - R_B(T)]$$

Now consider the more general problem of cumulating attributed returns, and just focus on the problem of cumulating the portfolio returns (not active returns). For each period t,

$$R_P(t) = R_F(t) + \sum_j x_{Pj}(t) \cdot b_j(t) + u_P(t) \quad (17A.5)$$

and hence

$$R_P(1,T) = \left[R_F(1) + \sum_j x_{Pj}(1) \cdot b_j(1) + u_P(1) \right] \quad (17A.6)$$

$$\cdots \left[R_F(T) + \sum_j x_{Pj}(T) \cdot b_j(T) + u_P(T) \right]$$

Equation (17A.6) contains many cross-product terms. We would like to write this as

$$R_P(1,T) = R_F(1,T) + \sum_j x_{Pj}(1,T) \cdot b_j(1,T) + u_P(1,T) + \delta_{CP}, \quad (17A.7)$$

attributing the cumulative return linearly to factors plus a cross-product correction δ_{CP}. There are two straightforward approaches to defining the cumulative attributed returns, one based on a bottom-up view and the other based on a top-down view. The bottom-up view cumulates each attributed return in isolation:

$$x_{Pj}(1,T) \cdot b_j(1,T) \quad (17A.8)$$
$$= [R_F(1) + x_{Pj}(1) \cdot b_j(1)] \cdots [R_F(T) + x_{Pj}(T) \cdot b_j(T)] - R_F(1,T)$$

The top-down view attributes cumulative returns by deleting each factor in turn from the cumulative total return and observing the effect:

$$x_{Pj}(1,T) \cdot b_j(1,T) \qquad\qquad\qquad\qquad\qquad\qquad (17A.9)$$
$$= R_P(1,T) - [R_P(1) - x_{Pj}(1) \cdot b_j(1)] \cdots [R_P(T) - x_{Pj}(T) \cdot b_j(T)]$$

We recommend the top-down approach [Equation (17A.9)], which often leads to smaller cross-product correction terms δ_{CP} in Eq. (17A.7). Given that the cross-product term is usually small, and that intuition for it is limited, we often attribute the cross-product term back to the factors, proportional to either the factor risk or the factor return.

Risk Estimates for Performance Analysis

We observe returns over T periods $t = 1, \ldots, T$ and wish to analyze performance. Prior to the period, the estimated risk of these returns was $\sigma_{prior}(0)$. The realized risk for the returns is σ_{real}. Both risk numbers are sample estimates of the "true" risk. What is the best overall estimate of risk, given these two estimates?

According to Bayes, if we have two estimates, x_1 with standard error σ_1 and x_2 with standard error σ_2, and the estimation errors are uncorrelated, then the best linear unbiased estimate, given these two estimates, is

$$x = \left(\frac{\sigma_2^2}{\sigma_1^2 + \sigma_2^2}\right) x_1 + \left(\frac{\sigma_1^2}{\sigma_1^2 + \sigma_2^2}\right) x_2 \qquad (17A.10)$$

Equation (17A.10) provides the overall estimate with minimum standard error σ.

We also know that the standard error of a sampled variance is approximately

$$SE\{variance\} = variance \cdot \sqrt{\frac{2}{T}} \qquad (17A.11)$$

where T is the number of observations in the sample and we assume that the distribution of the underlying variable is normal.

Combining Eqs. (17A.10) and (17A.11), our best risk estimate is

$$\sigma^2 = \sigma^2_{prior}(0) \cdot \left[\frac{T_0}{T + T_0} \right] + \sigma^2_{real} \left[\frac{T}{T + T_0} \right] \qquad (17A.12)$$

where T_0 measures the number of observations[11] used for the estimate of $\sigma_{prior}(0)$.

Valuation-based Approach to Performance Analysis

The theory of valuation (Chap. 8) defined valuation multiples v such that

$$p(0) = \frac{E^*\{cf(T)\}}{(1 + i_F)^T} = \frac{E\{v \cdot cf(T)\}}{(1 + i_F)^T} \qquad (17A.13)$$

where $p(0)$ is the current value of the asset based on its possible future values $cf(T)$ at time T. Defining total returns as

$$R = \frac{cf(T)}{p(0)} \qquad (17A.14)$$

we see that

$$1 = \frac{E\{v \cdot R\}}{(1 + i_F)^T} \qquad (17A.15)$$

One aspect of the valuation multiples, which is shown by Eq. (17A.15), is that they fairly price all assets. Within the context of the CAPM and APT, all returns are fairly priced with respect to portfolio Q. A manifestation of this is that under this adjusted measure, they all have the same value. Equation (17A.15) states that the set of possible returns R should be worth $1.00 using the valuation multiples v.

In the valuation-based approach to performance analysis, the benchmark plays the role of portfolio Q. We determine the valuation multiples by the requirement that they fairly price the benchmark and the risk-free asset. The observed set of benchmark returns and

---

[11]We can define T_0 implicitly using $SE\{\sigma^2_{prior}(0)\} = \sqrt{2/T_0}$ if we have an estimate of the standard error of $\sigma^2_{prior}(0)$.

the observed set of risk-free returns will each be priced at $1.00. How much will the observed portfolio returns be worth then?

How do we choose the valuation measure? We could use the results from Chap. 8, that

$$v = 1 - \frac{f_Q}{\sigma_Q^2} \cdot (r_Q - f_Q) \qquad (17A.16)$$

This has certain problems, as discussed before; for instance, it isn't guaranteed to be positive. Alternatively, we can use a result from continuous time option theory, that

$$v(r_B(t), i_F(t)) = \delta \cdot \exp \left\{ \frac{-(\ln[R_B(t)/R_F(t)] + \sigma^2 \cdot \Delta t/2)^2}{2 \cdot \sigma^2 \cdot \Delta t} \right\} \qquad (17A.17)$$

where we use δ here as a proportionality constant. Given Eq. (17A.17), the valuation multiples are guaranteed to be positive, and we can choose δ and σ by the requirement that they fairly price the observed set of benchmark returns and risk-free returns:

$$\sum_t \frac{v \cdot R_B(t)}{R_F(t)} = 1 \qquad (17A.18)$$

$$\sum_t \frac{v \cdot R_F(t)}{R_F(t)} = \sum_t v = 1 \qquad (17A.19)$$

Once we have used Eqs. (17A.18) and (17A.19) to determine δ and σ, we can calculate the value added of the portfolio as

$$\text{Value added} = \sum_t \frac{v \cdot R_P(t)}{R_F(t)} - 1 \qquad (17A.20)$$

We can apply Eq. (17A.20) to attributed returns, as well as to the total portfolio returns, to calculate value added factor by factor:

$$\text{Value added} = \sum_t \frac{v \cdot \left[R_F(t) + \sum_j r_{P_j}(t) \right]}{R_F(t)} - 1 \qquad (17A.21)$$

Now, using Eq. (17A.19) and switching the summation order leads to

$$\text{Value added} = \sum_j \sum_t \frac{v \cdot r_{Pj}(t)}{R_F(t)} \qquad (17A.22)$$

Exercise

1. Over a 60-month period, the forecast market variance was (17 percent)^2, with a standard error of (5.1 percent)^2, and the realized (sample) variance was (12 percent)^2. What is the best estimate of market variance over this period?

Applications Exercises

1. Compare the Major Market Portfolio to the S&P 500 over the past 60 months. What were the best and worst policies of this active portfolio?
2. What are the largest and smallest attributed returns in the most recent month?

Asset Allocation

INTRODUCTION

In Chap. 4 we developed a utility function for active management which separated benchmark timing from asset selection. The intervening chapters have focused on asset selection, postponing treatment of benchmark timing to Chap. 19. Before moving on to that treatment, we want to focus separately on a style of investment—asset allocation—which lies somewhere between asset selection and benchmark timing.

Asset allocation comes in several varieties: strategic versus tactical, and domestic versus global. The process of selecting a *target asset allocation* is called *strategic asset allocation*. The variation in asset allocation around that target is called *tactical asset allocation*. There is an analogy between strategic asset allocation and the choice of a benchmark in a single equity market, and between tactical asset allocation and active management within the equity market. We do not address the important question of strategic asset allocation in this book.[1] We assume that we have simply been presented with the benchmark.

This chapter explicitly addresses tactical asset allocation. Domestic tactical asset allocation typically involves actively choosing allocations to at least three asset classes—stocks, bonds, and cash—

---

[1] For a discussion of strategic asset allocation issues, see Ambachtsheer (1987) or Sharpe (1987).

and possibly more. Global asset allocation involves actively choosing allocations to typically 20 or so global equity and bond markets.

The principles for actively managing asset selection in one market apply to tactical asset allocation. The main difference is in the number of assets. There are typically from 3 to 20 in tactical asset allocation and from 100 to several thousand for portfolio management in a single market. Given this important difference, the fundamental law of active management implies that tactical asset allocation will have to surmount a high skill hurdle to compete with asset selection.

Asset allocation differs from asset selection in other ways as well. Asset allocation strategies often involve time series, rather than cross-sectional analysis, and rely on different types and sources of information. Currencies are more central to global asset allocation than even to international asset selection. Finally, traditional asset allocation managers have eschewed the explicit acknowledgement of a benchmark in portfolio construction.

Given the relatively small number of bets, why pursue asset allocation? These strategies have several desirable features: new opportunities for enhanced returns, often beyond national boundaries; the possibility of increased diversification; and the control of the major determinant of total returns. The asset allocation decision incurs large risks and offers large potential returns. Global asset allocation is the largest source of differences in performance among global portfolios.[2]

This chapter will present a practical framework for researching global asset allocation strategies, and will include examples of global asset allocation to clarify the discussion. Major points will include the following:

- Researching asset allocation strategies is a three-step process: forecasting returns, building portfolios, and analyzing out-of-sample performance.
- The procedure for forecasting returns for asset allocation differs from that for asset selection in its focus on time series instead of cross-sectional analysis. In spite of this,

---

[2]See Solnik (1993b).

asset allocation, like asset selection, adds value through identifying relative performance.

- Traditional asset allocation ignores any explicit benchmark, simply trading off expected excess return against total risk. This causes substantial problems. We will implicitly include a benchmark in the expected returns, a procedure complicated by the presence of currencies.

THE THREE-STEP PROCESS

Researching asset allocation strategies for institutional investors is a three-step process: forecasting asset-class expected returns, building optimal portfolios, and testing their out-of-sample performance.

The forecasts may come from a quantitative model, a qualitative model, or a combination of the two. We will demonstrate a quantitative model of expected returns.

The quantitative framework will differ somewhat from that for individual security selection in that it will build a separate time series model for each asset class, as opposed to a cross-sectional model of differences between individual securities.

There are two related reasons to focus on separate time series models rather than a cross-sectional model. First, to the extent that these asset classes exhibit low correlations as compared to asset returns (which usually include a strong market factor), a time series approach makes better sense. Second, the typical explanatory variables for asset-class returns focus on the individual time series rather than on cross-sectional comparisons, and aren't always comparable across countries and asset classes. There may still be a place for cross-sectional models, especially focusing on a smaller set of correlated asset classes (e.g., European equities), but we will not deal with such models here.

Even though asset allocation forecasting uses time series analysis, asset allocation strategies add value by identifying relative performance. They bet on the relative performance of asset class A versus asset class B this month, not on the performance of asset class A this month versus last month. Underlying the reliance on time series models is the idea that accurate time series forecasts provide accurate relative valuations.

Given the expected excess return forecasts, step 2 is to build optimal mean/variance portfolios. A problem with traditional asset allocation is its trade-off of expected excess returns against total risk, without regard to any benchmark. The resulting optimal portfolio weights are extremely sensitive to small changes in expected returns, and often vary widely from benchmark weights. A Bayesian approach (following the principles discussed in Chap. 10 and dependent on a benchmark) can control this problem.

The final step is out-of-sample performance analysis on our optimal portfolios. We must test these strategies out-of-sample to determine the information content of the expected return models.

Out-of-sample testing is always critical for researching investment strategies. For time series–based approaches, even the in-sample period must include explicit testing of forecasting ability. Let's say we fit a time series model over a period from T_1 to T_2. The model's estimates for times $t < T_2$ will then generally include information from times all the way through T_2. In particular, the estimated regression coefficients will depend on all the data through T_2. Hence the in-sample testing must include estimating the model from T_1 to T_2 and looking at its forecasting ability beyond T_2. We will measure forecasting ability using the information coefficient (IC), the correlation of forecasts and realizations. After an in-sample look at forecasting ability to choose appropriate explanatory variables, out-of-sample testing will validate the performance of the model.

Step 1: Forecasting Returns

We will illustrate step 1 by building a model to forecast monthly excess returns for the German, Japanese, U.K., and U.S. equity markets using data from January 1985 through December 1992. In this example, we will build a linear, regression-based model

$$r(t) = \sum_j x_j(t) \cdot b_j + \epsilon(t) \tag{18.1}$$

where we attempt to explain asset-class excess monthly returns $r(t)$ using a set of explanatory variables $\{x_j(t)\}$. The information used to forecast $r(t)$, the explanatory variables $\{x_j(t)\}$, are available at the beginning of period t. We estimate coefficients b_j to relate the explanatory variables to the returns.

As described before, we will estimate model coefficients over part of the in-sample data, and then test forecasting ability through the remainder of the in-sample period. In fact, our initial regression will use the first 30 months of data to forecast returns over the 31st month. Our next regression will use the first 31 months of data to forecast returns over the 32nd month. We will expand our regression window until we reach 60 months of data, after which we will always use the past 60 months of data to forecast returns over the next month.

In this example, our 8 years of in-sample data will allow us to estimate information coefficients using 5.5 years of in-sample forecasts. These in-sample information coefficients help us choose appropriate explanatory variables.

Later on, we will test model performance in an out-of-sample period, looking at the performance of portfolios built using the model. Building portfolios will require the information coefficient for each country, which we will estimate using the available history of forecasts and realizations (which start in month 31).

We will use the same five explanatory variables for each market.[3] These explanatory variables are the predicted dividend yield for the market, the short-term interest rate in the market, the difference between that short rate and the U.S. short-term interest rate, the exchange rate to U.S. dollars, and a January dummy variable. Two of these variables drop out for the U.S. model.

Table 18.1 displays the statistical results for the markets, based on model estimation as of January 1993, the beginning of our out-of-sample period. Table 18.1 displays the coefficients b_j and their t statistics, as well as the adjusted R^2 statistics for each market. We can first make some overall observations about the performance of the model, and then focus in on some details to compare it to intuition.

Overall, the explanatory power of the model varies widely from country to country over this mainly in-sample period. The

---

[3]See the references of Solnik (1993b), Emanuelli and Pearson (1994), and Ferson and Harvey (1992) for more details.

T A B L E 18.1

Country	Intercept	Dividend Yield	Short Rate	Relative Short Rate	Exchange Rate	January	Adjusted R Squared
Germany	-0.24	19.7	2.52	-0.96	-0.58	0.03	0.24
	-1.4	4.0	2.3	-1.8	-2.8	1.2	
Japan	-0.47	24.7	2.03	-2.28	26.10	-0.01	0.03
	-1.7	2.0	1.5	-2.2	0.9	-0.4	
United Kingdom	-0.10	6.9	0.65	-1.92	-1.10	0.02	0.09
	-0.9	3.1	1.5	-2.5	-1.6	0.8	
United States	-0.08	4.0	-0.56			0.00	0.01
	-1.6	1.8	-1.4			-0.1	

average adjusted R^2 is roughly 9 percent, ranging from close to zero for the United States to over 20 percent for Germany. For a model of returns, these results are on average good.

Looking at the estimated coefficients, we can first see that the coefficients for dividend yield are always positive. Higher dividend yields imply higher expected returns. In the United States, for example, the coefficient is 4.0. Each 1 percent increase in predicted dividend yield in the United States raises our expected monthly U.S. equity market excess return by 4.0 percent.

The coefficients for the short interest rate are sometimes positive and sometimes negative. Looking again at the example of the United States, each 1 percent increase in the short rate lowers the expected monthly market excess return by 0.56 percent.

The coefficients for the difference between short interest rates in the local market and in the United States are negative. In the United Kingdom, a 1 percent rise in this differential implies a decrease of 1.92 percent in the expected monthly market excess return.

The intuition here is perhaps that both higher short rates and higher rate differentials to the United States should lower expected equity market returns. Our results for the short-rate effect do not entirely agree with this intuition. However a more detailed analysis of this model shows a high correlation between these two variables in some countries for the 60 months ending January 1993. Given this high correlation of exposures, coupled very often with coefficients of differing signs, the net result may well be that higher short rates do indeed imply lower market returns. If we were interested in pursuing this model further, the natural solution would be to delete one of these explanatory variables, given its high correlation with other explanatory variables.

The coefficients for the local exchange rate (U.S. dollars per unit of local currency) is negative for Germany and the United Kingdom, and positive for Japan. Only the result in Germany is statistically significant. The negative coefficient means that as the local currency depreciates relative to the dollar (as the dollars per unit of local currency increases), the expected return increases. For example, if the dollars per deutsche mark decreases from $0.59 to $0.58, the expected monthly excess return to the German market will increase by $-0.58 \cdot (\$0.58 - \$0.59) = .0058 = 0.58$ percent.

The January effect is positive for Germany and the United Kingdom. The coefficient for Germany implies that the expected monthly excess return is higher by 2.89 percent in January than in the other months.

In our implementation of this example, we have used the raw values for all the explanatory variables. This can lead to estimated coefficients of widely differing magnitudes. It is only $x_j b_j$ that has the units and magnitude of returns. If the dollar value of a U.K. pound has a very different magnitude from the U.K. short interest rate, then the estimated coefficients associated with these explanatory variables will have compensatingly different magnitudes. This can obscure our insight into the relative importance of these effects (although the t statistics will help). A variant of our implementation is to linearly rescale the explanatory variables—subtract the sample mean and divide by the sample standard deviation—to put all the variables on an equal footing. This linear transformation will have no effect on explanatory power. However, after the transformation, the magnitude of the estimated coefficients will identify which variables explain most of the monthly variation in asset-class returns.

This example is quantitative, yet it also provides qualitative insight and intuition into market behavior. It explicitly connects economic variables to expected returns. These connections should be intuitive. It can identify which economic variables are relatively more important for market returns, and help in predicting market direction.

The above discussion shows that this simple model exhibits reasonable explanatory power, with coefficients that generally conform to our intuition. The next step is to implement these forecasts in optimal mean/variance portfolios. Before doing that, however, we should briefly discuss alternatives for maximizing the explanatory power of these models.

Our simple model constrained the explanatory variables to be the same in each market. An obvious extension would be to allow different variables in different markets based on how well they forecast returns in those markets (and accounting for colinearities in some markets). We could extend the explanatory variables to include macroeconomic variables and previous or lagged monthly returns (to capture mean reversion or trends). We could add analysts' forecasts or even forecasts of political risks. We can combine the forecasts from a quantitative model with forecasts from the more qualitative sources that are traditional in global asset allocation. We can even use the insights of the model into the size and sign of these coefficients to help the traditional analyst make better-informed qualitative forecasts. And, of course, we can extend the analysis to include bond markets as well as equity markets.

Step 2: Building Optimal Portfolios

Our estimated model [Eq. (18.1)] provides monthly expected excess returns to a set of equity markets. But mean/variance optimal portfolios that trade off expected excess return and total risk are extremely sensitive to these expected returns. Whereas active or residual asset returns exhibit relatively low correlations, asset-class excess returns exhibit high correlations.

We could handle this problem by using expected active or residual returns relative to an asset allocation benchmark. This is the approach of the rest of the book. Instead, for this chapter, we will stick to the traditional asset allocation methodology, and describe how to avoid the sensitivity problem. To do this, we will effectively sneak the benchmark into our expected excess return forecasts.[4]

Our approach will be the methodology we developed in Chap. 10, refining these "raw" expected returns $\hat{r}$. The basic forecasting formula is

$$E\{r|\hat{r}\} = E\{r\} + \text{Cov}\{r,\hat{r}\} \cdot \text{Var}^{-1}\{\hat{r}\} \cdot (\hat{r} - E\{\hat{r}\}) \qquad (18.2)$$

where $E\{r|\hat{r}\}$ is the refined expected return conditional on the forecast $\hat{r}$. This simplifies to the forecasting rule of thumb

$$E\{r|\hat{r}\} = E\{r\} + \text{IC} \cdot \text{STD}\{r\} \cdot \text{Score} \qquad (18.3)$$

When we implement our simple model, each market will have its own information coefficient, which may vary over time depending on the model's forecasting ability in that market. Only for

---

[4]Note that the problem involving the trade-off between active or residual return and risk differs from the standard global asset allocation methodology in that it involves the aversion to active or residual risk, not to total risk.

markets with significant information coefficients will our forecast returns differ from consensus expectations.

To use Eq. (18.3) in our example model, we must analyze one further detail: Where do we find the consensus expected excess returns? Here is where we will sneak a benchmark into the problem: We will use the consensus returns implied by our benchmark portfolio. Given a benchmark, then, as we saw in Chap. 2, the consensus expected excess returns are just

$$E\{r\} = \beta \cdot f_B \qquad (18.4)$$

where β is the beta of the asset class relative to the benchmark and f_B is the consensus expected return to the benchmark.

This approach is more complex with multiple currencies, especially if we want consensus expected excess returns that are reasonable from many different currency perspectives.[5]

INTERNATIONAL CONSENSUS EXPECTED RETURNS

So what is the problem with backing out consensus expected returns in the international context? If we aren't careful, the results will look very different from different perspectives. Part of the problem is the home bias. If we start by assuming, for example, that the standard asset allocation of a U.S. pension fund, with at most about 20 percent invested outside the United States, is optimal, Eq. (18.4) leads to artificially low expected excess returns for foreign assets.

Perhaps more surprising, we can't solve the problem by simply reweighting the assets in the presumed efficient portfolio so that, for example, 60 percent of the holdings are outside the United States and 40 percent are within the United States, more in line with global capital market weights. At this level, Eq. (18.4) implies consensus expected excess returns for foreign assets that are too large.[6] But this domestic view is only part of the problem.

---

[5]If your focus is solely on asset allocation for investors from a single country, and their benchmark is imposed externally, then you may not require "sensible" expected returns. You can use the expected returns consistent with the imposed benchmark, whether they appear sensible or not. In that case, the discussion in the next section is just a cultural diversion.

[6]See Grinold (1996) for details.

An Aside: Currency Semantics

We should be aware of a semantic pitfall. Currency has a double meaning: It can be either a numeraire of perspective or an asset. It is this double nature that gives a theological aspect to that old conundrum: "Is currency an asset?" We will maintain that short-term, default-free, interest-bearing bills held in foreign countries are indeed assets. The return on such a bill is known in its home country; the only uncertainty in its return for a foreign investor is the exchange rate risk. Thus, when we speak loosely of currency as an asset, we actually mean a short-term, default-free, discount bill in that particular country.

On the other hand, we use the notion of currency to indicate an investment perspective—i.e., how we keep score. Phrases like "for the yen-based investor" or "this is not as attractive from a sterling perspective" indicate that we are using the currency as a numeraire.

We will use currency in both its meanings. We start with an example of consensus expected returns viewed from several numeraire perspectives. We will examine stocks and bonds in the four major countries treated in our expected return model: Germany, Japan, the United Kingdom, and the United States. Our presumed efficient portfolio is 60 percent stocks and 40 percent bonds in each country. The country weights are Germany, 10 percent; Japan, 30 percent; the United Kingdom, 20 percent; and the United States, 40 percent. We estimate risk from historical data for 1970 through 1995.

Table 18.2 shows the consensus expected returns from each of the four different currency perspectives.

The wide range of expected excess returns suggests a major inconsistency. For example, a Frankfurt-based investor holding dollars will expect 4.80 percent excess return, while a New York–based investor holding deutsche marks (or Euros, post 1999) will expect a 1.93 percent excess return. While win/win is a laudable concept, this seems to carry the notion too far. In fact, as we show below, it is not possible to have numbers this high in a consistent scheme.

This example suggests two questions. First, how do we consistently transform expected excess returns from one currency perspective to another? If we know the expected excess returns for a

T A B L E   18.2

Asset	Numeraire Perspective			
	Germany	Japan	United Kingdom	United States
German stocks	5.10%	5.18%	5.48%	6.27%
Japan stocks	9.70%	5.36%	7.27%	7.54%
U.K. stocks	10.76%	7.41%	6.49%	7.63%
U.S. stocks	10.62%	6.62%	7.49%	5.54%
German bonds	0.46%	1.05%	1.56%	2.73%
Japan bonds	4.15%	0.36%	2.36%	2.08%
U.K. bonds	4.64%	2.18%	0.91%	2.97%
U.S. bonds	5.96%	2.44%	3.40%	1.87%
Deutsche marks	0.00%	0.47%	0.75%	1.93%
Yen	3.80%	0.00%	1.75%	1.30%
Sterling	3.31%	0.97%	0.00%	1.48%
Dollars	4.80%	0.83%	1.78%	0.00%

London-based investor, how do we deduce the expected excess returns for a New York– or Tokyo-based investor? Second, how do we determine a "reasonable" ex ante efficient portfolio? In particular, what role will currency play in that portfolio?

The first question has a definite answer, as discussed in Black (1990) [also Black (1989)]. International returns, by their nature, involve products of the return in the local market and changes in the level of exchange rates. This type of relationship will hold between any two countries and for any asset. We illustrate using U.S. and U.K. investors and the Australian stock BHP:

$$R_{BHP}(\text{U.S.}|0,t) = \frac{[(\$/\pounds)(t)]}{[(\$/\pounds)(0)]} \cdot R_{BHP}(\text{U.K.}|0,t) \qquad (18.5)$$

where $R_{BHP}(\text{US}|0,t)$ refers to the cumulative total return[7] to BHP over the period from 0 to t from the U.S. dollar perspective, and we represent a 3.5 percent return as 1.035. Suppose a British investor observes a 3.5 percent return to BHP between 0 and t. Furthermore, the exchange rate at time 0 is $1.50 per pound, and the exchange

---

[7]We are assuming reinvestment of any cash flows.

rate at time t is \$1.52 per pound. Then the U.S. investor will observe a 4.88 percent return over the interval.

From that simple relationship, we can derive a rule linking excess rates of return in different locales. We always measure returns in excess of the *investor's* risk-free alternative; i.e., the excess return on BHP for a U.S. investor is relative to the risk-free return in the U.S. market:

$$r_{BHP}(\text{U.S.}) = r_{BHP}(\text{U.K.}) - r_{\$}(\text{U.K.}) + \sigma_{BHP,£}(\text{U.S.}) \qquad (18.6)$$

So the excess return to BHP from the U.S. perspective equals the excess return to BHP from the U.K. perspective, less the excess return to U.S. Treasury bills from the U.K. perspective, plus the covariance between BHP and U.K. Treasury bills from the U.S. perspective (see Appendix C for details).

Equation (18.6) deals with realized returns. We can also take expectations to derive a link between the expected returns:

$$E\{r_{BHP}(\text{U.S.})\} = E\{r_{BHP}(\text{U.K.})\} - E\{r_{\$}(\text{U.K.})\} + \sigma_{BHP,£}(\text{U.S.}) \qquad (18.7)$$

This result answers our first question about moving expected excess returns from one locale to another. It requires both expected return and risk forecasts.

The second question, concerning a reasonable presumed efficient portfolio, has no totally acceptable answer in the domestic case. It will only get harder in the global case. We will have to be satisfied with a reasonable way to treat currency in the global context. Here is the procedure from Grinold (1996).

How can we get rid of the exchange rates? One way is to envision a world with a single currency. Suppose we had a composite country that we will call COM. The currency for COM is a mixture of the currencies of all the countries, a composite currency. A portfolio called BSK (for basket) determines the makeup of the composite currency. For example, the basket could be 40 percent dollars, 30 percent yen, 20 percent sterling, and 10 percent deutsche marks. Recall the double nature of currency. The currency portfolio, BSK, defines the composite currency numeraire, COM. It is also an asset. It serves as the risk-free asset from the COM perspective, and German, Japanese, U.K., and U.S. investors can hold BSK.

We can rewrite Eq. (18.7) using this new currency asset and numeraire:

$$E\{r_{\mathrm{BHP}}(\mathrm{U.S.})\} = E\{r_{\mathrm{BHP}}(\mathrm{COM})\} - E\{r_{\$}(\mathrm{COM})\} + \sigma_{\mathrm{BHP,BSK}}(\mathrm{U.S.}) \quad (18.8)$$

Now, we can't expect the consensus expected returns procedure to work perfectly from the COM perspective, since it doesn't work perfectly in a pure domestic setting. We are striving for a relative measure of satisfaction rather than an absolute measure. The best way to judge is to look at the improvement we get over using the naïve procedure. To do that, we will observe the improvement in our example. But first, we will trace the presumed efficient portfolio as we move from one locale to the other. We'll see that the presumed efficient portfolio changes.

Let's start from the COM currency perspective and presume that portfolio Q is efficient. Now, from the COM perspective, portfolio Q explains all expected excess returns. For example,

$$E\{r_{\mathrm{BHP}}(\mathrm{COM})\} = \beta_{\mathrm{BHP}}(\mathrm{COM}) \cdot f_Q(\mathrm{COM}) \quad (18.9)$$

and for a U.S. risk-free instrument from the COM currency perspective,

$$E\{r_{\$}(\mathrm{COM})\} = \beta_{\$}(\mathrm{COM}) \cdot f_Q(\mathrm{COM}) \quad (18.10)$$

We can use Eqs. (18.9) and (18.10) for the expectations in Eq. (18.8).

Furthermore, we can use this approach to calculate an effective efficient portfolio from other perspectives. The idea is to transform the betas from the COM perspective to the dollar perspective. Then we can solve for the portfolio, $Q_{\mathrm{U.S.}}$, that explains excess returns from the U.S. perspective. The technical appendix contains the details.

We find that the only change required in order to move from Q to $Q_{\mathrm{U.S.}}$, or from $Q_{\mathrm{U.S.}}$ to $Q_{\mathrm{U.K.}}$, comes in the currency position. For example, to move from Q to $Q_{\mathrm{U.S.}}$, we partially hedge against changes in the value of the currency basket. Portfolio $Q_{\mathrm{U.S.}}$ will be long dollars and short the basket currency, relative to portfolio Q. As the technical appendix will show, to move from Q to $Q_{\mathrm{U.S.}}$, we subtract a fraction $[1 - (\sigma_Q/\mathrm{SR}_Q)]$ of the portfolio that is long the basket currency (e.g., 40 percent dollars, 30 percent yen, 20 percent deutsche marks, 10 percent pounds) and short (-100 percent) dollars. That fraction is roughly 65 percent, assuming a Sharpe ratio of about 0.35 and a volatility of about 12 percent for the global asset allocation portfolio Q.[8]

Our presumed efficient portfolio from the COM perspective will have 60 percent stock and 40 percent bond allocations in each country, with country weights 40 percent in the United States, 30 percent in Japan, 20 percent in the United Kingdom, and 10 percent in Germany. It contains no explicit currency positions.

Table 18.3 displays the consensus expected returns from varying perspectives, including the composite currency. Notice the very low expected excess returns for holding currency.

The forecasts of expected excess returns for the currencies are more reasonable and the expected excess returns for stocks and bonds more consistent across countries than in Table 18.2. In particular, let's look at the German investor holding U.S. T-bills and the U.S. investor holding German T-bills. Using Eq. (18.7), and

T A B L E 18.3

| Asset | Numeraire Perspective | | | | |
	Germany	Japan	United Kingdom	United States	Composite
German stocks	4.72%	4.59%	4.68%	4.96%	4.51%
Japan stocks	6.81%	5.70%	6.15%	6.32%	5.89%
U.K. stocks	7.51%	6.62%	6.45%	6.80%	6.49%
U.S. stocks	6.79%	5.76%	5.98%	5.65%	5.60%
German bonds	0.65%	0.64%	0.77%	1.14%	0.61%
Japan bonds	1.52%	0.53%	1.00%	1.04%	0.67%
U.K. bonds	2.14%	1.45%	1.19%	1.75%	1.33%
U.S. bonds	2.64%	1.71%	1.95%	1.71%	1.60%
Deutsche marks	0.00%	−0.04%	0.05%	0.41%	−0.09%
Yen	0.99%	0.00%	0.41%	0.42%	0.09%
Sterling	0.85%	0.19%	0.00%	0.43%	0.06%
Dollars	1.08%	0.06%	0.29%	0.00%	−0.07%

---

[8]In other chapters, we discussed portfolio Q volatilities in the range of 15 to 20 percent. Those numbers assume only equity investments. The lower volatility quoted here reflects the significant exposure to fixed income.

remembering that the excess return for a German investor on German T-bills is, by definition, zero,

$$E\{r_{DM}(U.S.)\} + E\{r_{\$}(GER)\} = \sigma^2_{DM}(U.S.) \qquad (18.11)$$

In Table 18.3, the 0.41 percent return for a U.S. investor holding German bills and 1.08 percent for a German investor holding U.S. bills are consistent with a 12.2 percent exchange rate volatility. By contrast, the expectations in Table 18.2—a large 1.93 percent for a U.S. investor holding German bills and an enormous 4.80 percent for a German investor holding U.S. bills—are consistent with a huge exchange rate volatility of 25.9 percent. The realized volatility of this exchange rate over any sizable period in the last 20 years has consistently been in the 11 to 13 percent range.

Step 3: Analyzing Out-of-Sample Portfolio Performance

The last step in our methodology involves analyzing the out-of-sample performance of our optimized portfolios. Remember that a fair test of these time series models requires this out-of-sample testing. Focusing on excess returns to the strategy, we can examine the cumulative return plots and compare portfolio performance to benchmark performance. We can calculate the Sharpe ratios for the portfolio and the benchmark.

We can also look at the portfolio's active returns. We can examine the cumulative active returns, the information ratio, and the t statistics. A more detailed performance analysis would also look at turnover, performance in up markets versus down markets (defined by the benchmark or the numeraire market), the number of up and down months, and which particular markets contributed the most to the outperformance. Performance dominated by one particular market would be a worrisome sign.

The goal of this out-of-sample performance analysis step is to fairly measure the value added of the strategy, and possibly identify research directions for model improvement. Note that this final step of analysis of asset allocation performance measures how well we identify relative value among asset classes, since we overweight some and underweight others. Our return forecasts use time series models. To add value, those time series models must forecast cross-sectional returns.

SUMMARY

We have discussed a three-step procedure for researching practical asset allocation strategies. These steps include forecasting expected asset class returns, building optimal portfolios, and analyzing the out-of-sample performance of those portfolios.

We saw that asset allocation strategies, unlike asset selection strategies, rely on time series analysis to forecast returns. We discussed how traditional asset allocation trades off expected excess returns against total risk in building portfolios. We showed how to retain that traditional approach, but avoid its problems, by refining the expected excess returns based on a benchmark. This process is complicated for global investors by the presence of currencies.

This framework has importance far beyond quantitative strategies for global asset allocation. It can provide intuition and control for quantitative or qualitative approaches to this critical element of global investing.

NOTES

There are two distinct strands of research concerning asset allocation. One involves building models to forecast expected returns for different asset classes. The other focuses on appropriate methods for constructing portfolios.

Let's start with the research on international expected returns. Solnik has worked extensively on modeling expected returns to international equity and bond markets. In his 1993 *Journal of Empirical Finance* paper, he models expected returns to nine equity and nine bond markets using three fundamental variables—dividend yield, the short interest rate, and the long interest rate—plus a January dummy variable. Solnik's 1993 monograph, *Predictable Time-Varying Components of International Asset Returns*, extends his model by including the spread between short interest rates and the U.S. short interest rate and lagged market returns as additional explanatory variables. Emanuelli and Pearson (1994) also use IBES earnings forecast data to help explain market returns. In particular, they define an earnings forecast revision ratio based on the number of up and down earnings forecast revisions in the market as a predictor of future market returns. Ferson and Harvey (1992) have also built models of expected returns to 18 different international equity markets. The review paper by Solnik includes an extensive bibliography of these and other efforts to build models of expected returns.

Black and Litterman's work on portfolio construction for global asset allocation focuses on an entirely different challenge of global investing. Starting with the traditional mean/variance framework, they discuss a well-known problem for global asset allocation: The optimal portfolio weights can be extremely sensitive to small changes in expected returns. The underlying cause is the high correlation of many asset classes. To an optimizer, they appear as reasonable substitutes.

Because of this, optimized portfolios can often exhibit weights that vary greatly from global benchmarks. Exposures may be restricted to only a very few assets. Black and Litterman describe a Bayesian approach to portfolio construction. Instead of using raw expected returns and mean/variance optimization, they back out the consensus expected returns which will lead exactly to benchmark portfolio weights, and then move away from those consensus forecasts toward the raw expected forecasts in proportion to the information content of the model. Grinold (1996) also covers this territory, describing how to back out consistent and reasonable expected excess returns for multiple currency perspectives. This is especially important for institutional portfolios, which require not only an optimal return/risk trade-off, but also low risk relative to a benchmark.

PROBLEMS

1. You are researching an asset allocation strategy among global equity markets using price/earnings and price/book ratios. What difficulties might you encounter in trying to implement this with cross-sectional analysis?

2. Why might you expect to see differing January effects across countries?

3. Suppose a U.K. investor observes a BHP return of 3.5 percent, but the pound depreciates relative to the dollar by 3.5 percent over the period (e.g., from $1.50 to $1.4475). Does a U.S. investor observe a net BHP return of zero? Why or why not?

4. Evidently (from examining Table 18.3), the sample data have produced a Q(GER) for Germany that has a high correlation with currencies and a Q(JPN) for Japan that has a low correlation with currencies. How would you explain the lack of symmetry between the Japanese relationship with other currencies and the German relationship with other currencies?

REFERENCES

Ambachtscheer, Keith P. "Pension Fund Asset Allocation: In Defense of a 60/40 Equity/Debt Asset Mix." *Financial Analysts Journal*, vol. 43, no. 5, 1987, pp. 14–24.

Black, Fischer. "Capital Market Equilibrium with Restricted Borrowing." *Journal of Business*, vol. 45, 1972, pp. 444–455.

———. "Universal Hedging: Optimizing Currency Risk and Reward in International Equity Portfolios." *Financial Analysts Journal*, vol. 45, no. 4, 1989, pp. 16–22.

———. "Equilibrium Exchange Rate Hedging." *Journal of Finance*, vol. 65, no. 3, 1990, pp. 899–907.

Black, Fischer, and Robert Litterman. "Asset Allocation: Combining Investor Views with Market Equilibrium." Goldman Sachs Fixed Income Research Publication, September 1990.

———. "Global Asset Allocation with Equities, Bonds, and Currencies." Goldman Sachs Fixed Income Research Publication, October 1991.

Emanuelli, Joseph F., and Randal G. Pearson. "Using Earnings Estimates for Global Asset Allocation." *Financial Analysts Journal*, vol. 50, no. 2, 1994, pp. 60–72.

Ferson, Wayne E., and Campbell R. Harvey. "The Risk and Predictability of International Equity Returns," *Review of Financial Studies*, vol. 6, no. 3, 1992, pp. 527–566.

Grinold, Richard C. "Alpha Is Volatility Times IC Times Score." *Journal of Portfolio Management*, vol. 20, no. 4, 1994, pp. 9–16.

———. "Domestic Grapes from Imported Wine." *Journal of Portfolio Management*, Special Issue December 1996, pp. 29–40.

Kahn, Ronald N., Jacques Roulet, and Shahram Tajbakhsh. "Three Steps to Global Asset Allocation." *Journal of Portfolio Management*, vol. 23, no. 1, 1996, pp. 23–32.

Sharpe, William F. "Capital Asset Prices: A Theory of Market Equilibrium under Conditions of Risk." *Journal of Finance*, vol. 19, no. 3, 1964, pp. 425–442.

————. "Integrated Asset Allocation." *Financial Analysts Journal*, vol. 43, no. 5, 1987, pp. 25–32.

Singer, Brian D., Kevin Terhaar, and John Zerolis. "Maintaining Consistent Global Asset Views (with a Little Help from Euclid)." *Financial Analysts Journal*, vol. 54, no. 1, 1998, pp. 63–71.

Solnik, Bruno. "The Performance of International Asset Allocation Strategies Using Conditioning Information." *Journal of Empirical Finance*, vol. 1, 1993a, pp. 33–55.

Solnik, Bruno. *Predictable Time-Varying Components of International Asset Returns.* (Charlottesville, Va.: Research Foundation of Institute of Chartered Financial Analysts, 1993b).

TECHNICAL APPENDIX

In this appendix, we will derive the link between excess returns from different perspectives [Eq. (18.6)], and also the transformation of portfolio Q from the COM perspective to other perspectives.

To derive the result connecting excess returns from different perspectives, we will continue the tradition of this chapter and focus on BHP from the U.K. and U.S. perspectives. The generalization of the approach is obvious, and by using a specific example, we avoid having to remember which subscript or superscript refers to numeraire versus local market, etc. Let's begin this treatment with Eq. (18.5) from the main text:

$$R_{\text{BHP}}(\text{U.S.}|0,t) = \frac{[(\$/\pounds)(t)]}{[(\$/\pounds)(0)]} \cdot R_{\text{BHP}}(\text{U.K.}|0,t) \qquad (18\text{A}.1)$$

Just to understand the logic of this starting point, imagine taking \$1 at time 0 and converting it to U.K. pounds. You will have $1/[(\$/\pounds)(0)]$ pounds. Invest that amount in BHP from $t = 0$ to t. You then have $1/[(\$/\pounds)(0)] \cdot R_{\text{BHP}}(\text{U.K.}|0,t)$ pounds. Converting back to dollars leads to Eq. (18A.1).

To account for the multiplicative relationship between local returns and currency returns, we will use a slightly unusual definition of cumulative excess return:

$$R_{\text{BHP}}(\text{U.S.,excess}|0,t) = \frac{R_{\text{BHP}}(\text{U.S.}|0,t)}{R_{\$}(\text{U.S.}|0,t)} \qquad (18\text{A}.2)$$

where $R_{\$}(\text{U.S.}|0,t)$ is the value at time t of a U.S. money market account starting with \$1 at $t = 0$. We can similarly define excess returns to BHP from the U.K. perspective, and excess returns to U.K. pounds from the U.S. perspective. In fact,

$$R_{\text{BHP}}(\text{U.S.,excess}|0,t) = \frac{R_{\text{BHP}}(\text{U.K.,excess}|0,t)}{R_{\$}(\text{U.K.,excess}|0,t)} \qquad (18\text{A}.3)$$

Now we want to look at instantaneous excess returns r:

$$r(t) = \frac{dR(\text{excess} \mid 0,t)}{R(\text{excess} \mid 0,t)} \qquad (18\text{A}.4)$$

The calculation of this from Eq. (18A.3) is complicated by the ratio of two stochastic terms. We can apply Ito's lemma, to show that, in general, for

$$F = \frac{X}{Y} \qquad (18\text{A}.5)$$

we find $\qquad \dfrac{dF}{F} = \dfrac{dX}{X} - \dfrac{dY}{Y} + \text{Var}\left\{\dfrac{dY}{Y}\right\} - \text{Cov}\left\{\dfrac{dX}{X}, \dfrac{dY}{Y}\right\} \qquad (18\text{A}.6)$

Ito's lemma effectively tells us to expand dF in a Taylor series and keep all terms up to second order. Applying this to Eq. (18A.3), we find

$$\begin{aligned}
r_{\text{BHP}}(\text{U.S.},t) = \; & r_{\text{BHP}}(\text{U.K.},t) - r_{\$}(\text{U.K.},t) \qquad (18\text{A}.7)\\
& + \text{Var}\{r_{\$}(\text{U.K.},t)\} - \text{Cov}\{r_{\text{BHP}}(\text{U.K.},t),r_{\$}(\text{U.K.},t)\}
\end{aligned}$$

We will need one more step to derive the result in the main text. In general, for any asset n,

$$\begin{aligned}
\text{Cov}\{r_{\text{BHP}}(\text{U.S.}), r_n(\text{U.S.})\} \qquad (18\text{A}.8)\\
= \text{Cov}\{r_{\text{BHP}}(\text{U.K.}) - r_{\$}(\text{U.K.}), r_n(\text{U.K.}) - r_{\$}(\text{U.K.})\}
\end{aligned}$$

If we set $n = $ U.K. pounds, we can simplify this because the excess return to U.K. pounds from the U.K. perspective is zero:

$$\begin{aligned}
\text{Cov}\{r_{\text{BHP}}(\text{U.S.}), r_{£}(\text{U.S.})\} \qquad (18\text{A}.9)\\
= \text{Cov}\{r_{\text{BHP}}(\text{U.K.}) - r_{\$}(\text{U.K.}), - r_{\$}(\text{U.K.})\}\\
= \text{Cov}\{r_{\text{BHP}}(\text{U.K.}), - r_{\$}(\text{U.K.})\} + \text{Var}\{r_{\$}(\text{U.K.})\}
\end{aligned}$$

Substituting this into Eq. (18A.7) leads to

$$r_{\text{BHP}}(\text{U.S.}) = r_{\text{BHP}}(\text{U.K.}) + r_\$(\text{U.K.}) + \text{Cov}\{r_{\text{BHP}}(\text{U.S.}), r_\pounds(\text{U.S.})\}$$
$$(18\text{A}.10)$$

This is Eq. (18.6) in the main text.

Transforming Portfolio Q

We saw in the main text that

$$E\{r_{\text{BHP}}(\text{U.S.})\} = E\{r_{\text{BHP}}(\text{COM})\} - E\{r_\$(\text{COM})\} + \sigma_{\text{BHP,BSK}}(\text{U.S.})$$
$$(18\text{A}.11)$$

We also saw that

$$E\{r_n(\text{COM})\} = \beta_n(\text{COM}) \cdot f_Q(\text{COM}) \qquad (18\text{A}.12)$$
$$= a \cdot \sigma_{n,Q}(\text{COM})$$

where
$$a = \frac{f_Q(\text{COM})}{\sigma_Q^2(\text{COM})} \qquad (18\text{A}.13)$$

Here we are using Q to refer to the efficient portfolio from the COM perspective. We are seeking a portfolio we will call $Q_{\text{U.S.}}$. If we apply standard (not international) CAPM analysis to this portfolio from the U.S. perspective, we will find the same consensus expected excess returns as if we had used Q in the full international context.

First, we will use Eq. (18A.8) to convert the necessary covariances from Eqs. (18A.12) and (18A.11) to the U.S. perspective:

$$\sigma_{\text{BHP},Q}(\text{COM}) \qquad (18\text{A}.14)$$
$$= \sigma_{\text{BHP},Q}(\text{U.S.}) - \sigma_{\text{BSK},Q}(\text{U.S.}) - \sigma_{\text{BHP,BSK}}(\text{U.S.}) + \sigma_{\text{BSK}}^2(\text{U.S.})$$

and
$$\sigma_{\$,Q}(\text{COM}) = -\sigma_{\text{BSK},Q}(\text{U.S.}) + \sigma_{\text{BSK}}^2(\text{U.S.}) \qquad (18\text{A}.15)$$

Substituting Eqs. (18A.12), (18A.14), and (18A.15) into Eq. (18A.11) leads to

$$E\{r_{\text{BHP}}(\text{U.S.})\} = a \cdot [\sigma_{\text{BHP},Q}(\text{U.S.}) - \sigma_{\text{BHP,BSK}}(\text{U.S.})] + \sigma_{\text{BHP,BSK}}(\text{U.S.})$$
$$(18\text{A}.16)$$

If we define $Q_{U.S.}$ such that

$$E\{r_{BHP}(U.S.)\} = a \cdot [\sigma_{BHP,Q_{U.S.}}(U.S.)] \qquad (18A.17)$$

then $\sigma_{BHP,Q_{U.S.}}(U.S.) = \sigma_{BHP,Q}(U.S.) - \left(1 - \dfrac{1}{a}\right) \cdot \sigma_{BHP,BSK}(U.S.)$ (18A.18)

Hence, we can define $Q_{U.S.}$ as

$$\mathbf{h}_{Q_{U.S.}} = \mathbf{h}_Q - \left(1 - \dfrac{1}{a}\right) \cdot (\mathbf{h}_{BSK} - \mathbf{h}_\$) \qquad (18A.19)$$

We can freely add or subtract $\mathbf{h}_\$$ without influencing the covariances. We have used this property to preserve the investment level (e.g., fully invested) of Q. Note that the only adjustment in moving from Q to $Q_{U.S.}$ involves a shift in currency exposure. We are lowering our exposure to the currency basket, i.e., hedging our international currency exposure.

CHAPTER 19

Benchmark Timing

INTRODUCTION

In Chap. 4 we separated active management into benchmark timing and stock selection and postponed consideration of benchmark timing until a later chapter. We can postpone it no longer. In this chapter we will explore benchmark timing as another avenue for adding value.

The main conclusions of this chapter are as follows:

- Successful benchmark timing is hard. The potential to add value is small, although it rises with the number of independent bets per year.
- *Exceptional* or unanticipated benchmark return is the key to the benchmark timing problem. Forecasts of exceptional benchmark return lead to active beta positions.
- We can generate active betas using futures or stocks with betas different from 1. There is a cost—measured in unavoidable residual risk and transactions costs—associated with relying on stocks for benchmark timing.
- Performance measurement schemes exist to evaluate benchmark timing skill.

We'll start with the definitions.

DEFINING BENCHMARK TIMING

As discussed in Chap. 4, benchmark timing is an active management decision to vary the managed portfolio's beta with respect

541

to the benchmark. If we believe that the benchmark will do *better than usual,* then beta is increased. If we believe the benchmark will do *worse than usual,* then beta should be decreased. Notice the relative nature of our expectations—better than usual and worse than usual. We will need some feeling for what we should expect in the usual circumstances.

In its purest sense, we should think of benchmark timing as choosing the correct mixture of the benchmark portfolio and cash. This is a one-dimensional problem, and variations along that dimension should not cause any active residual bets in the portfolio; i.e., all the active risk will come from the active beta. This type of benchmark timing is akin to buying or selling futures contracts[1] on the benchmark.

Benchmark timing is not asset allocation. As we saw in Chap. 18, asset allocation focuses on aggregate asset classes rather than specific individual stocks, bonds, etc. In the simplest case, the aggregates may be domestic equity, domestic bonds and cash. In more complicated cases, the asset allocation may include several kinds of equity and bonds as well as international equities and bonds, real property, and precious metals. International managers betting on several country indices are engaged in global asset allocation, not benchmark timing. The motivation for asset allocation is to simplify an extremely complicated problem.

While tactical asset allocation involves 5 to 20 assets, benchmark timing involves only 1. This makes adding value through benchmark timing very difficult, as we can see from the fundamental law of active management. Remember that the information ratio for benchmark timing arises from a combination of forecasting skill, the benchmark timing information coefficient IC_{BT}, and breadth BR, the number of independent bets per year:

$$IR_{BT} = IC_{BT} \cdot \sqrt{BR} \qquad (19.1)$$

An independent benchmark timing forecast every quarter leads to a breadth of only 4. Then, according to Eq. (19.1), to generate a

[1]A forward contract is equivalent to being long the benchmark and short cash, i.e., borrowing to buy the benchmark. A futures contract is very similar to a forward contract.

benchmark timing information ratio of 0.5 requires an information coefficient of 0.25—extremely high! The fundamental law of active management captures exactly why most institutional managers focus on stock selection.

Stock selection strategies can diversify bets cross-sectionally across many stocks. Benchmark timing strategies can diversify only serially, through frequent bets per year. The fundamental law quantifies this. Significant benchmark timing value added can arise only with multiple bets per year. To keep this point clear, this chapter will monitor the forecast frequency: first once per year and later multiple times per year.

FUTURES VERSUS STOCKS

Benchmark timing is choosing an active beta. We can implement benchmark timing with futures. We can also implement an active beta without modifying the cash/benchmark mix. For example, if we think the benchmark will be exceptionally strong this month, then we might overemphasize the higher-beta stocks in our portfolio. However, this has three drawbacks. First, we have to take on residual risk as a result of emphasizing one group of stocks over another. Second, we must have faith that we have identified the betas of the stocks correctly. Even the best forecasts of beta are subject to error. There is no error in the pure cash/benchmark trade-off. The beta of cash is exactly 0, and the beta of the benchmark is exactly 1. Third, the transactions costs involved in trading many individual securities are generally much greater than for a forward or futures contract.

We can push the residual risk problem a bit further with the following analysis. Let's build the minimum-risk, fully invested portfolio with beta constrained to be β_P. Given the beta constraint, the portfolio which minimizes total risk will also minimize residual risk. As shown in the technical appendix, the optimal portfolio is a weighted combination of the benchmark and portfolio C. Its residual variance—the lowest possible residual variance for a fully invested portfolio with specified active beta $\beta_{PA} = \beta_P - 1$—is

$$\omega_P^2 = (\beta_{PA} \cdot \sigma_B)^2 \cdot \left(\frac{\beta_C}{1 - \beta_C}\right) \tag{19.2}$$

Assuming a benchmark risk of 18 percent and a portfolio C risk of 12 percent, and remembering that the beta of portfolio C is:

$$\beta_C = \frac{\sigma_C^2}{\sigma_B^2} \qquad (19.3)$$

an active beta of 0.1 leads to a residual risk of at least 1.6 percent. With a moderate level of residual risk aversion ($\lambda_R = 0.1$), this corresponds to a penalty of about 0.25 percent.

This analysis of the benefits of using futures rather than stocks to implement benchmark timing strategies has clear implications for situations where the benchmark has no closely associated futures contract. In that case, the potential for adding value through benchmark timing is very small.

VALUE ADDED

In Chap. 4 we derived an expression for the value added by benchmark timing. The key ingredients in this formula are

β_{PA} = the portfolio's active beta with respect to the benchmark. This is the decision variable.

Δf_B = the forecast of exceptional benchmark return. This is the departure, positive or negative, from the *usual* level of benchmark return. If μ_B is the usual annual expected excess return on the benchmark and f_B is our refined forecast of the expected excess return on the benchmark over the next year, then $\Delta f_B = f_B - \mu_B$ is the *exceptional* benchmark return in the next year.

σ_B = the volatility of the benchmark portfolio.

λ_{BT} = a measure of aversion to the risk of benchmark timing.

We will start with the simple case in which we only make one benchmark timing decision per year. In Chap. 4 we determined that the value added by benchmark timing is

$$VA\{\beta_{PA}|\Delta f_B\} = \beta_{PA} \cdot \Delta f_B - \lambda_{BT} \cdot \beta_{PA}^2 \cdot \sigma_B^2 \qquad (19.4)$$

T A B L E 19.1

Active Beta

	Aversion to Timing Risk λ_{BT}		
Exceptional Forecast Δf_B	High, 0.14	Medium 0.09	Low, 0.06
4.00%	0.05	0.08	0.12
2.00%	0.02	0.04	0.06
0.00%	0.00	0.00	0.00
−2.00%	−0.02	−0.04	−0.06
−4.00%	−0.05	−0.08	−0.12

The optimal level of active beta, β_{PA}^*, is determined by setting the derivative of Eq. (19.4) with respect to beta equal to zero. We find

$$\beta_{PA}^* = \frac{\Delta f_B}{2 \cdot \lambda_{BT} \cdot \sigma_B^2} \tag{19.5}$$

Table 19.1 shows how β_{PA}^*, will vary with changes in the exceptional forecast Δf_B and the aversion to benchmark timing risk λ_{BT}. Table 19.1 assumes a 17 percent annual volatility for the benchmark.

The value added at the optimal beta β_{PA}^* is

$$VA^*\{\Delta f_B\} = VA\{\beta_{PA}^* | \Delta f_B\} = \frac{(\Delta f_B)^2}{4 \cdot \lambda_{BT} \cdot \sigma_B^2} \tag{19.6}$$

Table 19.2 displays this value added, assuming a benchmark volatility of 17 percent. Given only one active decision per year, this corresponds to basis points *per year*.

We can take this analysis a step further by looking in depth at the forecast deviation Δf_B and the risk aversion λ_{BT}. In particular, we want to reformulate this analysis to

- Avoid the need to forecast the usual expected excess return on the market μ_B
- Make it easier to build up a forecast of exceptional return Δf_B
- Avoid having to determine the risk aversion parameter λ_{BT}

T A B L E   19.2

Value Added

Exceptional Forecast Δf_B	Aversion to Timing Risk λ_{BT}		
	High, 0.14	**Medium 0.09**	**Low, 0.06**
4.00%	9.9	15.4	23.1
2.00%	2.5	3.8	5.8
0.00%	0.0	0.0	0.0
−2.00%	2.5	3.8	5.8
−4.00%	9.9	15.4	23.1

To begin with, we can see from Eq. (19.5) that the difference Δf_B between the forecast f_B and the usual μ_B drives the optimal active beta. Hence, we can greatly simplify matters by not worrying about either μ_B or f_B and forecasting the exceptional return Δf_B directly. However, we must adjust our thinking from an absolute framework (e.g., f_B) to a relative framework (e.g., Δf_B).

This view is completely consistent with the approach to forecasting discussed in Chap. 10. Recall that the refined forecast of exceptional benchmark return is

$$\Delta f_B = \sigma_B \cdot IC \cdot S \qquad (19.7)$$

where IC = the information coefficient, the correlation between our forecasts and subsequent exceptional benchmark returns. It's a measure of skill.

  S = score, a normalized signal with mean 0 and standard deviation equal to 1 over time.

What is an appropriate level of benchmark timing skill? With sufficient data on past forecasts, you can calculate the IC directly. Without those data, or if you think that the past is not an accurate guide to the future, then reasonable IC estimates are 0.05, 0.1, or 0.15 depending on whether you are good, very good, or terrific. This is where humility should enter the game. Benchmark timing skill is rare. If you assume that you have this skill that most others lack, you may be misleading yourself. As a crude test, consider your ability to forecast whether the benchmark will do better than

T A B L E 19.3

Scores for Benchmark Timing

View	Probability	Score
Very positive	0.11	1.73
Positive	0.22	0.87
No view	0.33	0.00
Negative	0.22	-0.87
Very negative	0.11	-1.73

average.[2] With a correlation of IC = 0.1, you would expect to be correct 55 percent of the time.

Table 19.3 shows one way to translate qualitative views into quantitative scores. The scores in Table 19.3 have an average of 0 and a standard deviation of 1. The probability column indicates that we should be, on average, very positive one time in nine.

Using $\Delta f_B = \sigma_B \cdot IC \cdot S$, we can calculate the optimal active beta and value added as a function of the score:

$$\beta_{PA}^*(S) = \left(\frac{IC}{2 \cdot \lambda_{BT} \cdot \sigma_B} \right) \cdot S = \kappa \cdot S \qquad (19.8)$$

$$VA^*\{S\} = \left(\frac{IC^2}{4 \cdot \lambda_{BT}} \right) \cdot S^2 = \left(\frac{\kappa \cdot \sigma_B \cdot IC}{2} \right) \cdot S^2 \qquad (19.9)$$

Table 19.4 displays these relationships, assuming an IC of 0.10, a 17 percent benchmark volatility, and a risk aversion of 0.06.

To make the benchmark timing process more transparent, we would like to ignore the risk-aversion parameter and find a more direct way to determine aggressiveness. We can do this using κ, defined in Eq. (19.8). Assuming that the score is normally distributed, a κ of 0.06 implies that the portfolio's beta will lie between 0.94 and 1.06 two-thirds of the time, falling above 1.06 one time in six and below 0.94 one time in six. If that seems too aggressive, then decrease κ. This implies an increase in risk aversion and/or a decrease in information coefficient, but we can also deal with κ

---

[2]This does not mean better than the risk-free rate.

T A B L E   19.4

View	Probability	Score	Forecast	Active Beta	Value Added
Very positive	0.11	1.73	2.94%	0.09	0.12%
Positive	0.22	0.87	1.47%	0.04	0.03%
No view	0.33	0.00	0.00%	0.00	0.00%
Negative	0.22	−0.87	−1.47%	−0.04	0.03%
Very negative	0.11	−1.73	−2.94%	−0.09	0.12%

directly. Table 19.5 shows how κ depends on risk aversion and information coefficient.

Using κ, we can also examine value added in more detail. Equation (19.9) writes the value added conditional on the score S. The unconditional value added then is

$$VA^* = E\{VA^*\{S\}\} = \left(\frac{\kappa \cdot \sigma_B \cdot IC}{2}\right) \cdot E\{S^2\} = \left(\frac{\kappa \cdot \sigma_B \cdot IC}{2}\right) \quad (19.10)$$

using the condition that the scores have mean 0 and standard deviation 1. A very good forecaster, with an IC = 0.10, given a benchmark volatility of 17 percent and a κ of 0.05, can produce a not very impressive expected value added of 4.2 basis points.[3] And

T A B L E   19.5

κ

Skill Level	IC	Aversion to Timing Risk		
		High, 0.14	Medium, 0.09	Low, 0.06
Good	0.05	0.01	0.02	0.02
Very good	0.10	0.02	0.03	0.05
World class	0.15	0.03	0.05	0.07

---

[3]The situation is even worse if the forecaster implements the timing bet using stock selection as opposed to futures. The technical appendix will show that even a low aversion to the unavoidable residual risk of that approach will shave 2.9 basis points off that 4.2 basis points.

with only one forecast per year, this is 4.2 basis points per year. However, we shouldn't give up yet. The way to add more value with benchmark timing is to make high-quality forecasts more frequently.

FORECASTING FREQUENCY

The analysis to this point has assumed a 1-year investment horizon. That 1-year horizon is mainly responsible for the vanishing contribution of benchmark timing to value added. The strategy's information ratio and value added depend on skill and breadth, according to the fundamental law of active management, and benchmark timing once per year sets the lower positive bound on breadth (1 bet per year). To add more value, we must forecast more frequently.[4]

Assume that we can make T forecasts per year. Divide the year into T periods, indexed by $t = 1, 2, \ldots, T$, with each period of length $1/T$ years. For quarterly forecasts, $T = 4$; for monthly forecasts, $T = 12$; for weekly forecasts, $T = 52$; and for daily forecasts, $T = 250$ trading days. The volatility of the benchmark over any period t will be

$$\sigma_B(t) = \frac{\sigma_B}{\sqrt{T}} \tag{19.11}$$

Period by period, the forecasting rule of thumb still applies:

$$\Delta f_B(t) = \sigma_B(t) \cdot IC \cdot S(t) = \frac{\sigma_B \cdot IC \cdot S(t)}{\sqrt{T}} \tag{19.12}$$

Now the IC is the correlation of the forecast and return over the period of length $1/T$.

Since we ultimately keep score on an annual basis, we must analyze the annual value added generated by these higher-

---

[4]Consider the plight of a gambler who has a 65 percent chance to "beat the spread" on the Super Bowl (once per year) compared to another gambler who has a 55 percent chance to beat the spread on each of the 480 (as of 1999) regular season and playoff games.

frequency forecasts. It is the sum of the value added for each period. So, appropriately extending Eq. (19.4), we find

$$VA = \sum_{t=1}^{T} \beta_{PA}(t) \cdot \Delta f_B(t) - \lambda_{BT} \cdot \sum_{t=1}^{T} \beta_{PA}^2(t) \cdot \sigma_B^2(t) \qquad (19.13)$$

Using Eq. (19.12), this becomes

$$VA = \left(\frac{\sigma_B \cdot IC}{\sqrt{T}}\right) \cdot \sum_{t=1}^{T} \beta_{PA}(t) \cdot S(t) - \lambda_{BT} \cdot \left(\frac{\sigma_B^2}{T}\right) \cdot \sum_{t=1}^{T} \beta_{PA}^2(t) \qquad (19.14)$$

and therefore the optimal active beta in period t becomes

$$\beta_{PA}^*(t) = \sqrt{T} \cdot \left(\frac{IC}{2 \cdot \lambda_{BT} \cdot \sigma_B}\right) \cdot S(t) \qquad (19.15)$$

If we forecast once per year, this reduces to Eq. (19.8). If we forecast more frequently, we can be more aggressive. So, according to Eq. (19.15), other things being equal, our active betas will double if we forecast quarterly instead of annually. However, we will also see later that the IC may shrink as we move to shorter time periods.

Given the optimal active betas in each period, the annual value added conditional on the sequence of scores $\{S(1), S(2), \ldots, S(T)\}$ is

$$VA^*\{S(1),S(2), \ldots, S(T)\} = \left(\frac{IC^2}{4 \cdot \lambda_{BT}}\right) \cdot \sum_{t=1}^{T} S^2(t) \qquad (19.16)$$

and the unconditional expected annual value added is

$$VA^* = \left(\frac{IC^2}{4 \cdot \lambda_{BT}}\right) \cdot T \qquad (19.17)$$

This is a form of the fundamental law of active management: The optimal value added is proportional to the breadth T of the strategy. Table 19.6 shows this potential for value added for various numbers of forecasts per year and various IC levels. We have assumed a medium aversion to risk of $\lambda_{BT} = 0.09$.

These results assume that each forecast is based on new information. The forecasts must be independent. If you make one yearly forecast, then divide it by 4 and use that for the four quarterly forecasts, you have added no new information. It still counts as only one forecast per year.

T A B L E 19.6

Value Added

IC	Number of Forecasts per Year			
	1	4	12	52
0.1	2.78	11.11	33.33	144.44
0.05	0.69	2.78	8.33	36.11
0.02	0.11	0.44	1.33	5.78
0.01	0.03	0.11	0.33	1.44

To see this concretely, let us represent the benchmark's exceptional return over the year using a binary model:

$$r_B(t) - \mu_B = \theta_1 + \theta_2 + \cdots + \theta_{399} + \theta_{400} \tag{19.18}$$

where the θ_j are independent and equally likely to be $+1$ or -1. We will further specify this model in the following particular way: Of those 400 components, the first 100 occur in the first quarter, the second 400 occur in the second quarter, etc.[5] According to this model, the benchmark exceptional return has annual variance of 400 and annual risk of 20 percent, with quarterly variance of 100 and quarterly risk of 10 percent.

First assume that we make only one forecast g per year:

$$g = \theta_1 + \theta_2 + \theta_{101} + \theta_{102} + \theta_{201} + \theta_{202} + \theta_{301} + \theta_{302} + \sum_{j=1}^{8} \eta_j \tag{19.19}$$

where g includes elements of signal, the θ_k; and elements of noise, the η_j, which are independent of the θ_k and of each other. Each η_j is equally likely to equal $+1$ or -1. The variance of this raw forecast is 16; its standard deviation is 4 percent. Using Eq. (19.19), we can calculate both an annual and a quarterly information coefficient

---

[5]Alternatively, we could label these binary elements as θ_{ij}, with $i = 1, \ldots, 4$ and $j = 1, \ldots 100$. The label i would denote the quarter. We prefer the notation in the text because it emphasizes that without additional information, we will not know which binary element influences which quarter.

by correlating the forecast g with the annual and quarterly return, respectively. We find

$$IC_a = \frac{8}{20 \cdot 4} = 0.10 \tag{19.20}$$

$$IC_q = \frac{2}{10 \cdot 4} = 0.05 \tag{19.21}$$

We can substitute these results into Eq. (19.17) and see that the value added is identical whether we consider the forecast g annually or quarterly.

In contrast, suppose that we receive the same information, but in parcels each quarter. The quarterly forecasts are

$$g_1 = \theta_1 + \theta_2 + \eta_1 + \eta_2 \tag{19.22}$$

$$g_2 = \theta_{101} + \theta_{102} + \eta_3 + \eta_4 \tag{19.23}$$

$$g_3 = \theta_{201} + \theta_{202} + \eta_5 + \eta_6 \tag{19.24}$$

$$g_4 = \theta_{301} + \theta_{302} + \eta_7 + \eta_8 \tag{19.25}$$

The IC in each quarter is

$$IC_q = \frac{2}{10 \cdot 2} = 0.10 \tag{19.26}$$

and we get the full benefit of the four separate forecasts, according to Eq. (19.17). We can also observe that breaking the annual forecast g into four appropriate quarterly forecasts g_1 through g_4 requires information on precisely which components of our signal apply to which quarters. The signal g in Eq. (19.19) contains only the *sum* over all the quarterly information.

PERFORMANCE ANALYSIS

We have already discussed performance analysis generally in Chap. 17, where we even presented approaches to benchmark timing performance analysis. If we are limited to returns-based performance analysis, Chap. 17 showed how to estimate benchmark timing skill by distinguishing up-market betas from down-market betas.

For portfolio-based performance analysis (or for benchmark timing so long as we have ex ante estimates of portfolio betas), we can separate the achieved active systematic return into three components: expected active beta return, active beta surprise, and active benchmark timing return. To do this, we require two parameters: the expected benchmark return μ_B and the average active beta.

The ex ante analysis takes μ_B as given and assumes that the average active beta is 0. In an ideal world, these parameters would be part of the prior agreement between the manager and the client. With these two parameters, we can attribute the systematic active return, $\beta_{PA}(t) \cdot r_B(t)$, over the time interval $\{t, t + \Delta t\}$ as

$$\beta_{PA}(t) \cdot r_B(t) = \beta_{PA}(t) \cdot \mu_B \cdot \Delta t + \beta_{PA}(t) \cdot [r_B(t) - \mu_B \cdot \Delta t] \quad (19.27)$$

We can interpret these components as

1. The expected active return $\beta_{PA}(t) \cdot \mu_B \cdot \Delta t$
2. Benchmark timing $\beta_{PA}(t) \cdot [r_B(t) - \mu_B \cdot \Delta t]$

The benchmark timing component measures whether the portfolio's active beta is positive (negative) when the benchmark's excess return is greater (less) than $\mu_B \cdot \Delta t$. This benchmark timing term is the realization of exactly what we are hoping for in the benchmark timing utility, Eq. (19.4).

The ex post approach to portfolio-based performance attribution is very similar, except that it establishes the average market return and beta target ex post. Let

$$\bar{\beta}_{PA} = \left(\frac{1}{T}\right) \cdot \sum_{t=1}^{T} \beta_{PA}(t) \quad (19.28)$$

and

$$\bar{r}_B \cdot \Delta t = \left(\frac{1}{T}\right) \cdot \sum_{t=1}^{T} r_B(t) \quad (19.29)$$

Then we separate the active systematic return as follows:

$$\beta_{PA}(t) \cdot r_B(t) = \beta_{PA}(t) \cdot \bar{r}_B \cdot \Delta t + \bar{\beta}_{PA} \cdot [r_B(t) - \bar{r}_B \cdot \Delta t] \quad (19.30)$$
$$+ [\beta_{PA}(t) - \bar{\beta}_{PA}] \cdot [r_B(t) - \bar{r}_B \cdot \Delta t]$$

$$\text{or } \beta_{PA}(t) \cdot r_B(t) \quad (19.31)$$
$$= \beta_{PA}(t) \cdot \bar{r}_B \cdot \Delta t + \bar{\beta}_{PA} \cdot [r_B(t) - \bar{r}_B \cdot \Delta t] + \delta\beta_{PA}(t) \cdot \delta r_B(t)$$

This ex post approach is similar in spirit to the ex ante approach. The two approaches would be identical if we had specified ex ante an average return of $\bar{r}_B$ and an average beta of $\overline{\beta}_{PA}$.

Over the entire period, the first term averages to $\overline{\beta}_{PA} \cdot \bar{r}_B \cdot \Delta t$. The second term averages to zero. The third term, the benchmark timing contribution, when averaged, captures the in-sample covariance between the active beta and the benchmark returns.

We can also invent hybrid approaches, with one of the parameters set ex ante and the other ex post.

As a final, general comment, the forecasting frequency can also affect this ex post component of benchmark timing. A one-forecast-per-year strategy will exhibit not only a low information ratio and value added, but also a low t statistic. It may require many years of observations to prove with statistical confidence the existence of any benchmark timing skill.

SUMMARY

Benchmark timing strategies adjust active portfolio betas based on forecasts of exceptional benchmark returns. Benchmark timing is a one-dimensional problem, so whereas stock selection strategies can benefit from diversifying bets cross-sectionally across stocks, benchmark timing strategies can diversify bets only serially, by frequent forecasts per year. Benchmark timing can realistically generate significant value added only through such frequent forecasts per year. The most efficient approach to implementing benchmark timing is through the use of futures, as opposed to the use of stocks with betas different from 1. Performance analysis techniques exist that can measure benchmark timing contributions.

PROBLEMS

1. Given a risk aversion to benchmark timing of 0.09, an exceptional market return forecast of 5 percent, and market risk of 17 percent, what is the optimal portfolio beta?

2. Bob is a benchmark timer. His IC is 0.05, he bets once per year, and he has a low aversion to benchmark timing risk $\lambda_{BT} = 0.06$. What is his value added? What is his optimal level of active risk?

3. How many years of active returns would you require in order to determine that Bob has statistically significant (95 percent confidence level) benchmark timing skill?

4. How would the answers to problems 1 and 2 change if Bob bet 12 times per year?

REFERENCES

Ambachtsheer, Keith P. "Pension Fund Asset Allocation in Defense of a 60/40 Equity/Debt Asset Mix." *Financial Analysts Journal*, vol. 43, no. 5, 1987, pp. 14–24.

Brocato, Joe, and P. R. Chandy. "Does Market Timing Really Work in the Real World?" *Journal of Portfolio Management*, vol. 20, no. 2, 1994, pp. 39–44.

———. "Market Timing Can Work in the Real World: A Comment." *Journal of Portfolio Management*, vol. 21, no. 3, 1995, pp. 39–44.

Cumby, Robert E., and David M. Modest. "Testing for Market Timing Ability." *Journal of Financial Economics*, vol. 19, no. I, 1987, pp. 169–189.

Gennotte, Gerard, and Terry A. Marsh. "Variations in Economic Uncertainty and Risk Premiums on Capital Assets." Berkeley Research Program in Finance Working Paper 210, May 1991.

Henriksson, Roy D., and Robert C. Merton. "On Market Timing and Investment Performance II. Statistical Procedures for Evaluating Forecasting Skills." *Journal of Business*, vol. 54, no. 4, 1981, pp. 513–533.

Larsen, Glen A., Jr. and Gregory D. Wozniak. "Market Timing Can Work in the Real World." *Journal of Portfolio Management*, vol. 21, no. 3, 1995.

Modest, David. "Mean Reversion and Changing Risk Premium in the U.S. Stock Market: A Survey of Recent Evidence." Presentation at the Berkeley Program Finance Seminar, April 3, 1989.

Rudd, Andrew, and Henry K. Clasing, Jr. *Modern Portfolio Theory*, 2d ed. (Orinda, Calif.: Andrew Rudd 1988).

Sharpe, William F. "Likely Gains from Market Timing." *Financial Analysts Journal*, vol. 43, no. 2, 1975, pp. 2–11.

———. "Integrated Asset Allocation." *Financial Analysts Journal*, vol. 43, no. 5, 1987, pp. 25–32.

Wagner, Jerry, Steve Shellans, and Richard Paul. "Market Timing Works Where It Matters Most . . . in the Real World." *Journal of Portfolio Management*, vol. 18, no. 4, 1992, pp. 86–92.

TECHNICAL APPENDIX

This technical appendix will investigate how to implement a benchmark timing strategy using stocks instead of futures. It will show that such an approach leads to unavoidable residual risk.

Consider the problem of constructing a fully invested portfolio with beta β_{BT} and minimum residual risk.

Proposition 1

1. The portfolio BT,

$$\mathbf{h}_{BT} = \left(\frac{\beta_{BT} - \beta_C}{1 - \beta_C}\right) \cdot \mathbf{h}_B + \left(\frac{1 - \beta_{BT}}{1 - \beta_C}\right) \cdot \mathbf{h}_C \qquad (19A.1)$$

is the minimum-risk, fully invested portfolio with $\beta = \beta_{BT}$. As is clear from Eq. (19A.1), it is a linear combination of the benchmark and portfolio C.

2. Portfolio BT is also the minimum-*residual*-risk, fully invested portfolio with $\beta = \beta_{BT}$.

3. Portfolio BT has residual risk ω_{BT}:

$$\omega_{BT}^2 = (\beta_{PA} \cdot \sigma_B)^2 \cdot \left(\frac{\beta_C}{1 - \beta_C}\right) \qquad (19A.2)$$

where β_{PA} is portfolio BT's active beta: $\beta_{PA} = \beta_{BT} - 1$.

Proof To prove item 1, start with the observation that portfolio BT is clearly fully invested, since the weights in Eq. (19A.1) sum to 1, and the benchmark and portfolio C are fully invested. We can also quickly verify that portfolio BT has $\beta = \beta_{BT}$. More generally, we can show that portfolio BT is the solution to the problem

$$\text{Min}\{\mathbf{h}^T \cdot \mathbf{V} \cdot \mathbf{h}\} \qquad (19A.3)$$

Subject to
$$\mathbf{h}^T \cdot \mathbf{e} = 1 \qquad (19A.4)$$

$$\mathbf{h}^T \cdot \boldsymbol{\beta} = \beta_{BT} \qquad (19A.5)$$

It is the minimum-risk portfolio, subject to the constraints of full investment and $\beta = \beta_{BT}$. To derive Eq. (19A.1), we must solve the minimization problem, use the definition of portfolio C, and use the definition of the vector $\boldsymbol{\beta}$ in terms of the benchmark portfolio.

To prove item 2, for any portfolio P, we can decompose total risk as

$$\sigma_P^2 = \beta_P^2 \cdot \sigma_B^2 + \omega_P^2 \qquad (19A.6)$$

Among the universe of all portfolios with $\beta = \beta_P$, the minimum-total-risk portfolio is also the minimum-residual-risk portfolio.

To prove item 3, we can calculate the residual holding for portfolio BT:

$$\mathbf{h}_{BTR} = \mathbf{h}_{BT} - \beta_{BT} \cdot \mathbf{h}_B \tag{19A.7}$$

$$\mathbf{h}_{BTR} = \left(\frac{\beta_{PA} \cdot \beta_C}{1 - \beta_C}\right) \cdot \mathbf{h}_B + \left(\frac{1 - \beta_{BT}}{1 - \beta_C}\right) \cdot \mathbf{h}_C \tag{19A.8}$$

Using Eq. (19A.8), we can directly calculate residual variance and verify Eq. (19A.2).

We can use this result to analyze further the value-added implications of this unavoidable residual risk. Assuming T forecasts per year, we will incur expected residual risk over the year of

$$E\{\omega_{BT}^2\} = \sum_{t=1}^{T} E\{\omega_{BT}^2(t)\} \tag{19A.9}$$

The expected residual variance each period is

$$E\{\omega_{BT}^2(t)\} = \left(\frac{\sigma_B^2}{T}\right) \cdot \left(\frac{\beta_C}{1 - \beta_C}\right) \cdot E\{\beta_{PA}^2(t)\} \tag{19A.10}$$

where the benchmark total variance over period t is σ_B^2/T. Using Eq. (19.14) from the main text, which solves for the active beta each period, Eq. (19A.10) becomes

$$E\{\omega_{BT}^2(t)\} = \left(\frac{\sigma_B^2}{T}\right) \cdot \left(\frac{\beta_C}{1 - \beta_C}\right) \cdot \sum_{t=1}^{T} \left(\frac{T \cdot IC^2}{4 \cdot \lambda_{BT}^2 \cdot \sigma_B^2}\right) \cdot E\{S^2(t)\} \tag{19A.11}$$

$$E\{\omega_{BT}^2(t)\} = \left(\frac{\beta_C}{1 - \beta_C}\right) \cdot \left(\frac{T \cdot IC^2}{4 \cdot \lambda_{BT}^2}\right) \tag{19A.12}$$

Subtracting the value-added cost of this expected unconditional residual variance from the expected unconditional value added from benchmark timing [Eq. (19.16)] leads to

$$VA \rightarrow \left(\frac{T \cdot IC^2}{4 \cdot \lambda_{BT}^2}\right) \cdot \left[1 - \left(\frac{\beta_C}{1 - \beta_C}\right) \cdot \left(\frac{\lambda_R}{\lambda_{BT}}\right)\right] \tag{19A.13}$$

As we discussed in the main text, remembering that $\beta_C = \sigma_C^2/\sigma_B^2$ and assuming $\sigma_B = 18$ percent and $\sigma_C = 12$ percent leads to $\beta_C = 4/9$. Equation (19A.13) then shows that benchmark timing via stock selection leads to positive net value added only if the investor's aversion to residual risk is significantly less than his or her aversion to benchmark timing risk.

Exercise

1. Prove Eq. (19A.1), the formula for the minimum-risk, fully invested portfolio with $\beta = \beta_{BT}$.

Applications Exercises

Using the MMI stocks, build portfolio BT, the minimum-risk, fully invested portfolio with $\beta = 1.05$ relative to the (benchmark) CAPMMI. Also build portfolio C from MMI stocks.

1. What is the beta of portfolio C?
2. Compare portfolio BT to the linear combination of portfolio C and portfolio B (the CAPMMI) according to Eq. (19A.1).
3. What is the residual risk of portfolio BT? Compare the result to Eq. (19A.2).

CHAPTER 20

The Historical Record
for Active Management

INTRODUCTION

What makes for successful active management? We have argued that the process of successful active management consists of efficiently utilizing superior information. It has two key elements: finding superior information, and efficiently building portfolios based on that information.

Some sections of this book have described the meaning of superior information: better than the consensus, high information ratio, positive information coefficient, and, most likely, high breadth. We have also devoted many chapters to efficiently utilizing superior information. We showed how to process raw signals into alphas, how to build alphas into portfolios, how to trade off alphas against risk, and the cost of transacting.

We now want to step away from our prescriptions and view the historical record for active management. Ultimately we will want to see the historical evidence for our view of successful active management.

Finance academics have a fairly long history of studying active manager performance. Their motivation has typically been in the context of efficient markets theory. According to the strong version of the theory, active management is impossible. There is no source of superior information. Hence, efficient utilization is irrelevant. Of course some active managers will outperform and others will underperform, but no more so than at the roulette wheel, where some gamblers win through sheer luck.

STUDIES OF PERFORMANCE

As we discussed in Chap. 17, studies of active managers' performance began soon after the development of the CAPM, which provided a framework for performance analysis. Pioneers in this field included Jensen (1968), Sharpe (1966), and Treynor (1965).

Studies of managers' performance have focused on three separate questions: Has the average active manager outperformed, are the top performers skillful or lucky, and does performance persist? Note that a negative answer to the first of these questions would not prove that successful active management is impossible.

Let's start with the first question, about average manager performance. The early studies found that on average, mutual funds underperformed the index on a risk-adjusted basis, and that there existed a direct relationship between the level of fund expenses and the amount of underperformance. Subsequent work, summarized by Ippolito (1993), found that the performance of the average fund, net of expenses and on a risk-adjusted basis, is statistically indistinguishable from that of the index. At best, the performance of the average fund only matches the index.

More recent academic work on this question has extended the previous work in three directions: overcoming survivorship bias, controlling for style, and looking at portfolio holdings. Brown, Goetzmann, Ibbotson, and Ross (1992) demonstrate that survivorship bias in manager databases can significantly affect the results of performance studies. Several subsequent studies have very carefully built databases free of survivorship bias by including all funds that are no longer in business. Malkiel (1995), for example, shows that from 1982 through 1991, the average equity mutual fund *still existing in 1991* underperformed the S&P 500 by 43 basis points per year. But when he includes all funds that existed over that period, even those no longer in business in 1991, the average underperformance drops to 1.83 percent per year. Survivorship bias is important, and the average U.S. equity manager significantly underperforms the S&P 500.

Several more recent academic studies analyzing manager performance have controlled for style and for publicly available information. Chapter 17 has described these methods. For example, Ferson and Schadt (1996) and Ferson and Warther (1996) control for publicly available information—namely, interest rates and market dividend yields—in analyzing 67 U.S. equity mutual funds[1] from 1968 through 1990. Their approach improves average manager performance from below the market to matching the market. While their database suffers from survivorship bias, they claim that this should not affect their result concerning the improvement in average manager performance.

From a slightly different perspective, Jones (1998) has analyzed median institutional manager performance. He finds that he can explain median performance relative to the S&P 500 almost entirely with three variables: market return, small-capitalization stocks versus large-capitalization stocks, and value stocks versus growth stocks. The average manager owns some cash, has a bias toward small stocks, and has a bias toward growth stocks. Hence, the average manager tends to underperform when the market is up, large-capitalization stocks outperform, and/or value stocks outperform growth stocks.

Daniel, Grinblatt, Titman, and Wermers (1997) control for size, book-to-price, and one-year momentum effects, and use quarterly portfolio holdings for more than 2500 U.S. equity mutual funds from 1975 through 1994 in their analysis. Their approach begins by estimating quarterly asset-level returns beyond the effects of size, book-to-price, and momentum. They do this by assigning all assets to 1 of 125 groupings based on quintile rankings for these three characteristics, and then looking at each asset's active return relative to its (capitalization-weighted) group return. To analyze mutual fund returns, they use the quarterly holdings and these active asset returns. They find statistically significant evidence for positive average performance of 1 to 1.5 percent, but only for growth and aggressive growth funds over the entire period. Most of this arises from performance from 1975 through 1979.

But we must view even this small evidence for average outperformance sceptically, since the study ignored both fees *and* transactions costs. The study used not the actual mutual fund returns, but returns to quarterly buy-and-hold portfolios with no quarterly rebalance charges. There is little reason to believe that the average

---

[1]Ferson and Warther examine 63 funds.

growth or aggressive growth fund delivered any of that outperformance to investors.

Overall, there is no evidence for average active management's producing exceptional returns. Fortunately, this says nothing about the possibility of successful active management. Why would we expect the *average* manager to outperform?

To focus more on the possibility of successful active management, Marcus (1990) looked at whether top-performing mutual funds exhibited statistically significant positive performance, given the large number of funds in existence. The Marcus study is a rigorous version of the classic (and anecdotal) defense of active management: "Look at Peter Lynch, look at Warren Buffet." Using statistics for the maximum of a sample, he shows that the very top funds do outperform. Peter Lynch and Warren Buffet don't appear to be just the two out of tens of thousands of investors who are lucky enough to flip heads 10 or 15 times in a row. So this is one study that demonstrates that successful active management is possible.

But beyond whether the average fund outperforms or whether the top fund outperforms, the question concerning the possibility of successful active management that has received the most attention is whether performance persists. We now turn to this question.

PERSISTENCE OF PERFORMANCE

Do the winners in one period remain winners in a subsequent period? After 30 years of intensive research, the results fall into two camps: those that do not find persistence, and those that do.

Several studies have shown, based on different asset classes and different time periods, that performance does not persist. Jensen (1968) looked at the performance of 115 mutual funds over the 1945–1964 period and found no evidence for persistence. Kritzman (1983) reached the same conclusion after examining the 32 fixed-income managers retained by AT&T for at least 10 years. Dunn and Theisen (1983) found no evidence of persistence in 201 institutional portfolios from 1973 to 1982. And Elton, Gruber, and Rentzler (1990) showed that performance did not persist for 51 publicly offered commodity funds from 1980 to 1988.

Several other diverse studies, however, have found that performance does persist. Grinblatt and Titman (1988) found evidence of persistence in 157 mutual funds over the period 1975 to 1984. Lehmann and Modest (1987) report similar results from looking at 130 mutual funds from 1968 to 1982. In the United Kingdom, Brown and Draper (1992) demonstrated evidence for persistence using data on 550 pension managers from 1981 to 1990. Hendricks, Patel, and Zeckhauser (1993) documented persistence of performance in 165 equity mutual funds from 1974 to 1988. Goetzmann and Ibbotson (1994) showed evidence for persistence using 728 mutual funds over the period 1976 to 1988. Bauman and Miller (1994) showed evidence for persistence using as many as 608 institutional portfolios from December 1972 through September 1991, but only when using periods corresponding to complete market cycles.

Kahn and Rudd (1995), after accounting for style effects, fees and expenses, and database errors, found no evidence for persistence of performance for 300 equity funds from October 1988 through September 1994. They did, however, find evidence for persistence of performance for 195 bond funds from October 1991 through September 1994. Unfortunately, this persistence was insufficient to support an outperforming investment strategy: It could not overcome the average underperformance of bond mutual funds (especially after fees and costs). Kahn and Rudd (1997a, b, c) find similar results when they extend the analysis to additional time periods and to institutional portfolios as well as mutual funds, and when they focus on managers rather than just on mutual funds.

Now remember that Brown, Goetzmann, Ibbotson, and Ross (1992) showed that survivorship bias could significantly affect performance studies. In particular, they demonstrated that survivorship bias would generate the appearance of significant persistence. This calls into question several of the studies that found evidence for persistence. The recent work on persistence has carefully utilized databases free of survivorship bias.

Looking at all U.S. equity mutual funds from 1971 through 1991, Malkiel (1995) found evidence for persistence of performance in the 1970s, but it disappeared in the 1980s. However, Gruber (1996), also looking at 270 U.S. equity mutual funds from 1985 to 1994, found persistence so strong, that, he argued, it explained the growth in active mutual funds. Malkiel measured performance using simple CAPM regressions, while Gruber also controlled for size, book-to-price, and bond market effects. Finally, Carhart (1997) looked at 1892 diversified equity mutual funds from 1962 through 1993, controlling for size, book-to-price, and 1-year momentum effects. The only significant persistence he found was for the strong underperformance of the very worst mutual funds.

In summary, the past 30 years of research on persistence of performance has generated at best a mixed record. These data have been tortured mercilessly, analyzed in as many different ways as there have been studies, and with widely varying results even among recent studies produced by highly respected academics. In spite of mutual fund advertising (though consistent with proxy statements), the connection between historical performance and future performance is weak. The probability that a winner will repeat is not 90 percent but perhaps 55 percent, with academics strongly arguing about the statistical significance of such a result.[2]

What does the limited connection between historical performance and future performance tell us about the possibility of successful active management?

A SIMPLE MODEL OF THE MANAGER POPULATION

The mixed results on persistence of performance clearly show that a simple strategy of picking last year's winners (above-median performers) will not have much (if any) more than a 50 percent chance of being a winner (outperforming the median) this year. These results do not definitively say that active management is impossible. At the same time, they are hardly a dramatic vindication of active management. These results do say that it isn't easy to find successful active managers from their track records alone.

We can better understand this with a simple model. Instead of investments, we will consider flipping coins. Imagine that the

---

[2]Goetzmann and Ibbotson (1994), in one of the more optimistic studies, find, for example, that the probability of equity mutual fund winners' (defined by above-median alphas) repeating, on average, year by year from 1978 through 1987, is 62 percent. The more pessimistic studies find numbers like 50 percent. That roughly defines the range of the academic argument.

population consists of two different groups. There are the "persistent winners," who consistently call heads or tails correctly. They exhibit the ultimate in skill: They are correct every time.

Then there are the "coin tossers," who call heads or tails at random. Since we want to rig this to be a zero-sum game, we will set up the coin tossers to be correct slightly less than half the time. Then, when we average over the entire population, with persistent winners always correct and coin tossers correct slightly less than half the time, the calls are correct exactly half the time. We will assume that most of the population are coin tossers.

We will analyze our overall population using a 2 × 2 contingency table, Fig. 20.1. Every member of the population will call a coin toss. Half will be correct (winners), and half will be incorrect (losers). The experiment will then be repeated. Each member of the population will be either a winner or a loser on the first toss and either a winner or a loser on the second toss. A contingency table records how many members of the population are winners on both tosses, losers on both tosses, winners then losers, and losers then winners.

The persistent winners will show persistence. They will all appear in the two-time winner category. The coin tossers will show up in all four categories. Some, through sheer luck, will be consistent winners. The rest will be scattered through the other categories.

If there are no persistent winners—if coin tossers constitute the entire population—then we expect one-quarter of the population in each category. The probability of a winner repeating is exactly 50

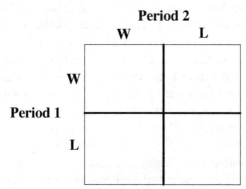

Figure 20.1 Contingency tables.

percent. In this simple model, any deviations from this random pattern result from the presence of the persistent winners. In fact, we can relate the probability p of winners repeating to the fraction δ of consistent winners in the population:

$$\delta = 1 - \frac{1}{2 \cdot p} \tag{20.1}$$

If the probability of winners repeating is just 50 percent, then $\delta = 0$. If the probability of winners repeating is 100 percent, then $\delta = 50$ percent. The consistent winners represent half the entire population. Note that in a zero-sum game, the winners can't make up more than 50 percent of the population.

Now, if the probability of winners repeating is 60 percent, which corresponds to about the highest claimed probability of investment winners' repeating in any academic study, then Eq. (20.1) implies that about 17 percent of the population is skilled.

Note that this model implies a way to identify the persistent winners: Look over more periods. This effectively divides the population into more groups. If we look at the players who call coin tosses correctly three periods in a row, these will consist of all the persistent winners, plus the few coin tossers who were lucky three times in a row. Even fewer coin tossers will be lucky four times in a row. In this way, we can filter out the persistent winners.

But this simple model does not perfectly capture the investment world. Even skilled managers do not outperform every day, or every month, or even every year. We can never escape some element of noise in historical performance numbers, and the shorter the horizon, the more that noise is a significant factor. Hence, Eq. (20.1) will underestimate the fraction of skillful managers.

Put another way, we would be happy to be able to identify managers with information ratios of 0.5. But given the levels of noise in performance numbers, in any 1-year period, such a manager has only a 69 percent chance of ouperforming (assuming normal distributions). The probability of outperforming in two consecutive periods is 48 percent. If we look at 5-year periods, then these probabilities change to 87 percent and 75 percent, respectively. Even if we choose two consecutive 5-year periods and build a contingency table as described before, only 75 percent of our target pool of managers (those with information ratios above 0.5) will show up as repeat winners. And that is if their skill (and their career with one firm) has lasted 10 years.

This simple model of the population of active managers leads to two conclusions. First, the limited evidence for persistence of performance does not rule out the possibility of successful active management. It simply puts a rough bound on the fraction of skillful managers in the population. Second, the levels of noise in performance numbers imply that historical performance will never precisely identify skillful managers.

WHAT DOES PREDICT PERFORMANCE?

After 30 years, the academics have beaten to death this question of persistence of performance. It's time to frame the question more broadly: What, if anything, does predict performance?

Here, we can rely on some results given in this book. The fundamental law of active management shows that high information ratios depend on skill and breadth. We might expect to see high information ratios for managers who hold more positions or exhibit more turnover, both of which are proxies for breadth. Of course, higher turnover also implies higher transactions costs, so the connection may not be very strong.

Stewart (1998) examined 1527 U.S. institutional equity products from January 1978 through March 1996, and found just such a connection. Rather than looking at information ratios, he grouped all managers into quintiles based on their fraction of monthly positive active returns, a measure he labeled "consistency of performance." This fraction should be a monotonic function of the information ratio,[3] and so this should correspond to information ratio quintiles as well. He found that the number of holdings, and the turnover, increases as we move to the more consistent (higher information ratio) quintiles. Furthermore, Stewart found that the more consistent performers in one period had higher active returns in the next period.

---

[3]Assuming normally distributed active returns, this fraction is just

$$1 - N\left\{\frac{-\text{IR}}{\sqrt{12}}\right\}$$

Kahn and Rudd (1997c) have presented similar results for 367 institutional equity portfolios from October 1993 through December 1996. After controlling for style effects, they regressed information ratios in the second half of the period cross-sectionally against a set of possible explanatory variables from the first half of the period. While the information ratio in the first half of the period does not show up as statistically significant, the number of assets in the portfolio does have statistically significant forecasting power, consistent with Stewart's results.

These results may be the clearest empirical evidence of the importance of the precepts in this book.[4]

WHY BELIEVE IN SUCCESSFUL ACTIVE MANAGEMENT?

We have reviewed the empirical results. The references include a long list of learned studies. We have compiled some evidence that successful active managers exist. We have encouraging evidence that the approaches outlined in this book help. But the evidence for successful active management isn't overwhelming, and besides, all this evidence looks backward. Why should we believe in active management, looking forward?

First, we know that markets aren't perfectly efficient, because market participants are human. Humans are not perfectly rational. Perhaps more surprising, humans are irrational in consistent and specific ways. The field of behavioral finance has developed to understand these persistent human behaviors and their impact on financial markets.[5]

Behavioral finance has claimed that markets are not efficient because of human behavior. Until evolution cooperates, market inefficiencies will remain available for successful active management.

---

[4]In a more flattering vein, Chevalier and Ellison (1997) have uncovered a positive connection between active returns and manager SAT scores. We naturally believe that the followers of the ideas in this book represent the high end of the active manager intelligence spectrum.

[5]One seminal article is Tversky and Kahneman (1974). See also DeBondt and Thaler (1985) and Kahneman and Riepke (1998).

Second, and perhaps paradoxically, only active management can make markets efficient. Since the development of the CAPM and efficient markets theory in the 1960s, passive management has grown in popularity. According to Ambachtsheer (1994), in the 1970s, 100 percent of institutional assets were actively managed. That fraction had dropped significantly. As he points out, if only 10 percent or 1 percent of assets were actively managed, then elementary investment research, not even efficiently implemented, should pay off. As the fraction of active management increases, some inefficiencies will remain, but they will be exploitable only with an efficient implementation. Moreover, that exploitation will be exactly at the expense of managers with inefficient processes and/or inferior information.

Ambachtsheer argues that successful active management must be possible, because efficient markets require it. Furthermore, successful active management will require both superior information and efficient implementation.

Looking forward, there are compelling arguments for believing in successful active management. But, not surprisingly, successful active management will require cleverness and hard work: to uncover information superior to that of other managers, and to implement more efficiently than other managers.

REFERENCES

Ambachtsheer, Keith P. "Active Management That Adds Value: Reality or Illusion." *Journal of Portfolio Management*, vol. 21, no. 1, 1994, pp. 89–92.

Bauman, W. Scott, and Robert E. Miller. "Can Managed Portfolio Performance Be Predicted?" *Journal of Portfolio Management*, vol. 20, no. 4, 1994, pp. 31–40.

Bello, Zakri, and Vahan Janjigian. "A Reexamination of the Market-Timing and Security-Selection Performance of Mutual Funds." *Financial Analysts Journal*, vol. 53, no. 5, 1997, pp. 24–30.

Bogle, John C. "The Implications of Style Analysis for Mutual Fund Performance Evaluation." *Journal of Portfolio Management*, vol. 24, no. 4, 1998, pp. 34–42.

Brown, G., and P. Draper. "Consistency of U.K. Pension Fund Investment Performance." University of Strath Clyde Department of Accounting and Finance, Working Paper, 1992.

Brown, Stephen J., William N. Goetzmann, Roger G. Ibbotson, and Stephen A. Ross. "Survivorship Bias in Performance Studies." *Review of Financial Studies*, vol. 5, no. 4, 1992, pp. 553–580.

Brown, Stephen J., William N. Goetzmann, and Alok Kumar. "The Dow Theory: William Peter Hamilton's Track Record Reconsidered." *Journal of Finance*, vol. 53, no. 4, 1998, pp. 1311–1333.

Brown, Stephen J., William N. Goetzmann, and Stephen A. Ross. "Survival." *Journal of Finance*, vol. 50, no. 3, 1995, pp. 853–873.

Carhart, Mark M. "On Persistence in Mutual Fund Performance." *Journal of Finance*, vol. 52, no. 1, 1997, pp. 57–82.

Chevalier, Judith, and Glenn Ellison. "Do Mutual Fund Managers Matter? An Empirical Investigation of the Performance, Career Concerns, and Behavior of Fund Managers." National Bureau of Economic Research Preprint, 1997.

Christopherson, Jon A., and Frank C. Sabin. "How Effective Is the Effective Mix?" *Journal of Investment Consulting*, vol. 1, no. 1, 1998, pp. 39–50.

Daniel, Kent, Mark Grinblatt, Sheridan Titman, and Russ Wermers. "Measuring Mutual Fund Performance with Characteristic-based Benchmarks." *Journal of Finance*, vol. 52, no. 3, 1997, pp. 1035–1058.

DeBondt, W. F. M ., and Richard Thaler. "Does the Stock Market Overreact?" *Journal of Finance*, vol. 40, no. 3, 1985, pp. 793–805.

Dunn, Patricia C., and Rolf D. Theisen. "How Consistently Do Active Managers Win?" *Journal of Portfolio Management*, vol. 9, no. 4, 1983, pp. 47–50.

Elton, E., Martin Gruber, and J. Rentzler. "The Performance of Publicly Offered Commodity Funds." *Financial Analysts Journal*, vol. 46, no. 4, 1990, pp. 23–30.

Ferson, Wayne E., and Rudi W. Schadt. "Measuring Fund Strategy and Performance in Changing Economic Conditions." *Journal of Finance*, vol. 51, no. 2, 1996, pp. 425–461.

Ferson, Wayne E., and Vincent A. Warther. "Evaluating Fund Performance in a Dynamic Market." *Financial Analysts Journal*, vol. 52, no. 6, 1996, pp. 20–28.

Goetzmann, William N., and Roger Ibbotson. "Do Winners Repeat?" *Journal of Portfolio Management*, vol. 20, no. 2, 1994, pp. 9–18.

Grinblatt, Mark, and Sheridan Titman. "The Evaluation of Mutual Fund Performance: An Analysis of Monthly Returns." Working Paper 13-86, John E. Anderson Graduate School of Management, University of California at Los Angeles, 1988.

Gruber, Martin J. "Another Puzzle: The Growth in Actively Managed Mutual Funds." *Journal of Finance*, vol. 51, no. 3, 1996, pp. 783–810.

Hendricks, Darryll, Jayendu Patel, and Richard Zeckhauser. "Hot Hands in Mutual Funds: Short-Run Persistence of Relative Performance, 1974–1988." *Journal of Finance*, vol. 48, no. 1, 1993, pp. 93–130.

Ippolito, Richard A. "On Studies of Mutual Fund Performance 1962–1991." *Financial Analysts Journal*, vol. 49, no. 1, 1993, pp. 42–50.

Jensen, Michael C. "The Performance of Mutual Funds in the Period 1945–1964." *Journal of Finance*, vol. 23, no. 2, 1968, pp. 389–416.

Jones, Robert C. "Why Most Active Managers Underperform (and What You Can Do About It)." In *Enhanced Index Strategies for the Multi-Manager Portfolio*, edited by Brian Bruce (New York: Institutional Investor, 1998).

Kahn, Ronald N., and Andrew Rudd. "Does Historical Performance Predict Future Performance?" *Financial Analysts Journal*, vol. 51, no. 6, 1995, pp. 43–52.

———. "The Persistence of Equity Style Performance: Evidence from Mutual Fund Data." In *The Handbook of Equity Style Management*, 2d ed., edited by J. Daniel Coggin, Frank J. Fabozzi, and Robert D. Arnott (New Hope, Pa. Frank J. Fabozzi Associates, 1997a).

———. "The Persistence of Fixed Income Style Performance: Evidence from Mutual Fund Data." In *Managing Fixed Income Portfolios*, edited by Frank J. Fabozzi (New Hope, Pa: Frank J. Fabozzi Associates, 1997b), chap. 18.

———. "The Persistence of Institutional Portfolio Performance." BARRA International Research Seminar, Montreux, Switzerland, September 1997c.

Kahneman, Daniel, and Mark W. Riepke. "Aspects of Investor Psychology." *Journal of Portfolio Management*, vol. 24, no. 4, 1998, pp. 52–65.

Kritzman, M. "Can Bond Managers Perform Consistently?" *Journal of Portfolio Management*, vol. 9, no. 4, 1983, pp. 54–56.

Lehmann, Bruce N., and David M. Modest. "Mutual Fund Performance Evaluation: A Comparison of Benchmarks and Benchmark Comparisons." *Journal of Finance*, vol. 42, no. 2, 1987, pp. 233–265.

Malkiel, Burton G. "Returns from Investing in Equity Mutual Funds 1971 to 1991." *Journal of Finance*, vol. 50, no. 2, 1995, pp. 549–572.

Marcus, Alan J. "The Magellan Fund and Market Efficiency." *Journal of Portfolio Management*, vol 17, no. 1, 1990, pp 85–88.

Sharpe, William F. "Mutual Fund Performance." *Journal of Business*, vol. 39, no. 1, Part II, 1966, pp. 119–138.

Stewart, Scott D. "Is Consistency of Performance a Good Measure of Manager Skill?" *Journal of Portfolio Management*, vol. 24, no. 3, 1998, pp. 22–32.

Treynor, Jack L. "How to Rate Management of Investment Funds." *Harvard Business Review*, vol. 43, January–February 1965, pp. 63–75.

Tversky, Amos, and Daniel Kahneman. "Judgment under Uncertainty: Heuristics and Biases." *Science*, vol. 185, 1974, pp. 1124–1131.

Open Questions

INTRODUCTION

For 20 chapters, we have aspired to be magicians. We have attempted to present a comprehensive and seamless theory: covering every aspect of active portfolio management, and smoothly flowing from foundations to expected returns and valuation to information processing to implementation.

We must now confess—if you don't already know—that the theory isn't seamless. We have swept aside, ignored, or simply assumed away the poorly understood aspects of portfolio management—the open questions—that require additional work.

Successful active management efficiently utilizes superior information. The search for the next source of superior information is an inherent open question all the time for every active manager, but it isn't an open question for active management. We will not deal here with any specifically focused valuation questions (e.g., what combination of accounting variables correlates most closely with future returns?).

Instead, we wish to highlight open questions for the process of active management. Our goal is to emphasize that we haven't completed the theory of active portfolio management. It is still fertile ground for research.[1]

---

[1] In 1900, the mathematician David Hilbert presented a now-famous list of important open questions as a challenge and a research plan for the mathematics community for the twentieth century. This book is appearing at the beginning of the twenty-first century, but we cannot claim ambitions quite as lofty.

These open questions will cover the general topics of

- Dynamics
- Transactions costs
- Liabilities, asset allocation, and risk over time
- Nonlinearities
- After-tax investing
- Behavioral finance

DYNAMICS

Active portfolio management is a dynamic problem. We manage portfolios over time. We confront a flow of information (and noise). Risk changes as volatilities change and as our exposures change over time. (Benchmark timing is just the most obvious example.) Transactions costs change over time and with our speed of trading.

Active portfolio management confronts these changing parameters simultaneously. With a proper frame, managers should make investment decisions now, accounting for these dynamics and interactions now and in the future.

This full dynamic problem is both complicated and important. One simple open question is, when should we trade? This simple question demands more than just a static analysis. If transactions costs were zero, the solution would be obvious: Trade every time the alpha changes. But transactions costs aren't zero. When should we trade, given the dynamics of returns, risks, and costs over time?

Another open question concerns dynamic strategies and risk. Even if single-period returns are normal or lognormal, dynamic strategies can generate skewed and optionlike return patterns. Portfolio insurance is one example. So another open question is, how should we decide on an appropriate dynamic strategy, and what are its implications for our return distribution?

TRANSACTIONS COSTS

As we stated in Chap. 16, there is no CAPM or Black-Scholes model of transactions costs. A complete and practical model of transactions costs would cover three important aspects: tightness, depth, and resiliency. Tightness measures the bid/ask spread. Depth measures market impact. Resiliency measures how depth or market impact evolves over time. An investor buys a large block and pushes up the price. How long will it take for the price to sink back to equilibrium? What factors influence resiliency? One open question is, how do we model tightness, depth, and resiliency? A second open question is, how do transactions costs in one stock influence transactions costs in other stocks?

LIABILITIES, ASSET ALLOCATION, AND RISK OVER TIME

Investors choose assets based on their future liabilities. This is most obvious in strategic asset allocation. Accurate liability modeling is one open question. Liabilities aren't certain. They are often contingent on other factors (e.g., inflation, dead or alive). Another question concerns managing assets against fixed-horizon liabilities. How should our asset allocation change as we approach retirement, and move past it?

NONLINEARITIES

Nonlinearities arise in at least two contexts in finance. We empirically observe nonlinear responses to certain exposures, particularly size. Relative behavior along the size dimension is still poorly understood. How do small stocks behave relative to midcap, large, and megacap stocks? Size is a pervasive issue in portfolio management. It enters into benchmarks and market averages. It is linked to the typical long-only constraint. The open question is, How do we adequately capture the nonlinear (and multidimensional) behavior of size?

Quite separately, researchers have investigated the applicability of nonlinear dynamic models like chaos or catastrophe theory to finance. An open question: Do nonlinear models offer any predictive power for understanding financial market behavior?

AFTER-TAX INVESTING

Managing after-tax returns is extremely complicated. It combines all the intricacies of dynamic portfolio management with wash sale rules, multiple tax rates dependent on holding periods, and even calendar date dependencies. We should respond differently to a set of alphas we receive in January from the way we respond to one we receive in December. We will never solve this problem exactly.

The current approaches to after-tax investing are reasonable but simplistic. Most analyze the one-period problem, placing a penalty on net realized capital gains each period. There are two open questions here: How good are these simple approaches, and how much better can we do?

BEHAVIORAL FINANCE

Our final question touches on a topic related to valuation, but from a very broad perspective.

Traditional finance theories assume perfectly rational investor behavior. Underneath that assumption is perhaps the idea that while investors aren't perfectly rational, their departures from rationality are unique and random and should wash out across the marketplace.

Investment psychologists have now demonstrated, however, that investors are irrational in systematic and predictable ways. They have even named and cataloged these systematic effects.

So far, behavioral finance has mainly served as an argument for why some anomalies (e.g., residual reversal) continue to work over time. It has helped explain several known market phenomena.

The open question for behavioral finance is whether it has predictive ability. Can first principles of psychology lead to new investment strategies?

SUMMARY

We have presented several open questions concerning the process of active management. Many of them involve the interaction of several separately solvable phenomena (e.g., changing alphas and transactions costs), often dynamically over time. Others involve the potential application of new methodologies to finance. Some of these open questions are technical. All have important implications. The process of active portfolio management is still a vibrant area of research.

Summary

In *Active Portfolio Management*, we have attempted to provide a comprehensive treatment of the process of active management, covering both basic principles and many practical details. In summary, we will review what we have covered, the major themes of the book, and what is now left for the active manager to do.

WHAT WE HAVE COVERED

The book began by covering the foundations: the appropriate framework for active management, and the basic portfolio theory required to navigate in that framework. The active management framework begins with a benchmark portfolio and defines exceptional returns relative to that benchmark. Active managers seek exceptional returns, at the cost of assuming risk. Active managers trade off their forecasts of exceptional return against this additional risk. We measure value added as the risk-adjusted exceptional return. The key characteristic measuring a manager's ability to add value is the information ratio, the amount of additional exceptional return he or she can generate for each additional unit of risk. The information ratio is both a figure of merit and a budget constraint. A manager's ability to add value is constrained by her or his information ratio.

Given this framework, portfolio theory connects exceptional return forecasts—return forecasts which differ from consensus expected returns—with portfolios that differ from the benchmark. If a manager's forecasts agree with the consensus, that manager will hold the benchmark. To the extent that a manager's forecasts differ from the consensus, and to the extent that his or her information ratio is positive, that manager will hold a portfolio that differs from the consensus.

The information ratio arises repeatedly as the variable governing active management, and the fundamental law of active management provides insight into its components. High information ratios require both skill and breadth. Skill is captured by information coefficients—correlations between a manager's forecasts of exceptional return and their subsequent realization. Breadth measures the manager's available number of independent forecasts per year. Breadth allows the manager to diversify his or her imperfect forecasts of the future. High information ratios may combine low skill with large breadth, high skill with small breadth, or something in between.

With the framework, basic theory, and insights in place, the book went on to cover the process of active management. Day-to-day active management begins with the processing of raw signals into exceptional return forecasts and moves on to implementation: portfolio construction, trading, and subsequent performance analysis. The forecasting process may depend on a factor model (like APT) or on individual stock valuation models. Forecasting includes the processing of raw information into refined alpha forecasts. Active management also requires research in order to find valuable information. Once again, a process exists for analyzing the information content of potential signals and refining them for use in active management.

THEMES

We hope that several themes have strongly emerged from the text and the equations. First, active management is a process. Active management begins with raw information, refines it into forecasts, and then optimally and efficiently constructs portfolios balancing those forecasts of return against risk. Active management should consist of more than merely buying a few stocks you think will go up. The raw information may be the list of stocks you think will go up, and it certainly need not be derived from a quantitative model. But starting with this information, active management is a disciplined approach to acting on that information, based on a rigorous analysis of its content.

A second theme of the book is that active management is forecasting, and a key to active manager performance is superior information. In fact, most of this book describes the machinery for processing this superior information into portfolios. If your forecasts match the consensus, or if your forecasts differ from the consensus but contain no information, this machinery will lead you back to the benchmark. Only as you develop superior information will your portfolio deviate from the benchmark.

The third strong theme of the book is that active managers should forecast as often as possible. The fundamental law shows that the information ratio depends on both skill and breadth, the number of independent forecasts or bets per year. Given the realities (and difficulties) of active management, the best hope for a large information ratio is to develop a small edge and bet very often—e.g., forecast returns to 500 stocks every quarter. In this search for breadth, we also advocate using multiple sources of information—the more the better. In line with this theme of breadth, the reader should also notice that we are not strong proponents of benchmark timing. The fundamental law shows that benchmark timing is seldom fruitful.

A fourth, and to some readers surprising, theme that we hope has emerged is that mathematics cannot overcome ignorance. If your raw information is valueless, no mathematical transformation will help. In this book, we have presented the mathematics for investing efficiently based on superior information from any source. We have tried to avoid wherever possible the use of mathematics to obscure lack of information.

WHAT'S LEFT?

We have described the process and machinery of active management, starting from superior information. Much of this machinery is available from vendors, or available to implement on your own, if you wish. But clearly, the focus of the active manager, and what this book ultimately can't help with, is the search for superior information.

Seeking superior information in this zero-sum game is lonely. Jack Treynor once described the process this way: If he identifies a stock he thinks will go up, he talks to his wife about it. If she is enthusiastic, he asks his barber. From there, he discusses the idea with his accountant and his lawyer. If they all agree it's a great idea—he doesn't buy the stock. If everyone agrees with him, the price must already reflect his insight.

We have covered where to look for superior information, we have discussed forecasting factor returns and forecasting asset specific returns, and we have described particular information sources that have proven valuable in the past. These may still be valuable now, but over time they must begin to inform the consensus expected returns. New, clever ideas will always help the active manager.

Once you have found superior information, this book provides the best path to success with active management.

Standard Notation

This appendix covers standard notation used repeatedly throughout the book. It does not cover notation introduced and used only in one particular section.

In general, we represent vectors in lowercase bold letters and matrices in uppercase bold letters. To refer to an element of a vector or matrix, we use subscripts and do not use bold, e.g., r_n, the excess return to asset n, is the nth element of $\mathbf{r}$, the vector of asset excess returns.

REALIZED RETURNS

$\mathbf{R}$	total returns $[(P_{\text{new}} + \text{dividend})/P_{\text{old}}]$
i_F	risk-free rate of return
R_F	risk-free total return
$\mathbf{r}$	excess returns
$\boldsymbol{\theta}$	residual returns
$\mathbf{b}$	factor returns
$\mathbf{u}$	specific returns

EXPECTED RETURNS

$\mathbf{f}$	expected excess returns
$\boldsymbol{\mu}$	long-term expected excess returns
$\boldsymbol{\alpha}$	expected residual returns
$\boldsymbol{\phi}$	expected exceptional returns
$\mathbf{m}$	expected factor returns

RISK

σ	total risk
ω	residual risk
ψ	active risk
$\boldsymbol{\beta}$	asset betas
β_P	portfolio beta (exposure to benchmark risk)
β_{PA}	active portfolio beta

V   asset-by-asset covariance matrix
F   factor covariance matrix
Δ   specific variance matrix

PORTFOLIOS AND ASSETS

$\mathbf{h}_P$ portfolio holdings
$\mathbf{h}_{PR}$ residual portfolio holdings
$\mathbf{h}_{PA}$ active portfolio holdings
X   matrix of all assets' exposures to factors
$\mathbf{x}_P$ vector of portfolio P's exposure to factors

PERFORMANCE AND VALUE ADDED

λ_T total risk aversion
λ_{BT} benchmark timing risk aversion
λ_R residual risk aversion
λ_A active risk aversion
λ_S short-term risk aversion
SR   Sharpe ratio
IR   information ratio
IC   information coefficient
BR   breadth

PORTFOLIO NAMES

B benchmark portfolio
M market portfolio
Q fully invested portfolio with maximum Sharpe ratio
C fully invested portfolio with minimum risk
q minimum-risk portfolio with expected return $= 1$
A minimum-risk portfolio with $\alpha = 1$
S portfolio with minimum expected $\{R_P^2\}$

OTHER

e   vector of 1s

Glossary

This glossary defines some of the most commonly used terms in the book.

Active management The pursuit of investment returns in excess of a specified benchmark.

Active return Return relative to a benchmark. If a portfolio's return is 5 percent, and the benchmark's return is 3 percent, then the portfolio's active return is 2 percent.

Active risk The risk (annualized standard deviation) of the active return. This is also called the tracking error.

Alpha The expected residual return. Outside the pages of this book, alpha is sometimes defined as the expected exceptional return and sometimes as the realized residual or exceptional return.

Arbitrage To profit because a set of cash flows has different prices in different markets.

Benchmark A reference portfolio for active management. The goal of the active manager is to exceed the benchmark return.

Beta The sensitivity of a portfolio (or asset) to a benchmark. For every 1 percent return to the benchmark, we expect a β percent return to the portfolio.

Breadth The number of independent forecasts available per year. A stock picker forecasting returns to 100 stocks every quarter exhibits a breadth of 400 if each forecast is independent (based on separate information).

Certainty equivalent return The certain (zero-risk) return an investor would trade for a given (larger) return with an associated risk. For example, a particular investor might trade an expected 3 percent active return with 4 percent risk for a certain active return of 1.4 percent.

Characteristic portfolio A portfolio which efficiently represents a particular asset characteristic. For a given characteristic, it is the minimum-risk portfolio with the portfolio characteristic equal to 1. For example, the characteristic portfolio of asset betas is the benchmark. It is the minimum-risk $\beta = 1$ portfolio.

Common factor An element of return that influences many assets. According to multiple-factor risk models, the common factors determine correlations between asset returns. Common factors include industries and risk indices.

Descriptor   A variable describing assets, used as an element of a risk index. For example, a volatility risk index, distinguishing high-volatility assets from low-volatility assets, could consist of several descriptors based on short-term volatility, long-term volatility, systematic and residual volatility, etc.

Dividend discount model   A model of asset pricing, based on discounting the future expected dividends.

Dividend yield   The dividend per share divided by the price per share. Also known as the yield.

Earnings yield   The earnings per share divided by the price per share.

Efficient frontier   A set of portfolios, one for each level of expected return, with minimum risk. We sometimes distinguish different efficient frontiers based on additional constraints, e.g., the fully invested efficient frontier.

Exceptional return   Residual return plus benchmark timing return. For a given asset with $\beta = 1$, if the residual return is 2 percent and the benchmark portfolio exceeds its consensus expected returns by 1 percent, then the asset's exceptional return is 3 percent.

Excess return   Return relative to the risk-free return. If an asset's return is 3 percent and the risk-free return is 0.5 percent, then the asset's excess return is 2.5 percent.

Factor portfolio   The minimum-risk portfolio with unit exposure to the factor and zero exposure to all other factors. The excess return to the factor portfolio is the factor return.

Factor return   The return attributable to a particular common factor. We decompose asset returns into a common factor component, based on the asset's exposures to common factors times the factor returns, and a specific return.

Information coefficient   The correlation of forecast returns with their subsequent realizations. A measure of skill.

Information ratio   The ratio of annualized expected residual return to residual risk, a central measurement for active management. Value added is proportional to the square of the information ratio.

Market   The portfolio of all assets. We typically replace this abstract construct with a more concrete benchmark portfolio.

Normal   A benchmark portfolio.

Passive management   Managing a portfolio to match (not exceed) the return of a benchmark.

Payout ratio   The ratio of dividends to earnings. The fraction of earnings paid out as dividends.

Regression   A data analysis technique which optimally fits a model based on the squared differences between data points and model fitted points. Typically, regression chooses model coefficients to minimize the (possibly weighted) sum of these squared differences.

Residual return   Return independent of the benchmark. The residual return is the return relative to beta times the benchmark return. To be exact, an asset's residual return equals its excess return minus beta times the benchmark excess return.

Residual risk   The risk (annualized standard deviation) of the residual return.

Risk-free return   The return achievable with absolute certainty. In the U.S. market, short-maturity Treasury bills exhibit effectively risk-free returns. The risk-free return is sometimes called the time premium, as distinct from the risk premium.

Risk index   A common factor typically defined by some continuous measure, as opposed to a common industry membership factor defined as 0 or 1. Risk index factors include size, volatility, value, and momentum.

Risk premium   The expected excess return to the benchmark.

R squared   A statistic usually associated with regression analysis, where it describes the fraction of observed variation in data captured by the model. It varies between 0 and 1.

Score   A normalized asset return forecast. An average score is 0, with roughly two-thirds of the scores between -1 and 1. Only one-sixth of the scores lie above 1.

Security market line   The linear relationship between asset returns and betas posited by the capital asset pricing model.

Sharpe ratio   The ratio of annualized excess returns to total risk.

Skill   The ability to accurately forecast returns. We measure skill using the information coefficient.

Specific Return   The part of the excess return not explained by common factors. The specific return is independent of (uncorrelated with) the common factors and the specific returns to other assets. It is also called the idiosyncratic return.

Specific risk   The risk (annualized standard deviation) of the specific return.

Standard error   The standard deviation of the error in an estimate; a measure of the statistical confidence in the estimate.

Systematic return   The part of the return dependent on the benchmark return. We can break excess returns into two components: systematic and residual. The systematic return is the beta times the benchmark excess return.

Systematic risk The risk (annualized standard deviation) of the systematic return.

t **statistic** The ratio of an estimate to its standard error. The *t* statistic can help test the hypothesis that the estimate differs from zero. With some standard statistical assumptions, the probability that a variable with a true value of zero would exhibit a *t* statistic greater than 2 in magnitude is less than 5 percent.

Tracking error See *active risk.*

Value added In the context of this book, the utility, or risk-adjusted return, generated by an investment strategy: the return minus a risk aversion constant times the variance. The value added depends on the performance of the manager and the preferences of the owner of the funds.

Volatility A loosely defined term for risk. In this book, we define volatility as the annualized standard deviation of return.

Yield See *dividend yield.*

Return and
Statistics Basics

This appendix will very briefly cover the basics of returns, statistics, and simple linear regression. We provide a list of basic references at the end.

RETURNS

We define returns over a period t, of length Δt, which runs from t to $t + \Delta t$. If the asset's price at t is $P(t)$ and at $t + \Delta t$ is $P(t + \Delta t)$, and the distributions[1] over the period total $d(t)$, then the asset's total return is

$$R(t) = \frac{P(t + \Delta t) + d(t)}{P(t)} \tag{C.1}$$

The asset's total rate of return is

$$rr(t) = R(t) - 1 \tag{C.2}$$

We can also calculate a total return R_F and total rate of return i_F for the risk-free asset (e.g., a Treasury bill of maturity Δt). Then we define the asset's excess return as

$$r(t) = R(t) - R_F(t) \tag{C.3}$$

or
$$r(t) = rr(t) - i_F(t) \tag{C.4}$$

Throughout this book, we focus mainly on excess returns and decompositions of excess returns. We occasionally use total returns, and never explicitly use total rates of return.

Return calculations become more difficult where they involve stock splits, stock dividends, and other corporate actions. We will not explicitly treat those critical details here.

---

[1]We label the distributions over the period $d(t)$. If the period Δt is relatively long and a cash distribution occurs in midperiod, we could assume reinvestment of the distribution over the rest of the period at either the risk-free rate of return or the asset rate of return.

STATISTICS

Here we will briefly define how to calculate means, standard deviations, variances, covariances, and correlations, and briefly discuss their standard errors. Let's start with a set (a sample) of observed excess returns to stock n, $r_n(t)$, where $t = 1, \ldots, T$. So we have observed stock n for T months. The mean return over the period (the sample mean) is $\bar{r}_n$:

$$\bar{r}_n = \left(\frac{1}{T}\right) \cdot \sum_{t=1}^{T} r_n(t) \tag{C.5}$$

The sample variance is

$$\text{Var}\{r_n\} = \left(\frac{1}{T-1}\right) \cdot \sum_{t=1}^{T} [r_n(t) - \bar{r}_n]^2 \tag{C.6}$$

and the sample standard deviation is

$$\text{Std}\{r_n\} = \sqrt{\text{Var}\{r_n\}} \tag{C.7}$$

Note the use of $T - 1$ in the denominator of Eq. (C.6). We use $T - 1$ instead of T to calculate an unbiased estimate of the variance, on the assumption that we are estimating both the sample mean and the sample variance. If we knew the mean with certainty, independent of the sample mean, we would use T in the denominator of Eq. (C.6). We recommend limited use of statistics in very-small-sample situations, where using T versus $T - 1$ can lead to very different results.

To complete our discussion of basic statistical calculations, consider the excess returns to another asset m, $r_m(t)$, $t = 1, \ldots, T$. The covariance of returns to assets n and m is

$$\text{Cov}\{r_n, r_m\} = \left(\frac{1}{T-1}\right) \cdot \sum_{t=1}^{T} [r_n(t) - \bar{r}_n] \cdot [r_m(t) - \bar{r}_m] \tag{C.8}$$

Note that $\qquad\qquad \text{Cov}\{r_n, r_n\} = \text{Var}\{r_n\} \tag{C.9}$

and $\qquad\qquad\qquad \text{Cov}\{r_m, r_n\} = \text{Cov}\{r_n, r_m\} \tag{C.10}$

Finally, the correlation of returns to assets n and m is

$$\mathrm{Corr}\{r_n, r_m\} = \frac{\mathrm{Cov}\{r_n, r_m\}}{\mathrm{Std}\{r_n\} \cdot \mathrm{Std}\{r_m\}} \qquad (\text{C.11})$$

STANDARD ERRORS

The standard error of an estimate is the standard deviation of the errors in its estimation, a basic measure of its accuracy. Assuming that the errors in the estimate are normally distributed, the standard error for the estimated mean is

$$\mathrm{SE}\{\bar{r}\} = \frac{\mathrm{Std}\{r\}}{\sqrt{T}} \qquad (\text{C.12})$$

The standard error of the estimated standard deviation is approximately

$$\mathrm{SE}\{\mathrm{Std}\{r\}\} \approx \frac{\mathrm{Std}\{r\}}{\sqrt{2 \cdot T}} \qquad (\text{C.13})$$

and the standard error of the estimated variance is approximately

$$\mathrm{SE}\{\mathrm{Var}\{r\}\} \approx \mathrm{Var}\{r\} \cdot \sqrt{\frac{2}{T}} \qquad (\text{C.14})$$

These approximations become more exact in the limit of large sample size, i.e., very large T.

SIMPLE LINEAR REGRESSION

Throughout the book, we make extensive use of regression analysis. The simplest type of regression in the book estimates betas by regressing excess returns against market returns:

$$r_n(t) = \alpha_n + \beta_n \cdot r_{\mathrm{mkt}}(t) + \epsilon_n(t) \qquad (\text{C.15})$$

Simple linear regression (OLS, or ordinarily least squares) estimates α_n and β_n by minimizing the sum of squared errors (ESS):

$$\mathrm{ESS} = \sum_{t=1}^{T} \epsilon_n^2(t) \qquad (\text{C.16})$$

The estimate of β_n is

$$\beta_n = \frac{\text{Cov}\{r_n, r_{\text{mkt}}\}}{\text{Var}\{r_{\text{mkt}}\}} \qquad (C.17)$$

and that of α_n is $\qquad \alpha_n = \bar{r} - \beta_n \cdot \bar{r}_{\text{mkt}} \qquad (C.18)$

These results use sample estimates of means, variances, and covariances. In the book, we generally define betas using Eq. (C.17), but with variances and covariances *forecast* using a covariance matrix.

The R^2 of the regression is defined as

$$R^2 = 1 - \frac{\text{Var}\{\epsilon_n\}}{\text{Var}\{r_n\}} \qquad (C.19)$$

Another useful result of basic regression is that the errors $\epsilon_n(t)$ are uncorrelated with the excess returns $r_n(t)$:

$$\text{Cov}\{r_n, \epsilon_n\} = 0 \qquad (C.20)$$

More general regression analysis can involve more independent variables and use weighted sums of squares, but the basic idea is the same. The procedure estimates model parameters by minimizing the (possibly weighted) sum of squared errors. The resulting errors are uncorrelated with the returns. The definition of R^2 remains the same. For a thorough introduction to regression analysis, see the texts of Hoel, Port, and Stone; Hogg and Craig; and Neter and Wasserman.

REFERENCES

Hoel, Paul G., Sidney C. Port, and Charles J. Stone. *Introduction to Probability Theory* (Boston: Houghton Mifflin, 1971).
———. *Introduction to Statistical Theory* (Boston: Houghton Mifflin, 1971).
Hogg, Robert V., and Allen T Craig. *Introduction to Mathematical Statistics* (New York: Macmillan, 1970).
Neter, John, and William Wasserman. *Applied Linear Statistical Models* (Homewood Ill.: Richard D. Irwin, 1974).
Pindyck, Robert S., and Daniel L. Rubinfeld. *Econometric Models & Economic Forecasts*, 3d ed. (New York: McGraw-Hill, 1991).

INDEX

Achievement, information ratio as measure of, 112
Active management, 1–2
  as dynamic problem, 574
  as forecasting, 261
  and information, 316–318
  information ratio as key to, 125
  objective of, 119–121
  as process, 578–579
Active returns, 89, 102–103
Active risk, 50
After-tax investing, 575–576
Allocation (see Asset allocation)
Alpha(s), 91–92
  benchmark-neutral, 384–385
  characteristic portfolio of, 134
  definition of, 111–112
  and event studies, 331–332
  extreme values, trimming, 382–383
  and information horizon, 357–359
  and information ratio, 127–129
  and portfolio construction, 379–385, 411–413
  risk-factor-neutral, 385
  scaling, 311–312, 382
American Express, 20–21, 67
Arbitrage pricing theory (APT), 13, 26, 173–192
  applications of, 187–190
  assumptions of, 177–178
  examples using, 178–181
  and factor forecasting, 185–190, 194–197, 304
  and Portfolio Q, 182–185
  rationale of, 181–182
  and returns-based analysis, 249
  and valuation, 203–205, 207, 208, 218–220
  and weaknesses of CAPM, 174–177
ARCH, 279–280
Asset allocation, 517–532
  asset selection vs., 518
  and construction of optimal portfolios, 525–532
  and forecasting of returns, 520–525

Asset allocation (*Cont.*)
  and international consensus expected returns, 526–532
  and liability, 575
  out-of-sample portfolio performance, 532–533
  technical aspects of, 536–539
  as three-step process, 519–520
  types of, 517
Asset valuation, 6–7
AT&T, 67
Attributed returns, cumulation of, 510–512
Attribution, performance, 498–503
Attribution of risk, 78, 81–83
Autocorrelation, 491
Aversion to total risk, 96

BARRA, 4, 51, 60, 63, 73, 184–186, 188, 252, 284, 435, 438, 449, 454, 500
Behavioral finance, 576
Benchmark risk, 100–101
Benchmark timing, 101–102, 491–493, 541–554
  defining, 541–542
  and forecasting frequency, 549–552
  with futures, 543–544
  and performance analysis, 552–554
  technical aspects of, 555–558
  and value added, 544–549
Benchmarks, 5, 88–90, 426–428
Beta, 13–16
  forecasts of, 24
  and information ratio, 125–127, 140
  a priori estimates of, 493
Biased data, 450
Book-to-price ratios, 322, 323
Breadth, 6, 148

Capital asset pricing model (CAPM), 11–40, 487–489, 494, 496, 503, 560
  assumptions of, 13–16, 27–28
  characteristic portfolios in, 28–35
  and efficient frontier, 35–37
  and efficient markets theory, 17–18
  example of analysis using, 20–21
  and expected returns, 11, 18–19

About the Authors

Richard C. Grinold, Ph.D., is Managing Director, Advanced Strategies and Research at Barclays Global Investors. Dr. Grinold spent 14 years at BARRA, where he served as Director of Research, Executive Vice President, and President; and 20 years on the faculty at the School of Business Administration at the University of California, Berkeley, where he served as the chairman of the finance faculty, chairman of the management science faculty, and director of the Berkeley Program in Finance.

Ronald N. Kahn, Ph.D., is Managing Director in the Advanced Active Strategies Group at Barclays Global Investors. Dr. Kahn spent 11 years at BARRA, including over seven years as Director of Research. He is on the editorial advisory board of the *Journal of Portfolio Management* and the *Journal of Investment Consulting*.

Both authors have published extensively, and are widely known in the industry for their pioneering work on risk models, portfolio optimization, and trading analysis, equity, fixed income, and international investing; and quantitative approaches to active management.

Printed in the USA
CPSIA information can be obtained
at www.ICGtesting.com
JSHW011933230824
68578JS00010B/162